SPECIAL ADVERTISING SECTION

Diversity and Inclusion in Action

At Schering-Plough, we thrive on diversity. In fact, diversity and inclusion are key drivers of our work to create new medicines for the future.

The more than 33,500 men and women who work for Schering-Plough around the world represent a range of racial, ethnic and cultural backgrounds, ages, gender orientations and physical abilities. Our diversity and inclusion strategy recognizes the value of the various perspectives our colleagues bring. By learning from each other, we are better able to serve the doctors, patients and other customers who are counting on us.

Schering-Plough Corporation
2000 Galloping Hill Road
Kenilworth, NJ 07033-0530
www.schering-plough.com

An Equal Opportunity Employer Committed to Diversity

 Schering-Plough

ACHIEVEMENT STARTS WHEN
YOU HARNESS THE POWER
OF MANY PERSPECTIVES.

WE KNOW GREATNESS IS OFTEN THE PRODUCT OF PEOPLE BRINGING FRESH PERSPECTIVES TO THE TABLE

Achievement can take you places. Northrop Grumman professionals work on the cutting edge of global defense and technology, and at every level we've made strong commitments to workforce diversity – because we know that diversity fuels innovation, and innovation fuels achievement. Our commitment is visible – Northrop Grumman was recently selected #7 in Woman Engineer magazine's Top 50 Companies Hiring Women Engineers, and 15th in NSBE's Top 50 Preferred Employers. At Northrop Grumman, we foster a breadth of perspectives to power our world-class projects. Perspectives like yours.

Achievement never ends.

NORTHROP GRUMMAN

DEFINING THE FUTURE™

HCA

Hospital Corporation of America

It takes **all of us.**

As a member of the HCA family, your **career growth** comes with added value – the personal reward of the impact you can have on the lives of others. If you're interested in a position with a corporation that shares your goal to truly make a difference, visit our website at **www.hcahealthcare.com** to find out which opportunity is right for you.

At HCA, the nation's leading provider of healthcare services, we strive to deliver the best care in our 173 hospitals throughout the US and Europe.

Our diverse and inclusive workforce of over 186,000 dedicated employees is vital to our mission and commitment to the care and improvement of human life.

www.hcahealthcare.com

make your
mark

Archer Daniels Midland Company is a world leader in BioEnergy and has a premier position in the agricultural processing value chain. We count on the ambition and creativity of our colleagues to help us enhance our position as a global leader in the development of food, feed and fuel products.

Whether you are looking to further your career or are a recent college graduate, ADM is the place to be. As a Fortune 100 company, we are committed to providing opportunities, training and benefits that exceed expectations.

At ADM, the opportunity is yours.

Visit us online at www.adm.jobs.

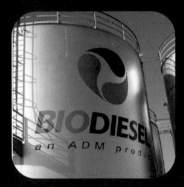

ADM

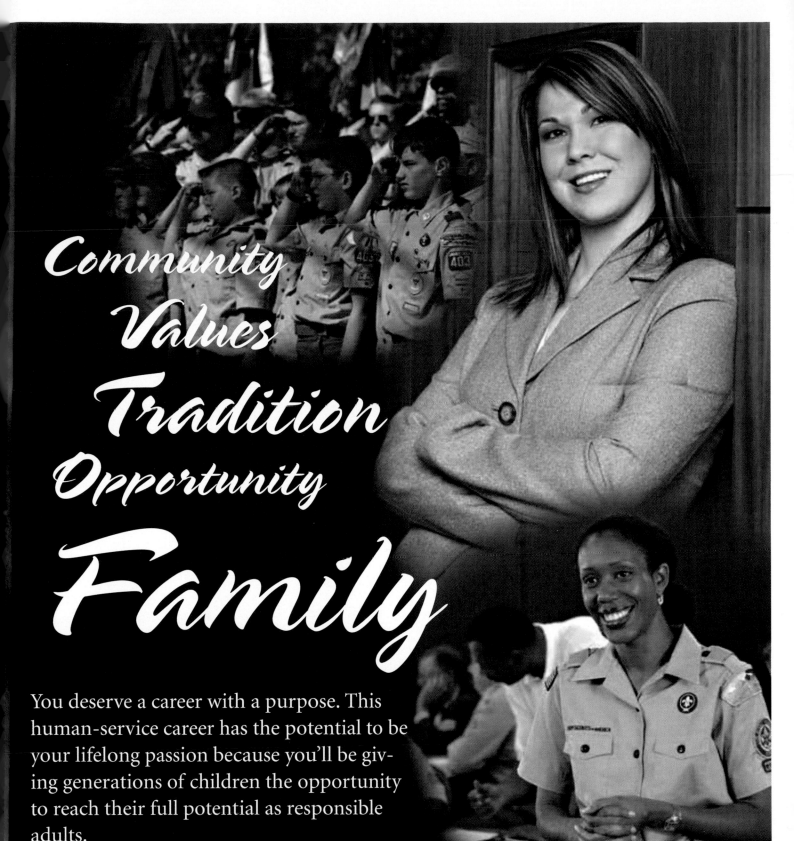

Community
Values
Tradition
Opportunity
Family

You deserve a career with a purpose. This human-service career has the potential to be your lifelong passion because you'll be giving generations of children the opportunity to reach their full potential as responsible adults.

Visit www.scouting.org for information on employment opportunities in Scouting.

BOY SCOUTS OF AMERICA®

THE VAULT INROADS GUIDE TO
CORPORATE DIVERSITY PROGRAMS 2008 EDITION
is made possible through the generous support of the following sponsors:

THE VAULT INROADS GUIDE TO
CORPORATE DIVERSITY PROGRAMS 2008 EDITION
is made possible through the generous support of the following sponsors:

 imagination at work

HCA

INROADS.

THE VAULT INROADS GUIDE TO
CORPORATE DIVERSITY PROGRAMS 2008 EDITION
is made possible through the generous support of the following sponsors:

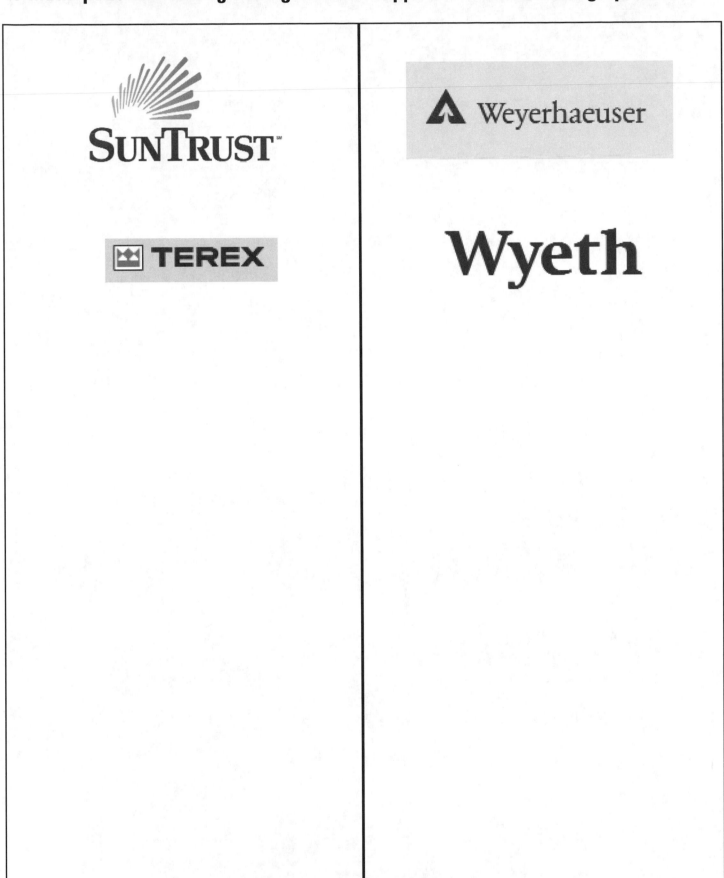

The media's watching Vault!
Here's a sampling of our coverage.

"For those hoping to climb the ladder of success, [Vault's] insights are priceless."
– *Money magazine*

"The best place on the web to prepare for a job search."
– *Fortune*

"[Vault guides] make for excellent starting points for job hunters and should be purchased by academic libraries for their career sections [and] university career centers."
– *Library Journal*

"The granddaddy of worker sites."
– *US News and World Report*

"A killer app."
– *The New York Times*

One of Forbes' 33 "Favorite Sites"
– *Forbes*

"To get the unvarnished scoop, check out Vault."
– *Smart Money Magazine*

"Vault has a wealth of information about major employers and job-searching strategies as well as comments from workers about their experiences at specific companies."
– *The Washington Post*

"Vault has become the go-to source for career preparation."
– *Crain's New York*

"Vault [provides] the skinny on working conditions at all kinds of companies from current and former employees."
– *USA Today*

THEN:
INROADS Intern
NOW:
Steven Davis, Bob Evans President, CEO, and Chairman of the Board

OUR INTERNS ARE YOUR FUTURE LEADERS

With **INROADS®** you can give a college student, like Steve, an opportunity to learn and grow, while at the same time, giving your company early access to talented minds interested in contributing to your bottom line.

INROADS Interns are high achievers, make top grades, have the edge on leadership, and have a burning desire to become part of the corporate structure. In addition to our expert recruiting and training, **INROADS** partners with you to mentor your Interns through a customized career development plan. **INROADS** graduates are more productive, advance faster, and are more loyal.

Find your next CEO RIGHT NOW. Visit us at www.INROADS.org.

VAULT/INROADS GUIDE TO

CORPORATE DIVERSITY PROGRAMS

CIT is a leading commercial and consumer finance company and a leader in the financial industry. We are committed to the development of our employees and invite you to explore the opportunities we have available. Whether you are just beginning your career or are a seasoned professional, there are a variety of current opportunities that could be right for you. We offer competitive salaries and comprehensive benefits as well as programs for educational assistance, Work/Life and internal training. For more information about a career at CIT, visit us at www.cit.com.

CIT
One CIT Drive
Livingston, NJ 07039

It is the policy of CIT to be an Equal Opportunity Employer. CIT maintains a policy of nondiscrimination with employees and applicants for employment. no aspect of employment with CIT will be influenced in any manner by race, color, religion, age, sex, national origin, marital status, disability, citizenship, veteran status, sexual orientation or any other basis prohibited by applicable law.

VAULT/INROADS GUIDE TO

CORPORATE DIVERSITY PROGRAMS

ANGELA ENTZMINGER AND THE STAFF OF VAULT

Acknowledgments

Acknowledgments from Vault

We are extremely grateful to Vault's entire staff for all their help in the editorial, production and marketing processes. Vault would also like to acknowledge the support of our investors, clients, family, and friends for enabling this guide to become a reality.

Acknowledgments from INROADS

INROADS would like to thank the entire staff of Vault for their work in completing this very useful resource. In addition, a warm thank you goes to President & CEO Charles Cornelius, Wilson Martinez del Rio, Tanza Pride, Javona Braxton, Tamika Curry, and all of our corporate sponsors who so willingly donated time, funding, and efforts to support this publication.

Special thanks also from Vault and INROADS to the committee members who assisted in finalizing the survey: Rod Adams of PricewaterhouseCoopers, Jen Carmody of Deloitte & Touche USALLP, Steve Canale of GE, Joelle Hayes of United Technologies Corporation, Rachel Rende of IBM, Ann Nowak of Liberty Mutual Insurance Company, Tracey Sumner of MetLife, Tamika Curry of Target Corporation, Melissa Aboytes of Kaiser Permanente, and Shaneen Tatum of Lockheed Martin.

ADI
Asian Diversity, Inc

2008 Asian Diversity

CAREER EXPO

May 2, 2008 New York
Madison Square Garden

Join one of the largest recruiting events for
Asian Americans in the U.S.! Last year, our
expo drew a record 101 exhibitors and over
4,000 job candidates. Here are just some of
the highlights to expect at the career expo:

- Meet hundreds of qualified Asian
  American job seekers
- Recruit candidates interested in
  working in Asia
- Connect to working professionals
  in a wide range of industries
- Find bilingual and bicultural talent
- Recruit, market, and reach out to
  the Asian American community

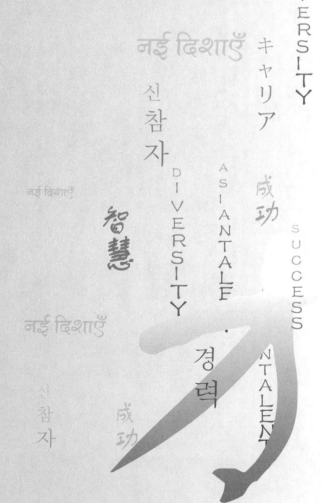

www.adiversity.com

Table of Contents

UNLEASH YOUR POTENTIAL

TEREX, the third largest equipment manufacturer in the world, strives to recruit, employ and develop highly talented and motivated individuals.

We believe that having a diverse group of employees stimulates ideas and creative thinking, a key to both our success and yours.

For more information about TEREX internships and career opportunities, please visit us at www.terex.com.

THE STRENGTH OF MANY. THE POWER OF ONE.

 TEREX

FOUND:
A job where the paycheck is only half the reward.

Do you want more out of your job than just a paycheck? Do you want to be challenged and learn new things? Do you want your talents to be recognized? Put your career in a position to grow at State Farm,® a Fortune 500® company. With a variety of jobs and placement opportunities all across the U.S., go ahead and reward yourself and your career. Join the State Farm team.

LIKE A GOOD NEIGHBOR, STATE FARM IS THERE.®

Introduction

Vault is proud to partner with INROADS, a top nonprofit organization that trains and develops talented minority youth for professional careers in business and industry, for the third annual edition of the *Vault/INROADS Guide to Corporate Diversity Programs*. Vault and INROADS make ideal partners to bring students, young professionals and educators the most recent, accurate and up-to-date information on corporate diversity planning, representation, strategies and programs.

For this third annual guide, 188 top companies and organizations shared their actions and goals in the crucial area of corporate diversity in self-reported profiles. By participating in the guide, companies are not endorsing Vault or INROADS, and there is no requirement that they be, have been or plan to be an INROADS partner. Rather, they are expressing their commitment to, and appreciation of, the importance of diversity in the 21st century workplace.

We thank all the participants in the third annual *Vault/INROADS Guide to Corporate Diversity Programs* and we hope that its readers will find it instructive and useful in evaluating potential employers and partners.

The Editors
Vault, Inc.

Letter from Charles Cornelius

Welcome to the third edition of the *Vault/INROADS Guide to Corporate Diversity Programs*. It is an honor to once again partner with Vault, Inc., the premier career resource publisher, to create this valuable tool.

For 37 years, the INROADS mission has been to place talented minority youth in business and industry. It is not only our mission, but our passion. In 1970, when Frank Carr founded our organization, he did so because of the lack of ethnic minorities in management and executive roles in corporate America. While there is still much work to be done, INROADS is proud to have been instrumental in changing the face of America's professional workforce. To date, we have graduated over 21,000 leaders and each year INROADS places 5,000 young men and women into salaried corporate internships.

Vault and INROADS understand that diversity is about more than the number of people of color on a company's roster. It is about creating a work environment that welcomes and embraces diversity. That is why this guide is essential to students, interns, young professionals, parents, counselors and corporations.

As a young person of color entering the corporate world, the *Vault/INROADS Guide to Corporate Diversity Programs* will provide you with critical data to help you in your search for opportunities.

For corporate leaders, I want to encourage you to use this guide as a resource to launch proactive programs that will not only help you attract, but also retain, the best and brightest minority talent in the country.

It is truly an honor for INROADS to work with Vault to produce this publication and we are excited about the opportunities it holds.

Sincerely,

Charles Cornelius
President & CEO
INROADS, Inc.

Letter from Tamika Curry

On behalf of Target, we are thrilled to be a part of the 2008 *Vault/INROADS Guide to Corporate Diversity Programs*.

Target's partnership with INROADS began in 1982 with a small group of talented interns at our headquarters location in Minneapolis, Minn. With the help of our partners at INROADS, and hundreds of outstanding interns, we have been able to expand our internship program nationwide with great success. Today, we are proud to be INROADS number one sponsoring company in the world.

At Target, we continue to integrate diversity into all aspects of our business—from how we relate to each other as team members, to how we serve our guests and communities, to the way we deliver for our shareholders by pursuing the right business strategies.

Our guiding principle is that Target is a performance-based company with equal opportunities for all who perform. We are focused on attracting the best talent, creating an environment where those who contribute are valued, and utilizing best practices to build a competitive advantage and drive towards a shared vision.

Our commitment to INROADS supports that objective and aligns with our business needs. Our goal is to build a strong pipeline of future leaders, help current leaders grow through mentorship and development activities, and create a pathway for new ideas and innovation.

We are honored and excited to be partnering with INROADS and Vault, Inc. to bring you this year's publication. As the world and workforce become increasingly diverse, we remain committed to developing young professionals who will become our future leaders.

Sincerely,

Tamika Curry

Tamika Curry
Director of Diversity
Target Corporation

Life. Enhanced.

New Breakthroughs, New Opportunities.

If you're looking for an exciting place to work with a future full of opportunities, consider Bristol-Myers Squibb.

In just over three years, we have introduced several major medicines to treat serious diseases. And we have a robust pipeline of investigational medicines in full development.

Help us fulfill our mission *to extend and enhance human life*. You'll not only help enrich the lives of others, but also have the opportunity for a rewarding career with personal and professional advancement in a high-caliber, team-oriented environment.

Please see our website at
www.bms.com/career
for a complete listing of opportunities

BMS offers opportunities for MBA students and graduates to join Summer and Full-Time Associate Programs in the following areas: Marketing, Finance, Information Management, and Technical Operations.

Undergraduate-level students and other advanced-degree graduates may also pursue internship, co-op and permanent job opportunities in many business divisions and functions across BMS and its family of companies.

 Bristol-Myers Squibb

Bristol-Myers Squibb
P.O. Box 4000, Princeton, NJ 08543-4000

Bristol-Myers Squibb is an equal opportunity employer.

© 2007 Bristol-Myers Squibb Company ZN-K0112 11/07

How to Use this Guide

Over the past few years, most U.S. companies have devoted increasing resources to diversity initiatives as well as to the management and administration of these efforts. Nearly all have developed their own unique cultural approach and methods of administration. The *Vault/INROADS Guide to Corporate Diversity Programs* was developed to provide students with the essential objective information necessary to meaningfully evaluate corporate diversity initiatives and programs. We hope that the information contained within this guide will enable students to match their interests and career objectives with an appropriate company.

The guide format presents the same information for all companies in a user-friendly way, addressing the degree to which several widely-recognized "best practices" are incorporated into a company's diversity program.

The complete survey sent to each company is printed in the guide. In cases where a company did not respond to a question, the unanswered question is not reprinted in their profile; it is simply left out. For questions where companies had the option of choosing one or more options to answer a question, we listed the choices the company chose; to see which answers the company did not choose, you can refer to the full text of the survey.

We encourage you to use the information in the guide as a springboard to ask constructive questions and open a dialogue that will empower you to define your relationship with the company. In the case of students evaluating potential employers, it may be whether the company's efforts measure up to your personal goals and developmental needs.

The survey upon which the *Vault/INROADS Guide to Corporate Diversity Programs* is based was finalized by the efforts of a committee composed of representatives from top companies in 2007. Participants included Rod Adams of PricewaterhouseCoopers, Jen Carmody of Deloitte & Touche USA LLP, Steve Canale of GE, Joelle Hayes of United Technologies Corporation, Rachel Rende of IBM, Ann Nowak of Liberty Mutual Insurance Company, Tracey Sumner of MetLife, Tamika Curry of Target Corporation, Melissa Aboytes of Kaiser Permanente, and Shaneen Tatum of Lockheed Martin.

Definitions

The survey refers to full-time or permanent exempt employees in the U.S. Entry-level college graduate hires are new full-time, professional or white-collar hires made directly from undergraduate institutions. The survey also covers interns, who typically work during the summer months, and co-ops, who typically work for more extended periods of time during the school year.

For this survey, diversity is defined as male and female minorities and white women but does not include gay and lesbian employees.

For this survey, minorities are defined as those whose ethnic background is other than White/Caucasian (e.g., African-American/Black, Latino/Hispanic, Asian and Native American).

Firm Contact Info

This section contains basic information, including the contact person for diversity hiring. Offices and revenue, also in this section, give a sense of the size of the company.

Recruitment

This section explores how to get hired at the company of your choice. It contains useful information on schools at which the company recruits (for new hires) as well as other outreach efforts, including participation in conferences, career panels and scholarship programs. Similar info is available for professional hires, as well as insight on whether the company uses women and/or minority-owned executive search firms to make hires.

Internships and Co-ops

Internships and co-op programs are a key way to be hired by any top company. This section describes the type of internships and co-op programs (there may be more than one) offered by the company, as well as contact information.

Scholarships

Many companies offer special scholarship programs for qualified minority students. You'll find the details, including the amount, the deadline to apply and contact information in this section for companies that offer scholarships.

Affinity Groups

If you're thinking of joining a company you may wish to join an affinity group or employee network, which is an internal organization that addresses the needs and interests of specific minority groups, and other employee groups.

Entry-Level Programs/Full-Time Opportunities/Training Programs

Looking for a place to work after graduation that may differ from the place where you did your internship? This section gives an overview of the type of entry-level positions at the company, including training and any kind of educational perks, like tuition reimbursement.

Strategic Plan and Diversity Leadership

Once a company has committed to work at being more diverse, there are various ways in which the company can advance that commitment. It may be helpful for the reader to pay attention to what steps the company's management has taken to communicate its diversity commitment widely and to develop a clear action plan for progress. Is diversity progress a goal that has been set with company-wide responsibility and accountability? Do diversity leaders have a voice on management issues? You can begin to explore some of those issues in this section.

The Stats

Find out how large your potential employer is, and see its revenue growth. Companies may choose to add additional information on minority and male/female demographics if they choose.

Retention and Professional Development

This section covers retention rates of women and minorities, as well as the steps the company is taking to reduce attrition.

Diversity Mission Statement

Many companies have a guiding credo that shapes their approach to employment diversity issues; you'll find it in this section (if the company has one).

Additional Information

This section of the diversity profile is comprised of a narrative composed by the company. There were no requirements regarding what had to be addressed (although we admit to having made a few suggestions). For example, some companies chose to list diversity awards. This section offers a great place for the company to elaborate on some of its answers to the survey questions and discuss things they are doing that we may have failed to cover.

In conclusion, we hope that this book assists you in identifying companies that are a good match to your diversity values and needs. Remember: although you can get a quick impression by flipping through these pages and looking at diversity program overviews, and yes/no responses, the most important factor is the commitment of the company to diversity goals. We hope you find what you're looking for in the *Vault/INROADS Guide to Corporate Diversity Programs*.

Survey Invitation Letter from Vault and INROADS

Dear Employer,

We are writing to invite you to participate in an exciting project and to ask for your involvement in the third edition of the *Vault/INROADS Guide to Corporate Diversity Programs,* an effective means to explore corporate performance in the critical area of diversity.

INROADS, a nonprofit organization that trains and develops talented minority youth for professional careers in business and industry, and Vault Inc., a premier source of employment information for MBAs, JDs, college students and grad students, have partnered to develop the attached Corporate Diversity Survey. We finalized this year's survey with the advice and assistance of a committee of representatives from top employers. We are requesting that all firms listed below complete the survey, which we believe represents the best way to stimulate diversity progress and achieve a measure of consistency in how diversity information is reported.

Vault compiles all of the completed surveys into a directory called the *Vault/INROADS Guide to Corporate Diversity Programs.* The guide's purpose is to educate the business and career center communities, as well as interested students and recent graduates, on the commitment and types of diversity programs in place at approximately 600 major corporations (see list below). The objectives of publishing the guide are:

• To provide a consistent profile of current corporate diversity planning, implementation and representation;

• To identify the best practices for the design and implementation of diversity initiatives in companies; and

•To outline the strategies, programs, and metrics that top companies use to increase the recruitment, retention and promotion of minority and women employees.

This guide differs from some of Vault's other publications, such as the *Vault Guide to the Top 100 Law Firms* and the *Vault Guide to the Top 50 Banking Employers,* in two significant ways:

•**There are no rankings.** Rather, Vault is simply gathering and presenting information about each company's diversity efforts. Firm profiles will appear in alphabetical order.

•**All information is self-reported by each firm.** Each employer's data will be published virtually as submitted, with only minor editing from Vault for clarity and length, and all edits will be reviewed and approved by the employer prior to publication.

Please return the survey to Angela Entzminger at aentzminger@vault.com.

The *Vault/INROADS Guide to Corporate Diversity Programs* will be distributed in print and electronic form free of charge to every firm that submits a completed survey, to 10,000 current and recent INROADS interns, and to the career center offices at approximately 800+ colleges and universities in the United States. This is our third edition. Please let Vault VP of Content Marcy Lerner, at mlerner@vault.com or Editor Angela Entzminger, at aentzminger@vault.com know if you would like to see last year's edition.

We hope that you will join us in this effort by completing and returning the attached survey in a timely manner.

If you have any questions, please direct them to Marcy Lerner, Angela Entzminger or INROADS Sr. Marketing & Communications Manager, Tanza Pride, at TPride@INROADS.org.

Best regards,

Charles Cornelius
President & CEO
INROADS
www.INROADS.org

Samer Hamadeh
Co-founder & CEO
Vault
www.vault.com

Vault/INROADS Diversity Survey

Survey Introduction

Thank you for taking the Vault/INROADS Corporate Diversity Survey (2008 edition). Following are a few pointers on completing the survey. If you have any questions about the survey or how to answer a question, please contact Vault VP of Content Marcy Lerner, at mlerner@vault.com or at (212) 366-3724, Vault Editor Angela Entzminger, at aentzminger@vault.com, or at (212) 366- 4212 ext. 213, or Tanza Pride, INROADS Sr. Marketing & Communications Manager, at tpride@INROADS.org. We thank you for your understanding and welcome comments and feedback as we seek to improve the survey for future editions.

The Process

Participation is entirely FREE of charge. We ask that a representative or group of representatives from your firm complete the attached questionnaire (in MS Word format) within the next five weeks. Please note that each firm should complete and return only one questionnaire. Do not handwrite or PDF survey responses. Please submit your form by March 2, 2007.

Distribution

The *Vault/INROADS Guide to Corporate Diversity Programs* (15,000 total print copies) will be distributed free of charge to every employer that submits a completed survey, to over 10,000 former and current INROADS interns, and to the undergraduate career office of approximately 500 colleges and universities in the United States. The guide will also be sold through college and university bookstores and on the Internet. Excerpts from the guide will also be available free at www.vault.com. At no additional charge, moreover, the entire guide will be available to Vault Gold subscribers and to the 800+ colleges and universities worldwide that have subscribed to the Vault Online Career Library. (1,000,000 total PDF copies.)

Instructions

1. You may opt to skip any question. If you skip a question, we will not publish the question in your completed entry.

2. The survey covers only U.S. internship, co-op and entry-level hiring, although we do ask for your worldwide locations, employee numbers and revenue figures.

3. The survey refers to full-time exempt employees in the U.S.

   - Entry-level college graduate hires are new full-time, professional or white-collar hires made directly from undergraduate institutions.
   - Exempt employees are employees who are not temporary, hourly or contract.

4. Under section I, Diversity Team Leader/Diversity Campus Recruiting Team Leader, please list the person or persons heading the diversity recruiting efforts at your organization.

5. Under section I, Office Locations, feel free to list the exact locations or supply the number of locations, to list your headquarters plus the number of offices, or to use any other method you prefer of listing locations.

6. Under section XII, Additional Information, points you may wish to address in the narrative include:

- More detail on diversity scholarships for interns, co-ops or entry-level college hires
- More detail on part-time/flex-time programs
- More detail on the workings of your diversity committee
- The names of minority associations with which you have relationships
- A list and description of diversity awards and honors
- Any financial support or service donated to minority public interest organizations and the names of such organizations.

We very much appreciate your participation and look forward to your response.

Vault/INROADS Diversity Survey

I. Firm Info

Contact Person: _____ Title: _____

Diversity Team Leader/Diversity Campus Recruiting Team Leader: (name & title):

_____

Firm Name: _____

Address: _____

City: _____ State: _____ Zip: _____

Phone: _____ Fax: _____ E-mail: _____

Office Locations (worldwide): _____

_____

Career web site address _____

II. Recruitment of Interns, Co-ops and Entry-Level College Graduate Hires

1. Does your firm annually recruit at any of the following types of institutions? (Check all that apply and list the schools).

☐ Ivy League schools: _____

☐ Other private schools: _____

☐ Public state schools: _____

☐ Historically Black Colleges and Universities (HBCUs): _____

☐ Hispanic Serving Institutions (HSIs): _____

☐ Native American Tribal Universities: _____

☐ Other predominantly minority and/or women's colleges: _____

2. Of the schools that you listed above, do you have any special outreach efforts directed to encourage <u>minority</u> students to consider your firm?

☐ Hold a reception for minority students

☐ Conferences.   Please list: _____

☐ Advertise in minority student association publication(s)

☐ Participate in/host minority student job fair(s)

☐ Sponsor minority student association events

☐ Firm's employees participate on career panels at schools

☐ Outreach to leadership of minority student organizations

☐ Scholarships or intern/fellowships for minority students

☐ Other. Please specify: _____

3. What activities does the firm undertake to attract minority and women employees?

☐ Partner programs with women and minority associations

☐ Conferences. Please list: _____

☐ Participate at minority job fairs

☐ Seek referrals from other employees

☐ Utilize online job services

☐ Other. Please specify: _____

(a) Do you use executive recruiting/search firms to seek to identify new diversity hires? Yes ☐ No ☐

(b) If yes, list all women- and/or minority-owned executive search/recruiting firms to which the firm paid a fee for placement services in the past 12 months: _____

_____

II. Internships and Co-ops

For the following section, please repeat this template as necessary for all of your U.S.-based internships and co-ops, including those aimed at minority undergraduate students and non-minority undergraduate students (i.e., INROADS)

Name of internship/co-op program: _____

Deadline for application: _____

Number of interns in the program in summer 2006 (internship) or 2006 (co-op): _____

Pay ($US) _____ (indicate if by week, by month, or for entire program)

Length of the program (in weeks): _____

Percentage of interns/co-ops in the program who receive offers of full-time employment

_____

Web site for internship/co-op information

_____

Please describe the internship program or co-op, including departments hiring, intern/co-op responsibilities, qualifications for the program and any other details you feel are relevant.

IV. Scholarships

For the following section, please repeat this template as necessary if you have more than one scholarship aimed at minority undergraduate students.

Name of scholarship program: _____

Deadline for application for the scholarship program: _____

Scholarship award amount ($US) _____ (indicate if by week, by month, or for entire scholarship)

Web site or other contact information for scholarship

_____

Please describe the scholarship program, including basic requirements, eligibility, length of program and any other details you feel are relevant.

V. Affinity Groups

For the following section, please repeat this template as necessary if you have more than one affinity group at your organization.

Name of affinity group

Please describe the affinity group/employee network, including its purpose, how often it meets, web site, etc.

VI. Entry-Level Programs/Full-Time Opportunities/Training Programs

For the following section, please repeat this template as necessary if you have more than one full-time, entry-level program, training program or management/leadership program at your organization.

Name of program: _____

Length of program _____

Geographic location(s) of program _____

Please describe the training/training component of this program _____

Please describe any other educational components of this program (i.e., tuition reimbursement)

_____

VII. Strategic Plan and Diversity Leadership

1. What trends in your industry affect your corporate diversity goals, strategies and/or internal or external alliances?

2. How does the firm's leadership communicate the importance of diversity to everyone at the firm? (e.g., e-mails, web site, newsletters, meetings, etc.)

3. Who has primary responsibility for leading diversity initiatives at your firm? Name of person and his/her title:

_____

4. (a) Does your firm currently have a diversity committee? Yes ☐ No ☐

If yes, please describe how the committee is structured, how often it meets, etc.

_____

(b) If yes, does the committee's representation include one or more members of the firm's management/executive committee (or the equivalent)? Yes ☐ No ☐

(c) If yes, how many executives are on the committee, and in 2006, what was the total number of hours collectively spent by the committee in furtherance of the firm's diversity initiatives? How many employees are on the committee, and how often does the committee convene in furtherance of the firm's diversity initiatives?

Total Executives on Committee: _____

5. Does the committee and/or diversity leader establish and set goals or objectives consistent with management's priorities?

Yes ☐ No ☐ Partially (explain): _____

Please elaborate, if you wish.

6. Has the firm undertaken a formal or informal diversity program or set of initiatives aimed at increasing the diversity of the firm?

Yes, formal ☐ Yes, informal ☐ No ☐

Please elaborate, if you wish.

7. (a) How often does the firm's management review the firm's diversity progress/results?

☐ Monthly

☐ Quarterly

☐ Twice a year

☐ Annually

☐ Does not review/measure progress/results

☐ Other, please specify_____

(b) How is the firm's diversity committee and/or firm management held accountable for achieving results?

_____

VIII. The Stats

	Total in the U.S.		Total outside the U.S.		Total worldwide	
	2006/2005		2006/2005		2006/2005	
1. Number of employees						
2. Revenue						

Please elaborate on your firm's demographic profile, including the percentage of minorities in the U.S., number of minorities in the U.S., percentage of male/female employees, percentage of minorities and/or women on the executive team, and any other figures you may wish to reveal.

IX. Retention and Professional Development

1. How do 2006 minority and female attrition rates generally compare to those experienced in the prior year period?

☐ Higher than in prior years

☐ Lower than in prior years

☐ About the same as in prior years

☐ Please elaborate if you wish.

2. Please identify the specific steps you are taking to reduce the attrition rate of minority and women employees. (It is suggested that you elaborate on this issue in the final question of this survey.)

☐ Develop and/or support internal employee affinity groups (e.g., minority or women networks within the firm)

☐ Increase/review compensation relative to competition

☐ Increase/improve current work/life programs

☐ Adopt dispute resolution process

☐ Succession plan includes emphasis on diversity

☐ Work with minority and women employees to develop career advancement plans

☐ Review work assignments and hours billed to key client matters to make sure minority and women employees are not being excluded

☐ Strengthen mentoring program for all employees, including minorities and women

☐ Professional skills development program, including minority and women employees

☐ Other. Please specify

XI. Diversity Mission Statement

Please state your organization's diversity mission statement if applicable.

XII. Additional Information

In a narrative of 500 words or less, please provide any additional information regarding your firm's diversity initiatives that you wish to share. See instructions for details and suggestions.

Firms invited to participate in the Vault/INROADS Diversity Survey

3M

84 Lumber Company

AAA Automotive Club

Abbott Laboratories

Abercrombie & Fitch

ABN AMRO Holding N.V.

Accenture

Advance Auto Parts

Advanced Micro Devices (AMD)

AdvancePCS

AES

Aetna Inc.

Affiliated Computer Services

Aflac

AGCO

A.G. Edwards, Inc.

Agilent Technologies, Inc.

AIG

Air Products and Chemicals, Inc.

AK Steel Holdings

Albertsons

Alcatel-Lucent

Alcoa, Inc.

Allegheny Energy, Inc.

Allergan, Inc.

Allen & Company, Inc.

Allied Waste Industries

Allmerica Financial

Allstate Insurance Company

Alltel

Altria Group, Inc.

Amazon.com

Amerada Hess

Ameren Corporation

American Airlines, Inc.

American Axle & Mfg.

American Cancer Society

American Cast Iron Pipe Co.

American Electric Power (AEP)

American Express Company

American Family Insurance

American Financial Grp.

American Greetings

American Home Products

American Red Cross, The

American Standard

AmerisourceBergen

Ametek

Amgen

AMR

AmSouth Bancorporation

Anadarko Petroleum Corporation

Anheuser-Busch Companies, Inc.

Aon

Apache

Apple Inc.

Applied Materials, Inc.

Applied Signal Technology, Inc.

Aramark

Archer Daniels Midland Company

Armstrong Holdings

Arrow Electronics, Inc.

ArvinMeritor

Asbury Automotive Group

Asea Brown Boveri Inc.

Ashland Inc

AstraZeneca PLC

A.T. Kearney

Atlanta Life Financial Group

AT & T

AT&T Wireless Services

Aurora Health Care Inc.

Autoliv

Automatic Data Processing (ADP)

AutoNation

Auto-Owners Insurance

AutoZone

Avaya Inc.

Avery Dennison

Avnet

Avon Products

BAE Systems

Bain & Company

Baker Hughes

Ball Aerospace & Technologies Corp.

BancWest Corporation

Bank of America

Bank of New York

Barclays Capital

Barnes & Noble

BASF Corporation

Baxter International

Baystate Medical Center

Bayer CropScience

BB&T Corporation

BE&K, Inc

Bear Stearns

Becton, Dickinson, and Company

Bed Bath & Beyond

Bell Atlantic

BellSouth

Berkshire Hathaway

Best Buy

Big Lots

BJC Health System

BJs Wholesale Club

Black & Decker

Blackwell Sanders Peper Martin LLP

Blue Cross and Blue Shield Association

BNP Paribas

Boeing Company, The

Boise Cascade

Bonneville Power Administration

Borders Group

Boston Consulting Group

Boston Scientific Corporation

Boy Scouts of America

BP North America

Bridgestone Americas Holding, Inc.

Briggs & Stratton

Brinker International, Inc.

Brinks

Bristol-Myers Squibb

Broadcom

Brown Brothers Harriman & Company

Brunswick

Bunzl Distribution

Burger King Corporation

Burlington Northern Santa Fe Railway Co.

Burlington Resources

C. R. Bard, Inc.

C.H. Robinson Worldwide

Cablevision Systems

Caesars Entertainment

Calyon Securities

Campbell Soup Company

Cap Gemini Ernst & Young

Capital One Financial Corporation

Cardinal Health Inc

Caremark Rx

Cargill

CarMax

Cascadia Capital LLC

Caterpillar

CDW Computer Centers, Inc.

Cendant Corporation

CenterPoint Energy, Inc.

Centex Homes

Central Intelligence Agency

Central Parking Corporation

Cerner Corporation

CGI-AMS

Chanin Capital Partners

Charles Schwab

Charter Communications

ChevronTexaco

CHS

Chubb Corporation, The

CIGNA

Cinergy Corporation

Cintas Corporation

Circuit City Stores

Cisco Systems, Inc.

CIT

Citi (Citigroup Inc.)

City National

Clarian Health

Clear Channel Communications

Cleveland Clinic

Clorox Company, The

CNA Insurance

CNF

Coca-Cola

Coca-Cola Bottling Company

Coca-Cola Enterprises

Colgate-Palmolive

Collins & Aikman

Colorado Springs Utilities

Columbia St. Mary's, Inc.

Comcast Cable Communications, LLC

Comerica, Inc.

Compass Bancshares, Inc.

Computer Associates Internation

Computer Sciences Corporation

ConAgra Foods, Inc.

ConocoPhillips

Conseco

Consolidated Edison Company of New York

Constellation Energy

Consumers Energy Corporation

Continental Airlines

Convergys Corporation

Cooper Tire & Rubber

Coors Brewing Company (Adolph Coors)

Corn Products International Inc

Corning Incorporated

Costco Companies

Countrywide Financial

Coventry Health Care

Cox Enterprises

CPC International Inc.

Credit Suisse

Crown Holdings

CSX Corporation, Inc.

Cummins

CVS

D&K Healthcare Resources Inc

D.R. Horton

DaimlerChrysler Corporation

Dana Corporation

Danaher

Darden Restaurants

Daymon Worldwide, Inc.

Dean Foods

Dell

Deloitte & Touche USA LLP

Delphi Automotive

Delphi Corporation

Delta Air Lines

Deluxe Corporation

DENTSPLY International

Deutsche Bank

Devon Energy Corporation

Dial Corporation

Dillards

Dole Foods

Dollar General

Dominion

Domino's Pizza, Inc.

Donaldson Company

Dover

Dow Chemical Company

Dresdner Kleinwort

DTE Energy

Duke Energy Corporation

Duke Realty Corporation

Dun & Bradstreet

DuPont

Dynegy Inc.

E.W. Scripps Company, The

Eastman Chemical

Eastman Kodak Company

Eaton Corporation

EBay Inc.

Echostar Communications Corp.

Ecolab, Inc.

Edison International

El Paso Corporation

El Paso Electric

Electronic Data Systems

Eli Lilly

EMBARGQ

EMC Corporation

Emcor Group

Emerson Electric

Energy East

Engelhard

Entergy Corporation

Enterprise Products Partners

Enterprise Rent-A-Car Company

Equitable Life Assurance Society of the Equity Office Properties Trust

Erie Insurance Group

Ernst & Young LLP

Estee Lauder

Exelon Corporation

Express Scripts

ExxonMobil Corporation

Family Dollar Stores

Fannie Mae

Farmland Industries

Federal Aviation Administration

Federal Reserve Bank of NY

Federal-Mogul Corporation

Federated Department Stores

FedEx

Fidelity Investments

Fidelity National Financial

Fifth Third Bancorp

First American Corp.

First Data Corporation

FirstEnergy Corporation

First National Bancshares, Inc.

Fisher Scientific

Fluor

FMC Corporation

Foot Locker Inc

Ford Motor

Fortune Brands, Inc.

FPL Group, Inc.

Frank Russell & Company

Freeport-McMoRan Copper & Gold Inc.

Gannett Corporation

Gap Inc.

Gateway

GE

GEICO

General Dynamics Land Systems

General Growth Companies

General Mills Inc.

General Motors Corporation

Genuine Parts

Georgia-Pacific Corporation

Gillette

GlaxoSmithKline plc

Golden West Financial Corporation

Goldman Sachs & Co.

Goodrich Corporation

Goodyear Tire & Rubber

Graybar Electric

Great Plains Energy, Inc.

Group 1 Automotive

Guardian Life of America

Guradian Life Insurance Company of Ameri

H&R Block

H.J. Heinz

Halliburton

Hallmark Cards, Inc.

Harley-Davidson

Harleysville Group, Inc.

Harrahs Entertainment

Hartford Financial Services Group Inc, T

HCA, Hospital Corporation of America

HDR, Inc.

Health Insurance Plan of Greater New York

Health Net

Hearst Corporation

Henry Schein

Hershey Company, The

Hewlett-Packard

Hibernia

Hilton Hotels

Hitachi

Home Depot

Honeywell International Inc.

Hormel Foods

Household International

HSBC

Hughes Supply

Humana Health Plans

Huntington Bancshares

IAC/InterActiveCorp

IKON Office Solutions

Illinois Tool Works

IMS Health Incorporated

ING Americas

Ingram Industries

Intel Corp.

International Business Machines Corporation (IBM)

International Council of Shopping Center

International Paper

International Steel Group

Interpublic Group of Companies

Interstate Bakeries

ITT Industries, Inc.

J.C. Penney Company, Inc.

Jabil Circuit

Jacobs Engineering Grp.

JEA

Jefferson-Pilot

JM Family Enterprises

Jo-Ann Stores Inc

John Deere

John Hancock

Johnson & Johnson

Johnson Controls Inc.

Jones Apparel Group

JPMorgan Chase

Kaiser Permanente

KB Home

Kellogg Company

Kelly Services

Kerr McGee Corporation

Key Bank

KeySpan

Kiewit Corporation

Kimberly-Clark

Kinder Morgan Energy

Kindred Healthcare

Kmart Holding

Kohl's Corporation

KPMG LLP

Kraft Foods

Kroger Company

L-3 Communications

Laidlaw International

Land OLakes Inc.

LandAmerica Financial

Lear Corporation

Leggett & Platt

Lehman Brothers

Lennar

Level 3 Communications, Inc.

Levi Strauss

Lexmark International

Liberty Mutual Insurance Company

Limited Brands

Lincoln Financial Group

Liz Claiborne, Inc.

Lockheed Martin Corporation

Loews Corporation

Longs Drug Stores

L'Oreal USA

Lowes Companies, Inc.

Lyondell Chemical

Manpower

Marathon Oil

Marriott International, Inc.

Marsh Inc.

Marshall & Ilsley Corporation

Masco

Massachusetts Mutual Life

Mattel Inc.

Maxtor

Mayo Foundation

MBNA Corporation

McDonald's Corporation

McGraw-Hill

McKesson Corporation

MeadWestvaco Corporation

Medco Health Solutions

Medtronic, Inc.

Mellon Financial

Merck

Merrill Lynch & Co Inc

METLIFE

MGIC Investment Corporation

MGM Mirage

Michelin North America

Microsoft

Middle Tennessee State University

Minnesota Mutual Life Insurance

Mirant

Mohawk Industries

Monsanto Company

MONY-Mutual of New York

Moodys Corporation

Motorola

Murphy Oil

Mutual of Omaha Insurance

Nash Finch

National City Corporation

National Fuel Gas

Nationwide

Navistar Corporation

NBC Universal

NCR Corp

NetBank

New York Life Insurance Company

New York Times

Newell Rubbermaid

Newmont Mining

Nextel Communications, Inc.

Nike Inc.

NiSource

Nissan Motor Corporation

Nokia

Nordstrom, Inc.

Norfolk Southern

Nortel Networks Corporation

North Carolina Office of State Personnel

Northeast Utilities

Northern Trust Company (The)

Northrop Grumman Corporation

Northwest Airlines

Northwestern Mutual Financial Network

NTL

Nucor

NVR

Occidental Petroleum

Office Depot, Inc.

OGE Energy

Ohio State University Hospitals

Old Republic Intl.

Olin Corporation

OM Group

Omaha Public Schools

Omnicare

Omnicom Group

Oracle

OSRAM SYLVANIA

Owens & Minor

Owens Corning

Owens-Illinois

Oxford Health Plans, Inc.

Paccar

Pacific Life Insurance Company

PacifiCare Health Sys.

Parker Hannifin Corp.

Pathmark Stores

Pearson Education

Pepco Holdings

Pepsi Bottling (PBG)

Pepsi North America

PepsiAmericas

PepsiCo Inc.

Performance Food Group

PETsMART Inc

Pfizer Inc

PG&E Corp.

Phelps Dodge Corporation

Philip Morris Companies, Inc.

Phillips-Van Heusen

Pinnacle West Capital

Pitney Bowes

Plains All American Pipeline

PNC Financial Services Group, Inc.

PPG Industries

PPL Corporation

Praxair

Premcor

PricewaterhouseCoopers

Principal Financial Group

Procter & Gamble Company, The

Progress Energy

Progressive

Protective Life Corporation

Prudential Financial

PSEG

Publix Super Markets

Pulte Homes Inc.

Qualcomm Incorporated

Quest Diagnostics

Qwest Communications International Inc.

R. J. Reynolds Tobacco Holdings, Inc.

R.J. Reynolds Tobacco

R.R. Donnelley

RadioShack Corporation

Raytheon

Reebok International

Regions Financial Corporation

Reliant Energy

Rite Aid

Robert Half International Inc.

Roche Pharmaceuticals

Rockwell Automation Inc.

Rockwell Collins

Rohm & Haas

Ross Stores

Roundys

Royal Bank Of Canada

Royal Dutch/Shell group of Companies

Russell Corporation

Ryder Systems, Inc.

Ryland Group Inc., The

Safeco Corp.

Safeway, Inc.

Saks Incorporated

Sanmina-SCI

Sara Lee Corporation

SBC Communications, Inc.

SC Johnson & Son

SCANA

Schering-Plough Corporation

Schlumberger

Science Applications International Corp.

Sealed Air

Sears Roebuck

SEI Investments

Sempra Energy

ServiceMaster

Shaw Group

Shell Oil Company

Shell Trading

Sherwin-Williams Co.

Siemens

Simmons Company

SLM Corporation

Smith International

Smithfield Foods

Smurfit-Stone Container Corporation

Sodexho

Solectron Corporation

Sonic Automotive

Southern Company

SouthTrust Corporation

Southwest Airlines

Southwest Gas Corporation

Spartan Stores

Sprint Nextel Corporation

SPX

St. Paul Travelers Companies, Inc., The

Staples, Inc.

Starbucks Coffee Company

Starwood Hotels & Resorts Worldwide

State Farm Insurance

State Street Corporation

Steelcase Inc.

Storage Technology Corporation

Stryker

Sun MicroSystems

Sunoco Inc

SunTrust Banks, Inc.

SUNY Upstate Med Univ

SUPERVALU Inc

Symbol Technologies, Inc.

Synovus Financial Corp.

Sysco

T. Rowe Price

Target Corporation

Teachers Insurance & Annuity (TIAA-CREF)

Tech Data Corporation

TECO Energy

Telephone & Data Sys.

Temple-Inland

Tenet Healthcare Corporation

Tenneco Automotive

Terex Corporation

Tesoro Petroleum

Texas Instruments

Textron

Thrivent Financial for Lutherans

Time Warner, Inc.

Timken

TJX Companies, The

Toyota Motor Company

Toys 'R' Us

TransMontaigne

Travelers Corporation (The)

Triad Hospitals

Tribune Company

Turner Corporation (The)

TXU

Tyco International

Tyson Foods

UAL

UBS AG

Unilever USA

Union Bank of California

Union Pacific Corporation

Union Planters Corporation

UNISYS

United Auto Group

United Defense Industries Inc

United HealthCare

United Parcel Service (UPS)

United Rentals, Inc

United Stationers

United Technologies Corporation

Universal Health Services

University Hospitals/Cleveland

Unocal

UnumProvident

US Airways

US Bancorp

USAA

USG Corporation

United States Steel Corporation

USX

Valero Energy Corporation

Verizon Communications

Verizon Wireless

VF Corporation

Viacom

Visteon

Vulcan Materials Co.

W.R. Berkley

W.W. Grainger, Inc.

Wachovia Corporation

Walgreens

Wal-Mart Stores, Inc.

Walt Disney Company

Washington Mutual Savings Bank

Waste Management Inc

WellChoice

Wellpoint Health Networks Inc.

Wells Fargo & Company

Wesco International

Western & Southern Financial

Weyerhaeuser

Whirlpool Corporation

Williams Companies, The

Winn-Dixie Stores

Wisconsin Energy

Wisconsin Public Service Corporation

Wyeth Pharmaceuticals

Xcel Energy

Xerox Corporation

YMCA of the USA

York International

Yum! Brands, Inc.

Zions Bancorporation

Zurich North America

DIVERSITY PROFILES

84 Lumber Company

1019 Route 519
Eighty Four, PA 15330
Phone: (800) 664-1984

Locations
500 offices in 40 states in the US.

Diversity Leadership
Position currently being filled.

Employment Contact
Angeles Valenciano
Director of Diversity & Inclusion
1019 Route 519
Eighty Four, PA 15330
Phone: (800) 664-1984 ext. 2180
www.84lumber.com/About84/careers.asp

Recruiting

Please list the schools/types of schools at which you recruit.

- Private schools
- Public state schools
- Historically black colleges and universities (HBCUs)
- Other predominantly minority and/or women's colleges

Do you have any special outreach efforts directed to encourage minority students to consider your firm?

- Hold a reception for minority students
- Advertise in minority student association publication(s)
- Participate in/host minority student job fair(s)
- Sponsor minority student association events
- Firm's employees participate on career panels at schools
- Outreach to leadership of minority student organizations
- Scholarships or intern/fellowships for minority students

What activities does the firm undertake to attract minority and women employees?

- Partner programs with women and minority associations
- Participate at minority job fairs
- Seek referrals from other employees
- Utilize online job services

Do you use executive recruiting/search firms to seek to identify new diversity hires?

No

Internships and Co-ops

Select Intern Program

Deadline for application: May 1st

Number of interns in the program in summer 2006 (internship) or 2006 (co-op): 2006 is the first year

Pay: $7.42 to $9.42 per hour

Length of the program: 12 weeks

Percentage of interns/co-ops in the program who receive offers of full-time employment: New program/no data yet

The internship program is an elite opportunity for freshmen interested in recurring summer internships. Interns will learn all aspects of 84 Lumber over three summer internships. They will also gradually focus on an area of interest with the ultimate goal of full-time employment upon graduation and fast-track to leadership.

Corporate Internships

Deadline for application: May 1st

Number of interns in the program in summer 2006 (internship) or 2006 (co-op): 2006 was the first year

Pay: Varies by department

Length of the program: Flexible

Percentage of interns/co-ops in the program who receive offers of full-time employment: New program/no data yet

Internships are available for all majors at our corporate headquarters in Eighty Four, Pa.

Scholarships

School of Business & Public Administration

Scholarship award amount: $1,000.

The scholarship is awarded to the University of D.C. to be given to two students.

Entry-Level Programs, Full-time Opportunities and Training Programs

84 Lumber Manager Trainee

Length of program: Six to 12 months

Geographic location(s) of program: U.S. nationwide

Please describe the training/training component of this program:
Paid training includes OJT, Self-Study CD, Early Development Program and Team Headquarters Training.

84 Lumber Inventory Manager

Length of program: Six to 12 months

Geographic location(s) of program: Corporate headquarters, Eighty Four, Pa.

Please describe the training/training component of this program:
Paid training includes OJT, Self-Study CD, Early Development Program, and Team Headquarters Training.

Strategic Plan and Diversity Leadership

How does the firm's leadership communicate the importance of diversity to everyone at the firm?

The firm communicates the importance of diversity by using our inter-company web site, e-mails and holding meetings.

Who has primary responsibility for leading diversity initiatives at your firm?

The manager of diversity initiatives position is being filled.

Does your firm currently have a diversity committee?

No

Has the firm undertaken a formal or informal diversity program or set of initiatives aimed at increasing the diversity of the firm?

Yes, formal

How often does the firm's management review the firm's diversity progress/results?

Monthly

How is the firm's diversity committee and/or firm management held accountable for achieving results?

Results are calculated and are then shared with the senior management team at weekly meetings.

The Stats

	NUMBER OF EMPLOYEES		REVENUE	
	2006	2005	2006	2005
Total in the U.S.	N/A	8,850	N/A	$3.9 billion

Retention and Professional Development

Please identify the specific steps you are taking to reduce the attrition rate of minority and women employees.

• Adopt dispute resolution process

• Work with minority and women employees to develop career advancement plans

• Professional skills development program, including minority and women employees

Diversity Mission Statement

In addition to 84 Lumber's success through teamwork, we strive to have the best associates and improve our standing as an employer of choice. We hire talented, dedicated go-getters and we embrace their different cultural backgrounds, skills, talents, abilities and experiences. At 84 Lumber Company we understand that diversity brings us many benefits.

INROADS

Accenture

1345 Avenue of the Americas
New York, NY 10105
Phone: (917) 452-4400
www.accenture.com
www.uscareers.accenture.com

Locations

Offices and operations in more than 150
cities in 49 countries.

Diversity Leadership

Erika L. Myrthil
US Entry-Level Diversity Recruiting
Phone: (678) 657-5414
E-mail: erika.l.myrthil@accenture.com

Recruiting

Please list the schools/types of schools at which you recruit.

- Ivy League schools
- Other private schools
- Public state schools
- *Historically black colleges and universities (HBCUs):* Howard, Morehouse, Spelman, FAMU, NC A&T, Prairie View A&M, Clark Atlanta, North Carolina A&T
- *Hispanic serving institutions (HSIs):* UPR - Rio Piedras, UPR - Mayaguez, UPR - Polytechnic

Do you have any special outreach efforts directed to encourage minority students to consider your firm?

- *Hold a reception for minority students:* Diversity-focused open house in Atlanta, New York, Chicago and Washington, D.C., and hold receptions at all our targeted schools
- *Conferences:* Candidate Five Conference, National Black MBA Association, National Society of Black Engineers, National Society of Hispanic MBAs, Out for Work Conference, Reaching Out MBA Conference, Society of Hispanic Professional Engineers, Society of Women Engineers, Women for Hire, Women in Technology
- Advertise in minority student association publication(s)
- *Participate in/host minority student job fair(s):* National Black MBA Association, National Society of Black Engineers, National Society of Hispanic MBAs, Society of Hispanic Professional Engineers, Society of Women Engineers, Women for Hire, Women in Technology.
- Sponsor minority student association events

- Firm's employees participate on career panels at schools
- Outreach to leadership of minority student organizations
- *Scholarships or intern/fellowships for minority students:* Accenture American Indian Scholarship Fund, Accenture Junior and Community College Scholarship, Accenture Scholarship Program for Minorities and the Thurgood Marshall College Fund
- *Other:* Accenture has created several programs aimed at attracting and retaining ethnic minority and women employees, including Accenture's Women's Networking Forum, Student Leadership Conference and the Accenture Student Empowerment Program for female and diverse students.

What activities does the firm undertake to attract minority and women employees?

- *Partner programs with women and minority associations:* Catalyst, INROADS, National Black MBA Association, National Society of Black Engineers, National Society of Hispanic MBAs, Society of Hispanic Professional Engineers, Society of Women Engineers
- *Conferences:* Candidate Five Conference, National Black MBA Association, National Society of Black Engineers, National Society of Hispanic MBAs, Out for Work Conference, Reaching Out MBA Conference, Society of Hispanic Professional Engineers, Society of Women Engineers, Women for Hire, Women in Technology
- *Participate at minority job fairs:* National Black MBA Association, National Society of Black Engineers, National Society of Hispanic MBAs, Society of Hispanic Professional Engineers, Society of Women Engineers, Women for Hire, Women in Technology
- Seek referrals from other employees

• Utilize online job services

• *Other:* Accenture hosts exclusive open house and networking events for ethnic minority, female and GLBT employees.

Do you use executive recruiting/search firms to seek to identify new diversity hires?
Yes

Internships and Co-ops

Accenture Internship Program

Deadline for application: Applications are due in the early winter time frame.

Pay: Accenture offers market-competitive wages for interns.

Length of the program: They last for a period of at least 10 weeks—typically from late May/early June and ending in mid-August/early September.

Percentage of interns/co-ops in the program who receive offers of full-time employment: Approximately 90 to 95 percent of interns receive offers for employment

Web site for internship/co-op information:
campusconnection.accenture.com

Aside from our overall internship program, Accenture has been a strong supporter of INROADS interns since the organization began in 1970 in Chicago, and was one of the original 17 corporate sponsors. We also have a limited number of internships available through the National Action Council for Minorities in Engineering (NACME) and the Accenture On-Campus Internship program. Interesting fact: Accenture partner Andrew Jackson from the Cleveland office was the first inductee into the INROADS Alumni Hall of Fame.

We also provide internship opportunities to students participating in our Accenture Student Empowerment Program.

Intern analysts participate in a variety of roles, including those of an actual full-time analyst. As an intern, you may participate in client or internal engagements with an emphasis on the planning, design and installation of management information systems.

Assignments may include:

• Defining user requirements

• Programming

• Coding and testing applications

• Analyzing, designing and implementing business process improvements

• Project administration

• Researching work on a proposal

• Developing an array of technology-based solutions to improve business performance—from interactive, virtual technologies to object-oriented, client/server and Internet applications

• Developing training and human performance management programs

Additionally, all students interning with us the summer before their rising senior year attend a three-day leadership conference during the summer. The agenda for the conference includes team-building exercises, meeting our executives, diversity presentations, networking opportunities, motivational speakers and a showcase of our clients.

Scholarships

Accenture is committed to providing financial support for a variety of programs at institutions of higher education. We are also very serious about the advancement of minorities. We believe that there are tremendous opportunities for bright, hardworking individuals who wish to apply their skills to the advantage of businesses on a global scale. We also believe that education helps individuals reach their maximum potential.

At Accenture, we have made a commitment to help support meritorious minority students in pursuit of their dreams. That's why we have established a series of scholarship programs:

Accenture Scholarship Program For Minorities

Deadline for application for the scholarship program:
Applications are due in the month of February each year.

Scholarship award amount: Scholarship awards of $2,500 are awarded to outstanding students for undergraduate study.

Web site or other contact information for scholarship:
careers3.accenture.com/Careers/US/DiversityInclusion/Scholarships/Scholarships_Minorities.htm

The Accenture Scholarship Program for Minorities was created to encourage minorities to pursue degrees in engineering, computer science, and a variety of programs related to information systems and decision or management sciences. Scholarships of $2,500 are awarded to outstanding students for undergraduate study. Scholarship recipients are selected solely on merit, based on academic achievement, leadership, participation in school and community activities, work experience, statement of education and career goals, personal essay and an outside appraisal. This scholarship program is administered by Scholarship Management Services, a department of Scholarship America.

Accenture Junior and Community College Scholarship

Deadline for application for the scholarship program:
Applications are due in the month of February each year.

Scholarship award amount: Scholarship awards of $5,000 each

Web site or other contact information for scholarship:
careers3.accenture.com/Careers/US/DiversityInclusion/Scholarships/communitycollege

The Accenture Junior and Community College Scholarship Fund was recently created to support junior and community college students seeking four-year degrees in high technology and business. These scholarships are part of our commitment to providing access to higher education and developing a competitive U.S. workforce.

The scholarship fund will award up to 20 scholarships of $5,000 each, renewable up to one year or until a bachelor's degree is earned. In addition to the scholarship funds, recipients at the junior-year undergraduate level may be eligible for summer internships at Accenture.

Accenture American Indian Scholarship Fund

Deadline for application for the scholarship program:
Applications are due during the May/June time frame each year.

Scholarship award amount: Accenture awards three types of scholarships ranging in amounts of $1,000 to $20,000.

Web site or other contact information for scholarship:
http://careers3.accenture.com/Careers/US/DiversityInclusion/Scholarships/aigc

Accenture awards three types of scholarships to high-achieving American Indian and Alaskan Native students seeking degrees and careers in the professional, teaching, social services, high technology or business fields:

Accenture Scholars: Three undergraduate scholarships of $20,000 each will be awarded to high school seniors pursuing a four-year undergraduate program at a U.S. university or college.

Accenture Fellows: Two graduate scholarships of $15,000 each will be awarded to undergraduate students pursuing an advanced degree at a U.S. accredited university or college.

Finalist Scholarships: Two undergraduate scholarships of $1,000 per year for four years and one graduate scholarship of $2,500 per year for two years will be awarded to candidates for the Accenture Scholars and Fellows scholarships.

In addition to the funding, scholarship recipients are eligible for summer internships with Accenture, as first-year graduate students or junior-year undergraduate students. Applicants are evaluated based on academic excellence, demonstrated leadership ability, commitment to preserving American Indian culture and communi-

ties, and proof of enrollment in a federally recognized American Indian/Alaskan Native tribe.

Thurgood Marshall College Fund

Deadline for application for the scholarship program:
Application deadlines vary.

Scholarship award amount: Accenture awards $2,500 for each semester.

Web site or other contact information for scholarship:
www.thurgoodmarshallfund.org/scholarships/scholarships.htm

Through the Thurgood Marshall College Fund, Accenture awards scholarships directly to students at participating member schools. The Thurgood Marshall College Fund is a 501(c)(3) organization, which provides scholarship money to historically black colleges and universities for the purpose of helping students complete their education.

Affinity Groups

Through a national networking program, Accenture provides the structure and guidance necessary to develop, maintain and grow the following local networking groups in each office location:

• African-American
• American Indian
• Asian-American
• Gay and Lesbian
• Hispanic American/Latino
• Military
• Multicultural
• Women
• Work/Life Strategy

These groups provide individuals who share a common purpose an opportunity to come together to discuss specific issues related to workplace diversity, such as:

• Present members with networking opportunities
• Foster a means for individuals with similar backgrounds to discuss similar challenges and opportunities
• Offer professional direction
• Promote diversity throughout the company
• Support national and local recruiting activities
• Provide employees with heritage packets that highlight various cultural celebrations throughout the year

Accenture currently has 32 U.S. offices with active local office diversity programs. In locations that lack critical mass of the demographic groups above, or where the location does not have formalized interest groups, multicultural groups have been put in place.

Entry-Level Programs, Full-Time Opportunities and Training Programs

Accenture professionals are encouraged to understand the value in differences. Diversity training programs are available to all Accenture employees to raise their awareness of cultural diversity and help them more fully appreciate the differences in everyone.

Here are just some of the diversity training programs Accenture offers:

Appreciating Gender Differences: This three-hour instructor-led course heightens the awareness of gender differences and demonstrates the importance of appreciating and valuing the dynamics between men and women. This helps create an inclusive workplace, which increases team innovation and productivity. The course is available to all U.S. people at Accenture.

Cultural Awareness Guides: These information briefs (available for individual study) provide information to help Accenture employees increase their cultural awareness and provide insight on work styles and behaviors across specific cultures, including appropriate salutations, communications etiquette, preferred modes of communication, meeting styles and respect.

The Diversity Principle: This one-hour course is designed to empower each individual to have a positive impact on Accenture through diversity awareness. Employees learn how they can create a work environment rich in diversity that celebrates the valuable contributions of every team member. The presentation defines diversity at Accenture, establishes diversity as a key company priority and demonstrates how negative stereotypes and related situations can contribute to a nonproductive working environment.

The Diversity Principle In Motion: Presented in a group setting, this workshop takes a further in-depth examination of people's perceptions and behaviors regarding individuals who are different from them. It helps participants recognize inappropriate behaviors related to differences in the workplace and become fully aware of the vehicles in place to address these behaviors, presents Accenture's commitment to the diversity initiatives and makes participants aware of relevant Accenture policies related to diversity.

Accenture also offers other training resources for teams to use at a local or organizational level.

Diversity Ice Breakers are fun, educational activities that teams and communities can use to demonstrate the importance of diversity at Accenture.

Mentoring Toolkit: Accenture has developed a "mentoring toolkit" to help individuals foster their own mentoring relationships on a formal or informal and ongoing basis. These mentoring relationships are in addition to mentoring activities established through our two national programs, the Mentoring Program for Women and the Minority Mentoring Program.

Strategic Plan and Diversity Leadership

How does the firm's leadership communicate the importance of diversity to everyone at the firm?

Accenture communicates regularly with employees on our global inclusion program. Some of the vehicles we leverage are:

• Executive memos

• Internal web site

• Local memos

• U.S.-wide newsletter

• Networking meetings

• Conference calls

Who has primary responsibility for leading diversity initiatives at your firm?

Accenture's chief leadership officer chairs the Accenture Diversity Council and provides global oversight of our inclusion and diversity agenda. At a local level, each of our 13 geographic units has a human capital and diversity lead that is accountable for strengthening our focus on inclusion and diversity at the geographic level.

In the United States, there is also a dedicated diversity recruiting team, which is responsible for recruiting and hiring a diverse workforce. There are recruiters dedicated at the entry and experienced hire levels to ensure we recruit women and minorities across all levels and workforces.

Does your firm currently have a diversity committee?

Yes

If yes, please describe how the committee is structured.

In the United States, Accenture's diversity initiatives are led by three primary groups:

U.S. Diversity Advisory Council: This is a group of leadership partners with representation from several of the operating units and capability groups. The diversity advisory council confirms priorities, helps set strategic direction and takes a leadership role in implementing key initiatives.

U.S. Women's Steering Group: This is comprised of a committee of Accenture female partners. The U.S. women's steering group manages, implements and leads different women's initiatives across the U.S.

Workforce Diversity Leads: Within each of the Accenture entities, there is a lead dedicated to ensuring that diversity is embraced by all Accenture people.

If yes, does the committee's representation include one or more members of the firm's management/executive committee (or the equivalent)?

Yes

Does the committee and/or diversity leader establish and set goals or objectives consistent with management's priorities?

Yes. Accenture's diversity efforts continue to align with the company's top global priorities of engaging senior leadership, improving retention of senior executive women and focusing on the U.S. minority pipeline.

Has the firm undertaken a formal or informal diversity program or set of initiatives aimed at increasing the diversity of the firm?

Yes, formal

Here are some of the key initiatives for this year:

Leading a Diverse Workforce: This is a new program designed for senior executives to focus on the complexities of a global work environment and the actions we can take to promote inclusiveness.

Global Inclusion Advisory Council: To further expand the infrastructure of our global network, we are assembling key senior executives from around the world to serve on an advisory council. The council's mission is to further ensure the integration of global inclusion concepts into each area of our business from both a geographic and operating group perspective.

International Women's Day: Accenture hosts this global women's event on March 8th—universally known as International Women's Day. A series of events around the world brought together thousands of Accenture clients and professionals to focus on the advancement of women in the workforce and included local panels, workshops and a global web cast featuring top women business leaders. The development of women and our commitment to attract, retain and advance them has become part of Accenture's culture and is a key factor in the future success of our organization.

How often does the firm's management review the firm's diversity progress/results?

Quarterly

The Stats

	NUMBER OF EMPLOYEES		REVENUE	
	2007[1]	2006[2]	2006[3]	2005[4]
Total	146,000	133,000	$16.65 billion	$15.55 billion

[1]*Approximately as of Februrary 2007*
[2]*As of July 2006*
[3]*Fiscal year ended Aug. 31, 2006*
[4]*Fiscal year ended Aug. 31, 2005*

Retention and Professional Development

Please identify the specific steps you are taking to reduce the attrition rate of minority and women employees.

• Develop and/or support internal employee affinity groups (e.g., minority or women networks within the firm)

• Increase/improve current work/life programs

• Work with minority and women employees to develop career advancement plans

• Strengthen mentoring program for all employees, including minorities and women

• Professional skills development program, including minority and women employees

Diversity Mission Statement

Accenture is a global management consulting, technology services and outsourcing company. With approximately 146,000 people in 49 countries, we bring together the unique experiences and perspectives of a diverse workforce to deliver cutting-edge technologies and solutions to companies around the world to help them become high-performance businesses. Accenture strives to attract and retain the best people and provide an environment where they can all develop professionally and build a rewarding career. As a result, we have an environment rich in diversity that acknowledges each individual's uniqueness, values his or her skills and contributions, and promotes respect, personal achievement and stewardship. Learn more about our diversity efforts at http://diversity.accenture.com.

Additional Information

Accenture is committed to helping build tomorrow's leaders. We sponsor various workshops and forums for minorities and women to help foster their growth and development. The events also serve as an excellent opportunity for college students of similar backgrounds to get to know each other and learn more about a career in consulting.

Here are three of Accenture's key programs:

Accenture Student Empowerment Program

This three-year program is targeted toward diverse and female rising sophomores with majors in business, computer science and engineering. Participating students will:

• Shadow Accenture personnel for a day at a local office

• Attend networking lunches to help establish a mentoring relationship

• Participate in the End of Year Forum to understand how to meet long-term career goals

• Attend the Leadership Conference the summer following their second mentoring year

• Intern with Accenture for two summers, as rising juniors and rising seniors

• Gain valuable exposure to the business world, explore the consulting career path and understand what companies are looking for

Accenture Student Leadership Conference

This three-day conference is held for a limited number of outstanding seniors at our education center in St. Charles, Ill. (near Chicago). This helps participants further develop and refine leadership skills and experience the same learning environment as full-time employees.

Accenture's Women's Networking Forum

This program is a series of one-day networking events at Accenture local offices for top female students in their junior or senior year. Selected women will attend a one-day event at the local Accenture office closest to their university and:

• Network and build relationships with top Accenture female employees, along with top women from other universities

• Gain valuable exposure to the business world and build leadership skills to use in any business setting

• Get a realistic preview of what it's like to be an Accenture employee

• Explore career paths within Accenture and understand what we are seeking in future employees

• Learn how to successfully overcome challenges women face in the workplace

In 2006, Accenture made *Working Mother* magazine's list of 100 Best Companies for Working Mothers for the fourth consecutive year, ranked as one of 25 notable companies in diversity by *DiversityInc* and was named as a Top 10 Employer for African-Americans by *Black Collegian* magazine.

Aetna Inc.

151 Farmington Avenue
Hartford, CT 06156
Phone: (860) 273-0123
Fax: (860) 273-3971
www.aetna.com

Diversity Recruiting Leadership
Caroline Wilke
University Relations Lead
151 Farmington Avenue, RSAA
Hartford, CT 06156
Phone: (860) 273-7831
Fax: (860) 273-1757
E-mail: college@aetna.com

Recruiting

Please list the schools/types of schools at which you recruit.

- Ivy League schools
- Other private schools
- Public state schools
- Historically black colleges and universities (HBCUs)
- Hispanic serving institutions (HSIs)
- Native American tribal universities
- Other predominantly minority and/or women's colleges

Do you have any special outreach efforts directed to encourage minority students to consider your firm?

- Hold a reception for minority students
- *Conferences:* NSHMBA, ALPFA, NABA, NBMBAA, HACU (Hispanic Association of Colleges and Universities) and TMCF (Thurgood Marshall College Fund)
- Advertise in minority student association publication(s)
- Participate in/host minority student job fair(s)
- Sponsor minority student association events
- Outreach to leadership of minority student organizations

What activities does the firm undertake to attract minority and women employees?

- Partner programs with women and minority associations
- Participate at minority job fairs
- Seek referrals from other employees
- Utilize online job services

Do you use executive recruiting/search firms to seek to identify new diversity hires?

Yes

Internships and Co-ops

Aetna's Summer Internship Program

Deadline for application: We post new dates every year

Number of interns in the program in summer 2006 (internship) or 2006 (co-op): 110 interns, 20 co-ops

Pay: $10 to $18 per hour

Length of the program: 12 to 14 weeks

Web site for internship/co-op information: www.aetna.com/working

Our internship and cooperative education programs give you the practical experience needed to build your resume. You'll be able to use what you've learned in school and apply it to productive work assignments. Our programs offer a great opportunity to use your creativity and fresh viewpoint while exploring career possibilities.

Aetna intern: You can be employed as an intern in a pre-professional assignment throughout the summer (usually late May through early August—the perfect time for college students). Our summer intern program provides students with a depth of experience in functional area assignments, as well as a breadth of experience through company-wide programs including classroom and e-based training, an executive speaker series, social and community service events, and a cross-functional final project.

Aetna co-op: As a co-op student, you'll be employed for a minimum of five months and work at least 20 hours a week. Most co-op students work full time in six month blocks (January through June, or June through December).

How to qualify for a co-op or internship:

- Complete at least 45 semester hours (second semester sophomore)
- Maintain good grades—a 3.0 GPA or above is preferred
- Follow your interests—education or career aspirations in the hiring area is a must

Affinity Groups

The following are a listing of employee networks offered at Aetna.

Aetna African-American Employee Network (AAEN)

Mission: Provide opportunities for our members to develop and enhance their professionalism through programs, workshops and networking opportunities; and develop a strong business partnership between Aetna and AAEN that supports strategic business initiatives.

Aetna Hispanic Network (AHN)

Mission: The Aetna Hispanic Network (AHN) is an inclusive Aetna employee network organized for the purpose of providing professional and career development, and for advocacy in the areas of cultural awareness and community service. The AHN strives to promote Aetna's internal and external business and diversity initiatives while ensuring that its members receive cultural and professional support at Aetna.

Aetna Native-American Employee Network (A-Native)

Mission: To support Aetna's diversity initiatives and also provide support to Native American issues.

Aetna Network of Gay, Lesbian, Bisexual and Transgender Employees (Angle)

Mission: To contribute to Aetna's business and diversity strategies by providing networking support to our members and resources to the corporation.

Aetna Women's Network (AWN)

Mission: To support Aetna's values and diversity initiatives and programs by facilitating professional and personal development and advancement opportunities.

Aetna Working Mothers' Network (AWMN)

Mission: To bring working parents together to help support, develop and retain talent for Aetna.

Asian-American Network (AsiaNet)

Mission: To support Aetna's diversity initiatives and programs, assist Aetna in achieving its goals in the global and Asian-American markets, and assist network members with their personal and career development.

Aetna Teleworker Community Network (TCN)

Mission: To provide a forum for telework employees, and employees who work with teleworkers, to come together to network and provide mutual support, to develop personally and professionally, and to serve as a business resource to the company in support of Aetna's strategic telework business initiative.

Entry-Level Programs, Full-Time Opportunities and Training Programs

Aetna's Actuarial Training Program

Aetna's Actuarial Training Program, which includes a student program and an intern program, provides participants with the experience, training and support necessary to become a future financial leader within the company. The program offers a challenging and supportive environment in which the actuarial student can attain fellowship and grow professionally.

Actuaries are considered the financial engineers and the leading professionals in finding ways to manage risk. They lay the foundation for long-term success by designing and pricing new products, as well as ensuring that existing products are financially sound. They also ensure that the company's reserves are sufficient to meet its future obligations.

What's Required?

• 3.0 GPA or above is desired, with a concentration in actuarial science, mathematics, statistics or economics
• Demonstrated ability to successfully complete actuarial exams
• Strong analytical, critical thinking and communication skills
• Demonstrated leadership and initiative

Aetna Information Services Leadership Development Program

The Aetna Information Services (AIS) Leadership Development Program (LDP) is a three-year, fast-track program whose purpose is to recruit, hire and develop talented new graduates into the future technology leadership at Aetna. This is more than just a job—it's a career path.

LDP participants contribute to a series of challenging projects and technical assignments within Aetna Information Services and other selected Aetna business areas in our Pennsylvania and Connecticut offices. These assignments last approximately eight months each, with one rotation outside the participant's home office location expected.

Rotational stops may include assignments in the following disciplines:

• Infrastructure and networking
• Application development
• IT architecture
• Software testing
• Database management
• Project management
• Strategic planning

LDP participants are trained, coached and evaluated to achieve optimum performance. Participants are assigned a carefully selected career mentor, who provides development opportunities and guidance through career-related experiences. LDP participants also attend formal leadership and skills training and have the opportunity to participate in various networking events and activities. Participants work with the program manager to find the right full-time leadership opportunity within AIS upon completion of the program.

Preferred Qualifications:

• BS or BA in computer science or management information systems, other business majors are also considered

• 3.3 GPA

• Demonstrated strong communication, analytical, team, interpersonal and problem-solving skills

• Previous intern/co-op work experience

The E.E. Cammack Group School Sales Professional Training Program

Aetna is looking for people who want to make a difference. As an Aetna sales professional, you will represent our values and product portfolio to customers and members every day. If you are career-oriented, have strong communication and interpersonal skills and are interested in working with senior decision makers in a dynamic environment, then the E.E. Cammack Group School Training Program can be a bridge to your future.

The E.E. Cammack Group School provides a transition from college to your career. It is a highly selective, fast-track training program that has earned a reputation for producing world-class executives. This intensive program includes classroom and on-the-job learning. In addition, an assigned mentor will support you as you contribute to Aetna's business results.

Group School alumni hold high-profile positions both at Aetna and throughout the industry. Aetna has a commitment to excellence that has existed throughout many generations. Since Group School began in 1924, 100 classes have graduated from this prestigious program. A career at Aetna is strongly rooted in history, with a promising future through innovation and integrity. Be a part of history. Be a part of the future. Be a part of Aetna.

What's Preferred:

• BS or BA

• *Leadership skills:* Demonstrate the ability to lead and influence others

• *Communication skills:* Interact effectively with groups of people at all levels

• *Problem solving:* Focused and skilled at identifying the business problem, identifying options to resolve and is effective at working through complex resolution scenarios

• *Work ethic:* Demonstrate a strong work ethic, sense of urgency and a strong competitive drive; be willing to go the extra mile; take initiative and handle a fast pace

• *Decision making:* Seek out information to support actions and takes responsibility for own actions

• *Teamwork:* Demonstrate the ability to work independently and as part of a team; has strong interpersonal skills that demonstrate approachability and appreciation for others

• *Learning:* Listen and retain key information and translate information to comparable situations; willing to admit knowledge gaps and identify learning opportunities in order to grow quickly; learn complex information quickly and can apply to problem resolution

• *Management of resources:* Use available resources efficiently and is well organized; demonstrate effective time management skills, the ability to handle multiple assignments and a high volume of work

• *Analytical skills:* Able to analyze business processes, assess risk, identify problems, make decisions and use data to support decisions and actions

• *Computer skills:* Use technology to deliver a more effective and efficient service solution

Strategic Plan and Diversity Leadership

How does the firm's leadership communicate the importance of diversity to everyone at the firm?

A combination of e-mails, web site, newsletter, meetings and we have just produced our first annual company-wide diversity report.

Who has primary responsibility for leading diversity initiatives at your firm?

Raymond Arroyo, chief diversity officer, Aetna

Does your firm currently have a diversity committee?

Yes, several. Two high-level companywide committees/boards mentioned below, as well as various diversity councils within business segments.

The Aetna Diversity Board

A senior management group of 18 executives and chaired by our CEO and president to:

• Provide governance, resources and visibility

• Drive actions and increase accountability

• Monitor enterprise-wide program (review workforce representation and supplier diversity progress on quarterly basis)

• Evaluate results and impact

• Report progress during quarterly meetings and to entire organization

Aetna Diversity Alliance

Mission Statement: The Aetna Diversity Alliance is a multidisciplinary team that leverages and integrates each other's resources to maximize Aetna's diversity-related presence and reach, internally and externally. Its goal is to help Aetna earn the distinction, financially and by reputation, of being the preferred benefits company for all of our constituents.

If yes, does the committee's representation include one or more members of the firm's management/executive committee (or the equivalent)?

Yes

How many employees are on the committee?

The Aetna Diversity Board has 18 executive members and the Aetna Diversity Alliance has 23 in a combination of executives and middle management.

Does the committee and/or diversity leader establish and set goals or objectives consistent with management's priorities?

Yes

Has the firm undertaken a formal or informal diversity program or set of initiatives aimed at increasing the diversity of the firm?

Yes, formal

How often does the firm's management review the firm's diversity progress/results?

Quarterly

How is the firm's diversity committee and/or firm management held accountable for achieving results?

Each business segment has diversity milestone objectives appropriate to that business consisting of workforce representation goals, workplace environment and culture, and supplier diversity targets, and is built into the business scorecard. Aetna uses a diversity index to measure inclusive culture through responses to employee survey questions regarding inclusion and supervisory behavior. Scorecard achievements are directly tied to compensation.

The Stats

	NUMBER OF EMPLOYEES		REVENUE	
	2006	2005	2006	2005
Total	30,050	27,677	$25.1 billion	$22.5 billion

Retention and Professional Development

How do 2006 minority and female attrition rates generally compare to those experienced in the prior year period?

About the same as in prior years.

Please identify the specific steps you are taking to reduce the attrition rate of minority and women employees.

• Develop and/or support internal employee affinity groups (e.g., minority or women networks within the firm)

• Increase/review compensation relative to competition

• Increase/improve current work/life programs

• Adopt dispute resolution process

• Succession plan includes emphasis on diversity

• Work with minority and women employees to develop career advancement plans

• Professional skills development program, including minority and women employees

Diversity Mission Statement

Aetna fosters an inclusive work environment through collaboration and partnerships to increase employee engagement, strengthen business relationships, encourage innovation, influence multicultural markets and ultimately enhance our business results.

Additional Information

Diversity is a brand imperative that helps to bring Aetna's health and related benefits to the attention of the fastest-growing segments of the U.S. population—the African-American and Hispanic/Latino markets, as well as the Asian market. In addition, Aetna's ongoing commitment to diversity builds greater competency among Aetna's employees. As a result, diversity is an important element of Aetna's strategic initiatives.

We deliver on Aetna's brand promise by valuing and respecting the strengths and differences among our employees, customers and communities because they reflect our continued future success. Our customers, suppliers and strategic partners are increasingly diverse and multicultural. We must be positioned to understand, interface, relate to and meet their needs. Our challenge is to seek out and use our diversity in ways that bring new and richer perspectives to our jobs and to our business.

We are currently concentrating on the following:

• Recognizing diversity as a business imperative in increasing our business opportunities and partnerships with key external markets, communities and suppliers

• Creating a work environment that engages, enables and empowers people to do their best work

• Focusing specifically on recruitment, retention and development of diverse talent at all levels in the organization

• Establishing and supporting programs that increase the understanding and appreciation of cultural differences through the Aetna Foundation and charitable giving

• Providing diversity education to all employees

Aflac

1932 Wynnton Road
Columbus, GA 31999
Phone: (706) 323-3431
Fax: (706) 660-7253
www.aflac.com

Location

Columbus, GA

Employment Contact
Keyla Cabret
University Relations Coordinator
E-mail: kcabret@aflac.com

Recruiting

Please list the schools/types of schools at which you recruit.

• Private schools

• Public state schools

• Historically black colleges and universities (HBCUs)

Do you have any special outreach efforts directed to encourage minority students and graduates to consider your firm?

• Participate in/host minority student job fair(s) or other minority-focused job events

• Sponsor minority student association events

• Firm's employees participate on career panels at schools

What activities does the firm undertake to attract minority and women employees?

• Seek referrals from other employees

• Utilize online job services

Do you use executive recruiting/search firms to seek to identify new diversity hires?

No

Internships and Co-ops

Aflac Internship/Co-op Program

Number of interns in the program in summer 2006 (internship) or 2006 (co-op): 16 for the internship, seven for the co-op

Pay: $10 to $16 hourly

Length of the program: 10 to 16 weeks

Web site for internship/co-op information: www.aflac.com

Principal Duties and Responsibilities:

• Performs assigned duties, under direction of experienced personnel, to gain knowledge and experience in preparation for a professional opportunity within the information technology, actuarial, sales support and administration, communications, accounting, finance, human resources or other assigned business units.

• Provides assistance on specific projects, including analysis of departmental business practices or procedures, case studies, data analysis, time-defined projects, or ad hoc project of some facet of the industry/department structure or process.

• Receives training and performs duties to become familiar with division functions, operations, management skills or style, and company policies and practices affecting each phase of business; observes experienced workers to acquire knowledge of methods, procedures and standards required for performance of departmental duties.

Education and Experience:

• Must be currently enrolled in a university pursuing a bachelor's or master's degree in the specific field required by the participating division, such as information technology, business administration, accounting, finance, communications, journalism, broadcasting or marketing.

• Minimum 3.0 GPA

The Stats

	NUMBER OF EMPLOYEES		REVENUE	
	2006	2005	2006	2005
Total in the U.S.	4,347	4,208	$4 billion	$3.7 billion
Total outside the U.S.	4,561	3,396	$10.5 billion	$10.4 billion
Total worldwide	8,908	7,604	$14.6 billion	$14.3 billion

Retention and Professional Development

Please identify the specific steps you are taking to reduce the attrition rate of minority and women employees.

• Increase/review compensation relative to competition

• Increase/improve current work/life programs

• Adopt dispute resolution process

• Professional skills development program, including minority and women employees

Diversity Mission Statement

The Aflac Diversity Council develops, supports and implements diversity-related initiatives that help Aflac better achieve its business objectives.

Additional Information

Aflac is continuously making efforts to build stronger relationships with our employees, customers and community. Aflac strives to be an employer of choice, but we also strive to be recognized as a company of inclusion and opportunity. Women make up the majority of the company's entire workforce, accounting for nearly 70 percent of all employees. More than half of the employees in management and close to 30 percent of upper management are women. Minorities make up 42 percent of the company and hold 24 percent of our leadership positions.

Work/life balance and flexibility are avenues that we continue to promote. We have incorporated many family-friendly policies, including flex-time, child care for first and second shifts and telecommuting. We continue to create a corporate culture that encourages the retention and promotion of its female employees.

In support of our corporate diversity initiatives, Aflac's diversity department and the Aflac Diversity Council were formed. The diversity department's primary purpose is to develop and support our diversity strategies. The diversity department also partners with the Diversity Council to host one of its biggest events each year, Celebrate Our Diversity Day. This event helps employees learn about other cultures by sampling food, visiting educational booths and enjoying entertainment from employees around the world.

Aflac created Mentoring Matters in June 2002 to provide additional training and support to minority associates within the sales force. Not only do minority sales associates face the traditional challenges of prospecting and securing business, they also face cultural chal-

lenges that can hinder their success. These challenges may include employers' discriminatory practices, lack of training and lack of document translations into languages other than English. Aflac's multicultural recruiting and market development (MRMD) department reviewed surveys and numerous correspondences from the sales force about their challenges and compiled data from other organizations using benchmarking and primary and secondary research. They discussed findings with divisional and various departmental management. Since the program's inception, African-American associates have increased by approximately 50 percent and Hispanic associates have increased by more than 100 percent. Together, these two minority groups have sold more than $2.6 million in new insurance policies.

Aflac is also taking strides in the small-business sector to offer resources such as our small business web site. Through the web site and other vehicles, we hope to proactively engage and address the specific challenges, concerns and needs of small-business owners nationwide from varying socioeconomic and demographic backgrounds.

Supplier diversity is an extremely important initiative to our organization. Aflac has increased its spending with minority-owned vendors from three million in 2003 to 34 million (9.3 percent of the corporate spend) by year-end 2006. In addition, Aflac hosted "Moving Your Business Forward: The Power of Technology" workshop. The purpose of the workshop was to give small- to medium-sized business owners the opportunity to participate in educational workshops as well as the opportunity to introduce their products and services to an array of potential clients and customers. The workshops also provided the opportunity for them to network and obtain valuable information and instructional tactics from successful entrepreneurs.

Aflac plays a major part in the surrounding communities. Building cross-cultural relationships is key to our success. We have formed an alliance with the Latino Coalition to honor Hispanic contributors with the newly created Aflac Civic Awards. This award identifies and rewards Hispanic small-business owners for their civic contributions and provides support and promotion for causes served by the winning entrepreneurs. In addition, we provide donations to groups involving scholarships for multicultural students, including the Jackie Robinson Foundation, the Thurgood Marshall Scholarship Fund, the NAMIC (National Association for Multi-ethnicity in Communications) and the HBCU (historically black colleges and universities). Major donations have included $1 million contributions to the Martin Luther King, Jr. Memorial Project Foundation and the National Museum of African American History and Culture. We sponsor numerous events and efforts in support of the African-American, Latino, Asian-American and Native American communities to include the Urban League of Greater Columbus, the NAACP and One Columbus, which is an organization that operates a wide variety of programs in the community designed to encourage bridge building through dialogue among individuals and groups using formal and informal techniques.

Our people are our greatest asset. Each one brings a small piece that makes up the success of Aflac. We take care of all of our employees and those employees have taken care of the business for more than 50 years.

Agilent Technologies, Inc.

5301 Stevens Creek Boulevard
Santa Clara, CA 95051
Phone: (408) 345-8830
Fax: (734) 533-6779
www.agilent.com/go/jobs

Locations

US:

Alabama • Arizona • California • Colorado
• Connecticut • Delaware • District of
Columbia • Florida • Illinois • Indiana •
Iowa • Louisiana • Maryland •
Massachusetts • Minnesota • Mississippi
• Missouri • New Jersey • New Mexico •
New York • North Carolina • Ohio •
Oklahoma • Oregon • Pennsylvania •
Tennessee • Texas • Vermont •
Washington • West Virginia • Wisconsin

Asia Pacific:

Australia • China • India • Japan • Korea
• Malaysia • Singapore

Europe:

Belgium • France • Germany •
Netherlands • United Kingdom

Diversity Leadership

Nury Plumley
Diversity Recruiting Program Manager
5301 Stevens Creek Boulevard
Santa Clara, CA 95051
Phone: (408) 345-8830
Fax: (734) 533-6779
E-mail: nury_plumley@agilent.com

Recruiting

Please list the schools/types of schools at which you recruit.

• *Ivy League schools:* Cornell University.

• *Other private schools:* Stanford University, Carnegie Mellon

• *Public state schools:* UC Berkeley, UC Davis, UC Santa Barbara, UC San Francisco, CalPoly, SLO, Colorado State University, University of Colorado at Boulder, Penn State University, University. of Michigan, University. of Illinois, Auburn University, Santa Clara State University, Purdue University, Sonoma State University, University Of Delaware

• *Historically Black Colleges and Universities:* North Carolina A&T State University

• *Hispanic Serving Institutions:* New Mexico State University

Do you have any special outreach efforts directed to encourage minority students to consider your firm?

• *Conferences:* CGSM, SWE, NSBE, SHPE

• Advertise in minority student association publication(s) (sometimes)

• Participate in/host minority student job fair(s)

• Sponsor minority student association events

• Firm's employees participate on career panels at schools

• Outreach to leadership of minority student organizations

• Scholarships or intern/fellowships for minority students

What activities does the firm undertake to attract minority and women employees?

• Partner programs with women and minority associations

• *Conferences:* SWE, WITI

• Participate at minority job fairs

• *Seek referrals from other employees:* Employee Referral Program

• Utilize online job services

Do you use executive recruiting/search firms to seek to identify new diversity hires?

No (very rarely)

Internships and Co-ops

INROADS is one of our sourcing channels for the U.S. internship program. Students from INROADS are incorporated into the companywide internship program.

Agilent Intern Program

Deadline for application: Applications for the U.S. internship program are accepted throughout the year. Most of our offers for internship assignments are presented to candidates during the months of January through May, and often into June.

Number of interns in the program in summer 2006 (internship) or 2006 (co-op): From a reporting standpoint, we do not distinguish the difference between an intern and co-op. In 2006, we had 122 interns.

Pay: Varies by job, level and location.

Length of the program: Varies. Minimum is 10 weeks, although some do go beyond the 10 weeks time frame.

Percentage of interns/co-ops in the program who receive offers of full-time employment: Rate of eligible interns who receive offers from Agilent is approximately 70 percent. Eligible interns are those who are scheduled to graduate and who have received favorable performance evaluations by their managers.

Web site for internship/co-op information:
www.agilent.com/go/jobs

Agilent's U.S. internship program is designed for those who really want to contribute and gain practical experience in their area of interest. The goal of this program is to hire students into regular jobs after graduation. To qualify, a student must:

• Have completed his/her freshman year in college

• Have strong academic achievement in a technical or business curriculum pursuing a BS, BA, MS, MBA or PhD

• Be majoring in:

> Electrical engineering
> Mechanical engineering
> Industrial engineering
> Computer science
> Computer engineering
> Chemical engineering
> Chemistry
> Bioscience
> Materials science
> Physics
> Management information systems
> Computer information systems
> Information technology
> Master's in business administration

Affinity Groups

Asian Employee Network (AEN)—Bay Area

Mission: To help create a company in which all members of a diverse, global workforce can contribute to their highest potential in meeting the business needs of Agilent, its partners and customers. We seek to actively involve Asian-American employees in this ongoing process. AEN has an executive sponsor, an internal web site, and monthly and quarterly events. The group also hosts some events with other similar network groups from other local companies.

Bay Area Women's Network (BAWN)

Mission:

• To exemplify and celebrate the strength, citizenship and diversity of Agilent's women

• To promote professional development and personal/life skills development for Agilent women

• To advocate for the growth and development of women leaders within Agilent

BAWN is an employee network group that works to achieve its mission statement via public forums, video viewings, roundtable discussions, communications programs and attending events of interest together. While we are focused on issues that impact women, our forums provide skills and knowledge development for all Agilent employees. Having men join our organization and participate in our forums encourages an open dialogue and better learning for all. The group has an internal web site and quarterly events.

Black Employee Network Forum (BEF)—Bay Area

Mission:

• To be at the forefront of helping Agilent meet its high-performance, high-growth goals

• To assist Bay Area African-Americans assume leadership roles within Agilent

• To assist Bay Area African-American employees in achieving their personal and professional development goals

• To promote a sense of belonging and unity within the Agilent environment

The BEF has monthly meetings and an executive sponsor.

Gay & Lesbian Employee Network (GLEN)—Sonoma County

Agilent Technologies' GLEN vision is an outgrowth of Agilent Technologies' organizational values and corporate objectives.

Agilent Technologies is a safe and pleasant work environment, free of harassment and discrimination, where all employees, regardless of their sexual orientation, are recognized for their individual achievements, gain a sense of satisfaction and accomplishment, are rewarded and promoted equally, and receive equal opportunities and benefits.

Agilent Technologies is a supportive environment for gay, lesbian, bisexual and transgender employees. At work, they feel comfortable to be open about their sexual orientation, and employees treat their families like they treat all other employees' families.

Glen has quarterly meetings and an executive sponsor.

(East) Indian Employee Network Group (INET)—Bay Area

INET envisions Agilent to be an organization that helps attract and retain a diverse workforce including people from different nations. The employees of Indian origin are organized to:

• Support, develop and grow as members of this organization to achieve their full professional potential.

• Offer a competitive advantage for Agilent through a diverse perspective on future challenges.

• Bring together employees of Indian origin in order to make meaningful contribution to Agilent by increasing knowledge of global and multicultural market place.

• Make Agilent a diverse and a better place to work for everyone.

INET has monthly meetings and occasional forums.

Management of Development and Advancement (MDA)—Sonoma County

Mission: To lead diversity initiatives across all Sonoma County Employee Network Groups and increase management's understanding of diversity as a critical and necessary factor for Agilent's long-term business success. The vision is to achieve strategic alignment and cooperation across all Sonoma County Employee Network Groups and foster an environment where all employees feel valued.

Women's Leadership Development (WLD)—Sonoma County

Mission: To provide a forum that gives women opportunities to practice leadership skills by coordinating various projects such as educating girls about careers in technology and science, professional skills development workshops and resolving workplace issues related to women.

The Physical Informational Emotional (PIE) Networking Group—Colorado

Mission: To provide information and support for all employees, and to help them enhance their physical and emotional capabilities by offering opportunities to:

• Increase functionality, productivity and happiness

• Improve personal development

• Maximize their contributions to Agilent's success

PIE is a great example of a successful grassroots effort. PIE formed in May 1989 as a result of a group of nonmanagement people who felt there was a need for a networking group for employees with physical and/or emotional disabilities.

Diversity is a critical area of focus for Agilent. In partnership with Agilent's Diversity Made Real Program, PIE's goals include informing and supporting all employees experiencing physical and/or emotional limitations.

Others:

• Abilities Network
• La Voz (Hispanic Network Group)
• Native American Employee Network
• Northern Colorado Diversity Team
• Celebrating Our Differences Group
• Spokane Inclusivity Taskforce

Entry-Level Programs, Full-Time Opportunities and Training Programs

Agilent has a yearlong global Next Generation Leadership Program, which has two strategic corporate programs designed to accelerate the readiness of Agilent's leadership pipeline by identifying and developing a pool of top talent capable of managing world-class emerging, growth and mature businesses. Participants in this program are nominated by management and selected by their respective businesses, and as such, the programs are not open for general enrollment.

Programs offered:

• LEAD is a strategic leadership development process designed to accelerate the readiness of high potential operating managers and individual contributors for integrating manager or expanded leadership roles.

• AIM is a strategic leadership development process designed to accelerate the readiness of high potential integrating managers for senior or expanded leadership roles.

Program objectives and benefits: increase leadership effectiveness, gain self and strategic business insights, establish global network, expand circle of influence and develop strategic business skills.

Program components include: 360 degree assessment, workshops, global leadership forums, leadership in action series, coaching, mentoring, networking and business project teamwork.

Both programs feature a proven accelerated development process which provides: 1) opportunities to build leadership skill and confidence in own abilities through involvement in action learning with peers in high potential, cross-functional, cross-business and cross-geographic teams, networking and virtual learning events; 2) a feedback-rich environment based on Agilent's leadership framework; and 3) alignment with a continuous leadership pipeline.

Strategic Plan and Diversity Leadership

How does the firm's leadership communicate the importance of diversity to everyone at the firm?

Agilent has several means to communicate the importance of diversity to everyone at the firm: internal web site, internal newsgram (INFOSPARK), coffee talks, forums, brown bags, employee network group sessions and more.

Who has primary responsibility for leading diversity initiatives at your firm?

We have a diversity council led by the senior VP of HR and one member of the executive team—the senior VP of one of our businesses.

Does your firm currently have a diversity committee?

Yes

If yes, does the committee's representation include one or more members of the firm's management/executive committee (or the equivalent)?

Yes

If yes, how many executives are on the committee?

Total Executives on Committee: Two

Does the committee and/or diversity leader establish and set goals or objectives consistent with management's priorities?

Yes

Has the firm undertaken a formal or informal diversity program or set of initiatives aimed at increasing the diversity of the firm?

Yes, formal and informal. Agilent has, since its inception, included diversity initiatives in its overall staffing plans; currently we are also developing a formal diversity recruiting and sourcing program.

How often does the firm's management review the firm's diversity progress/results?

Monthly—with diversity responsibility.

Quarterly—executives review quarterly.

The Stats

	NUMBER OF EMPLOYEES	
	2006	2005
Total in the U.S.	7,321	8,602
Total outside the U.S.	11,879	12,582
Total worldwide	19,202	21,184

Retention and Professional Development

How do 2006 minority and female attrition rates generally compare to those experienced in the prior year period?

About the same as in prior years.

Please identify the specific steps you are taking to reduce the attrition rate of minority and women employees.

- Develop and/or support internal employee affinity groups (e.g., minority or women networks within the firm)

- Work with minority and women employees to develop career advancement plans (some mentoring)

- Strengthen mentoring program for all employees, including minorities and women

- Professional skills development program, including minority and women employees

Diversity Mission Statement

Harness Global Diversity as Agilent's competitive advantage

At Agilent, we believe that our global competitiveness will be accomplished not only by designing, manufacturing, marketing and selling superior products, but also by leveraging the diversity of our customers, stakeholders, employees and partners all around the world.

Our success is achieved through:

• An environment that enables all to develop and contribute to their full potential

• Leaders that engage, focus, mobilize and leverage all cultures

• Strategies that direct our diverse, collective intelligence to solve urgent business challenges

• Excellent resources and tools that enable our people to excel

• Systems and processes that align and support our vision for success

Additional Information

At Agilent, we recognize the business value of integrating diversity and inclusion into our normal business practices. While we still maintain a distinct Diversity Compliance/AA program, beyond that, diversity and inclusion is everyone's responsibility and thus, you will find aspects of it throughout the company. For example, there is a diversity component in the staffing organization where we work to increase the diversity of our pipeline; there is a diversity component to our corporate affairs activities where we work in diverse communities around the world with our Agilent After School Initiative; and there is a diversity component in our global leadership and learning function where we have tools and resources to help our employees, managers and leaders work more effectively across cultural boundaries. Also, within each business, there is the focus on how to unleash and focus the diverse ideas of all of our global population to contribute to innovation and business success for our company.

A statement from our CEO:

Agilent's inclusive environment and workforce, and our acceptance of diverse ideas, help us achieve global success in several ways: we attract and retain top talent; we create an environment of diversity of thought and insight, which will only improve our ability to be innovative in everything we do. The bottom line is that diversity and inclusion give us a powerful business advantage, and we want to make sure they remain a part of our business philosophy, planning and practice.

– Bill Sullivan, president and CEO

Air Products and Chemicals, Inc.

7201 Hamilton Boulevard
Allentown, PA 18195-1501
Phone: (610) 481-4911
Fax: (610) 481-5900
E-mail: info@airproducts.com

Location

Allentown, PA

Diversity Leadership

Stacy Halliday
Recruiter, Engineering & IT
7201 Hamilton Boulevard
Allentown, PA 18195
E-mail: hallidsb@airproducts.com
www.airproducts.com/careers

Recruiting

Please list the schools/types of schools at which you recruit.

• Ivy League schools

• Other private schools

• Public state schools

Do you have any special outreach efforts directed to encourage minority students to consider your firm?

• Hold a reception for minority students

• *Conferences:* NSBE, SWE, Consortium

• Participate in/host minority student job fair(s)

• Sponsor minority student association events

• Scholarships or intern/fellowships for minority students

What activities does the firm undertake to attract minority and women employees?

• Partner programs with women and minority associations

• Participate at minority job fairs

Do you use executive recruiting/search firms to seek to identify new diversity hires?

No

Internships and Co-ops

INROADS, GEM, Air Products

Deadline for application: Varies based on assignment

Pay: Varies based on experience

Length of the program: 10 to 26 weeks

Percentage of interns/co-ops in the program who receive offers of full-time employment: Approximately 67 percent of the interns who are returning to school for their senior years

Web site for internship/co-op information:
www.airproducts.com/Careers/NorthAmerica/UniversityRecruiting/Co-OpInternProgram.htm

Affinity Groups

Employee networks are part of an overall diversity program intended to make Air Products a more inclusive, creative, responsive and efficient organization—one that recognizes and captures all the potential of its people.

Air Products has six employee networks:

• All Asian-Americans at Air Products Network

• Ethnically Diverse Employee Network

• Gay and Lesbian Empowered Employees

• Hispanic Organization of Latinos and Amigos (HOLA)

• Parents Association

• Women in Business

Web site for more information:

www.airproducts.com/Careers/NorthAmerica/Diversity/EmployeeNetworks.htm

Entry-Level Programs, Full-Time Opportunities and Training Programs

Career Development Program

The Career Development Program (CDP) is a strategic investment in the future of Air Products. Since this program began in 1959, it has provided a steady flow of talent including BS and MS engineers, PhD engineers and scientists, BS and MS information technology

(IT) specialists, and financial and commercial MBAs into our company.

In this program, participants are given an opportunity to develop their skills and interests through various positions in different areas of the company. This normally involves the completion of three different assignments during the first two to three years of employment. Every individual is encouraged to take an active role in influencing his or her career path.

Over the years, many past and current leaders of Air Products, including our current CEO John P. Jones, have joined the company through the Career Development Program. We're looking for people who will help shape the future of Air Products.

Engineering Career Development Program

The Engineering Career Development Program (CDP) is designed for entry-level chemical and mechanical engineers (zero to two years of experience). The program provides entry-level chemical and mechanical engineers with experience in various areas of the company in various types of positions. While in the program, participants are able to develop their engineering and professional skills while achieving a better understanding of their interests and strengths.

The program consists of three rotations that include different locations and assignments with durations of 10 to 12 months. Typical assignments for chemical engineers in the program may include manufacturing, environmental health and safety, operations, process, production, project, research and startup roles. Typical assignments for mechanical engineers in the program may include manufacturing, safety, operations, maintenance, reliability and design roles.

Program Requirements

Academic Record: Air Products hires candidates with outstanding academic records. A baseline GPA is one of the factors we consider, in addition to work experience and activity involvement.

Disciplines: Recent graduates or rising seniors who have received or are pursuing a BS or MS in the following majors will be considered:

- Chemical engineering
- Mechanical engineering

Assignment Descriptions

Air Products offers you a world of engineering opportunities in our Career Development Program (CDP). Numerous engineering positions are available in both our world headquarters in the Lehigh Valley, Penn., area, and in our many field locations throughout the United States. Typical engineering roles are:

- *Design Engineers:* Responsible for the design, analysis, specification and troubleshooting of mechanical equipment for use by various operating groups. Typical equipment items are valves, piping, pressure vessels, heat exchangers and packaged process units. Other specialty items such as blend panels, burners, food freezers and gas cabinets are also within the scope of design engineers.

- *Machinery Engineers:* Involved with the design, application, selection and long-term operation of compressors, turbines, pumps and expanded systems, including auxiliaries such as lubrication and seal systems, heat exchangers, piping, and instrumentation and control systems.

- *Maintenance Engineers:* Provide a variety of support services to our production facilities. Preventive and predictive maintenance programs, troubleshooting, work order systems, planning and scheduling, lubrication programs and work sampling are among their responsibilities.

- *Manufacturing and Operations Engineers:* Involved in all phases of manufacturing and plant operations. Assignments for chemical and mechanical engineers are found in Air Products' maintenance, process, production, project engineering and quality assurance functions. Their assignments are either at our corporate headquarters or domestic plants.

- *Process Engineers:* Responsible for optimum process design and improvement of our facilities. This includes not only the development of a thermodynamically efficient process, but also the economic design of each piece of equipment. Process engineers apply engineering principles to the design, development and operation of chemical and gas separation plants across a wide range of businesses—specialty chemicals, cryogenic air separation, high-temperature process for the production of hydrogen and carbon monoxide, electronic specialty gases (ESG), liquefied natural gas (LNG) and hydrocarbon separation processes.

- *Process Control Engineers:* Ensure that the production plants we build can be monitored and controlled to optimum efficiency. Depending on its size and complexity, a plant may employ a simple PLC (programmable logic controller) or more sophisticated DCS (distributed control system), each of which must be configured to perform appropriate control and monitor display functions. Advanced control applications such as MPC (model predictive control) also fall within their realm of responsibility.

- *Process Systems Engineers:* Responsible for developing P&IDs (process and instrumentation diagrams) that provide the definitive scope of equipment, valves, flowmeters, safety devices, etc., for a new facility. They also ensure that all startup, shutdown and other operational and maintenance requirements are included in the facility's design.

- *Product Development Engineers:* Responsible for the technical, economic and business aspects of new market development from conception through commercialization and, ultimately, to customer acceptance. They become involved in equipment design and testing, process development, economic and market studies, and sales and profit forecasts.

• *Production Engineers:* Responsible for monitoring the production process to ensure sound operation and the efficient use of raw materials and energy. Their work typically includes resolving technical operating problems to minimize production costs and to improve on-stream time.

• *Project Engineers:* Manage and coordinate the efforts of our various engineering groups and other departments in the design and construction of a facility. As a project engineer, you must be both a capable engineer and administrator, using critical path methods and computer cost control as tools in taking the facility or equipment from the contract signing to startup.

• *Project Development Engineers:* Responsible for capital cost estimates and profitability analyses for major capital expenditures. They are involved throughout the project cycle, coordinating all engineering input for the initial bid to the customer, preparing a detailed project budget and managing final execution of the project's cost.

• *Research and Development Engineers:* Support a broad spectrum of research activities, from long-range fundamental programs to more market-driven applied R&D efforts. Significant resources of the company are committed to numerous areas, including cryogenic and noncryogenic gas separation technologies, wastewater treatment, liquid natural gas processing, polymers, industrial and specialty chemicals and environmental controls.

• *Safety Engineers:* Ensure that we are applying the highest degree of technology to maximize safety in the laboratory and field environments. Responsibilities include leading HazOp reviews for specific projects, developing fault trees for safety-relief scenarios and analyzing incidents for root cause failures.

• *Start-up Engineers:* Responsible for the startup and commissioning of all new production facilities. They inspect all equipment, perform operational readiness inspections, commission equipment and conduct performance testing of the entire facility.

The Information Technology Career Development Program

Program Overview

The Information Technology Career Development Program (CDP) is designed for entry-level IT specialists (zero to two years of experience) joining Air Products. The program provides entry-level IT specialists with experience in various areas of the company in various types of positions. While in the program, participants are able to develop their technical and professional skills while achieving a better understanding of their areas of interests and strengths.

The program consists of three rotations that include different assignments with durations of approximately 10 months. Typical assignments for IT specialists in the program may include business process, e-business, infrastructure, data and regional execution services.

Program Requirements

Academic Record: Air Products hires candidates with outstanding academic records. A baseline GPA is one of the factors we consider, in addition to work experience and activity involvement.

Disciplines: Recent graduates or rising seniors who have received or are pursing a BS or MS in the following areas will be considered:

• Computer science
• Computer engineering
• Information systems
• Information technology
• Management sciences and information systems

Assignment Descriptions

Air Products' Global Information Technology Group is dedicated to serving the company's worldwide businesses, and plays a key role in achieving strategic objectives. IT Products and Services cover the spectrum of business functions, allowing participants of the IT Career Development Program to gain a broad knowledge of company activities. Typical roles for IT CDP participants are discussed below.

IT Business Process Services incorporates the application development and support activities for our global gases and chemicals businesses and provides liaison and support to the enterprise business process activities, as well as applied engineering, modeling and computer aided engineering services for engineering. Business process services consists of four primary process groups with three supporting centers of expertise: offering and customer relationship management (CRM), supply chain management (SCM), asset creation and improvement, and enabling processes. The centers of expertise include the ERP/SAP (enterprise resource planning/systems and applications in data processing) program management office, decision sciences and application delivery services across the global IT organization.

E-Business IT Services includes such diverse activities as APDirect, our online ordering system, as well as solutions services, value-added services, web business, business-to-business applications, application technical standards, and systems integrity support and testing —all with a global focus and all aimed at enhancing the way business is done. By understanding the needs and capabilities of its customers, Air Products is creating applications that deliver value, strengthen businesses and ultimately strengthen the industries in which it participates. Several years in a row, Air Products e-business initiatives have been recognized by InternetWeek as one of the top 100 e-business programs in the U.S.

IT Infrastructure Services is responsible for global telecommunications and network services, the service operations center and the client server organizations. Consolidated infrastructure services standardize the desktop, the server environment and mainframe services, and provide focused, rapid advancement in telecommunications and data networks. IT infrastructure services organization provides an ideal opportunity to develop and apply in-depth technical knowledge across a variety of technologies.

IT planning, business relationship, and data services includes the office of the chief information technologist, which is responsible for planning the IT architecture, managing the introduction of new computer technology into Air Products and creating the architecture design for new applications. In addition, this office runs projects to evaluate and introduce step-out computer technology, which has a high potential to deliver business value to Air Products. IT planning, business relationship and data services also includes data resource management services, decision support services; IT strategy development, operational planning, budgeting, and forecasting; IT work portfolio and process management; change management; communications and resource management; and strategic alliance management. Knowledge management services is also a part of this function and addresses the expanding requirements for best practices sharing, team collaboration and self-help through an effective, responsive Intranet.

IT country clusters and regional execution provides development and business analysis resources as well as functional leadership of IT personnel in key global regions, including Asia, Latin America, Eastern Europe and South Africa for all gases, chemicals and corporate functions in those geographies.

Web site for more information:

www.airproducts.com/Careers/NorthAmerica/UniversityRecruiting/WelcomeAndOverview.htm

Strategic Plan and Diversity Leadership

Who has primary responsibility for leading diversity initiatives at your firm?

Victoria Boyd, director of diversity

Does your firm currently have a diversity committee?

Yes

If yes, does the committee's representation include one or more members of the firm's management/executive committee (or the equivalent)?

Yes

Does the committee and/or diversity leader establish and set goals or objectives consistent with management's priorities?

Yes

Has the firm undertaken a formal or informal diversity program or set of initiatives aimed at increasing the diversity of the firm?

Yes, formal

How often does the firm's management review the firm's diversity progress/results?

Quarterly

The Stats

	NUMBER OF EMPLOYEES		REVENUE	
	2006	2005	2006	2005
Total	20,700	N/A	$8.9 billion	N/A

Allergan

Employment Contact
www.allergan.com/site/careers

Recruiting

Please list the schools/types of schools at which you recruit.

Public state schools: UCI, UCLA, UCSD, CSULG, CSUF, Pepperdine

Do you have any special outreach efforts directed to encourage minority students to consider your firm?

Other: Via the on-campus college minority clubs/groups.

What activities does the firm undertake to attract minority and women employees?

Utilize online job services

Do you use executive recruiting/search firms to seek to identify new diversity hires?

Yes

Strategic Plan and Diversity Leadership

Who has primary responsibility for leading diversity initiatives at your firm?

Alice White, senior director HR

Does your firm currently have a diversity committee?

No

Does the committee and/or diversity leader establish and set goals or objectives consistent with management's priorities?

Yes

Has the firm undertaken a formal or informal diversity program or set of initiatives aimed at increasing the diversity of the firm?

Yes, informal

How often does the firm's management review the firm's diversity progress/results?

Twice a year

Retention and Professional Development

Please identify the specific steps you are taking to reduce the attrition rate of minority and women employees.

• Increase/review compensation relative to competition
• Increase/improve current work/life programs

Allstate Insurance Company

<table>
<tr><td>

2775 Sanders Road
Northbrook, IL 60062
www.allstate.com

Locations
Nationwide

</td><td>

Employment Contact
Rodney Daniels
2775 Sanders Road, Suite A1
Northbrook, IL 60062
E-mail: rdaniels@allstate.com
Phone: (847) 402-6829

</td></tr>
</table>

Recruiting

Please list the schools/types of schools at which you recruit.

• Ivy League schools

• Other private schools

• Public state schools

• Historically black colleges and universities (HBCUs)

• Hispanic Serving Institutions (HSIs)

Do you have any special outreach efforts directed to encourage minority students to consider your firm?

• Advertise in minority student association publication(s)

• Participate in/host minority student job fair(s)

• Sponsor minority student association events

• Firm's employees participate on career panels at schools

What activities does the firm undertake to attract minority and women employees?

• Partner programs with women and minority associations

• Participate at minority job fairs

• Seek referrals from other employees

Do you use executive recruiting/search firms to seek to identify new diversity hires?

Yes

Internships and Co-ops

Allstate Internship Program

Deadline for application: Rolling

Number of interns in the program in summer 2006 (internship) or 2006 (co-op): 108 interns

Pay: Weekly

Length of the program: 12 weeks

Percentage of interns/co-ops in the program who receive offers of full-time employment: 25 percent

Web site for internship/co-op information: www.allstate.jobs

Scholarships

Education Support Programs

Allstate continues to see excellent results through its partnership with the ConSern Education Program. This program assists employees or members of their families with securing educational funding for private (K-12), undergraduate and professional education.

In 2005, 3,191 employees used the ConSern program for education loans or assistance, receiving $140,446 in the form of educational loans. Also, the program had awarded free scholarships to four of our employees.

Entry-Level Programs, Full-Time Opportunities and Training Programs

Learning and Development

A high-performance work environment requires continuous learning. Allstate invested more than $14.8 million in 2006, helping employees cultivate new skills leading to new job opportunities through a variety of programs:

The Learning Resource Network (LRN): An e-learning platform for interpersonal, technical and leadership development courses—available 24/7 at virtually every employee's workstation. The LRN total usage for 2006 was 1,297,941 hours with over 568,000 courses completed.

Professional education programs that offer industry and professional designations as well as tuition reimbursement for undergraduate and graduate degree programs.

On site open enrollment undergraduate and MBA programs at the corporate headquarters in Northbrook, as well as online undergraduate and graduate degree programs supported by tuition reimbursement and available to all eligible employees through the University of Phoenix.

Workshops

The other 50 percent of Allstate's job-related education is accounted by instructor-led workshops. In addition to its corporate headquarters, instructional facilities are located in all regional offices, call centers, processing centers and other facilities. Allstate facilitators, as well as outside vendors, in order to provide a full range of topic coverage and a variety of viewpoints within the workshops.

Strategic Plan and Diversity Leadership

How does the firm's leadership communicate the importance of diversity to everyone at the firm?

For Allstate's corporate culture, a commitment to communication is fundamental, and it begins at the top. Edward M. Liddy, Allstate chairman and CEO, describes a deceptively simple modus operandi: "At Allstate, we invest in truthful communication in a multitude of ways, through our people and through our processes. The result is a culture in which people are free to express their opinions, challenge the status quo and help guide the company with a sound moral compass."

Mr. Liddy believes that open, honest, two-way communication is the bedrock of ethical standards. "How much time you invest in communication is equally important," he notes. "An independent study showed that Allstate annually devotes an estimated two million man-hours to communication in all forms—face-to-face, electronic and print. These hours not only reflect corporate and departmental communications, but also local communication efforts throughout the company by individual units and offices that dedicate resources to communication."

Methods of Communicating Diversity Issues

The flow of information from Allstate's senior management to all employees is ongoing, and it is accomplished through a multitude of vehicles and media:

• Quarterly communication meetings hosted by Mr. Liddy.

• Town hall meetings conducted by Mr. Liddy and fellow senior leaders.

• *Allstate NOW:* This popular company communications vehicle has been published continually since the 1970s, and is now an online publication directed to all employees and agents. *Allstate NOW* features news, information and interviews designed to inform and align employees and agencies behind company strategies and key

initiatives, and also to foster pride in working for Allstate. The site recorded more than 1.2 million visits in 2004, which attests to its popularity and value as a communications source.

• "Helping Hands" volunteer opportunities: This ongoing schedule of events is posted prominently near each cafeteria.

• *Broadcast Bulletins:* From weekly *Allstate NOW* broadcast e-mails—providing employees with updates on everything from company and industry news, upcoming programs, events and volunteer opportunities—to voice mail broadcasts communicating messages around safety security and stability, Allstate believes in using all mediums to communicate thoroughly, honestly and frequently with employees.

Intranet web site

Company management and department leaders disseminate information on an ongoing basis via departmental/group meetings, e-mail and video messages, memoranda and publication articles.

External company communications: These include press releases and media/trade publication articles, as well as speeches delivered by company leaders to a variety of audiences.

Mr. Liddy is convinced of the value of employee communications in fostering understanding, enthusiasm and a sense of belonging. "I believe that when employees are well informed and understand the business and their roles," he notes, "it shows in their performance—and in their commitment to the company and its standards."

Mr. Liddy is a champion for diversity and uses all of the above venues to discuss the importance of diversity and work/life.

Who has primary responsibility for leading diversity initiatives at your firm?

Anise Wiley-Little, AVP and chief diversity officer

Does your firm currently have a diversity committee?

Yes, Allstate currently has a diversity committee. In 2005, Allstate formed a Corporate Diversity Council to further expand on the company's commitment and great strides with regard to diversity and to ensure that Allstate continues to meet the changing demographic needs of both customers and employees.

The diversity council will strive to assess all the diversity initiatives throughout the company with a futuristic focus on three long-term initiatives that will strengthen our unified approach to diversity and the measurement behind it.

Allstate also has a diversity and work/life team dedicated to improving diversity and work/life, meeting affirmative action goals, ergonomics, equal pay and external recognition. The team is comprised of six full-time staff members reporting in to a director.

INROADS®

If yes, does the committee's representation include one or more members of the firm's management/executive committee (or the equivalent)?

Yes, the committee's representation does include one or more members of the firm's management/executive committee (or the equivalent). The diversity council consists of 14 senior-level decision-makers—including representatives from the diversity team, supplier diversity, marketing, corporate relations, selection and leadership—dedicated to integrating diversity within Allstate business strategy. Chairman and CEO Ed Liddy is the executive sponsor of the council.

Does the committee and/or diversity leader establish and set goals or objectives consistent with management's priorities?

Yes. The mission of the Corporate Diversity Council is to identify, recommend and champion the implementation of strategies and initiatives to effectively drive high performance for all, maximizing productivity of Allstate's workforce. At Allstate, managing diversity is a strategy for leveraging differences in the workplace and marketplace to gain a competitive advantage.

Has the firm undertaken a formal or informal diversity program or set of initiatives aimed at increasing the diversity of the firm?

The firm has undertaken a formal diversity program or set of initiatives aimed at increasing its diversity.

For many years, Allstate has been a recognized diversity leader in the marketplace and in the workplace. The company's diversity strategy has proven to be a sound business practice that has contributed to Allstate's growth and profitability goals.

A core component of the diversity strategy at Allstate continues to be effective education for all employees. Since its inception, the diversity education program has reached more than 40,000 employees delivering a message that focuses on inclusion and managing personal behavior in order to maximize performance.

In 2003, Allstate introduced a new diversity curriculum that includes updated material and a new format utilizing classroom and online training. This training is called Diversity—Allstate's Competitive Edge (ACE) and it is required for all employees. In 2005, 2,347 employees completed this training.

In 2004, Allstate rolled out a new leader's diversity training curriculum, Creating an Environment for Success. This facilitated workshop is required for new managers with direct reports. As part of Allstate's diversity initiative, workshop participants develop specific actions to increase their effectiveness through self-assessment, shared best practices, and an increased understanding of the importance of differences and their implications on management/leadership style. This course is also available as an optional refresher for existing managers with direct reports who have previously completed other diversity training. In 2005, 260 participants completed this course.

Additionally in 2005, 651 employees completed the diversity and work/life course on the learning resource network (LRN) as a part of the Allstate management curriculum.

A diversity video is also used in training. In this video, Ed Liddy, chairman, president and CEO; Tom Wilson, president, Allstate Protection; and Casey Sylla, president, Allstate Financial, share their vision of diversity.

How often does the firm's management review the firm's diversity progress/results?

The firm's management reviews the firm's diversity progress/results annually.

How is the firm's diversity committee and/or firm management held accountable for achieving results?

Measurement is a key to understanding the overall effectiveness of our diversity and work/life strategy.

In 2004, we launched a new employee retention survey to help us better understand the factors that engage and retain our employees. Its purpose is to collect and centrally retain data from existing employees about what impacts their decision to join, stay or leave the company. The survey, which is available on the Internet, is conducted with new employees at 90 days and at the one-, three- and five-year anniversary dates—points in time that are high risk for turnover.

Allstate conducts workforce assessments on an annual basis for all its major business units/shared service areas to provide leadership with information to aid in making decisions regarding human capital strategies. The assessments include information on new hires, turnover and performance ratings, as well as a summary of survey results. Assessment data is analyzed for differences by demographics, such as gender, ethnicity, job level, age and tenure.

Allstate also has an enhanced employee feedback system that includes an annual survey (QLMS—Quality, Leadership, Measurement System) to collect data on the work environment and the effectiveness of leadership. The data helps us to shape leadership actions and enhance existing programs.

Beginning in 2001, we included questions in the survey to assess the impact of elder care on our employee population. Survey results indicate this is a growing area of concern for employees. Our ongoing strategy is to ask a random sampling of diversity and work/life questions to continue to assess the issues and challenges faced by employees.

Retention and Professional Development

Please identify the specific steps you are taking to reduce the attrition rate of minority and women employees.

• Develop and/or support internal employee affinity groups (e.g., minority or women networks within the firm)

• Increase/review compensation relative to competition

• Increase/improve current work/life programs

• Adopt dispute resolution process

• Succession plan includes emphasis on diversity

• Work with minority and women employees to develop career advancement plans

• Review work assignments and hours billed to key client matters to make sure minority and women

• Strengthen mentoring program for all employees, including minorities and women

• Professional skills development program, including minority and women employees

Diversity Mission Statement

The diversity, inclusion and work/life team partners with business clients to create an effective work environment to drive a high performance culture that enables higher productivity, higher morale, more innovation and risk taking, and a better work environment. Our policies, procedures, programs and interventions are designed to promote inclusion, work/life balance, dignity and respect, commitment to affirmative action and leveraging differences to maximize innovation and creativity.

American Airlines, Inc.

4333 Amon Carter Boulevard
Fort Worth, TX 76155
Phone: (817) 963-1234
www.aacareers.com

Locations
Dallas/Fort Worth, TX (HQ)

Recruiting

Please list the schools/types of schools at which you recruit.

- Ivy League schools
- Other private schools
- Public state schools
- Historically black colleges and universities (HBCUs)
- Hispanic Serving Institutions (HSIs)

Do you have any special outreach efforts directed to encourage minority students to consider your firm?

- *Conferences:* NSHMBA, NBMBAA, SHPE, NSBE, BDPA, ALPFA, NABA
- Participate in/host minority student job fair(s)
- Sponsor minority student association events
- Firm's employees participate on career panels at school
- Outreach to leadership of minority student organizations
- *Other:* INROADS

What activities does the firm undertake to attract minority and women employees?

- Partner programs with women and minority associations
- *Conferences:* WAI, NAWMBA
- Participate at minority job fairs
- Seek referrals from other employees

Do you use executive recruiting/search firms to seek to identify new diversity hires?

No

Internships and Co-ops

- INROADS
- Monster DLP

Affinity Groups

- African-American Employee Resource Group
- Asian Cultural Association
- Caribbean Employees
- Christian Resource Group
- Employees with Disabilities
- Gay, Lesbian, Transgender and Bisexual Employees
- Indian Employees
- Jewish Resource Group
- Latin Employee Resource Group
- Muslim Resource Group
- Native American Employee Resource Group
- Women in AAviation
- Work and Family Balance
- 40 Plus/Senior Employees

Strategic Plan and Diversity Leadership

How does the firm's leadership communicate the importance of diversity to everyone at the firm?

American Airlines communicates diversity initiatives through e-mails, the firm web site, newsletters and meetings.

Who has primary responsibility for leading diversity initiatives at your firm?

Debra Hunter Johnson, VP, diversity and corporate leadership

Does your firm currently have a diversity committee?

Yes

If yes, please describe how the committee is structured, how often it meets, etc.

Employee Resource Group (ERG) leadership and executive officers

If yes, does the committee's representation include one or more members of the firm's management/executive committee (or the equivalent)?

Yes

How many employees are on the committee?

There is one employee for each ERG.

Total Executives on Committee: 14

Does the committee and/or diversity leader establish and set goals or objectives consistent with management's priorities?

Yes

Retention and Professional Development

Please identify the specific steps you are taking to reduce the attrition rate of minority and women employees.

• Develop and/or support internal employee affinity groups (e.g., minority or women networks within the firm)

• Increase/improve current work/life programs

• Succession plan includes emphasis on diversity

Diversity Mission Statement

At American, we are committed to diversity. With diversity comes opportunities for success which is good for our employees, our customers, our communities, and ultimately our business. We also do more than state our commitment to diversity. Our commitment is displayed in numerous ways and frequently sets the standard for other companies. Our many achievements include:

• Top diversity employer

• First major commercial airline to hire a female pilot

• First U.S. airline to provide a Spanish and Portuguese language onboard magazine, *Nexos*

• First airline to create a targeted sales team focused specifically on ethnic and GLBT markets

• Award winning diversified supplier program

• Ongoing employee and company involvement in diverse community affairs and charitable organizations

• 14 ERGs and diversity advisory council that take an active role in business solutions

• ERGs are an important part of AMR's efforts to foster an inclusive work environment. Through our ERGs, we've created opportunities for employees to have a voice in business, support each other and share their unique perspectives, cultures and experiences with employees.

Together, we create the team that delivers the best air travel service in the world. Our employees are proud to be American Airlines.

American Cancer Society

1599 Clifton Road
Atlanta, GA 30329
www.cancer.org

Locations

All 50 states and Washington, DC

Diversity Leadership

Ree Stanley
Chief Diversity Officer

Employment Contact

Recruitment Department
1599 Clifton Road
Atlanta, GA 30329
Phone: (404) 320-3333
Fax: (404) 982-3677
E-mail: acs.jobs3@cancer.org

Recruiting

Please list the schools at which your firm recruits.

• Ivy League schools
• Other private schools
• Public state schools
• Historically black colleges and universities (HBCUs)
• Hispanic serving institutions (HSIs)
• Native American tribal universities
• Other predominantly minority and/or women's colleges

Do you have any special outreach efforts directed to encourage minority students to consider your firm?

• *Conferences:* NAACP, NUL
• Participate in/host minority student job fair(s)

What activities does the firm undertake to attract minority and women employees?

• *Conferences:* NAACP, NUL
• Participate at minority job fairs
• Seek referrals from other employees
• Utilize online job services
• *Other:* Advertise in diversity magazines

Do you use executive recruiting/search firms to seek to identify new diversity hires?

No

Internships and Co-ops

Various internships are available at the American Cancer Society.

Entry-Level Programs, Full-Time Opportunities and Training Programs

Various full-time opportunities available nationwide

Strategic Plan and Diversity Leadership

Who has primary responsibility for leading diversity initiatives at your firm?

Ree Stanley, chief diversity officer

Does your firm currently have a diversity committee?

Yes

If yes, please describe how the committee is structured, how often it meets, etc.

We have 13 divisions and one HR representative from each division meets quarterly to discuss initiatives and progress with COO of organization.

If yes, does the committee's representation include one or more members of the firm's management/executive committee (or the equivalent)?

Yes

Does the committee and/or diversity leader establish and set goals or objectives consistent with management's priorities?

Yes. We have a diversity staff of five employees whose focus is on diversity strategies in employment, in volunteerism and in communicating our message to diverse populations.

Has the firm undertaken a formal or informal diversity program or set of initiatives aimed at increasing the diversity of the firm?

Yes, formal

How often does the firm's management review the firm's diversity progress/results?

Quarterly

How is the firm's diversity committee and/or firm management held accountable for achieving results?

Diversity initiatives are part of every VP's performance objectives.

The Stats

	NUMBER OF EMPLOYEES
	2005
Total in the U.S.	7,000
Total worldwide	7,000

Retention and Professional Development

Please identify the specific steps you are taking to reduce the attrition rate of minority and women employees.

• Increase/improve current work/life programs

• Adopt dispute resolution process

• Succession plan includes emphasis on diversity

• Strengthen mentoring program for all employees, including minorities and women

• Professional skills development program, including minority and women employees

Diversity Mission Statement

We know too well that cancer does not discriminate. It reaches across all populations to claim thousands of diverse lives each year. This unequivocal truth is the compass that guides our fight against cancer. To continue making progress toward our goals, we must have a professional and volunteer staff as diverse as the millions of people who are touched by cancer each year.

The American Cancer Society is committed to waging war against the disease. Through research, education, advocacy and service, we are winning battles and saving lives. Our volunteers, staff and supporters make every victory possible—by discovering scientific breakthroughs, by building public awareness and educating the public, by raising money to support the services we provide to thousands of cancer patients and survivors, and by ensuring that cancer is a top priority with our nation's lawmakers.

Our ability to value each other's differences is vital to our mission. At the heart of the Society's diversity plan is the belief that we can meet our organizational goals if we leverage diversity as an organizational resource. Creating an inclusive environment where all people are appreciated and have opportunities to learn will prepare our greatest asset—our people—to continue meeting and exceeding our lifesaving goals in the future.

American Electric Power (AEP)

1 Riverside Plaza
Columbus, OH 43215
Phone: (614) 716-1000
Fax: (614) 716-1823

Locations

Arkansas • Indiana • Kentucky •
Louisiana • Michigan • Ohio • Oklahoma •
Tennessee • Texas • Virginia • West
Virginia

Diversity Leadership

Mary Cofer
Director, Diversity/Culture

Employment Contact

Peggy Sibila Buck
Senior College Relations Coordinator
1 Riverside Plaza
Columbus, OH 43215
Phone: (614) 716-1856
Fax: (614) 716-4800
E-mail: psbuck@AEP.com
www.AEP.com/careers

Recruiting

Please list the schools/types of schools at which you recruit.
• Private schools
• Public state schools
• Historically black colleges and universities (HBCUs)
• Hispanic serving institutions (HSIs)
• Other predominantly minority and/or women's colleges

Do you have any special outreach efforts directed to encourage minority students to consider your firm?
• *Conferences:* Black Engineer of the Year, AABE, NSBE, etc.
• Participate in/host minority student job fair(s)
• Sponsor minority student association events
• Firm's employees participate on career panels at school
• Outreach to leadership of minority student organizations
• Scholarships or intern/fellowships for minority students

What activities does the firm undertake to attract minority and women employees?
• Partner programs with women and minority associations
• Conferences
• Participate at minority job fairs
• Seek referrals from other employees
• Utilize online job services

Do you use executive recruiting/search firms to seek to identify new diversity hires?
Yes

Internships and Co-ops

Length of the program: 12 weeks

Percentage of interns/co-ops in the program who receive offers of full-time employment: 25 to 85 percent

Web site for internship/co-op information: www.AEP.com/careers

Co-op Requirements:

• Students be in their sophomore year at college (a minimum of 50 credit hours) and preferably have completed at least one core class
• Are available to co-op for a minimum of two nonconsecutive terms
• Are willing to rotate to different work sites to expand knowledge and experience with differing projects
• 3.0 GPA or better preferred
• Preferably U.S. citizens or permanent residents

Internship Requirement:

• Students be in their junior or senior year of college
• Work one or two sessions, typically only during the summer
• 3.0 GPA or better preferred
• Preferably U.S. citizens or permanent residents

Scholarships

AEP scholarships are awarded annually on a competitive basis to children of AEP employees who are high school seniors planning to pursue a baccalaureate degree. AEP does not offer college scholarships to our customers or their children. However, AEP does have a long history of support for K-12 education, as well as for colleges and univer-

sities, including grants for teachers and workshops. Read more about it on our web site at www.aep.com under the "About Us" tab.

Entry-Level Programs, Full-Time Opportunities and Training Programs

(Full-time) Associates (MBA)

Requirements:

- MBA graduates
- Prefer one to five years of related experience
- Are willing to rotate to different work assignments for a more complete understanding of the business for a duration of approximately one to two years

(Full-time) Associates (Engineering)

Requirements:

- Hold a bachelor's degree in engineering from an ABET accredited school/program
- Prefer one to three years of related experience
- Are willing to rotate to different work assignments for a more complete understanding of the business for a duration of approximately one to two years

(Full-time) Analysts

Requirements:

- Must have completed their undergraduate degree in a business-related area
- Prefer one to three years of related experience
- Are willing to rotate to different work assignments for a more complete understanding of the business for a duration of approximately one to two years

Strategic Plan and Diversity Leadership

How does the firm's leadership communicate the importance of diversity to everyone at the firm?

The firm communicates diversity information through e-mails, the company web site, newsletters, meetings and mandatory training.

Who has primary responsibility for leading diversity initiatives at your firm?

Mary Cofer, director personnel services and EEO. (Please contact her for diversity-related specifics.)

Does your firm currently have a diversity committee?

Yes

Diversity Mission Statement

AEP is committed to providing and fostering an inclusive business environment that leverages the unique talents, perspectives and experiences of each employee.

Additional Information

Our Commitment to Diversity

Like fingerprints, every human being is different. Beyond obvious differences such as race, gender, age, height and weight, there are more subtle dissimilarities: personality, motivation, education, work ethic and goals.

At AEP, we recognize and respect the differences among those who contribute to the success of our company: our investors, our shareholders, our customers and our employees. We know that together, we make up one great organization—a company that produces a product that allows each and every one of us to pursue success in life, in business and in everything that we do.

Recently, we launched a series of diversity initiatives under the theme Everyone Counts. These initiatives are ongoing and dedicated to the philosophy that each of us has something valuable to contribute to the good of the organization. We encourage different points of view, all working together toward AEP's common goals. We value unique thinking within the context of teamwork.

We understand that to truly succeed, all of us must stretch beyond our own personal comfort zones of the familiar and embrace the similarities and differences of others who contribute to the success of our company.

American Express Company

200 Vesey Street
Mail Drop 01-35-01
New York, NY 10285
www.americanexpress.com

Diversity Leadership

Linda S. Hassan
Director, Diverse Talent Acquisition
200 Vesey Street
Mail Drop 01-35-01
New York, NY 10285
www.americanexpress.com/diversity

Crystal E. Hunt
Diversity Recruiter, Diverse Talent Acquisition
200 Vesey Street
Mail Drop 01-35-01
New York, NY 10285
www.americanexpress.com/diversity

Recruiting

Please list the schools/types of schools at which you recruit

• Ivy League schools
• Other private schools
• Public state schools
• *Historically black colleges and universities (HBCUs):* Clark Atlanta University, Morehouse College, Spelman, Howard University
• Other predominantly minority and/or women's colleges

Do you have any special outreach efforts directed to encourage minority students to consider your firm?

• *Conferences:* National Black MBA Association, National Society of Hispanic MBAs, National Association of Black Accountants, National Association of Asian American Professionals
• Advertise in minority student association publication(s)
• Participate in/host minority student career fair(s)
• Sponsor minority student association events
• Firm's employees participate on career panels at school
• Outreach to leadership of minority student organizations
• Scholarships or intern/fellowships for minority students
• Host targeted reception to minority student groups

What activities does the firm undertake to attract minority and women employees?

• Partner programs with women and minority associations
• *Conferences:* Please see conferences listed above
• Participate at minority job fairs

• Seek referrals from other employees through employee referral program
• Utilize online job services

Do you use executive recruiting/search firms to seek to identify new diversity hires?

No, not for entry-level roles.

Internships and Co-ops

Summer Internship Program

Length of the program: 10 to 12 weeks

Percentage of interns/co-ops in the program who receive offers of full-time employment: Varies year to year, on average 85 to 90 percent.

Web site for internship/co-op information: www.americanexpress.com/campus

Marketing BA summer interns at American Express are responsible for contributing to strategy development and value-added benefits for targeted customer segments including both current and prospective customers. Focus may include new customer segments as well as established customer bases.

Individuals have specific goals that directly support key business unit metrics and have the authority and accountability to manage critical projects that drive results for both our customers and shareholders.

American Express is a leader in the financial services arena and is considered one of the premier marketing companies. With over 150 years of history, the Amex blue box is one of the most recognizable logos in the world. The American Express Campus Internship Program is best in class and offers a realistic job preview, project ownership, opportunity to impact the bottom line, exposure to executives, networking and fun!

Potential Responsibilities

• Support American Express' strategic relationship with service establishments and/or partners

• Assist in the conceptualization of creative marketing strategies and campaigns

• Demonstrate strategic thought leadership to drive results and maintain the integrity of the Amex brand

• Increase profitability and success of business through effective, targeted marketing strategies

• Identify new and underserved market segments to drive business growth

• Manage analytics associated with evaluating cost/benefit and profitability of marketing initiatives, establishing appropriate metrics for success and demonstrating results

• Work with cross-functional partners to leverage organizational synergies to execute programs from concept through launch

Relevant Background

• Undergraduate degree, marketing or business concentration helpful

• Experience in consulting, marketing, business analysis, or general management

• Experience in one of our target industries (charge/credit card, finance, retail, travel, services, interactive) which can be utilized in the development of strategy

• Full lifecycle project management experience

Valued Skills

• Strong customer focus and fully developed project management skills

• Ability to conceptualize and sell ideas internally

• Strong negotiation, communication and presentation skills

• Team player/individual contributor with a desire to function in a flexible, changing environment

• Strong analytics

• Demonstrated ability to drive results

Affinity Groups

• AHORA—Hispanic Employee Network

• EWEX Exchange—Asian Employee Network

• BEN—Black Employee Network

• CHAI—Jewish Employee Network

• DAN—Disabilities Awareness Network

• PRIDE—Gay, Lesbian, Bisexual and Transgender Employee Network

• NATION—Native American, Tribal and Indigenous Organizational Network

• PEACE—Muslim Employee Network

• Passages—Employees Over 40 Network

• SALT—Christian Employee Network

• WIN—Women's Interest Network

In support of American Express' corporate policy "to establish a work environment that encourages and supports each person to reach his or her full potential—regardless of any nonwork related factor such as age, race, gender, sexual orientation, religion, disabilities or other differences," 49 employee network chapters have been formed within the company. They are initiated and driven by employees. While separately they may each represent a different segment of the population, they all share common goals. The intent of employee networks is not to highlight differences but to enlighten and make us more sensitive to the unique workplace issues confronting persons of different backgrounds. It is for this reason that networks must be open to all employees so that the knowledge of each group can be shared with all colleagues.

Employee networks sponsor programs that enhance professional and personal growth. Participants engage in educational activities, including job fairs and cultural events; act as liaisons to management and to the community; participate in outreach and volunteer programs; support employee recruitment and retention initiatives; and enhance marketing efforts in targeted communities. Participation in networks also offers employees a supportive environment in which to expand their skills and develop leadership capabilities.

Entry-Level Programs, Full-Time Opportunities and Training Programs

Full-Time Opportunities: Marketing

Training Programs: Global Finance Undergraduate Development Program

Geographic location(s) of program: Marketing—New York only; finance—New York, Phoenix, Salt Lake City

We look at our campus hires as future leaders within the organization. Professional development and training are critical to achieving these goals. Marketing analysts create a development plan and work with

their leader to participate in a number of training and development courses, including valuing diversity and practicing inclusion, personal presence, situational self leadership and project management. In addition to the course listed above, participants in the Global Finance Development Program take classes to enhance their accounting, audit and analytical skills.

Strategic Plan and Diversity Leadership

How does the firm's leadership communicate the importance of diversity to everyone at the firm?

American Express leadership communicates the importance of diversity via corporate communications, company Intranet, web site, meetings, new hire orientation and training programs.

Who has primary responsibility for leading diversity initiatives at your firm?

Melinda Wolfe, SVP and chief diversity officer

Does your firm currently have a diversity committee?

Yes, the committee meets quarterly

If yes, does the committee's representation include one or more members of the firm's management/executive committee (or the equivalent)?

Yes

Does the committee and/or diversity leader establish and set goals or objectives consistent with management's priorities?

Yes, the committee's goals are established based on American Express overall diversity goals and objectives.

Has the firm undertaken a formal or informal diversity program or set of initiatives aimed at increasing the diversity of the firm?

Yes, formal

How often does the firm's management review the firm's diversity progress/results?

Quarterly

The Stats

	NUMBER OF EMPLOYEES	REVENUE
	2006	2006
Total in the U.S.	65,500	$27 billion

Retention and Professional Development

How do 2006 minority and female attrition rates generally compare to those experienced in the prior year period?

About the same as in prior years.

Please identify the specific steps you are taking to reduce the attrition rate of minority and women employees.

• Develop and/or support internal employee affinity groups (e.g., minority or women networks within the firm)

• Increase/improve current work/life programs

• Succession plan includes emphasis on diversity

• Work with minority and women employees to develop career advancement plans

• Review work assignments and hours billed to key client matters to make sure minority and women employees are not being excluded

• Strengthen mentoring program for all employees, including minorities and women

Diversity Mission Statement

The diversity and global inclusion vision is to be the premium provider of solutions that leverage diverse talent in creating an inclusive work environment and competitive advantage in the global marketplace.

American Express' employees around the world represent many age groups, ethnicities, family structures, races, religions, sexual orientations, nationalities, and levels of mental and physical ability. While all American Express employees possess essential core competencies, we also speak many languages, come from a wide array of cultures, and comprise diverse educational backgrounds and life experiences. When it comes to the broad horizon of human experience, diversity encompasses all facets of imagination and innovation.

Additional Information

"Diversity is absolutely critical to the success of American Express, from a business and value standpoint. We must cultivate an environment in which people want and are able to contribute to their fullest potential because employees are examining the values of the institution and the values of their leaders. People are looking for companies and institutions that have strong values. Diversity is a business imperative and is central to the success of the company."

– Ken Chenault, CEO, American Express

American Family Insurance

6000 American Parkway
Madison, WI 53783
Phone: (608) 249-2111
Fax: (608) 243-6529
www.americanfamilyinsurance.jobs

Locations

18 states

Diversity Leadership

Jeff Close
Strategic Staffing Specialist
6000 American Parkway
Madison, WI 53783
Phone: (608) 249-2111

Employment Contact

Teresita Torrence
Staffing Manager
6000 American Parkway
Madison, WI 53783
Phone: (608) 249-2111
Fax: (608) 243-6529
E-mail: ttorrenc@amfam.com

Recruiting

Please list the schools/types of schools at which you recruit.

• *Private schools:* Edgewood College in Madison and all other private Wisconsin colleges

• *Public state schools:* University of Wisconsin-Madison and University of Wisconsin System Schools, Madison Area Technical College and Technical Colleges throughout Wisconsin, Hertzing College, Northern Illinois University, University of Illinois, Illinois State University, Drake University, Iowa State University, Northern Iowa University

Do you have any special outreach efforts directed to encourage minority students to consider your firm?

• *Conferences:* NEON (National Economic Opportunity Network), MSLC (Multicultural Student Leadership Conference)

• Advertise in minority student association publication(s)

• Participate in/host minority student job fair(s)

• Sponsor minority student association events

• Firm's employees participate on career panels at schools

• Outreach to leadership of minority student organizations

• Scholarships or intern/fellowships for minority students

What activities does the firm undertake to attract minority and women employees?

• Partner programs with women and minority associations

• Participate at minority job fairs

• Seek referrals from other employees

• Utilize online job services

Do you use executive recruiting/search firms to seek to identify new diversity hires?

Yes

If yes, list all women- and/or minority-owned executive search/recruiting firms to which the firm paid a fee for placement services in the past 12 months:

Consultis, New Directions and several other firms

Internships and Co-ops

I/S Summer Internship Program

Deadline for application: March 1st

Pay: $16.60 per hour

Length of the program: 12 weeks

Percentage of interns/co-ops in the program who receive offers of full-time employment: About 10 percent

Web site for internship/co-op information:
www.amfam.com/careers

Those who intern in applications development work side-by-side with a mentor and other full-time technologists to provide application planning, design, development, enhancements and maintenance. We work with a variety of web, client server and mainframe development tools. We provide professional and technical services for the development and ongoing support of both our end users and the I/S division. In this developmental position, interns gain experience as they program, test and debug applications and subroutines under the leadership of our mentor and senior technologists. Other possible opportunities may be available in base technology support areas such as database adminis-tration, networking, security, peripheral components, customer sup-port, desktop platforms, server support and end user computing.

Actuarial Internship Program

Deadline for application: March 1st

Pay: $19.00 per hour plus a $1,500 hiring bonus

Length of the program: 12 weeks. There may be opportunities to work part time during the school year and over the semester breaks as well.

Percentage of interns/co-ops in the program who receive offers of full-time employment: About 25 percent

Web site or other contact information for scholarship: www.amfam.com/careers

The American Family property/casualty and life/health actuarial summer internship programs are designed to involve the student in a variety of actuarial activities, including assistance in modeling projects and development of rate indications. These activities will provide the student with valuable experience in the type of work they could be involved with in their future career.

Requirements

Pursuit of a bachelor's degree in actuarial science, math or a related field such as risk management, statistics, or computer science

Depending on the position, there may be a requirement that the can-didate has sat for at least one of the actuarial exams.

The candidates should be at least in their second year of school at a university.

Depending on the position, courses in interest theory and/or actuar-ial mathematics may be required.

Experience with Microsoft Office and programming languages such as Visual Basic is considered a plus.

Corporate Internship Program

Deadline for application: Ongoing

Pay: Hourly rate varies depending on year in school

Length of the program: 12 weeks in the summer. There may be opportunities to work part time during the school year and to work over the semester break as well.

Percentage of interns/co-ops in the program who receive offers of full-time employment: Four percent overall

Web site for internship/co-op information: www.amfam.com/careers

All of the above programs fall under the umbrella of the corporate internship program at American Family Insurance. In addition to matching students to positions aligned with their majors and career goals, each student is assigned a mentor, provided meaningful work, opportunities to interact with fellow interns, a performance apprais-al and the opportunity to provide feedback on their internship expe-rience with American Family.

Strategic Plan and Diversity Leadership

How does the firm's leadership communicate the importance of diversity to everyone at the firm?

All new employees participate in a diversity workshop. New man-agers receive more in-depth training. There are numerous e-mails, presentations, etc., promoting diversity throughout the year.

Does your firm currently have a diversity committee?

Yes

If yes, please describe how the committee is struc-tured, how often it meets, etc.

Committees are located at our major offices. The teams consist of HR representatives, employees and managers.

If yes, does the committee's representation include one or more members of the firm's management/exec-utive committee (or the equivalent)?

No

Does the committee and/or diversity leader establish and set goals or objectives consistent with manage-ment's priorities?

Yes. At the core of our diversity efforts is the PEOPLE Plan. To us, "PEOPLE" stands for "Partnership in Equal Opportunity Producing Leadership Excellence." Included within the PEOPLE Plan are ini-tiatives that enrich and support not only our employees but also the communities we serve. These initiatives include internships, educa-tional programs, scholarships, neighborhood and community involvement activities, support of emerging market development and active participation in cultural celebrations.

Has the firm undertaken a formal or informal diversity program or set of initiatives aimed at increasing the diversity of the firm?

Yes, formal and informal. The firm's goal is for our workforce to reflect the population of the communities in which we do business. On a less formal level, the strategic staffing area of HR has devel-oped a community outreach program to offer job seeking and career planning services to our local minority communities.

How often does the firm's management review the firm's diversity progress/results?

Quarterly

How is the firm's diversity committee and/or firm management held accountable for achieving results?

It has become part of our management's annual performance plan.

Retention and Professional Development

Please identify the specific steps you are taking to reduce the attrition rate of minority and women employees.

• Increase/review compensation relative to competition

• Increase/improve current work/life programs

• Succession plan includes emphasis on diversity

• Strengthen mentoring program for all employees, including minorities and women

• Professional skills development program, including minority and women employees

• *Other:* The advancement of women and minorities is a major corporate goal

Diversity Mission Statement

American Family Insurance is dedicated to fostering a culture that is welcoming, diverse and inclusive—a culture that supports our goal of attracting and retaining "the best and the brightest."

Additional Information

We promote a culture of diversity and inclusion through ongoing efforts that include a variety of initiatives designed to promote awareness and understanding of the value that inclusion and diversity bring to us all.

Our commitment to inclusion and diversity enables our employees to contribute to our business in a way that enhances their performance and helps them provide world-class service to our diverse customers. And by ensuring that inclusion and diversity are woven throughout our culture and business practices, we are creating the foundation for future success.

We strive to build the most talented workforce possible—one that mirrors the communities we serve. We believe it is motivating for employees to work in an inclusive environment where they feel respected and valued for their individuality. That's why we embrace and celebrate our unique differences and similarities.

At American Family, inclusion and diversity are a part of our very foundation. From a strong foundation, there are no limits to what we can achieve.

American Family Insurance is an equal opportunity employer.

American Red Cross, The

2025 E St. NW
Washington, DC 20006
Phone: (202) 303-5665
Fax: (202) 303-0200
www.redcross.org

Diversity Leadership

D. Eric (Rick) Pogue
Senior VP for HR, Chief Diversity Officer
2025 E St. NW
Washington, DC 20006
Phone: (202) 303-5665
Fax: (202) 303-0200
E-mail: diversity@usa.redcross.org

Recruiting

Please list the schools/types of schools at which you recruit.

• Ivy League schools

• Other private schools

• Public state schools

• Historically black colleges and universities (HBCUs)

• Hispanic serving institutions (HSIs)

• Other predominantly minority and/or women's colleges

Do you have any special outreach efforts directed to encourage minority students to consider your firm?

Participate in/host minority student job fair(s) or other minority-focused job events.

What activities does the firm undertake to attract minority and women employees?

• Participate at minority job fairs

• Seek referrals from other employees

Internships and Co-ops

American Red Cross Presidential Internship Program

Deadline for application: January 15, 2007

Number of interns in the program in summer 2006 (internship) or 2006 (co-op): 42 interns

Pay: $480 to 800/week depending on experience and education level

Length of the program: 10 weeks

Web site for internship/co-op information:
www.redcross.org/services/diversity/0,1082,0_517_,00.html

The American Red Cross offers paid internships during the summer months through the Presidential Internship Program. These positions are open to students currently enrolled in undergraduate and graduate studies or who have recently graduated during the spring immediately prior to their appointment.

The goal of the Presidential Internship Program is to increase the diversity of the organization by identifying and recruiting minority students as interns. By providing a meaningful summer internship opportunity to undergraduate and graduate students, the American Red Cross increases the age and ethnic/racial diversity of its workforce. Through paid internships in key professional areas, interns can develop lifelong associations with the Red Cross and the organization will increase its overall diversity and inclusiveness.

Throughout the program, information is disseminated to interns about available career opportunities at the American Red Cross. Significant projects are presented to interns that require students to apply their previous knowledge and develop critical skills in a professional work environment. By taking part in this experience and drawing on their experience, it is our hope that students greatly enhance their ability for securing employment at an organization or corporation after graduation.

Strategic Plan and Diversity Leadership

What trends in your industry affect your corporate diversity goals, strategies and/or internal or external alliances?

Changing demographics in our communities reflecting an increase in diversity and multiculturalism are critical factors that drive our diversity goals and strategies. It's not enough for us to have a presence in these communities; it's critical that we reflect these communities in our volunteers, employees, donors, partners and suppliers. Advances in technology will allow—and require—us to reach and communicate with different populations in more innovative and immediate ways. Diversity is a necessary goal for the American Red Cross and it is critical to our success. It allows us to connect to our communities, better engage these communities and serve these communities to more effectively fulfill our mission of saving lives. Diversity is not an obligation for the American Red Cross—it is truly an opportunity.

How does the firm's leadership communicate the importance of diversity to everyone at the firm?

The corporate diversity department works closely with the American Red Cross communication and marketing department to develop communications strategies and platforms to promote our diversity goals to increase our organizational diversity. Using broadcast e-mails to American Red Cross volunteers and staff, internal and external web sites and various two-way communication mechanisms, the corporate diversity department communicates the American Red Cross's diversity programs, resources and initiatives to its employees and volunteers.

Who has primary responsibility for leading diversity initiatives at your firm?

The corporate diversity department (CDD) under the leadership of the Chief Diversity Officer (CDO), Mr. Rick Pogue, provides diversity-related leadership, resources and technical expertise for the American Red Cross enterprise-wide.

Does your firm currently have a diversity committee?

Yes

If yes, please describe how the committee is structured, how often it meets, etc.

This year, the National Diversity Council is being transformed into a regional structure to more effectively facilitate the integration of diversity into all Red Cross business operations. Regional Diversity Councils (RDCs) are being developed and will include representatives from American Red Cross Biomedical services units, chapters and external partner organizations. These RDCs provide opportunities for the sharing of best practices, communication of any needs/concerns and encourage improved coordination of activities nationally.

If yes, does the committee's representation include one or more members of the firm's management/executive committee (or the equivalent)?

No, however, executives at the regional level will work closely with the diversity councils and may appoint key paid staff and volunteers appointed to work with the councils.

Does the committee and/or diversity leader establish and set goals or objectives consistent with management's priorities?

Yes

Has the firm undertaken a formal or informal diversity program or set of initiatives aimed at increasing the diversity of the firm?

Yes, formal

Building our Language Capacity

The American Red Cross and the American Translators Association (ATA) maintain a successful partnership in which interpreters from ATA work with the American Red Cross during times of disaster. This partnership allows the Red Cross to improve its outreach to linguistically diverse communities with emergency preparedness materials, health and safety classes, and other important information. The American Translators Association (ATA) is a professional association founded to advance the translation and interpreting professions and foster the professional development of individual translators and interpreters. Its 9,500 members in more than 70 countries include translators, interpreters, teachers, project managers, web and software developers, language company owners, hospitals, universities and government agencies. Association membership is available to both individuals and organizations.

Increasing the Diversity of our Volunteers

The American Red Cross has actively pursued partnerships with organizations that serve diverse constituencies. Last year, we developed opportunities to more effectively engage and include our partners in our service delivery. The NAACP, African Methodist Episcopal Church, and the Progressive National Baptist Convention, have coordinated special training sessions with the American Red Cross where members have been trained to become disaster response volunteers. Through this combined effort, over 1,300 volunteers have been trained to respond to disasters. We are currently planning similar opportunities with other partner organizations in order to increase the diversity of our volunteers and improve our ability to reach diverse communities.

Serving the Disability Community

The American Red Cross has Statements of Understanding with the American Council of the Blind, National Federation of the Blind,

American Association of the Deaf-Blind, Through the Looking Glass and the American Association of People with Disabilities. An enterprise-wide committee meets regularly to discuss opportunities to more effectively serve the disability community. Members of this committee also meet regularly with external partners to address issues/concerns and to better engage our partners in service delivery.

Presidential Internship Program

Created and implemented in 1997, the goal of the Presidential Intern Program is to bring diverse undergraduate and graduate college students into the Red Cross in key professional areas by providing paid internships. The 2007 group, with 43 paid internships, is the largest group of presidential interns since the inception of the program. Thanks to an intensified marketing and outreach effort to colleges and universities, the 4,200 applications we received—a remarkable 700 percent increase over last year—represent the most talented and competitive applicant pool to date.

NAIA & American Red Cross Collaboration

The American Red Cross is embarking on an exciting pilot program with the National Association of Intercollegiate Athletics (NAIA) thanks to the generous financial support from State Farm. The NAIA is the governing body for the athletic programs of nearly 300 colleges and universities throughout the U.S. and Canada and reaches 650,000 students annually. Additionally, NAIA is the only intercollegiate athletic organization with a consistent emphasis on character development and an outreach program to extend student reach beyond its campuses into the community. This pilot program will put selected student athletes on the advisory board of ARC blood regions. Red Cross leaders will act as mentors to the selected students as they serve as ARC ambassadors on their campuses and in their communities, connecting the ARC to a new generation of volunteers and leaders.

How often does the firm's management review the firm's diversity progress/results?

Annually

How is the firm's diversity committee and/or firm management held accountable for achieving results?

The president and CEO sets performance goals, including diversity goals, for each direct report and evaluates that performance against all of these goals in determining merit increases.

The Stats

The American Red Cross headquarters is a majority female organization with a broad range of minority representation.

Diversity Mission Statement

To inspire a new generation of volunteers and supporters to enrich our traditional base of support. Our presence and services will reflect the diversity of America's communities. This requires a renewed focus to engage a broader constituent and client base than we currently have. We will engage more Americans in the mission of the Red Cross and undertake aggressive outreach efforts to underserved populations. We will reach out to diverse populations, developing opportunities for youth and broadening our donor and volunteer base by asking them to help the American Red Cross help individuals, families and communities.

Additional Information

As we work to make the American Red Cross a more inclusive organization, it is important to reaffirm our commitment to diversity. Recognizing that the Red Cross stands firm by its fundamental principles, diversity must be integrated into the organization to guarantee that it remains neutral and impartial. Our humanitarian mission requires us to reflect the communities we serve—not only in our employee and volunteer base, but also in our donors, partners, and suppliers.

Diversity is imperative to our business of serving those in need. Embracing a diversity of people, programs and services allows us to reach deeper into the communities we serve, improving our ability to carry out our mission and uphold the trust of the American public. And as the American public continues to evolve, so must the Red Cross.

Because of this, every Red Cross unit must work to integrate diversity into all services in order for us to fulfill our humanitarian mission.

DISCOVER ANADARKO

At Anadarko Petroleum Corporation, our vision for the future is clear.

We understand the importance of discovering the talents of our youth today and preparing them to become the leaders of tomorrow.

We award scholarships to promising college students, provide internships, sponsor organizations that help develop our youth and volunteer our time to mentoring students who attend at-risk schools in math, science, reading and free enterprise.

We believe in the value of education, equal opportunity and supporting the INROADS program.

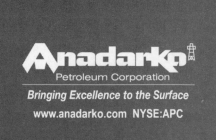

Anadarko
Petroleum Corporation

Bringing Excellence to the Surface
www.anadarko.com   NYSE:APC

Anadarko Petroleum Corporation

1201 Lake Robbins Drive
The Woodlands, TX 77380
www.anadarko.com

Locations
US
UK

Employment contact
E-mail: employment@anadarko.com

Diversity Mission Statement

Anadarko's vision for employment is to create the premier diversified employment culture incorporating industry best practices, effective sourcing vehicles, efficient processes and strong networking relationships to maintain Anadarko's competitive human capital advantage.

In an effort to continue our diversity program and ensure that the best available candidates are secured and retained for future company growth, we plan to take a three-pronged approach:

1. Strategically impact our mid-career hiring with an aggressive program that is designed to fill the gaps in our competencies and has a positive impact on our demographics from a diversity perspective.

2. Enhance our selection of candidates in our college hiring practices that will give us a diverse population of employees with the different technical skill sets and business acumen we need for the future.

3. Continue to leverage and more effectively utilize the INROADS program for internships, with the goal to convert INROADS students to full-time employment with Anadarko.

Anheuser-Busch Companies, Inc.

1 Busch Place
St. Louis, MO 63118
Phone: (314) 577-2000
Fax: (314) 577-2900
Toll Free: (800) 342-5283
www.anheuser-busch.com

Locations

St. Louis, MO (corporate office)
Offices worldwide

Diversity Leadership
Arturo Corral
Director of Diversity

Employment Contact
Alene Becker
Senior Director
Phone: (314) 577-3971
Fax: (314) 577-0719
E-mail: alene.becker@anheuser-busch.com

Recruiting

Please list the schools/types of schools at which you recruit.

• Public state schools
• Historically black colleges and universities (HBCUs)
• Hispanic serving institutions (HSIs)

Do you have any special outreach efforts directed to encourage minority students to consider your firm?
• Participate in/host minority student job fair(s)
• Firm's employees participate on career panels at school
• Outreach to leadership of minority student organizations
• Scholarships or intern/fellowships for minority students

What activities does the firm undertake to attract minority and women employees?
• Participate at minority job fairs
• Seek referrals from other employees
• Utilize online job services

Do you use executive recruiting/search firms to seek to identify new diversity hires?
Yes

Internships and Co-ops

INROADS
Pay: Varies
Length of the program: Varies
Web site for internship/co-op information: www.buschjobs.com

Scholarships

Hispanic Scholarship Fund and Urban Scholarship Fund
Scholarship award amount: Varies
Web site or other contact information for scholarship:
www.anheuser-busch.com

Entry-Level Programs, Full-Time Opportunities and Training Programs

The company has a wide variety of training programs available to all employees.

Strategic Plan and Diversity Leadership

How does the firm's leadership communicate the importance of diversity to everyone at the firm?
We have communication meetings across the country where diversity is one of the many topics discussed with employees. Also, a diversity page is now available through our company's Intranet.

Who has primary responsibility for leading diversity initiatives at your firm?
Arturo Corral, director of diversity

Does your firm currently have a diversity committee?
Yes

Please describe how the committee is structured, how often it meets, etc.:

We have a corporate committee that is structured by representation across business units with human resource generalists and specialists. This group meets on a monthly basis and is led by the diversity team.

Does the committee's representation include one or more members of the firm's management/executive committee (or the equivalent)?

Yes, the committee includes a number of executives.

Diversity Mission Statement

A diversified workforce is made up of individuals with a variety of backgrounds and ethnic makeup and experiences that translate into different perspectives.

Aon

200 East Randolph
Chicago, IL 60601
Phone: (312) 381-1000
www.aon.com

Locations
Worldwide

Diversity Leadership
Corbette Doyle
Chief Diversity Officer

Employment Contact
Beth Pelling
Senior Human Resources Manager, Early
Career Development

Ronnette Jenkins,
Senior HR Specialist

Recruiting

Please list the schools/types of schools at which you recruit.

- *Ivy League schools:* Cornell, UPenn
- *Other private schools:* USC, Northwestern, Notre Dame, BYU, Howard, St. John's, Temple
- *Public state schools:* Illinois, Wisconsin, Miami, Berkeley, Georgia, UNC, Texas
- *Historically black colleges and universities (HBCUs):* Howard

Do you have any special outreach efforts directed to encourage minority students and graduates to consider your firm?

- Hold a reception for minority students
- Participate in/host minority student job fair(s) or other minority-focused job events.
- Sponsor minority student association events
- Firm's employees participate on career panels at school
- Outreach to leadership of minority student organizations (postings)
- Scholarships or intern/fellowships for minority students
- *Other:* 21st Century Advantage Program (CAP 21), a retention program for School of Business at Howard University. The program creates learning environment involving teamwork to improve college experience for all undergraduate levels. Aon's role within CAP 21 is in the Corporate Adoption Program. Here Aon "adopts" students and focuses on educating and developing them with real-life business guidance.

What activities does the firm undertake to attract minority and women employees?

- Partner programs with women and minority associations

- *Conferences:* National Society of Hispanic MBAs Annual Conference, National Association of Insurance Women Annual Conference, National Black MBA Annual Conference
- Participate at minority job fairs
- Seek referrals from other employees
- Utilize online job services
- *Other:* Aon attends and sponsors women's networking events as well as partners with various minority groups on campus

Do you use executive recruiting/search firms to seek to identify new diversity hires?

Yes

If yes, list all women- and/or minority-owned executive search/recruiting firms to which the firm paid a fee for placement services in the past 12 months:

Mack & Associates, SV Search Insurance Recruiting

Internships and Co-ops

Business Internship Program

Deadline for application: March 1, 2007

Number of interns in the program in summer 2006 (internship) or 2006 (co-op): 50

Pay: Hourly rate discussed only at time of offer; hourly rate determined by geographic location.

Length of the program: 10 weeks

Percentage of interns/co-ops in the program who receive offers of full-time employment: 2006 internship class yielded 80 percent offer statistic, however offers are granted based on performance only.

Web site for internship/co-op information:
www.aon.com/us/about/careers/early_career_opp/bip/default.jsp

The Business Internship Program is a 10-week program that provides college students the opportunity to gain firsthand experience while also providing Aon the opportunity to develop relationships with potential future employees. Aon will provide all interns with a variety of training and development opportunities, which include: business etiquette, communication and presentation skills, Aon business line speaking events, performance management and Aon's corporate education system. Interns will work in one of nine different business tracks: Aon Risk Service, Aon Consulting, finance/accounting, actuary, Aon's underwriting managers, human resources, corporate communications, combined insurance and Aon reinsurance. To qualify for Aon's Business Internship Program, you must be a rising college senior enrolled and working toward an undergraduate degree of any type with a minimum GPA of 3.0. Interns are selected from partnership universities and aon.com based on previous job experience, professional goals and alignment with skills and competencies required for the job.

Affinity Groups

African American Networking Group, Asian Pacific Islander Networking Group, Aon Pride (Gay, Lesbian, Bisexual & Transgender) Networking Group, Latino Networking Group, People with Disabilities Networking Group and Women's Networking Group.

Each affinity group listed above is an independent, voluntary, non-profit association of people with a common interest in working together to enhance Aon's culture. By cultivating unique thinking, teamwork and value within our workplace, business networking groups and local diversity councils play a valuable role in individual development, as well as supporting communication among staff, community partners and company management. Each group shares a common objective which is to support Aon's three-pronged diversity strategy: talent development, talent recruitment and adding client value.

Entry-Level Programs, Full-Time Opportunities and Training Programs

Early Career Development Program

Length of program: 18 months

Geographic location(s) of program: U.S.-based locations differ each year

Participants within the Early Career Development Program aggressively learn the business and Aon culture through on-the-job experience and a formal training curriculum to develop concentrated skills within one of Aon's major lines of business. Depending on the line of business, a participant may be required to obtain the associate in

risk management designation, a property/casualty license, pass the Society of Actuaries exams, etc. The program includes the following different lines of business: risk services, consulting, finance and accounting, actuarial, underwriting and human resources.

Study materials and exam costs are covered for curriculum required components. Actuarial study time is awarded to actuaries, predetermined based upon exam pursued.

Strategic Plan and Diversity Leadership

What trends in your industry affect your corporate diversity goals, strategies and/or internal or external alliances?

The insurance industry is one of the least diverse sectors of the financial institutions industry, per the EEOC. Given our primary focus on hiring experienced professionals, this means we must focus on early career recruiting and development strategies to meet our diversity goals.

How does the firm's leadership communicate the importance of diversity to everyone at the firm?

Aon's leadership views diversity as an integral part of its business strategy. Therefore, diversity communications are integrated into all communication vehicles, including posters, company-wide e-mails, highlighted portions of our internal and external web sites, a diversity-focused blog and, most recently, a global diversity web cast with our chief executive officer and chief diversity officer.

Who has primary responsibility for leading diversity initiatives at your firm?

Corbette Doyle, global chief diversity officer

Does your firm currently have a diversity committee?

Yes

If yes, please describe how the committee is structured, how often it meets, etc.

Our firm has two separate development councils: the Minority Development Council and the Women's Development Council. The councils provide strategic oversight for our six national business networking groups, act as the primary executive advocates for our talent development strategies and provide feedback on various other diversity initiatives. The membership of both councils consists of senior leaders from all parts of our organization committed to building Aon's future talent pool. Both groups meet in person at least once a month.

We also have a global diversity advisory board that determines the global dimensions of diversity we will focus on and local best practices.

If yes, does the committee's representation include one or more members of the firm's management/executive committee (or the equivalent)?

Yes

How many employees are on the committee, and how often does the committee convene in furtherance of the firm's diversity initiatives?

We replaced our U.S.-based diversity council last year (consisted of 16 leaders) with two global and one U.S./Canadian between September 2006 and February 2007. Each has approximately 10 members and each meets in person quarterly with conference calls in between for a total of eight meetings.

Does the committee and/or diversity leader establish and set goals or objectives consistent with management's priorities?

Yes

Has the firm undertaken a formal or informal diversity program or set of initiatives aimed at increasing the diversity of the firm?

Yes, formal

How often does the firm's management review the firm's diversity progress/results?

Quarterly

How is the firm's diversity committee and/or firm management held accountable for achieving results?

Diversity goals for senior managers are linked to performance management. Senior executives have an upside bonus potential for meeting or exceeding goals.

The Stats

	NUMBER OF EMPLOYEES		REVENUE	
	2006	2005	2006	2005
Total in the U.S.	18,321	20,590	$4,185 million	$3,932 million
Total outside the U.S.	24,914*	26,161*	$4,769 million	$4,564 million
Total worldwide	43,069*	46,580*	$8,954 million	$8,496 million

* International and worldwide figures are based upon FTE's and U.S. figures based upon headcount

Our most recent EEO-1 report indicates that we have a total workforce representation of minorities at 23 percent and women at 54.7 percent

of managers; our minority representation is 11.1 percent and women 37.2 percent.

Retention and Professional Development

How do 2006 minority and female attrition rates generally compare to those experienced in the prior year period?

For women, lower than in prior years; for minorities, about the same as in prior years.

Please identify the specific steps you are taking to reduce the attrition rate of minority and women employees.

• Develop and/or support internal employee affinity groups (e.g., minority or women networks within the firm)

• Increase/review compensation relative to competition

• Increase/improve current work/life programs

• Succession plan includes emphasis on diversity

• Work with minority and women employees to develop career advancement plans

• Strengthen mentoring program for all employees, including minorities and women

• Professional skills development program, including minority and women employees

Diversity Mission Statement

The Diversity and Inclusion Group ensures that its employees have the tools and support necessary to build and maintain an inclusive environment at Aon.

Aon's diversity strategy is founded on four key objectives:

Talent supply and development: Supporting Aon's campus recruiting efforts and job fairs; assisting with mentoring, sponsoring and identification of talent; assisting with attracting, retaining and developing talent; and succession planning.

Cultural competence: Assisting Aon in developing a more inclusive approach and mindset, communicating with senior leadership to encourage different ideas and perspectives and to promote culture coaching.

Strengthening the business: Helping to identify strategic sourcing opportunities for diverse suppliers and supporting diversity initiatives throughout each business unit.

Connecting with the community: Helping Aon build community relationships that create a welcoming and inclusive environment for Aon and its constituencies, participate in diverse community service activities to increase cultural awareness, play a role in community events and initiatives to enhance Aon's corporate image and reputation, and provide social sponsorship of newly hired employees to create a sense of belonging at Aon.

Additional Information

"Hire the Best, Build the Best, Be the Best." That statement captures both Aon's promise and our potential with respect to creating an inclusive environment that nurtures the unique background, skills and creativity that each of our colleagues brings to the Aon table.

The only way Aon can live up to its goals and potential is to attract, develop and retain the best talent in the world. Therefore, talent is the foundation for all of our diversity initiatives. These initiatives include developing new and aggressive strategies for sourcing employees from places we haven't looked before, offering robust strategies to mentor them and build their skills, and offering them challenges that keep them loyal to Aon. And we do the same for our current employees through our networking groups and formal development programs, because they are even more important to our future.

As a client-focused organization, we understand that when you deliver the best to a client, they will realize and appreciate your value. The same holds true for our talent. By providing them with the best opportunities, we create an environment where they value Aon and, in turn, provide the best service possible to our clients.

Applied Materials, Inc.

3050 Bowers Avenue
Santa Clara, CA 95054
www.appliedmaterials.com

Locations
Countries:
China • Europe • India • Israel • Japan •
Korea • Malaysia • Singapore • Taiwan •
US

Continents:
Asia • Europe • North America

Employment Contact
Daniella Del Vento
University Relations Representative
Global Staffing
9700 US Highway 290 E
Austin, TX 78724
Phone: (512) 272-6798
Fax: (512) 272-0918
E-mail: Daniella_Del_Vento@amat.com
www.appliedmaterials.com/careers/index.html

Recruiting

Please list the schools/types of schools at which you recruit.

• *Ivy League schools:* Cornell

• *Other private schools:* Stanford, MIT, Cal Tech

• *Public state schools:* Berkeley, University of Texas-Austin, Texas A&M, University of Illinois, Purdue University, Georgia Tech, Arizona State University, University of Texas-El Paso, Michigan State University, Santa Clara University and San Jose State University

Do you have any special outreach efforts directed to encourage minority students to consider your firm?

• Participate in/host minority student job fair(s)

• Outreach to leadership of minority student organizations

What activities does the firm undertake to attract minority and women employees?

• Partner programs with women and minority associations

• *Conferences:* SWE, NSBE, NABA and SHPE

• Participate at minority job fairs

• Seek referrals from other employees

• Utilize online job services

Do you use executive recruiting/search firms to seek to identify new diversity hires?

No

Internships and Co-ops

College Programs Intern/Co-Op Program

Deadline for application: Open

Pay: Pay is by the hour and varies

Length of the program: Varies

Percentage of interns/co-ops in the program who receive offers of full-time employment: 30 to 40 percent

Web site for internship/co-op information: www.appliedmaterials.com/careers/intern_coop_prog.html?menuID=1_3

Applied Materials offers various internship and co-op programs designed to provide students with hands-on experience, an opportunity to develop skills in an area of interest and the ability to gain knowledge about the company and the semiconductor industry while enhancing their education. Paid internships and co-ops are offered throughout the company, in multiple divisions and vary in both duration and location.

Students seeking an internship or co-op assignment must:

• Be enrolled in a degree-seeking program.

• Be enrolled in a minimum nine-hour class load or three-quarters of the full-time load during the fall and spring semesters. (Course requirements do not apply to summer internships or co-op assignments.)

• Possess a 2.5 GPA or above on a 4.0 scale and a 4.0 on a 5.0 scale.

Students who wish to be considered for a co-op assignment must register through their university co-op office.

Affinity Groups

LEAD (Leadership Encouraging Achievement through Diversity)

LEAD provides the opportunity for the corporation and its African-American employee base in Austin to team up to create a general sense of community and emphasize corporate citizenship among all employees, ultimately reinforcing Applied Materials' standing as an employer of choice.

HIP (Hispanics in Partnership)

HIP's mission is to create networking opportunities for employees, to cultivate leadership and to promote career growth, thus enabling a corporate partnership for diversity. The group's members aim to serve as role models by promoting educational opportunities within the Hispanic population, while also encouraging all AMAT employees to participate in the opportunities provided by Hispanics in Partnership.

WPDN (Women's Professional Development Network)

The mission of the Austin WPDN is to inspire and enable a community of women to reach their full potential while strengthening Applied Materials' goal to be an employer of choice.

Entry-Level Programs, Full-Time Opportunities and Training Programs

College to Corporate Development Program

Length of program: One year

Geographic location(s) of program: U.S.

Applied Materials' College to Corporate Development Program (CCDP) includes training courses that help new employees transition seamlessly from academia to a corporate environment. We provide networking, leadership and team-building opportunities, giving participants both valuable business contacts and practical skills.

Each graduate will be matched with the Applied Materials division that is best suited with his or her background and aligned with current company needs. We're looking for strong, enthusiastic candidates with a minimum 3.0 GPA. Internships and other relevant experiences are helpful, but not required.

Training

Each college hire within CCDP will receive a customized training plan. Participants also receive technical and professional development training that is specifically relevant to their full-time employment.

To learn more about the program, please visit our web site: www.appliedmaterials.com/careers/ccdp.html?menuID=1_1

Applied Signal Technology, Inc.

400 W. California Avenue
Sunnyvale, CA 94086
Fax: (408) 617-3617
Apply online at APPSIG.com

Locations

Allen, TX • Anaheim Hills, CA • Annapolis
Junction, MD • Arlington, VA • Herndon,
VA • Salt Lake City, UT • Sunnyvale, CA
• Torrance, CA

Diversity Leadership

Diane Cusano
Human Resources Department Manager

Employment Contact

Todd Penns
Senior Recruiter

Experienced Hire Contact

Todd Penns
Senior Recruiter

Recruiting

Please list the schools/types of schools at which you recruit.

• *Private schools:* University of Santa Clara, Stanford, BYU, John Hopkins, Rice

• *Public state schools:* University of Pacific, Cal Tech, UC Davis, UC Santa Cruz, Cal Poly Pomona, UC San Diego, UC Santa Barbara, Cal Poly San Luis Obispo, San Jose State, UC Berkeley, UCLA, Oregon State University, University of Utah, Utah State

Do you have any special outreach efforts directed to encourage minority students and graduates to consider your firm?

• Advertise in minority student association publication(s) or other minority-focused publications.

What activities does the firm undertake to attract minority and women employees?

• Participate at minority job fairs

• Seek referrals from other employees

Do you use executive recruiting/search firms to seek to identify new diversity hires?

No

Internships and Co-ops

Applied Signal does not have a structured internship program. We do offer internships on an as-needed basis for the company.

Strategic Plan and Diversity Leadership

How does the firm's leadership communicate the importance of diversity to everyone at the firm?

Meetings with managers on the company's AAP each year (e.g., e-mails, web site, newsletters, meetings, etc.).

Who has primary responsibility for leading diversity initiatives at your firm?

Diane Cusano, human resources department manager

Does your firm currently have a diversity committee?

No

Does the committee and/or diversity leader establish and set goals or objectives consistent with management's priorities?

Yes. Objectives are set from our AAP plan.

Has the firm undertaken a formal or informal diversity program or set of initiatives aimed at increasing the diversity of the firm?

No

How often does the firm's management review the firm's diversity progress/results?

Annually

The Stats

	NUMBER OF EMPLOYEES		REVENUE	
	2006	2005	2006	2005
Total worldwide	647	677	$162 million	$156 million

We have a total of 641 employees in the U.S. On the West Coast, we have 30 percent minority, 16 percent female, 54 percent male. On the East Coast, we have 17 percent minority, 18 percent female, 64 percent male.

Retention and Professional Development

How do 2006 minority and female attrition rates generally compare to those experienced in the prior year period?

About the same as in prior years.

ARAMARK

Aramark Tower
1101 Market Street
Philadelphia, PA 19107
www.Aramark.com

Locations

Headquartered in Philadelphia, ARAMARK has approximately 242,500 employees serving clients in 20 countries.

Employment Contact

Phone: 1 (800) 999-8989 ext. 3184
E-mail: college-relations@aramark.com
Web site: www.aramarkcollegerelations.com

Recruiting

Please list the schools/types of schools at which you recruit.

- Public state schools
- Other private schools
- Historically black colleges and universities (HBCUs)
- Hispanic serving institutions (HSIs)
- Native American tribal universities

Do you have any special outreach efforts directed to encourage minority students to consider your firm?

- Participate in/host minority student job fair(s)
- Sponsor minority student association events
- Outreach to leadership of minority student organizations

What activities does the firm undertake to attract minority and women employees?

- *Conferences:* National Society of Minorities in Hospitality, National Black MBA, National Hispanic MBA, INROADS, Multicultural Food Service Alliance (MFHA)

- Seek referrals from other employees

- Utilize online job services

Do you use executive recruiting/search firms to seek to identify new diversity hires?

Yes

Internships and Co-ops

ARAMARK is a great place to start your career. As part of the ARAMARK team, you will get a chance to learn hands-on from the best in the business. These individuals are interested in developing you as a person and as a professional.

A variety of internship opportunities are available in the following areas:

- Accounting
- Engineering
- Facilities management
- Food and beverage
- Human resources
- IT
- Lodging
- Sales

To apply, please visit our web site at www.aramarkcollegerelations.com.

Entry-level Programs, Full-time Opportunities and Training Programs

Pathways To Leadership

Length of program: Depends on the line of business (six to 13 weeks)

Geographic location(s) of program: Nationwide

Strategic Plan and Diversity Leadership

How does the firm's leadership communicate the importance of diversity to everyone at the firm?

The firm's leadership communicates diversity initiatives through its web site, e-mails, newsletters and extensive online and in-person training programs.

Who has primary responsibility for leading diversity initiatives at your firm?

VP of diversity

Does your firm currently have a diversity committee?

Yes

If yes, does the committee's representation include one or more members of the firm's management/executive committee (or the equivalent)?

Yes

The Stats

	NUMBER OF EMPLOYEES		REVENUE	
	2006	2005	2006	2005
Total in the U.S.	150,000	170,000	N/A	$8 .6 billion
Total outside the U.S.	N/A	70,000	N/A	$2.2 billion
Total worldwide	240,000	242,000	$11.6 billion	$10.8 billion

Diversity Mission Statement

Kaleidoscope, ARAMARK's Commitment to Diversity

ARAMARK understands that a mosaic of backgrounds, styles, perspectives, values and beliefs adds value to our workforce, our workplaces and our business partners.

We are comprised of unique individuals who, together, make the company what it is and what it can be in the future. Only when all individuals contribute fully can the strength and vision of ARAMARK be realized.

Our Principles for Valuing Diversity

Because we are committed to being a company where the best people want to work, we champion a comprehensive diversity initiative.

Because we thrive on growth, we recruit, retain and develop a diverse workforce.

Because we succeed through performance, we create an environment that allows all employees to contribute to their fullest potential.

make your
mark

Archer Daniels Midland Company is a world leader in BioEnergy and has a premier position in the agricultural processing value chain. We count on the ambition and creativity of our colleagues to help us enhance our position as a global leader in the development of food, feed and fuel products.

Whether you are looking to further your career or are a recent college graduate, ADM is the place to be. As a Fortune 100 company, we are committed to providing opportunities, training and benefits that exceed expectations.

At ADM, the opportunity is yours.

Visit us online at www.adm.jobs.

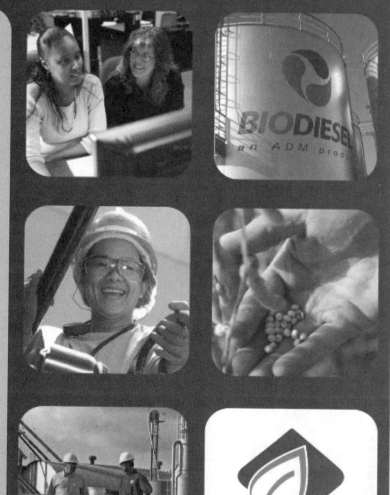

BIODIESEL an ADM product

ADM

Archer Daniels Midland Company

P.O. Box 1470
Decatur, IL 62525
Phone: (800) 637-5843
 or (217) 424-5200
Fax: (217) 451-4383
www.admworld.com

Diversity Leadership
John Taylor, CDP
Director of Diversity

Case McGee

Employment Contact
www.adm.jobs

Recruiting

Please list the schools/types of schools at which you recruit.

• *Ivy League schools:* Cornell University

• *Other private schools:* Rose-Hulman Institute of Technology, Millikin University, Bradley University, Illinois Weslyan University, Illinois College, Culver-Stockton College, University of Dayton

• *Public state schools:* Eastern Illinois University, Illinois State University, Iowa State, Kansas State, Michigan State University, Michigan Tech University, New Mexico State, Northern Illinois University, North Dakota State, Ohio State University, Oklahoma State, Purdue University, South Dakota School of Mines, Southern Illinois University Carbondale & Edwardsville, Texas A&M, Truman University, University of Illinois, University of Illinois in Chicago & Springfield, University of Iowa, University of Kansas, University of Michigan, University of Minnesota, University of Missouri Columbia, University of Missouri Rolla, University of Nebraska, University of North Dakota, University of Wisconsin and Western Illinois University

• *Historically black colleges and universities (HBCUs):* North Carolina A&T; Clark Atlanta University

• *Hispanic serving institutions (HSIs):* New Mexico State; Texas A&M

Do you have any special outreach efforts that are directed to encourage minority students to consider your firm?

• Hold a reception for minority students

• Conferences

• Advertise in minority student association publication(s)

• *Participate in/host minority student job fair(s):* Minorities in Agriculture, Natural Resources and Related Sciences (MANRRS), Society for Women Engineers (SWE), Women for Hire, National Society of Black Engineers (NSBE), Urban League Diversity Job Fair, National Association of Black Accountants, National Black MBA Association

• Sponsor minority student association events

• Firm's employees participate on career panels at school

• Outreach to leadership of minority student organizations

• Scholarships or intern/fellowships for minority students

What activities does the firm undertake to attract minority and women employees?

• Partner programs with women and minority associations

• Conferences

• Participate at minority job fairs

• Seek referrals from other employees

• Utilize online job services

Do you use executive recruiting/search firms to seek to identify new diversity hires?

Yes

Internships and Co-ops

ADM Internship Program

Deadline for application: We will accept students until April, but complete most recruiting by the end of fall semester.

Pay: Monthly salary dependent upon division where intern works.

Length of the program: 10 to 12 weeks

Percentage of interns/co-ops in the program who receive offers of full-time employment: 65 percent

Web site for internship/co-op information: www.adm.jobs

An internship with ADM allows students to work in a variety of different areas within the company: accounting, internal audit, engineering, IT, elevator management, grain terminal operations management, commodity trading and other specialty areas.

Students can find themselves in a variety of different locations across the Midwest. They can range from working in a manufacturing environment to a country grain elevator or even in a corporate setting. Our program promotes the development of the student while providing a training ground for potential employees. Our internship provides many benefits; including a monthly salary, housing arrangements, and a structured orientation and wrap-up ceremony. Students are required to have a minimum GPA of 2.8, be of junior status and be legally authorized to work in the United States.

Scholarships

ADM offers scholarships to the following universities:

• Iowa State University
• Kansas State University
• Ohio State University
• Purdue University
• University of Illinois at Urbana-Champaign
• University of Nebraska-Lincoln

Kansas State ADM Scholarship

The recipient of this scholarship will be a student properly enrolled in the College of Agriculture at Kansas State University from a diverse background pursing a degree in grain science, agriculture economics/agricultural engineering or food science. Successful applicants will have 60 hours of college credit with a GPA of 3.0/4.0 or better. Each scholarship award is valued at $10,000. Additional qualification criteria does apply. Interested students should contact the college relations department at ADM for full details.

Illinois State Department of Agriculture Minority Recruitment and Scholarship Program

The recipient of this scholarship will be a minority student who is interested in the food and agribusiness industries and enrolled in the department of agriculture at Illinois State University. In addition, applicants must be U.S. citizens and classified as new beginning freshmen or new transfer students with a transfer degree who have applied for and been admitted to the fall term with a major and sequence offered by the department of agriculture. Each scholarship is valued at $5,000 per year (at $2,500 per semester following certification of qualification) and is renewable for up to eight consecutive semesters (four semesters for transfer students). The total potential value of the scholarship is $20,000. Each scholarship recipient is required to maintain at least a 2.8 cumulative GPA. There may be additional qualification criteria and inter-

ested students should contact the college relations department at ADM for full details.

IL State—ADM Minority Scholars

The recipient of this scholarship will be an academically talented incoming freshman minority student. The recipient will preferably pursue a degree in business, agribusiness, international business, foreign language, finance, accounting, economics, chemistry or biology. Students must have a minimum 3.0/4.0 GPA for consideration and must maintain a 2.75/4.0 GPA for renewal of scholarship. The scholarship is valued at $5,000 per year for up to four years.

Affinity Groups

ADMWIN; ADM Women's Initiative Network

The ADM Women's Initiative Network (WIN) exists to facilitate the professional development of women at ADM, while helping them reach their individual goals and potential. One part networking, one part professional development, one part mentoring, WIN draws on the most important resource we have: each other. Working together, with the support of top ADM management, we'll help enhance the positive impact of women in our company through recruitment, retention and development efforts.

Entry-Level Programs, Full-Time Opportunities and Training Programs

Engineering (referred to as a production assistant)

Recent engineering graduates are assigned to a production unit where they gain first hand exposure to leadership of employees, equipment troubleshooting and dealing with the myriad of challenges faced routinely in a facility that operates around the clock, 365 days a year. The experience begins with on-the-job training through observation and typically progresses to full responsibility for a work group working rotating shifts during the first year. Production assistants experience a very hands-on environment and are placed at one of our processing facilities through the United States, primarily within the Midwest.

Commodity Training (referred to as a commodity trader trainee)

The position of commodity trader trainee is one of buying and selling commodities in the cash market, as well as making and coordinating arrangements for the transportation of the product. Our commodity traders learn the fundamentals of the business by embarking on an intense two-month training curriculum, which involves thorough classroom and on-site learning. Training occurs at our corporate headquarters, river terminals, country elevators and processing plants.

Grain Elevator Management

The grain elevator manager will manage the profitability of a grain facility through grain merchandising, accounting, operations, customer service, and staff supervision. The career focuses upon the ability of the manager to enhance value through the safe handling and merchandising of grain and providing outstanding customer service. ADM owns and/or operates a network of grain elevators stretching across the United States, South America, and Canada with a concentration in the Midwest. The manager's success will depend on their ability to perform in a fast paced, multi-task oriented environment and can provide a world of opportunity for career growth with ADM in position responsibilities, geographic location, and business units. The training program begins on the job at an assigned location, and includes hands-on web-based and classroom training. The manager will have exposure at other ADM facilities, including soy processing, river elevator and wheat milling. The first location placement is through a harvest season, and generally not more than 12 months.

Grain Terminal Operations Management (referred to as Grain Terminal Operations Management Trainee)

The employee will be stationed at one of approximately 50 elevators across the Midwest. The training program is hands-on; the trainee will learn by performing the work with proper safety and supervision. A trainee will be learning most of the activities at the elevator such as: loading and unloading grain trucks and railcars, sampling and grading grain, loading barges, overseeing hourly employees and assigning work, transferring, drying, storage, and blending of grain, repairs, troubleshooting and maintenance, preventative maintenance, implementation of safety programs and procedures.

Internal Audit (Staff Auditor I)

Recent accounting graduates will attend an internal audit orientation the first week of work at the Decatur, IL internal audit office. Upon completion of orientation, staff auditors begin their experience in a team atmosphere where they perform "risk based" audits of ADM entities throughout the world. On each audit assignment the staff auditor will review, assimilate, and logically document work procedures performed at ADM entities with a focus on the "inherent risks" associated with each entity. Upon completion of each audit assignment, staff auditors will work with team members to provide ADM management and the board of directors with analysis, information, and recommendations in an objective, accurate, and timely fashion.

Accounting Staff Development Program

The Accounting Staff Development Program is generally two to four years consisting of six month to one year assignments in rotational entry-level and experienced accounting positions. Areas of assignment include corporate, grain, operations and internal audit. Performance reviews are given at the end of each assignment. Our accounting department emphasizes promoting people from within the company, so advancement opportunities at ADM are excellent. Location opportunities included our corporate headquarters in Decatur, IL and Overland Park, KS. Candidates must be able to function independently, handle multiple tasks, meet deadlines, and use Microsoft Office software. Strong communication skills are critical in order to communicate effectively in different disciplines and varying levels of management.

Retention and Professional Development

Please identify the specific steps you are taking to reduce the attrition rate of minority and women employees.

• Develop and/or support internal employee affinity groups (e.g., minority or women networks within the firm)

• Increase/improve current work/life programs

Diversity Mission Statement

ADM remains committed to unlocking the potential of all of its people. To this end, we seek to recruit talent wherever it exists. This is an inclusive policy that recognizes the need for concerted efforts to tap into a diverse pool of human resources as we continue to serve and thrive in an increasingly diverse society. In this way, we can provide our suppliers, customers, shareholders and global community with maximum value now and into the future.

At ADM, we define diversity broadly—in keeping with the global perspective that comes from being a global business. We see diversity as a broad mix of people in our business—certainly gender, ethnicity and race...and also a variety of backgrounds, experiences, styles, cultures, skills and competencies.

Additional Information

Supplier Diversity

ADM places a high priority on its commitment to supplier diversity, in which we have significantly expanded our utilization of minority-owned, women-owned, disabled veteran-owned and HUBZone-located enterprises to provide products and services to ADM. We work with such groups as the National Minority Supplier Development Council (NMSDC) and the Women's Business Enterprise National Council (WBENC) in order to meet this commitment.

Arrow Electronics, Inc.

50 Marcus Drive
Melville, NY 11747
Phone: (631) 847-2000
www.arrow.com

Locations

260 locations in 55 countries & territories

Diversity Leadership

Sherry Snipes
Manager Compliance & Diversity
E-mail: ssnipes@arrow.com

Kristin Dortz
Diversity & Compliance Analyst
F-mail: kdortz@arrow.com

50 Marcus Drive
Melville, NY 11747
Phone: (631) 847-2000
Fax: (631) 847-2551
www.arrow.com/careers

Employment Contact

Patricia Signorelli
Corporate Staffing Analyst
E-mail: psignorelli@arrow.com

Recruiting

Please list the schools/lists of schools at which you recruit.

• *Private schools:* Stony Brook University, Baruch College, Texas A & M, New York Institute of Technology

• *Public state schools:* Hofstra University, St. Johns University, C.W. Post University

• *Historically black colleges and universities (HBCUs):* HBCU.com

Do you have any special outreach efforts directed to encourage minority students and graduates to consider your firm?

Outreach to leadership of minority student organizations.

What activities does the firm undertake to attract minority and women employees?

• Partner programs with women and minority associations

• Conferences

• Participate at minority job fairs

• Seek referrals from other employees

• Utilize online job services (diversityinc.com, iHispano.com, HBCU.com)

Do you use executive recruiting/search firms to seek to identify new diversity hires?

Yes

Internships and Co-ops

Corporate Internship Program – Melville, NY

Deadline for application: May, but varies by open position

Number of interns in the program in summer 2006 (internship): 15

Pay: $14 to $20 per hour (varies by position)

Length of the program: 12 weeks+ (some positions work full-time during the summer and part time throughout the year)

Percentage of interns/co-ops in the program who receive offers of full-time employment: 20 percent

Web site for internship/co-op information: www.arrow.com/careers

Arrow Electronics employs interns in various corporate departments, such as corporate accounting, tax, internal audit, finance, communications, human resources and law.

Strategic Plan and Diversity Leadership

What trends in your industry affect your corporate diversity goals, strategies and/or internal or external alliances?

We look at our internal growth, hiring trends and external workforce demographics.

How does the firm's leadership communicate the importance of diversity to everyone at the firm?

Web casts, e-mails, diversity web site and e-newsletters

Who has primary responsibility for leading diversity initiatives at your firm?

Sherry Snipes, manager, compliance and diversity

Does your firm currently have a diversity committee?

Yes

If yes, please describe how the committee is structured, how often it meets, etc.

We are a cross-functional team, which operates strategically, and oversees several subteams. We meet biweekly to update and measure progress against team goals.

If yes, does the committee's representation include one or more members of the firm's management/executive committee (or the equivalent)?

Yes

If yes, how many executives are on the committee, and in 2006, what was the total number of hours collectively spent by the committee in furtherance of the firm's diversity initiatives?

There are five to 10 employees on the committee, who collectively met for 3,640 hours in 2006.

Does the committee and/or diversity leader establish and set goals or objectives consistent with management's priorities?

Yes, goals are aligned with the organization's strategic plans.

Has the firm undertaken a formal or informal diversity program or set of initiatives aimed at increasing the diversity of the firm?

Arrow Electronics has established a formal diversity program. We are formally developing an education and awareness program, as well as embedding diversity into our employment brand. In addition, we have formally developed recruitment outreach strategies and are embedding diversity and inclusion thinking into our processes, including succession planning.

How often does the firm's management review the firm's diversity progress/results?

Biannually

How is the firm's diversity committee and/or firm management held accountable for achieving results?

Reports results and status periodically to the CEO and C-Suite.

The Stats

	NUMBER OF EMPLOYEES		REVENUE	
	2006	2005	2006	2005
Total in the U.S.	6,000	6,000	N/A	N/A
Total outside the U.S.	6,000	5,400	N/A	N/A
Total worldwide	12,000	11,400	$13.6 billion	$11.2 billion

Retention and Professional Development

Please identify the specific steps you are taking to reduce the attrition rate of minority and women employees.

• Succession planning
• Individual development plans

Diversity Mission Statement

Arrow Electronics strives to foster and grow a diverse and inclusive environment that encourages an open exchange of ideas, where each individual is valued, respected and enabled to reach his or her potential. We firmly believe that embracing and learning from individual differences is a strength that will give Arrow a sustained, competitive advantage with customers and suppliers, and enable innovation for Arrow's continued success.

Aurora Health Care

2920 W. Dakota Avenue
Milwaukee, WI 53234-3910
www.aurorahealthcare.org

Locations

Aurora Health Care is a health care
provider in Wisconsin. Our corporate
office is located in Milwaukee.

Diversity Leadership

Rhonda Taylor-Parris
Director, Workforce Planning
2920 W. Dakota Avenue
Milwaukee, WI 53234-3910
Phone: (414) 647-3346
Fax: (414) 647-4878
E-mail: Rhonda.Taylor-Parris@Aurora.org

Recruiting

Please list the schools/types of schools at which you recruit.
- Private schools
- Public state schools

Do you have any special outreach efforts directed to encourage minority students to consider your firm?
- Participate in/host minority student job fair(s)
- Firm's employees participate on career panels at schools
- Scholarships or intern/fellowships for minority students

What activities does the firm undertake to attract minority and women employees?
- Participate at minority job fairs
- Seek referrals from other employees
- Utilize online job services

Do you use executive recruiting/search firms to seek to identify new diversity hires?
Yes

Internships and Co-ops

INROADS-Wisconsin

Deadline for application: Based on the INROADS program requirements

Pay: Pay is biweekly; rate depends on field and standing in school (range: $10.30 to 18.75)

Length of the program: 10-week minimum commitment

Percentage of interns/co-ops in the program who receive offers of full-time employment: Over 50 percent receive offers.

Web site for internship/co-op information: www.inroads.org
Internships are offered in the following career fields:

- *Business:* Finance, accounting, HR, marketing

- *Information service/technology:* MIS, IS, IT, computer science

- *Engineering:* Biomedical engineering

- *Medical:* Pre-med, physical therapy, occupational therapy, athletic training

- Nursing; pharmacy

All students must meet all INROADS program qualifications. (Many students who attend school in-state work throughout the school year.)

Scholarships

Jestene McCord INROADS Intern Scholarship
Deadline for application for the scholarship program: Mid-July
Scholarship award amount: $1,000 per year awarded

This scholarship is only offered to returning Aurora INROADS interns who meet the requirements and are nominated.

Stanley Kritzik Innovation and Technology Scholarship
Deadline for application for the scholarship program: None
Scholarship award amount: $1,000 per year awarded

This scholarship is only offered to information technology Aurora INROADS interns who meet the requirements.

Aurora Health Care INROADS Intern Book Scholarship
Deadline for application for the scholarship program: None
Scholarship award amount: Ten $200 scholarships awarded per year.

This scholarship is offered to 10 Aurora INROADS interns who meet the requirements.

Entry-Level Programs, Full-Time Opportunities and Training Programs

Aurora Leadership Academy

Length of program: 15 months

Geographic location(s) of program: Milwaukee, Wisc.

This program prepares employees with high potential for first-line management positions. Employees are nominated by their immediate supervisor and are paired up with a leader that serves as a mentor.

Strategic Plan and Diversity Leadership

How does the firm's leadership communicate the importance of diversity to everyone at the firm?

The importance of diversity and Aurora's commitment to diversity is captured in our values. Aurora's values consist of accountability, teamwork and respect, setting the standard for service, continually improving our quality, controlling our costs and "The Power of Diversity." We communicate the commitment to diversity in our management bulletin, *Aurora Today* (employee newsletter) and the Aurora diversity plan.

Who has primary responsibility for leading diversity initiatives at your firm?

Rhonda Taylor-Parris, director of workforce planning

Does your firm currently have a diversity committee?

Yes

Please describe how the committee is structured, how often it meets, etc.

The committee consists of Aurora's seven senior leaders and they meet on a quarterly basis.

Does the committee's representation include one or more members of the firm's management/executive committee (or the equivalent)?

Yes

How many employees are on the committee, and how often does the committee convene in furtherance of the firm's diversity initiatives?

The committee members consist of Aurora's seven senior leaders and they meet on a quarterly basis. Meetings are held more frequently if needed.

Total Executives on Committee: Seven

Does the committee and/or diversity leader establish and set goals or objectives consistent with management's priorities?

Yes. Goals and objectives are set annually and added to the annual strategic plan. Departments throughout the organization draft their business plans according to the goals and objectives set forth in the strategic plan.

Has the firm undertaken a formal or informal diversity program or set of initiatives aimed at increasing the diversity of the firm?

Yes, formal. Diversity education modules are placed on our internal diversity web site for managers to facilitate with their staff. The diversity modules are resources that provide an opportunity for employees to learn more about diversity and provide a forum for the expression of concerns and the sharing of experiences. Aurora also provides classes in the "Managing Diversity Education Series" for managers to learn how to effectively manage in a diverse environment.

How often does the firm's management review the firm's diversity progress/results?

Quarterly

How is the firm's diversity committee and/or firm management held accountable for achieving results?

Employees' attitudes around diversity are captured in an annual survey that Aurora conducts. The results of the survey determine our diversity index, which is what leaders are held accountable for improving/maintaining. Achievement of outcomes is included in the incentive and merit increases as a part of the annual performance review process.

The Stats

2005 Employees: 25,000

Retention and Professional Development

Please identify the specific steps you are taking to reduce the attrition rate of minority and women employees.

The attrition rate of minority and women employees is not a critical issue for us.

Diversity Mission Statement

In order to provide the best health care and achieve the desired health outcomes for all that we serve, a diverse and culturally competent workforce is essential.

Avaya Inc.

211 Mt. Airy Road
Basking Ridge, NJ 07920

Locations

Basking Ridge, NJ (HQ)
Avaya has multiple locations throughout
the United States and over 90 locations
worldwide.

Diversity Leadership

University Relations
211 Mt. Airy Road
Basking Ridge, NJ 07920
Fax: (303) 538-4144
Web site: www.avaya.com/careers

Recruiting

Please list the schools/types of schools at which you recruit.

• Ivy League schools
• Other private schools
• Public state schools

What activities does the firm undertake to attract minority and women employees?

• Utilize online job services

Do you use executive recruiting/search firms to seek to identify new diversity hires?

Yes

If yes, list all women- and/or minority-owned executive search/recruiting firms to which the firm paid a fee for placement services in the past 12 months.

We only use firms for executive hiring.

Affinity Groups

4A—Asian/Pacific Americans at Avaya

The charter of the 4A organization is to support Avaya's efforts to achieve the goal of a diverse workforce and to address concerns related to Asian/Pacific American employees. In addition, 4A provides several opportunities for networking and mentoring: we host employment candidates during their interviews, provide mentoring to those new employees who request it and represent 4A concerns to upper management.

Members of 4A-Avaya come together and work together for these purposes:

• To advance the educational and professional development of APAs

• To promote the importance of diversity in the workplace

• To educate Avaya employees on the rich heritage, diverse cultures and valued traditions of APAs

• To recognize and publicize the achievements and accomplishments of APAs

• To serve as a resource to promote Avaya's objectives and mission

• To foster the advancement of APAs in the business through mentorship, professional development and education

• To build a supportive network to communicate issues for APAs in business

• To create opportunities for personal and professional growth

• To be a positive presence within the business and throughout the communities in which we work

EQUAL! Home

Company Without Closets ...

The SAFE Place to Work and Grow

EQUAL! is an educational and support group that addresses workplace environment issues affecting employees who are gay, lesbian, bisexual or transgendered, or who have family, friends or colleagues who are gay, lesbian, bisexual or transgendered. Our mission is to advocate a work environment that is inclusive and supportive of gay, lesbian, bisexual and transgendered employees—enabling all employees to perform to their fullest potential. EQUAL! is a resource serving our customers, shareholders, colleagues, families and the global community in which we work and live. EQUAL! commits to advancing change that will help people respect and value differences, thus allowing employees to achieve Avaya's vision.

HISPA—The Hispanic Association of Avaya

HISPA-Avaya is a nonprofit organization that serves many different purposes professionally and socially.

HISPA provides:

- The opportunity to mentor others
- The opportunity to a very valuable network
- Exposure beyond your local sphere of influence
- The chance to be part of "Una segunda familia"

NOVA—Natives Offering Value at Avaya

NOVA stands for Natives Offering Value at Avaya. NOVA is an organization open to all employees committed to the career advancement, educational needs and general understanding of Native Americans and equality of all employees. By developing our Native American resources as employees, business partners and customers, we support Avaya in leveraging diversity as a competitive advantage. As we move to strengthen corporate diversity, we aid in achieving global business results.

Other Affinity Groups

- Alliance of Black Leaders at Avaya (ABL)

- Individuals with Disabilities Enabling Advocacy Link (IDEAL)

- Women at Avaya Valuing Excellence (WAVE)

Entry-Level Programs, Full-Time Opportunities and Training Programs

We have tuition reimbursement and Avaya University, which provides in-house training at all levels.

Strategic Plan and Diversity Leadership

How does the firm's leadership communicate the importance of diversity to everyone at the firm?

The firm communicates the importance of diversity through e-mails and the company web site.

Has the firm undertaken a formal or informal diversity program or set of initiatives aimed at increasing the diversity of the firm?

Yes, informal

How often does the firm's management review the firm's diversity progress/results?

Annually

Diversity Mission Statement

Our value as a company is realized by recognizing the value of each individual. Our strategic intent is to create a culture of unity and global community, where every employee feels included, supported and respected.

We align around common business objectives—revenue, cost, people and process—and within that framework, we acknowledge and support diverse groups. We are a global company in every sense—geographically, strategically and culturally. We embrace diversity as a competitive advantage. Harmonizing and leveraging the diversity of our people will realize our full potential. In the spirit of global community, our diversity will unite us, and it will enhance the quality of our work and our work lives.

Barclays Capital

200 Park Avenue
New York, NY 10166
Phone: (212) 412-4000
Fax: (212) 412-6795
Barclayscapital.com/campusrecruitment

Locations

London (HQ)

Additional offices in:

Europe, Middle East and Africa:
Amsterdam • Birmingham • Dubai •
Dublin • Frankfurt • Geneva •
Johannesburg • Lisbon • Lugano • Madrid
• Manchester • Milan • Munich • Paris •
Reading • Zurich

Americas:
Boston • Calgary • Chicago • Los Angeles
• Mexico City • Miami • New York • San
Francisco • São Paulo • Washington, DC
• Whippany

Asia Pacific:
Bangkok • Beijing • Hong Kong • Jakarta
• Kuala Lumpur • Labuan • Mumbai •
Seoul • Shanghai • Singapore • Sydney •
Taipei • Tokyo

Diversity Leadership

Mark Kurman
Head of Diversity, Americas

Alison Lipman
Diversity Manager, Americas

Employment Contact

Jennie Ashley
Diversity Recruiter, Americas

Recruiting

Please list the schools/types of schools at which you recruit.

• Ivy League schools

• Public state schools

• Private schools

• Historically black colleges and universities (HBCUs)

• Hispanic serving institutions (HSIs)

• Other predominantly minority and/or women's colleges

Active partners with Sponsors for Educational Opportunity Program, INROADS and Toigo.

Do you have any special outreach efforts directed to encourage minority students to consider your firm?

• Hold a reception for minority students

• Conferences

• Advertise in minority student association publication(s)

• Sponsor minority student association events

• Firm's professionals participate on career panels at schools

• Outreach to leadership of minority student organizations

• Scholarships or intern/fellowships for minority students

• Contest/challenge

• Outreach to sororities, fraternities and other minority student clubs

What activities does the firm undertake to attract women and minorities?

• Partner programs with women and minority banking associations

• Conferences

• Seek referrals from other professionals

• Utilize online job services

Do you use executive recruiting/search firms to seek to identify new diversity hires?

Yes

Internships and Co-ops

At Barclays Capital, we have built our name in the industry as a result of our strong track record. We have focused primarily on the debt markets and, in the past eight years, our reputation has grown due to our strength and our people. The firm seeks to distinguish itself by the skills and excellence of its debt capital markets, origination, sales, trading, research and advisory services supported by the Barclays' balance sheet—one of the strongest in the global banking industry. Barclays Capital acts internationally as intermediary and adviser to major corporations, financial institutions and governments, and has the global reach and distribution power to meet the needs of issuers and investors worldwide.

Barclays Capital Summer Program

The Barclays Capital Summer Program is designed to provide summer analysts with broad exposure to the Barclays Capital businesses. This program consists of practical work assignments and various other learning opportunities throughout the summer. Through a variety of activities, summer analysts will have the opportunity to network with line professionals and with their peers. The goal of the summer program is to enable the summer analysts to achieve a solid understanding of the strength and capabilities of our global platform, its businesses and its culture. Specific details of the program include:

• 10-week summer program beginning in early June and ending in early August

• Day One Orientation in an effort to get you acclimated to Barclays Capital

• Technical training (Excel, Bloomberg), communication skills and business-specific training

• Product knowledge sessions taught by line professionals

• Social and networking opportunities throughout the summer

• Mentors provided for all summer analysts

Barclays Capital believes strongly in giving our graduates the opportunity to grow and develop over their career, and building a strong foundation is the key to making this successful. Our program is designed to provide a broad overview of investment banking and of the position and involvement of Barclays Capital's business and its products. It gives participants a solid grounding in key technical competencies and the skills required to perform in their specific role. Additionally, it is a critical way to embed the graduates into the culture of the firm, while creating a cohort of participants who will continue to network with each other throughout their careers with the organization. This initial training creates a strong platform on which to build more in-depth specialist expertise relevant to your chosen area. The training program takes place in London and lasts approximately five weeks. The Graduate Program takes learning one step further, incorporating practical applications through a variety of case

studies, workshops and presentations. Once you have completed the initial training program, you will participate in our continuous professional education program which includes product knowledge sessions, online tutorials and our mentor program.

Qualifications

• Strong-to-superior verbal, quantitative and analytical skills

• Resourcefulness, team orientation, enthusiasm and an entrepreneurial spirit

• Proven leadership qualities, a strong work commitment and high ethical standards

• Minimum GPA of 3.2

Commercial Mortgage Backed Securities (CMBS)

Barclays Capital is looking to hire qualified rising seniors for summer intern positions in commercial mortgage backed securities, which is a business that originates, underwrites, structures, securitizes and trades in commercial real estate loans and commercial mortgage-backed securities.

The intern position offers exposure to a breadth of real estate capital markets activities, including fundamentals of real estate investing, loan underwriting and structuring, securitization and trading.

Compliance

At Barclays Capital, our reputation is a key asset of the firm. That is why we place great emphasis on evaluating and managing the regulatory risks that the firm encounters from day to day. The compliance function not only assists business units and their supervisors in complying with the rules and regulations that govern our industry, but also provides expert advice on where "the line" may be drawn in the future.

Compliance is responsible for ensuring that Barclays Capital adheres to the financial regulations that are prescribed by a variety of sources, including regulators, exchanges, central banks, governments and supranational institutions. We work closely with internal divisions to ensure timely and pragmatic implementation of appropriate systems and controls and then monitor compliance with the regulations as they come into force. We also actively engage with external bodies to ensure that the impact of proposed regulations on the orderly functioning of the market in general, and our firm in particular, is clearly understood.

Finally, compliance has a crucial responsibility to safeguard the firm's reputation: protecting it against adverse risk as well as enhancing its profile in the eye of public stakeholders.

Corporate Communications

The corporate communications team is responsible for maintaining the firm's reputation and public image.

The division consists of three main teams:

- Advertising and brand creates the advertising strategy, manages the advertising campaigns and ensures all internal and external collateral and materials are consistent with the firm's visual identity.

- Internal communications informs and inspires our people to turn strategy into action, sharing views across Barclays Capital and the wider Barclays group. This includes developing appropriate and effective channels for communications, including the company Intranet, presentations, newsletters, posters and display-stand material.

- Media relations handles all media communications. This includes writing and distributing press releases, organizing interviews and briefings, preparing awards submissions, and providing strategic PR planning and advice for the businesses.

Working with the corporate communications team will give you a good overall understanding of how a global investment bank operates, and for graduates looking for a career in financial communications or financial PR, a position here will provide great experience. You will need to be a good communicator and be well organized with excellent interpersonal skills.

Corporate Real Estate Services (CRES)

Corporate real estate services is a vital strategic discipline because it "translates" the high-level, strategic change required by senior decision makers into day-to-day reality for people in their work or living space. CRES provides a world-class service, meeting the needs of an increasingly sophisticated range of clients. The success of our business is built on high levels of customer service, staff training and quality facilities. These elements combine together to ensure we deliver a world-class experience around our offices, time after time. Our extensive responsibilities range from property strategy, space management and supply chain management to building maintenance, engineering, administration and contract management.

Finance

Finance is divided into two groups: financial control and product control. The financial control group is responsible for the financial records and reporting of our business activity. Providing accurate information, they enable us to react to opportunities and focus on critical business issues. They also provide information to senior management as well as external fiscal bodies.

Product control provides explanations of business revenue, attributing any movements to market positions, inherent risk and new deals. It is, like operations, also responsible for ensuring the integrity of the balance sheet for revenue products. This function is key to our reporting and control infrastructure, and the information provided by the group gives us the means to assess business performance. In addition, the group coordinates all global finance controls and procedures.

Both areas allow you to build a thorough understanding of our business and enable you to add value in the reporting and analysis of

financial information. As the function supports different products in a constantly changing marketplace, you'll need to be able to respond to that change.

Finance requires people with a passion for improving existing processes to deliver a better service. You should be highly analytical and confident under pressure. If you have a proactive approach to resolving problems and the ability to work well in a team, you could well be the ideal person. Opportunities exist for candidates who would like to 1) improve or streamline existing business processes, 2) deliver a high-quality, innovative service and add a proactive approach to resolving unstructured problems. Opportunities for placement are New York and New Jersey.

Human Resources

The role of HR is to partner with the business to ensure we maintain our competitive advantage by attracting, developing and retaining the best people. We are responsible for delivering integrated and innovative HR solutions, which allow our people to provide outstanding service to our clients.

The HR unit is organized around core business units with client relationship teams who are overall responsible for service delivery and manage the ongoing HR needs of the business. Specialist teams provide specific expertise and project management across a range of HR topics, including compensation, diversity, learning and development, and recruiting.

Key requirements for anyone looking for a career in human resources include an understanding of investment banking and the markets we operate in and how to attract and develop talent. You will spend time identifying the human capital issues faced by our business units and working across the HR disciplines to create and execute solutions.

You will develop a wide range of competencies, from communicating and influencing to critical thinking and problem solving. You will quickly gain exposure to senior members of the firm as you work on a wide range of both transactional and strategic initiatives. Building relationships so you can advise and consult whilst executing at pace are prerequisites for a role within HR.

Investment Banking and Debt Capital Markets

This business area exists to provide effective global "multiproduct" solutions for clients seeking to raise capital or manage their risk exposure. As a result, associates within the team work in close contact with our client groups, which are structured by geography and sector. Extensive research, internal briefings and presentations are involved in the search for a client solution. Once these solutions are approved, models are built that provide the client with accurate projections. This role involves creative thinking, maintaining relationships and providing the full range of the firm's services to the client—government agencies or corporate clients looking to raise capital.

Generating new business is an important part of the role. It demands an understanding of complex products and their pricing, as well as looking at issues from different angles and creating alternative ideas. Looking at the bigger picture in terms of client needs and wider market issues is also important. As such, you may spend your time developing ideas and solutions to pitch to clients. Following that, you may work on live deals involving products such as bonds, equity and credit derivatives, securitization, loans, foreign exchange, interest rates and commodities.

Fundamental analysis and research into companies and markets is the starting point in investment banking and debt capital markets. This offers an opportunity to work with teams across the firm, delivering more integrated solutions for our clients and across all areas of financing and risk management services. As relationship management skills develop, you will be given more responsibility for client relationships.

Operations

Operations is involved in the full spectrum of financial products, from bonds and equity derivatives to swaps and options. Traders execute financial transactions, but it is the operations function that ensures all trades are settled as quickly and efficiently as possible. Operations provides effective cash management and is responsible for ensuring the integrity of the balance sheet. It is also responsible for the global integrity of client data, as well as full compliance monitoring of all transactions. Due to technological progress and globalization, operations is evolving—certain functions and processes have now been centralized to increase business efficiency and enhance the control environment. E-commerce is also changing the way we work. As more and more clients interface with dealer screens in their own offices, they need to be able to call operations directly for support, rather than traders or salespeople.

Working in operations involves dealing with established and emerging markets worldwide. This leads to constant dialogue with professionals, both internally and externally. It also presents a unique opportunity as it allows you to see and learn about a significant number of functions throughout Barclays Capital.

Initially, you would spend your time familiarizing yourself with departmental functions within the firm. People who work in operations coordinate and streamline all the bank's processes. To do this, you'd deal with a range of people, internally and externally, across all trading regions. You'd enjoy a high profile within the bank as your advice is needed for all operational matters. As you progress, you would be given responsibility for new projects and initiatives. Managing such initiatives demands creative thinking and the ability to work well within a wider team. Certain skills would be developed through formal education programs and others are better developed on the job, through practical experience. There are opportunities to specialize in one particular product or to build more general expertise across several areas.

Research

As Barclays Capital is primarily a fixed-income house, research has a bigger profile than at some other investment banks. We believe that original thinking in the analysis of financial information empowers our business and drives our market strategies for clients. So, essentially, the purpose of research is to provide clients and internal teams with a wide range of financial thoughts and ideas to help them to make the best investment decisions. Our research vision is best described as "differentiation and integration"—we produce differentiated market analysis and viable investment ideas to a range of clients around the globe, integrated across geographies and financial products or asset classes. To provide this information, our research group is divided into credit research and economics and market strategy.

The credit research team provides fundamental analysis as well as strategic and quantitative analysis. The fundamental analysis focuses on individual corporate/financial issuers and sectors and the drivers of investment performance for each. Dedicated research teams cover investment grade, high-yield, emerging market, asset-backed and convertible bonds as well as providing equity derivatives research and credit derivatives/index strategies. Credit strategy looks at major drivers for the credit market, quantitative model-driven investment strategies and relative value between different asset classes, currencies, maturities, etc.

The economics and market strategy team provides commentary on the macroeconomic environment. Our economists issue key global and regional economic data forecasts as well as regular analyses of economic themes. The Market Strategy Group is a recognized leader in foreign exchange and fixed-income strategy, especially inflation-linked bonds research.

At Barclays Capital, the research role is essential and is expected to contribute toward revenue generation. As an analyst, we would expect you to gather and analyze data on companies and markets. As you progress, you may be expected to convert that analysis into trade ideas. You would also be expected to write analyses and present findings to clients, as well as colleagues in sales and trading. We look for high levels of analytical capability and a desire for responsibility and firmwide levels of exposure. You would also need the ability to learn to think like a trader or portfolio manager.

Sales

Barclays Capital's global sales force provides corporate and institutional clients with a highly focused, round-the-clock, team-based service. This service includes coverage on rates, credit, foreign exchange, commodities (both precious metals and energy), mortgages and equity derivatives, often with innovative solutions leading to complex structured transactions. As an organization and as a sales team, we need to build strong, effective and continuous global partnerships with clients, keeping them updated on international markets and new products. (Clients vary and may include banks, asset managers, pension funds, hedge funds, central banks, insurance companies and corporations—essentially, institutional clients with capital to invest.) These relationships are not just about selling the firm's services; salespeople also act as an intelligence-gathering network. The salesperson is, in many ways, the cornerstone of our business model. Salespeople are responsible for delivering the services of the firm to the client. They also deliver the client's business to the firm. The sales relationship is the means by which we can go both deeper and broader in terms of product penetration with our clients, thus maximizing our revenue potential. Salespeople need to be good communicators and very good at building relationships; they must also have strong analytical abilities.

Structuring

Sitting between and working in cooperation with derivatives trading and sales, our mission is to develop and deliver customized products and solutions to investors and financial institutions. The Global Structuring Group is split into various product areas, including commodities, credit derivatives, equity derivatives, emerging markets, fund derivatives, FX and interest rates.

Structurers are responsible for creating and pricing structured derivatives and assisting in the marketing and execution of transactions. They work closely with salespeople, traders, research analysts and quantitative analysts, and with divisions such as legal, compliance and operations in order to complete a transaction.

Structurers learn how the markets work through research and working with traders. Structurers also learn how to build and use pricing models, which requires strong analytical ability and advanced qualifications in technical subjects such as engineering and financial markets.

Technology

For technically capable people with an interest in finance, Barclays Capital presents an opportunity to learn about various aspects of the business. Positions are available for bachelor's, master's and doctoral candidates. Openings are located at our offices in New York City (Midtown) and Whippany, New Jersey (candidates should indicate if they have a preference for N.J.).

Analysts will work as members of various teams on either the application development side or the infrastructure side. You may begin your career in an IT development group working closely with the "front office." Analysts in application areas will develop, test and deploy software for many different areas of the firm such as trading, sales, research, risk, finance, clearance and settlements. We also have opportunities in our IT infrastructure area that manage servers, networks and operating systems. Your first rotation could be improving the design and structure of databases, which help to increase the speed and efficiency of the firm's day-to-day operations. Our technical environment is quite varied and includes Windows, Unix, C++, Java, C#, VB, VBA, SQL Server, Oracle, Linux, scripting languages, grid computing and real-time systems. Apart from technical knowledge, the analyst role demands a strong

sense of initiative and the ability to prioritize workloads. We offer excellent training to those in the technology role and expect them to liaise with traders and product control to optimize their input to the business.

Trading

Traders buy and sell financial instruments and must be ready to quote "bid and offer" prices to clients and counterparties. Our traders work in global markets and global credit products; the two trading businesses cover diverse areas, including commodities, emerging markets, credit and equity derivatives, fixed income, FX, corporate bonds, high yield and asset-backed securities. The success of these businesses is unsurpassed; we have been named *Risk* magazine's "Derivatives House of the Year 2005." Traders add value by thinking on their feet, knowing where liquidity lies and building strong client relationships. As part of this, traders work very closely with the sales teams in order to ensure we meet the clients' needs. The role of a trader requires significant focus and strong analytical skills. To be a good trader, you need to be well informed; able to read the direction of the market; a quick, accurate decision-maker and have a strong yet measured appetite for risk. As a trader, you would monitor breaking news and price fluctuations and provide analysis and trade ideas. To be successful requires motivation and resilience. Traders are also expected to operate in a team environment while coping in stressful situations; trading requires keeping your head while working in a hectic and dynamic atmosphere. Traders are given a lot of responsibility and expected to rise to the challenge.

Affinity Groups

We have four active employee forums in the Americas and two in the U.K., with several others being formed in the U.K.

Americas

• Barclays Cultural Alliance—Ethnicity networking group

• GLBT Network—Gay and lesbian networking group

• Women's Leadership Forum—Women's networking group

• Disability Champions Network—Disability networking group

U.K.

• Women's Internal Network—Women's networking group

• GLBT Network—Gay and lesbian networking group

Employee forums are open to all employees and are recognized by the firm for their support of business and diversity goals.

Strategic Plan and Diversity Leadership

How does the firm's leadership communicate the importance of diversity to everyone at the firm?

Erin Mansfield, managing director, U.S. compliance and chairperson of the U.S. diversity committee, is one of the primary communicators of our commitment to diversity. She and Michael Evans, head of global HR (see below), are responsible for ensuring that diversity is part of Barclays Capital's culture and that it is incorporated in the day-to-day business activities at the firm.

The importance of diversity is further communicated through our diversity committee, employee forums and sponsorships. Employees can access information via the diversity web site, e-mails and monthly diversity and employee forum group meetings.

Who has primary responsibility for leading overall diversity initiatives at your firm?

Michael Evans, as the head of global human resources, leads the primary business group responsible for supporting and facilitating all the efforts of the individuals in diversity initiatives throughout the firm.

Tara Udut, head of campus recruiting, Americas, and her group work with regional campus recruiting committees as well as targeted campus teams to ensure that diversity is an important business consideration. Each team has an executive charged with ensuring specific focus on diverse student representation.

Our U.S. Diversity team consists of Alison Lipman, diversity manager, and Jennie Ashley, diversity campus recruiter. They have responsibility for ensuring that diversity-related recruiting initiatives are integrated into the campus recruiting, the experienced hire arena, and the overall firm agenda. They regularly reinforce our commitment to diversity with our partners and review how their performance contributes to furthering our diversity agenda.

Does your firm currently have a diversity committee?

Yes

If yes, does the committee's representation include one or more members of the firm's management/executive committee (or the equivalent)?

Yes, the committee consists of senior representation from all areas of the firm.

If yes, how many senior managers are on the committee, and how often did the committee convene in furtherance of the firm's diversity initiatives in 2005?

Total Executives on Committee: 11 senior managers

Number of diversity meetings annually: 12, once a month

Does the committee(s) and/or diversity leader establish and set goals or objectives consistent with management's priorities?

Yes, we use a model that focuses our initiatives along three key work streams—recruit, develop and retain—with a designated senior manager responsible for progress along each stream.

Has the firm undertaken a formal or informal diversity program or set of initiatives aimed at increasing the diversity of the firm?

Yes, formal. To reiterate, a broad range of staff are committed to initiatives within each of three major work streams.

Diversity Mission Statement

At Barclays Capital, we are committed to providing creative and innovative solutions for our clients, and the attraction and retention of world-class professionals enables us to fulfill that commitment. We actively promote diversity to sustain continued business success, and therefore we:

• Seek to build a workforce that reflects the communities in which we live and work so that we are best able to meet the needs of our clients.

• Strive to ensure that the talents of all our employees are fully utilized and that no job applicant or employee will receive less favorable treatment on the grounds of race, religion, gender, age, physical ability, sexual orientation or nationality.

• Aim to provide our employees with a working environment that encourages dignity and respect and is free from discrimination and harassment.

• Aspire to be an employer that has a reputation for fairness, integrity, innovation and creativity in order to attract and retain clients as well as potential and existing employees.

Diversity is a business imperative and we are committed to being an organization that values diversity and promotes the inclusion of all people who share the firm's aspirations and performance expectations.

Additional Information

Barclays Capital supports the National Black MBA Association Metro-Chapter, Toigo, Sponsors for Educational Opportunity and INROADS

The National Black MBA is a business organization that leads in the creation of economic and intellectual wealth from the African-American community. One of the main operating principles of the NBMBA is to establish and maintain an effective information and

communication network. Additionally, the NBMBA enhances the membership's professional and career development goals that link black business professionals.

Toigo is the only graduate-level program with a specialized focus on leadership development and career services for minority MBAs pursuing careers in finance. Each year, this organization selects the best and brightest minority business school students to become Toigo fellows and assist them in joining the top firms on Wall Street.

INROADS is a program whose mission to develop and place talented students of color in business and industry to prepare them for corporate and community leadership

Sponsors for Educational Opportunity is a program that places outstanding college students of color in substantive internships that are designed to lead to full-time jobs with Wall Street firms.

BASF Corporation

100 Campus Drive
Florham Park, NJ 07932
Phone: (973) 245-6000
Toll Free: (800) 526-1072
www.basf.com/careers

Locations
Florham Park, NJ (US HQ)
Ludwigshafen, Germany (Global HQ)

Diversity Leadership
Ingrid Abreu
Manager, Management Development &
Diversity

Employment Contact
Catharina King
Recruitment Specialist
University Recruiting

Recruiting

Please list the schools/types of schools at which you recruit.

• Ivy League schools
• Other private schools
• Public state schools

Do you have any special outreach efforts directed to encourage minority students to consider your firm?

• Hold a reception for minority students
• *Conferences:* NSBE, NSHMBA, Reaching Out, SHPE, SWE
• Participate in/host minority student job fair(s)
• Sponsor minority student association events
• Firm's employees participate on career panels at school
• *Scholarships or intern/fellowships for minority students:* TMSF and the Jackie Robinson Foundation
• *Other:* Monster Diversity Leadership Program sponsor

What activities does the firm undertake to attract minority and women employees?

• Partner programs with women and minority associations
• Conferences
• Participate at minority job fairs
• Seek referrals from other employees
• Utilize online job services

Internships and Co-ops

Internship
Deadline for application: Ongoing
Number of interns in the program in summer 2006 (internship) or 2006 (co-op): 17

Pay: Competitive
Length of the program: 12 weeks
Percentage of interns/co-ops in the program who receive offers of full-time employment: 80 percent
Web site for internship/co-op information: www.basf.com/careers

MBA Internship Professional Development Program

The BASF MBA Internship Program provides MBA graduates with the opportunity to apply their education and background to challenging assignments, develop technical and managerial expertise, network at senior levels throughout BASF and explore possible careers with the company. Individual assignments in your field of expertise will be designed and planned to enhance your career development and deliver immediate value to BASF. The program focuses on financial management and consists of assignments in business groups, financial functions and logistics. Projects include preparing operational plans, break-even analysis, acquisitions and divestitures. A technical undergraduate degree is desirable but not necessary.

Requirements:

• First-year MBA students only
• Demonstrated academic achievement: GPA 3.0+
• International perspective required, international experience preferred
• Three to five years of work experience prior to MBA/international experience preferred
• Undergraduate finance or technical degree preferred (e.g. chemistry, engineering, etc.)
• Bilingual preferred, German fluency preferred
• Intercultural orientation, business acumen
• Authorization to work in the U.S. without restriction

Logistics/Customer Care Internship

The qualified candidate will be responsible for the management of customer orders through the entire order fulfillment process. The

intern will ensure complete customer satisfaction through timely, thorough follow-through—keeping the customer appraised of their account status. The intern will function in a team environment while retaining the ability to empower themselves to perform their specific job functions and make decisions that are in the best interests of the customer and BASF. Additional responsibilities include, but are not limited to, assisting in the resolution of outstanding credit issues, nonconformances and various supply chain-related projects. This position will interface with various functions within the business, such as marketing, sales and logistics, at all levels of the organization.

Requirements:

- Knowledge of MS Office
- Must be a self-starter and able to make key decisions in a fast-paced dynamic work environment
- Action-oriented, with good problem solving and analytical skills
- Excellent communication skills
- Demonstrated academic achievement
- A desire to advance career within the business
- Rising seniors only
- Authorization to work in the U.S. without restriction

Desired Skills:

- A bachelor's degree in supply chain, business, logistics or finance preferred
- Experience in customer service account management or internal sales preferred
- Bilingual (French, German and/or Spanish a plus)
- APICS-certified a plus (production and inventory management)
- Knowledge of SAP preferred

Chemical Engineering Internship Professional Development Program

We offer junior chemical engineering students the opportunity to spend a summer working at a North American BASF site or at BASF AG's international headquarters in Ludwigshafen, Germany, where the company operates the world's largest integrated chemical complex. Interns will partake in various chemical engineering projects/practical assignments and an opportunity to apply what you've learned in school. Competitive salary, round-trip travel to Ludwigshafen, Germany (if selected for the Germany program).

Requirements:

- Excellent communication skills
- Outstanding work ethic
- Demonstrated academic achievement
- College juniors only (rising seniors)
- German language skills preferred for those interested in the Germany program

- Mobile-minded
- International orientation (a plus)
- Bilingual (a plus)

Accounting Internship Professional Development Program

We offer rising seniors the opportunity to spend a summer working at BASF's North American headquarters site in Florham Park, N.J., in the corporate financial planning and controlling department. Interns will receive exposure to various corporate-level accounting functions, which include monthly financial closings, accounting procedure reviews, accounting research, financial statement development and financial system integrations.

Requirements:

- Excellent communication skills
- Outstanding work ethic
- Demonstrated academic achievement: GPA 3.0+
- College juniors only (rising seniors)
- Authorization to work in the U.S. without restrictions

Affinity Groups

- African-American Employee Group (AAEG)
- Women and Business Issues (W&BI)
- Gay Lesbian Bisexual Transgender and Friends (GLBT&F)
- Latin American Employee Group (LAEG)
- Emerging Professionals and Friends (EP&F)

Groups of BASF employees committed to a long-term strategy that contributes to the overall values and goals of the corporation. They each define their mission, which supports BASF's overall strategy. They convene frequently and use different means for communication, including e-mails and feature stories/events on their web sites hosted in the BASF Intranet.

Entry-Level Programs, Full-Time Opportunities and Training Programs

MBA Professional Development Program

The Professional Development Program (PDP) provides MBA graduates with the opportunity to apply their education and background to challenging assignments, develop technical and managerial expertise, network at senior levels throughout BASF and explore possible career tracks with the company. Two domestic six-month assignments in your field of expertise will be designed for your first year in the program. In the second year, PDP participants will be

required to participate in a minimum of a three-month assignment in Germany and an additional nine-month international assignment with the sponsoring group. These assignments will be designed and planned to enhance your career development and deliver immediate value to BASF.

Requirements:

• Must be willing to relocate—various job locations within the United States

• International perspective required, international experience preferred

• Three to five years of work experience prior to MBA/international experience preferred

• Undergraduate finance or technical degree preferred (e.g., chemistry, engineering, etc.)

• Bilingual preferred, German fluency preferred

• Intercultural orientation, business acumen

Accounting Professional Development Program

BASF Corporation's Accounting Professional Development Program is a high-profile, fast-track program for accounting graduates who demonstrate strong potential. The program's goal is to develop future accounting managers and business controllers for a world-class chemical company, BASF Corporation—the chemical company.

The 18-month program consists of training assignments in each of the following accounting areas:

• Accounting services

• Business/managerial accounting

• Corporate accounting

• Corporate financial planning and analysis

Site accounting (a four-month assignment at a major production facility either in Geismar, La.; Freeport, Texas; or Wyandotte, Mich.)

Upon successful completion of the program, the incumbent will, based upon existing opportunities at that time, be eligible for a two-year assignment within one of the above accounting functions. Subsequent to that, opportunities for advancement will be based upon performance and will include not only the above area but also other opportunities within BASF Corporation.

During the course of the program, the incumbent will be exposed to a wide array of technical and personal growth opportunities. Additionally, the incumbent will be expected to pursue an MBA degree and/or CPA. We seek bright, geographically mobile, well-rounded individuals who are searching for an excellent entrance opportunity into private sector accounting.

Logistics/Customer Care Representative

Qualified candidates will be responsible for the management of customer orders through the entire order fulfillment process. The customer care representative will ensure complete customer satisfaction through timely, thorough follow-through—keeping the customer appraised of their account status. The customer care representative will function in a team environment while retaining the ability to empower themselves to perform their specific job functions and make decisions that are in the best interests of the customer and BASF. Additional responsibilities include, but are not limited to, assisting in the resolution of outstanding credit issues, nonconformances and various supply chain-related projects. This position will interface with various functions within the business, such as marketing, sales and logistics, at all levels of the organization.

BASF Corporation offers a comprehensive program of employee benefits, including insurance coverage for medical, dental, life and long-term disability, tuition reimbursement and retirement savings plan.

Requirements:

• Knowledge of MS Office

• Must be a self-starter and able to make key decisions in a fast-paced dynamic work environment

• Action-oriented, with good problem-solving and analytical skills

• Excellent communication skills

• Demonstrated academic achievement

• A desire to advance career within the business

• College seniors only

• Authorized to work in the U.S. without restrictions

Desired Skills:

• A bachelor's degree in supply chain, business, logistics or finance preferred

• Experience in customer service account management or internal sales preferred

• Bilingual (French, German, and/or Spanish a plus)

• APICS-certified a plus (production and inventory management)

• Knowledge of SAP preferred

Chemical Engineering Professional Development Program

This comprehensive program provides new college graduates with the opportunity to gain an understanding of BASF from different perspectives and to apply their expertise through real-world assignments. PDP participants explore career options and develop technical and professional decision-making skills, while fulfilling specific business needs through two nine-month rotational assignments at different sites. PDP participants gain valuable exposure to BASF culture and values and have the opportunity to live and work in a wide range of locations, including some of our major sites in

Louisiana, Michigan, New Jersey, North Carolina, South Carolina and Texas.

The program may consist of assignments in the following areas:

• Corporate engineering (process/project)
• Ecology and safety
• Maintenance
• Manufacturing/operations
• Research and development

BASF Corporation offers a comprehensive program of employee benefits, including insurance coverage for medical, dental, life and long-term disability, tuition reimbursement and retirement savings plan.

Requirements:

• Authorization to work in the U.S. without restrictions
• Bilingual (a plus)
• Chemical engineering degree required
• College seniors only
• Demonstrated academic achievement
• Excellent communication skills
• International orientation (a plus)
• Mobile-minded
• Outstanding work ethic

Strategic Plan and Diversity Leadership

How does the firm's leadership communicate the importance of diversity to everyone at the firm?

The firm communicates diversity initiatives by sending quarterly communications to the senior management team and spotlighting stories on the BASF Intranet.

Who has primary responsibility for leading diversity initiatives at your firm?

Ingrid Abreu, manager, management development and diversity

Does your firm currently have a diversity committee?

Yes. The diversity team (DT) is comprised of 11 members who review diversity-related information and make recommendations to the HR Leadership Committee. The team meets once a month virtually and once a year in person.

If yes, does the committee's representation include one or more members of the firm's management/executive committee (or the equivalent)?

Yes

How many employees are on the committee, and how often does the committee convene in furtherance of the firm's diversity initiatives?

The BASF diversity team has been designed to include representatives from a wide cross-section of the corporation. The team is comprised of 11 members from various sites in the North American region. We have taken years of service and experience levels into consideration in the composition of the team. Members represent a variety of communities: manufacturing and engineering, sales and marketing, purchasing, customer service, finance, research and development, human resources, PMU and legal. Each team member serves at least two years. We have two executive women in the team, and we meet once a month for an hour via virtual teleconference and also for two days in person for our annual diversity strategy meeting.

Total Executives on Committee: Two

Does the committee and/or diversity leader establish and set goals or objectives consistent with management's priorities?

Yes

Has the firm undertaken a formal or informal diversity program or set of initiatives aimed at increasing the diversity of the firm?

Yes, informal

How often does the firm's management review the firm's diversity progress/results?

Quarterly

The Stats

	NUMBER OF EMPLOYEES	REVENUE
	2006	2006
Total in the U.S.	15,500	$14.3 billion
Total worldwide	95,000	$66.1 billion

Diversity Mission Statement

Vision

At BASF NAFTA, we value the differences in our workforce, as they are key to the success of our business and to the achievement of our status as partner of choice. Consistent with our values, BASF has an inclusive environment that promotes respect and dignity for all in the workplace.

Resources

Diversity alliance consists of the diversity team (cross-functional group from various sites and backgrounds), employee groups (African-American Employees Group—AAEG; Women & Business Issues—W&BI; Gay, Lesbian, Bisexual, Transgender & Friends—GLBT&F; Latin American Employee Group—LAEG; and Emerging Professionals and Friends—EP&F) and extended alliance members that represent other HR functions including staffing, etc.

2006 Strategy

Focus on recruitment and retention, talent development and community outreach.

Goals

• To attract diverse candidates to work at BASF

• To maximize the development of the diverse talent in BASF

• To strengthen BASF's visibility and presence in the diverse communities we serve

Bayer CropScience

2 T.W. Alexander Drive
Research Triangle Park, NC 27709
Phone: (866) 992-2937
www.bayerjobs.com

Diversity Leadership

Summer Busto
Manager, Talent Acquisition & Domestic
 Relocation
P.O. Box 12014
Research Triangle Park, NC 27709
Phone: (919) 549-2437
E-mail: summer.busto@bayercropscience.com
www.bayerjobs.com

Recruiting

Please list the schools/types of schools at which you recruit.

• Public state schools

Do you have any special outreach efforts directed to encourage minority students to consider your firm?

INROADS Program

What activities does the firm undertake to attract minority and women employees?

• Seek referrals from other employees

• Utilize online job services

Do you use executive recruiting/search firms to seek to identify new diversity hires?

No

Internships and Co-ops

INROADS

Length of the program: 14

Web site for internship/co-op information: www.bayerjobs.com

We hire interns in various departments based on need and availability of projects. For the past three summers we've had interns in O&I, supply chain, marketing, HR, government regulatory affairs and accounts payable.

The Stats

2005 Revenue: $7.396 billion

Baystate Medical Center

759 Chestnut Street
Springfield, MA 01199
Phone: (413) 794-5655
Fax: (413) 794-8274
www.baystatehealth.com/jobs

Diversity Leadership
The director of recruitment is responsible for all recruitment initiatives.

Employment Contact
Nadrah McKenzie
E-mail: Nadrah.McKenzie@bhs.org

Recruiting

Please list the schools/types of schools at which you recruit.
• Private schools
• Public state schools
• Hispanic serving institutions (HSIs)
• Other predominantly minority and/or women's colleges

Do you have any special outreach efforts directed to encourage minority students to consider your firm?
• Conferences
• Sponsor minority student association events
• Firm's employees participate on career panels at school
• Outreach to leadership of minority student organizations
• Scholarships or intern/fellowships for minority students

What activities does the firm undertake to attract minority and women employees?
• Partner programs with women and minority associations
• Conferences
• Participate at minority job fairs
• Seek referrals from other employees
• Utilize online job services

Do you use executive recruiting/search firms to seek to identify new diversity hires?
Yes

Internships and Co-ops

INROADS; Clinical Externships
Number of interns in the program in summer 2006: 20 internships
Pay: $11.50 to $16 per hour, based on program and year in school

Length of the program: INROADS, eight to 10 weeks. Externships depend on specialty

Percentage of interns/co-ops in the program who receive offers of full-time employment: 100 percent of the INROADS students who successfully have completed the program have been offered full-time employment.

We are a major medical center and teaching hospital that offer internships with the INROADS program. We offer internship opportunities in a variety of areas both clinical and nonclinical. The INROADS program runs for 10 weeks in the summer and prepares students to become skilled professionals in a variety of areas. The internship offers a progressive program throughout the student's four years of college. When the students graduate, they are fully prepared to begin their health care career. During their senior year, our students may take advantage of any Baystate services offered, which includes our forgivable loan program and early sign on bonuses.

Strategic Plan and Diversity Leadership

How does the firm's leadership communicate the importance of diversity to everyone at the firm?
Our monthly news publication publishes articles; our internal web site offers information about educational programs and updates; global e-mails go out to management alerting them to information that they can share with their staffs; in-services are provided; diversity is part of our annual Knowledge Refreshers for staff.

Who has primary responsibility for leading diversity initiatives at your firm?
Senior VP of Human Resources Paula S. Dennison; currently hiring a chief diversity officer.

Does your firm currently have a diversity committee?
Yes

If yes, please describe how the committee is structured, how often it meets, etc.

Made up of staff and management employee representatives from spiritual services, interpreter services, staff development, professional and organizational development, staff RNs and nursing managers.

If yes, does the committee's representation include one or more members of the firm's management/executive committee (or the equivalent)?

Yes

If yes, in 2006, what was the total number of hours collectively spent by the committee in furtherance of the firm's diversity initiatives?

54 hours

If yes, how many employees are on the committee, and how often does the committee convene in furtherance of the firm's diversity initiatives?

The committee has regularly scheduled meetings.

Does the committee and/or diversity leader establish and set goals or objectives consistent with management's priorities?

Yes

Has the firm undertaken a formal or informal diversity program or set of initiatives aimed at increasing the diversity of the firm?

Yes, formal—affirmative action recruitment processes, JCAHO initiatives, magnet hospital initiatives and our internal customer service program.

The Stats

DEMOGRAPHIC PROFILE	
2006 Employees	6,579
Number of minorities	1,391
Minorities	21.1 percent
Minority executives	9.1 percent
Males	20.9 percent
Females	79.1 percent
Female executives*	68.3 percent

From supervisor level through CEO

Retention and Professional Development

How do 2006 minority and female attrition rates generally compare to those experienced in the prior year period?

Lower than in prior years.

Please identify the specific steps you are taking to reduce the attrition rate of minority and women employees.

• Increase/review compensation relative to competition
• Increase/improve current work/life programs
• Adopt dispute resolution process: In place for 22 years
• Work with minority and women employees to develop career advancement plans
• Professional skills development program, including minority and women employees

Additional Information

We are very much involved with community outreach, which includes collaborative efforts for minority students from grammar school through senior year in high school. We have a department that is solely responsible for collaborating with school systems as well as working closely with community groups such as the Urban League, etc. We have grown our INROADS internship program over the past several years and hope to increase our commitment in the future. We offer "career ladders" for the majority of our staff nurses (who are predominately women) as well as recognition for clinical certifications and tuition reimbursement to support further education. Our work/life department continually reviews its programs and has expanded its services offered to employees.

Black & Decker

701 E. Joppa Road
Towson, MD 21286
Phone: (410) 716-3900
Fax: (410) 716-2933
Toll Free: (800) 544-6986
www.bdk.com
www.bdksales.com

Locations

Towson, MD (HQ)
Campbellsville, KY • Charlotte, NC;
Chesterfield, MI • Danbury • CT • Decatur,
AR • Denison, TX • Ft. Lauderdale, FL • Fort
Mill, SC • Hopkinsville, KY • Jackson, TN •
Lake Forest, CA • Mira Loma, CA •
Montpelier, IN • Reading, PA • Rialto, CA •
Shelbyville, KY • Shelton, CT • Tampa, FL

Additional Information

Black and Decker was founded in 1910 when Duncan Black and Alonzo Decker invested $1,200 to operate a machine shop. Their first designs included a vest pocket adding machine and a candy dipping machine. Since that time, Black & Decker has grown to be a leading global manufacturer and marketer of quality power tools and accessories, hardware and home improvement products and technology based fastening systems. Our products and services are marketed in more than 100 countries, and we have manufacturing operations in 11 countries. Throughout our businesses, we have established a reputation for product innovation, quality, end-user focus, design and value. Our strong brand names and new product development capabilities enjoy worldwide recognition, and our global distribution is unsurpassed in our industries.

In 2005, Black & Decker had annual sales of over $6 billion and the company employs approximately 25,000 people around the world. The corporate headquarters is located in Towson, Maryland.

Black & Decker is made up of three business segments. They are as follows:

Power Tools: Headquartered in Towson, Maryland. Product categories include: corded and cordless power tools and equipment, outdoor tools, home products, accessories and product service. Major brand names include: Black & Decker, DeWalt, Firestorm, Workmate, Porter-Cable, and Delta.

Home and Hardware Improvement: Headquartered in Lake Forest, California. Product categories include: security hardware, commercial and residential door locksets, door hardware and plumbing products. Major product categories are Kwikset, Baldwin, Weiser, and Price Pfister.

Fastening and Assembly Systems: Headquartered in Shelton, Connecticut. Product categories include: assembly systems, specialty screws, metal and plastic fasteners, self-piercing riveting systems and platform-management services. Major brand names include Emhart Teknologies, Autoset, Gripco, Heli-Coil and Ultra-Grip.

Diversity Mission Statement

We are committed to developing a culture and environment in which all employees are respected and their differences are fully utilized toward meeting our organization's goals. This will allow us to provide a stimulating, challenging and satisfying environment for our employees and to improve returns to our investors through increased innovation and creativity and consistent improvement in the quality and profitability of our businesses. Our policies, practices and accountabilities reflect our belief that inclusion is a core value that will allow us to achieve higher levels of customer and employee satisfaction.

One of the ways in which we are working to achieve our diversity and inclusion objectives is through the Workplace Advisory Council that has been established in our power tools and accessories business. The mission of the Council is to provide advice and recommendations on workplace issues directly to our business heads.

For more information on career opportunities with Black & Decker, please visit our web site at www.bdk.com.

Blackwell Sanders Peper Martin LLP

4801 Main Street, Suite 1000
Kansas City, MO 64112
Phone: (816) 983-8782
Fax: (816) 983-8080
www.blackwellsanders.com

Locations

Belleville, IL • Kansas City, MO • Lincoln, NE • Omaha, NE • Overland Park, KS • Springfield, MO • St. Louis, MO • Washington, DC • London

Employment Contact

Stacie Cronberg
Manager of Legal Recruiting
E-mail: scronberg@blackwellsanders.com

Peter Sloan
Recruiting & Career Development Partner

Diversity Leadership

Kimberly Jones
Partner

Recruiting

Please list the schools/types of schools at which you recruit.

- Ivy League schools
- Other private schools
- Public state schools
- Historically black colleges and universities (HBCUs)
- Other predominantly minority and/or women's colleges

Do you have any special outreach efforts directed to encourage minority students and graduates to consider your firm?

- Hold a reception for minority students
- Advertise in minority student association publication(s) or other minority-focused publications
- Participate in/host minority student job fair(s) or other minority-focused job events
- Sponsor minority student association events
- Firm's employees participate on career panels at schools
- Outreach to leadership of minority student organizations
- Scholarships or intern/fellowships for minority students

What activities does the firm undertake to attract minority and women employees?

- Partner programs with women and minority associations
- Participate at minority job fairs
- Seek referrals from other employees
- Utilize online job services

Do you use executive recruiting/search firms to seek to identify new diversity hires?

No

Internships and Co-ops

INROADS

Deadline for application: February/March

Number of interns in the program in summer 2006 (internship) or 2006 (co-op): Eight total, among three of our offices

Pay: $17 per hour in Kansas City and St. Louis; $14 per hour in Omaha

Length of the program: 10 weeks

Web site for internship/co-op information: www.blackwell-sanders.com

The INROADS internship process increases business career opportunities and knowledge for outstanding, ethnically diverse young people, while giving employers the opportunity to develop diverse management talent. We offer an administrative track and a legal track at Blackwell Sanders for INROADS interns.

KCMBA Diversity Clerkship Program

Deadline for application: January

Number of interns in the program in summer 2006 (internship) or 2006 (co-op): One in Kansas City

Pay: $17 per

Length of the program: 12 weeks

Given the historic underrepresentation of diverse lawyers in greater Kansas City law firms, the pilot program seeks to provide a means for exposing diverse law students to area law firms and vice versa. The objective is to establish a vehicle through which participation of diverse students in law firm clerkship programs is increased with the long-term goal of increasing diverse hiring.

SLIP (Summer Law Internship Program)

Deadline for application: March

Number of interns in the program in summer 2006 (internship) or 2006 (co-op): Two total among offices (one in Kansas City, one in St. Louis)

Pay: $8 per hour

Length of the program: Eight weeks

SLIP is a law firm internship program for high school students interested in a legal career. Sponsored by the Kansas City Metropolitan Bar Association and the Kansas City School District, the SLIP program provides its participating students professional attire, information on working in a professional environment and several summer outings to area courts and law schools.

St. Louis Minority Clerkship Program

Deadline for application: February/March

Number of interns in the program in summer 2006 (internship) or 2006 (co-op): One in St. Louis

Pay: $17 per hour

Length of the program: 12 weeks

Blackwell Sanders and other St. Louis law firms partner with the law schools of Washington University, St. Louis University, the University of Missouri-Columbia and Southern Illinois University-Carbondale to place minority first-year law students in summer internships at participating firms.

Scholarships

We do contribute to law school minority scholarship programs at three universities.

Affinity Groups

True North

True North: Women with Direction is a Blackwell Sanders-sponsored initiative that showcases dynamic women, enhances leadership potential and establishes relationships for professional women in the community. Blackwell Sanders lawyers and area businesswomen interact at events and also benefit from enrichment programs on leadership topics.

The Mamas and the Papas

Blackwell Sanders recognizes the unique stresses the practice of law places on young lawyers, their spouses and their families. To support parenting lawyers and their families, Blackwell Sanders attorneys started the informal affinity group called the Mamas and the Papas, which gathers for monthly coffees and periodic events with children.

Entry-Level Programs, Full-Time Opportunities and Training Programs

Professional Development Program

Length of program: Trainings are on-going for all levels

Geographic location(s) of program: Our offices

Our Professional Development Program provides enrichment for lawyers at various stages of their careers on such topics as legal writing skills, presentation skills, time management skills, supervisor and project management skills, client relationship and business development skills, mentoring and coaching skills, technology skills and substantial legal practice skills.

Strategic Plan and Diversity Leadership

What trends in your industry affect your corporate diversity goals, strategies and/or internal or external alliances?

• An increase in demand by clients for both law firm and legal team diversity

• An increase in competition for diverse recruiting candidates

How does the firm's leadership communicate the importance of diversity to everyone at the firm?

We use e-mails, our web site, our *Mentoring Matters* newsletter, meetings and we offer diversity training opportunities to communicate the importance of diversity.

Who has primary responsibility for leading diversity initiatives at your firm?

Kimberly Jones, partner

Does your firm currently have a diversity committee?

Yes

If yes, please describe how the committee is structured, how often it meets, etc.

The Diversity Committee meets monthly and has a retreat annually. The committee is comprised of attorneys from four of our offices; eight partners, three associates, the director of human resources and the manager of legal recruiting.

If yes, does the committee's representation include one or more members of the firm's management/executive committee (or the equivalent)?

Yes

If yes, how many executives are on the committee, and in 2006, what was the total number of hours collectively spent by the committee in furtherance of the firm's diversity initiatives? How many employees are on the committee, and how often does the committee convene in furtherance of the firm's diversity initiatives?

Total Executives on Committee: One

The committee spent 731 hours in 2006. There are 13 employees on the committee, which convenes once a month.

Does the committee and/or diversity leader establish and set goals or objectives consistent with management's priorities?

Yes

Has the firm undertaken a formal or informal diversity program or set of initiatives aimed at increasing the diversity of the firm?

Yes, formal

How often does the firm's management review the firm's diversity progress/results?

Annually

How is the firm's diversity committee and/or firm management held accountable for achieving results?

The committee reports directly to the firm's chairman, with periodic measurement of progress toward goals.

The Stats

	NUMBER OF EMPLOYEES		REVENUE	
	2006	2005	2006	2005
Total in the U.S.	523	507	$115,810,000	$102,495,000
Total outside the U.S.	1	1	$856,000	$1,245,000
Total worldwide	524	508	$116,666,000	$103,740,000

DEMOGRAPHIC PROFILE	
Minorities in U.S. (not women)	65 (9.18 percent)
Minorities in U.S. (counting women)	430 (60.70 percent)
Male	41.28 percent
Female	58.72 percent
Executive Team	2 women (28 percent) 1 other minority (14 percent)

OTHER INFORMATION	
INTERNS IN THE LAST CALENDAR YEAR	
African-American	31.37 percent
Latino	3.92 percent
Asian	7.84 percent
Women	47.06 percent
Other ethnic group	1.96 percent
NEW HIRES IN THE LAST CALENDAR YEAR	
African American	13.38 percent
Latino	1.91 percent
Asian	5.73 percent
Women	57.32 percent
Other ethnic group	1.27 percent
NEW WOMEN HIRES IN THE LAST CALENDAR YEAR	
African American	10 percent
Latino	3 percent
Asian	5 percent
Women	90 percent
Other ethnic group	2 percent

Retention and Professional Development

How do 2006 minority and female attrition rates generally compare to those experienced in the prior year period?

Lower than in prior years.

Please identify the specific steps you are taking to reduce the attrition rate of minority and women employees.

• Develop and/or support internal employee affinity groups

• Increase/review compensation relative to competition

• Increase/improve current work/life programs

• Adopt dispute resolution process

• Work with minority and women employees to develop career advancement plans

• Review work assignments and hours billed to key client matters to make sure minority and women employees are not being excluded

• Strengthen mentoring program for all employees, including minorities and women

• Professional skills development program, including minority and women employees

Diversity Mission Statement

Blackwell Sanders is committed to recruiting, developing, retaining and promoting talented attorneys and staff with diverse backgrounds and experiences. At Blackwell Sanders, diversity encompasses a variety of characteristics, lifestyles and perspectives, including race, national origin, religion, gender, sexual orientation, gender identity, age, education, family and marital status. We firmly believe this diversity is essential to enhancing the quality of service to our clients, and to ensuring the personal satisfaction of our attorneys and staff.

Boeing Company, The

100 North Riverside
Chicago, IL 60606
Phone: (312) 544-2000
www.boeing.com/collegecareers

Employment Contact
Robert Poole
Senior Manager, College & Diversity Programs

Recruiting

Please list the schools/types of schools at which you recruit.

- Ivy League schools
- Other private schools
- Public state schools
- Historically black colleges and universities (HBCUs)
- Hispanic serving institutions (HSIs)
- Native American tribal universities
- Other predominantly minority and/or women's colleges

Do you have any special outreach efforts directed to encourage minority students to consider your firm?

- Hold a reception for minority students
- *Conferences:* National Society of Black Engineers, Society of Hispanic Professional Engineers, National Association of Asian-American Professionals, Hispanic Engineer National Achievement Awards Conference, Society of Women Engineers, Women of Color in Technology
- Advertise in minority student association publication(s)
- Participate in/host minority student job fair(s)
- Sponsor minority student association events
- Firm's employees participate on career panels at school
- Outreach to leadership of minority student organizations
- Scholarships or intern/fellowships for minority students

What activities does the firm undertake to attract minority and women employees?

- Partner programs with women and minority associations
- *Conferences:* See above list
- Participate at minority job fairs
- Seek referrals from other employees
- Utilize online job services

Internships and Co-ops

Deadline for application: Positions are posted from September through April

Number of interns in the program in summer 2006 (internship) or 2006 (co-op): 1,500

Length of the program: 12 to 14 weeks for internships; six months for co-ops

Percentage of interns/co-ops in the program who receive offers of full-time employment: 50 to 60 percent

Web site for internship/co-op information: www.boeing.com/collegecareers

Scholarships

Scholarship money is given to selected universities that select the scholarship recipients on Boeing's behalf.

Affinity Groups

- Boeing Asian-American Association
- Boeing Black Employees Association
- Boeing Employee Ability Awareness Association
- Boeing Employee Association for Gays and Lesbians
- Boeing Employee Association for Sexual Minorities
- Boeing Hispanic Employees Network

Strategic Plan and Diversity Leadership

We can accomplish much more if we are able to bring varied viewpoints and experience to the workplace. This will allow us to come up with the innovative products, services, and solutions we need to be competitive in a global environment.

We also want to be an employer of choice. We must be able to offer present and future employees the advantages of a creative, harmonious, inclusive workplace.

This will allow us to attract talent, improve quality performance and increase our market share in a global economy.

Retention and Professional Development

Please identify the specific steps you are taking to reduce the attrition rate of minority and women employees.

• Develop and/or support internal employee affinity groups (e.g., minority or women networks within the firm)

• Increase/review compensation relative to competition

• Increase/improve current work/life programs

• Adopt dispute resolution process

• Succession plan includes emphasis on diversity

• Work with minority and women employees to develop career advancement plans

• Review work assignments and hours billed to key client matters to make sure minority and women employees are not being excluded

• Strengthen mentoring program for all employees, including minorities and women

• Professional skills development program, including minority and women employees

Bonneville Power Administration

905 NE 11th Avenue
Portland, OR 97208
Phone: (503) 230-3000
www.bpa.gov

Locations
Portland OR (HQ)
Various jobs located in:
Idaho • Montana • Oregon • Washington

Employment Contact
www.jobs.bpa.gov

Recruiting

Please list the schools/types of schools at which you recruit.
- Ivy League schools
- Other private schools
- Public state schools
- Historically black colleges and universities (HBCUs)
- Hispanic serving institutions (HSIs)
- Native American tribal universities
- Other predominantly minority and/or women's colleges

Do you have any special outreach efforts directed to encourage minority students to consider your firm?
- Advertise in minority student association publication(s)
- Participate in/host minority student job fair(s)
- Sponsor minority student association events
- Firm's employees participate on career panels at school
- Outreach to leadership of minority student organizations
- Scholarships or intern/fellowships for minority students

What activities does the firm undertake to attract minority and women employees?
- Partner programs with women and minority associations
- Participate at minority job fairs
- Seek referrals from other employees
- Utilize online job services

Do you use executive recruiting/search firms to seek to identify new diversity hires?
Yes

Internships and Co-ops

STEP (Student Temporary Employee Program) and SCEP (Student Career Experience Program)
Deadline for application: Rolling

Pay: Range is from $10 to $25 per hour, depending on the type of position.

Length of the program: STEP participants generally work in one-year increments but could work during the summer only. For SCEP, if program requirements are met and FTE (manpower authorization) and budget are available, a participant can be eligible for a permanent position upon graduation.

Percentage of interns/co-ops in the program who receive offers of full-time employment: SCEP participants only are eligible for possible conversion to full-time employment.

Web site for internship/co-op information: www.jobs.bpa.gov (Click on "student" and you will get info on our two programs.)

Any organization within BPA can recruit students if they have the FTE (manpower authorization) and budget to fund the position.

Entry-Level Programs, Full-Time Opportunities and Training Opportunities

High Voltage Power System Electrician, Line Worker and Substation Operator Apprentice Program
Length of program: Three-and-a-half to four years

Geographic location(s) of program: Washington, Oregon, Montana and Idaho

Intensive classroom study, homework and on-the-job-training. End-of-Step presentations, exams and reviews are required every six months and if successful, the apprentice will be promoted to the next step of the apprenticeship program and finally to journeyman.

Pay starts out at $20.91 per hour. To join the company as a SCEP, you must meet all the student eligibility requirements, be enrolled in a two-year college in a course of study leading to a degree or certificate related to the electric utility industry, such as electrical theory, electronics, industrial arts or industrial technology. Watch for the vacancy announcements at our web site each fall for complete details.

Strategic Plan and Diversity Leadership

Who has primary responsibility for leading diversity initiatives at your firm?

Currently, Godfrey Beckett, manager diversity and EEO

Does your firm currently have a diversity committee?

Yes

If yes, does the committee's representation include one or more members of the firm's management/executive committee (or the equivalent)?

Yes

Does the committee and/or diversity leader establish and set goals or objectives consistent with management's priorities?

Yes

Has the firm undertaken a formal or informal diversity program or set of initiatives aimed at increasing the diversity of the firm?

Yes, formal and informal

The Stats

2006 Employees: 3,035

Diversity Mission Statement

The office of human resources, diversity and EEO provides leadership and serves as a principal advisor to the senior vice president, employee and business resources, the BPA administrator and chief executive officer and executive committee members on the impact and use of policies, proposals and programs related to human capital management, diversity management, equal employment opportunity and achievement of a high-performing organization.

The office staff develops, facilitates, administers and oversees and evaluates effective strategies, programs, policies and reports that support the BPA mission through:

• Strategic agency-wide Human Capital Management Program, which includes alignment of BPA mission and people measurement of management accountability and organizational improvements and semiannual reports to DOE headquarters

• Human resources, diversity and EEO policy development, evaluation and oversight

• Legislative proposal development and analysis

• Labor relations, including technical assistance to, and coordination of, the Partnership Council

• EEO Title VI and VII compliance and resolution programs, which includes affirmative employment planning and reporting

• Alternative dispute resolution programs

• Diversity management strategy and program support, including technical assistance to, and support of, the pluralism council

• Workforce statistics and analysis

Borders Group

100 Phoenix Drive
Ann Arbor, MI 48108
Phone: (734) 477-1100
Fax: (734) 477-1965
www.bordersgroupinc.com

Location

Ann Arbor, MI

Diversity Leadership

Leah Maguire
Director, Diversity Programs
100 Phoenix Drive
Ann Arbor, MI 48108
Phone: (800) 243-7510
Fax: (734) 477-1127

Recruiting

Please list the schools/types of schools at which you recruit.

• Public state schools

Do you have any special outreach efforts directed to encourage minority students to consider your firm?

• Participate in/host minority student job fair(s)
• *Other:* Network with student and professional organizations which support minority students

What activities does the firm undertake to attract minority and women employees?

• Participate at minority job fairs
• Seek referrals from other employees
• Utilize online job services
• *Other:* Built relationship with HACE (Hispanic Alliance for Career Enhancement)

Do you use executive recruiting/search firms to seek to identify new diversity hires?

Yes

Internships and Co-ops

Borders Group Summer Intern Program

Deadline for application: January 1st

Length of the program: 12 weeks

Percentage of interns/co-ops in the program who receive offers of full-time employment: It depends on the year

Web site for internship/co-op information: www.borders-groupinc.com

We continue to build upon the success of our Summer Internship Training Program. The program is intended to provide meaningful work experience to rising college seniors who would then become candidates for our College Graduate Training Program after graduation. Interns are placed in positions in finance, marketing/merchandising, information technology and human resources for a 12- to 14-week summer experience with Borders Group. In addition, our summer interns participate in an informative and interactive training program that is designed to help prepare them for their career.

Affinity Groups

• African-American Employee Action Group
• Women's Employee Action Group
• GLBT Employee Action Group
• Enlace Latino Employee Action Group

Employee action groups are a vehicle to better understand and support the complexity of varying employee and customer cultures and backgrounds. EAGs represent the diversity of and within a unique constituency, and are employee-driven teams composed of individuals at varying levels and with different functions. The purpose of the employee action groups is to explore and construct meaning on a range of issues that support diversity efforts in the workplace, marketplace and the local community. These groups meet on a monthly basis.

Entry-Level Programs, Full-Time Opportunities and Training Programs

College Grad Training Program

Length of program: Six months

Geographic location(s) of program: Ann Arbor, MI

We have had great success with our College Graduate Training Program. The goal of the program is to hire and develop college graduates in order to build a strong foundation of future leaders within Borders Group. College grads are placed in meaningful roles throughout our organization in the following functional areas: finance, marketing/merchandising, information technology and human resources. In addition, participants go through an informative and interactive training program that is designed to help prepare them for success at Borders Group. The College Graduate Training Program consists of the following elements:

Mentorship Guidance: College grads are partnered with a mentor who is a leadership team member.

Cross-Functional College Grad Team Project: College grads work together in cross-functional group projects that provide the company with predetermined deliverables at the end of the training period.

Operational Activities: College grads spend time training in our stores and distribution centers in order to see how our internal customers operate.

Professional Development Series: College grads participate in a number of training sessions that are designed to build their professional skills.

Functional Learning Lessons: College grads participate in a number of meetings with departmental leaders who share more specific information on how Borders Group operates.

Strategic Plan and Diversity Leadership

How does the firm's leadership communicate the importance of diversity to everyone at the firm?

The firm uses its web site, electronic newsletters, *Quarterly Scoop* newsletter, Intranet, meetings and training programs to showcase the importance of diversity.

Who has primary responsibility for leading diversity initiatives at your firm?

Dan Smith, senior vice president of HR and Leah Maguire, director—diversity programs

Does your firm currently have a diversity committee?

Yes. The committee meets monthly. Borders Group has developed a diversity task force to focus on building strategic initiatives that drive diversity awareness throughout the organization. The task force establishes the focus for diversity efforts throughout our business units, and develops strategies with the help of advisory committees made up of employees from the corporate offices, the field and the distribution facilities. Using various methods like those listed below, the diversity task force and the advisory committees have improved our overall business and nurtured Borders Group's commitment to diversity. The diversity task force focuses on the areas

of employee awareness, customer outreach, supplier diversity and recruiting/retention.

If yes, does the committee's representation include one or more members of the firm's management/executive committee (or the equivalent)?

Yes

How many employees are on the committee, and how often does the committee convene in furtherance of the firm's diversity initiatives?

Total Executives on Committee: One executive and five directors/senior managers

The DTF leaders provide formal updates to our executive team and our external diversity council once a year.

Does the committee and/or diversity leader establish and set goals or objectives consistent with management's priorities?

Yes

Has the firm undertaken a formal or informal diversity program or set of initiatives aimed at increasing the diversity of the firm?

Yes, formal

How often does the firm's management review the firm's diversity progress/results?

Monthly

Retention and Professional Development

Please identify the specific steps you are taking to reduce the attrition rate of minority and women employees.

- Develop and/or support internal employee affinity groups (e.g., minority or women networks within the firm)

- Increase/improve current work/life programs

- Succession plan includes emphasis on diversity

- Work with minority and women employees to develop career advancement plans

- Professional skills development program, including minority and women employees

- *Other:* We have our Pacesetters Programs at the corporate level and in the field, which are specifically dedicated to employee development. Both divisions of the program place an emphasis on minority recruitment and retention initiatives.

Diversity Mission Statement

At Borders Group, diversity is who we are. Our commitment to diversity extends to progressive policies, which uphold the right to personal dignity and fairness.

Every person has the right to be treated with respect and dignity, regardless of race, religion, color, creed, national origin, age, gender, gender identity, sexual orientation, disability, veteran or military sta-tus, marital status or citizenship status and other categories protect-ed by applicable federal, state and local laws.

Borders Group supports the individualism of each employee and encourages all who wish to grow to explore their talents and seek expanded opportunities. This deep-rooted enthusiasm for diversity of people and perspectives extends far beyond the walls of our stores. It reaches from our corporate office into our stores, distribu-tion centers and into every community we serve around the world.

Boy Scouts of America

P.O. Box 152079
1325 W. Walnut Hill Lane
Irving, TX 75015-2079
Phone: (972) 580-2118
Fax: (972) 580-2549
www.scouting.org

Diversity Leadership
Carolyn Altemus
Director, Diversity & Executive Recruiting
E-mail: caltemus@netbsa.org

Recruiting

Please list the schools/types of schools at which you recruit.
- Private schools
- Public state schools
- Historically black colleges and universities (HBCUs)
- Hispanic serving institutions (HSIs)
- Native American tribal universities
- *Other predominantly minority and/or women's colleges:* Asian serving universities

Do you have any special outreach efforts directed to encourage minority students to consider your firm?
- *Conferences:* LULAC, HACU, Asian Inc., NCLR, Alpha Phi Alpha, Professional Women, NACE, Job Choices Diversity Edition
- Advertise in minority student association publication(s)
- Participate in/host minority student job fair(s)
- Sponsor minority student association events
- Firm's employees participate on career panels at schools
- Outreach to leadership of minority student organizations
- Scholarships or intern/fellowships for minority students
- *Other:* Internship Mentoring Program

What activities does the firm undertake to attract minority and women employees?
- Participate at minority job fairs
- Seek referrals from other employees
- Utilize online job services
- *Other:* Internal ads in *Scoutreach Newsletter*, *Black EOE Journal*, *Hispanic Network Magazine*, *Job Choices Diversity Edition*, *Hispanic Career World*

Do you use executive recruiting/search firms to seek to identify new diversity hires?
No

Internships and Co-ops

Local Council Internship Model
Deadline for application: Varies by location
Pay: Pay varies by location
Length of the program: Semester
Percentage of interns/co-ops in the program who receive offers of full-time employment: Approximately 70 percent or more
Web site for internship/co-op information: Each local council has their own internship program.

The local college internship program is designed to be a unique, educational work and interpersonal relationship program especially and specifically designed to increase practical knowledge of the role and responsibilities of professional scouting. Students can receive academic credit for their internship from their college or university, and your local council receives another opportunity to extend scouting's relationships.

A local council internship program for college students will provide your council with the opportunity to develop a pool of qualified entry-level professionals and the ability to focus on serving an increasingly diverse population.

Scholarships

Each local council has its own procedure and options.

Entry-Level Programs, Full-Time Opportunities and Training Programs

Professional Development I, II, III
Length of program: One to two weeks
Geographic location(s) of program: Texas and regionally by area

The Boy Scouts of America realizes that in order for employees to grow and be productive, people need opportunities to learn. The fact that more than 75 percent of the BSA's professionals receive training each year is a testimony to the commitment by local councils and the national organization. Training courses, with set periods of time to acquire specific information, are part of our overall plan of development.

Professional scouters receive continuous instruction through formal as well as informal training. The BSA fosters an environment of continuous learning to nurture the collective creativity and skills that will benefit both professionals and the organization. We share knowledge, ideas and experience to create a workforce that is involved in decision-making and an inclusive work environment that ensures the success of scouting in the local area.

BSA is committed to the training and development of individuals because we fully recognize the benefits of mutual growth and development.

Strategic Plan and Diversity Leadership

How does the firm's leadership communicate the importance of diversity to everyone at the firm?

The chief scout executive of the Boy Scouts of America continually emphasizes the strategic need to increase and retain a diverse workforce as well as membership in the organization; we continually communicate the importance of diversity through BSA's "Who Are We" web page, monthly diversity newsletters, editorials and advertising in internal and external publications; we've established diversity communications committees who will review, educate, govern and enforce the need to increase and retain diverse employees, members and volunteers.

Who has primary responsibility for leading diversity initiatives at your firm?

Carolyn Altemus, director, diversity and executive recruiting

Does your firm currently have a diversity committee?

Yes

If yes, please describe how the committee is structured, how often it meets, etc.

The Communications Committee meets monthly; the Workforce Committee meets annually; and the Training Committee meeting quarterly. Each committee is lead by an advisor and is made up of employees of all levels, ethnicities and genders.

If yes, does the committee's representation include one or more members of the firm's management/executive committee (or the equivalent)?

Yes

Does the committee and/or diversity leader establish and set goals or objectives consistent with management's priorities?

Yes

Has the firm undertaken a formal or informal diversity program or set of initiatives aimed at increasing the diversity of the firm?

Yes, formal

Boy Scouts of America established strategies and goals to recruit and retain the number of minorities and women executives.

How often does the firm's management review the firm's diversity progress/results?

Quarterly

How is the firm's diversity committee and/or firm management held accountable for achieving results?

Critical achievements are assigned to diversity committees and their performance in serving on the committee is reviewed annually as part of their yearly performance evaluation.

Retention and Professional Development

Please identify the specific steps you are taking to reduce the attrition rate of minority and women employees.

• Increase/improve current work/life programs
• Succession plan includes emphasis on diversity
• Work with minority and women employees to develop career advancement plans
• Strengthen mentoring program
• Increase professional skills development program

Diversity Mission Statement

More than 90 years ago, the Boy Scouts of America (BSA) was founded on the premise of teaching boys moral and ethical values through an outdoor program that challenges them and teaches them respect for nature, one another and themselves. Scouting has always represented the best in community, leadership and service.

The Boy Scouts of America has selected its leaders using the highest standards because strong leaders and positive role models are vitally important to the healthy development of youth. Today, the organization still stands firm that their leaders exemplify the values outlined in the "Scout Oath and Law."

On June 28, 2000, the United States Supreme Court reaffirmed the Boy Scouts of America's standing as a private organization with the right to set its own membership and leadership standards.

The BSA respects the rights of people and groups who hold values that differ from those encompassed in the "Scout Oath and Law," and the BSA makes no effort to deny the rights of those whose views differ to hold their attitudes or opinions.

Scouts and scouters come from all walks of life and are exposed to diversity in scouting that they may not otherwise experience. The Boy Scouts of America aims to allow youth to live and learn as children and enjoy scouting without immersing them in the politics of the day.

We hope that our supporters will continue to value the Boy Scouts of America's respect for diversity and the positive impact scouting has on young people's lives. We realize that not every individual nor organization subscribes to the same beliefs that the BSA does, but we hope that all Americans can be as respectful of our beliefs as we are of theirs and support the overall good scouting does in American communities.

BP North America

501 WestLake Park Boulevard
Houston, TX 79079
Phone: (281) 366-2000
www.bp.com/uscollegecareers

Locations
Alabama • Alaska • California • Illinois •
Indiana • New Jersey • Ohio • South Carolina
• Texas • Washington

Internships and Co-ops

BP Summer Intern Program

Deadline for application: Candidates are interviewed on campus in the fall

Number of interns in the program in summer 2007 (internship) or 2007 (co-op): 281

Length of the program: Approximately 12 weeks

Percentage of interns/co-ops in the program who receive offers of full-time employment: 90 percent

Web site for internship/co-op information: www.bp.com/careers/US

As part of our recruiting continuum, BP works closely with top colleges and universities around the country to give talented students hands-on experience in their chosen field. This allows both students and BP the opportunity to evaluate future career possibilities. You will earn a competitive salary to help pay your educational expenses while gaining invaluable experience that will pay off throughout your career.

To be considered for our Cooperative Education Program or the Internship Program, you need to be in good academic standing with exceptional leadership, communication and self-motivational skills. These programs are a primary source for hiring regular full-time employees.

Entry-Level Programs, Full-Time Opportunities and Training Programs

Early Experience Programs

Geographic location(s) of program: BP North American operations

Programs and program lengths vary depending on the business unit and business need.

BP's Early Experience Programs are journeys of education, exploration, and discovery. These programs give our new hires a chance to get to know us. Along the way, you'll gain a greater understanding of how energy moves through the global marketplace from producer to consumer, and you'll develop the essential skills you'll need to achieve your long-term career goals.

Through the Early Experience Programs, you'll have a chance to experience what life is like in a variety of different roles throughout BP. Whether you're headed toward exploration, refining, marketing or trading, you'll discover the complex, interrelated nature of energy as you work on real projects with real applications and real responsibilities. It's a collaborative process that emphasizes individual growth and achievement. The program is built around six core elements that ensure you get the greatest benefit possible from your time in the Early Experience Programs:

Access to a buddy and mentor: Folks who can guide you through your early days on the job, provide a seasoned perspective on your specific role and give you tips on how to be successful at BP.

A structured induction: The opportunity to learn more about how the petroleum industry functions and where you fit into the overall picture.

Training programs: You'll have the opportunity to continue your learning through formal courses, conferences, and on-the-job experiences.

Managed job rotation: Your path through an Early Experience Program is specifically designed to broaden your exposure to the many facets of BP's operations while building your knowledge in your chosen discipline.

Networking: Early Experience Programs provide you with an automatic connection to others in the program at your site and across the company.

Development plans and competency assessment: You'll be involved in personal development planning and assessment of your progress as you rotate through different jobs.

The Stats

	NUMBER OF EMPLOYEES		REVENUE	
	2006	2005	2006	2005
Total worldwide	96,400	96,200	$262 billion	$262 billion

How do 2006 minority and female attrition rates generally compare to those experienced in the prior year period?

About the same as in prior years.

Bridgestone Americas Holding, Inc.

535 Marriott Drive
Nashville, TN 37214
Phone: (615) 937-1485
Fax: (615) 937-1807
www.bsanavigator.com

Locations

Nashville, TN

Diversity Leadership

Devra Courneya
HR Rep, Compliance & Diversity

Employment Contact

Jessica Garza
HR – College Relations
E-mail: garzajessica@bfusa.com

Recruiting

Do you use executive recruiting/search firms to seek to identify new diversity hires?
No

Internships and Co-ops

INROADS

Entry-Level Programs, Full-Time Opportunities and Training Programs

Navigator Training Program
Length of program: Six months
Geographic location(s) of program: North America

Travel to different business units to learn about the company. Completion of two nine-week projects within different business units.

Strategic Plan and Diversity Leadership

How does the firm's leadership communicate the importance of diversity to everyone at the firm?
Training modules, meetings and newsletters

Who has primary responsibility for leading diversity initiatives at your firm?
Devra Courneya, HR rep, compliance and diversity

Does your firm currently have a diversity committee?
No

Retention and Professional Development

How do 2006 minority and female attrition rates generally compare to those experienced in the prior year period?
Lower than in prior years.

Please identify the specific steps you are taking to reduce the attrition rate of minority and women employees.
- Develop and/or support internal employee affinity groups
- Increase/review compensation relative to competition
- Adopt dispute resolution process
- Succession plan includes emphasis on diversity
- Work with minority and women employees to develop career advancement plans
- Strengthen mentoring program for all employees, including minorities and women
- Professional skills development program, including minority and women employees

Additional Information

Promoting diversity within the workplace at all levels ensures our global competitiveness. Our teammates come from many different countries, cultures and ethnicities. By blending the strengths of our diverse workforce, we've created a team that's uniquely qualified to serve the needs of our customers and the communities we call home.

Brinker International, Inc.

6820 LBJ Freeway
Dallas, TX 75240
Phone: (972) 770-9824
www.brinkerjobs.com

Locations

Dallas, TX (HQ)
Global operations

Diversity Leadership

Mark King
Director, Diversity & Inclusion
6820 LBJ Freeway
Dallas, TX 75240
Phone: (972) 770-9824
E-mail: mark.king@brinker.com

Employment Contact

Kathleen Prawdzik
Staffing Manager—Home Office

Martin Riggs
Director, Recruiting—Field

Recruiting

Please list the schools/types of schools at which you recruit.

Schools with National Society of Minorities in Hospitality (NSMH) chapters.

Do you have any special outreach efforts directed to encourage minority students to consider your firm?

• Hold a reception for minority students

• Advertise in minority student association publication(s)

• Participate in/host minority student job fair(s)

• Sponsor minority student association events

• Outreach to leadership of minority student organizations

• Scholarships or intern/fellowships for minority students

What activities does the firm undertake to attract minority and women employees?

• Partner programs with women and minority associations

• *Conferences:*   National Society of Minorities in Hospitality; Professional Women Leadership

• Participate at minority job fairs

• Seek referrals from other employees

• Utilize online job services

Do you use executive recruiting/search firms to seek to identify new diversity hires?

Yes

Internships and Co-ops

INROADS

Deadline for application: January

Number of interns in the program in summer 2006 (internship) or 2006 (co-op): Six

Pay: $10 per hour

Length of the program: 10 weeks

Percentage of interns/co-ops in the program who receive offers of full-time employment: 25 percent (one out of four)

Strategic Plan and Diversity Leadership

What trends in your industry affect your corporate diversity goals, strategies and/or internal or external alliances?

• Labor shortage

• Awareness of the numerous career opportunities in the restaurant/hospitality industry

How does the firm's leadership communicate the importance of diversity to everyone at the firm?

Comprehensive approach to communications. Diversity messaging is aligned with quarterly employee meetings, key brand meetings, diversity e-mails, company newsletters, diversity section on Intranet and external web site, leadership talks (open forums), etc.

Who has primary responsibility for leading diversity initiatives at your firm?

Mark King, director, office of diversity and inclusion

Does your firm currently have a diversity committee?

Yes

If yes, please describe how the committee is structured, how often it meets, etc.

The team is strategically comprised of senior leadership representatives from home office and brands. The team meets quarterly or more frequently as needed. Meetings are facilitated by the office of diversity and inclusion.

If yes, does the committee's representation include one or more members of the firm's management/executive committee (or the equivalent)?

Yes

Does the committee and/or diversity leader establish and set goals or objectives consistent with management's priorities?

Yes. Collaborative approach; goals are set from recommendations by the office of diversity and inclusion and senior leadership vision and expectations

Has the firm undertaken a formal or informal diversity program or set of initiatives aimed at increasing the diversity of the firm?

Yes, formal diversity initiative in place

How often does the firm's management review the firm's diversity progress/results?

Quarterly

How is the firm's diversity committee and/or firm management held accountable for achieving results?

All officers have diversity goals included in performance management structure.

33 percent female—Brinker senior leadership team

The Stats

	NUMBER OF EMPLOYEES	REVENUE
	2005	2005
Total worldwide	120,000	$3.9 billion

Retention and Professional Development

How do 2006 minority and female attrition rates generally compare to those experienced in the prior year period?

Same

Please identify the specific steps you are taking to reduce the attrition rate of minority and women employees.

• Increase/improve current work/life programs

• Succession plan includes emphasis on diversity

• Work with minority and women employees to develop career advancement plans

• Professional skills development program, including minority and women employees

Diversity Mission Statement

We believe in celebrating the differences that make a good company great and in leveraging individual strengths to create an innovative, inclusive and unified team.

Bristol-Myers Squibb

345 Park Avenue
New York, NY 10154-0037
Phone: (212) 546-4000
www.bms.com

The Stats

	NUMBER OF EMPLOYEES	WORLDWIDE SALES
	2006	2006
Total	43,000	$17.9 billion

Additional Information

Different perspectives make it possible. At Bristol-Myers Squibb, we're a diverse team of talented and creative people—each with a different perspective. We value each person's unique contributions and inspire each other to develop the innovative solutions that extend and enhance the lives of our patients around the world.

Flexibility makes it possible. At Bristol-Myers Squibb, our people find fulfillment in their work, extending and enhancing the lives of patients around the world. And they have fulfilling lives at home too. Bristol-Myers Squibb offers a flexible range of work/life programs that help our employees at each stage of their lives. We're proud to be ranked in the top 100 of *Working Mother* magazine's Best Companies for Working Mothers.

Opportunities make your growth possible. Ask yourself—how far do you want to go? At Bristol-Myers Squibb, we're determined to be the company where our employees can achieve their career goals. We offer a range of opportunities to help you get there. It's simple. Your growth helps us to better extend and enhance the lives of patients around the world.

Brown Brothers Harriman & Co.

140 Broadway
New York, NY 10005
Phone: (212) 493-8945
Fax: (212) 493-7287

Locations
US:
Boston, MA • Charlotte, NC • Chicago, IL • Jersey City, NJ • New York, NY • Palm Beach, FL • Philadelphia, PA

International:
Dublin • Grand Cayman • Hong Kong • London • Luxembourg • Tokyo • Zurich

Diversity Leadership
Jim Minogue
Head of Human Resources

Employment Contact
Laura Scherban
Director of Recruiting

Recruiting

Please list the schools/types of schools at which you recruit.

- *Public state schools:* Rutgers University, Baruch College

- *Private schools:* Connecticut College, Northeastern University, Bryant College, Holy Cross College, Boston College, Stonehill College, St. Peter's College, Pace University, Dartmouth College, Providence College, etc.

Do you have any special outreach efforts directed to encourage minority students to consider your firm?

Yes

What activities does the firm undertake to attract women and minorities?

We utilize a wide variety of activities to attract women and minorities. We partner with a number of affinity organizations to develop strong relationships and networks to attract a wide range of candidates. We work with the INROADS organization to sponsor summer interns, and have a number of regional outreach efforts in our various locations.

Do you use executive recruiting/search firms to seek to identify new diversity hires?

Yes

Internships and Co-ops

Brown Brothers Harriman offers summer internship programs in our New York, New Jersey and Boston locations. Students are selected via an interview process for a specific role, then participate in a number of networking events throughout the summer. We sponsor INROADS interns, as well as interns from other local organizations in the communities in which we operate.

Entry-Level Programs, Full-Time Opportunities and Training Programs

Banking and Finance Training Program
Length of program: 18 weeks

Geographic location(s) of program: New York

The Brown Brothers Harriman Banking and Finance Training Program is an 18-week intensive program for new undergraduate hires in corporate banking and treasury. The program includes class instruction, case studies and presentations by BBH business leaders. Classes are conducted by instructors from top business schools. Subjects include financial accounting (introduction and advanced), money and banking, and corporate finance. All participants are joined with a mentor to give additional guidance and professional insight.

Corporate banking analysts will attend our 18-week Banking and Finance Training Program, after which they will join one of the regional or product specialty groups within the corporate banking group, under the leadership of a senior relationship manager. Initial responsibilities will include:

Financial analysis in support of new business initiatives

Credit analysis, including preparation of financial spreadsheets and written credit reports

Client relations support

As their experience develops over time, analysts are expected to take on relationship management and business development responsibilities.

Tuition reimbursement and additional internal training classes are available.

Investor Services-Client Service Training Program

Length of program: Two and a half weeks

Geographic location(s) of program: Boston

This program is designed for new hires new to the industry and will run for two-and-a-half weeks with each day including a full day of training. Incorporated into the program are different learning modules that include a variety of two- to three-hour training sessions. Modules include the basics of investment products, the global trade process and the fund accounting process at BBH.

Tuition reimbursement, on-the-job training and additional internal training classes are available.

Strategic Plan and Diversity Leadership

How does the firm's leadership communicate the importance of diversity to everyone at the firm?

BBH's employee handbook outlines very clearly BBH's commitment to diversity and equal employment opportunities. In addition, BBH's commitment to diversity is constantly reinforced throughout the entire recruitment process—from stressing our diversity efforts to external vendors, to conveying the importance to hiring managers.

Who has primary responsibility for leading overall diversity initiatives at your firm?

Head of Human Resources, Jim Minogue

Who has primary responsibility for diversity recruiting initiatives at your firm?

Director of Recruiting, Laura Scherban

Does your firm currently have a diversity committee?

No, but the firm does have a diversity leader.

Does the committee(s) and/or diversity leader establish and set goals or objectives consistent with management's priorities?

Yes

Has the firm undertaken a formal or informal diversity program or set of initiatives aimed at increasing the diversity of the firm?

Yes, informal

How often does the firm's management review the firm's diversity progress/results?

Ongoing

How are the firm's diversity committee(s) and/or firm management held accountable for achieving results?

There are annual reviews of promotions and compensation recommendations in which management reviews the progress of minorities and women within BBH. Senior managers challenge direct line managers to review when statistics do not show progress.

Additional Information

Work/Life Balance

Brown Brothers Harriman has thrived for almost 200 years on the strength of its people. Our employees' innovative ideas, commitment to quality and excellence and focus on client service have all contributed to the success of the firm.

Attracting the best people and providing them with a supportive environment in which they can grow, develop and contribute to the firm's success in a meaningful way has been and will continue to be a primary focus of the firm. This supportive environment is, in part, achieved by our offering a suite of benefits, programs and resources to our employees. Whether our employees are working to balance their work and personal life, are looking for a way to give back to the community, are seeking information about elder care services, or are looking for ways to save money through payroll deductions or profit sharing plans, BBH offers the resources to help.

Achieving our mission is accomplished through our people. We believe that our people deserve a premier environment in which to work with the appropriate benefits, programs and resources. We intend to support our employees and their changing needs for years to come.

Flexible Work Arrangements (FWAs)

We value our employees, and our support of FWAs reflects our trust in them. We seek to be an employer of choice, attracting the best

people and retaining employees who are committed to the firm. We recognize that there are differences among BBH employees and encourage creativity and initiative in addressing employee needs while simultaneously meeting or exceeding client expectations.

Excellent client service is critical to our continued success. At BBH, we are committed to achieving excellence and consider flexible work arrangements to be part of our business strategy that supports superior client service. FWAs need to fit with our business priorities and the nature of the job.

FWAs support the individuality of BBH employees without compromising teamwork, collaboration and mutual flexibility. Ongoing communication and collaboration of employees, managers and work groups is critical in all aspects of our business, including the effective implementation of FWAs. A mutual give and take occurs as needed, without taking advantage of an employee's or a manager's willingness to make periodic schedule adjustments in accessibility.

BBH Cares

BBHcares works to provide change in our communities—to transform peoples' lives through the power of collective effort, and to inspire a spirit of citizenship and social responsibility. The key focus of our mission is to offer our employees opportunities to give back to their communities and in the process, build a more rewarding workplace. Through volunteer projects that include reading books to children, feeding the hungry and building homes for low-income families, employees are working together to bring new possibilities to underprivileged people. As our volunteer efforts multiply and touch the lives of more and more people worldwide, BBH's employees are not only experiencing a more meaningful and unified workplace, they are helping to shape generations to come—leaving a legacy of social leadership, generosity and compassion for the future.

Bunzl Distribution

701 Emerson Road Suite 500
St. Louis, MO 63141
Phone: (314) 997-5959
Fax: (314) 228-0002
www.bunzldistribution.com

Locations

US:
Atlanta, GA • California • Dallas, TX •
Denver, CO • Kansas City, MO • North
Brunswick, NJ • Philadelphia, PA • St.
Louis, MO

International:
Canada • Mexico • UK

Employment Contact

Dana Jett
Employment Administrator
701 Emerson Road Suite 500
St. Louis, MO 63141
Phone: (314) 997-5959
Fax: (314) 228-0002
E-mail: dana.jett@bunzlusa.com

Recruiting

Do you have any special outreach efforts directed to encourage minority students to consider your firm?

• Participate in/host minority student job fair(s)

• Sponsor minority student association events

• Outreach to leadership of minority student organizations

• Scholarships or intern/fellowships for minority students

What activities does the firm undertake to attract minority and women employees?

• Participate at minority job fairs

• Seek referrals from other employees

Do you use executive recruiting/search firms to seek to identify new diversity hires?

Yes

If yes, list all women- and/or minority-owned executive search/recruiting firms to which the firm paid a fee for placement services in the past 12 months:

We haven't placed any candidates as of yet.

Internships and Co-ops

INROADS

Length of the program: Summer, winter and spring breaks

Percentage of interns/co-ops in the program who receive offers of full-time employment: 100 percent

Entry-Level Programs, Full-Time Opportunities and Training Programs

Management Trainee Program (i.e., Sales, Sales Management, Warehouse, Distribution, Logistics)
Length of program: Six to 12 months
Geographic location(s) of program: Worldwide

We customize and diversify our business in all segments with highly skilled and self-driven candidates in the above core areas. Also, we make sure our candidates understand our entire business scope. We offer tuition reimbursement for undergraduate and graduate degrees. Also, we offer four-year scholarships for all Bunzl employee dependents.

Strategic Plan and Diversity Leadership

How does the firm's leadership communicate the importance of diversity to everyone at the firm?
We conduct diversity training along with communicating the diversity initiatives to the employees through our Intranet.

Who has primary responsibility for leading diversity initiatives at your firm?
Robin Pokoik, VP HR and benefits

Does your firm currently have a diversity committee?

No

Has the firm undertaken a formal or informal diversity program or set of initiatives aimed at increasing the diversity of the firm?

We are in the process of creating a diversity program within our organization.

Burger King Corporation

5505 Blue Lagoon Drive
Miami, FL 33126
Phone: (305) 378-3000
www.bk.com

Diversity Leadership
Cirabel Olson
Director, Diversity

Employment Contact
Luis Almodovar
Human Resources Specialist

Marcia Ise
Manager, Talent Acquisition

Recruiting

Please list the schools/types of school at which you recruit.

- Ivy League schools
- Other private schools
- Public state schools
- Historically black colleges and universities (HBCUs)

Do you have any special outreach efforts directed to encourage minority students and graduates to consider your firm?

- *Conferences:* NBMBAA and NSHMBA
- Participate in/host minority student job fair(s) or other minority-focused job events
- Firm's employees participate on career panels at school
- Outreach to leadership of minority student organizations

What activities does the firm undertake to attract minority and women employees?

- Conferences
- Participate at minority job fairs
- Seek referrals from other employees
- Utilize online job services

Do you use executive recruiting/search firms to seek to identify new diversity hires?

Yes

Internships and Co-ops

Summer Internship Program

Deadline for application: For Summer 2008, the deadline is 03/28/2008.

Number of interns in the program in summer 2007 (internship): 30

Number of interns in the program in summer 2006 (internship): 26

Length of the program: 10 weeks

Web site for internship/co-op information: www.bkcareers.com

Our internship program will provide a great opportunity to get hands-on experience working with some of the best talent around in the following areas:

- Accounting/finance
- Communications
- Diversity
- Human resources
- Information technology
- Legal
- Marketing
- Operations

Internship details:

- Positions available at our global headquarters in Miami, Fla.
- 10-week paid program
- Presentation to functional leadership team
- Lunches with the BKC executives
- Social/networking events with interns and cross-functional hiring managers

Requirements:

- Undergraduate or graduate student
- Minimum 3.2 GPA

Entry-Level Programs, Full-Time Opportunities and Training Programs

Information Technology Leadership Program, ITLP

Length of program: Two years

Geographic location(s) of program: Miami, Florida

Position Summary:

- This exclusive opportunity is available to an individual who wants to build a strong technical foundation, gain leadership and communication skills, and attain cross-functional business knowledge.
- Two-year program consisting of four assignments lasting six months each
- Assignments in IT operations, development/programming and outside of the IT department designed to help you develop leadership skills, technical acumen and gain project management experience
- Formal and on-the-job training during the program in BKC-focused information technology systems, project management, communication skills, finance and career development
- Consistent feedback and development plans to ensure growth

Benefits:

- Great work/life balance programs
- On-site weight room, cafeteria and concierge services
- Competitive salary
- Opportunity for professional growth and development

Qualifications:

- Undergraduate student with a graduation date between May 2007 and December 2007
- Bachelor's degree in MIS, computer science or computer engineering preferred
- Minimum GPA of 3.5
- Demonstrated leadership skills
- Strong interest in a career in information technology
- Sharp business acumen
- Strategic plan and diversity leadership

What trends in your industry affect your corporate diversity goals, strategies and/or internal or external alliances?

Because our customer base skews highly ethnic, we are committed to giving back to the communities of which our customers are a part.

Diversity is the foundation of Burger King Corporation (BKC) in creating an environment that values and respects differences in employees, consumers, franchisees and business partners because it supports the mission and core values of the company.

Areas of focus:

- Community involvement
- Franchising
- Hiring
- Marketing
- People development
- Supplier diversity

How does the firm's leadership communicate the importance of diversity to everyone at the firm?

Diversity is a philosophy we embrace here at Burger King Corporation. Our CEO sends out a monthly newsletter in which our diversity initiatives are disseminated to all our employees and franchisees. Our CEO is also a member of our Diversity Action Council.

Who has primary responsibility for leading diversity initiatives at your firm?

Director, Diversity, Cirabel Olson

Does your firm currently have a diversity committee?

Yes

If yes, please describe how the committee is structured, how often it meets, etc.

We have a Diversity Action Council (DAC), which is an advisory council for Burger King Corporation in the formulation and evaluation of diversity development goals.

The DAC's mission is to help facilitate business development and trade between Burger King Corporation and ethnic business communities and to remove barriers that impede good business relationships.

The DAC members include:

- BKC executives in the areas of focus, including our CEO and our president of North America
- Franchisee representatives from our national association as well as from our three franchisee affinity groups
- Community leaders representing each one of the ethnic groups in the DAC
- CEO of our purchasing co-op, Restaurant Services, Inc.

Burlington Northern Santa Fe Railway Co.

2500 Lou Menk Drive
Fort Worth, TX 76131-2828
Phone: (817) 352-6008
Fax: (817) 352-7108

Locations

Fort Worth, TX (corporate office)
Operations in a total of 28 states and two
Canadian provinces.

Diversity Leadership

Pamela Sherlock
Director Staffing

Employment Contact

Susan Hutchison
E-mail: susan.hutchison@BNSF.com

Recruiting

Please list the schools/types of schools at which you recruit.

- Private schools
- Public state schools
- Historically black colleges and universities (HBCUs)

Do you have any special outreach efforts directed to encourage minority students to consider your firm?

- *Conferences:* NSBE, NSHBA, NBMBA, NACE (local, regional and national)
- Participate in/host minority student job fair(s)
- Outreach to leadership of minority student organizations
- Scholarships or intern/fellowships for minority students

What activities does the firm undertake to attract minority and women employees?

- *Conferences:* NSBE, NSHBA, NBMBA, NACE
- *Other:* BOLD Initiative

Do you use executive recruiting/search firms to seek to identify new diversity hires?

No

Internships and Co-ops

BNSF Railway

Deadline for application: Early spring

Pay: Varies

Length of the program: Varies; typically eight to 10 weeks

Web site for internship/co-op information: www.bnsf.com/jobs

The BNSF internship program gives college students practical, on-the-job experience in a business environment.

Candidates for internships are typically full-time students currently enrolled at a college or university who are pursuing an undergraduate degree or a graduate degree in a field of study that supports BNSF's business objectives. BNSF recruits candidates from college campuses, minority student referral programs, the Internet, employee referrals and unsolicited resumes.

Interns are assigned to a department that will then direct the intern's activities on specific projects and work assignments.

BNSF departments that seek interns include: accounting/finance, corporate audit services, engineering, human resources, marketing, mechanical, safety, technology services, transportation/operations and other support departments. While most assignments are at BNSF's corporate headquarters (Fort Worth, Texas), some interns are placed in field locations across the BNSF system. Field assignments are predominantly for the transportation/operations, engineering and mechanical departments.

The program includes an orientation with an overview of corporate policies and appropriate conduct. Interns participate in several key activities throughout their program, including:

- Presentations by various department leaders
- Midterm and final activity status reports prepared by the intern
- Intern team presentations at the end of the program
- Midterm and final performance evaluations by supervisors
- Exposure to some BNSF management trainee program activities
- Networking opportunities

Scholarships

BNSF Diversity Scholarships

Deadline for application for the scholarship program: Students apply through their universities by March of each year.

Scholarship award amount: Honored recipients receive $5,000 (payable in two annual installments of $2,500 for students' junior and senior years).

Five scholarships are established at four predesignated universities. Students must have at least a 3.0 GPA, be well rounded and pass a skills assessment exam. A facility review panel recommends the top two to three sophomore students. Students all receive two summer internships with BNSF.

Affinity Groups

- African-American
- Asian-American
- Native American
- Hispanic
- Women's

The purpose is to promote the professional and personal development of its members. Meet at least monthly. All have internal web sites.

Entry-Level Programs, Full-Time Opportunities and Training Programs

BNSF Railway Management Trainee Program

BNSF recruits candidates from college campuses, the Internet, BNSF's former interns and internal job postings. As part of the selection process, a potential candidate visits BNSF's corporate headquarters to participate in panel interviews and a comprehensive skills assessment. Candidates for the program must be team players who value diversity and who drive for results. They should also have a good scholastic record, a history of leadership roles in school or the community, previous internship experience, ability to analyze problems logically, and excellent oral and written communication skills.

Length of program: Six to 12 months

Geographic location(s) of program: Across BNSF system, with a large number at corporate headquarters

Management trainees receive cross-functional, departmental training during their six or 12-month training period, as well as exposure to all departments through an initial one month corporate orientation. Each trainee can request a BNSF mentor for career and personal guidance. The training itself is tailored to the individual and monitored by the sponsoring business group and human resources department.

Strategic Plan and Diversity Leadership

What trends in your industry affect your corporate diversity goals, strategies and/or internal or external alliances?

The most significant trend is the aging workforce in our industry and company. The baby boomer bubble is very real, which has created the necessity to find ways to brand ourselves in order to attract future diverse applicants and provides opportunities for employees, particularly people of color and women to compete for positions vacated by retirees.

How does the firm's leadership communicate the importance of diversity to everyone at the firm?

BNSF communicates through internal diversity conferences, diversity councils, affinity groups, newsletters, departmental meetings, awareness training sessions and various written forms of communication.

Who has primary responsibility for leading diversity initiatives at your firm?

Ed McFalls, assistant vice president, human resources and diversity

Does your firm currently have a diversity committee?

Yes, There are two types of diversity committees:

Executive diversity council: Consists of BNSF's CEO, his six direct reports, VP of corporate relations and the AVP of human resources and diversity. Group meets quarterly to review diversity successes and opportunities. In 2004, this group spent at least eight hours as a council, but they address initiatives throughout the year during weekly executive meetings.

16 regional diversity councils (across our system): Consist of both union and management employees that are responsible for resolving diversity tensions in their respective locations.

In 2004, each council spent approximately 36 hours furthering diversity initiatives (monthly meetings of approximately three hours each).

If yes, does the committee's representation include one or more members of the firm's management/executive committee (or the equivalent)?

Yes

Does the committee and/or diversity leader establish and set goals or objectives consistent with management's priorities?

Yes. Each committee's goals are established based upon BNSF's overall diversity strategy.

Has the firm undertaken a formal or informal diversity program or set of initiatives aimed at increasing the diversity of the firm?

Yes, formal. BNSF has a robust formal diversity strategy that addresses executive/leadership support, recruiting and enhancing talent, community involvement and continual education and awareness.

How often does the firm's management review the firm's diversity progress/results?

Quarterly: CEO and senior VPs perform a detailed review quarterly.

Annually: VP and AVP are provided an overview/update at annual management meeting.

The Stats

	NUMBER OF EMPLOYEES		REVENUE	
	2006	2005	2006	2005
Total in the U.S.	41,396 (year end)	40,537 (year end)	$15.0 billion	$13.0 billion

Diversity Mission Statement

We view diversity as a business necessity, a business opportunity and a moral imperative. To achieve diversity, BNSF has undertaken strategies and actions that recognize, accept, value and utilize the differences and similarities among all applicants, employees, customers, suppliers and the community.

To advance our vision, we have a diversity business purpose. Embracing diversity helps BNSF to: recruit, hire and promote the best diverse talent; create a collaborative workforce that functions as a team; understand and market to a diverse customer base; procure from a diverse supplier base; and provide quality service that meets our customers' needs and requirements.

Additional Information

By design, BNSF's diversity definition is simple: respecting and valuing the differences and similarities of people. Too often, diversity is defined by the traditional terms of race, gender, age, religion and culture. At BNSF, we have expanded the definition to include diversity of mind, experience, education, skills and thought.

BNSF affinity groups share a vision to advance the personal and professional development of their members, expose their members to increased leadership opportunities, provide support and networking for members, participate in community service and work with corporate diversity to achieve other BNSF people initiatives, including employee recruitment and retention. Nevertheless, they are unique when they address the particular needs of their group. Currently, there are five active affinity groups at BNSF: BNSF Asian American Network; Hispanic Leadership Council; African-American Networking Group; Women's Network; and the Council of Native Americans.

Hundreds of BNSF people throughout the railway have volunteered for the regional diversity councils, and they work tirelessly to educate co-workers about different cultures and backgrounds. They are also responsible for identifying and resolving local diversity tensions, before formal resolutions have to be implemented. They host diversity celebrations such as Martin Luther King Jr. Day, Veteran's Day, Cinco de Mayo and Women's Month, among others. Lastly, they promote community advocacy initiatives by getting involved with the communities in which they live and work.

BNSF has hosted annual diversity forums and summits to bring together 200 to 300 employees and the leadership team to share ideas and identify ways for BNSF to enhance its diversity efforts. Invitees include a broad representation of BNSF departments and are randomly selected to allow opportunity for more BNSF people to participate in the conferences. At each event, participants have the opportunity to talk with BNSF leaders, brainstorm ideas on how to make BNSF a more diverse community, listen to experts' insights and perspectives on success in corporate America, network with employees from throughout the company and participate in experiential learning.

BNSF offers a variety of alternative work arrangements on a limited basis, informally administered by each department, for certain positions including traditional flex-time, daily flex-time, compressed work week and telecommuting/working from home.

Campbell Soup Company

1 Campbell Place
Camden, NJ 08103-1701
Phone: (856) 342-4800 ext. 2225
www.campbellsoupcompany.com

Campbell Soup Company is a global manufacturer and marketer of high-quality, branded convenience food products. With sales exceeding $7 billion, Campbell Soup Company is the world's largest manufacturer and marketer of soup and a leading producer of sauces, juice beverages, biscuits and confectionery products.

At Campbell, we define diversity as the vast array of human differences and similarities, inclusive of everyone. In order to compete and succeed in a changing marketplace we must cultivate and embrace a diverse employee population that fuels our growth and enriches our global culture. As part of our Campbell's Vision, "together we will do extraordinary things in the workplace and marketplace," our commitment to building and strengthening teams has the greatest focus of our leadership. We must have diverse perspectives, talents and teams to meet this business challenge. You won't find a better place for your talent, ideas and experience than at Campbell Soup Company.

Campbell Soup Company is an equal opportunity employer by choice, and supports the principles of hiring a diverse workforce. EEO/AA/D/V

Visit our web site at careers.campbellsoupcompany.com.

Capital One Financial Corporation

1680 Capital One Drive
McLean, VA 22012
Phone: (703) 720-1000
www.capitalone.com/careers

Locations

US:

California • Connecticut • Florida •
Louisiana • Massachusetts • New York •
Texas • Virginia • Washington, DC

International:
Canada • UK

Diversity Leadership

Rob Keeling
Vice President of Diversity

Employment Contact

Lisa Metrinko
Senior Recruiting Manager
Phone: (703) 720-3665
E-mail: lisa.metrinko@capitalone.com
www.capitalone.com/careers

Recruiting

Please list the schools/types of schools at which you recuit.

- *Ivy League schools:* Brown, Cornell, Harvard, Stanford, University of Pennsylvania
- *Other private schools:* Boston College, Carnegie Mellon, Columbia, Dartmouth, Duke, Emory, Georgetown, Johns Hopkins, MIT, Notre Dame, Vanderbilt
- *Public state schools:* University of Virginia, Virginia Tech, George Washington University, Georgia Tech, Indiana University, University of Chicago, UT-Austin, University of Michigan, University of Maryland, Case Western, Penn State, Ohio State, Rutgers, University of Illinois, University of North Carolina, Purdue, Washington University, William & Mary, University of Florida, University of Wisconsin
- Other predominantly minority and/or women's colleges

Do you have any special outreach efforts directed to encourage minority students to consider your firm?

- Advertise in minority student association publication(s)
- Sponsor minority student association events
- Firm's employees participate on career panels at school

What activities does the firm undertake to attract minority and women employees?

- *Conferences:* Simmon's School of Management Leadership Conference, Linkage Women in Leadership, Wharton's Whitney M. Young Conference, HBS Women's Leadership Conference

- *Participate at minority job fairs:* NAACP, NSBE, NBMBAA, NSHMBA, National Association of Women MBAs, Reaching Out, MBA, MEAC/SWAC job fair, SWE
- Seek referrals from other employees
- Utilize online job services

Do you use executive recruiting/search firms to seek to identify new diversity hires?

No

Internships and Co-ops

Capital One Summer Intern Program

Deadline for application: March 10th

Pay: Based on full time competitive salary

Length of the program: 12 weeks

Percentage of interns/co-ops in the program who receive offers of full-time employment: 90 percent

Web site for internship/co-op information:
www.capitalone.com/careers/campusrecruiting.shtml

If you're looking to put your education to the test in real business situations, beef up your resume, add to your skills, and have fun too, then our Summer Intern Program may be perfect for you! As an intern, you'll get involved in and be responsible for challenging projects that can have a significant impact on our business—no making coffee or picking up dry cleaning here! Your projects will typically be team-oriented, and you'll gain new skills in a positive learning environment. Other great benefits of our intern program include the following: executive speaker series, team building events, intern-specific training class.

Affinity Groups

Five Associate Networks:
• African-American Network
• Asian Network
• Hispanic Network
• LGBT (Lesbian, Gay, Bisexual and Transgender) Network
• Women's Network

Capital One's associate networks have shared objectives of recruitment, retention, development and community outreach. These networks provide support in the form of programs, resources and tools that enable our associates to achieve their full potential in an environment that values the differences we bring to the workplace.

Diversity Councils

Across Capital One, several Diversity Councils have formed within specific lines of business to drive our diversity strategy at the local level. From education to flexible work arrangements and mentoring to advancement, our Diversity Councils bring together business leaders to ensure success.

Diversity Mission Statement

At Capital One, diversity means finding associates with different backgrounds, life and work experiences, beliefs and communication styles. Diversity means seeking and embracing our differences because of the richness those differences add to our lives and the many advantages they provide to our business.

– Rich Fairbank, Chairman and Chief Executive Officer

Charter Communications

12405 Powerscourt
St. Louis, MO 63116
www.chartercom.com

Locations
United States

Recruiting

Please list the schools/types of schools at which you recruit.
- Private schools
- Public state schools
- Historically black colleges and universities (HBCUs)
- Hispanic serving institutions (HSIs)
- Other predominantly minority and/or women's colleges

Do you have any special outreach efforts directed to encourage minority students to consider your firm?
- *Conferences:* NAMIC, WICT, NAACP
- Advertise in minority student association publication(s)
- Participate in/host minority student job fair(s)
- Sponsor minority student association events
- Firm's employees participate on career panels at school
- Outreach to leadership of minority student organizations
- Scholarships or intern/fellowships for minority students

What activities does the firm undertake to attract minority and women employees?
- Partner programs with women and minority associations
- *Conferences:* NAMIC, WICT, NAACP
- Participate at minority job fairs
- Seek referrals from other employees
- Utilize online job services

Do you use executive recruiting/search firms to seek to identify new diversity hires?
Yes

Internships and Co-ops

Emma Bowen Foundation
Deadline for application: Potential interns apply to the Emma Bowen Foundation directly.

Length of the program: Three to six months

Percentage of interns/co-ops in the program who receive offers of full-time employment: 85 percent

Web site for internship/co-op information:
www.emmabowenfoundation.com

Strategic Plan and Diversity Leadership

How does the firm's leadership communicate the importance of diversity to everyone at the firm?
The firm's leadership communicates diversity's importance through membership drives with NAMIC, WICT, and other e-mails, newsletters and outreach opportunities within the community.

Who has primary responsibility for leading diversity initiatives at your firm?
Sandra Young, vice president of corporate human resources

Heather Reynolds, senior recruiting generalist and Lamont Orange, vice president enterprise security

Does your firm currently have a diversity committee?
Yes, we have a strong presence in NAMIC and WICT, where we have several members throughout the organization involved in.

If yes, please describe how the committee is structured, how often it meets, etc.
NAMIC and WICT, both meet monthly.

If yes, does the committee's representation include one or more members of the firm's management/executive committee (or the equivalent)?
Yes

The Stats

2005 Employees: 16,000

Retention and Professional Development

Please identify the specific steps you are taking to reduce the attrition rate of minority and women employees.

- Develop and/or support internal employee affinity groups (e.g., minority or women networks within the firm)
- Increase/review compensation relative to competition

- Succession plan includes emphasis on diversity
- Work with minority and women employees to develop career advancement plans
- Professional skills development program, including minority and women employees

Diversity Mission Statement

It takes all kinds of people to bring it all together.

CIGNA

1601 Chestnut Street
Philadelphia, PA 19192

Locations

Philadelphia, PA (HQ)
Bloomfield, CT, and other offices nationwide.

Diversity Leadership

Priti Dheer
Director of Diversity

Employment Contact

careers.cigna.com

Recruiting

Please list the schools/types of schools at which you recruit.

• Ivy League schools
• Other private schools
• Public state schools
• Historically black colleges and universities (HBCUs)

Do you have any special outreach efforts directed to encourage minority students to consider your firm?

• Participate in/host minority student job fair(s)
• Sponsor minority student association events
• Outreach to leadership of minority student organizations
• Scholarships or intern/fellowships for minority students
• *Other.* Black Executive Exchange Program

What activities does the firm undertake to attract minority and women employees?

• Partner programs with women and minority associations
• Participate at minority job fairs
• Seek referrals from other employees
• Utilize online job services

Do you use executive recruiting/search firms to seek to identify new diversity hires?

Yes

Internships and Co-ops

Actuarial Executive Development Program, Technology Early Career Development Program, HealthCare

Leadership Program and Financial Development Program

Deadline for application: We recruit for these programs from September through April

Pay: $18 to $35/hour (depends whether undergrad or grad level)

Length of the program: 11 to 13 weeks

Percentage of interns/co-ops in the program who receive offers of full-time employment: 70 percent

Please describe the internship program or co-op, including departments hiring, intern/co-op responsibilities, qualifications for the program and any other details you feel are relevant.

Varies based on program.

Affinity Groups

No affinity groups, however, CIGNA has partnered with BEEP, BDPA, NABA, IABA & MCCA as a resource for employees.

Entry-Level Programs, Full-Time Opportunities and Training Programs

Actuarial Executive Development Program

Length of program: 18 to 24 months

Geographic location(s) of program: Philadelphia, Pa.; Bloomfield, Conn.; Claymont, Del.

Please describe the training/training component of this program:

Given study time for actuarial exams separate from vacation time, cover cost of SOA exams, study materials/notes etc., cost of review seminars plus travel expenses.

Accounting Development Track

Length of program: Three rotations each about 18 months in length

Geographic location(s) of program: Philadelphia, Pa.; Bloomfield, Conn.;

Please describe the training/training component of this program:

Obtain valuable hands-on experience in diverse accounting and audit-focused environments.

Business Sales and Leadership Training Program

Length of program: 13 to 15 weeks

Geographic location(s) of program: Nationwide

Please describe the training/training component of this program:

The program is an extensive learning opportunity that consists of on-the-job and classroom training, coaching and mentoring.

Financial Development Program

Length of program: Three to four rotations of 18 to 24 months

Geographic location(s) of program: Hartford, Conn.; Philadelphia, Pa. and other various field locations nationwide.

Please describe the training/training component of this program:

Training will be competency-based rotational assignments, training and mentoring.

HealthCare Leadership Program

Length of program: Three 12 to 24 month rotations

Geographic location(s) of program: First rotation in Bloomfield, Conn.

Please describe the training/training component of this program:

Training will be a multifaceted approach, using a required set of Corporate Training programs, self-study and special projects.

Service Emerging Leadership Development Program

Length of program: Two-and-a-half-year program

Geographic location(s) of program: Field locations nationwide

Please describe the training/training component of this program:

Formal, individual, and on-the-job training is provided. Training will be focused on these main topics: six sigma, project management, customer service and leadership.

Sales Optimization, Acquisition and Retention Program

Length of program: 13 to 15 weeks

Geographic location(s) of program: Field locations nationwide

Please describe the training/training component of this program:

On-the-job and classroom training, coaching and mentoring.

Technology Early Career Development Program

Length of program: Rotations every 12 to 18 months over three years

Geographic location(s) of program: Hartford, Conn. and some available in Philadelphia, Pa.

Please describe the training/training component of this program:

Training will be a multifaceted approach, using a required set of Corporate Training programs, self-study and special projects.

Underwriting Leadership and Risk Assessment Program

Length of program: 12 weeks

Geographic location(s) of program: Philadelphia, Pa.

Please describe the training/training component of this program:

Classroom training and on-the-job–experience.

Strategic Plan and Diversity Leadership

How does the firm's leadership communicate the importance of diversity to everyone at the firm?

Communication is sent through internal newsletters, company Intranet, cultural competency training and e-learning.

Who has primary responsibility for leading diversity initiatives at your firm?

Priti Dheer, director of diversity in partnership with HR directors and business partners.

Does your firm currently have a diversity committee?

Yes

If yes, please describe how the committee is structured, how often it meets, etc.

Each of the individual business units (finance, group, etc.) at CIGNA are currently in the process of developing their own diversity plans; they have chosen individuals to be on their diversity councils, to develop partnerships and plans, specifically relating to their own needs. We also have diversity councils in various field offices.

If yes, does the committee's representation include one or more members of the firm's management/executive committee (or the equivalent)?

No

Does the committee and/or diversity leader establish and set goals or objectives consistent with management's priorities?

Yes, the committee sets goals consistent with their business unit's demographic information.

Has the firm undertaken a formal or informal diversity program or set of initiatives aimed at increasing the diversity of the firm?

Yes, formal. The executive management team has had education provided by Roosevelt Thomas Consulting, conducting cultural competency training and internal diversity education.

How often does the firm's management review the firm's diversity progress/results?

Twice a year

The Stats

	NUMBER OF EMPLOYEES		REVENUE	
	2006	2005	2006	2005
Total in the U.S.	23,858	25,391	$16.5 billion	N/A

Retention and Professional Development

Please identify the specific steps you are taking to reduce the attrition rate of minority and women employees.

• Succession plan includes emphasis on diversity

• Work with minority and women employees to develop career advancement plans

• Strengthen mentoring program for all employees, including minorities and women

• Professional skills development program, including minority and women employees

• *Other:* Develop partnerships with external organizations.

Diversity Mission Statement

Our mission is to create and support a work environment that attracts and retains the most talented, ethical, knowledgeable, mutually supportive and diverse people.

Cintas Corporation

6800 Cintas Blvd
Cincinnati, OH 45262
Phone: (513) 459-1200

Locations
Throughout North America

Diversity Leadership
Marsha Thornton

Employment Contact
Rick Johnson

Recruiting

Please list the schools/types of schools at which you recruit.

• Ivy League schools
• Other private schools
• Public state schools
• Historically black colleges and universities (HBCUs)
• Hispanic serving institutions (HSIs)
• Native American tribal universities
• Other predominantly minority and/or women's colleges

Do you have any special outreach efforts directed to encourage minority students to consider your firm?

• Hold a reception for minority students
• Advertise in minority student association publication(s)
• Participate in/host minority student job fair(s)
• Sponsor minority student association events
• Firm's employees participate on career panels at school
• Outreach to leadership of minority student organizations
• Scholarships or intern/fellowships for minority students

What activities does the firm undertake to attract minority and women employees?

• Partner programs with women and minority associations
• Participate at minority job fairs
• Seek referrals from other employees
• Utilize online job services

Do you use executive recruiting/search firms to seek to identify new diversity hires?
No

Entry-Level Programs, Full-Time Opportunities and Training Programs

Management Trainee
Length of program: 24 months
Geographic location(s) of program: Nationwide

Cisco Systems, Inc.

170 West Tasman Drive
San Jose, CA 95134
Phone: (408) 526-4000
www.cisco.com

Locations
San Jose, CA (HQ)
Bedfont Lakes, UK

Contact Person
James Brooks
Director, World Wide Diversity & Inclusion

Recruiting

Please list the schools/types of schools at which you recruit.

- Ivy League schools
- Public state schools
- Historically black colleges and universities (HBCUs)
- Other predominantly minority and/or women's colleges

Do you have any special outreach efforts directed to encourage minority students to consider your firm?

- Hold a reception for minority students
- *Conferences:* Anita Borg, NBMBAA, NSBE, SWE, SHPE, NSHMBA
- Advertise in minority student association publication(s) or other minority-focused publications.
- Participate in/host minority student job fair(s) or other minority-focused job events
- Sponsor minority student association events
- Outreach to leadership of minority student organizations
- Scholarships or intern/fellowships for minority students

What activities does the firm undertake to attract minority and women employees?

- Partner programs with women and minority associations
- *Conferences:* Anita Borg, NBMBAA, NSBE, SWE, SHPE, NSHMBA
- Participate at minority job fairs
- Seek referrals from other employees

Do you use executive recruiting/search firms to seek to identify new diversity hires?

Yes

Internships and Co-ops

Cisco Internet Generation Scholars (CIGS)

Number of interns in the program in summer 2006 (internship) or 2006 (co-op): 25

Pay: Based upon market rate/location

INROADS

Number of interns in the program in summer 2006 (internship) or 2006 (co-op): Two

Pay: Based upon market rate/location

Length of the program: 12 weeks during the summer

Scholarships

Hispanic Scholarship Fund, UNCF, Grace Hopper, Women in Computing

Scholarship award amount in U.S. dollars; amount varies depending upon requirements.

Affinity Groups

Network groups may hold monthly meetings as well as host various programs throughout the year to support the business needs and foster the organization's mission.

Cisco Asian Affinity Network (CAAN)

Mission
Cisco Asian Affinity Network is an inclusive forum to develop a professional network of Cisco employees with a special focus on the interests of Asian Cisco community worldwide.

Cisco Black Employee Network (CBEN)

Mission:

Create and develop a dynamic environment for black employees that cultivates career growth, community involvement and business excellence.

Latino Employee Network (Conexión)

Mission:

Conexión is the employee network that bridges Cisco to the Latino community and enables Cisco to reach and impact the global community through collaborative efforts with our partners, suppliers, customers and top talent.

Indians Connecting People (ICON)

Vision:

Connecting people to maximize Cisco's growth through leveraging the diversity of our community.

Mission:

ICON is an employee association that connects the Cisco Indian community to facilitate professional development and networking for our employees, drive business growth and market the Cisco brand to advance the success of Cisco business objectives and give back to targeted communities in need around the world.

Women's Action Network (WAN)

Vision:

The Women's Action Network contributes to a strategic effort to enhance Cisco's success in attracting, developing and retaining talented female employees.

Mission:

Enable Cisco to increase its competitive advantage by capitalizing on the talents and skills of its female employees.

Gay, Lesbian, Bisexual, Transgender (GLBT)

Vision

To create a climate where GLBT individuals are embraced as part of the Cisco family, and are valued for their contributions to Cisco and their local and global communities.

Mission:

Partnering with Cisco to ensure a safe work environment for GLBT individuals—asserting support for, and establishing a widespread understanding of, nondiscrimination policies related to sexual orientation, gender identity, and gender expression.

Reaching out to the GLBT and advocates community and beyond to improve awareness and advocacy of GLBT issues, and promote education, philanthropy and professional development opportunities.

Entry-Level Programs, Full-Time Opportunities and Training Programs

Associate Systems Engineer (ASE)/ Associate Sales Representative (ASR)

Length of program: 12 months

Geographic location(s) of program: United States, Latin America, Europe, Middle East, Africa

ASE

Join the Sales Associates Program as an ASE and take advantage of a blend of classroom and guided discovery learning that uses case studies, sales simulations, competitive debates, and field shadowing to develop your ability to articulate business and technical solutions. Start on the track to becoming a Cisco systems engineer today.

ASR

Start on the track to becoming an account manager at Cisco. Become an ASR in the Sales Associates Program, and you will develop your ability to articulate business and technical solutions. You'll learn using case studies, sales simulations, competitive debates, and field shadowing in a blend of classroom and guided discovery learning. University graduate applicants who meet the criteria should be willing to relocate to Raleigh, N.C., or Amsterdam for 12 months, and available to fill any job position according to Cisco business needs.

Strategic Plan and Diversity Leadership

How does the firm's leadership communicate the importance of diversity to everyone at the firm?

Our diversity strategy and initiatives are communicated via the website, telecast, training sessions and e-mail correspondences.

Who has primary responsibility for leading diversity initiatives at your firm?

The global inclusion and diversity council

Does your firm currently have a diversity committee?

Yes

If yes, does the committee's representation include one or more members of the firm's management/executive committee (or the equivalent)?

Yes

Citi (Citigroup, Inc.)

(i.e., Citigroup, Inc., its subsidiaries and their affiliates) 399 Park Avenue New York, NY 10043 Phone: (800) 285-3000 **Locations** National and international locations	**Employment Contact** www.oncampus.citi.com

Recruiting

Please list the schools/types of schools at which you recruit.

Citi recruits at a number of schools both in the United States and internationally. At these schools, our businesses host presentations and on-campus interviews and/or participate in career fairs.

Do you have any special outreach efforts directed to encourage minority students and graduates to consider your firm?

Citi is engaged in a variety of outreach efforts directed toward minority students. Citi's level of engagement ranges from sponsoring student receptions, attending diversity conferences and career fairs, supporting programming toward financial education, participating on panels and offering scholarships to qualifying interns/fellows and outreach to the leadership of minority student organizations.

What activities does the firm undertake to attract minority and women employees?

Citi's ability to attract and retain diverse undergraduate, graduate and professional talent is fundamental to our success. To recruit the best talent, we continue to strengthen our partnerships with organizations such as: MLT, NSHMBA, NBMBAA, The Robert Toigo Foundation, The Consortium for Graduate Studies (CGSM), The National Association of Women MBAs, Reaching Out MBA and Global MBA.

Internships and Co-ops

INROADS

Deadline for application: The deadline is established by INROADS.

Number of interns in the program in summer 2006 (internship) or 2006 (co-op): 71 INROADS interns participated in Citi's 2006 summer internship program.

Pay: $12 to $18 per hour

Length of the program: 10 weeks

Web site for internship/co-op information: www.oncampus.citi.com

Please refer to our on-campus web site listed above for further information.

Scholarships

Citi awards a total of $15,000 in scholarships to outstanding INROADS interns in New York City, Dallas, Jacksonville, St. Louis and California. Scholarship criteria is determined by the INROADS staff in that location.

Affinity Groups

Citi's employee networks are employee-initiated and employee-led affinity groups open to all employees to provide an opportunity to share common experiences and build awareness of diverse cultures and communities. Citi's employee networks exist in 15 cities in the U.K. and the U.S. In 2006, 11 new networks were formed, bringing our total to 37. Recognized U.S. groups include: African Heritage, Asian Pacific Heritage, Hispanic, Pride (a group focused on the lesbian, gay, bisexual and transgender communities), Women, and Working Parents. In the U.K., disABILITY (a group focused on people with disabilities and the caregivers of people with disabilities), Pride, Women, Parents and a multicultural network called Roots have been recognized.

Entry-Level Programs, Full-Time Opportunities and Training Programs

Citibank North America Management Associate Program

Length of program: Two years

Geographic location(s) of program: Boston, Philadelphia, Conneticut, Maryland, New Jersey, New York, Virginia and Washington D.C.

Two-year rotation through various retail banking functions.

Citi Operations and Technology Management Associate Program

Length of program: Operations program is three years—three 12-month rotations; technology program is two years—two 12-month rotations

Geographic location(s) of program: New York-metro area, Tampa, Dallas

Leadership development is the goal. Formal on-boarding orientation plus two- to three-year training curriculum to build and develop soft skills.

Citi's tuition reimbursement policy applies.

Global Transaction Services Analyst Program

Length of program: Two years

Geographic location(s) of program: New York

Classes are taught by a combination of Citi professionals and public accounting and business school professionals

Four- to five-week training program in New York: two weeks accounting, one week finance; one to two weeks of overview of Citi businesses

Accounting, finance and general business concepts taught; computer training—financial modeling, utilizing Excel and word processing

Each analyst is assigned an analyst buddy as well as a junior and senior mentor.

Finance Analyst Program

Length of program: Two years

Geographic location(s) of program: New York

The analyst training program is approximately 10 weeks in duration and focuses on the specific skill sets and substantive knowledge needed to succeed at Citi. This program offers classes in financial accounting, corporate finance, analytics, cash flow modeling, risk and credit analysis, and capital markets. Additionally, the training

provides an understanding of the industry groups with whom analysts will work. Classes are taught by a combination of world-class consultants, university professors and banking professionals. Additionally, all analysts are assigned a junior and senior mentor.

Technology Leadership Program (TLP)

Length of program: Two years

Geographic location(s) of program: New York

The program is designed to bring technical and leadership talent into the IT organization and to accelerate the development of the participants through the program elements. The program lasts two years and includes four rotational assignments with project and people management, as well as periods of high-intensity classroom training, self-instruction and exposure to different senior managers and operating styles, which enhances the leadership development experience.

Strategic Plan and Diversity Leadership

How does the firm's leadership communicate the importance of diversity to everyone at the firm?
- Company Intranet
- Diversity annual report
- E-mail
- Employee cultural heritage month programs
- Newsletter
- Town hall meetings

Who has primary responsibility for leading diversity initiatives at your firm?
Ana Duarte McCarthy, chief diversity officer, global workforce diversity

Does your firm currently have a diversity committee?
Yes

If yes, please describe how the committee is structured, how often it meets, etc.
Citi's Diversity Operating Council, which formed in 2000, is comprised of senior diversity and human resources leaders from core businesses and regions. The council meets biweekly to review progress against our strategy, share best practices and align policies globally.

If yes, does the committee's representation include one or more members of the firm's management/executive committee (or the equivalent)?
No

Does the committee and/or diversity leader establish and set goals or objectives consistent with management's priorities?

Yes

Has the firm undertaken a formal or informal diversity program or set of initiatives aimed at increasing the diversity of the firm?

Yes, formal

How often does the firm's management review the firm's diversity progress/results?

Quarterly

How is the firm's diversity committee and/or firm management held accountable for achieving results?

Since 2002, Citi businesses and managers have been required to develop annual diversity plans and, through quarterly reviews, have been held accountable for progress against these plans. These reviews culminate in an annual review of our franchise efforts with Citigroup Inc.'s full board of directors. In total, 155 diversity reviews were conducted in our businesses in 2006.

The Stats

	NUMBER OF EMPLOYEES		REVENUE	
	2006	2005	2006	2005
Total worldwide	325,000 (approx.)	300,000 (approx.)	$89.6 billion	$83.6 billion

Diversity Mission Statement

Employer of choice

Citi values a work environment where diversity is embraced, where people are promoted on their merits and where people treat each other with respect and dignity. Around the world, we are committed to being a company where the best people want to work, where opportunities to develop are widely available, where innovation and an entrepreneurial spirit are valued and where employees are encouraged to fulfill their professional and personal goals.

Service provider of choice

Citi strives to deliver products and services to our clients that reflect both our global reach and our deep local roots in every market where we operate. The diversity of our employees enables us to better understand our clients, while the breadth of our product offerings allows us to serve them better.

Business partner of choice

Citi works to create mutually beneficial business relationships with minorities, women, disabled veterans and other people with disabilities. We recognize that working with a wide range of professionals, suppliers and consultants strengthens the communities we serve while creating value for our shareholders.

Neighbor of choice

Citi believes it has a responsibility to make a difference in the neighborhoods in which we live and work around the world. We reach out to and form relationships with nonprofit organizations, civic groups, educational institutions and local governments representing the diverse nature of these communities.

Cleveland Clinic

9500 Euclid Avenue
Cleveland, OH 44195
Phone: (216) 445-7323
Fax: (216) 444-3469
www.ClevelandClinic.org

Locations
Cleveland, OH (HQ)

Diversity Leadership
Deborah L. Plummer, PhD
E-mail: diversity@ccf.org

Employment Contact
Executive Director

Recruiting

Please list the schools/types of schools at which you recruit.

• *Private schools:* Case Western Reserve University
• Public state schools
• Historically black colleges and universities (HBCUs)

Do you have any special outreach efforts directed to encourage minority students and graduates to consider your firm?

• Hold a reception for minority students
• Advertise in minority student association publication(s) or other minority-focused publications
• Participate in/host minority student job fair(s) or other minority-focused job events
• Sponsor minority student association events
• Firm's employees participate on career panels at schools
• Outreach to leadership of minority student organizations
• Scholarships or intern/fellowships for minority students

What activities does the firm undertake to attract minority and women employees?

• Partner programs with women and minority associations
• Conferences
• Participate at minority job fairs

Do you use executive recruiting/search firms to seek to identify new diversity hires?

Yes

If yes, list all women- and/or minority-owned executive search/recruiting firms to which the firm paid a fee for placement services in the past 12 months:

The Prout Group

Internships and Co-ops

Division of Surgery Internship

Deadline for application: Ongoing throughout the year

Number of interns in the program in summer 2006 (internship) or 2006 (co-op): Six to 12 throughout the year

Pay: Unpaid

Length of the program: Eight to 10 weeks

Percentage of interns/co-ops in the program who receive offers of full-time employment: 75 percent

Division of Surgery hires interns. Intern responsibilities include data analysis, exposure to different areas of the department and researching information. They also attend and observe meetings and attend business events by the department. Qualifications include bachelor's or master's candidates for health or business administration. This program is used to identify high potentials for future employment at Cleveland Clinic.

Cleveland Clinic Fellowship Program

Deadline for application: October 15th

Number of interns in the program: Four

Pay: Stipend

Length of the program: 12 weeks; the fellowship year begins July 1st and ends on July 31st of the following year

Percentage of interns/co-ops in the program who receive offers of full-time employment: 75 to 100 percent

The Administrative Fellowship Program has been coordinated by the division of operations for over 25 years. While the fellowship is housed within the division of operations, it is supported clinic-wide, which gives fellows numerous opportunities to participate in projects within other divisions.

The program is geared to the self-starter who has had some practical experience in the health care environment. Qualified applicants will have a master of health administration (MHA) or equivalent course work completed from a program accredited by the Accrediting Commission on Education for Health Services Administration (ACEHSA). With the support of the preceptor and chief operations officer, during the 13-month fellowship, the administrative fellow will have the opportunity, as well as responsibility, to explore areas of personal interest.

Weatherhead Scholar Program

Number of interns in the program: Four

Pay: Stipend

Length of the program: 12 to 16 months

The Weatherhead Scholar Program goal is to attract top MBA candidates to Cleveland Clinic internships and serve as a pool for future hires.

INROADS Program

Number of interns in the program: 10 slots per year

Pay: Hourly pay depending on education

Length of the program: Varies

The mission of the INROADS Program is to identify and prepare talented minority students for positions of leadership.

Affinity Groups

Women's Professional Staff Association (WPSA), Gay and Lesbian Employee Resource Group, Gen X/Y Employee Resource Group, Philippine's Nursing Employee Group, Asian Employee Group, Black Employee Resource Group, Men's Health Care Employee Group.

WPSA meets regularly throughout the year and assists the women professional staff in mentoring, career development, training and networking. The Gay and Lesbian Employee Resource Group meets monthly on gay and lesbian issues as they relate to the mission, vision and values of Cleveland Clinic.

Entry-Level Programs, Full-Time Opportunities and Training Programs

Center for Leadership and Learning (CLL)

Length of program: Continuous

Geographic location(s) of program: Cleveland, Ohio

The CLL builds the organization's management and leadership team and select competencies of the general workforce that increases workforce performance and in turn builds Cleveland Clinic's business.

There is no charge for all classes at the Center for Leadership and Learning.

Strategic Plan and Diversity Leadership

What trends in your industry affect your corporate diversity goals, strategies and/or internal or external alliances?

Diversity plays a key role not only at Cleveland Clinic, but in all health care organizations, because it impacts interactions between staff and patients as well as among employees. As a global health care provider and the largest employer in Northeast Ohio, diversity is inherent in Cleveland Clinic's patients, employee base and the communities we serve.

How does the firm's leadership communicate the importance of diversity to everyone at the firm?

Mailings, e-mails, leadership makes appointments to the Diversity Councils, CEO communicates diversity through Intranet videos, senior leadership receives weekly updates and senior leadership also receives diversity updates and information via memos.

Who has primary responsibility for leading diversity initiatives at your firm?

Deborah L. Plummer, PhD, executive director, office of diversity.

Does your firm currently have a diversity committee?

Yes

If yes, please describe how the committee is structured, how often it meets, etc.

Cleveland Clinic has 23 Diversity Councils for each of its regional hospitals, family medical centers and the main campus. Councils are a diagonal cross-section of Cleveland Clinic staff and employees. Each of the 23 councils is chaired by a member of the senior leadership. Councils meet monthly.

If yes, does the committee's representation include one or more members of the firm's management/executive committee (or the equivalent)?

Yes

If yes, in 2006, what was the total number of hours collectively spent by the committee in furtherance of the firm's diversity initiatives? How many employees

are on the committee, and how often does the committee convene in furtherance of the firm's diversity initiatives?

Each of Cleveland Clinic's 23 diversity councils is chaired by a member of the executive staff. Each council has approximately 20 members. Committees meet monthly. Total approximate hours time in 2006 in diversity council meetings was over 150 hours.

Does the committee and/or diversity leader establish and set goals or objectives consistent with management's priorities?

Yes. All diversity council initiatives are driven by Cleveland Clinic's mission, vision and values.

Has the firm undertaken a formal or informal diversity program or set of initiatives aimed at increasing the diversity of the firm?

Yes, formal. Cleveland Clinic has a formalized supplier diversity program with targeted goals to increase the number of diverse suppliers. Cleveland Clinic also collaborates with minority organizations to facilitate minority professional staff recruitment. For example, Cleveland Clinic has hosted meet and greet events for organizations such as the Black MBAs, Black Data Processors, Cleveland Medical Association (black physicians), Cuarenta/Cuarenta Club (Hispanic emerging leaders), 40/40 Club (African American Emerging Leaders) and minority- and women-owned business enterprises.

How often does the firm's management review the firm's diversity progress/results?

Monthly

How is the firm's diversity committee and/or firm management held accountable for achieving results?

The executive director of the office of diversity is a member of the executive management team and therefore reports out on the progress of all diversity initiatives at the weekly staff meeting. Progress is measured by the CAO using a series of metrics and benchmark standards; for example, we have established targeted goals for minority- and women-owned businesses on several of our half-a-billion-dollar construction projects.

The Stats

	NUMBER OF EMPLOYEES		REVENUE	
	2006	2005	2006	2005
Total in the U.S.	36,000	35,000	$4.4 billion	N/A

2006 DEMOGRAPHIC PROFILE	
Female	70 percent
White	70 percent
Black	21 percent
Asian	6.5 percent
Latino	2 percent
SENIOR MANAGEMENT	
White	90 percent
Black	6.6 percent
Latino	3.25 percent
MANAGEMENT	
Female	57 percent

Retention and Professional Development

How do 2006 minority and female attrition rates generally compare to those experienced in the prior year period?

About the same as in prior years.

Please identify the specific steps you are taking to reduce the attrition rate of minority and women employees.

• Develop and/or support internal employee affinity groups

• Increase/improve current work/life programs

• Succession plan includes emphasis on diversity

• Work with minority and women employees to develop career advancement plans

• Strengthen mentoring program for all employees, including minorities and women

• Professional skills development program, including minority and women employees

Diversity Mission Statement

The Cleveland Clinic Office of Diversity provides strategic support for creating an inclusive organizational culture. Through education, recruitment of minority talent, employee development and internal/external collaborations on diversity-related initiatives, we reinforce our cornerstone values of service, quality, innovation and teamwork.

Additional Information

As a global health care provider and one of Northeast Ohio's largest employers, diversity is inherent in Cleveland Clinic's patients, staff, employee base and the communities we serve. Supported by the office of diversity, all Cleveland Clinic leaders are expected to develop a best-in-class, inclusive organizational structure. The office of diversity was established in January 2006 and, in the short span of one year, has transformed the culture of Cleveland Clinic.

Our efforts address diversity through:

• *Representation:* our staff and employees represent the communities we serve.

• *Inclusion:* we create conditions by which we learn from differences.

• *Economic empowerment:* we enhance teamwork for innovation and the best care and outcomes for our patients.

• *Equity:* we organize our business process to promote minority participation reflective of the diverse business community and enhance economic growth.

Cleveland Clinic broad initiatives include:

• Cultural competency training
• Diversity councils and affinity networks
• Minority talent acquisition and management
• Supplier Diversity Program

Concurrent and/or additional programs include:

• Business internships and mentoring programs
• Emerging leader (minority) meet and greet events
• Family-friendly work environment
• Minority Business Mentoring Program
• Women in Medicine Mentoring Dinners
• Women professional staff roundtables

Business and Civic Organization we collaborate with include:

• Black Contractors Association
• CAAO (Consortium of African American Organizations)
• Links, Incorporated (National Civic organization of over 10,000 African-American Women)
• Mayor's Contractor Assistant Program
• NAACP
• NOMBC (Northern Ohio Minority Business Council)
• President's Council (organization of business executives dedicated to the economic development of black-owned businesses)
• Urban League

In 2006, Cleveland Clinic provided approximately $100,000 in sponsorships for minority civic and business organizations.

Diversity plays a key role not only at Cleveland Clinic, but in all healthcare organizations, because it impacts interactions between staff and patients as well as among employees. The Cleveland Clinic Office of Diversity was created to promote an inclusive organizational culture through diversity education, consultation and programs that leverage differences to enhance innovation, quality of care, teamwork and economic impact.

Clorox Company, The

1221 Broadway
Oakland, CA 94612
Phone: (510) 271-7000
www.thecloroxcompany.com

Locations

Oakland, California (HQ)
Various global locations

Employment Contact

Rosa dela Resma
Senior Recruiting Manager, Marketing/Sales
1221 Broadway
Oakland, CA 94612
Phone: (510) 271-7122
Fax: (510) 271-6593
E-mail: rosa.dela.resma@clorox.com

Recruiting

Please list the schools/types of schools at which you recruit.

• Ivy League schools
• Public state schools

Do you have any special outreach efforts directed to encourage minority students to consider your firm?

• *Conferences:* ALPHA, NBMBAA, NSHMBA, NSN, LGBT MBA, Reaching Out, SHPE, SIFE, SWE
• *Conventions:* ALPFA, NABA, NSBE
• *Receptions:* NAASA, NABA, NBMBAA, NSBE

What activities does the firm undertake to attract minority and women employees?

• Partner programs with women and minority associations
• Conferences, receptions, conventions (see above)
• Seek referrals from other employees

Do you use executive recruiting/search firms to seek to identify new diversity hires?

Yes

Internships and Co-ops

INROADS

Deadline for application: April for summer internship
Number of interns in the program in summer 2006 : 10
Pay: $14 to $18 per hour depending on level
Length of the program: Eight to 12 weeks

The Clorox Company offers three different internship programs: there are eight to 10 interns hired for marketing, eight to 10 hired for research and development and 10 to 12 INROADS interns hired for various other functions (i.e., human resources, product supply, information services, and finance and accounting). Interns work closely with full-time professionals on a variety of projects. Marketing looks for associate marketing managers and associate marketing intelligence managers for interns. To intern in marketing, a business administration degree with a marketing focus and other marketing internships are pluses. Other qualifications include: demonstrated outstanding leadership/results orientation skills and strong analytical/problem-solving abilities.

Research and development looks for process core technology, corporate packaging and consumer applied technology interns. To intern with research and development, students must have completed their junior year with a minimum 3.0 GPA. Recommended majors include a bachelor's of science in either packaging sciences engineering or chemical engineering. INROADS interns must have a cumulative GPA of 2.8 or better as a sophomore or junior at a four-year school with at least two summers remaining prior to graduation. Prefer degrees in: business, engineering, information and computer sciences, sales and marketing.

Affinity Groups

The company is focused on nurturing and growing five Employee Resource Groups (ERGs):

• African-American ERG
• Asian ERG
• Clorox Pride (gay, lesbian, bisexual and transgender ERG)
• Latinos for Excellence, Advancement and Development (LEAD)
• Support, Heart and Opportunity for Women (SHOW)

Entry-Level Programs, Full-Time Opportunities and Training Programs

Diamond Leadership Foundation

Length of program: Depending on module, three to seven days

Geographic location(s) of program: General offices (Oakland, Calif.)

Strategic Plan and Diversity Leadership

What trends in your industry affect your corporate diversity goals, strategies and/or internal or external alliances?

The business case for diversity is real and is based on two fundamental beliefs:

• We believe we can improve business results through growing minority market share.

• We believe we can improve organizational effectiveness by developing a more diverse workforce and inclusive environment.

How does the firm's leadership communicate the importance of diversity to everyone at the firm?

Web site, newsletters, meetings, events and functions, diversity and inclusion leadership team.

Who has primary responsibility for leading diversity initiatives at your firm?

Erby Foster, director, diversity and inclusion

Does your firm currently have a diversity committee?

The firm has a diversity and inclusion leadership team of 20 cross-functional leaders who meet quarterly.

If yes, does the committee's representation include one or more members of the firm's management/executive committee (or the equivalent)?

Yes

Does the committee and/or diversity leader establish and set goals or objectives consistent with management's priorities?

Yes, business and organizational effectiveness goals

Has the firm undertaken a formal or informal diversity program or set of initiatives aimed at increasing the diversity of the firm?

Yes, formal

How often does the firm's management review the firm's diversity progress/results?

Quarterly

How is the firm's diversity committee and/or firm management held accountable for achieving results?

It is tied to their compensation.

Retention and Professional Development

Please identify the specific steps you are taking to reduce the attrition rate of minority and women employees.

• Develop and/or support internal employee affinity groups (e.g., minority or women networks within the firm)

• Increase/improve current work/life programs

• Succession plan includes emphasis on diversity

• Work with minority and women employees to develop career advancement plans

• Strengthen mentoring program for all employees, including minorities and women

• Professional skills development program, including minority and women employees

Columbia St. Mary's, Inc.

4425 N. Port Washington Road
Glendale, WI 53212
Phone: (414) 326-2661
Fax: (414) 291-1427
www.columbia-stmarys.org

Diversity Leadership

Cynthia R. Stewart
Director, Diversity Resources & Language
Services
4425 N. Port Washington Road
Glendale, WI 53204
Phone: (414) 326-2661
Fax: (414) 291-1427
E-mail: cstewart@columbia-stmarys.org

Brenda Buchanan
Manager, Community Career Development
INROADS Coordinator
4425 N. Port Washington Road
Glendale, WI 53204
Phone: (414) 326-2655
Fax: (414) 291-1427

Internships and Co-ops

INROADS

Pay: $11.20 per hour

Length of the program: 10 weeks

Percentage of interns/co-ops in the program who receive offers of full-time employment: 90 percent

Qualifications for the program vary.

Scholarships

Estil Strawn Scholarship Program

Scholarship award amount: $1,500 for entire scholarship

Web site or other contact information for scholarship: Only open to company employees

To apply, you must be an employee in good standing, be studying in a field that would fit within a health care environment and have successfully completed an application process including an interview.

Strategic Plan and Diversity Leadership

How does the firm's leadership communicate the importance of diversity to everyone at the firm?

The firm communicates the importance of diversity through e-mails, leadership meetings, education sessions for staff and leadership, the diversity scorecard and our newsletter.

Who has primary responsibility for leading diversity initiatives at your firm?

The director of diversity resources

If yes, please describe how the committee is structured.

The council meets monthly. Two committees report to the council and they meet as necessary, usually one or more times per month. The council is made up of individuals from all levels of the organization, including executive leadership and is headed by an executive leader.

The Stats

2005 Demographic Profile	
Total employees	5,600
Minority	21 percent
Female	83.9 percent
Female executives	60 percent
Minority executives	7 percent

Diversity Mission Statement

The Columbia Saint Mary's Diversity Resources Council promotes the unique perspectives provided by distinctions of age, culture, ethnicity, family status, gender, physical/cognitive ability, race, religion, sexual orientation and socioeconomic status.

The council exists to support the overall vision and mission of CSM by advocating an inclusive environment that both respects and leverages the rich diversity of our employees, physicians, patients and surrounding community.

Our purpose is:

• To identify strategies and accountabilities related to diversity for CSM

• To educate the organization on how diversity is integral to achieving our mission

• To provide educational opportunities to continuously build cultural competence at all levels

• To strengthen the organization through valuing and promoting a diverse workforces

Additional Information

The organization has a position dedicated to targeting youth at the high school and college level to provide coaching, mentoring, internships, etc. The goal is to increase the interest in health care and to provide growth opportunities for students.

Our scorecard is designed to build accountability across the organization and at all levels.

We have a strong language services program with an emphasis on education and service to populations with limited or no English speaking abilities. We are also working to build programs or processes to hire more bilingual staff in positions at all levels in the organization and to utilize the skills of bilingual employees who have the skills necessary to serve as interpreters and translators.

We maintain affiliations and programs with community organizations to build community strength. We also own several clinics (medical and dental) that provide outreach to uninsured and underinsured persons and the homeless.

Comcast Cable Communications, LLC

1500 Market Street
Philadelphia, PA 19102
Phone: (215) 981-7783
Fax: (215) 981-8501
www.comcast.com

Locations

Philadelphia, PA (HQ)
Locations in 42 states

Employment Contact

Mary Pennington
Senior Director Recruitment & Career
Development
E-mail: Mary_Pennington@cable.comcast.com

Recruiting

Please list the schools/types of schools at which you recruit.

- Ivy League schools
- Other private schools
- Public state schools
- Historically black colleges and universities (HBCUs)

Do you have any special outreach efforts directed to encourage minority students to consider your firm?

- Hold a reception for minority students
- *Conferences:* National Black MBAs (NBMBAA), National Society of Black Engineers (NSBE), National Society of Hispanic MBAs (NSHMBA)
- Advertise in minority student association publication(s)
- Participate in/host minority student job fair(s)
- Firm's employees participate on career panels at school
- Outreach to leadership of minority student organizations
- Scholarships or intern/fellowships for minority students
- *Other:* Comcast recruitment efforts are not only national, but regional in scope. Recruiters for specific locations will develop partnerships with local colleges and universities and may become involved in any of the above activities on a regional or local level.

What activities does the firm undertake to attract minority and women employees?

- Partner programs with women and minority associations
- *Conferences:* NABA, National Society for Black Engineers, National Association of Black MBAs, National Women of Color Technology Conferences, Urban League, Hispanic Bar Association, National Society for Hispanic MBAs and other regional and local conferences throughout the country

- Participate at minority job fairs
- Seek referrals from other employees
- Utilize online job services
- *Other:* Internship programs in partnership with organizations including Emma Bowen, Work Ready Philadelphia, National Puerto Rican Coalition, Congressional Black Caucus and Congressional Hispanic Caucus Institute

Do you use executive recruiting/search firms to seek to identify new diversity hires?

Yes

If yes, list all women- and/or minority-owned executive search/recruiting firms to which the firm paid a fee for placement services in the past 12 months:

Selected firms include Criterion, David Gomez, Marci Dwyer, Carlsen Resources, API, ACE, Advanced Staffing Inc., Aquent, Banner Personnel Service, Inc., Barbara Davis Employment Services, Brandywine Technology Partners, CBI Group Limited Liability Company, Diverse Staffing Inc., Mercer Staffing and PDQ Personnel Services Inc.

Internships and Co-ops

Comcast Summer Intern Program

Pay: $12 to $15 per hour

Length of the program: 12 weeks if summer

Web site for internship/co-op information: www.comcast.com

Comcast offers part-time and full-time summer employment to students enrolled in, or who have recently graduated from, college or graduate degree programs.

In partnership with the Philadelphia Youth Network and WorkReady Philadelphia, Comcast will also offer opportunities to high school students who are employed by these organizations.

The Summer Internship Program affords students a solid introduction to the workforce through on-the-job learning and mentoring by Comcast leaders. At the same time, Comcast is able to further its commitment to diversity and community investment, while benefiting from the energy and knowledge of our summer interns. Summer internship programs afford us the ability to build lasting relationships with students, learning institutions and community organizations that will assist Comcast in building its next generation of Comcasters.

Departments hiring include:

HR, IT, accounts payable, marketing, real estate, finance, Comcast programming, investor relations, public affairs and corporate communications.

Qualifications for the program:

Must be a full-time student.

Emma Bowen Foundation

Deadline for application: March 31st

Number of interns in the program in summer 2006 (internship) or 2006 (co-op): 229

Pay: $10 per hour, plus a scholarship each year

Length of the program: Eight to 10 weeks

Web site for internship/co-op information: www.emmabowen-foundation.com

The Emma L. Bowen Foundation was created in 1989 to prepare minority youth for careers in the media industry. The foundation's program is unlike traditional intern programs in that students work for partner companies during summers and school breaks from the summer following their junior year in high school until they graduate from college. During the five-year program, students have an opportunity to learn many aspects of corporate operations and develop company-specific skills. Corporations have an opportunity to train and mentor students with the option of full-time employment upon completion of their college degrees.

Scholarships

Comcast Leaders and Achievers Scholarship Program

Deadline for application for the scholarship program: December

Scholarship award amount: $1,000

Web site or other contact information for scholarship: www.comcast.com/inthecommunity

The Leaders and Achievers® Scholarship Program recognizes high school seniors for their academic achievement, community service

activities and leadership skills. Qualified seniors must be nominated for the Leaders and Achievers Scholarship Program by their high school principal. All nomination information is mailed to principals at eligible schools at the end of each calendar year. Scholarship materials are not available through any Comcast office or the Comcast Foundation, and the scholarship program administrators cannot accept applications submitted by students on their own.

Affinity Groups

Senior Women's Group

The purpose of the forum is to provide senior-level women at Comcast an environment in which to enhance business acumen and business savvy, share information and feedback among peers and leverage each other as resources, advocates and sounding boards. In order to strengthen the relationships at the highest levels, the group is focused on vice president-level and above in cable and senior director-level and above in corporate. Events are held each quarter, and while the purpose of the group is primarily focused on bringing together the company's most senior women leaders, the goal also is to leverage this group for insight regarding leadership development opportunities for the next generation of women leaders.

Entry-Level Programs, Full-Time Opportunities and Training Programs

Entry-level training program in engineering, Associate Electrical Engineering Program

Other entry-level opportunities in the following departments: accounting, administration, customer service, HR and marketing.

Length of program: One to two years

Geographic location(s) of program: Philadelphia, PA

In the Associate Electrical Engineering Program, the individual is assigned to a VP of engineering. They have exposure to various aspects of field operations, engineering, plant operations, plant upgrades, testing of equipment and vendor negotiations.

Strategic Plan and Diversity Leadership

How does the firm's leadership communicate the importance of diversity to everyone at the firm?

Through diversity training, intranet and part of interview training. In addition, the Diversity Committee provides quarterly reports. There is a Monthly Leadership Link communication by executive officers to senior leadership throughout the company and diversity is promoted in leadership development programs. Diversity initiatives are also incorporated into annual goals for senior leaders.

Who has primary responsibility for leading diversity initiatives at your firm?:

David L. Cohen, EVP, Comcast Corporation

Payne Brown, vice president of outreach strategies, Comcast Corporation

Charisse Lillie, vice president of human resources, Comcast Corporation and senior vice president, human resources, Comcast Cable Communications

Does your firm currently have a diversity committee?

Yes

If yes, please describe how the committee is structured, how often it meets, etc.

In the last few years, Comcast has established two committees as part of its commitment to diversity. The first committee is the Diversity Council. The council is responsible for meeting quarterly and reviewing the company's overall progress in terms of 1) employee diversity, 2) diversity programming, 3) supplier diversity and 4) external and public affairs. The council takes a critical look at progress in these areas of the business and discusses and outlines means of holding executives in all markets accountable for reaching established milestones.

The second committee committed to diversity in the workplace is the Diversity Working Committee. The mission of this committee is to identify field best practices as they relate to diversity. This group meets monthly to share with each other progress being made in local markets relative to our outreach efforts. Another important responsibility of this group is to identify internal talent worthy of nomination for various industry publications and awards. It is important to note that Comcast does not "put itself out there" relative to bragging about its own. One of the tasks of this committee is to identify the diverse talent in the workforce and look for opportunities to showcase this talent through publications, panel discussions, speaking engagements and industry awards.

If yes, does the committee's representation include one or more members of the firm's management/executive committee (or the equivalent)?

Yes

If yes, how many executives are on the committee, and in 2006, what was the total number of hours collectively spent by the committee in furtherance of the firm's diversity initiatives?

Total Executives on Committee: 12 on the Diversity Council, four on the Diversity Working Committee.

How many employees are on the committee, and how often does the committee convene in furtherance of the firm's diversity initiatives?

Diversity Council: 12 employees on committee

Diversity Communications Committee: 25 employees on committee

The Diversity Council meets quarterly and the Working Committee meets monthly. Additional meetings are held as needed.

Does the committee and/or diversity leader establish and set goals or objectives consistent with management's priorities?

Yes. The key focus is in areas of programming, corporate communication, recruitment/retention, supplier diversity and external affairs and public policy.

Has the firm undertaken a formal or informal diversity program or set of initiatives aimed at increasing the diversity of the firm?

Yes, formal. There are specific initiatives and goals established for each area listed above.

How often does the firm's management review the firm's diversity progress/results?

Quarterly

How is the firm's diversity committee and/or firm management held accountable for achieving results?

Diversity goals are tied into the management achievement component of objectives for all leadership. This is ultimately tied into the bonus.

The Stats

2006 DEMOGRAPHIC PROFILE	
Minority	39 percent
Female	37 percent
Executive team (female)	22 percent
Executive team (minority)	11 percent

	NUMBER OF EMPLOYEES		REVENUE	
	2006	2005	2006	2005
Total in the U.S.	76,615	64,911	$24,966 billion	$22,255 billion
Total outside the U.S.	N/A	N/A	N/A	N/A
Total worldwide	76,615	64,911	$24,966 billion	$22,255 billion

Retention and Professional Development

How do 2006 minority and female attrition rates generally compare to those experienced in the prior year period?

About the same as in prior years.

Please identify the specific steps you are taking to reduce the attrition rate of minority and women employees.

- Increase/review compensation relative to competition
- Adopt dispute resolution process
- Succession plan includes emphasis on diversity
- Work with minority and women employees to develop career advancement plans
- Strengthen mentoring program for all employees, including minorities and women
- Professional skills development program, including minority and women employees

Diversity Mission Statement

Keeping Cultures, Communities, and Customers Connected

Respecting the individuality and dignity of others by appreciating their differences and similarities is a tradition deeply rooted in the Comcast credo. Our commitment to diversity is woven into every aspect of our business and reflected through our workforce, our suppliers and our social responsibility. We know that to complete the big picture, we must focus on the many diverse pieces that it comprises.

To learn about the culture at Comcast Cable, you need only read our credo. Developed by our own employees, representing all levels throughout the organization, the credo gives us focus and direction in an ever-changing, high-growth environment.

The Comcast Credo: "We will be the company to look to first for the communications products and services that connect people to what's important in their lives."

Comcast Promise We will entertain, inform and empower our customers while enriching our communities. To keep this promise, we will commit to:

An ongoing introduction of new communications products and services

Consistent financial results that define the industry's best

An enjoyable work environment that allows people to grow personally as well as professionally

A belief that consistent, professional and respectful customer service is everybody's job

Comcast Touchstones Our company, reputation and true success are founded on the following core values:

- *Ethics:* we will be true to the highest standards of honesty, fairness and integrity
- *Quality:* we will commit ourselves to excellence in our products and personal relationships
- *Flexibility:* we will maintain our ability to adapt to an ever-changing world
- *Diversity:* we will respect and reflect the customers, communities and cultures we serve
- *Employee focus:* we will invest in people with the belief that our company can only be as strong as its work force
- *Enthusiasm:* we will work with an unbridled passion for our business

Additional Information

Diversity comes in many forms. Race and gender are ones that easily come to mind; however, there is also diversity of interests, skills and talents, personalities—all of which comprise diversity at Comcast. Diversity is key to the success of our organization. Diversity is, in fact, one of the Comcast touchstones a part of our credo which defines who we are as a company. Simply stated, "We will respect and reflect the customers, communities and cultures we serve."

To support this, we are involved in a number of recruiting initiatives that allow us to build upon our current success. As an organization, we work with over 100 organizations to ensure that we are attracting and retaining a diverse workforce. Nationally, we have participated in events sponsored by the National Society for Black Engineers, the National Black MBA Association, the National Hispanic MBA Association, among others. Comcast is an active participant in the Emma Bowen Internship Program, targeted to helping minority students gain experience in the field of telecommunications. Over the past two years, Comcast has increased student placements by over 100 percent. Students work in locations throughout the country and are invited to spend several days at the Philadelphia headquarters, meeting with Comcast's senior executives. More recently, through the work of Comcast's Diversity Council, we have strengthened our partnerships with organizations including La Raza, LULAC and the National Hispanic Chamber of Commerce.

Many of our diversity initiatives are driven at the local and regional level, and include ongoing efforts to partner with associations and

community organizations to identify diverse talent for our organization. We have funded student scholarships for members of professional associations. Working through our public affairs and community investments teams, Comcast connects with the community through support of organizations including local chapters of the NAACP, Urban League, Boys and Girls Clubs and the YWCA.

Another of the Comcast touchstones is employee focus—we invest in people with the belief that our company can only be as strong as its workforce. We support continuous development of our workforce, including involvement in professional associations. Our employees are actively involved in groups including the National Association of Multicultural Ethnicity in Communications and Women in Cable and Telecommunications. Our employees have been recognized and have received awards, including Women to Watch from Women in Cable and Telecommunications, 50 Most Important Hispanics by *Hispanic Engineer and Information Technology Magazine,* Top 50 Most Influential Minorities in Cable by *CableWorld* and Distinguished Achiever Award from the National Women of Color.

Whether it is individual employees or the company as a whole, Comcast is honored to be regularly recognized by local publications and national associations for our diversity efforts. Our diversity initiatives, our efforts in the community and our commitment to our employees are all keys to this success.

ConAgra Foods, Inc.

1 ConAgra Drive
Omaha, NE 68102-5001
Phone: (402) 595-4000
Fax: (402) 595-4707
www.conagrafoods.com

Locations
Various

Employment Contact
Staffing Support Team, College Recruiting
One ConAgra Drive 1-252
Omaha, NE 68102
Phone: (402) 595-4000
Fax: (402) 595-4707
www.conagrafoods.com

Recruiting

Please list the schools/types of schools at which you recruit.

- *Private schools:* Too numerous to list
- *Public state schools:* Too numerous to list
- *Historically black colleges and universities (HBCUs):* Xavier New Orleans, NCA&T, Howard
- *Hispanic serving institutions (HSIs):* UTEP

Do you have any special outreach efforts directed to encourage minority students to consider your firm?

- *Conferences:* Black MBA, Hispanic MBA, NHBA, Women's MBA, INROADS, MANRRS, Urban League, etc.
- Participate in/host minority student job fair(s)
- Sponsor minority student association events
- Firm's employees participate on career panels at school
- Outreach to leadership of minority student organizations
- Scholarships or intern/fellowships for minority students

What activities does the firm undertake to attract minority and women employees?

- Partner programs with women and minority associations
- *Conferences:* see above
- Participate at minority job fairs
- Seek referrals from other employees
- Utilize online job services

Internships and Co-ops

INROADS
Deadline for application: April
Pay: Varies
Length of the program: Varies

Web site for internship/co-op information: www.conagrafoods.com

Strategic Plan and Diversity Leadership

Who has primary responsibility for leading diversity initiatives at your firm?

Vivian Ayuso, diversity director

Does your firm currently have a diversity committee?

Yes

If yes, does the committee's representation include one or more members of the firm's management/executive committee (or the equivalent)?

Yes

Does the committee and/or diversity leader establish and set goals or objectives consistent with management's priorities?

Yes

Has the firm undertaken a formal or informal diversity program or set of initiatives aimed at increasing the diversity of the firm?

Yes, formal

The Stats

	NUMBER OF EMPLOYEES	REVENUE
	2005	2005
Total in the U.S.	40,000	$14 billion

Retention and Professional Development

Please identify the specific steps you are taking to reduce the attrition rate of minority and women employees.

• Develop and/or support internal employee affinity groups (e.g., minority or women networks within the firm)

• Increase/review compensation relative to competition

• Increase/improve current work/life programs

• Succession plan includes emphasis on diversity

• Strengthen mentoring program for all employees, including minorities and women

• Professional skills development program, including minority and women employees

Consolidated Edison Company of New York

4 Irving Place
New York, NY 10003
Phone: (212) 460-4314
Fax: (646) 654-2679
www.coned.com

Locations

New York, NY (HQ)
Westchester, NY
Orange & Rockland Counties

Diversity Leadership

Joan Jacobs
Director, Equal Employment Opportunity
Affairs (EEOA)

Timothy Indiveri
Section Manager, Recruitment

Employment Contact

Joanne Colosi
Secretary

Recruiting

Please list the schools/types of schools at which you recruit.

- *Ivy League schools:* Columbia University, Cornell University, University of Pennsylvania

- *Other private schools:* Cooper Union, Drexel University, Fordham University, Lafayette College, Lehigh University, Manhattan College, Marist College, New York Institute of Technology, New York University, Pace University, Polytechnic University, Rensselaer Polytechnic Institute, Stevens Institute of Technology, St. John's University, Howard University, Wesleyan University

- *Public state schools:* Baruch College, City College of New York, Brooklyn College, Lehman College, Morgan State University, Rutgers University, SUNY Maritime, University of Buffalo, Stony Brook University & Penn State

- *Historically black colleges and universities (HBCUs):* Atlanta Center University (Morehouse, Spellman and Clark Atlanta University) Howard University, Morgan State University

- *Hispanic serving institutions (HSIs):* City College of New York, Baruch College, Vaughn College of Aeronautics and Technology, Lehman College, New York City College of Technology & Bronx Community College

- *Other predominantly minority and/or women's colleges:* Columbia University, Cornell University, University of Pennsylvania, Drexel University, Rensselear Polytechnic Institute & Rutgers University

Do you have any special outreach efforts directed to encourage minority students and graduates to consider your firm?

- Hold a reception for minority students

- *Conferences:* American Association of Blacks in Energy (AABE), Women in Construction (WIC), Non-Traditional Employment for Women (NEW) Black Executive Exchange Program (BEEP) Asian Diversity Career Fair, Veteran Job Fair
- Advertise in minority student association publication(s) or other minority-focused publications
- Participate in/host minority student job fair(s) or other minority-focused job events
- Sponsor minority student association events
- Firm's employees participate on career panels at school
- Outreach to leadership of minority student organizations
- Scholarships or intern/fellowships for minority students
- *Other:* We use Parker Advertising Service, Inc., to place our ads through *The New York Times*. Parker Advertising is a certified woman-owned business.

What activities does the firm undertake to attract minority and women employees?

- *Partner programs with women and minority associations:* NEW, AABE, Seedco, BEEP, Hispanic Professional Engineers, National Society of Black Engineers
- *Conferences:* Center for Women in New York Career Fair, Women for Hire Career Fair
- Participate at minority job fairs
- Seek referrals from other employees
- Utilize online job services

Do you use executive recruiting/search firms to seek to identify new diversity hires?

Yes

If yes, list all women- and/or minority-owned executive search/recruiting firms to which the firm paid a fee for placement services in the past 12 months:
Buckner & Associate and Sairam Consultants.

Internships and Co-ops

High School Weekly Co-op Program

Number of interns in the program in summer 2006 (internship) or 2006 (co-op): 14

Web site for internship/co-op information: www.coned.com

Con Edison continues to provide New York City high school students with a variety of work experiences that add another dimension to the technical skills they learn in the classroom. Through the High School Weekly Co-op Program, students benefit from career development information, teamwork experiences and skills development.

In 2006, 14 students, including nine minorities (64.3 percent) and three women (21.4 percent), were participants. Fourteen of the co-op students were employed by various organizations within the company and held positions that were engineering- and computer-related. Since 2002, 85 students have participated in the program, of whom 61 (71.8 percent) were minorities and 11 (12.9 percent) were women.

Co-op Intern Program

Number of interns in the program in summer 2006 (internship) or 2006 (co-op): 51

Web site for internship/co-op information: www.coned.com

The Co-op Intern Program invites college students, many of whom had previously worked for the company as summer interns, to supplement their studies with hands-on work during the school year.

In 2006, of this program's 51 participants, 35 were minorities (68.6 percent) and 11 were women (21.6 percent). Since 2002, 247 students have participated in the program, including 150 minorities (60.7 percent) and 60 women (24.3 percent).

Summer Intern Program

Number of interns in the program in summer 2006 (internship) or 2006 (co-op): 90

Web site for internship/co-op information: www.coned.com

Con Edison's Summer Intern Program provides high school and college students with work experiences that help them bring textbook knowledge to real-world settings and gain an understanding of the way we work at Con Edison. With this program, Con Edison identifies students who demonstrate high energy, strong intellect and a genuine thirst for learning and who, upon graduation from college, may qualify as candidates for the company's Growth Opportunities for Leadership Development (GOLD) program.

Students must be involved in the study of engineering, environmental science or business, such as accounting or finance.

In 2006, 90 interns participated in the program; 53 were minorities (58.9 percent) and 19 were women (21.1 percent). Since 2000, 58.1 percent of all participants were minorities and 32.5 were women.

Scholarships

Con Edison Scholarship Program

Deadline for application for the scholarship program: November 10th

Scholarship award amount: $2,500 per student for 10 students—for entire scholarship

Web site or other contact information for scholarship: For Con Edison employees only—internal web site. The Scholarship & Recognition Program, a nonprofit organization, administers this program.

Thurgood Marshall Scholarship Fund (TMSF)

Scholarship award amount: $15,000 per student for three students—for entire scholarship

The TMSF is the only national organization that awards four-year merit scholarships, programmatic and capacity-building support to 45 historically black public colleges and universities and the students who attend them. Con Edison supports this fund, and the two scholarships are named for Con Edison and are for minority students majoring in the physical sciences and/or engineering.

The United Negro College Fund (UNCF)

Scholarship award amount: $5,000 per student for four students—for entire scholarship

The UNCF is the nation's oldest and most successful higher education assistance organization. The Con Edison Scholarship is awarded to students who are majoring in the fields of accounting, computer science, electrical, mechanical or nuclear engineering.

This program fosters long-term relationships among the corporation, the students and the participating institutions. It increases student interest in the corporation and ultimately enlarges the pool of prospective minority employees.

The Hundred Year Association of New York

Scholarship award amount: $3,000 per student for two students—for entire scholarship

This program offers scholarships to the sons and daughters of career city employees. Con Edison has participated in this program since 1994. The selection committee receives 150 applications from diverse high school seniors each year and selections are based on scholastic achievement, leadership, commitment and community service.

CUNY Program for the Retention of Engineering Students (PRES)

This program was established in 1987 to provide academic support and guidance to underrepresented minorities and women in the engineering field, thereby reducing attrition. PRES currently serves more than 550 students and continues to effectively increase the performance of minority engineering students. Con Edison supports this program with an annual grant of $10,000.

Affinity Groups

American Association of Blacks in Energy (AABE)

AABE is a national association of energy professionals founded and dedicated to ensure the input of African-Americans and other minorities into the discussions and developments of energy policies regulations, R&D technologies and environmental issues.

Web site: http://aabe-nymac.org/home.html

LGBT Pride

This newly formed Con Edison group represents lesbian, gay, bisexual and transgender (LGBT) employees. LGBT Pride meets on a monthly basis to discuss providing opportunities for employee networks and mentoring. They also raise diversity awareness, share experiences, and promote personal and professional growth.

Entry-Level Programs, Full-Time Opportunities and Training Programs

Growth Opportunities for Leadership Development (GOLD)

Length of program: 18 months

Geographic location(s) of program: New York

This program develops high-caliber college graduates for positions of increasing responsibility and leadership within the company during the course of an 18-month period. Through a series of practical, rotational job assignments, mentoring and senior-management guidance, GOLD program participants tackle challenging supervisory and project-based jobs that provide valuable work experience insight into Con Edison's practices and operations. Upon successful completion of the program, participants are poised to advance into Con Edison's management ranks. In the past six years, we have hired 77 GOLD associates who had previously participated in the co-op and/or summer intern programs.

The program continues to be successful in recruiting and retaining minorities and women. In 2006, it enabled 61 college graduates, 42 of whom were minorities (68.9 percent) and 22 of whom were women (36.1 percent), to begin careers at Con Edison. Since 2002, 269 GOLD associates have participated in the program, including 156 minorities and 96 women.

Over the past six years, 75.8 percent of our GOLD program employees have remained with the company. Significantly, 76.3 percent of the minority participants and 69.8 percent of the women participants are continuing their careers at Con Edison. Such retention rates are solid signs of a successful program.

Tools for Employees Advancing into Management (TEAM)

Length of program: Approximately 12 months

Geographic location(s) of program: New York

The TEAM Program is a developmental experience designed to provide recently promoted union employees with the tools necessary to make a successful transition into a management role. The program's goal is to develop the participants into quality supervisors or individual contributors.

Tuition Aid Program

Length of program: As long as the employee is going to college

Geographic location(s) of program: New York

The Tuition Aid Program continues to be a noteworthy feature of Con Edison's benefit package. The program offers reimbursement to eligible employees who pursue courses or programs that maintain or improve their present career skills. Upon the successful completion of a degree, the employee is provided with up to 100 percent reimbursement of tuition costs.

In 2006, 469 employees participated in the program; more than half of the participants were minorities and 27.9 percent were women.

Strategic Plan and Diversity Leadership

Chairman's Message

TO: All Employees

FROM: Kevin Burke, Chairman of the Board

DATE: June 30, 2006

SUBJECT: Reaffirmation of Our Commitment to Equal Employment Opportunity and Affirmative Action

At Con Edison, we have long supported the principles of equal employment opportunity and affirmative action. We acknowledge and reaffirm that these values are integral to the foundation of our society, our workplaces and our communities. Con Edison's commitment to these principles is reflected in our diverse employees—one of our greatest strengths.

We recognize that our company's success depends on how effectively we develop and utilize the talents of the men and women who make up our workforce. Therefore, we remain dedicated to maintaining an environment that is free of discrimination, and a workplace where all employees are afforded the opportunity to develop, perform and reach their full potential without regard to race, color, religion, gender, age, national origin, gender identity, marital status, sexual orientation, citizenship, disability, or Vietnam-Era, special disabled, and/or other qualified veteran status.

Our commitment to these principles is set forth in further detail in Corporate Policy Statements 500-4 (EEO Policy), 500-12 (Employment of Individuals with Disabilities and Veterans' Policy) and 500-14 (Sexual Harassment Policy), which complement our standards of business conduct. I encourage you to read these policies, as it is every employee's job to do his or her share to maintain a workplace that is free of discrimination, harassment and retaliation. Fulfilling this obligation means that we must promptly report any such behavior to the corporate EEOA office, an immediate supervisor or one with higher authority, or your human resources representative. You may also report violations using the EEO complaint line, (212) 460-1065, or the complaint form on the EEO web site (http://intranet/eeo). All complaints will be promptly investigated, and employees who are found to have violated our EEO polices are subject to discipline up to and including termination.

Con Edison stands behind its EEO policies. By sustaining and enhancing our outstanding diversity record, we will provide the best service to our customers and achieve our full potential as a responsible company.

In addition to the chairman's message, Con Edison sends out occasional e-mails to remind employees about the importance of diversity to all of us. We also post diversity messages on our elevator screens and bulletin boards at all our company locations. Finally, we encourage all employees to visit our internal EEOA website, which contains information regarding the importance of diversity.

Who has primary responsibility for leading diversity initiatives at your firm?

Joan Jacobs, director, equal employment opportunity affairs (EEOA).

Does your firm currently have a diversity committee?

Yes

If yes, please describe how the committee is structured, how often it meets, etc.

The committee comprises primarily upper-level members of the line organizations that meet once each month.

If yes, does the committee's representation include one or more members of the firm's management/executive committee (or the equivalent)?

Yes

If yes, how many executives are on the committee, and in 2006, what was the total number of hours collectively spent by the committee in furtherance of the firm's diversity initiatives?

Total Executives on Committee: The committee comprises of nine executives that meet once a month for three hours.

Does the committee and/or diversity leader establish and set goals or objectives consistent with management's priorities?

Yes

Has the firm undertaken a formal or informal diversity program or set of initiatives aimed at increasing the diversity of the firm?

Yes, formal

How often does the firm's management review the firm's diversity progress/results?

Monthly

The Stats

	NUMBER OF EMPLOYEES		REVENUE	
	2006	2005	2006	2005
Total in the U.S.	13,441	13,145	$8.6 billion	$9 billion
Total worldwide	13,441	13,145	$8.6 billion	$9 billion

2005 DEMOGRAPHIC PROFILE	
Minority	5,576 (41.5 percent)
Female	2,125 (15.8 percent)
Minority executives	6 (15.4 percent)
Female executives	10 (25.6 percent)

Retention and Professional Development

How do 2006 minority and female attrition rates generally compare to those experienced in the prior year period?

About the same as in prior years.

Please identify the specific steps you are taking to reduce the attrition rate of minority and women employees.

• Succession plan includes emphasis on diversity

• Work with minority and women employees to develop career advancement plans

• Strengthen mentoring program for all employees, including minorities and women

• Professional skills development program, including minority and women employees

Diversity Mission Statement

As our industry and our workforce continue to evolve in the new marketplace, we face challenges in maintaining and expanding our role as an industry leader and an employer of choice. To that end, our diverse workforce will continue to be one of our greatest strengths.

Con Edison has a long-standing commitment to the principles of equal employment opportunity and affirmative action, not just because it is a good business practice, but also because it is the right thing to do. Indeed, our company's success is tied to how effectively we develop and maximize the potential of our most valuable resources—the men and women of Con Edison.

At Con Edison, employment and personnel decisions, including hiring, job assignments, promotions and compensation are based on ability and merit, without regard for race, color, religion, gender, age, national origin, disability, marital status, gender identity, sexual orientation, citizenship or military service status. In today's business world, workplace diversity and business accomplishment go hand in hand and we regard Con Edison's commitment to diversity as a key element in our company's ongoing success.

Our equal employment opportunity (EEO) policies set forth our commitment to these principles. Maintaining a workplace free of discrimination is an integral part of each employee's job. Each of us must contribute to a safe, productive and harmonious work environment, and we must respect every individual's dignity and well-being.

Our compliance with these policies is one of our most effective means of attracting and retaining highly qualified employees, pro-

viding the best service to our customers and achieving our full potential as a responsible, concerned and competitive company.

Additional Information

The success of our 2006 recruitment and diversity initiatives is clear. More than 50 percent of all new hires consisted of minorities, and 21.6 percent were women. Marketing career opportunities through the Internet was a primary means of reaching diverse populations. The company posted job openings through leading sites, such as HotJobs.com, Careerbuilder.com and Monster.com, allowed us to reach diverse audiences in technical fields through links to a broad range of diversity web sites, including America's Job Bank, the U.S. Department of Labor, DisabilityJobs, GayJobs, Womenlinks, Network of Indian Professionals, GayWork, Hispanic Online and NAACP.

Con Edison also posted jobs on the Society for Human Resource Management web site, which is linked to a broad array of professional associations, including American Indian Native, National Disability, the American Association of Blacks in Energy, the Society of Hispanic Professional Engineers, the Society of Women Engineers and the National Action Council for Minorities in Engineering. We also participated in a luncheon sponsored by the Black Executive Exchange program.

In our continuing efforts to increase women hires, our recruitment office has strengthened our partnership with Nontraditional Employment for Women (NEW), an organization that trains and secures employment for women in trades. The Con Edison Learning Center trained 200 women enrolled with NEW in 2006. They learned basic electricity, carpentry, plumbing and math, and were given an introduction to transmission and distribution systems. Seven women from NEW were hired—six into the titles of general utility worker and mechanic B, and one as a customer service representative. Since 2000, we have recruited 53 women from NEW. As career opportunities arise, we will continue to consider NEW graduates for employment.

In addition, Con Edison participated in many New York City job fairs in 2006 that introduced us to a diverse pool of qualified applicants. Some career fairs were sponsored by the New York State Department of Labor, New York City Housing Authority, NEW, Women for Hire, the NAACP National Convention Diversity Job Fair, the CUNY Big Apple Job Fair, the Disabled Career Exposition, the Gay Life Exposition, the World of Working Women Job Fair and the Dress for Success Job Fair. We also participated in several college-sponsored career fairs including the Society of Women Engineers at Cornell University, the National Society of Black Engineers and the Society of Hispanic Professional Engineers at Rensselaer Polytechnic Institute. Con Edison was also represented at career fairs at historically black colleges and universities

Additional information regarding item VI: Con Edison offers a variety of programs geared to assist all employees, including minorities and women, in mastering their job functions, advancing their careers and furthering their education. Classes and presentations are held at Con Edison's Learning Center, a multimillion-dollar facility devoted to providing employees with practical training and personal development courses.

Whether it is training new customer service representatives or upgrading the skills of field workers, The Learning Center staff works closely with operating departments to develop training programs that enable us to maintain our system, run more effective operations, improve customer service and nurture employee leadership skills. Courses are provided in electric, gas and steam systems; customer operations; environment, health and safety information technology; and leadership. Additionally, Strategic Issues Seminars are designed to help employees gain the leadership skills necessary to run the Con Edison of tomorrow. These seminars are held frequently and cover a wide range of topics. Con Edison is also a corporate member of the Institute for Management Studies and the American Management Association, where employees can find classes and seminars covering many different topics. The company also provides web-based, self-study programs that employees are able to take at their convenience. The programs offered at The Learning Center are available to all employees and are particularly useful to individuals who may need to advance their skill level or want to try a new career path.

Con Edison has received the following corporate and individual awards in the past three years:

2006

- *Diversity Inc's* Top 50 Best Companies for Diversity
- *Hispanic* magazine's Corporate 100 List
- The *LATINA Style* Top 50
- *Black Enterprise's* 40 Best Companies for Diversity
- Human Rights Campaign Foundation, Best Places to Work for GLBT Equality

2005

- *Diversity Inc's* Top 50 Best Companies for Minorities
- The *LATINA Style* Top 50
- New York Urban League Champions of Diversity
- *Black Enterprise's* Top 40 Companies for Diversity

2004

- *Fortune* magazine's 50 Best Companies for Minorities
- *Hispanic* magazine's Corporate 100
- The *LATINA Style* Top 50
- *Diversity Inc's* Top 50 Companies for Diversity
- Asian American Business Development Center's Outstanding 50 Asian Americans in Business

- Leadership Institute for African-American Female Executives
- Top 10 Queens Women in Business
- *The Network Journal* magazine's 25 Influential Black Women in Business

The following are organizations with diversity-initiative programs that received Con Edison support in 2006:

- 100 Hispanic Women, Inc.
- Abyssinian Development Corporation
- African American Men of Westchester
- Agudath Israel of America
- American Association of Blacks in Energy
- American Civil Rights Education Services
- Arthur D. Phillips Scholarship Fund, Inc.
- Asia Society
- Asian American Business Development Center
- Asian American Federation of New York
- Asian American/Asian Research Institute
- Asian American Legal Defense and Education Fund
- Asian Americans for Equality, Inc.
- Asian Professional Extension, Inc.
- Asian Women in Business
- ASPIRA of New York, Inc.
- Associated Black Charities
- Association of Minority Enterprises of New York
- AYUDA for the Arts
- Ballet Hispanico of New York
- Barnard College
- Black Agency Executives
- Bottomless Closet
- Bronx Hispanic Foundation, Inc.
- Brooklyn Chinese-American Association, Inc.
- Caribbean American Chamber of Commerce and Industry, Inc.
- Casita Maria, Inc.
- Catalyst
- Chinese-American Planning Council, Inc.
- Coalition of Asian Pacific Americans
- Coalition For Hispanic Family Services
- Comite Noviembre Mes De La Herencia Puertorriquena
- Committee for Hispanic Children and Families, Inc.
- Congressional Black Caucus Foundation, Inc.
- Council of Jewish Organizations of Flatbush, Inc.
- Dominican American National Roundtable
- Dominican Women's Development Center, Inc.
- Dominico American Society of Queens, Inc.
- El Carnaval del Boulevard
- El Museo del Barrio

- Foundation for Ethnic Understanding, Inc.
- Girl Scout Council of Greater New York, Inc.
- Hispanic Federation of New York City, Inc.
- Hong Kong Dragon Boat Festival in New York, Inc.
- Instituto Arte Teatral Internacional, Inc.
- Jewish Community Relations Council of New York, Inc.
- Jewish Museum
- Korean-American Counseling Center, Inc.
- Latino Commission on AIDS
- Latino Gerontological Center
- Latino Job ServiceEmployer Committee
- Latinos in Information Sciences and Technology and Association, Inc.
- League of Women Voters of the City of New York
- League of Women Voters of Westchester
- Lewis H. Latimer Fund, Inc.
- Martin Luther King Jr. Concert Series, Inc.
- Metropolitan New York Coordinating Council on Jewish Poverty
- Metropolitan Jewish Geriatric Foundation
- Museum of Chinese in the Americas
- Musica de Camara, Inc.
- NAACP
- NAACP ACT-SO Coalition of NYC Branches
- NAACP Legal Defense and Education Fund
- National Action Council for Minorities in Engineering
- National Association for Female Executives Women's Foundation
- National Council of Jewish Women, Inc.
- National Hispanic Business Group
- National Puerto Rican Forum, Inc.
- National Urban Fellows, Inc.
- New York Association of Black Journalists
- New York State Assembly/Senate Puerto Rican/Hispanic Task Force
- New York State Association of Black and Puerto Rican Legislators, Inc.
- New York State Federation of Hispanic Chambers of Commerce
- New York Women's Agenda
- Nontraditional Employment for Women
- Northern Manhattan Coalition for Economic Development

- One Hundred Black Men, Inc.
- Operation Exodus Inner City, Inc.
- Organization of Chinese Americans – Westchester & Hudson Valley Chapter
- Pregones Touring Puerto Rican Theatre Collection, Inc.
- Professional Women in Construction
- Promesa Foundation
- Puerto Rican Bar Association Scholarship Fund, Inc.
- Puerto Rican Bar Association Women's Committee
- Puerto Rican Family Institute, Inc.

Puerto Rican Legal Defense and Education Fund
- Puerto Rican Traveling Theatre Company
- Queens Women's Center, Inc.
- Queens Women's Network
- Redhawk Indian Arts Council
- Regional Aid for Interim Needs, Inc.
- Resource Center For Community Development
- Repertorio Español
- Russian Ethnic Bilingual Educational and Cultural Association
- San Juan Fiesta/Archdiocese of N.Y.—Office of Hispanic Affairs
- Society of Hispanic Professional Engineers
- Society of the Educational Arts, Inc./SEA
- Spanish Repertory Theatre
- Teatro Circulo, Ltd.
- Thalia Spanish Theatre, Inc.
- Thurgood Marshall Scholarship Fund
- Tomchei Torah Chaim Birnbaum
- Uja-Federation of New York
- United Negro College Fund
- Washington Heights-Inwood Coalition, Inc.
- West Indian-American Day Carnival Association, Inc.
- Wien House (YWHA)
- Women in Communications and Energy
- Women's City Club of New York, Inc.
- Women's Research and Education Fund
- Yeshiva University (Albert Einstein College Of Medicine Of Yeshiva University)
- YWCA

Convergys Corporation

201 E. 4th Street
Cincinnati, OH 45202
Phone: (513) 723-7000
Fax: (513) 421-8624
www.convergys.com/turnyourfutureon

Locations

Cincinnati, OH (HQ)
Jacksonville, FL
Orlando, FL
Various other national and global locations.

Diversity Leadership

Tommie Lewis
Senior Manager of Global Diversity

Employment Contact

Jim Hartman
Director of Human Resources

Diane Wall
Sr. Associate of Recruiting

Recruiting

Does your firm annually recruit at any of the following types of institutions?

We recruit at the following schools:

Bowling Green State University, Brigham Young University, Carnegie Mellon University, Florida A&M University, Florida International University, Florida State University, Georgia Institute of Technology, Miami University of Ohio, Northern Kentucky University, Purdue University, Ohio University, The Ohio State University, University of Central Florida, University of Cincinnati, University of Dayton, University of Florida, University of Illinois, University of Michigan, University of North Florida, University of Texas-Austin, University of Utah, Xavier University

Do you have any special outreach efforts directed to encourage minority students and graduates to consider your firm?

• Hold a reception for minority students

• *Conferences:* Catalyst Conference, Most Important Hispanics in Business and Technology Conference, Black Engineer of the Year Conference, MatchMaker Supplier Diversity Conference, INROADS Leadership Development Institute & Corporate Conference, Women of Color Awards Conference

• Advertise in minority student association publication(s) or other minority-focused publications: Black Enterprise magazine, Black Career Women, National Society for Hispanic Professionals, Society of Hispanic Professional Engineers, Employer Assistance and Recruiting Network, National Association of African-Americans in Human Resources, Women in Technology International, National Society for Hispanic MBAs, National Society for Black MBAs

• Participate in/host minority student job fair(s) or other minority-focused job events.

• Sponsor minority student association events

• Firm's employees participate on career panels at school

• Outreach to leadership of minority student organizations

• Scholarships or intern/fellowships for minority students

• *Sit in on affiliate boards:* BDPA, INROADS, Jobs for American Graduates

• Host the Women in Technology Conference

What activities does the firm undertake to attract minority and women employees?

• Partner programs with women and minority associations

• *Conferences:* See above

• Participate at minority job fairs

• Seek referrals from other employees

• Utilize online job services

• Host the Women in Technology Conference

Do you use executive recruiting/search firms to seek to identify new diversity hires?

Yes

Internships and Co-ops

Convergys Intern Program

Deadline for application: Continuous

Number of interns in the program in summer 2006: 75

Pay: $9 to $18 per hour (housing stipends available for summer)

Length of the program: 12 weeks

Percentage of interns/co-ops in the program who receive offers of full-time employment: 60 percent

Web site for internship/co-op information:
www.convergys.com/turnyourfutureon

Through the intern program, we strive to recognize those students that excel in their personal and academic lives so that they may excel in their professional lives as well. Convergys offers full-time summer internships as well as part-time, year-round internships in various locations, with Cincinnati, Ohio, and Jacksonville and Orlando, FL, being the primary locations of hiring activity. We focus on a wide range of disciplines and skills to fit into our program, including accounting/finance, business, human resources, information systems technology and marketing. We also work closely with INROADS to bring in the best and most diverse candidates.

Scholarships

Convergys Academic Achievement Recognition Program

Deadline: June 22, 2007

Pay: $5,000 per recipient (amount may vary according to school)

Web site for scholarship information: www.convergys.com/turnyourfutureon, "Scholarship Awards"

Purpose of Program

To acknowledge and reward academically successful students who have chosen a field of study related to Convergys' business and its industry. Scholarships will be granted to students enrolled at selected universities based on specific criteria. Each university will select a number of qualified candidates to be approved by Convergys.

Objectives/Summary

Convergys is seeking to award academically based scholarships to:

Recognize academic achievement

Assist in positioning Convergys as an employer of choice

Assist in the recruitment of academically successful candidates for hiring needs

Appropriate designees of the educational facility will select the award recipients, with final review by Convergys-appointed designees. Payment of the awards will be sent directly to the attending university for the purpose of tuition and tuition-related expenses.

For each scholarship recipient, Convergys presently intends to offer a meaningful, developmental, paid internship experience that ultimately would position a candidate to accept a potential offer of full-time employment upon graduation.

Affinity Groups

- Global Women's Network (GWN)
- Convergys Hispanic Initiatives in Motion (CHIIM)
- Asian Employee Network (AEN)
- Gays, Lesbians and Allies at Convergys (GLAC)
- Black Employee Network (BEN)
- Convergys Ability Resource Team (CART)

Purpose

Convergys affinity groups are corporately-sanctioned, employee-led diversity initiatives designed to enhance open communication, business problem solving and employee development. Ultimately, our affinity groups add value to the business and help develop a more inclusive work environment.

Each group meets monthly.

Strategic Plan and Diversity Leadership

What trends in your industry affect your corporate diversity goals, strategies and/or internal or external alliances?

Global market and workforce trends in various industry verticals impact our strategy and our approach toward diversity solutions.

How does the firm's leadership communicate the importance of diversity to everyone at the firm?

The firm's leadership showcases the importance of diversity using the following: company corporate communications, business unit newsletters, organizational development, weekly diversity e-news stories, diversity action teams and office of diversity communications such as e-mail, company Intranet, desk-drops and the web.

Who has primary responsibility for leading diversity initiatives at your firm?

Senior Manager of Global Diversity, Tommie Lewis

Does your firm currently have a diversity committee?

Yes

If yes, please describe how the committee is structured, how often it meets, etc.

The Global Diversity Steering Committee is comprised of the most senior officers (CEO, CFO, etc.) and meets annually. The business Unit Global Diversity Council is comprised of representatives from the business units/resources units, chaired by business unit leaders and meets once per month. The office of global diversity sets the

diversity agenda, oversees the strategic plan, monitors progress and keeps units informed and aligned with business goals.

If yes, does the committee's representation include one or more members of the firm's management/executive committee (or the equivalent)?

Yes

If yes, how many executives are on the committee, and in 2006, what was the total number of hours collectively spent by the committee in furtherance of the firm's diversity initiatives? How many employees are on the committee, and how often does the committee convene in furtherance of the firm's diversity initiatives?

30 percent of the Global Diversity Council consists of business unit leaders. The council consists of 90 members contributing two to four hours per month.

Does the committee and/or diversity leader establish and set goals or objectives consistent with management's priorities?

Yes

Has the firm undertaken a formal or informal diversity program or set of initiatives aimed at increasing the diversity of the firm?

Yes, formal

How often does the firm's management review the firm's diversity progress/results?

Executive Steering Committee and office of global diversity reviews progress against diversity goals.

How is the firm's diversity committee and/or firm management held accountable for achieving results?

The global diversity council is segmented into five key areas to which members of these "subcommittees" participate in business meetings aligned with the key areas. Accountability is achieved through business unit metrics around cultural diversity, diversity education and training, and representation.

The Stats

	NUMBER OF EMPLOYEES		REVENUE	
	2006	2005	2006	2005
Total worldwide	75,000	66,000	$2.8 billion	$2.6 billion

Retention and Professional Development

Please identify the specific steps you are taking to reduce the attrition rate of minority and women employees.

• Develop and/or support internal employee affinity groups

• Increase/review compensation relative to competition

• Increase/improve current work/life programs

• Adopt dispute resolution process

• Succession plan includes emphasis on diversity

• Work with minority and women employees to develop career advancement plans

• Review work assignments and hours billed to key client matters to make sure minority and women employees are not being excluded

• Strengthen mentoring program for all employees, including minorities and women

• Professional skills development program, including minority and women employees

Diversity Mission Statement

"We believe the effective management of diversity is one of the components that is key to our success as a leader in our industry. At Convergys, diversity encompasses all facets of our workforce."

—*Jim Orr, Chairman*

Diversity Principles

Through our diversity initiatives, we will establish and maintain an environment that:

• Values individual differences.

• Fosters consistent, mutual respect and open communication of ideas.

• Attracts, develops, supports and retains a diverse workforce with the ability to compete in the global market.

• Increases our competitive advantage by leveraging the knowledge, skills and unique talents of our employees.

• Enhances career opportunities for all employees by working to develop each employee to his or her full potential.

• Provides a richer, more fertile climate for creative thinking and innovation.

• Is recognized by employees, clients and the community as a fair and rewarding place to work..

Additional Information

Company Overview

The global leader in providing customer care, human resources and billing services, Convergys combines specialized knowledge and expertise with solid execution to deliver outsourced solutions, consulting services and software support. Clients in more than 70 countries speaking nearly 35 languages depend on Convergys to manage the increasing complexity and cost of caring for customers and employees. Convergys serves the world's leading companies in many industries including communications, financial services, technology and consumer products.

Convergys is a member of the S&P 500 and a *Fortune* Most Admired Company for seven consecutive years. Headquartered in Cincinnati, Ohio, Convergys has approximately 75,000 employees in 75 customer contact centers, three data centers and other facilities in the United States, Canada, Latin America, Europe, the Middle East and Asia. For more information, visit www.convergys.com.

Credit Suisse

11 Madison Avenue
New York, NY 10010
Phone: (212) 325-2000
www.credit-suisse.com

Locations

Worldwide

Employment Contact

Julie Kalish
Vice President, US Head of Firmwide Campus
 Recruiting

Freda Campbell
Assistant Vice President, Diversity Lateral
 Talent

Career web site address:
www.credit-suisse.com/careers

Recruiting

Please list the schools/types of schools at which you recruit.

• Ivy League schools

• Other private schools

• Public state schools

• Historically black colleges and universities (HBCUs)

• Hispanic serving institutions (HSIs)

Do you have any special outreach efforts directed to encourage minority students and graduates to consider your firm?

• Hold a reception for minority students-

• *Conferences:*   National Black MBA Associates, NSHMBA, Reaching Out, National Association of Women MBAs, MBA Jump Start, Society of Hispanic Engineers

• Advertise in minority student association publication(s) or other minority-focused publications

• Participate in/host minority student job fair(s) or other minority-focused job events

• Sponsor minority student association events

• Firm's employees participate on career panels at school

• Outreach to leadership of minority student organizations

• Scholarships or intern/fellowships for minority students

What activities does the firm undertake to attract minority and women employees?

• Partner programs with women and minority associations

• Conferences

• Participate at minority job fairs

• Seek referrals from other employees

• Utilize online job services

Do you use executive recruiting/search firms to seek to identify new diversity hires?

Yes—for experienced hires only.

Internships and Co-ops

Credit Suisse Overview

As one of the world's leading banks, Credit Suisse provides its clients with investment banking, private banking and asset management services worldwide. Credit Suisse offers advisory services, comprehensive solutions and innovative products to companies, institutional clients and high-net-worth private clients globally, as well as retail clients in Switzerland. Credit Suisse is active in over 50 countries and employs approximately 40,000 people. Credit Suisse Group's registered shares (CSGN) are listed in Switzerland and, in the form of American Depositary Shares (CSR), in New York.

Investment Banking

Credit Suisse offers a broad range of investment banking and securities products and services to meet the needs of institutional clients, companies and government bodies.

Private Banking

Credit Suisse provides expert advice and a comprehensive range of investment products and services tailored to the complex needs of high-net-worth individuals globally as well as private and business clients in Switzerland.

Asset Management

Credit Suisse serves clients by offering products across the full range of investment classes, from equities, fixed income and multiple-asset class products to alternative.

Qualifications for all Internships

Credit Suisse is noted for the diversity of its employees, but seeks candidates with a common set of abilities—highly motivated and creative individuals who have demonstrated academic achievement, specifically in finance and accounting and have the ability to work independently and as a member of a team. We look for intelligent, driven and hardworking candidates with consistent leadership involvement in school activities and athletics, and a solid interest in the financial sector.

Interested candidates must be between their junior and senior years at a four-year college or university. Please apply though the career center and at www.credit-suisse.com/careers.

Program Structure

Credit Suisse's summer programs begin with an intense one-week training period in New York. The training curriculum varies by program but summer analysts will participate in a capital markets overview, accounting classes, a bond math review and a library tour. You'll be trained on Bloomberg and learn Credit Suisse technology systems and databases.

Your learning experience will continue through the summer speaker series, where you'll hear from senior employees across the divisions. In addition, you'll participate in networking events and firmwide events that will help ensure that you are exposed to all the areas within the bank and understand the big picture of a global investment bank. You'll also enjoy interacting with the other summer analysts and full-time employees at a variety of social events throughout the summer.

To help you determine your strengths and plan your career, summer analysts are matched with mentors, who provide advice and guidance throughout the summer.

Summer Analyst: Investment Banking

Our 10-week Summer Analyst Program for rising college seniors gives you outstanding exposure to business and the financial services industry.

Whether you're working alongside a full-time analyst or staffed as the only analyst on a deal team, our summer program gives you the tools you'll need to jumpstart your career in finance and investment banking. Responsibilities may include analyzing companies using financial modeling and valuation techniques, examining the impact of a transaction on a client's capital structure and analyzing the consequences of a merger or acquisition.

Summer analysts will be placed directly into an industry or product group. As a summer program participant, you will have the opportunity to work on deals in your group/desk, gaining hands-on experience and working on all aspects of advising and transacting business for our clients. Summer analysts are formally reviewed at the mid and endpoints of the summer, and offers are made on the last day of the program, enabling you to return to school with a full-time position secured.

Our U.S. regional breadth offers unique opportunities to execute transactions from conception to close, which differentiates Credit Suisse from our competitors.

Summer Analyst: Alternative Investments

Credit Suisse Alternative Investments (AI) is a leading global alternative asset manager involved in private equity, hedge funds and related activities. The AI businesses include the fund and alternative solutions hedge fund of funds group, quantitative strategies and Volaris as well as a diverse family of private equity funds, including leveraged buyout funds, mezzanine funds, core and opportunity real estate funds, secondary funds, CDOs and fund of fund businesses. With over $130 billion in assets under management and exceptional investment performance, Credit Suisse is one of the world's largest and most successful managers of alternatives. Credit Suisse AI is also the world's leading placement agent in alternative assets, raising capital for third-party managers through its Private Fund Group and Real Estate Private Fund Group. The AI businesses have a 20-year history of strong investment performance, with leading market share positions. The funds that typically hire are multi-manager portfolios, leveraged investments, Real Estate Private Fund Group, Private Fund Group, strategic partners, and funds management.

Summer Analyst: Global Markets Solutions

The Global Markets Solutions Group (GMSG) is a global innovative coverage initiative focused on delivering creative financial solutions to our clients. The group combines originations efforts across equity capital markets (ECM), debt capital markets (DCM), private placements and structured origination. GMSG professionals coordinate with industry and coverage bankers to provide a single interface for all of the firm's capital markets, funding and structured products.

Summer analysts are placed directly onto a desk within a product area of Global Markets Solutions Group. As a summer program participant, you will have the opportunity to develop your analytical skills by using various financial techniques, gain hands-on experience and interact with both internal and external clientele.

Summer analysts are formally reviewed at the mid and end points of the summer. Summer analyst opportunities vary per product area and will be available in our New York office.

Summer Analyst: Fixed Income or Equity Sales and Trading

The fixed income and equities departments at Credit Suisse offer two separate, 10-week summer programs—one in equity sales and trading and one in fixed income sales and trading. If chosen for a first-round interview, students will interview for both the equity sales and trading and the fixed income sales and trading programs—please only drop your resume once for these programs. Second-round interviews are held separately and will be equity-specific or fixed-income specific. This will be determined based on your first-round interviews. In both programs, you'll spend one week in training, followed by three three-week rotations on either fixed income or equity desks.

Sales Rotation: You'll spend three weeks working within one sales product area. In equity, this rotation will give you the chance to work with the coverage sales, institutional sales, international sales, automated execution systems, prime services, convertible sales or derivative sales teams. In fixed income, you'll work with the corporate, structured products, interest rates, structuring, global foreign exchange, emerging markets, CDO Group or derivatives sales teams.

Trading Rotation: You'll spend three weeks working within one trading product area. In equity, it will include the cash trading, derivative trading, program trading, international sales trading and exchange traded funds teams. In fixed income, these groups include the corporate, structured products, interest rates, global foreign exchange, emerging markets, or interest rate products trading teams.

Sales or trading rotation: You'll spend your final three weeks on one of the above-mentioned sales or trading desks in either fixed income or equity.

These programs are a great way to become familiar to the sales and trading arena, as well as the overall investment process, gaining a broad and varied view of several potential career paths.

Summer Analyst: Equity Research

If you're a dynamic undergraduate looking for an intense and valuable introduction to the equity research arena, the Equity Research Summer Analyst Program may be for you. By working with one of our top-ranked senior research analysts, you'll gain an in-depth understanding of company analysis as well as the overall investment process. You will also have exposure to other divisions at Credit Suisse, including Credit Suisse global sales force, equity traders and institutional clients.

We offer our summer analysts a solid one-week training program to provide you with the skills to join one of our outstanding research teams. Throughout the summer, you may work on projects involving financial analysis and investigative research. Equity research summer analysts also have the opportunity to learn financial modeling and forecasting skills and to help produce research reports. In order to fully understand equity research's role at Credit Suisse, every summer intern will spend time with equity salespeople and equity traders. In addition to your day-to-day responsibilities, you'll be assigned an industry-specific project to work on throughout the summer.

Summer Analyst: HOLT

The HOLT division of Credit Suisse is offering a summer internship program, based in Chicago, for undergraduate students interested in learning and applying advanced business strategy analysis and buy-side valuation methodologies.

Through theoretical and applied research, HOLT has developed a framework that better explains the dynamic relationship between corporate financial performance and stock market pricing. HOLT's central premise is that the stock market sets prices based on cash flows, not traditional accounting measures of corporate performance.

As a summer analyst, you will gain exposure to multiple global industries, interact with numerous areas of the bank, engage in strategic initiatives for key clients around the globe, carry out in-depth analysis of the factors underlying corporate financial performance and valuation, enhance your ability to structure and present persuasive analyses, and gain financial analysis skills of leading investment management and management consulting firms.

Summer Analyst: Real Estate Finance and Securitization

The Real Estate Finance & Securitization Group's (REFS's) main product areas fall into the broad categories of real estate and real estate-related financial products—commercial mortgage-backed securities, for example. This group operates in a principal capacity as well as providing investment banking services to corporate clients, institutions and publicly traded real estate companies.

REFS is organized into several operating teams:

Origination Group: Organized on a geographic basis in both the New York and Los Angeles offices, origination teams invest in debt and equity and combination financing for office, industrial, retail, hotel and multifamily, single tenant and other property types. Loans can be made for "whole loan" sale, securitization or balance sheet purposes.

Investment banking: Provides advisory services for companies and institutions regarding their real estate activities. The work involves sale mandates, securitization, mergers and acquisitions, and other transactions.

Structured finance: Focuses on securitization transactions and other "financially engineered" exits for REFS's investments.

Trading: Encompasses several units involving whole loans, commercial mortgage-backed securities (CMBS) and derivatives.

As a summer analyst, you will develop your understanding of the field by working on a variety of transactions. Summer analyst positions are located in New York

Summer Analyst: Fixed Income Research

The experience, knowledge and commitment to serving the interests of our clients make Credit Suisse's fixed income and economics research one of the most innovative and insightful in the industry. Credit Suisse is particularly known for its excellence in global

macro-economics, strategy and foreign exchange, in both developed and emerging markets. In addition, the firm has pre-eminent U.S. high-grade and securitized asset research.

By working with one of our widely respected senior research analysts in emerging markets, structured products or credit research, you'll become knowledgeable about a research group and learn the fundamentals of research analysis. You will also gain exposure to other divisions of Credit Suisse including our sales force, fixed income traders, investment bankers and institutional clients.

Summer Analyst: Asset Finance Capital Markets

Asset finance capital markets summer analysts are investment bankers within the Fixed Income Division (FID). As a member of the Asset Finance Group, you will work within a team to help develop funding strategies for our clients. You'll also act as a liaison between our clients and the capital markets division, and execute transactions backed by a variety of asset classes, including auto loans, credit card receivables, home equity loans and student loans. Our clients cover many different industries and range from specialty finance firms to Fortune 500 companies.

During the 10-week program, summer analysts will have the opportunity to participate in all aspects of transaction execution: working with the client, performing due diligence, communicating with the FID trading floor and managing the accountants, rating agencies and attorneys. They will also help perform any cash flow or financial analyses involved in completing the transaction. Finally, summer analysts will support the ongoing effort to build and strengthen client relationships by preparing marketing materials to pitch the ABS product to new clients as well as presenting new ideas to current clients. Summer analyst positions are located in New York.

Scholarships

Douglas L. Paul Scholarship for Achievement

Credit Suisse will offer $5,000 scholarships to a number of college sophomores of African, Latino and Native American descent. Recipients of the scholarships will be selected based on their academic excellence, leadership abilities and interest in the financial services industry. In addition to monetary resources, Doug Paul scholars will have the chance to participate in our 10-week rotational program in New York. This program provides students with an educational opportunity to learn about the various areas of an investment bank, with rotations in equities, fixed income and investment banking. Scholars will receive a stipend for the duration of the 10-week program. During the program, students are given mentors to provide valuable insight into Credit Suisse, Wall Street and financial services.

Affinity Groups

Credit Suisse Employee Networks

Credit Suisse's Global Employee Networks bring people together from across the bank to share information, ideas and experiences. These diverse groups help employees balance their work and personal lives and promote career development through networking, informal mentoring, education and access to senior management. Activities include panel discussions, lecture series, seminars, presentations and study groups, as well as workplace support groups that raise awareness of a wide array of diversity issues. Every site-based network is inclusive and open to all Credit Suisse employees who wish to participate.

Americas Women's Network

The Americas Women's Network is a cross-divisional network of Credit Suisse employees dedicated to developing careers, attracting talent, cultivating client relationships and promoting camaraderie between women. Their purpose is to support career development through educational and relationship building opportunities and to win business and advance Credit Suisse strategy.

Multicultural Resource Network

The Multicultural Resources Network (MRN) in the U.K. and the U.S. is a forum where employees with various ethnic backgrounds and experiences can work together to develop professionally. MRN special events include guest speakers, receptions, art exhibits, fund raisers and even cooking and dancing demonstrations that showcase the rich cultural heritage of our global community. MRN members are also active in the firm's recruitment efforts and volunteer with a number of community organizations.

Open Network

The Open Network in both the U.S. and U.K. highlights an inclusive work culture in which gay, lesbian, bisexual and transgender (GLBT) employees can advance and succeed. Open Network members regularly assist recruitment efforts and organize fund raising for local organizations serving the GLBT community. Speakers at Open Network events have included members of the U.S. Congress, actors and leading experts on issues facing the GLBT community in the workplace.

Parents Network

The Parents Network provides holistic programming around the parenting life cycle; caring for children, parents and grandparents. The Network supports employees who are caregivers depending on the type of care they are providing:

• Future and Expectant Parents

• Parents of Infants and Toddlers

• Parents of Middle School/HS

• Parents of Children With Special Needs

• Elder Care

Strategic Plan and Diversity Leadership

How does the firm's leadership communicate the importance of diversity to everyone at the firm?

Credit Suisse utilizes a variety of communication methods to convey the importance of diversity, including newsletters, marketing brochures, e-mail memorandums, meetings and a web site on the company Intranet.

Who has primary responsibility for leading diversity initiatives at your firm?

Credit Suisse's commitment to diversity and Inclusion begins with the most senior executives at the bank who manage diversity and inclusion as a business. Accordingly, Angie Casciato, managing director and Credit Suisse's global head of diversity and inclusion, reports directly to the chief executive.

Does your firm currently have a diversity committee?

Global diversity and inclusion includes the successful implementation of many initiatives set by Credit Suisse's diversity advisory board, which is responsible for setting and advancing our global diversity strategy.

If yes, does the committee's representation include one or more members of the firm's management/executive committee (or the equivalent)?

Ms. Casciato chairs this board, the members of which include managing directors from across the businesses and from all regions.

If yes, how many executives are on the committee, and in 2006, what was the total number of hours collectively spent by the committee in furtherance of the firm's diversity initiatives? How many employees are on the committee, and how often does the committee convene in furtherance of the firm's diversity initiatives?

The diversity advisory board consists of 27 members and meets quarterly. In addition, each division has a diversity advisory council to implement the bank's overall diversity and inclusion strategy. These members spend thousands of hours throughout the course of the year.

Does the committee and/or diversity leader establish and set goals or objectives consistent with management's priorities?

Cultivating and fostering an inclusive workplace is a top priority and an integral part of Credit Suisse's business strategy. We believe that diversity breeds innovation. As such, corporate citizenship inte-

grates with business strategy. The business driver is very clear—the first step in helping our clients meet their goals is making sure our employees meet theirs.

Has the firm undertaken a formal or informal diversity program or set of initiatives aimed at increasing the diversity of the firm?

Yes, formal

How often does the firm's management review the firm's diversity progress/results?

Quarterly

Diversity Mission Statement

Diversity and inclusion at Credit Suisse is about an inclusive culture across the bank where employees' differences are valued and leveraged for the benefit of the business, employees are given opportunities to realize their full potential and all employees are treated with dignity and respect.

Diversity and inclusion supports our business as it provides a competitive edge in attracting and retaining talent, diverse perspectives lead to innovative solutions for our clients and diversity and inclusion strengthen client relationships.

Global diversity and inclusion is an integral part of Credit Suisse's business strategy. Our approach leverages diversity and inclusion to attract, develop and retain top talent, continues to promote a culture of respect for individual differences, which breeds innovation and draws talent and ideas from around the world, and gives us a distinct competitive advantage which creates new and compelling business opportunities. This has enabled us to win business, strengthen relationships with existing clients and create inroads to new clients.

Additional Information

Credit Suisse is dedicated to attracting, developing and retaining the best people in the industry. We bring together individuals of different genders, races, ages, nationalities, religions, sexual orientations and disabilities to create a world-class team of financial service professionals.

At the core of the Credit Suisse philosophy of inclusion is the firm's Global Dignity at Work policy, a set of conduct guidelines that apply to all employees worldwide. This policy ensures that diversity, inclusiveness and dignity in the workplace are everyone's responsibility. These enduring values are part of the very fabric of our business. They shape the way we hire, develop and promote employees, and they guide us in the way we treat one another.

CSX Corporation, Inc.

500 Water Street
Jacksonville, FL 32202
Phone: (904) 359-3100
Fax: (904) 359-2459
E-mail: Susan_Hamilton@csx.com
www.CSX.com

Locations

All US/Largest Railroad in the eastern US operate east of the Mississippi River, with 10 operating divisions in:

Jacksonville, FL (HQ)

Albany, NY • Atlanta, GA • Baltimore, MD • Chicago, IL • Florence, SC • Huntington, WV • Indianapolis, IN • Louisville, KY • Nashville, TN

Diversity Leadership

Susan O. Hamilton
AVP Diversity & EEOC
500 Water Street
Jacksonville, FL 32202
Phone: (904) 366-4092
Fax: (904) 359-3728
E-mail: Susan_Hamilton@csx.com

Recruiting

Please list the schools at which you recruit.

We recruit at approximately 25 different colleges and universities, including several historically black schools, and have a booth every year at both the national black and national Hispanic MBA expositions (only railroad).

Do you have any special outreach efforts directed to encourage minority students to consider your firm?

• Hold a reception for minority students
• Conferences
• Advertise in minority student association publication(s)
• Participate in/host minority student job fair(s)
• Firm's employees participate on career panels at school
• Outreach to leadership of minority student organizations
• Scholarships or intern/fellowships for minority students

What activities does the firm undertake to attract minority and women employees?

• Partner programs with women and minority associations
• Conferences
• Participate at minority job fairs
• Seek referrals from other employees
• Utilize online job services

Do you use executive recruiting/search firms to seek to identify new diversity hires?

Yes

Internships and Co-ops

INROADS Interns

Deadline for application: April

Pay: We pay a $40,000 fee and a base rate of pay by department to each intern.

Length of the program: Two to three months, depending on return dates for school

We have hired 18 INROADS interns permanently. We have had 86 INROADS interns since 1991, many of them multiple years.

Affinity Groups

• African American
• Asian American
• Hispanic
• Working Parents
• Women's Network
• Military
• C.A.R.E (caring for elderly parents)
• Gay/Lesbian

• Young Professionals

Entry-Level Programs, Full-Time Opportunities and Training Programs

Management Training Program

Length of program: January/July and July/December

Geographic location(s) of program: Headquarters-based with some travel to field locations, assignments

Rotations through the company with orientation periodically.

Open to graduates, MBA graduates, successful internal candidates— we have a corporate tuition reimbursement program available to all management employees, not just new hires.

Strategic Plan and Diversity Leadership

How does the firm's leadership communicate the importance of diversity to everyone at the firm?

The CEO and his five direct reports have diversity goals in their overall performance management program. Diversity goals cascade within their organizations. Diversity is one of our core competencies.

Who has primary responsibility for leading diversity initiatives at your firm?

Susan Hamilton, senior vice president, AVP-diversity and EEOC, reporting to Senior Vice President Bob Haulter, who reports to the CEO.

Does your firm currently have a diversity committee?

Yes, the Global Diversity Council meets monthly, and there are 24 satellite diversity councils, including most operating divisions.

If yes, does the committee's representation include one or more members of the firm's management/executive committee (or the equivalent)?

Yes

If yes, how many executives are on the committee? How many employees are on the committee, and how often does the committee convene in furtherance of the firm's diversity initiatives?

There are 60 members, each spending a minimum of two to five hours per month.

Total Executives on Committee: One senior vice president, one vice president, three division managers, one state vice president, three assistant vice presidents

Does the committee and/or diversity leader establish and set goals or objectives consistent with management's priorities?

Yes

Has the firm undertaken a formal or informal diversity program or set of initiatives aimed at increasing the diversity of the firm?

Yes, formal

How often does the firm's management review the firm's diversity progress/results?

Quarterly

How is the firm's diversity committee and/or firm management held accountable for achieving results?

We report periodically to the board of directors. We have shared performance goals and shared competencies.

Retention and Professional Development

How do 2006 minority and female attrition rates generally compare to those experienced in the prior year period?

About the same as in prior years.

Please identify the specific steps you are taking to reduce the attrition rate of minority and women employees.

• Develop and/or support internal employee affinity groups (e.g., minority or women networks within the firm)

• Increase/review compensation relative to competition

• Increase/improve current work/life programs

• Adopt dispute resolution process

• Succession plan includes emphasis on diversity

• Work with minority and women employees to develop career advancement plans

• Review work assignments and hours billed to key client matters to make sure minority and women employees are not being excluded

• Strengthen mentoring program for all employees, including minorities and women

• Professional skills development program, including minority and women employees

• *Other:* Expanding our formal coaching/mentoring program to various field locations; partner with NABA (National Association of Black Accountants) and co-sponsor the local chapter

Diversity Mission Statement

To embrace and value the differences of all CSX employees, while blending them into one team.

DaimlerChrysler Corporation

1000 Chrysler Drive
Auburn Hills, MI 48326-2766
Phone: (248) 576-5741
Fax: (248) 576-4742
www.daimlerchrysler.com

Additional Information

DaimlerChrysler Corporation's Chrysler Group is a North American-based unit of DaimlerChrysler AG. At the Chrysler Group, we design, manufacture and sell vehicles under the Chrysler, Jeep® and Dodge brand names. Through our fourth brand, Mopar®, we offer original equipment and performance quality parts.

The Chrysler Group's strategy is to grow product leadership by constantly building innovative and segment-defining vehicles, and to continue to improve operating performance by leveraging the technology, purchasing and production synergies made possible by DaimlerChrysler's global reach.

DaimlerChrysler is committed to fostering an inclusive work environment where all employees are treated with dignity and respect. Our company policies and standards of conduct reinforce this commitment. In doing so, we recognize the value that diverse perspectives bring to business success in enabling innovation and robust decision making.

As stated in our corporate diversity statement and through the leadership commitment to diversity, DaimlerChrysler Corporation is proud of and committed to our diversity initiatives that create and maintain an inclusive work environment, which encourages and values teamwork. One of the greatest strengths of our company is its diversity. We value our employees for their different talents, backgrounds, cultures, experiences and lifestyles, and strive to achieve the diversity in our workplace that reflects the diversity of our customers and the communities in which we do business. Further, we are committed to encouraging diversity among our dealers, suppliers and partners throughout the business enterprise.

As such, DaimlerChrysler Corporation has a diversity council, consisting of the company's top management, which provides leadership on corporate actions and programs fostering diversity. Furthermore, DaimlerChrysler supports a rich community of diverse employee resource groups that are initiated and chartered by employees. These self-organized groups provide support and networking opportunities, such as mentoring, working in the community, career development and assisting in other activities that promote cultural awareness.

Additionally, DaimlerChrysler offers a number of programs that help employees to better balance their work and personal lives. Some examples of these programs include a resource and referral program, discounted child care and home services providers, a no-cost employee assistance program and flexible work arrangements.

From our cadres of diverse designers, engineers and staff, to the men and women on the factory floor, to our network of dealers and suppliers, we're dedicated to creating the best cars and trucks possible. To find out more about DaimlerChrysler and career opportunities throughout its facilities, visit us at www.careers.chrysler-group.com.

Daymon Worldwide, Inc.

700 Fairfield Avenue
Stamford, CT 06902
Phone: (203) 352-7500
www.daymon.com

Locations

30+ states in the US
International
China • Czech Republic • England •
Germany • Hong Kong • Indonesia •
Japan • Malaysia • New Zealand •
Portugal • Singapore • South Africa •
South Korea • Taiwan

Diversity Leadership

Clint Sollenberger
Director of Talent Management
700 Fairfield Avenue
Stamford, CT 06902
Phone: (203) 352-7500
Fax: (203) 352-7947

Recruiting

Does your firm annually recruit at any of the following types of institutions?

• Ivy League schools

• Public state schools

• Other private schools

• Historically black colleges and universities (HBCUs)

Do you have any special outreach efforts directed to encourage minority students to consider your firm?

• Scholarships or intern/fellowships for minority students

• Other: Seek referrals from current Daymon employees

What activities does the firm undertake to attract minority and women employees?

Partner programs with women and minority associations.

Do you use executive recruiting/search firms to seek to identify new diversity hires?

Yes

Internships and Co-ops

INROADS

Deadline for application: March/April

Length of the program: Eight to 12 weeks

Percentage of interns/co-ops in the program who receive offers of full-time employment: 75 to 100 percent (depending on performance and fit)

The goal of Daymon's internship program is to expose interns to as much of the business as possible and to help them find an area that piques their interest. The internship positions are project-based and can be found in our field locations, HR, finance, IT and many other departments in the organization, including the executive branch. Candidates for our program must possess the following competencies to be successful in this role: strategic agility, drive for results, priority setting, interpersonal savvy, customer focus, business acumen, informing and personal learning.

Entry-Level Programs, Full-Time Opportunities and Training Programs

Management Development Program

Length of program: One year

Geographic location(s) of program: Throughout the country

Three-month rotations in different areas of the business.

Strategic Plan and Diversity Leadership

How does the firm's leadership communicate the importance of diversity to everyone at the firm?

• Communication with senior management to incorporate into business units

• Regular articles in company's daily online news publication and quarterly newsletter

• Company-wide quarterly conference calls

• New associate orientations

Who has primary responsibility for leading diversity initiatives at your firm?

Kelly Bruce, general manager

Does your firm currently have a diversity committee?

Yes

If yes, please describe how the committee is structured, how often it meets, etc.

The council is comprised of a chair, a vice chair, a vice president liaison, 13 members and numerous project participants throughout the company. The executive sponsors of the council are the company's president and human resources vice president. Currently, the council members are located in three countries, so meetings are held via conference call once per month. Subcommittees are formed for each project, and those teams meet on a calendar determined by each project lead. Projects are defined and then the appropriate research is conducted to provide a recommendation to the company with regard to the specific initiative. The executive sponsors review the recommendations and present them to the officer group for consideration.

If yes, does the committee's representation include one or more members of the firm's management/executive committee (or the equivalent)?

Yes

If yes, how many executives are on the committee?

Total Executives on Committee: Four—two executive sponsors, one vice president liaison and one member who is a vice president.

Does the committee and/or diversity leader establish and set goals or objectives consistent with management's priorities?

Yes

Has the firm undertaken a formal or informal diversity program or set of initiatives aimed at increasing the diversity of the firm?

Yes, formal— Diversity Metrics or Measures

How often does the firm's management review the firm's diversity progress/results?

Quarterly

The Stats

	U.S. EMPLOYEES	WORLDWIDE EMPLOYEES
	205	2005
Total	1,446	10,700

Retention and Professional Development

Please identify the specific steps you are taking to reduce the attrition rate of minority and women employees.

• Develop and/or support internal employee affinity groups (e.g., minority or women networks within the firm)

• Succession plan includes emphasis on diversity

• Strengthen mentoring program for all employees, including minorities and women

• Professional skills development program, including minority and women employees

Diversity Mission Statement

Daymon Worldwide is a global company working in diverse markets and with diverse customers. Our company's motto of "Noble, Profitable and Fun" states our first value as being noble. Our company's greatest asset has always been—and will always be—our associates. Continuing to respect and support the diversity of our associates will increase the value of our company and will always be our greatest opportunity for growth as a business and as individuals. Our commitment to our associates and principals also extends to the communities where we conduct business, and we strive to be a responsible and contributing member.

Deloitte & Touche USA LLP

1633 Broadway
New York, NY 10019
Phone: (212) 492-4680
Fax: (212) 653-4059
www.deloitte.com

Locations
See web site for complete listing of all office locations.

Employment Contact
Kaplan Mobray
US Diversity Recruiting Leader
E-mail: kmobray@deloitte.com
www.deloitte.com/careers

Recruiting

Please list the schools/types of schools at which you recruit.

• Ivy League schools
• Other private schools
• Public state schools
• Historically black colleges and universities (HBCUs)
• Hispanic serving institutions (HSIs)
• Native American tribal universities
• Other predominantly minority and/or women's colleges

We actively recruit at over 250 colleges and universities across the United States including many HBCUs and HSIs.

Do you have any special outreach efforts directed to encourage minority students and graduates to consider your firm?

• Hold a reception for minority students
• *Conferences:* NABA, ALPFA, NBMBAA, NSHMBA, Reaching OUT MBA, NSBE, SHPE, Consortium for Graduate Studies (CGSM), Out & Equal
• Advertise in minority student association publication(s) or other minority-focused publications
• Participate in/host minority student job fair(s) or other minority-focused job events
• Sponsor minority student association events
• Firm's employees participate on career panels at school
• Outreach to leadership of minority student organizations
• *Scholarships or intern/fellowships for minority students:* INROADS, Jackie Robinson Foundation, Deloitte Future Leaders Apprentice Program
• *Other:* Southeast Case Study Program in conjunction with HBCUs, Deloitte INROADS Leadership Development Program, host Diversity and Professional Development Forums, Monster Diversity Leadership Program

What activities does the firm undertake to attract minority and women employees?

• Partner programs with women and minority associations: INROADS, HACE, ALPFA, NABA, CGSM
• *Conferences:* NABA, ALPFA, NSHMBA, NBMBAA, NSBE, NAWMBA, ReachingOut MBA, SHPE, NSBE, CGSM.
• Participate at minority job fairs
• Seek referrals from other employees
• Utilize online job services
• *Other:* Deloitte National Leadership Conference (takes place in July). Over 450 students attend this three-day leadership and networking program. See website for more details: http://careers.deloitte.com/students_internships.aspx

Do you use executive recruiting/search firms to seek to identify new diversity hires?
Yes

Internships and Co-ops

Deloitte U.S. Firms Internship Program
Takes place during winter and summer.

Deadline for application: Ongoing/varies
Number of interns in the program in summer 2006 (internship) or 2006 (co-op): 2,000 interns
Pay: Varies by program and location
Length of the program: 10 to 12 weeks
Percentage of interns/co-ops in the program who receive offers of full-time employment: 90 percent
Web site for internship/co-op information:
careers.deloitte.com/students_internships.aspx

Departments:

- *Deloitte & Touche LLP:* Audit and enterprise risk services (summer and winter internship opportunities)

- *Deloitte Consulting LLP:* Summer Scholars Program; systems analysts, business analysts and human capital analysts

- *Deloitte Financial Advisory Services LLP:* Summer intern opportunities available within forensic and dispute services

- *Deloitte Tax LLP:* Summer and winter intern opportunities available in over 10 tax specialty areas

- *Deloitte Services LP:* Intern and co-op opportunities available year-round within office services and technology, human resources, and clients and markets

Responsibilities/Qualifications:

- Strong analytical skills
- Team player
- Demonstrated leadership in extracurricular activities
- Mature interpersonal relationship and communication skills
- Strong performance in major field of study

Our goal is to provide our interns with a meaningful and hands-on experience giving them insight into a career in professional services. You will play a pivotal role with responsibilities that range from analyzing client issues and interviewing key personnel to developing recommendations and preparing presentations. You will be part of an active collaborative engagement team providing our clients with solutions that are practical as well as visionary. Your internship will enhance your team and networking skills as you will participate in a number of team-building activities and office-wide meetings.

Please see our career site for specific job description information: http://careers.deloitte.com/students_internships.aspx

Scholarships

Deloitte Future Leaders Apprentice Program

Deadline for application for the scholarship program: Varies

Scholarship award amount: Ranges from $2,500 to $10,000 for entire award

The Deloitte Future Leaders Apprentice Program (FLAP) is a pre-packaged entry-level leadership development program and recruiting tool to attract high potential campus and experienced minority candidates to the organization. The program consists of three components: mentoring, scholarship and customized leadership and professional development training. Candidates will also gain exposure to senior leadership at the Deloitte U.S. firms via informal and formally scheduled networking opportunities. We also provide scholarships through specific colleges/universities and organizations including ALPFA and NABA.

Affinity Groups

- Asian American Alliance (AAA)
- Association of Hispanic and Latino(a) Employees (HNet)
- Black Employee Network (BEN)
- Deloitte Parent's Network (DPN)
- DisABILITY Business Resource Group (DABRG)
- Gay, Lesbian, Bisexual, Transgender and Allies (GLOBE)
- International Business Resource Group (International BRG)
- Women's Initiative (WIN)

For all Affinity Groups:

- Open to all people, in all businesses
- Key driver in supporting diversity and inclusion goals with focus on professional relationships/business development, recruitment, retention/professional development and community involvement
- Part of the larger strategy to create a more inclusive culture by promoting a sense of community around a core identity
- Influencing themselves, influencing the organization, influencing the community
- Professional relationships
- Business development
- Stronger ties to professional associations (e.g., ALPFA, NABA, NAASA, etc.)
- Develop relationships with client and target BRGs
- Recruitment
- Function as a barometer of cultural nuances and real time organizational pulse
- Actively involved in targeted recruiting efforts
- Retention and professional development
- Foster advancement through coaching and mentoring
- Enhance effectiveness of employees at work
- Cross-functional interaction
- Resource to improve retention
- Community involvement
- Increase the reach of community activities
- Shape and direct local community involvement

Entry-Level Programs, Full-Time Opportunities and Training Programs

Efficacy Development: Maximizing Your Professional and Personal Development

Length of program: One-and-a-half days

Geographic location(s) of program: Held in conjunction with key professional association conferences (i.e., NABA, ALPFA, NBMBA), thus in various parts of the United States.

The seminar will allow participants to develop:

• An awareness of obstacles that can impede peak performance

• Sharpened skills and explore the use of feedback for continuous professional improvement

• Effective networking strategies for career management

Breakthrough Leadership Program (BLP)

Length of program: Eight-month program

Geographic location(s) of the program: Held in various locations across the United States

Comprehensive minority leadership development program for top performing managers and senior managers from all of our businesses. BLP components include face-to-face training, various self-assessments, 360-degree feedback and one-on-one coaching.

Howard University School of Business Center for Accounting Leadership Development Program for African Americans/Blacks

Length of program: One-week program

Geographic location(s) of the program: Held at Howard University

Participants receive support for the CPA exam and informal networking opportunities with key leaders from the profession and industry

Ellen P. Gabriel Fellows Program

Geographic location(s) of the program: Held in various locations across the United States

Participants are senior managers. Work on special projects of strategic significance for the organization, attend a leadership development seminar facilitated by Columbia University and visit the Institute for the Future in Silicon Valley.

Strategic Plan and Diversity Leadership

What trends in your industry affect your corporate diversity goals, strategies and/or internal or external alliances?

In 2010, the U.S. labor landscape is projected to show increases of 37 percent in Asians, 36 percent in Hispanics, 17 percent in African-Americans and six percent in Caucasians. It's clear to Deloitte that the more diverse our workforce and inclusive our culture are, the more top talent we'll be able to attract. Deloitte invests significant-

ly in bringing top talent through our doors but that's just the first step in realizing the promise of their potential. As our people grow, so grows our organization. If we want to fully benefit from their promise to us, we need to keep our promises to them and that includes significant development opportunities.

These days when we use the word "diversity," we mean all aspects of an individual—not just race, gender, age, sexual orientation and ethnicity. We also mean attributes like thinking styles, work habits, career aspirations and experiences. So our mission has grown to be more inclusive, valuing each of our people for all that they are as well as for what they can offer. You see, diversity and inclusion is something that matters to all of us—to our people, to our clients and to our businesses. Why? Because a diverse and inclusive workplace makes us stronger—as individuals, as an organization, as a profession and as a community. Through our renewed focus on people and demonstrated commitment to diversity and inclusion, the Deloitte U.S. firms are stronger because:

• We continue to challenge ourselves.

• We invest in our people.

• We foster an inclusive culture.

• We demonstrate our commitment.

Ultimately, our goal is to unleash the power of our diverse perspectives, experiences and talents to make us all stronger. But to do that, we need everyone's commitment. So this year's annual report not only talks about what we've done and what we're going to do, it highlights some things that each of us can do to help foster a more inclusive environment. The more successful we are in creating a truly inclusive workplace, the more competitive and more profitable we will be. In short, we will be stronger.

How does the firm's leadership communicate the importance of diversity to everyone at the firm?

• Our vision is "to be the standard of excellence," which we achieve, in part, by being "the first choice of the world's most coveted talent ... drawn by our eminence, culture and diversity"

• One of the Deloitte U.S. firms' four values—strength from diversity

• Periodic, regional office visits by our U.S. managing partner, chief diversity officer (CDO), and National Diversity and Inclusion Leadership Council members

• Live road trip or town hall presentations by our C-suite national executives, including our CDO and the diversity leaders and councils for each of our regions and audit, tax, consulting and financial advisory businesses

• Limited access e-room where National Diversity and Inclusion Leadership Council members connect and share information

• Regular diversity and inclusion features in our business practices' weekly or biweekly newsletters

• E-mail and in-person communications to support the activities of our local Business Resource Groups (BRGs)

• BRGs' communications regionally about sponsored events and interactions with their Deloitte colleagues at these events

• New hire orientation and on-boarding sessions

• E-mail, online articles, digital video and other e-formats, and print literature (brochures, fliers, posters, etc.) about our diversity strategy, principles, goals and current programs offered

• E-learning courses, online books and other knowledge resources available from the Deloitte Learning Center website on our intranet

• New manager development schools

• National partner meetings

• Annual national diversity and inclusion report

• Bimonthly national diversity and inclusion newsletter

Who has primary responsibility for leading diversity initiatives at your firm?

Redia Anderson, chief diversity officer, diversity and inclusion.

Does your firm currently have a diversity committee?

Yes

If yes, please describe how the committee is structured, how often it meets, etc.

The National Diversity and Inclusion Leadership Council is composed of representatives from each geographic region and business unit. The council meets face-to-face on a quarterly basis and in between these meeting via conference calls.

If yes, does the committee's representation include one or more members of the firm's management/executive committee (or the equivalent)?

Yes

If yes, how many executives are on the committee? How many employees are on the committee, and how often does the committee convene in furtherance of the firm's diversity initiatives?

All representatives on the council are partners/principals/directors. Each representative is responsible for executing their respective D&I plan which is in alignment with the overall organization's D&I strategy. There are 121 members on the council including four members from the National Diversity Center.

Does the committee and/or diversity leader establish and set goals or objectives consistent with management's priorities?

Yes. The organization's diversity and inclusion goals support our people strategy, which is one of the organization's strategic choices and shared values.

Has the firm undertaken a formal or informal diversity program or set of initiatives aimed at increasing the diversity of the firm?

Yes, formal.

How often does the firm's management review the firm's diversity progress/results?

Quarterly

How is the firm's diversity committee and/or firm management held accountable for achieving results?

Each regional and business unit has a D&I scorecard with specific goals/objectives and metrics for measuring success which is monitored on a quarterly basis. As part of the individual's performance review, it is a factor considered.

The Stats

	NUMBER OF EMPLOYEES		REVENUE	
	2006	2005	2006	2005
Total in the U.S.	37,000	33,000	$8.77 billion	$7.81 billion

2006 DEMOGRAPHIC PROFILE (includes partners/principals and employees)	
Minority representation	32 percent
Female representation	45.7 percent
Minority hires	39.9 percent
Female hires	46.8 percent
2006 board of directors	23 percent women 9 percent minority

Retention and Professional Development

How do 2006 minority and female attrition rates generally compare to those experienced in the prior year period?

Lower than in prior years.

Please identify the specific steps you are taking to reduce the attrition rate of minority and women employees.

- Develop and/or support internal employee affinity groups (e.g., minority or women networks within the firm)
- Increase/review compensation relative to competition
- Increase/improve current work/life programs
- Adopt dispute resolution process
- Succession plan includes emphasis on diversity
- Work with minority and women employees to develop career advancement plans
- Review work assignments and hours billed to key client matters to make sure minority and women employees are not being excluded

- Strengthen mentoring program for all employees, including minorities and women
- Professional skills development program, including minority and women employees

Diversity Mission Statement

Our mission is to help our people and our clients benefit from a strong and active commitment to diversity and inclusion in the workplace and global marketplace.

Additional Information

In 2006, in an ongoing effort to meet the needs of our businesses, we examined new and emerging trends in the talent market, and addressed a number of crucial questions raised by the changing landscape. As a result, the overarching people strategy of the Deloitte U.S. firms will focus on: career enhancement, critical talent management, strength from diversity, and flexibility and choice. Within our commitment to diversity and inclusion, we will continue to strengthen our organization by:

- Growing our talent pipeline, with an immediate focus on recruiting and retention to meet the specific needs of our businesses

- Embracing diverse perspectives to achieve disproportionately higher team value

- Instilling a mindset of inclusion, rather than just removing barriers

When we do this, we will enhance our reputation in the marketplace and become known as the first choice of the most coveted talent and the provider of the most innovative solutions to clients. We will become the standard of excellence.

DENTSPLY International

Susquehanna Commerce Center
221 W. Philadelphia Street
P. O. Box 872
York, PA 17405
Phone: (800) 877-0020

Locations

22

Diversity Leadership
Ernest H. White
Manager
Corporate Diversity and Sales Staffing

Employment Contact
www.dentsply.com/careers

Recruiting

Please list the schools/types of schools at which you recruit.

• Private schools
• Public state schools
• Historically black colleges and universities (HBCUs)
• Other predominantly minority and/or women's colleges

Do you have any special outreach efforts directed to encourage minority students to consider your firm?

• Hold a reception for minority students
• Participate in/host minority student job fair(s)
• Firm's employees participate on career panels at schools
• Outreach to leadership of minority student organizations

What activities does the firm undertake to attract minority and women employees?

• Partner programs with women and minority associations
• Seek referrals from other employees
• Utilize online job services

Do you use executive recruiting/search firms to seek to identify new diversity hires?

Yes

Internships and Co-ops

DENTSPLY Internship Program

Deadline for application: End of each semester.
Number of interns in the program in summer 2006: Six internships and three co-ops
Pay: Up to $20/hour
Length of the program: 12 to 24 weeks

Percentage of interns/co-ops in the program who receive offers of full-time employment: Small

Web site for internship/co-op information: Career section on company web site

Affinity Groups

All of our affinity groups fall under our CARE Initiative:

• Create an inclusive environment
• Appropriately source for diverse talent
• Recruit, develop and retain diverse talent
• Engage community support and awareness

CARE fosters a diverse environment at DENTSPLY that will impact our community. CARE fosters a diverse environment at DENTSPLY that's similar to today's world.

Strategic Plan and Diversity Leadership

How does the firm's leadership communicate the importance of diversity to everyone at the firm?

E-mails and web site

Who has primary responsibility for leading diversity initiatives at your firm?

Ernest H. White

Does your firm currently have a diversity committee?

Yes

If yes, please describe how the committee is structured, how often it meets, etc.

Once a quarter

If yes, does the committee's representation include one or more members of the firm's management/executive committee (or the equivalent)?

Yes

Does the committee and/or diversity leader establish and set goals or objectives consistent with management's priorities?

Yes

Has the firm undertaken a formal or informal diversity program or set of initiatives aimed at increasing the diversity of the firm?

Yes, formal

How often does the firm's management review the firm's diversity progress/results?

Quarterly

The Stats

	NUMBER OF EMPLOYEES
	2006
Total in the U.S.	3,800
Total outside the U.S.	3,950
Total worldwide	7,750

Retention and Professional Development

How do 2006 minority and female attrition rates generally compare to those experienced in the prior year period?

About the same as in prior years.

Please identify the specific steps you are taking to reduce the attrition rate of minority and women employees.

• Increase/review compensation relative to competition

• Increase/improve current work/life programs

• Succession plan includes emphasis on diversity

• Work with minority and women employees to develop career advancement plans

• Strengthen mentoring program for all employees, including minorities and women

Diversity Mission Statement

As the global leader in our industry we understand the significance and importance of setting the industry standard in all that we do. This includes fostering an environment that puts our differences to work in the marketplace and in our communities. Our Employee CARE Program is designed to be a sequential program that when fully engaged drives the recruitment, development and retention of talent—supporting an environment that values and benefits from the differences our employees bring to the workplace to fully participate in our business success.

Additional Information

DENTSPLY defines diversity as the attracting, developing and retaining of a highly talented, globally diverse workforce. It is through creating an inclusive environment that values the differences and the unique contributions of our employees that we are able to sustain our business success. Through our different experience sets, perspectives and unique skills, we continue to develop and deliver innovative products to our customers around the world.

Deutsche Bank

---

60 Wall Street
New York, NY 10005
Phone: (212) 250-2500

Locations
1,814 offices

The Stats
Employees: 73,114 (March 31, 2007)
Revenue (2006): $28.3 billion

Diversity Mission Statement

Deutsche Bank is a leading global investment bank with a strong and profitable private clients franchise. A leader in Germany and Europe, the bank is continuously growing in North America, Asia and key emerging markets. With over 73,000 employees in 76 countries, Deutsche Bank offers unparalleled financial services throughout the world. The bank competes to be the leading global provider of financial solutions for demanding clients creating exceptional value for its shareholders and people.

Our drive to be the best financial services provider has gained us numerous accolades. In 2005, In recognition of our outstanding performance, we were awarded the title of Bank of the Year by *International Financing Review (IFR)* for the second time in three years—the only bank to have ever achieved this. In 2006, we won all the major deals of the year awards from IDD and in 2007, swept the board at the Lipper and ISR Awards.

At Deutsche Bank, we are committed to recruiting, retaining and developing diverse talent. We think of diversity in its broadest sense, embracing all of those differences that make up the exciting challenging world in which we live. These include age, culture, ethnicity, gender, nationality, personality type, physical ability, religion, sexual orientation and work style.

We believe that diverse perspectives foster innovation and creativity. They enable us to build teams with a unique range of capabilities that can win the trust of our most demanding clients. They enhance our ability to respond to global business issues and provide innovative, superior solutions. That's why, for us, diversity is a business imperative, improving performance for clients, employees and shareholders alike.

Recognizing diversity is important, but not enough on its own. That is why we have invested in diversity, embedding it into the fabric of our organization. Deutsche Bank leverages its diversity and fosters a work environment that attracts, develops and retains a diverse pool of talent. We include diversity as an important component in our leadership training and focus on utilizing a diverse group of speakers for internal and external events. Deutsche Bank's Women on Wall Street Conference, now in its 12th year, is an example of our commitment to developing and retaining talented women in our industry.

Our global graduate recruitment strategy aims to provide the bank with a diverse graduate pipeline. We partner with a number of organizations and student clubs on the graduate and undergraduate levels to source diverse talent. Through our internship programs, we offer talented minority and female students at the high school and undergraduate levels the opportunity to experience the world of investment banking by partnering with several minority organizations in various regions. Many of our sponsorships and activities are educational and aimed to increase industry awareness and enable us to reach a truly diverse audience who may not have previously considered a career in banking. We provide opportunities for an open exchange of experiences and ideas across all levels of the bank through our employee networks. For further information on our diversity initiatives and our firm, please visit our web site at www.db.com\careers. Expect the better career.

Dominion

120 Tredegar Street
Richmond, VA 23219

Locations

Richmond, VA (HQ)
Connecticut • North Carolina • Ohio •
Pennsylvania • Virginia • Wisconsin •
West Virginia

Diversity Leadership

James Eck
Vice President, Human Resources

Employment Contact

Lucy Rothnie
College Recruiter
POB 26666
Richmond, VA 23261-6532
Phone: (804) 771-5035
Fax: (804) 771-4843
E-mail: lucy.rothnie@dom.com
www.dom.com/jobs/index.jsp

Recruiting

Please list the schools/types of schools at which you recruit.

• Private schools
• Public state schools
• Historically black colleges and universities (HBCUs)

Do you have any special outreach efforts directed to encourage minority students to consider your firm?

Dominion actively participates in the career fairs of many HBCUs and the student chapters of professional organizations such as the National Society of Black Engineers and the Society of Women Engineers. Building stronger relationships with HBCUs is a priority for our company and we support many either directly or through our support of the United Negro College Fund. Dominion is also a supporter of the annual Black Engineer of the Year Award conference where, in 2005, one of our executives won the Black Engineer of the Year Award in Career Achievement. For the past three years, an annual survey by *U.S. Black Engineer & Information Technology* magazine has named Dominion as one of the private-sector organizations considered most supportive of the nation's historically black engineering schools.

Internships and Co-ops

Dominion Internship/Co-op Program

Pay: Amount varies based on assignment

Length of program: Generally, 10 to 12 weeks during the summer. Students may also have the option to work during breaks or part time in the regular school year.

Web site for internship/co-op information:
www.dom.com/jobs/intern.jsp

Dominion's intern program engages college or college-bound students for paid work sessions that involve projects or assignments that are closely related to the student's area of study. Work experiences generally are not required for college credit nor required to satisfy degree or graduation requirements.

Work sessions are structured, supervised, professional and relate to the student's area of study. These experiences allow students to sharpen their skills, develop a network of contacts, assess their strengths and test classroom theories in real-world settings.

In addition to working during school semesters or summer breaks, intern opportunities may include working during other school breaks or on a part-time basis while attending school if the company has opportunities available.

Students must maintain a GPA of 2.5/4.0 or above and must be currently enrolled and attending a four-year university.

Scholarships

Dominion Diversity Scholarship Program

Deadline for application for the scholarship program: February 28th of each year

Scholarship award amount: Currently $2,000 per year, in addition to an hourly salary during summer work sessions

Web site or other contact information for scholarship: www.dom.com/jobs/dsp.jsp

The Diversity Scholarship Program (DSP) was initially offered in 1988 as part of the company's commitment to equal opportunity and affirmative action. The DSP served as a recruiting tool to motivate minorities to pursue careers in engineering and other professions. Dominion is proud to continue to offer this unique opportunity and to expand the program to be more inclusive. The focus of the scholarship has changed from strictly seeking minority applicants to seeking candidates from more diverse backgrounds. Acceptance of the scholarship will require that the student agree to a 10-week work session during each summer of their eligibility. Interested students are encouraged to visit our diversity scholarship web page at www.dom.com/jobs/dsp.jsp, where they can learn more about the program and watch interviews with current interns and co-op students.

At the time of application, applicants must satisfy the following requirements:

• All applicants must currently have a 3.0 GPA or above on a 4.0 scale.

• All applicants must be enrolled or accepted for enrollment as a full-time student for the current academic year.

• At the time of applying, college applicants must be either a freshman or sophomore in a four-year program at an accredited institution. (If a student is pursuing a degree program that requires more than five years to complete, participation will be evaluated on a case-by-case basis.)

• Current high school applicants must have applied for admission as a full-time student at an accredited college or university.

• Applicants must be eligible to work in the U.S.

Strategic Plan and Diversity Leadership

How does the firm's leadership communicate the importance of diversity to everyone at the firm?

Dominion's leadership communicates the importance of diversity using a variety of methods. Our internal news magazine, *Connect,* regularly features articles that discuss various aspects of diversity at Dominion. Recent topics have included generations in the workplace, supplier diversity at Dominion, the impact of our community

relationships on our workforce diversity commitment and Dominion's overall diversity strategy. Our employee diversity councils publish newsletters and regularly update bulletin boards at our various locations with diversity-related news. The diversity and staffing team supports our leadership team with diversity-related data and research designed to assist them with meeting their business goals.

We also utilize our internal and external web pages to communicate specifics about our diversity initiatives. Our online multicultural calendar (www.dom.com/about/education/culture/index.jsp) features multicultural holiday information while highlighting some of our employees.

In May 2007, Dominion had its first "Dominion Diversity Month," which consisted of events sponsored by our employee councils, as well as corporately sponsored events. These events were designed to show how our different backgrounds and interests make Dominion a stronger company. Thousands of employees attended the festivities, which took place in Ohio, Pennsylvania, Virginia and West Virginia. During May Dominion was also recognized by the readers of *Diversity/Careers in Engineering and Information Technology* magazine as a Best Diversity Company.

Who has primary responsibility for leading diversity initiatives at your firm?

James Eck, vice president of human resources

Does your firm currently have a diversity committee?

Yes, Dominion has diversity councils at two levels. First, we have our executive diversity council consisting of vice presidents, senior vice presidents, directors and key contributors from each line of business and key business areas including:

• Corporate communications

• External affairs

• Finance

• Human resources

• Supplier diversity

The executive diversity council meets at least quarterly, and more often as needed to address particular initiatives. They are charged with the oversight and evaluation of Dominion's diversity strategic initiatives. The work of the executive diversity council is important to our president and CEO, Thomas F. Farrell, III, who has established his expectation for the council. Second, we have employee diversity councils in several of our business locations. Those councils consist of, on average, 20 to 22 employees from diverse backgrounds and work areas, union-represented and nonunion-represented, management and nonmanagement. The employee diversity councils meet monthly and support the work of the executive council through grassroots diversity-related activities. Participation is voluntary and each employee council has an executive sponsor who sits on the executive diversity council.

If yes, does the committee's representation include one or more members of the firm's management/executive committee (or the equivalent)?

Yes

If yes, how many executives are on the committee?

Total Executives on Committee: 23

Does the committee and/or diversity leader establish and set goals or objectives consistent with management's priorities?

Yes

Has the firm undertaken a formal or informal diversity of set of initiatives aimed at increasing the diversity of the firm?

Yes, Dominion's workforce diversity strategy focuses on four key areas:

• Communication and education

• Measurement and accountability

• Recruitment and retention

• Visible leadership

We believe that success in each of these areas is critical to our ability to manage diversity effectively. Each focus area has a series of supporting initiatives. Our diversity strategy has been communicated to all members of the organization through a series of articles in our internal news magazine *Connect.*

How often does the firm's management review the firm's diversity progress/results?

Quarterly

Retention and Professional Development

How do minority and female attrition rates generally compare to those experienced in the prior year period?

About the same

Please identify the specific steps you are taking to reduce the attrition rate of minority and women employees.

• Increase/review compensation relative to competition

• Increase/improve current work/life programs

• Succession plan includes emphasis on diversity

• Work with minority and women employees to develop career advancement plans

• Strengthen mentoring program for all employees, including minority and women employees

Diversity Mission Statement

Dominion's Philosophy

Valuing people creates and reinforces an inclusive, creative and productive environment in which each employee feels accepted, respected and believes it is possible to achieve his/her fullest potential.

Additional Information

Dominion recognizes the value of the diversity of its employees and considers it one of our organizational strengths. We consider diversity beyond those human characteristics that are easily seen to include those factors which are not so readily apparent: disability, education, ethnic background, sexual orientation, socioeconomic status and geographic region, to name a few.

Dominion is committed to creating and reinforcing an inclusive, creative and productive environment in which each employee feels accepted, respected and believes it is possible to achieve his/her fullest potential. We also believe in shared goals and a common vision, which guide the efforts of all employees.

Dominion's strategy for workforce diversity focuses on four key areas:

• Communication and education

• Measurement and accountability

• Recruitment and retention

• Visible leadership

Each is critical to our ability to achieve the inclusive environment that we aspire to. Our executive diversity council has primary responsibility for the corporate strategy.

It is the responsibility of each subsidiary and the Dominion Services Company to adopt action plans reflecting these principles and to incorporate diversity initiatives into ongoing business plans. This sound business practice will assist us in maintaining our position as an industry leader.

Successfully managing the diversity of our workforce is not the responsibility of one person or one area. Each employee's contribution to these efforts is essential to our success in this area.

Domino's Pizza, Inc.

30 Frank Lloyd Wright Drive
Ann Arbor, MI 48336
Phone: (734) 930-3030

Locations
Ann Arbor, MI • Atlanta, GA • Baltimore, MD • Los Angeles, CA • Phoenix, AZ

Employment Contact
Jessica Rowland
30 Frank Lloyd Wright Drive
Ann Arbor, MI 48336
Fax: (877) 801-4207
E-mail: recruiter3@dominos.com
www.dominos.com

Recruiting

Please list the schools/types of schools at which you recruit.
• Private schools
• Public state schools
• Historically black colleges and universities (HBCUs)
• Hispanic serving institutions (HSIs)

Do you have any special outreach efforts directed to encourage minority students to consider your firm?
• Advertise in minority student association publication(s)
• Participate in/host minority student job fair(s)
• Sponsor minority student association events
• Firm's employees participate on career panels at schools
• Outreach to leadership of minority student organizations

What activities does the firm undertake to attract minority and women employees?
• Participate at minority job fairs
• Seek referrals from other employees
• Utilize online job services

Do you use executive recruiting/search firms to seek to identify new diversity hires?
No

Internships and Co-ops

Domino's Pizza Summer Internship Program
Deadline for application: April 1st
Pay: $13 per hour
Length of the program: 16 weeks
Percentage of interns/co-ops in the program who receive offers of full-time employment: 60 percent
Web site for internship/co-op information: www.dominos.com

The Domino's Pizza Summer Internship Program is designed with the following objectives for students:

• Expand knowledge of a particular field of expertise
• Explore career options at Domino's
• Gain business experience in chosen field
• Have an opportunity to use their skills and expand their current skills
• Build their personal network

Not only does the Summer Internship Program at Domino's allow students to build on their professional skills, the program also includes a variety of activities to enhance their professional career, including lunch and learns with executives (including the CEO), interviewing and resume building workshops, company sponsored events (NASCAR racing, rock-climbing and other fun events), etiquette education dinners, etc.

The Summer Internship Program includes opportunities in the following disciplines:

• Accounting
• Communications
• Finance
• Human resources
• Information services
• Management
• Marketing
• Supply chain management

Affinity Groups

It's been proven that company performance is strongly linked to the ability to successfully attract, retain and develop a diverse employee population. Domino's Pizza supports the formation and operation of team member forums to support diversity. The company also welcomes and values the ideas and contributions of all team members.

Team member forums are groups of employees with common interests or backgrounds that share insights, different perspectives and contribute to each other's professional development as well as the company's mission.

Key focus areas for employee forums:

• *Employee development:* Provide personal and professional development and informal networking opportunities to team members

• *Workplace insight:* Provide viewpoints on company policies and workplace issues to aid our expansion into traditionally underrepresented communities through recruiting, employment practices and policies and marketing

Entry-Level Programs, Full-Time Opportunities and Training Programs

Domino's Pizza Leadership Development Program

Length of program: 12 to 18 months

Geographic location(s) of program: Nationwide

Domino's Pizza recognizes that to be "best in class" and maintain our position as the world leader in the pizza delivery industry, we need to have exceptional leaders. To prepare and develop future leaders, a development program known as Project People Pipeline was established.

The purpose of the people pipeline is to:

• Recruit and select early-career, high-potential team members

• Establish a rotational development program

• Provide broad organizational, business and leadership training

• Prepare for future leadership positions within Domino's Pizza

• Ensure workplace readiness, cross-functional knowledge and advanced leadership training to team members

During the program, the candidate will be fully integrated into new positions in a series of rotational assignments. Company-sponsored relocation to various business sites will be required in conjunction with completing various assignments. The assignments may include positions in the following areas of the business:

• Corporate store operations

• Finance and accounting

• Human resources

• Information services

• Marketing

• Public relations/communications

• Distribution/purchasing

• International

• Legal

Job responsibilities and objectives are established for each assignment and the candidate receives performance evaluations upon completion of each assignment. Typical position assignments are approximately six months in duration. The candidate will complete four to five various position assignments while in the people pipeline.

In addition to completing assignments, the candidate is also provided with leadership and organizational training defined in a customized plan known as a Learning Map. Mentors are assigned to aid in the development of the candidate. In addition, the candidate will complete leadership assessments during the program.

Each People Pipeline Program candidate graduates from the program once he/she has successfully completed all assignments and courses identified in the Learning Map, in approximately 18 to 24 months. The leadership team and PeopleFirst then work together to identify a permanent position for the candidate upon completion of the program that utilizes the skills, talents, interests and experiences gained throughout the program.

Strategic Plan and Diversity Leadership

How does the firm's leadership communicate the importance of diversity to everyone at the firm?

Web site, company meetings and targeted events

Who has primary responsibility for leading diversity initiatives at your firm?

Director, PeopleFirst, Eric Parsons

Does your firm currently have a diversity committee?

Yes

If yes, please describe how the committee is structured, how often it meets, etc.

The Diversity Committee is made up of members of the executive team who meet quarterly to review progress on diversity initiatives in the organization.

If yes, does the committee's representation include one or more members of the firm's management/executive committee (or the equivalent)?

Yes

If yes, how many executives are on the committee, and in 2005, what was the total number of hours collectively spent by the committee in furtherance of the firm's diversity initiatives? How many employees are on the committee, and how often does the committee convene in furtherance of the firm's diversity initiatives?

Eleven executives are in the committee, and in 2005, the total hours spent furthering Domino's diversity initiatives was 30. Subgroups of the committee meet monthly; this included over 40 team members in 2005.

Does the committee and/or diversity leader establish and set goals or objectives consistent with management's priorities?

Yes

Has the firm undertaken a formal or informal diversity program or set of initiatives aimed at increasing the diversity of the firm?

Yes, formal

How often does the firm's management review the firm's diversity progress/results?

Quarterly

How is the firm's diversity committee and/or firm management held accountable for achieving results?

These objectives are part of the business plan and measured through our performance appraisal process.

Retention and Professional Development

How do 2006 minority and female attrition rates generally compare to those experienced in the prior year period?

About the same as in prior years.

Please identify the specific steps you are taking to reduce the attrition rate of minority and women employees.

• Develop and/or support internal employee affinity groups (e.g., minority or women networks within the firm)

• Increase/improve current work/life programs

• Succession plan includes emphasis on diversity

• Professional skills development program, including minority and women employees

Diversity Mission Statement

Domino's Pizza is committed to an inclusive culture that values the contributions of our customers, team members, suppliers and neighbors.

The Stats

	NUMBER OF EMPLOYEES		REVENUE	
	2006	2005	2006	2005
Total in the U.S.	13,500	13,300	$3.2 billion	$3.3 billion
Total outside the U.S.	250	230	$1.87 billion	$1.68 billion
Total worldwide	13,750	13,530	$5.1 billion	$4.99 billion

Dresdner Kleinwort

Recruiting

Please list the schools/types of schools at which you recruit.

- Ivy League schools
- Public state schools

Do you have any special outreach efforts directed to encourage minority students to consider your firm?

- Conferences
- Participate in minority student job fair(s)
- Firm's professionals participate on career panels at schools
- Outreach to leadership of minority student organizations

What activities does the firm undertake to attract women and minorities?

- Conferences
- Participate at minority job fairs
- Seek referrals from other professionals
- Utilize online job services

Do you use executive recruiting/search firms to seek to identify new diversity hires?

Yes

Entry-level Programs, Full-Time Opportunities and Training Programs

Capital Markets and Global Banking full-time resume submission deadline: Friday, October 19, 2007

Capital Markets and Global Banking summer internship resume submission deadline: Friday, December 28, 2007

Cover letter and resume should be sent to: US.JOBS@dkib.com. E-mail subject header should indicate first and last name, school attending and position, i.e., "John Doe, University—GLOBAL BANKING Summer Analyst"

Capital Markets (CM)

CM positions are available in New York.

CM Summer Associate (12-week program) and CM Associate

Within capital markets, we recruit into trading, sales and structuring roles across the different divisions. Traders are decision makers; they need to be numerical and possess a thorough understanding of market dynamics to allow themselves to manage risk and reap rewards. Salespersons are sophisticated in determining the needs of the clients and identifying solutions with the products and services of the firm. Structurers have a dual function: take ideas that salespersons synthesize from the Street and incorporate them into a product that can be sold directly to the client or traded by the traders.

Requirements for full time and summer:

Dresdner Kleinwort is looking for candidates with an MBA from a leading university, with an outstanding academic record which places them in the top percentiles of their class. A background in finance, economics or accounting is preferred. It is to the applicant's advantage to have at least one year of professional experience in the front office trading environment. The individual must be able to work independently and alongside senior traders, salespersons and structurers. As a trading associate, one must be able to assess and execute trading ideas based on current market view and position. Sales associates need to have excellent interpersonal skills, exceptional product knowledge to effectively articulate solutions and ability to build institutional client relationships. Structurers are required to possess strong analytical and quantitative skills to evaluate opportunities and creatively provide value-added financing alternatives.

CM Summer Analyst (12-week program) and CM Analyst

Requirements for full time and summer:

Dresdner Kleinwort is looking for undergraduates from a leading university, with an outstanding academic record which places them in the top percentiles of their class. A strong academic and professional background in finance, economics or accounting is preferred. Previous internships that provided exposure to market dynamics are highly considered. We are looking for candidates who are inquisitive and tireless in their pursuit of product knowledge, and relationship management experience. We prize individuals who are committed to undergo the steep learning curve in order to grow within the firm.

Global Banking—Investment Banking (GBIB)

Global banking positions are available in New York.

GBIB Associate

Financial associates at Dresdner Kleinwort are responsible for all aspects of analysis and presentations relating to mergers, acquisitions, restructurings, divestitures, leveraged buyouts, privatizations and corporate finance. Associates are expected to be proficient with the fundamental analytical principles of mergers and acquisitions and general corporate finance. Associates will participate in structuring and negotiating various types of transactions and financings, and will gain increasing experience and responsibility as they develop expertise in these areas. In addition, associates will play a significant role in the firm's "new business" efforts and ongoing client relationships.

Requirements:

Dresdner Kleinwort expects to hire exceptionally accomplished, self-motivated individuals with the capability to work effectively in the high pressured, yet rewarding, environment of investment banking. The firm requires and expects the highest ethical and professional standards of its employees. An MBA or similar level qualification is preferred together with two years minimum work experience, preferably in investment banking or a related field. The firm is looking for students with an outstanding academic record that places them in the top percentiles of their class, as well as demonstrated leadership ability through involvement in extracurricular activities such as student government, athletics, and cultural and entrepreneurial activities.

GBIB Summer Associate

Summer associates at Dresdner Kleinwort are responsible for all aspects of analysis and presentations relating to mergers, acquisitions, restructurings, divestitures, leveraged buyouts, privatizations and corporate finance. The Summer Associate Program is intended to provide participants with a firm understanding of the fundamental analytical principles of mergers and acquisitions and general corporate finance. Summer associates will participate in structuring and negotiating various types of transactions and financings (including client interaction), and will gain increasing experience and responsibility as they develop expertise in these areas.

Requirements:

Dresdner Kleinwort expects to hire exceptionally accomplished, self-motivated individuals with the capability to work effectively in

the high pressured, yet rewarding, environment of investment banking. The firm requires and expects the highest ethical and professional standards of its employees. Working towards an MBA or similar level qualification is preferred together with two years minimum work experience, preferably in investment banking or a related field.

GBIB Analyst

Financial analysts at Dresdner Kleinwort are responsible for all aspects of analysis and presentations relating to mergers, acquisitions, restructurings, divestitures, leveraged buyouts, privatizations and corporate finance. Specifically, analysts are required to be proficient within a short period of time with fundamental accounting principles and various financial modeling and valuation techniques. It is expected that analysts will have significant opportunities to interact with clients and to take on additional responsibility based on performance.

Requirements:

Dresdner Kleinwort expects to hire exceptionally accomplished, self-motivated individuals with the capability to work effectively in the high pressured, yet rewarding, environment of investment banking. The firm requires and expects the highest ethical and professional standards of its employees. A background in finance, economics or accounting is preferred. The firm is looking for students with an outstanding academic record that places them in the top percentiles of their class, as well as demonstrated leadership ability through involvement in extracurricular activities such as student government, athletics, and cultural and entrepreneurial activities.

GBIB Summer Analyst

Summer analysts at Dresdner Kleinwort are responsible for all aspects of analysis and presentations relating to mergers, acquisitions, restructurings, divestitures, leveraged buyouts, privatizations and corporate finance. The Summer Analyst Program is intended to provide participants with an introductory understanding of the fundamental analytical principals of mergers and acquisitions and general corporate finance.

Requirements:

Dresdner Kleinwort expects to hire exceptionally accomplished, self-motivated individuals with the capability to work effectively in the high pressured, yet rewarding, environment of investment banking. The firm requires and expects the highest ethical and professional standards of its employees. A background in finance, economics or accounting is preferred. The firm is looking for students with an outstanding academic record that places them in the top percentiles of their class, as well as demonstrated leadership ability through involvement in extracurricular activities such as student government, athletics, and cultural and entrepreneurial activities.

Strategic Plan and Diversity Leadership

How does the firm's leadership communicate the importance of diversity to everyone at the firm?

• Employee forums

• Quarterly town hall meetings

• E-mail communication

• Quarterly diversity meetings

Who has primary responsibility for leading overall diversity initiatives at your firm?

Carrie Guillory, director and diversity committee chairperson

Who has primary responsibility for diversity recruiting initiatives at your firm?

Frances A. Lyman, director, recruitment

Does your firm currently have a diversity committee?

Yes

Has the firm undertaken a formal or informal diversity program or set of initiatives aimed at increasing the diversity of the firm?

Yes, informal

How often does the firm's management review the firm's diversity progress/results?

Quarterly

Diversity Mission Statement

In order to foster diversity throughout its North American operations, Dresdner Kleinwort has established a North American Diversity Committee. The diversity committee has been charged with identifying current needs and recommending practices and initiatives to promote diversity. The diversity committee's focus is the recruitment, retention and promotion of a diverse workforce and the creation of a work environment that is equally hospitable to all employees regardless of gender, race, ethnicity, language, religion, physical abilities or sexual orientation.

Additional Information

Overview of Dresdner Kleinwort

Dresdner Kleinwort is the investment banking division of Dresdner Bank AG and a member of Allianz, one of Europe's largest financial services groups. Alongside headquarters in London and Frankfurt,

Dresdner Kleinwort has an office network that spans five continents and 10 time zones and has over 5,500 employees around the globe.

We offer the full range of commercial and investment banking services to European and international clients through our global banking and capital markets business lines.

Dresdner Kleinwort operates an integrated business model, the elements of which are:

• Leading capital markets expertise

• An international cross-border advisory platform

• Innovative risk management solutions across all asset classes

• Strength in the home markets of Germany and the U.K., with an international presence and capability in key product areas to support a global client base

One of the first investment banks to remove traditional barriers between product and service lines, Dresdner Kleinwort delivers tailor-made solutions to clients' business problems and financing needs. The bank, backed by the resources of one of Europe's leading financial institutions, fosters an entrepreneurial culture that serves the interests of its clients.

On June 29, 2006, the firm changed its name to Dresdner Kleinwort.

Our new name, Dresdner Kleinwort, embraces two great assets. Firstly, the strength and strategic importance that comes from being part of the Dresdner Bank Group. Secondly, the enduring values that are rooted in our distinguished heritage. Together they reconfirm our international status.

Dresdner Kleinwort's size is viewed as a distinct advantage as it means that the bank is:

• Agile

• Flexible

• Innovative

• Creative

• Able to provide tailored solutions to our clients

• Able to provide greater opportunities and a wider range of experiences for our people and a chance to make a significant contribution

Dresdner Kleinwort's core values are:

• Communication

• Client first

• Teamwork

• Excellence

• Creativity

• Professionalism

Dresdner Kleinwort has created a culture where the best people have the freedom to think differently, to question convention and to address challenges in a fresh and creative way.

Dresdner Kleinwort adheres to current U.S. legislation and "best practice" in recruitment, including a conscious policy not to discriminate on the basis of age, race, color, religion, sex, national origin, disability, marital status, ancestry, medical condition, sexual orientation, citizenship, veteran status or any other basis proscribed by federal, state or local law.

Duke Energy Corporation

526 S. Church Street
Charlotte, NC 28202-2803
Phone: (704) 594-6200
Fax: (704) 382-3814
www.duke-energy.com

Locations

US:
Charlotte, NC • Cincinnati, OH • Houston TX • Plainfield, IN

International:
South America

Diversity Leadership
Colon McLean
Vice President HR Business Support

Employment Contact
Elizabeth (Beth) Britt
Managing Director, Recruiting and Staffing
400 S. Tryon Street
Charlotte, NC 28201
Phone: (980) 373-4317
Fax: (704) 382-1054
E-mail: epbritt@duke-energy.com

Recruiting

Please list the schools/types of schools at which you recruit.
- Ivy League schools
- Other private schools
- Public state schools
- Historically black colleges and universities (HBCUs)

Do you have any special outreach efforts directed to encourage minority students to consider your firm?
- Hold a reception for minority students
- Advertise in minority student association publication(s)
- Participate in/host minority student job fair(s)
- Sponsor minority student association events
- Firm's employees participate on career panels at school
- Outreach to leadership of minority student organizations
- Scholarships or intern/fellowships for minority students
- *Other:* Expose students to executives through round table discussions and organized events

What activities does the firm undertake to attract minority and women employees?
- Partner programs with women and minority associations
- *Conferences:* NSBE, SWE, NABA, SHPE, ALPFA, AABE
- Participate at minority job fairs
- Seek referrals from other employees
- *Other:* Strategies vary from year to year based on needs, but may include attendance at conferences for networking purposes and the possible use of online services

Do you use executive recruiting/search firms to seek to identify new diversity hires?
Yes

Internships and Co-ops

Co-op/Internship Program
Deadline for application: Currently we have no set deadlines, but post jobs at the schools when needed

Number of interns in the program in summer 2006 (internship) or 2006 (co-op): 120 interns, 120 co-op

Pay: Hourly, based on degree major and completed coursework

Length of the program: Approximately 12 weeks

Percentage of interns/co-ops in the program who receive offers of full-time employment: 6 percent

Web site for internship/co-op information: www.duke-energy.com

INROADS
Deadline for application: Determined by INROADS

Pay: Hourly, based on degree major and completed coursework. Students are paid biweekly

Length of the program: Approximately 12 weeks

Percentage of interns/co-ops in the program who receive offers of full-time employment: Not applicable at this time. For Charlotte, it depends on the number of opportunities; we use our interns/coops as a pipeline for our openings, but we look at all of our interns as a recruiting tool.

Web site for internship/co-op information: www.duke-energy.com

INROADS internships are designed to provide students with an opportunity to work in a variety of departments to gain a broad expe-

rience, or a specific area aligned with their career interests and goals. Our INROADS recruiting needs are primarily focused on students pursuing undergraduate degrees in accounting, finance, electrical, mechanical and chemical engineering. On occasion, a limited number of co-op/intern opportunities may be available for business and information technology majors.

Scholarships

Minority Professional Association Scholars

Awarded 12 renewable scholarships in 2006.

Helping Orient Minorities in Engineering (HOME)

Awarded four full scholarships at North Carolina A&T University.

National Association of Black Accountants (NABA)

Awarded two scholarships to accounting students.

Latin American Women's Association

Awarded five scholarships.

Affinity Groups

Employee Resource Groups

Employee resource groups have been in existence at Duke Energy for at least 10 years, and include the following ERGs whose mission is to increase employees' personal and professional success through collaborative initiatives. Through networking and development activities, the groups benefit from interaction with executive sponsors and mentors, as well as access to information about professional development opportunities and career advancement.

The African American Network (AAN)

Provides a supportive environment and facilitates the the advancement of African American employees at Duke Energy.

The Leadership Development Network (LDN)

Creates an environment where employees interested in developing leadership skills can interact with other employees to build their skills and abilities.

The Business Women's Network (BWN)

Supports Duke Energy's commitment to women's leadership development, provides employees an opportunity to engage in conversation with senior leaders concerning leadership skills specific to women's shared experiences and professional development needs, and enables employees to acquire and develop those skills.

Women In Nuclear (WIN)

Provides a network through which employees in the nuclear field can exchange knowledge about nuclear technologies and issues, while furthering their professional development.

The mission of the Women's Network is to motivate and support all women, as well as heighten awareness about women's issues in order to remove barriers and be recognized as a valued force within the company.

The Hispanic Heritage Network

The mission of the Hispanic Heritage Network is to promote and preserve the Hispanic culture while helping the company achieve its goals of leading a workforce that is truly balanced and a reflection of the people we serve; with this, we will lead in energizing the social, cultural and economic development of our community. Its vision is to help the company shape its future by improving its services and communications, and creating a dynamic relationship with the growing Hispanic/Latino community, attracting new talent who exhibit the drive, professional capabilities and desire to become part of the Duke Energy family.

NA-YGN (North American Young Generation in Nuclear)

NA-YGN's members are individuals age 35 and under working throughout the fields of nuclear science and technology. NA-YGN's members share a personal conviction that nuclear science and technology make important and valuable contributions to our society and will continue to do so in the future. NA-YGN brings together the different sectors of nuclear science and technology to speak with a united voice for a common goal, and to provide professional development opportunities for its members.

Strategic Plan and Diversity Leadership

How does the firm's leadership communicate the importance of diversity to everyone at the firm?

Work with the human resources staffing group and the consultants in the business units.

Who has primary responsibility for leading diversity initiatives at your firm?

Colon McLean, vice president HR business support

Does your firm currently have a diversity committee?

Yes

If yes, please describe how the committee is structured, how often it meets, etc.

The diversity council is comprised of 15 employees representing the executive level, director's level and ERG (employee resource

group) chairs. This group meets monthly. Please see "additional information" section for more details.

If yes, does the committee's representation include one or more members of the firm's management/executive committee (or the equivalent)?

Yes

How many employees are on the committee, and how often does the committee convene in furtherance of the firm's diversity initiatives?

The diversity council is comprised of 15 employees who meet monthly.

Does the committee and/or diversity leader establish and set goals or objectives consistent with management's priorities?

Yes

Has the firm undertaken a formal or informal diversity program or set of initiatives aimed at increasing the diversity of the firm?

Yes, formal

How often does the firm's management review the firm's diversity progress/results?

Quarterly

The Stats

Revenue

2006: $15 billion

Retention and Professional Development

How do 2006 minority and female attrition rates generally compare to those experienced in the prior year period?

About the same as in prior years.

Please identify the specific steps you are taking to reduce the attrition rate of minority and women employees.

• Develop and/or support internal employee affinity groups
• Increase/review compensation relative to competition
• Increase/improve current work/life programs
• Adopt dispute resolution process
• Succession plan includes emphasis on diversity

• Work with minority and women employees to develop career advancement plans
• Review work assignments and hours billed to key client matters to make sure minority and women employees are not being excluded
• Strengthen mentoring program for all employees, including minorities and women
• Professional skills development program, including minority and women employees

Note: Our turnover is fairly typical for the utility industry and relatively low for all employee groups.

Diversity Mission Statement

Diversity Vision Statement

Duke Energy's workforce is diverse in every facet and the company is prospering from the unique perspectives and contributions of every employee.

Additional Information

The purpose of the diversity council is to provide guidance to and oversight of diversity and inclusion efforts, including the recommendation of policies, programs and initiatives to management for implementation. Since talent development, staffing, workforce planning and work/life balance strategies are critical to the success of diversity and inclusion strategies, the diversity council may also provide input in these areas.

An ancillary purpose of the diversity council is to educate and raise awareness among council members themselves so they may role model and champion diverse perspectives and inclusive behaviors within their own work environment.

Vision

Duke Energy's workforce is diverse in every facet and the company is prospering from the unique perspectives and contributions of every employee.

Goals

• Institutionalize diversity and inclusion.

• Facilitate management's understanding that diverse representation in the most highly-valued jobs and at the most senior levels should increase.

• Drive the deployment of customer, community, and supplier diversity strategies to align with the company's business objectives.

• Ensure diverse and inclusive perspectives are reflected in communication, public recognition and outreach efforts.

Membership

The composition of the diversity council itself is intended to reflect the diversity that exists within our company and may include such aspects of diversity as race, gender, sexual orientation, ethnic origin, country of origin, age, legacy companies, level in organization, job function, location and business unit. We believe that a diversity council that reflects the composition of Duke Energy's workforce helps ensure that the council focuses on issues and opportunities relevant to the organization.

In addition to representatives from the executive level, members of the council are comprised of leaders from employee resource groups and diversity action teams.

Duke Realty Corporation

600 E. 96th Street, Suite 100
Indianapolis, IN 46240
Phone: (317) 808-6000
Fax: (317) 808-6794
www.dukerealty.com

Locations

Indianapolis, IN (HQ)
Atlanta, GA • Chicago, IL • Cincinnati,
OH • Cleveland, OH • Columbus, OH •
Dallas, TX • Minneapolis, MN • Nashville,
TN • Orlando, FL • Raleigh, NC • St.
Louis, MO • Tampa, FL • Weston, VA

Employment Contact

Jenny E. Bean
Assistant Vice President HR

Ginny Jackson
Staffing Manager

Recruiting

Please list the schools/types of schools at which you recruit.

- *Private schools:* Spelman, Clark Atlanta, Morehouse, Vanderbilt
- *Public state schools:* Indiana University, Purdue University, Indiana-Purdue University (IUPUI), Georgia Tech, Florida State, Georgia State, Emory
- *Historically black colleges and universities (HBCUs):* Spelman, Clark Atlanta, Morehouse

Do you have any special outreach efforts directed to encourage minority students to consider your firm?

- Hold a reception for minority students
- *Conferences:* AUC Job Fair
- Advertise in minority student association publication(s)
- Participate in/host minority student job fairs
- Firm's associates participate on career panels at school

What activities does the firm undertake to attract minority and women employees?

- Partner programs with women and minority associations
- *Conferences:* AUC, Black Expo, Career Forum for minorities and women
- Participate at minority job fairs
- Seek referrals from other associates
- Utilize online job services: Other media outlets—iHispano.com
- *Other:* Participants in Project REAP; Participants in INROADS in Indianapolis, Chicago and Atlanta

Internships and Co-ops

The Duke Realty Internship Program (INROADS and Non-INROADS)

Pay: $12 to $16 per hour for 12 weeks

Length of program: 12 weeks

Percentage of interns/co-ops in the program who receive offers of full-time employment: We have a conversion rate of 95 percent

Web site for internship/co-op information: www.Dukerealty.com

The Duke Internship Program is designed to be a multi-summer internship program with the ultimate goal of hiring the intern into a full-time position upon graduation. The interns will have one to four summers of in-house training with us prior to being offered a full-time position. During these summers, the intern will learn about our company culture, delivery system and the long term benefits of employment at Duke, with the expectation that their contributions and productivity are successively higher each summer.

PROJECT REAP (Real Estate Associate Program)

Pays: $40 to $45k per year

Length of program: 12-month program

Percentage of interns/co-ops in the program who receive offers of full-time employment: Conversion rate of 100 percent

Web site for internship/co-op information: www.REAP.ORG

REAP is an industry-backed, market driven program with a five-year track record. REAP finds, trains and places talented dedicated minority professionals with leading commercial real estate firms. The internship is for 12 months with the goal of converting the interns into full-time associates.

Entry-Level Programs, Full-Time Opportunities and Training Programs

Duke has two formal training programs available to interns and associates.

Career Development Training

Duke offers a variety of career development training courses to support associates in developing their work skills. Courses are available for interns and associates in all of our markets. Typical courses include:

• Communication between the genders
• Dealing with difficult people
• Effective interviewing
• Personality types in the workplace
• Stress management

ElementK

Computer-based training is available for all interns and associates. This online training solution provides training for select Microsoft products, sexual harassment, and diversity training.

In addition, associates participate in departmental training.

Strategic Plan and Diversity Leadership

How does the firm's leadership communicate the importance of diversity to everyone at the firm?

Quarterly associate conference calls, company newsletters, annual performance reviews, (including the CEO's annual review), e-mails, financial support for diversity council and other sponsored diversity activities, career development courses, quarterly diversity training activities and a diversity CD that new hires must review during their first few months at Duke.

Who has primary responsibility for leading diversity initiatives at your firm?

Denny Oklak, CEO and president, and his executive team

Does your firm currently have a diversity committee?

Yes

Duke Realty Corporation Diversity Council

It is the mission of the Duke Realty Corporation Diversity Council to educate, increase awareness and be advocates for diversity at Duke. The Diversity Council will lead the company in recognizing the value of respect and inclusiveness will foster Duke's core values and will promote the understanding and appreciation of our differences and similarities. In so doing, we strive to develop and nurture a strong, diverse workforce in order to produce exceptional customer satisfaction and shareholder value.

The Diversity Council is made up of 24 associates from every level (entry to executive) and from each of our 13 locations nationwide. The Diversity Council meets two to three times per year in person and via conference calls every other month.

The Diversity Council also provides diversity training to over 1,100 associates on a quarterly basis.

If yes, does the committee's representation include one or more members of the firm's management/executive committee (or the equivalent)?

Yes

Does the committee and/or diversity leader establish and set goals or objectives consistent with management's priorities?

Yes. Annually, corporate goals are set for management. These goals include increasing minority hires and decreasing minority turnover. Throughout the last few years, diversity was put on associates reviews, a minority vendor program was rolled out and associate satisfaction was measured with several questions pertaining to diversity at Duke. In addition, each intern has a career development plan in place.

Has the firm undertaken a formal or informal diversity program or set of initiatives aimed at increasing the diversity of the firm?

Yes, formal. Our diversity council was created to assist the company in furthering its diversity goals and initiatives. One major accomplishment that the council achieved was to propose to Duke's management committee that they add a diversity component on all associate performance review forms.

How often does the firm's management review the firm's diversity progress/results?

Quarterly

How is the firm's diversity committee and/or firm management held accountable for achieving results?

It is on both the CEO's performance review and all employee performance reviews.

The Stats

	NUMBER OF EMPLOYEES	REVENUE
	2005	2005
Total in the U.S.	1,065	$8 billion

Retention and Professional Development

Please identify the specific steps you are taking to reduce the attrition rate of minority and women employees.

- Increase/review compensation relative to competition
- Increase/review/improve current work/life programs
- Succession plan includes emphasis on diversity
- Strengthen mentoring program for all associates, including minorities and women
- Professional skills development program, including minority and women associates
- *Other:* Associate opinion survey—including diversity questions

Diversity Mission Statement

Company Statement

Diversity is an important strategic issue at Duke Realty Corporation involving our associates, our customers and our shareholders. As our work force and customer base continues to become more diverse, our challenge is to understand and value our individual differences and similarities and those of our customers and prospective customers. Our behaviors and actions must demonstrate and confirm our respect for each other and each other's contributions.

Diversity involves developing organizational processes that are inclusionary rather than exclusionary, and which create an environment for company contributions by everyone.

Our expectation is that by responding in a positive and proactive way to these diversity issues, we will be better prepared for our long-term future through continued commitment of our associates, ongoing and successful relationships with existing and potential customers and continued investment from existing and prospective shareholders.

The company, recognizing the very broad nature of the term "diversity," offers the following examples of the many dimensions of diversity:

- Age and experience
- Culture (individual, group, global)
- Economic status
- Education and training
- Gender and sexual orientation
- Marital and family status
- Personal style
- Disabilities
- Race, nationality and ethnicity
- Religion
- Veteran and active armed service status

To reinforce this commitment in our daily work, all company activities, policies, practices and procedures are to be carried out in accordance with this policy. Each associate is personally responsible and accountable for ensuring that her/his actions and behaviors reflect this policy.

Diversity Council Statement

It is the mission of the Duke Realty Corporation Diversity Council to educate, increase awareness and be advocates for diversity at Duke. The Diversity Council will lead the company in recognizing the value of respect and inclusiveness will foster Duke's core values and will promote the understanding and appreciation of our differences and similarities. In so doing, we strive to develop and nurture a strong, diverse workforce in order to produce exceptional customer satisfaction and shareholder value.

Additional Information

Duke's commitment to diversity in the workplace is paramount to the company's ability to attract and retain associates. The Duke Diversity Council was created to cultivate an environment in which all associates feel valued and have the opportunity to grow. This environment of inclusiveness helps make Duke an attractive culture for today's best and brightest.

To be able to attract and retain minority associates, the company offers a variety of diverse benefits. Here are just a few:

Adoption

Any full-time associate with at least 90 days' service receives 10 days' paid leave upon adopting a child. Duke offers an adoption assistance plan, which will reimburse any full-time associates with at least six months of service, for certain qualifying adoption expenses up to $7,500 per adoption.

EAP

Duke realizes that in today's world, balancing work and home can be a real test of an associate's time and energy. All associates and their immediate family, including spouses and dependent children, are immediately eligible to participate in Duke's Employee Assistance Program (EAP) and work/life benefit. The EAP is a free benefit, which provides confidential consultation and short-term counseling for most of the problems that can hinder happiness and effectiveness at work and home. Examples include, but are not limited to: marital difficulties, financial or legal problems, parenting concerns and other stress-related issues. Prenatal kits, child safety kits and elder care kits are also available at no cost.

Tuition Reimbursement

Duke reimburses associates (with at least six months of service) for 100 percent of the cost of tuition, registration fees and books to a maximum of $3,000 per year. Many Duke Associates have been able to achieve their goal of receiving a degree with the aid of the Tuition Reimbursement Program since Duke started offering it in 1998.

Health Insurance for Part-time Associates

Duke offers medical coverage to any part-time associate who has had at least three consecutive years of prior full-time service. In addition, there are additional paid benefits for part-time associates.

Employer Assisted Housing

The Employer Assisted Housing Program helps Duke associates realize the dream of home ownership. Any associate with at least six months' service and an annual salary of $57,000 or less (excluding bonus) may receive up to a $3,000 forgivable loan to use toward the purchase of their first home. Duke has been able to assist 70 associates with the purchase of their first home since the program began in 2001.

Career Resource Library

The Duke human resources department maintains the Career Resource Library, which contains many different resources for Duke associates to use when situations, needs or interests arise.

Currently, the library contains over 300 different resources, some of which are the most popular titles in business today. Topics such as leadership, diversity, personal growth, time management and organization, business writing, communication and career development are available, as well as many others. Duke has also just added How to Speak Spanish CDs to the library for associates to use.

Community Days

All associates receive two paid community days each year for use in volunteering in charitable community activities.

287 Associates at Duke utilized at least one Community Day in 2004. Volunteer activities have been performed for the following organizations:

- United Way
- Habitat for Humanity

- Big Brothers Big Sisters
- Cancer Society
- Juvenile Diabetes Foundation
- Race for the Cure
- Arthritis Foundation

Duke is committed to diversity and we show our commitment in various ways. Whether it's volunteer support or financial support, diversity at Duke is making a difference.

Over the last several years, Duke associates have received various honors in appreciation for their commitment. Associates were honored for the following awards:

INROADS

- Board member of the year—three years in a row
- Business coordinator of the year—two years
- Business advisor of the year
- Highest conversion rate
- Rainmaker of the year—two years

Finalist for Mayor's Diversity Award

Duke also supports various diverse organizations/associations. The following is a list of some of the organizations we support and participate in:

- INROADS in three cities
- Project REAP
- Asian Alliance
- Regional Black MBA
- CREW—Commercial Real Estate for Women

Along with the various honors, Duke contributes associate's time and company funding for various organizations and associations. Here is a small list:

- United Way in all 13 of our markets
- Big Brother Big Sisters
- Habitat for Humanity
- American Cancer Society
- American Diabetes Association

DuPont

1007 N. Market Street
Wilmington, DE 19898
Phone: (302) 774-1000
Fax: (302) 999-4399
www1.dupont.com/dupontglobal/corp/car
eers/index.html

Diversity Leadership
Sandra Lewis
Manager of Diversity and WorkLife

Employment Contact
Shannon Freeze-Flory
Manager of Recruitment and Selection
1007 N. Market Street
Room D 6156
Wilmington, DE 19898
Phone: (302) 774-2112

Recruiting

Please list the schools/types of schools at which you recruit.

- Ivy League schools
- Other private schools
- Public state schools
- Historically black colleges and universities (HBCUs)
- Hispanic serving institutions (HSIs)

Do you have any special outreach efforts directed to encourage minority students to consider your firm?

- Hold a reception for minority students
- *Conferences:* SWE, NSBE, SHPE, AISES, NSHMBA, NOBC-CHE, Consortium, NABA, WEPAN
- Participate in/host minority student job fair(s)
- Sponsor minority student association events
- Firm's employees participate on career panels at school
- Outreach to leadership of minority student organizations
- *Scholarships or intern/fellowships for minority students:* GEM, NACME

What activities does the firm undertake to attract minority and women employees?

- Partner programs with women and minority associations
- *Conferences:* SWE, NSBE, SHPE, AISES, NSHMBA, NOBC-CHE, Consortium, NABA, WEPAN
- Participate at minority job fairs
- Seek referrals from other employees
- Utilize online job services

Do you use executive recruiting/search firms to seek to identify new diversity hires?

No

Internships and Co-ops

Engineering Co-op/Intern Program

Deadline for application: Ongoing posting on the Web. We have three main terms: spring, summer and fall.

Pay: Pay is competitive, based on student's education level and degree.

Length of the program (in weeks): We offer terms of varying length, based on business need and student availability during the school year. Some students work the 12 to 16 weeks in the summer. We also have students who work six-month terms (spring/summer or summer/fall)

Percentage of interns/co-ops in the program who receive offers of full-time employment: About 50 percent

Web site for internship/co-op information:
www1.dupont.com/dupontglobal/corp/careers/univ_internships.html

Our co-op/internship program is a key part of DuPont's engineer recruiting strategy. The program provides an excellent pool of motivated, diverse, and well-prepared employees for DuPont. Assignments are located throughout the U.S. Minimum qualifications:

- Legal right to work in the United States without restrictions
- Attending an ABET accredited engineering school
- 3.3 minimum GPA preferred (3.0 as absolute minimum)
- Completed freshman year
- Prior work or volunteer experience
- Demonstrated leadership capability

Finance MBA Development Program

Deadline of Application: April, 2006

Pay: Monthly pay in the $5,000 to $6,000 range

Length of program: 12 to 14 weeks

Percentage of Interns/co-ops in the program who receive full time offers of employment: 90 percent

MBA Interns are placed throughout the finance areas in the businesses and in corporate finance. They are primarily functioning as business analysts. We attract MBA's from top U.S. business schools. We seek prior financial experience.

Sourcing & Logistics Co-op Program

Deadline for application: Recruit throughout the year based on need. There are two sessions for co-ops: May/June to December and January to June.

Number of co-ops in the program: 12 to 24 at any given time

Pay: Pay is competitive, based on student's education level and degree.

Length of the program: Approximately six months (24 weeks)

Percentage of interns/co-ops in the program who receive offers of full-time employment: Approximately 50 percent

Web site for internship/co-op information: www1.dupont.com/dupontglobal/corp/careers/univ_internships.html

The Sourcing & Logistics Co-op Program is a key part of our recruiting strategy. The program provides an excellent pool of motivated, diverse, and well-prepared employees for DuPont. Assignments are located in Wilmington, Del.

Requirements for the Sourcing & Logistics Co-op Program:

- Currently enrolled as a full-time, undergraduate student at an accredited college or university.
- *BA/BS candidates:* A specific major is not relevant although some preference will be given to candidates studying supply chain management, logistics, engineering, operations management, transportation or business administration.
- Minimum GPA of 2.8.
- Ability to relocate to Wilmington, Delaware for the duration of the co-op/internship program.
- Legal right to work in the United States without restrictions.
- Only those candidates who are able to complete the entire assignment will be considered.

In addition to these requirements, candidates must possess the following qualifications:

- *Business Knowledge:* Ability to learn about DuPont's various businesses and their unique purchasing agreements.
- *Computer Skills:* Experience with MS Office (WORD, Excel, Access, PowerPoint). Candidates must be able to work with the Internet and learn internal DuPont systems and tools.
- *Resourcefulness:* Candidates must be able to identify leveraging opportunities (the advantage of having businesses buy supplies and services collectively versus individually).
- *Implementation:* The ability to handle multiple priority assignments, as well as, the ability to work independently with minimal supervision.
- *Networking skills:* They must have the ability to network with different internal and external groups and contacts and be capable of working in a team environment.

Scholarships

We no longer give scholarships directly, however we provide funding through third parties (e.g., NACME, UNCF).

Affinity Groups

Corporate Black Employees Network (CBEN)

Web site: http://www1.lvs.dupont.com/networks/cben/

The purpose of CBEN is to link the individual sites networks into a unified network.

CBEN strives to:

Recognize, strengthen and support all black networks throughout the corporation.

- Create an atmosphere of nurturing and mentoring for all black employees.
- Allow the CBEN to partner with DuPont leadership in addressing issues affection black employees.
- Communicate information to all black employees in a timely manner.
- Encourage two-way communications among networks (sharing of best practices).
- Provide a more cohesive, concentrated and formalized effort to shape organizational decisions.
- Seek alignment and agreement to identify and implement initiatives affecting the greater whole.
- Help the corporate leadership understand issues affecting black employees.
- Serve as an agent for positive change within the DuPont Corporation, wholly owned subsidiaries and associated joint ventures.

By doing these things, we build a strong, united community ready to address issues and challenges to ensure that we can contribute to our fullest potential in the work environment and achieve business success.

DuPont Women's Network (DWN)

Web site: http://cdcrs58.lvs.dupont.com/DWN/default.htm

DWN's mission is to foster development of DuPont women (and DuPont as a whole) through the leveraging of tools and ideas; to enable retention and personal and business growth; and to improve the capability of the corporate intellectual asset base.

Hispanic Network (HISNET)

Web site: www1.lvs.dupont.com/networks/hisnet/

The mission of the Hispanic Network is to promote an environment across the corporation that empowers Hispanics to perform at their maximum potential and that recognizes and values the contribution of Hispanic employees.

The Hispanic Network will work toward accomplishing the following goals:

• Inclusion of Hispanics in all aspects of the businesses.

• Empowerment of all Hispanics to contribute, learn, grow, and advance.

• Recognition of Hispanic employees for their accomplishments and contributions.

• Fair and respectful treatment of Hispanic employees.

• A corporate work environment that welcomes and supports Hispanic employees.

DuPont Asian Group (DPAG)

Web site: http://dpag.es.dupont.com/

The purpose of DPAG is to:

• Promote a corporate environment that fully values and maximizes contributions of Asian-Americans.

• Encourage and support DuPont Asian-Americans in achieving business success and personal growth.

Bisexuals, Gays, Lesbians, Transgendered and Allies at DuPont Network (BGLAD)

Web site: www.dupontbglad.com/

BGLAD's mission is to help DuPont attract, utilize, and retain talented bisexual, gay, lesbian, and transgendered people by:

• Using its collective power to eliminate homophobia and heterosexism within DuPont businesses.

• Serving as a resource regarding bisexual, gay, lesbian and transgender issues, and as a point of contact between DuPont and the community at large.

• Partnering with Human Resources to address mental, emotional, and physical health issues, and to help design compensation and benefit plans accordingly.

• Providing opportunities to discuss and advance issues, to expand the network and increase the visibility of its members.

• Ensuring a safe, healthy, and supportive environment in the workplace that empowers bisexual, gay, lesbian and transgendered employees to be open and authentic about themselves.

• Partnering with DuPont businesses to identify and capitalize on the bisexual, gay, lesbian and transgendered market.

DuPont Part-Time Network (DPTEN)

The Global DuPont Part-time Employees Network exists to provide a community of support and information for all DuPont employees and businesses currently in or considering part-time roles. Our members are global, both men and women, working both full and part-time schedules.

DPTEN exists to maximize DuPont employee professional contribution, maximize personal life balance satisfaction, and maximize DuPont sustainable business results through valued employees.

DPTEN's purpose:

• To establish a community for full-service DuPont employees working part time or any interested supportive DuPont employee working full time.

• To provide a "voice" from this diverse work group.

• To define benefit/value of the part-time employee.

There are both corporately sponsored and site-sponsored affinity networks in DuPont. Corporately sponsored networks receive funding support for initiatives and activities that are driven through DuPont corporate headquarters. However, site and business units maintain autonomy in their support of local networks.

The networks conduct biannual conferences. BGLAD, DPAG, and HISNET included marketing segments during their last conference. Some networks conducted marketing surveys and used the information gathered to conduct sessions where conference participants helped business marketing managers identify opportunities for businesses covering automotive paints and refinishes, Corian® and Zodiaq® surfaces, and Solae™ products. The CBEN network identified an opportunity that provided future opportunity for the crop protection business, and CBEN collected funds during its last conference to help villagers in underdeveloped countries.

Entry-Level Programs, Full-Time Opportunities and Training Programs

Field Engineering Program

Length of program: Four years, minimum (two assignment minimum)

Geographic location(s) of program: U.S.-based program; locations throughout country

Web site:

www1.dupont.com/dupontglobal/corp/careers/univ_fieldprograms_engineering.html

Series of rotational assignments providing developmental experience in roles such as engineering, business, operations leadership, sales/marketing, R&D and Six Sigma. Strong emphasis on career development via tools, training and coaching throughout the year. Required participation in annual development meetings that offer: training (soft and hard skills), presentations on business initiatives and programs, networking opportunities (with peers, technical leaders and management), and exposure to senior leadership via keynote presentation(s). Six Sigma training required.

Tuition reimbursement supported via corporate program. Support for professional engineering society conferences and educational opportunities.

Finance Field Program

Length of program: Two to three rotational assignments/four to six years

Geographic location(s) of program: United States

Training would be aimed at providing:

• Three diverse work experiences

• *DFU Courses:* Ethics, DuPont Accounting, Internal Controls, etc.

• Support of certifications such as CPA, CIA and continuing education

Marketing Leadership Development Program

Length of program: Three years

Geographic location(s) of program: Start in Wilmington, Delaware (for U.S. hires), rotate within U.S. and potentially to one of our global markets.

Web site:

www1.dupont.com/dupontglobal/corp/careers/univ_fieldprograms_marketing.html

This is a development program comprised of many elements that could be considered training. For example, we have developed a performance assessment process unique to the program to ensure that our participants get the feedback they need to develop into potential business leaders. With regard to formal training, we have scheduled formal training, which includes:

• Six Sigma training in the first year

• LEAD II training (middle manager training in DuPont) the second year

At each of our semiannual meetings, we include topical training. Examples include: Myers-Briggs, "Strengthfinders," "The first 90 Days," etc.

We offer tuition assistance to those foreign students whom we localize outside the US. Additionally, DuPont offers tuition reimbursement for preapproved and agreed educational development opportunities.

DuPont Corporate IT Field Program

Length of program: Field members are required to complete three to five assignments from 18 to 30 months in length. On average, members are part of the program for six to eight years.

Geographic location(s) of program: Primarily within the contiguous states where DuPont is located, including Wilmington, Delaware

Web site:

www1.dupont.com/dupontglobal/corp/careers/paths_infotech.html

• Basic training and orientation for new employees

• DuPont targeted development discussion training

• Other training and education is based upon developmental gaps identified for each assignment

For qualified candidates; there is a tuition reimbursement program.

DuPont Human Resources Field Program

Length of program: Based upon the series of rotational development assignments designed for the individual, a participant may be associated with the program from three to five years.

Geographic location(s) of program: The program is focused within the United States. The rotational design entails relocation to DuPont sites throughout the U.S. and corporate headquarters located in Wilmington, Delaware. Participants gain global business experience and an understanding of human resource policies and strategies associated with a global workforce. Opportunities to work on global teams and interact with employees around the world are provided to participants.

The DuPont Human Resources Field Program provides participants with early-career development opportunities through a series of rotational assignments. Each rotational assignment is designed to give the individuals the opportunity to foster their skills in a variety of HR functional areas. Upon completion of the program, individuals will have a strong foundation on which to build an exciting career as an HR leader at DuPont. Program benefits include:

• Exposure to many of the businesses within the DuPont portfolio.

• Extensive contact with senior level HR and business leaders across the company.

• A support network of fellow program participants that will be beneficial to the individual throughout his/her career.

- Meaningful assignments designed to engage individual development goals and career objectives.

- Biannual development workshops created specifically for program participants.

Individual development is the foundation upon which the Human Resources Field Program is founded. The program has a listing of training programs that each individual is required to attend. Six Sigma training and certification is also required. Biannual development workshops designed specifically for program participants are also held. Individual development/training is identified through personal targeted development plans. As with all employees at DuPont, program participants may participate in our Assistance for Lifelong Learning (tuition refund) Program.

Strategic Plan and Diversity Leadership

Who has primary responsibility for leading diversity initiatives at your firm?

Willie C. Martin, vice president for diversity and work/life; Sandra Lewis, manager, diversity and work/life.

Does your firm currently have a diversity committee?

No

Does the committee and/or diversity leader establish and set goals or objectives consistent with management's priorities?

Yes

Has the firm undertaken a formal or informal diversity program or set of initiatives aimed at increasing the diversity of the firm?

Yes, formal

How often does the firm's management review the firm's diversity progress/results?

Monthly. Ongoing reviews vary according to drivers/processes

How is the firm's diversity committee and/or firm management held accountable for achieving results?

Management is held accountable for achieving results in several different ways including the annual assignment of critical operating tasks and as part of managers' normal performance. Managers are held accountable by leadership, which reviews succession plans at every level of the organization. The CEO and a representative from the diversity area review succession plans for directors and all levels above. DuPont's corporately sponsored affinity networks hold conferences biannually. The conferences are a forum for employees to meet, review past performance, and set new expectations for the coming

years. During these conferences, leadership is also held directly accountable by employees.

The Stats

	NUMBER OF EMPLOYEES	REVENUE
	2005	2005
Total in the U.S.	12,199	N/A
Total outside the U.S.	34,000	N/A
Total worldwide	60,000	$27.1 billion

Retention and Professional Development

Please identify the specific steps you are taking to reduce the attrition rate of minority and women employees.

- Develop and/or support internal employee affinity groups (e.g., minority or women networks within the firm)
- Increase/review compensation relative to competition
- Increase/improve current work/life programs
- Adopt dispute resolution process
- Succession plan includes emphasis on diversity
- Work with minority and women employees to develop career advancement plans
- Strengthen mentoring program for all employees, including minorities and women
- Professional skills development program, including minority and women employees

Diversity Mission Statement

To foster an inclusive environment in a way that unleashes the potential of people and enables winning businesses to deliver significant shareholder value.

Additional Information

DuPont believes in the power of our networks (affinity groups) and the role they play in helping employees realize their full potential and achieve business success. The six corporately sponsored networks—i.e., Corporate Black Employees Network (CBEN), DuPont Women's Network (DWN), Hispanic Network (HISNET), DuPont Asian Group (DPAG), Bisexual Gay Lesbian Transgendered and Allies in DuPont Network (BGLAD), and the DuPont Part-Time Network (DPTEN)—are critical to the success of the DuPont diversity strategic imperatives. The networks assist in recruiting, retention, representation, community relations, marketing and communications initiatives. They serve as sounding boards for the organization and are partners in helping DuPont achieve its diversity vision by improving performance feedback, employee development and retention, and marketing strategies to diverse customers. The networks provide a diverse perspective and, in some cases, drive company policy. Additionally, they are role models of an inclusive organization, as all networks are open to anyone who wants to join in support of their objectives.

The networks are helping DuPont gain a global competitive advantage. For example the DuPont Asian Network hosted the Glimpse of Asia/Business Expo during Asian Heritage Month 2004 to build cultural awareness as DuPont moves into emerging markets. The exposition was so successful that the Hispanic Network soon followed with an exposition as well. These events are examples of how diverse groups of employees have contributed to business success by helping leadership understand that as DuPont moves into new markets, and subsequently cultures, the appreciation for diversity within the business context is key to success.

Beginning as early as 1985, the results of several work/life surveys determined work balance issues were not only a concern for women, but also for men as well. DuPont concluded that work/life balance was a "mainstream business issue." Other work/life surveys have helped us gather information to implement programs that assist employees in becoming more productive. Follow-up surveys proved a direct correlation between work life supports and happy, healthy employees. Feedback indicated that those employees that had used our work/life programs or knew about our work/life programs felt more supported and less stressed. It also indicated that employees were more productive and more likely to go the "extra mile" for the company's success.

Our current work/life offerings include:

• Paid adoption leave
• Adoption assistance
• Dependent care spending accounts
• Dependent care reimbursement for overnight travel
• Family leave
• Flexible work practices
• Just in time care (backup dependent care program)
• LifeWorks (resource and referral service)
• Work/life committees/teams

Awards and Recognition

• DuPont was named among the 50 Best Employers in Argentina by *Apertura.*

• DuPont was named Corporation of the Year by the Minority Supplier Council.

• DuPont was inducted into the *Working Mother* Hall of Fame.

• Ellen Kullman was named to *Fortune's* 50 Most Powerful Women in Business.

• The Louisiana Chemical Association recognized DuPont Pontchartrain as The Best in Louisiana.

• DuPont Argentina was named among the 60 best companies to work for in Argentina, according to the 2005 Great Place to Work® survey.

• DuPont ranked 26th in the 2005 Harris Interactive Reputation Quotient (RQ) survey.

• *La Tribune de Genève* named DuPont as a most important employer in Geneva.

• DuPont was selected as one of the 100 Best Companies for Working Mothers in the United States by *Working Mother* magazine. (2005)

• The National Safety Council selected DuPont as the recipient of the 2006 Green Cross for Safety Medallion for corporate excellence in safety. (2005)

• *Fortune* ranked DuPont 188th on the Global 500 rankings, *Fortune's* annual list of the world's largest corporations. (2005)

• *The Scientist* magazine named Pioneer among the Best Places to Work for Scientists in Industry. (2005)

• DuPont Argentina was ranked among the Top Ten Companies to Work For in Argentina in a list published by The Great Place to Work Institute. (2005)

• DuPont Mexico was named a Best Place to Work in a survey published by the Mexican business magazine *EXPANSION* and The Great Place To Work Institute®. (2005)

• The DuPont Sabine River Works in Orange, Texas, was voted Best Place to Work in Orange County. (2005)

• The National Association for Female Executives (NAFE) named DuPont one of the Top 30 Companies for Executive Women. (2005)

Dynegy Inc.

1000 Louisiana Street
Suite 5800
Houston, TX 77002
Phone: (713) 507-6400
Toll Free: (877) 396-3499
www.dynegy.com

Diversity Mission Statement

Dynegy Inc. provides electricity, natural gas and natural gas liquids to markets and customers throughout the United States. Through its energy businesses, Power Generation and Natural Gas Liquids, the company owns and operates a diverse portfolio of assets. The company also strives to achieve diversity in its human capital assets, recognizing that diversity encompasses a great many factors such as ethnicity/race, gender, sexual orientation, language, religion, work status and social and economic status. One of the company's goals is to promote and maintain an inclusive environment free from discrimination.

Echostar Communications Corp.

9601 S. Meridian Boulevard
Englewood, CO 80112

Locations
Over 150 globally

Employment Contact
Holly Reed
Manager, Corporate Talent Acquisition
9601 S. Meridian Boulevard
Englewood, CO 80112

Career URL:
www.dishnetwork.com/careers

College Recruiting/Internship URL:
www.dishnetwork.com/college

Internships and Co-ops

EchoStar hosts one of the most competitive and comprehensive summer internship programs in the nation. If you have a thirst for adventure and the desire to prove yourself, consider joining EchoStar as a summer intern. EchoStar Communications Corp. is the parent company of DISH Network, and hires over 60 interns each summer, for positions throughout the company, including: accounting, internal audit and tax, customer service support, engineering/R&D, finance, human resources, information technology, legal, marketing, operations, public relations, sales, and training and development.

The summer-long program allows college and graduate students to interact with other interns from across the country while working with managers and executives on projects that receive wide exposure and have a lasting impact on the company. Our interns work to both enhance their education and open themselves up to the many full-time opportunities that EchoStar has to offer. In addition to working on substantial projects, interns participate in field trips, training and other enrichment activities, such as: executive team presentations, tours of our operations centers and digital broadcast centers, and social events like baseball games and hikes.

EchoStar offers exciting and challenging summer internship opportunities to:

• Students studying business, IT, engineering, liberal arts and other related areas (bachelor's and master's), with at least one more quarter of school left after the summer of their internship, and no more than two years of college or graduate school remaining

• DuPontStudents who demonstrate intelligence, drive and energy through a track record of extracurricular involvement, service, leadership, prior experience, honors and other achievements

• Students with exceptional communication, technical, analytical and problem-solving skills

• Students who pass our rigorous screening process, including assessment exams

An internship at EchoStar is much more than a summer job—it is an experience that will provide a lifetime of benefits!

Ecolab, Inc.

370 N. Wabasha Street
St. Paul, MN 55102-2233
Telephone: (651) 293-2233
Fax: (651) 293-2092

Locations

St. Paul, MN (HQ)
Ecolab operates in more than 160 countries worldwide.

Diversity Leadership

Betsy Rot
Manager, College Relations
370 N. Wabasha Street
St. Paul, MN 54022
Phone: (651) 293-4515
Fax: (651) 225-3304
E-mail: betsy.rot@ecolab.com
www.ecolab.com/carrers

Recruiting

Please list the schools/types of schools at which you recruit.

- *Public state schools:* University of Wisconsin – Madison, University of Wisconsin – Eau Claire, University of Minnesota, University of North Dakota, Michigan State University, Penn State, Purdue, Cal Poly Pomona, Cal Poly San Luis Obispo, University of Houston, Florida State, University of IL-Champaign/Urbana, Iowa State, Ohio State, Western Michigan University, University of Michigan, University of Chicago, Northwestern University, Indiana University, Mississippi State University
- *Historically black colleges and universities (HBCUs):* Morgan State University, UNC, North Carolina A&T
- *Other predominantly minority and/or women's colleges:* College of St. Catherine's

Do you have any special outreach efforts directed to encourage minority students to consider your firm?

- Receptions for minority students
- *Conferences:* National Black MBA, National Society for Minorities in Hospitality
- Sponsor student attendance at diversity conferences
- Participate in/host minority student job fair(s)
- Sponsor/donations to minority student associations
- Firm's employees participate on career panels at school
- Outreach to leadership of minority student organizations

What activities does the firm undertake to attract minority and women employees?

- Partner programs with women and minority associations
- *Conferences:* St Kate's career and development conferences, Woman's Food Service Forum
- Participate at minority job fairs
- Seek referrals from other employees

Do you use executive recruiting/search firms to seek to identify new diversity hires?

Yes

Internships and Co-ops

Territory Sales Intern

Deadline for application: May 1st

Number of interns in the program in summer 2006 (internship) or 2006 (co-op): 28

Pay: $13.00 per hour

Length of the program: 10 to 12 weeks

Percentage of interns/co-ops in the program who receive offers of full-time employment: 100 percent available; average 80 percent offer rate

Web site for internship/co-op information:
www.ecolab.com/careeers/collegerelations

As an Ecolab summer intern, you will develop your skills from the following:

- Work alongside a successful territory manager to learn customers' operations, understand their cleaning challenges, and devise solutions to meet their needs.

- Gain exposure to the entire hospitality industry including hotel, restaurants, hospitals, schools and dining facilities. You will also work with a wide customer base including large corporate chains as well as independent, single-unit organizations.

- Learn how to successfully prospect to find new leads, set up new accounts and generate new business for the territory.

- Receive training on how to provide excellent customer service by troubleshooting Ecolab dish machines, laundry equipment and dispensing systems.

• Work closely with the district sales manager to perfect your sales, presentation, and professional skills.

• Work for 10 weeks as part of an intern class to share feedback, resources, and experiences.

Successful Ecolab Interns will possess the following:

• Currently enrolled as a junior or senior undergraduate student

• Experience within the foodservice, hospitality or sales industry is preferred

• Well-developed interpersonal and customer relations skills

• Organizational skills

• Strong mechanical aptitude

• Ability to lift and/or carry 50 pounds and acceptable motor vehicle record

The objective of the internship program is to give you a hands-on, advanced level overview of Ecolab and the Institutional sales division. You will gain valuable sales and service experience by selling to and servicing our customers on a daily basis with an experienced salesperson. You will also be considered for long-term career opportunities within Ecolab through exposure to additional roles within the organization.

Undergraduate Finance Intern

Deadline for application: Early March

Number of interns in the program in summer 2006 (internship) or 2006 (co-op): 16

Pay: $16 per hour

Length of the program: 10 to 12 weeks

Percentage of interns/co-ops in the program who receive offers of full-time employment: 70 percent

Web site for internship/co-op information:
www.ecolab.com/careers/college relations

Responsibilities could include:

• Provide management with financial analysis

• Assess the performance of a business unit

• Identify areas of opportunity and risk

• Assist in the preparation of annual financial plans

• Produce management reports

• Perform regular month-end general ledger maintenance and reconciliations

• Assist in special projects

Requirements:

• Pursuing a BA or BS degree in a finance, accounting or a business related major

• Excellent analytical skills

• Strong communication skills

• Demonstrated project management skills

• Ability to work as a member of a team

• Well-developed organizational skills

• Extensive PC spreadsheet skills

Information Technology Intern

Deadline for application: Early March

Number of interns in the program in summer 2006 (internship) or 2006 (co-op): Three

Pay: $16 per hour

Length of the program: 10 to 12 weeks

Percentage of interns/co-ops in the program who receive offers of full-time employment: 85 percent

Web site for internship/co-op information:
www.ecolab.com/careers/collegerelations

Job duties and projects you could get involved in as an information technology intern at Ecolab include:

• Design and develop software products and tools

• Create and modify applications to provide vital system statistics to various parts of the technology organization

• Create custom web interface designs and change web site process

• Develop large content management systems including data repositories, web based data access and UI system

• Write system requirements and maintenance documentation

• Software testing in multiple phases of the development cycle for initiatives across multiple organizations

• Researching current industry software tools and technologies

Qualifications:

• Pursuing a bachelor's degree in MIS, business or related field

• Demonstrated track record in project management

• Must be able to work independently and as part of a team on multiple overlapping projects

• Self-motivation and strong communication and interpersonal skills

• Analysis skills and attention to details for coding, testing/troubleshooting and for building and configuring applications

Food & Beverage Intern

Number of interns in the program in summer 2006 (internship) or 2006 (co-op): One (proposing 10 for 2007)

Pay: $15 per hour

Length of the program: 10 to 12 weeks

Percentage of interns/co-ops in the program who receive offers of full-time employment: 70 percent

Web site for internship/co-op information:
www.ecolab.com/careers

R&D Intern

Deadline for application: Varies

Number of interns in the program in summer 2006 (internship) or 2006 (co-op): 16

Length of the program: 10 to 12 weeks

Web site for internship/co-op information: www.ecolab.com/careers

Affinity Groups

EcoMondo

EcoMondo is an inclusive business and social network that supports Ecolab's growth through the integration and promotion of global talent diversity, global talent mobility and the creation of professional opportunities for associates with international interests.

E3

E3: Empowered, engaged, energized, a women's group that focuses on mentoring, leadership development and community outreach for female associates of Ecolab. Activities include professional development series, community service project, book club and formal mentoring program.

EcoEssence

EcoEssence is an African-American network that encourages interaction with, and growth and understanding of the various ethnic minority cultures that are represented at Ecolab.

Entry-Level Programs, Full-Time Opportunities and Training Programs

Territory Sales Manager-in-Training

Length of program: Six months training

Geographic location(s) of program: U.S.; national

As a territory manager-in-training, you will be responsible for planning, developing, servicing and managing a territory of customers including hotels, restaurants, hospitals and schools, as well as prospecting for new customers to service. You will deal directly with our customers and your success depends not only on your ability to sell cleaning, sanitizing and maintenance products, but also your ability to provide each customer with prompt, professional and personal service, as well as mechanical troubleshooting and repair of our dispensing systems and equipment to maintain customer relationships. Intensive 10-day training session at the world headquarters in St. Paul, Minn. All new hires attend this training session. Tuition reimbursement is offered for all positions after one year of employment.

Undergraduate Finance Development Program

Length of program: Two years

Geographic location(s) of program: St. Paul, Minn.

This is a two-year program where the associates hold two to three positions. They begin their first term with our CareerStart, on-boarding program. Monthly development session, bimonthly update meetings and tuition reimbursement.

Operation Analyst—Engineering

Geographic location(s) of program: U.S.; national

Tuition reimbursement available.

Strategic Plan and Diversity Leadership

What trends in your industry affect your corporate diversity goals, strategies and/or internal or external alliances?

The hospitality industry is becoming an increasing global and diverse industry and workforce. In order to stay competitive and successful in this industry, Ecolab values having a global and inclusive workforce to serve the industry.

How does the firm's leadership communicate the importance of diversity to everyone at the firm?

• *Ecolab Express:* the employee web site

• Corporate diversity brochure

• Affinity group meeting notices

• Inclusion/diversity training sessions

Who has primary responsibility for leading diversity initiatives at your firm?

Diana Lewis, senior vice president of human resources

Does your firm currently have a diversity committee?

Yes

If yes, does the committee's representation include one or more members of the firm's management/executive committee (or the equivalent)?

Yes

Has the firm undertaken a formal or informal diversity program or set of initiatives aimed at increasing the diversity of the firm?

Yes, formal

How often does the firm's management review the firm's diversity progress/results?

Monthly

The Stats

	NUMBER OF EMPLOYEES		REVENUE	
	2006	2005	2006	2005
Total in the U.S.	13, 000	12,700	53 percent	51 percent
Total outside the U.S.	10,000	9,300	47 percent	49 percent
Total worldwide	23, 000	22, 000	$4.9 billion	$4.5 billion

Retention and Professional Development

Please identify the specific steps you are taking to reduce the attrition rate of minority and women employees.

• Develop and/or support internal employee affinity groups (e.g., minority or women networks within the firm)

• Support associate attendance at minority and women's development conferences

• Work with minority and women employees to develop career advancement plans

• Strengthen mentoring program for all employees, including minorities and women

• Professional skills development program, including minority and women employees

• *Other:* CareerStart onboarding process, Individual Development Plans, Ecolab University Training facilities/sessions

Diversity Mission Statement

We are committed to a culture that fully leverages our people's talents by promoting an environment where all people can make a difference, be heard, be supported, be developed and be rewarded for their contributions.

Additional Information

Ecolab associates possess shared expectations, which include a workplace built on respect, mutual values, trust and goodwill. Diversity is a core tenet that enables us to achieve a more rewarding professional atmosphere for all of our associates around the globe. At Ecolab, we believe that the success of our associates and the success of the company go hand in hand.

We support our diversity efforts by recruiting and hiring the best people of all backgrounds to represent our company. Some programs in which we participate include:

• National Black MBA

• INROADS, which develops and places talented minority youth in business and industry

• National Association of Minorities in Hospitality

• College of St. Catherine, Center for Sales Innovation for Female Sales Professionals

EMBARQ

5454 W. 110th Street
Overland Park, KS 66211-1204
www.embarq.com

Locations
Overland Park, KS (HQ)
Doing business in 18 states or territories
in the United States

Diversity Leadership
Vivian Tate
Manager, Office of Inclusion & Diversity

Tiffany Morley-Fercho
Diversity & College Recruitment Manager
www.embarq.com/careers

Employment Contact
Vivian Tate
Manager, Office of Inclusion & Diversity

Recruiting

Please list the schools/types of schools at which you recruit.

- Ivy League schools
- Public state schools
- Historically black colleges and universities (HBCUs)
- Hispanic serving institutions (HSIs)

Do you have any special outreach efforts directed to encourage minority students and graduates to consider your firm?

- *Conferences:* NBMBAA, NSHMBA
- Participate in minority student job fair(s) or other minority-focused job events
- Sponsor minority student association events
- Firm's employees participate on career panels at school
- Outreach to leadership of minority student organizations

What activities does the firm undertake to attract minority and women employees?

- Partner programs with women and minority associations
- *Conferences:* NBMBAA, NSHMBA
- Participate at minority job fairs
- Seek referrals from other employees
- Utilize online job services

Do you use executive recruiting/search firms to seek to identify new diversity hires?

No, not routinely

Internships and Co-ops

EMBARQ Summer Internship

Deadline for application: May of the school year

Number of interns in the program in summer 2006 (internship): 46 students in summer 2006

Pay: $8.62 an hour up to $43 an hour (most interns will work a 40 hour+ work week)

Length of the program: 10 to 12 weeks

Percentage of interns in the program who receive offers of full-time employment: 10 to 20 percent

Web site for internship information: www.embarq.com/careers

The EMBARQ Summer Internship is an open opportunity-based program that focuses on learning the industry, the company and the community. The students are slotted based on their areas of interest, qualifications, educational focus and business needs. The openings and projects vary from summer to summer.

Affinity Groups

Embrace

Embrace is an African-American-focused employee resource group, whose mission is to aid EMBARQ in the recruitment, retention, development and promotion of diverse employees, and in serving as ambassadors in the communities within which we reside.

Embrace meets once a month and periodically throughout the month for various volunteer projects and events.

They also meet to support internal EMBARQ business projects.

Juntos Podemos

Juntos Podemos is a Latino-focused employee resource group whose mission and vision is to develop and host a symbiotic relationship within the Latino community that promotes EMBARQ's products and services in addition to offering cultural, educational and employee development opportunities. Juntos Podemos is committed to supporting the partnership with EMBARQ and the Latino community. From community involvement, cultural enrichment to employee development and market initiatives, Juntos Podemos is dedicated to promoting diversity. Chapters are located in Kansas City and Las Vegas.

Juntos Podemos meets once a month and periodically throughout the month for various volunteer projects and events.

They also meet to support internal EMBARQ business projects.

The Alliance Council (TAC)

The Alliance Council is a multicultural employee resource group whose mission is to create and maintain a company culture in which diversity is valued, respect for each other is practiced in spirit and deed, and to assist in enabling and achieving consistency in the application of diversity policies and practices. Special emphasis is given to creating and maintaining positive changes within the culture of EMBARQ with respect to the professional growth and advancement of people of diverse cultures and to creating and maintaining a workforce that reflects the diversity of the customers and communities we serve. Chapters are located in Florida.

The Alliance Council meets once a month and periodically throughout the month for various volunteer projects and events.

They also meet to support internal EMBARQ business projects.

W.E. (Women Empowered)

Women Empowered is an organization committed to building a community supportive of women and their professional and personal development, as well as to help position EMBARQ as an "employee of choice."

Equal

An employee resource group dedicated to promoting an inclusive work environment where all EMBARQ employees are valued for contributions without regard to sexual orientation or gender identity.

Entry-Level Programs, Full-Time Opportunities and Training Programs

EMBARQ does not have a full-time entry-level program. Students that are hired for full-time opportunities both at the undergraduate and MBA level follow the EMBARQ internal Leadership Quality Development Program that is available for all employees. The process is customized to each employee and their career goals.

Strategic Plan and Diversity Leadership

What trends in your industry affect your corporate diversity goals, strategies and/or internal or external alliances?

Customer demographics and diverse vendors/suppliers, among others.

How does the firm's leadership communicate the importance of diversity to everyone at the firm?

CEO communications to all employees, letters and information on our diversity Intranet site, management newsletters, "all hands" meetings of the entire employee population and through frequent messages in all types of media from our corporate communications diversity team.

Who has primary responsibility for leading diversity initiatives at your firm?

Vivian Tate, manager of the office of inclusion and diversity

Does your firm currently have a diversity committee?

Yes

If yes, please describe how the committee is structured, how often it meets, etc.

Our Diversity Council is chaired by our CEO. All of his direct reports are members of the council, along with four other vice presidents who chair Diversity Council committees. The manager of the office of inclusion and diversity plans and serves as facilitator for council meetings. The Diversity Council meets once each quarter.

If yes, does the committee's representation include one or more members of the firm's management/executive committee (or the equivalent)?

Yes

If yes, how many executives are on the committee? How many employees are on the committee, and how often does the committee convene in furtherance of the firm's diversity initiatives?

Our CEO and all of his direct reports (13), four vice president committee chairpersons. Collective hours of time for this group spent dedicated to diversity initiatives exceeds 100 hours.

Does the committee and/or diversity leader establish and set goals or objectives consistent with management's priorities?

Yes. Placement goals have been established for all business leaders.

Has the firm undertaken a formal or informal diversity program or set of initiatives aimed at increasing the diversity of the firm?

Yes, formal—our minority internship program, succession planning process and diversity recruiting initiative.

How often does the firm's management review the firm's diversity progress/results?

Monthly

How is the firm's diversity committee and/or firm management held accountable for achieving results?

Through specific diversity competencies incorporated in our performance evaluation process.

The Stats

	NUMBER OF EMPLOYEES	REVENUE
	2006	2006
Total in the U.S.	20,023	Over $6 billion
Total worldwide	20,023	Over $6 billion

Retention and Professional Development

Please identify the specific steps you are taking to reduce the attrition rate of minority and women employees.

- Develop and/or support internal employee affinity groups (e.g., minority or women networks within the firm)

- Increase/review compensation relative to competition
- Succession plan includes emphasis on diversity
- Work with minority and women employees to develop career advancement plans
- Strengthen mentoring program for all employees, including minorities and women
- Professional skills development program, including minority and women employees
- *Other:* Micro-inequities training to help create a more inclusive corporate culture

Diversity Mission Statement

- To create an environment committed to inclusion and mutual respect wherein employee diversity is a catalyst for innovative thinking and productivity

- To gain competitive advantage and enhance organizational performance by providing culturally sensitive customer service

- To become an "employer of choice" and increase EMBARQ's ability to attract and recruit the "best and the brightest" talent by reflecting and valuing diversity at all levels of the organization

Additional Information

Our company was just established in May 2006 and we have already progressed beyond many established firms in our diversity initiatives. At EMBARQ, we recognize that diversity is not a program but an ongoing process. Diversity has been incorporated in most of our programs, policies and processes. Implementation of EMBARQ's diversity strategy and commitment plan will be accomplished through six primary areas of focus: communications, employees, suppliers, marketing, community and measurement.

Erie Insurance Group

100 Erie Insurance Place
Erie, PA 16530
Phone: (814) 870-2000
Fax: (814) 461-2694
www.erieinsurance.com

Locations

Illinois • Indiana • Maryland • North Carolina • New York • Ohio • Pennsylvania • Tennessee • Virginia • Wisconsin • West Virginia

Diversity Leadership

Ann K. Scott
Vice President & Strategic Sourcing Manager

Employment Contact

Lois K. Smith
Supervisor, Employment Operations
www.erieinsurance.com/Careers/Default.htm

Recruiting

Please list the schools/types of schools at which you recruit.

• Private schools

• Public state schools

• Historically black colleges and universities (HBCUs)

Do you have any special outreach efforts directed to encourage minority students and graduates to consider your firm?

• Hold a reception for minority students

• Participate in/host minority student job fair(s) or other minority-focused job events

• Sponsor minority student association events

• Firm's employees participate on career panels at school

• Outreach to leadership of minority student organizations

What activities does the firm undertake to attract minority and women employees?

• Seek referrals from other employees

• Utilize online job services

• *Other:* Sponsorship of diverse community organizations and events

Internships and Co-ops

Future Focus IT and Actuarial Internship Program

Deadline for application: March

Number of interns in the program in summer 2006 (internship) or 2006 (co-op): Five

Pay: Varies according to work performed—generally between $12 to $17 per hour

Length of the program: Varies according to student schedule and department need; most are full time from May to August. Opportunities may exist to continue part-time throughout the school year for students

Web site for internship/co-op information: www.erieinsurance.com

About the Internship

The Erie Insurance Group Future Focus Internship is available to students whose permanent residence is within approximately 250 miles of Erie's home office in the Erie, Penn., community. Applications are accepted from students who are completing their sophomore or junior year. Qualifications include a major in IT or computer science for the IT internship, and in math or actuarial science for the actuarial internship. A minimum cumulative GPA of 3.0 is required. For an IT internship, completion of the first class in COBOL is preferred. For an actuarial internship, passing at least one actuarial exam is preferred. Several interns are hired each year for this paid internship program. Relocation assistance is available for those who are eligible.

About the Special Features

The internship includes orientation to the company and the insurance industry through:

• A variety of challenging assignments in a stimulating work environment

• A personal mentor

• A welcome event for the interns and their supervisors and mentors

• Educational programs and round table lunches with company management

Planned social events and opportunities for a wide variety of recreational activities will round out the interns' experience in Pennsylvania's scenic city on the lake.

To apply

Visit our web site at www.erieinsurance.com, or contact:

Melissa DiGiacomo, Corporate Recruiter

Employment Department

Erie Insurance Group

100 Erie Insurance Place

Erie, PA 16530

Phone: (814) 870-4035

Entry-Level Programs, Full-Time Opportunities and Training Programs

ERIE University Claims Adjuster Training Program

Length of program: Four months

Geographic location(s) of program: Erie Insurance claims offices service territories; locations vary according to the needs of the company at the time of the training class

Erie University is an exciting, dynamic training program that prepares bright, independent, hardworking candidates for careers in insurance claims. Training consists of a combination of fieldwork at the branch of initial hire and travel to our state-of-the-art facility in Erie, Penn., for classroom training in an intense, supportive learning environment. Training lasts for approximately four months and covers a variety of topics, such as an overview of the insurance industry and Erie Insurance; ERIE's service philosophy and standards; ERIE's product lines; claims, marketing, underwriting and other functions and procedures; field/home office interactions; product and policy information and other related topics.

Trainees attend classes taught by insurance experts both on company time and after hours. They also independently complete a variety of assigned projects and handle claims hands-on in the field. Trainees are also assigned a mentor who is a senior claims representative. Insurance training through the Insurance Institute of America is also included.

The ERIE University program leads to a career path in insurance that could eventually lead to management opportunities. Adjusters start in the position of property or liability adjuster I. With experience and additional education, they may advance to property or liability adjuster II and III, then to claims examiner, claims supervisor, claims manager, etc.

We are seeking college graduates (BS/BA, any major) with some work experience beyond graduation who are willing to enroll in extensive training and commit to the challenging and rewarding career of claims adjusting. Insurance knowledge is not required.

Before entering ERIE University, candidates must commit to locating to an assigned territory as determined by the company's needs. Assigned territories will be in areas that report to the hiring office. For example, our Indianapolis branch serves the entire southern portion of the state of Indiana from Illinois east to Ohio and from the Kentucky border north to approximately Lafayette and Muncie. Our Rochester branch serves the entire state of New York. Candidates should be enthusiastic about relocating anywhere within their branch's service area.

A valid driver's license, good driving record and acceptable credit history are required—motor vehicle, credit and criminal history reports will be ordered. College degrees will also be verified.

Good communication, interpersonal, analytical and organizational skills are required, along with independence and self-motivation.

Strategic Plan and Diversity Leadership

How does the firm's leadership communicate the importance of diversity to everyone at the firm?

Our commitment to diversity is incorporated into all of our communications, both internally and externally. Our message of equal professional service is incorporated into all of our management and employee training.

Who has primary responsibility for leading diversity initiatives at your firm?

Michael Krahe, executive vice president, leadership development

Does your firm currently have a diversity committee?

No

Has the firm undertaken a formal or informal diversity program or set of initiatives aimed at increasing the diversity of the firm?

Yes, informal.

The Stats

	REVENUE	
	2006	2005
Total in the U.S.	$1,134 billion	$1,125 billion

Retention and Professional Development

Please identify the specific steps you are taking to reduce the attrition rate of minority and women employees.

• Strengthen mentoring program for all employees, including minorities and women

• Professional skills development program, including minority and women employees

Different perspectives. One Goal.

Join a team where
your contribution matters.

Grow. Succeed.
Visit us at ey.com/us/careers
and our Facebook.com group.

#25 on *FORTUNE*® magazine's
100 Best Companies to Work For list.

Ernst & Young LLP

5 Times Square
New York, NY 10036
Phone: (212) 773-3000
Fax: (212) 773-6350
www.ey.com
Visit us at our Facebook.com group

Locations

Offices in 140 countries worldwide

Diversity Leadership

Gioia Pisano, Diversity Recruiting Leader
Ernst & Young LLP
Associate Director, Office of Minority Recruiting
99 Wood Avenue South
Iselin, NJ 08830
Phone: (732) 516-4243
Fax: (732) 516-4277
E-mail: gioia.pisano@ey.com

Recruiting

Please list the schools/types of schools at which you recruit.

• Ivy League schools
• Other private schools
• Public state schools
• Historically black colleges and universities (HBCUs)
• Hispanic serving institutions (HSIs)
• Other predominantly minority and/or women's colleges

Do you have any special outreach efforts directed to encourage minority students to consider your firm?

• Host receptions for minority students
• *Conferences:* National Association of Black Accountants (NABA), Association of Latino Professionals in Finance and Accounting (ALPFA), Hispanic Student Business Association (HSBA)
• Advertise in minority student association publications
• Participate in/host minority student job fairs
• Sponsor minority student association events
• Firm's employees participate on career panels at schools
• Outreach to leadership of minority student organizations
• Scholarships or intern/fellowships for minority students
• *Other:* Accounting Career Awareness Program with high school students and various universities
• *Other:* See below

The Your Master Plan (YMP) program was developed by Ernst & Young in collaboration with the University of Notre Dame and the University of Virginia. The innovative master's of accounting pro-

gram, which is fully funded by the firm, is primarily for non-accounting business majors. Over the past seven years, we have attracted over 1,200 students to the profession—and over 40 percent of these students were ethnic minorities.

Discover Tax is a National Diversity Leadership Conference where 100 students will attend in January 2008. Last year the three-day conference held in NYC attracted top students from across the country, where they had the opportunity to learn more about a career in tax and the firm's culture. All participants were eligible for office internship visits and many are now interning with us. To learn more go to ey.com/us/careers and click on campus and student programs.

Our affinity groups are active in outreach to community groups and high schools throughout the country. This encounters give students the opportunity to meet financial services professionals and learn about career and Ernst & Young.

What activities does the firm undertake to attract minority and women employees?

• Partner programs with women and minority associations
• *Conferences:* National Association of Black Accountants (NABA), Association of Latino Professionals in Finance and Accounting (ALPFA), Hispanic Student Business Association (HSBA)
• Participate in minority job fairs
• Seek referrals from other employees
• Utilize online job services
• Forte Foundation
• *Other:* INROADS

Do you use executive recruiting/search firms to seek to identify new diversity hires?

Yes

Internships and Co-ops

At Ernst & Young, an internship is a great way to find out what a career here is all about.

Interns get an inside look at the people, methods and technologies of a large international firm. Get a sense of our environment. See how we carry out assignments. Understand the value we place on quality and integrity.

Interns may assist with research, help conduct audits, work on marketing strategies, and assist in capital-sourcing efforts. Interns also may assist with tax-planning engagements or learn about audit processes, then apply audit concepts—like internal control, cash, accounts payable, and current liabilities—to real-life situations.

Interns also get the chance to attend Ernst & Young's International Intern Leadership Conference, held in Orlando every August. This event helps thousands of interns from around the world experience the firm's teaming culture, learn leadership skills, and network with future colleagues. Plus, it's a lot of fun.

Ernst & Young strongly supports INROADS and continues to increase its commitment each year. Ernst & Young received top honors at the 9th Annual Best of Class Conference sponsored by INROADS, Inc. In FY 2006, Ernst & Young hired 158 INROADS interns, a 76 percent increase over FY 2005. Our retention rate of 94.4 percent of INROADS interns was the highest of any organization, and our firm was among the national sponsors with the highest percentage of INROADS interns who became full-time employees.

In addition to working closely with INROADS, Ernst & Young also identifies multiyear interns through recruiting efforts on campus, Discover Tax and from conventions. In 2007, the firm will have over 240 multiyear interns; some sourced through INROADS others through our own sourcing efforts.

To find out more about our internship program, go to ey.com/us/careers.

Scholarships

Ernst &Young and the Ernst &Young Foundation have committed more than $6.5 million since 1996 to fund programs and minority scholarships for undergraduate and graduate degree candidates who are majoring in disciplines related to the firm's service areas, such as accounting, information technology, computer science, taxation and finance. Scholarships are distributed through universities and national organizations.

In addition to providing scholarships to students, we also fund a Masters of Accounting Program through the Your Master Plan (YMP) program, which was developed by Ernst & Young in collaboration with the University of Notre Dame and the University of Virginia. The innovative Masters of Accounting program, which is fully funded by the firm, is primarily for non-accounting business majors. Over the past seven years, we have attracted over 1,200 students to the profession—and over 40 percent of these students were ethnic minorities.

Affinity Groups

Professionals all over the country have taken part in initiatives through affinity groups or People Resource Networks to foster diversity and underscore our commitment to provide an open, flexible and supportive workplace that values the contributions of all our people. Our People Resource Networks are action-oriented groups designed to provide an opportunity for minority professionals to network internally and externally with professionals in the same field, to create informal mentoring relationships, and strengthen leadership skills through their involvement. We have specific people resource networks for:

• African-Americans
• Asian/Pacific Islanders
• Hispanics
• Gay, Lesbian, Bisexual and Transgender (GLBT)
• Women
• People with Disabilities

Entry-Level Programs, Full-Time Opportunities and Training Programs

At Ernst & Young, our commitment to development starts day one at the firm with orientation, and continues throughout one's professional career. Our four-pronged approach includes:

• *Learning:* Expand one's knowledge through instructor-led courses and technology-enabled learning.

• *Experiences:* Build your resume with stretch assignments, role changes and opportunities to expand responsibilities.

• *Relationships:* Forge important connections now—and for life— through networking, mentoring, and counseling relationships.

• *Feedback:* Gain insights through performance feedback, goal-setting, development plans and self-assessment.

The personal and professional growth of our people is at the heart of our People First culture. People First is a series of principles—supported by programs, processes, and behaviors—that aim to make Ernst & Young a place where the best people want to come and build their careers. Thus, it is the mutual commitment between Ernst &

Young and our people in which our people achieve their full potential, our clients benefit, and our business prospers.

Strategic Plan and Diversity Leadership

The firm has a strong commitment to diversity that starts at the top—Steve Howe, our Americas managing partner, chairs the firm's Ethnicity Diversity Task Force. This task force, along with the firm's offices of diversity strategy and development and minority recruitment, works along parallel paths to help Ernst & Young achieve its goal "to be the employer of choice among professional services firms for all people."

The Ethnicity Diversity Task Force includes partners and directors representing Ernst & Young's practices and geographic areas. The Ethnicity Diversity Task Force is charged with translating the firmwide vision for inclusiveness into action-oriented goals. The task force also develops strategy and examines initiatives to enhance the development and advancement of minorities in the firm. The task force meets regularly with personnel throughout North America to examine needed initiatives and take ownership in ensuring those initiatives are launched successfully.

The office of diversity strategy and development concentrates on the creation of strategies supporting awareness, communication, leadership accountability and career development. Much focus is placed on education, mentoring and networking, which fully support the firm's People First culture and its commitment to creating lifelong relationships by providing its people with the opportunities and tools they need to succeed within the firm and beyond.

The information below highlights some of the firm's key initiatives around the development of our minority professionals:

Local Diversity Frameworks

To focus on the firm's career development activities, diversity frameworks at the local level have been created to support the firm's national strategies, with local leadership driving the diversity efforts. Local teams include a diversity coordinator, an advisory council of local leaders, and subcommittees that focus on minority recruitment, career development, business development, and communications. These groups serve as the nucleus in initiating, championing and implementing change initiatives that will assist in creating a truly inclusive environment.

Minority Leadership Conference

The Ernst & Young Minority Leadership Conference, held every 18 months, brings together all of the firm's minority partners, principals, executive directors, and directors—as well as the firm's senior leadership, including the entire executive board—to increase partners, principals, executive directors and directors' leadership and accountability. This leads to enhanced awareness of inclusiveness as a key element of the firm's strategy, stronger commitment to the execution of key diversity drivers, and increased results and behavior change. The conference provides an opportunity to increase our minority leaders' involvement in diversity initiatives, as well as to continue to dialogue around increasing minority representation in the firm's leadership. It also provides an excellent networking opportunity for our minority partners, principals, executive directors and directors to network with senior firm leadership and to continue integrating diversity into the firm leadership culture and the People First environment.

Inclusiveness Learning Curriculum

The Inclusiveness Learning Curriculum sets a foundation for the success of the People First strategy by promoting the development of an "inclusive" leadership culture that respects individual talents and allows people to fully contribute to the success of the firm. Inclusiveness: An Awareness Workshop, is an integral part of the inclusiveness curriculum. The workshop expands the learner's awareness of inclusiveness through facilitated discussions and activities. This curriculum is being used and delivered within the context of the firmwide- and geography-based efforts that are currently in place. In addition, in a continued effort to cascade the message to all professionals, A Seat at the Table was developed as a two-and-a-half-hour session designed to raise awareness of the firm's commitment to inclusiveness. It is being deployed at a local level to staff, seniors and CBS equivalents.

Career Watch

At the local level, a standing leadership team or Career Watch Committee helps ensure that high-potential minorities and women are assigned to top clients, sales opportunities and projects, and are receiving the development opportunities they need to grow and excel. In other cases, individuals' development paths are studied to ensure there are no barriers to mentoring or access to opportunities for growth. Efforts like these help ensure that our best performers continue to develop and that any needs women and minorities might have are factored into their individual plans for growth.

Ethnicity Initiatives: Executive Mentoring Program and Learning Partnerships

Ernst & Young supports a formal mentoring program, the Executive Mentoring Program (EMP), that creates mentoring relationships by pairing high-potential minority partners with Americas executive board members and an external coach to ensure that the firm fully capitalizes on the talent available in its leadership ranks.

In 2002, Ernst & Young launched a formal, yearlong mentoring program called Learning Partnerships, which targets ethnic minorities as mentees and introduces a structured approach to mentoring and development. The program provides minority professionals with greater access to senior leaders, facilitates mentoring relationships, and supports the creation of informal relationships across industries.

How often does the firm's management review the firm's diversity progress/results?

Quarterly

The Stats

	NUMBER OF EMPLOYEES		REVENUE	
	2006	2005	2006	2005
Total in the U.S.	38,000	25,000	N/A	N/A
Total worldwide	14,000	107,000	$18.4 billion	$16.9 billion

LOCATIONS	
2006 countries worldwide	140
2006 Americas locations	150
2005 countries worldwide	140
2005 U.S. locations	95

Retention and Professional Development

How do 2006 minority and female attrition rates generally compare to those experienced in the prior year period?

We are proud that our efforts and culture have contributed to the continued higher retention of our minority and women professionals.

Please identify the specific steps you are taking to reduce the attrition rate of minority and women employees.

• Develop and/or support internal employee affinity groups (e.g., minority or women networks within the firm)

• Increase/improve current work/life programs (e.g., flexible work arrangements, concierge services, lactation programs)

• Succession plan includes emphasis on diversity

• Work with minority and women employees to develop career advancement plans

• Review work assignments to determine that minority and women employees are equitably assigned to top clients, sales opportunities and projects

• Strengthen mentoring programs for all employees, including minorities and women

Professional skills development programs, including minority and women employees.

Fannie Mae

3900 Wisconsin Avenue, NW
Washington, DC 22066
Phone: (202) 752-7000
www.fanniemae.com/careers

Locations
Washington, DC (HQ)
Atlanta, GA • Chicago, IL • Dallas, TX •
Pasadena, CA • Philadelphia, PA
Plus 54 partnership offices across the US.

Diversity Leadership
Angie Padilla
Diversity Manager

Jenny Luecking
Campus Recruiter
3900 Wisconsin Avenue NW
Washington, DC 20016
Phone: (202) 752- 6734

Recruiting

Please list the schools/types of schools at which you recruit.
• Ivy League schools
• Public state schools
• Historically black colleges and universities (HBCUs)
• Hispanic serving institutions (HSIs)

Do you have any special outreach efforts directed to encourage minority students to consider your firm?
• *Conferences:* NSHMBA, NBMBA
• Participate in/host minority student job fair(s)
• Firm's employees participate on career panels at school
• Scholarships or intern/fellowships for minority students

What activities does the firm undertake to attract minority and women employees?
• Conferences
• Participate at minority job fairs
• Seek referrals from other employees
• Utilize online job services

Do you use executive recruiting/search firms to seek to identify new diversity hires?
Yes

Internships and Co-ops

D.C. Public High School Program
Deadline for application: June 1st
Number of interns in the program in summer 2006 (internship) or 2006 (co-op): 10

Pay: Minimum wage

Length of the program: Eight weeks

Percentage of interns/co-ops in the program who receive offers of full-time employment: None; it is for work experience in corporate.

Drexel Co-op Program
Deadline for application: July 1st and January 1st
Number of interns in the program: Four (two fall, two spring)
Length of program: Six months
Percentage of co-ops in the program who receive offers for full-time employment: 20 percent

Scholarships

MBA Scholarship
Deadline for application for the scholarship program: February 15th
Scholarship award amount: $2,000

Seeking MBA intern interested in housing finance and minority home ownership; first-year MBA with strong finance skills; strong academic performance; recommendation from professor and personal recommendation.

Affinity Groups

Fannie Mae has several affinity groups all intended to foster a culture in which employees recognize and appreciate the diversity of their co-workers. The groups are employee led and are encouraged to raise any issues and concerns to leadership. The employee networks include groups for those who identify themselves as the following:

• African-American

- Asian Pacific
- Catholic
- Christian Salt and Light
- Corporate alumni
- Foreign national
- Hispanic
- Hindu
- Jewish
- Gay/Lesbian/Bisexual/Transgender
- Muslim
- Parents and guardians with children with special needs
- Single parent
- Women

Entry-Level Programs, Full-Time Opportunities and Training Programs

Analyst Program

Length of program: 24 months

Geographic location(s) of program: Primarily D.C. or Bethesda, Md.

Internal Audit

Length of program: Full-time opportunities (MBA only)

Geographic location(s) of program: Washington, D.C.

This program provides on-the-job training and mentoring from internal audit and staff leaders.

Research Analyst Program

Length of program: Three month apprenticeship

Geographic location(s) of program: Washington, D.C.

Applicants typically have a liberal arts background

Enterprise Management System Program

Length of program: 24 months

Geographic location(s) of program: Reston, Va. and Urbana, Md.

Controllers

Length of program: Full-time opportunities

Geographic location(s) of program: Washington, D.C.

This program provides on-the-job training and mentoring from finance staff and leaders.

Strategic Plan and Diversity Leadership

How does the firm's leadership communicate the importance of diversity to everyone at the firm?

We have an office of diversity and they are responsible for many programs that promote a diverse work environment. Fannie Mae is very committed to the minority home ownership challenges and our business is providing liquidity to the mortgage finance market so that more lenders can offer loans to potential home buyers. We set minority home ownership goals each year. Every employee of Fannie Mae appreciates and contributes to that mission every day in the work they do.

Does your firm currently have a diversity committee?

Yes

If yes, does the committee's representation include one or more members of the firm's management/executive committee (or the equivalent)?

Yes

Does the committee and/or diversity leader establish and set goals or objectives consistent with management's priorities?

Yes. Diversity is one of 10 core commitments essential to our success.

Has the firm undertaken a formal or informal diversity program or set of initiatives aimed at increasing the diversity of the firm?

Yes, formal. We have an office of diversity whose primary mission is to foster a diverse culture and environment through policies, programs, thought leadership and partnerships. Our recruiting efforts are very focused on diversity efforts and we partner with many constituents both internally and externally to be successful in attracting a diverse workforce to Fannie Mae.

How often does the firm's management review the firm's diversity progress/results?

Quarterly

The Stats

2006 Employees: 5,800 (U.S.)

Retention and Professional Development

Please identify the specific steps you are taking to reduce the attrition rate of minority and women employees.

• Develop and/or support internal employee affinity groups (e.g., minority or women networks within the firm)

• Increase/improve current work/life programs

• Succession plan includes emphasis on diversity

• Strengthen mentoring program for all employees, including minorities and women

• Professional skills development program, including minority and women employees

• *Other:* Training class on diversity

Diversity Mission Statement

As a corporation, Fannie Mae is guided by a set of values that permeates the way we conduct our business. Honesty, integrity and respect for others must be central to everything we do. Just as they are at the core of the way we do business, these values are permanent.

In keeping with these values, our corporate philosophy on diversity is based on respect for one another and recognition that each person brings his or her own unique attributes to the corporation. We are committed to providing equal opportunity for all employees to reach their full potential; it is a fundamental value, and it makes good business sense. Fannie Mae will be most successful in meeting its public mission and our corporate goals when we fully capitalize on the skills, talents and potential of all our employees.

Fannie Mae's approach to diversity is based on a two-tiered business rationale driven by our mission to tear down barriers, lower costs and increase the opportunities for home ownership and rental housing for all Americans. By this we mean that we designed the program to create opportunities for all employees internally, which in turn empowers employees to create opportunities for all Americans externally. The reason we do this is simple: it makes good business sense, because it enables us to fulfill our mission. We must reflect the diversity of the society we serve in order to understand and address their home-buying needs.

FedEx

942 S. Shady Grove Road
Memphis, TN 38120
Phone: (901) 818-7500
Fax: (901) 395-2000
www.fedex.com

Diversity Leadership

Linda Carter
Manager Corporate Human Resources Support
FedEx Express
3660 Hacks Cross Road
Building F, 3rd Floor
Memphis, TN 38125
Phone: (901) 434-6182
Fax: (901) 434-6356
E-mail: lfcarter@fedex.com

Recruiting

Please list the schools/types of schools at which you recruit.

• Ivy League schools

• Other private schools

• Public state schools

• Historically black colleges and universities (HBCUs)

Do you have any special outreach efforts directed to encourage minority students and graduates to consider your firm?

• Advertise in minority student association publication(s) or other minority-focused publications

• Participate in/host minority student job fair(s) or other minority-focused job events

• Sponsor minority student association events

• Firm's employees participate on career panels at school

• Outreach to leadership of minority student organizations

• Scholarships or intern/fellowships for minority students

What activities does the firm undertake to attract minority and women employees?

• Partner programs with women and minority associations

• Participate at minority job fairs

• Seek referrals from other employees

• Utilize online job services

Do you use executive recruiting/search firms to seek to identify new diversity hires?

No

Internships and Co-ops

FedEx Express

Deadline for application: None

Number of interns in the program in summer 2006 (internship) or 2006 (co-op): 93

Pay: $2,755 per month

Length of the program: 10 to 12 weeks

Percentage of interns/co-ops in the program who receive offers of full-time employment: 7 percent in 2006

Departments that hire interns:

• Air operations

• Engineering

• Finance

• Human resources

• International

• Legal

• U.S. operations

Participants must be in undergraduate or graduate school.

Affinity Groups

Asian Network Group

Mission/Purpose: To promote cultural awareness, education and information regarding Asians at FedEx to ensure inclusion of all employees

• Web site—via the diversity web site homepage (Intranet)

• Meets monthly/quarterly

- Sponsors/co-sponsors at least one corporate diversity forum with CCA annually

- Partners with Dress for Success to provide resources to women in the community (i.e., cell phone drive, clothing, etc.)

African American Network Group

Mission/Purpose: To promote cultural awareness, education and information regarding African-Americans at FedEx to ensure inclusion of all employees

- Meets monthly/quarterly

- Web site—via the diversity web site homepage (Intranet)

- Sponsors/co-sponsors at least one corporate diversity forum with CCA annually

- Serve as mentors via Memphis City Schools Mentoring Program

- Sponsors INROADS talent interviewing session annually

Hispanic Network Group

Mission/Purpose: To promote cultural awareness, education and information regarding Hispanics at FedEx to ensure inclusion of all employees

- Web site—via the diversity web site homepage (Intranet)

- Meets monthly/quarterly

- Sponsors/co-sponsors at least one corporate diversity forum with CCA annually

Women's Network Group

Mission/Purpose: To promote cultural awareness, education and information regarding women's issues at FedEx to ensure inclusion of all employees

- Meets monthly/quarterly

- Web site— via the diversity web site homepage (Intranet)

- Sponsors/co-sponsors at least one corporate diversity forum with CCA annually

Lesbian, Gay, Bisexual, Transgender (LGBT) and Friends Network Group

Mission/Purpose: To promote cultural awareness, education and information regarding GLBT issues at FedEx to ensure inclusion of all employees

- Meets monthly/quarterly

- Web site—via the diversity website homepage (Intranet)

- Sponsors at least one corporate diversity event with CCA annually

- Each network group operates as a separate entity. Each group has a chairperson and other group officer positions as needed.

Strategic Plan and Diversity Leadership

What trends in your industry affect your corporate diversity goals, strategies and/or internal or external alliances?

As a global leader in the transportation industry, we continue to look for opportunities to attract, retain and development top talent. Global trends that may impact our corporate goals include, but are not limited to the following:

- Increased minority representation (i.e., more Spanish-speaking employees)

- Work/life balance and competitive pay and benefits

- Four generations in the workplace

- Globalization—people able to move around more freely. Adds value to the business; it means there is no longer a majority ethnic group in any area

How does the firm's leadership communicate the importance of diversity to everyone at the firm?

E-mails, web site, quarterly diversity newsletters, forums for affinity groups, meetings, etc.

Who has primary responsibility for leading diversity initiatives at your firm?

Linda Carter, manager corporate human resources support, affirmative action and diversity

Does your firm currently have a diversity committee?

Yes

If yes, please describe how the committee is structured, how often it meets, etc.

The VP Diversity Committee is made up of 13 FedEx Express executives and they meet bimonthly. Each operating company has its own diversity committee, including FedEx corporate.

If yes, does the committee's representation include one or more members of the firm's management/executive committee (or the equivalent)?

Yes

If yes, how many executives are on the committee and how often does the committee convene in furtherance of the firm's diversity initiatives?

Total Executives on Committee: 13 executives

Bimonthly meetings; approximately 2.5 hours in length. Additional hours spent via communication media and attendance at various diversity functions.

Does the committee and/or diversity leader establish and set goals or objectives consistent with management's priorities?

Yes. The committee sets diversity performance objectives for managers and reviews/recommends diversity-related initiatives (i.e., recruitment) as needed.

Has the firm undertaken a formal or informal diversity program or set of initiatives aimed at increasing the diversity of the firm?

Yes, formal. These aim to:

• Develop strategies that attract, promote and retain diverse talent at all levels of the corporation

• Create the best work environment for diverse groups through programs, services and benefits enhancements

• Educate and raise awareness about diversity at FedEx

• Support the use of diverse suppliers

• Promote FedEx as a neighbor and employer of choice by enhancing its image through community outreach programs and internal and external communication strategies

• Support the development and implementation of marketing strategies aimed at diverse customers

• Develop corporate diversity strategies, programs and goals and ensure that the corporation accomplishes its diversity objectives

How often does the firm's management review the firm's diversity progress/results?

Bimonthly

How is the firm's diversity committee and/or firm management held accountable for achieving results?

The VP Diversity Council has annual objectives tied to diversity initiatives for FedEx. In addition, managers have diversity-related objectives that are tied to their annual incentives.

The Stats

Note: Fiscal year is June through May. Revenues are reported for fiscal years FY05, year ended May 2005, and FY06, year ended May 2006.

	REVENUE	
	2006	2005
Total worldwide	$32,294 million	$29,363 million

Retention and Professional Development

How do 2006 minority and female attrition rates generally compare to those experienced in the prior year period?

About the same as in prior years.

Please identify the specific steps you are taking to reduce the attrition rate of minority and women employees.

• Develop and/or support internal employee affinity groups (e.g., minority or women networks within the firm)

• Increase/review compensation relative to competition

• Increase/improve current work/life programs

• Adopt dispute resolution process

• Succession plan includes emphasis on diversity

• Work with minority and women employees to develop career advancement plans

• Professional skills development program, including minority and women employees

Diversity Mission Statement

Our diverse workforce, supplier base and supporting culture enable FedEx to better serve our customers and compete more effectively in the global marketplace. We value the contributions and perspectives of all employees regardless of race, gender, culture, religion, age, nationality, disability or sexual orientation. We will strive in our workplace practices to deal with our employees, customers and suppliers in a fair and ethical manner.

Additional Information

We continue to be viewed as innovators and trendsetters in the business world and are often asked to share our progressive systems, programs and philosophies that have earned us our reputation as an employer of choice. FedEx has earned recognition as one of the World's Most Admired Companies (*Fortune* magazine). Other national awards include:

• 50 Best Companies for Minorities to Work—*Fortune* magazine

• America's Most Admired Companies—*Fortune* magazine

• World's Most Admired Companies—*Fortune* magazine

- 100 Best Companies for Working Mothers—*Working Mother* magazine

- 50 Best Companies in America for Asians, Blacks and Hispanics—*Fortune* magazine

- 20 Better Places to Work—*Mother Jones* magazine

- Outstanding Corporate Support Award—National Minority Business Council

- Award for Excellence in Corporate Community Services—Points of Light Foundation

- The Top 100 Companies Providing the Most Opportunities for Hispanics—*Hispanic* magazine

- Diversity 100 Recognition Award—*Next Step* magazine

Fidelity Investments

82 Devonshire Street
Boston, MA 02109
Phone: (617) 563-7000

Locations

Boston, MA (HQ)
Eight regional centers in the US and
Canada, and investor centers in more
than 91 US cities.

International locations include: Canada •
France • Germany • Hong Kong • India •
Ireland • Japan • UK

Employment Contact

Kim DiNicola
College Relations Director
82 Devonshire Street
Boston, MA 02109
Phone: (617) 563-8537
Fax: (617) 385-1457
E-mail: kim.dinicola@fmr.com
www.fidelitycareers.com

Recruiting

Please list the schools/types of schools at which you recruit.

• Ivy League schools
• Other private schools:
• Public state schools:
• Other predominantly minority and/or women's colleges

Do you have any special outreach efforts directed to encourage minority students to consider your firm?

• Advertise in minority student association publication(s)
• Participate in/host minority student job fair(s)
• Firm's employees participate on career panels at school

What activities does the firm undertake to attract minority and women employees?

• Partner programs with women and minority associations
• Participate at minority job fairs
• Seek referrals from other employees
• Utilize online job services

Do you use executive recruiting/search firms to seek to identify new diversity hires?

Yes

Internships and Co-ops

Fidelity Intern/Co-op Program
Deadline for application: April
Length of the program: 12 weeks
Percentage of interns/co-ops in the program who receive offers of full-time employment: 6 percent
Web site for internship/co-op information:
www.fidelitycareers.com

Qualifications for the Fidelity Intern/Co-op Program vary depending on the assignment.

The Stats

	NUMBER OF EMPLOYEES
	2005
Total in the U.S.	37,000
Total outside the U.S.	3,000
Total worldwide	40,000

Fifth Third Bancorp

38 Fountain Sq. Plaza
Fifth Third Center
Cincinnati, OH 45263
Phone: (513) 579-5300
Fax: (513) 534-0629
Toll Free: (800) 972-3030
www.53.com

Locations

Georgia • Florida • Indiana • Illinois •
Kentucky • Michigan • Missouri • Ohio •
Pennsylvania • Tennessee • West Virginia

Employment Contact

Vickie Mc Mullen, Campus Relations Leader
38 Fountain Square Plaza
Cincinnati, OH 45263
Phone: (513) 534-6264
Fax: (513) 534-4950
E-mail: vickie.mcmullen@53.com
www.53.com

Recruiting

Please list the schools/types of schools at which you recruit.

• *Private schools:* Xavier University (Ohio) and the University of Dayton (Ohio)

• *Public state schools:* University of Cincinnati, Ohio State University, Northern Kentucky University, Michigan State University, University of Illinois, Miami University of Ohio, Case Western Reserve University and other regional universities.

• *Historically black colleges and universities (HBCUs):* Wilberforce University, Florida A&M University

Do you have any special outreach efforts directed to encourage minority students to consider your firm?

• Sponsor Networking Receptions for minority students

• *Conferences:* National Black MBA, National Society of Hispanic MBAs

• Sponsor minority student association events

• Firm's employees participate on career panels at school

• Outreach to leadership of minority student organizations

• *Other:* Participate in the INROADS program; corporate sponsorship (local chapters)—National Association of Black Accountants and National Society of Hispanic MBAs

What activities does the firm undertake to attract minority and women employees?

• Partner programs with women and minority associations

• Participate at minority job fairs

• Seek referrals from other employees

• Utilize online job services: Post job opportunities on web sites targeting minorities

Do you use executive recruiting/search firms to seek to identify new diversity hires?

Yes

If yes, list all women- and/or minority-owned executive search/recruiting firms to which the firm paid a fee for placement services in the past 12 months:

We use majority-owned firms, but demand diverse slates of candidates.

Internships and Co-ops

Deadline for applications to internship/co-op program: We follow campus deadlines for applications for co-ops and interns.

Number of interns in the program in summer 2006 (internship) or 2006 (co-op): 20 interns

Pay: $12.00 to $14.00 an hour

Length of the program: Eight weeks

Percentage of interns/co-ops in the program who receive offers of full-time employment: 80 percent

A college recruiting web site is being developed that will provide internship/co-op information.

Co-ops and internship opportunities currently exist in: audit, finance, IT, tax, operations and asset management.

Applicants must have a GPA of 3.0 or above and a major in accounting, finance, IT, operation management or marketing. Additional desired characteristics include strong analytical skills, the ability to work in a team environment, good PC skills and good oral and written communication skills.

Affinity Groups

• Women's Network (Cincinnati, Cleveland, Columbus, Detroit, Grand Rapids, Tennessee, Naples)

• African American Network (Cincinnati, Cleveland, Toledo, Louisville, Indianapolis, Chicago, Detroit, Grand Rapids, Tennessee, Cincinnati, Tampa)

• Hispanic Network (Chicago, Detroit, Grand Rapids, Tampa)

• GLBT (Cincinnati, Detroit)

The affinity groups' purpose is to act as support networks, and to encourage and provide opportunities for professional development through mentors, seminars and networking. Meetings are held once a month.

Entry-Level Programs, Full-Time Opportunities and Training Programs

Programs offered:

• Commercial Associate Program

• Financial Leadership Program

• IT Leadership Program

• Operations Associate Program

• Retail Associate Program

Length of program: Varies from six to 24 months

Other opportunities:

• Financial auditors

• IT auditors

• Tax analysts

Geographic location(s) of program: Cincinnati only, with the exception of the Retail Associate Program which is available in most of our affiliate locations.

These programs demonstrate business practices, operations and procedures in each department rotation, acquiring the knowledge and skills and experience required for assuming a permanent role. All programs provide classroom and on-the-job training.

Fifth Third Bank offers classroom and online professional development courses for knowledge and skill development.

Tuition reimbursement is offered as a benefit for all employees.

Strategic Plan and Diversity Leadership

How does the firm's leadership communicate the importance of diversity to everyone at the firm?

The firm's leadership communicates diversity through its web site, company newsletters and the diversity board.

Who has primary responsibility for leading diversity initiatives at your firm?

Ed Owens, senior vice president, diversity and community affairs

Does your firm currently have a diversity committee?

Yes. The board meets on a bimonthly basis and is divided into four key committees.

If yes, does the committee's representation include one or more members of the firm's management/executive committee (or the equivalent)?

Yes

If yes, how many executives are on the committee?

Total Executives on Committee: 10

Does the committee and/or diversity leader establish and set goals or objectives consistent with management's priorities?

Yes. The purpose of the board is to insure strategic success on diversity priorities.

Has the firm undertaken a formal or informal diversity program or set of initiatives aimed at increasing the diversity of the firm?

Yes, formal

How often does the firm's management review the firm's diversity progress/results?

Quarterly

How is the firm's diversity committee and/or firm management held accountable for achieving results?

Each EVP and affiliate president is responsible for achieving success as laid out by the diversity plan. The plan has one objective affecting compensation.

Retention and Professional Development

How do 2006 minority and female attrition rates generally compare to those experienced in the prior year period?

About the same as in prior years.

Please identify the specific steps you are taking to reduce the attrition rate of minority and women employees.

• Develop and/or support internal employee affinity groups (e.g., minority or women networks within the firm)

• Increase/review compensation relative to competition

• Increase/improve current work/life programs

• Succession plan includes emphasis on diversity

• Work with minority and women employees to develop career advancement plans

Diversity Mission Statement

Fifth Third Bank has a strong commitment to respect each individual and value every employee's personal contribution to the business. At Fifth Third Bank, we create an environment where everyone can be fully engaged, leaving no one out. We value diversity as an asset and will provide an environment where all individuals can maximize their potential for development.

Additional Information

All affiliates and lines of business have diversity plans. These plans have clear and measurable goals and focus on key initiatives to support long-term results, particularly in the key areas of recruitment, retention, advancement and promotion. Each line of business and affiliate has its own plan so that there is a common level of expectation and performance.

FirstEnergy Corporation

76 South Main St
Akron, OH 44308
Corporate Reception Desk: (330) 761
 7897
www.firstenergycorp.com

Locations

Various locations throughout Ohio,
Pennsylvania and New Jersey.

Diversity Leadership

Deborah Sergi
Director, Talent Management

Employment Contact

Renee A. Spino
Manager, Recruiting

Recruiting

Please list the schools/types of schools at which you recruit.

• Public state schools

• Historically black colleges and universities (HBCUs)

Do you have any special outreach efforts directed to encourage minority students to consider your firm?

• Advertise in minority student association publication(s)

• Participate in/host minority student job fair(s)

• Sponsor minority student association events

• *Other:* Source students through INROADS

What activities does the firm undertake to attract minority and women employees?

• Partner programs with women and minority associations

• Participate at minority job fairs

• Seek referrals from other employees

• Utilize online job services

Do you use executive recruiting/search firms to seek to identify new diversity hires?

Yes

Internships and Co-ops

Co-op/Internship Professional Development Program

Deadline for application: We offer various co-op/internship opportunities year round. All open positions are posted on the company's web site.

Number of interns in the program in summer 2006 (internship) or 2006 (co-op): 116 co-ops/interns during summer 2006; 189 co-ops/interns during all of 2006.

Number of interns in the program in summer 2007: 158

Pay: $12.20 to $25 per hour. Compensation is dependent on the student's major, number of quarters/semesters of school completed and number of previous work sessions at FirstEnergy. Relocation and paid corporate housing is provided to students who meet company qualifications.

Length of the program: There are three sessions per year.

Percentage of interns/co-ops in the program who receive offers of full-time employment: Our conversion goal in 2006 was 55 percent.

Web site for internship/co-op information:
www.firstenergycorp.com/employment

To staff the FirstEnergy Co-op/Internship Professional Development Program, we hire students who are enrolled in a major applicable to FirstEnergy's business (such as engineering, computer/IT, finance and management) and who have a 2.5 overall grade point average or above. The largest business units employing co-ops/interns include Engineering, Finance, IT, and Supply Chain. Business units provide challenging work assignments that are related to the students' majors. We also source students through INROADS.

FirstEnergy participates in the Third Frontier Internship Program, sponsored by Governor Bob Taft in 2002, which is the state of Ohio's initiative designed to attract talented students from Ohio to remain in high-tech jobs in Ohio. Students who are Ohio residents and are enrolled in a high-tech curriculum containing mathematics, science, and engineering are eligible for the Third Frontier Internship Program once they complete their second year of school. The program reimburses FirstEnergy up to $3,000 per student.

Affinity Groups

A Young Professionals Group exists to maintain a spirit of cooperation and good fellowship among the employees by promoting, developing, and carrying out social, recreational, educational and service activities for members.

Entry-Level Programs, Full-Time Opportunities and Training Programs

Students who participate in the Co-op/Intern Professional Development Program attend development sessions designed to help students improve their skills in areas that are important for success at FirstEnergy, such as personal productivity, effective business writing, working with multigenerations, and more. In addition, students participate in a coaching/mentoring relationship where they are mentored by experienced employees who help them better understand FirstEnergy and its career opportunities, while also providing guidance and support throughout the students' work experiences to enhance their professional development. Students also participate in the performance management process where clear performance objectives and development goals are established. Prior to the end of each work session, students review a performance evaluation.

As part of the employee onboarding process, all new employees at FirstEnergy are provided with a "buddy" who assists with acclimating them to FirstEnergy, their department/business unit, and their specific work location.

Full-time entry-level engineers participate in a Rotation of Assignment Program, which provides them with experience in different engineering functions. The program provides engineers with on-the-job training, as well as technical and professional development classroom training. Upon completion of the program, engineers are placed in open positions based on interest, skills, and business needs, in one of the areas through which they formerly rotated.

The finance and IT departments also have Rotation of Assignment Programs designed to give participants experience in multiple areas of the respective disciplines. Upon completion of the program, employees are placed in open positions based on interest, skill, and business needs, in one of the areas through which they formerly rotated.

Strategic Plan and Diversity Leadership

What trends in your industry affect your corporate diversity goals, strategies and/or internal or external alliances?

Within the next five to 10 years, approximately half of FirstEnergy's workforce will be eligible for retirement. Attracting and retaining top minority and female talent in a technical industry will be critical for staffing hiring needs, especially as external competition for talent increases.

How does the firm's leadership communicate the importance of diversity to everyone at the firm?

"Respect Differences" is one of FirstEnergy's critical success factors. All non-bargaining unit employees will be rated on this beginning midyear 2007.

The strategic vision statement on the corporate web site includes the following statement that expresses FirstEnergy's commitment to diversity:

FirstEnergy will be a leading regional energy provider, recognized for operational excellence and customer service; the choice for long-term growth, investment value and financial strength; and a company committed to safety and driven by the leadership, skills, diversity and character of its employees.

Who has primary responsibility for leading diversity initiatives at your firm?

Director of Talent Management, Deborah Sergi

Does your firm currently have a diversity committee?

Yes. FirstEnergy has a Workforce Planning and Diversity Steering Committee. This committee, which meets monthly, is comprised of vice presidents and directors from various business units that meet monthly.

If yes, does the committee's representation include one or more members of the firm's management/executive committee (or the equivalent)?

Yes

If yes, how many executives are on the committee, and in 2006, what was the total number of hours collectively spent by the committee in furtherance of the firm's diversity initiatives? How many employees are on the committee, and how often does the committee convene in furtherance of the firm's diversity initiatives?

The committee meets monthly and discusses strategic staffing initiatives, including ways to attract and retain qualified minority and female talent. Collectively, the committee members, comprised of ten executives, invested approximately 20 hours each in 2006.

Does the committee and/or diversity leader establish and set goals or objectives consistent with management's priorities?

Yes

Has the firm undertaken a formal or informal diversity program or set of initiatives aimed at increasing the diversity of the firm?

Yes, "Diversity & Inclusion" and "Working with Multiple Generations" classes are offered to all employees.

How often does the firm's management review the firm's diversity progress/results?

Quarterly

The Stats

	NUMBER OF EMPLOYEES	REVENUE
	2005	2005
Total in the U.S.	14, 152	$11.989 million

2006 DEMOGRAPHIC PROFILE	
Minority	10 percent

Retention and Professional Development

How do 2006 minority and female attrition rates generally compare to those experienced in the prior year period?

Minority and female attrition remained steady in 2006.

Please identify the specific steps you are taking to reduce the attrition rate of minority and women employees.

At FirstEnergy, we:

• Engage in succession planning, with an emphasis on identifying high performing/high potential females and minorities

• Encourage mentoring relationships for high performing/high potential females and minorities

• Provide high performing minorities with development opportunities (e.g. - Executive Leadership Council's Institute for Leadership Development and Research)

• Offer professional skills development programs, including women's leadership initiatives

• Include managing diversity in new supervisor training

• Offer diversity and inclusion training classes as well as online training classes

Interns and co-ops participate in a coaching relationship where students are mentored by experienced employees who help them better understand FirstEnergy and its career opportunities, while also providing guidance and support throughout the students' work experiences. New hires at FirstEnergy are provided with an individual or "buddy" who can assist them in becoming acclimated to FirstEnergy, their individual department and business unit, and their specific work or reporting location. By doing so, a personal connection between the organization and the new employee is established the first day, which also assists the onboarding process.

Additional Information

We continually participate in salary surveys to ensure that employees are paid competitively and have a team that is reviewing our work life programs for enhancements. Additionally, FirstEnergy has a dispute resolution program and internal harassment/discrimination process that all employees can utilize without fear of retaliation. FirstEnergy provides numerous professional skills development programs across the company for all employees.

FPL Group, Inc.

700 Universe Boulevard
Juno Beach, FL 33408
Phone: (561) 694-4000
Fax: (561) 694-4620
www.fplgroup.com

Locations

Various cities in Florida and other cities in the US.

Diversity Leadership

Yolanda Cornell
Manager of EEO & Diversity

Employment Contact

Maritza Castano
College Recruiter
9520 W. Flagler Street
Miami, FL 33174
Phone: (305) 552-3348
Fax: (305) 552-3999
E-mail: maritza_castano@fpl.com

Recruiting

Please list the schools/types of schools at which you recruit.

• Ivy League schools

• Other private schools

• Public state schools

• Historically black colleges and universities (HBCUs)

Do you have any special outreach efforts directed to encourage minority students to consider your firm?

• *Conferences:* SWE, NSBE, NSHMBA, NSBMBA, AABE

• Sponsor minority student association events

What activities does the firm undertake to attract minority and women employees?

• *Conferences* (see above)

• Seek referrals from other employees

Do you use executive recruiting/search firms to seek to identify new diversity hires?

No

Internships and Co-ops

Internship Program

Number of interns in the program in summer 2006 (internship) or 2006 (co-op): 157

Pay: $870 to $1672 biweekly

Length of the program: Approximately 12 weeks

Web site for internship/co-op information: www.fpl.com

Interns are hired throughout the company in various different business units. Approximately 90 percent of the interns are in the engineering field. Qualifications usually entail working towards a relevant degree in the area of the internship and successful completion of a screening interview.

Entry-Level Programs, Full-Time Opportunities and Training Programs

Full-time new hires

Geographic location(s) of program: Various cities in Southeast Florida

The company provides tuition reimbursement for graduate and undergraduate degrees as well as on-the-job training.

Strategic Plan and Diversity Leadership

Who has primary responsibility for leading diversity initiatives at your firm?

Yolanda Cornell, manager of EEO and diversity

Does the committee and/or diversity leader establish and set goals or objectives consistent with management's priorities?

Yes

Has the firm undertaken a formal or informal diversity program or set of initiatives aimed at increasing the diversity of the firm?

Yes, formal. We have a team of diversity professionals whose main goal is to concentrate on minority recruiting and meet the guidelines of hiring minorities.

The Stats

Revenue
2006: $15.7 billion

Retention and Professional Development

How do 2006 minority and female attrition rates generally compare to those experienced in the prior year period?

About the same as in prior years.

Please identify the specific steps you are taking to reduce the attrition rate of minority and women employees.

• Increase/improve current work/life programs

• Succession plan includes emphasis on diversity

• Work with minority and women employees to develop career advancement plans

• Professional skills development program, including minority and women employees

Diversity Mission Statement

We will foster an inclusive business environment that values and leverages the diverse talents, perspectives and ideas of all employees.

Our employees all have something in common. Imagination.

GE employees are as diverse as our products and services. That's because we bring together the best imaginations from diverse people. We're 300,000 minds operating in 100 countries, making over 25,000 products. Without diversity, we just wouldn't be GE.

GE is proud to support and share in INROADS commitment to promoting diversity in the workplace.

To learn more, visit ge.com

 imagination at work

GE

3135 Easton Turnpike
Fairfield, CT 06828-0001
Phone: (203) 373-2211
Fax: (203) 373-3131
www.gecareers.com

Locations
100 countries

Employment Contacts
Judy Mebane
Manager, Diversity Recruiting
3135 Easton Turnpike
Fairfield, CT 06828
Phone: (203) 373-3771
Fax: (203) 373-3292
E mail: judy.mebane@ge.com

Recruiting

Please list the schools/types of schools at which you recruit.

• Ivy League schools

• Other private schools

• Public state schools

• Predominantly minority and/or women's colleges

GE actively recruits from over 100 schools across the U.S. with a focus on 40 executive schools. GE hires approximately 1,000 undergraduate, master's and PhD students each year in the U.S., and nearly an equal number outside the U.S.

Do you have any special outreach efforts that are directed to encourage minority students to consider your firm?

• Hold a reception for minority students

• *Conferences:* Consortium, INROADS, NSBE, SHPE, NBMBA, NSHMBA, SWE

• Advertise in minority student association publication(s)

• Participate in/host minority student job fair(s)

• Sponsor minority student association events

• Firm's employees participate on career panels at school

• Outreach to leadership of minority student organizations

• Scholarships or intern/fellowships for minority students

• *Other:* Jackie Robinson Foundation, National Action Council for Minorities in Engineering

What activities does the firm undertake to attract minority and women employees?

• Partner programs with women and minority associations

• *Conferences:* Consortium, INROADS, NSBE, SHPE, NBMBA, NSHMBA, SWE

• Participate at minority job fairs

• Seek referrals from other employees

• Utilize online job services

• *Other:* GE is a founding member of many of the organizations listed above. GE actively strives to recruit the best and brightest college students from all ethnic backgrounds.

Do you use executive recruiting/search firms to seek to identify new diversity hires?

No, not for entry-level college and MBA recruiting.

Internships and Co-ops

GE Early Identification (EID)

Deadline for application: Continuous

Number of interns in the program in summer 2006 (internship) or 2006 (co-op): 2,400

Pay: Varies by degree and college year

Length of the program: Typically 10 to 12 weeks

Percentage of interns/co-ops in the program who receive offers of full-time employment: 50 percent of those eligible (graduating seniors)

Web site for internship/co-op information: gecareers.com

Other qualifications for the GE Early Identification program:

• GPA minimum 3.0 (cumulative)

• Looking for bright students with demonstrated academic success, leadership skills and willingness to learn and grow professionally.

Scholarships

All scholarship inquiries should be directed to the GE Foundation. The foundation provides scholarships to NSBE, Jackie Robinson, SWE, NBMBA and Consortium scholars, to name a few.

Affinity Groups

- African-American Forum
- Asian Pacific American Forum
- Gay, Lesbian, Bisexual and Transgender Alliance
- Hispanic Forum
- Women's Network

The purpose of all affinity groups is to provide an organization that can provide coaching, networking and career advancement opportunities to its membership.

Entry-Level Programs, Full-Time Opportunities and Training Programs

Commercial Leadership Program (CLP)

As part of our strategy to achieve commercial excellence and drive organic growth, we are developing a pipeline of strong marketing and sales leaders at GE through the Commercial Leadership Program (CLP). CLP offers a core curriculum that fosters the development of commercial skills and techniques that are critical to success in all GE businesses. The structure, duration and additional training are determined at the business level to meet their specific development and industry needs. Although the approach may vary by business, the end result is the same—CLP prepares candidates for a successful career in sales or marketing by providing the opportunity to learn about our products, industry and customers while making valuable contributions to the organization.

Edison Engineering Development Program (EEDP)

EEDP is a total development program—participants bring the passion for technology, and EEDP supplies technical training and projects to excel on a world-class team. EEDP increases participants' technical problem-solving skills through advanced courses in engineering and real-life business experience.

EEDP is a two-year, entry-level program providing three or more rotational assignments. All assignments are engineering projects driven by real GE business priorities.

Diverse experiences may include systems, analysis, design, quality, reliability, integration and test technical problem-solving skills developed via advanced engineering coursework, formal reports and presentations to senior leadership.

Participants in the program will gain business skills developed in corporate leadership courses. They will also have the opportunity to earn credit towards a MS degree in engineering and in real-world application technology

Candidate Criteria:

- Passion for technology
- Demonstrated academic excellence
- Commitment to technology and quality
- Strong analytical, problem-solving and communication skills
- Engineering degree and relevant internship/co-op experience preferred
- Minimum GPA 3.0/4.0

Experienced Commercial Leadership Program (ECLP)

The Experienced Commercial Leadership Program (ECLP) accelerates the development of commercial-savvy talent through a structured program combining coursework, job assignments and interactive seminars.

ECLP is a two-year program consisting of four six-month, cross-segment rotational assignments within the commercial function of a GE business. Two rotations are marketing focused and two are sales focused. Program participants strengthen their commercial, business and leadership skills by completing an intensive curriculum consisting of eight weeks of classroom training, online training and in-residence global symposiums. International rotations are available based on performance and availability.

Candidate Criteria:

- Bachelor's degree with four to six years marketing or sales experience
- Demonstrated leadership, communication and analytical skills
- Geographic mobility
- MBA with two to four years marketing or sales experience
- Second language preferred (English required)
- Unrestricted work authorization in the United States, EMEA, China or Japan

Financial Management Program (FMP)

FMP is widely considered to be the premier program of its kind. It is the first step in many successful GE management careers. This intensive two-year, entry-level program spans four rotational assignments.

Hands-on experience may include:

- Accounting
- Auditing
- Commercial finance
- Financial planning
- Forecasting
- Operations analysis
- Six Sigma quality
- Treasury/cash management

The program combines coursework, job assignments and interactive seminars to equip you with exceptional technical, financial and busi-

ness skills. It is led by senior GE professionals and mentors and develops world-class financial leaders for exciting positions.

Candidate Criteria:

- Minimum cumulative GPA of 3.0 (no rounding)
- Undergraduate degree only; no MBA or master's degree
- Less than one year full-time external work experience
- Demonstrated interest or competency in finance
- Mobility
- Preferred criteria
- Leadership experience
- Communication skills
- Finance or business-related internship
- Finance or business-related major

Human Resources Leadership Program (HRLP)

HRLP prepares participants for a dynamic role in the human dimension of GE. As a true business partner, HRLP participants' work influences the direction of our company. HRLP accelerates development through two HR assignments and one cross-functional role.

The two-year program consists of three challenging eight-month assignments. Each participant will develop broad business skills via hands-on experience in two HR assignments, plus a third assignment in an area such as finance, quality or business development.

Other skills that participants will acquire include:

- Formal classroom training in HR leadership and business skills and concepts
- Extensive contact with peers and senior business leaders from around the world
- Expansion of your knowledge base, critical problem-solving skills and professional network

Candidate Criteria:

- Demonstrated academic excellence, business acumen and leadership ability
- Self-confidence, strong analytic problem-solving skills and exceptional communication skills
- MBA/MA in business or an HR-related discipline plus several years work experience preferred
- Geographic flexibility and global mindset; able to operate across cultures

Information Management Leadership Program (IMLP)

IMLP puts information management careers on the fast track. Program graduates are in tremendous demand throughout GE. IMLP develops strong technical and project management skills through coursework and meaningful assignments. The two-year program consists of four six-month rotational assignments through different areas of a GE business.

On-the-job training in business dynamics, career strategies, communication skills, problem solving, decision-making and project leadership

Formal coursework in advanced information technology and systems, and their strategic application within GE

Develops strong technical foundation, project management skills and process knowledge that cuts across functions to support GE's boundless culture

Candidate Criteria:

- Strong interest in information technology applications
- Solid analytical abilities and sharp business acumen
- Bachelor's degree in computer science, information systems or computer engineering preferred; business degree or other related experience may be applicable

Operations Management Leadership Program (OMLP)

OMLP is an ideal entry point for engineers with the energy and drive to define and deliver world-class manufacturing processes, products and services. It is an intensive two-year, entry-level program with at least three rotational assignments.

Possible assignments include:

- Manufacturing shop operations
- Process engineering, Six Sigma quality
- Materials management
- Supply chain management
- Environmental health and safety
- Mentoring, teamwork, ongoing reviews and defined deliverables
- Technical training in contemporary manufacturing, global supply chain management, APICS certification, Six Sigma quality training, environmental health and safety
- Business training and challenging experience in project management, team leading, negotiation, manufacturing and finance

Candidate Criteria:

- Academic excellence, business acumen and leadership ability
- Strong communication and analytical problem-solving skills
- Geographic flexibility and global mindset; able to operate across cultures
- Degree in engineering or a technical discipline and relevant internship/co-op experience preferred
- Minimum GPA 3.0/4.0

Strategic Plan and Diversity Leadership

How does the firm's leadership communicate the importance of diversity to everyone at the firm?

The firm's leadership communicates diversity initiatives through e-mails, the web site, newsletters, meetings, etc.

Who has primary responsibility for leading diversity initiatives at your firm?

Deb Elam, manager, global employer of choice

Does your firm currently have a diversity committee?

Diversity is reviewed annually at all levels during GE's formal HR refer process referred to as "Session C."

Retention and Professional Development

How do 2006 minority and female attrition rates generally compare to those experienced in the prior year period?

About the same as in prior years.

Please identify the specific steps you are taking to reduce the attrition rate of minority and women employees.

The most important thing that GE does to retain all top talent is to provide them challenging and rewarding work. In addition, GE provides the tools and networks that give all employees an equal opportunity to grow and advance in their careers.

The Stats

	NUMBER OF EMPLOYEES		REVENUE	
	2006	2005	2006	2005
Total in the U.S.	155,000	161,000	N/A	N/A
Total worldwide	319,000	316,000	$163 billion	$147 billion

Diversity Mission Statement

Diversity and Inclusiveness

People are GE's greatest asset. With more than 300,000 people with jobs that range from biochemist to finance specialist to wind energy engineer, GE's employees are passionate about making life better with new ideas and technologies. They're also diverse, giving back to communities in more than 140 countries.

With operations all over the world, diversity is not just an ideal. It is our heritage and our mandate for success in the future. GE nurtures its diverse culture with inclusion and cross-cultural collaboration. We accomplish this through a series of forums that provide opportunity for networking, support, learning, and opportunity.

African American Forum

The AAF provides employees with mentors, seminars, networking, and career discussion. The forum also contributes to the development of local African-American communities.

Asian Pacific American Forum

The APAF supports the Asian Pacific American community with a career development network while promoting broader awareness of differences in Asian and American cultures.

Women's Network

The rapidly growing Women's Network supports the professional development of women around the world by sharing the wisdom of successful women role models.

Hispanic Forum

The Hispanic Forum supports coaching, mentoring, role modeling and the recruitment of Hispanic talent. It also reaches out to Hispanic communities with service and corporate sponsorships.

GLBT Alliance

GE's commitment to the Gay, Lesbian, Bisexual and Transgender communities is supported by the GLBT Alliance, as well as our offering of benefits for domestic partners.

Additional Information

Recent Awards:

• World's Most Admired Companies, *Fortune,* 2007

• America's Most Admired Companies, *Fortune,* 2007

• Best Companies for Leaders, *Chief Executive Magazine,* 2007

• Most Innovative Company, *BusinessWeek,* 2007

• Top 100 Global Brands, *Financial Times,* 2007

• World's Most Ethical Companies, *Ethisphere,* 2007

GEICO

One GEICO Plaza
Washington, DC 20076
Phone: (800) 824-5404
Human Resources: (301) 986-2802

Locations

Washington, DC (HQ)
Buffalo, NY • Coralville, IA • Dallas, TX •
Fredericksburg, VA • Honolulu, HI •
Lakeland, FL • Macon, GA • San Diego,
CA • Tucson, AZ • Virginia Beach, VA •
Woodbury, NY

Diversity Leadership

Thea Jenkins
Director of Minority Recruiting

Employment Contact

Malcolm Tucker
College Recruiting Manager
One GEICO Plaza
1CE-HR
Washington, DC 20076
Phone: (301) 986-2802
Fax: (301) 986-3092
E-mail: jobs@geico.com and
 DConcampus@geico.com

Career web site addresses:
www.geico.com/careers
www.geico.com/oncampus

Recruiting

Please list the schools/types of schools at which you recruit.

• Private schools
• Public state schools
• Community Colleges
• Historically black colleges and universities (HBCUs)
• Hispanic serving institutions (HSIs)

Visit our complete list of schools online at www.geico.com/oncampus/schools.

Do you have any special outreach efforts directed to encourage minority students to consider your firm?

• Hold a reception for minority students
• Advertise in minority student association publication(s)
• Participate in/host minority student job fair(s)
• Sponsor minority student association events
• Firm's employees participate on career panels at school
• Outreach to leadership of minority student organizations
• Scholarships or intern/fellowships for minority students

What activities does the firm undertake to attract minority and women employees?

• Partner programs with women and minority associations
• Participate at minority job fairs

• Seek referrals from other employees
• Utilize online job services

Do you use executive recruiting/search firms to seek to identify new diversity hires?
Yes

Scholarships

GEICO Achievement Award Program

Deadline for application for the program: Varies—offered throughout the spring and fall semesters

Achievement award amount: GEICO offers over $50,000 in Achievement Awards every year to students from across the country at targeted colleges and universities, and through specific student organizations. Each award is valued at $1,000.

Web site or other contact information for scholarship: The Achievement Award Program is available through various target schools and student organizations.

Applicants will be sophomores or juniors majoring in business, information technology, mathematics or related degree programs, possess at least a 3.0 overall GPA and have demonstrated leadership skills within his or her campus and/or community. Each applicant is required to fill out an application and submit it along with a resume, official transcript, essay and letter of recommendation from a faculty or staff member.

Entry-Level Programs, Full-Time Opportunities and Training Programs

Emerging Leaders Management Development Program Operations Management Track

This career track is well suited for finance, accounting, economics, marketing, risk management, management and general business majors.

Are you looking for a program that will utilize your degree and further develop your leadership ability? GEICO is looking for high potential graduates to join our selective Emerging Leaders Management Development Program.

As an emerging leader in the operations management track, you will have opportunities to make real contributions to GEICO's bottom line. You'll work one-on-one with your mentor, and interact with senior executives and all levels of associates. We'll teach you the ins and outs of our industry-leading company, while you gain hands-on leadership experience.

Throughout your program, you will have the great fortune to experience various aspects of our operations, including sales, customer service, claims, underwriting and planning. A typical day will depend on the discipline in which you are currently working!

During your sales rotation, we'll show you what it takes to sell a GEICO policy. After completing the classroom training and obtaining your insurance license, you will begin offering rate quotes and selling our exceptional line of products. In your customer service rotation, you'll learn how we keep millions of policyholders satisfied and what makes our service associates remarkable. Your rotation through claims will teach you how to help customers resolve their claims, investigate minor to major accidents, identify fraud and manage risk. Each rotation will include a chance for you to job shadow other associates, develop your employee coaching skills and work on special projects.

When you successfully finish your program, you'll be ready for a future with enormous potential! Our goal is to place you in a position of significant responsibility within our business operations.

Requirements:
- Bachelor's degree in business or related field
- Master's degree and MBA graduates are encouraged to apply
- At least a 3.5 overall undergraduate GPA
- Very good analytical and problem-solving skills
- Effective written and verbal communication skills
- Demonstrated leadership experience
- High level of dependability
- Desire to one day become a manager
- Willingness to relocate

Emerging leaders in the operations management track work in our regional offices, including San Diego, Calif.; Woodbury, N.Y.; Buffalo, N.Y.; Fredericksburg, Va.; Virginia Beach, Va.; Dallas, Texas; Lakeland, Fla.; Macon, Ga.; and Tucson, Ariz.

Emerging Leaders Management Development Program Information Technology Track

This career track is well suited for computer science, computer engineering and information systems majors.

Are you graduating with a technical degree, but looking for a company that will help develop you into a business leader? If you answered yes, then our Emerging Leaders Program may be a great place for you to start your career!

As an emerging leader in the information technology track, you'll make real contributions to GEICO's bottom line, while interacting with senior executives and all levels of associates. This highly selective program will teach you the ins and outs of our industry-leading company, while you gain hands-on technical and management experience.

During your three-year program, you'll learn our business by working on projects, attending business meetings, leading teams and rotating through our information services, systems operations and Internet business departments. Projects you could work on include database upgrades and business analyses, development and design, new application rollouts, data migration and project management. Technologies we currently use include Java, C++, VB.net, Oracle, UNIX, J2EE and SQL.

Requirements:
- Bachelor's degree in a technical field
- At least a 3.5 overall undergraduate GPA
- Understanding of business practices
- Very good analytical and problem-solving skills
- Effective written and verbal communication skills
- Demonstrated leadership experience
- High level of dependability
- Desire one day to become a manager

Emerging leaders in the information technology track work at our corporate headquarters in the Washington, D.C., metro area.

GEICO's college recruiting team actively recruits for a variety of entry-level positions, including:

- Supervisory leadership programs
- Actuarial associates
- Senior business analysts
- Product management analysts
- Information technology professionals
- Accounting associates
- Information systems analysts

- Sales professionals
- Customer service counselors
- Claim representatives
- Auto damage adjuster trainees
- Service direct underwriters
- Internships are available in select offices

Strategic Plan and Diversity Leadership

Who has primary responsibility for leading diversity initiatives at your firm?

Thea Jenkins, director of management development and minority recruiting.

Does your firm currently have a diversity committee?

Yes

If yes, does the committee's representation include one or more members of the firm's management/executive committee (or the equivalent)?

Yes

If yes, how many executives are on the committee and in 2006, what was the total number of hours collectively spent by the committee in furtherance of the firm's diversity initiatives?

Three executives, two attorneys and two managers. The committee meets at least once a month.

Does the committee and/or diversity leader establish and set goals or objectives consistent with management's priorities?

Yes

Has the firm undertaken a formal or informal diversity program or set of initiatives aimed at increasing the diversity of the firm?

Yes, formal

The Stats

	NUMBER OF EMPLOYEES	REVENUE
	2007	2007
Total in the U.S.	More than 21,500	$21.9 billion in assets as of 12/31/06

Other facts:

- GEICO is the fourth-largest private passenger auto insurer in the United States

- The third-largest property/casualty insurer in the world (Berkshire Hathaway/GEICO global revenues 2005)

- The fastest-growing major auto insurer in the U.S., with policies-in-force growth of 10 percent in 2006

Retention and Professional Development

Please identify the specific steps you are taking to reduce the attrition rate of minority and women employees.

- Increase/review compensation relative to competition
- Increase/improve current work/life programs
- Succession plan includes emphasis on diversity
- Work with minority and women employees to develop career advancement plans
- Strengthen mentoring program for all employees, including minorities and women

Diversity Mission Statement

GEICO is dedicated to assuring that all associates have an equal opportunity to achieve their full potential. The development and training of associates is vital to the success of the company. It is crucial that GEICO associates partner with the company in taking the initiative to look for opportunities to grow in their jobs, and to learn the skills that will help prepare them for greater growth and advancement. We are committed to providing an environment in which associates are recognized and rewarded, based on results and their contributions to the organization's success.

Goldman, Sachs & Co.

85 Broad Street
New York, NY 10004
Phone: (212) 902-1000
Fax: (212) 902-3000

Locations

US: Atlanta, GA • Boston, MA •
Chicago, IL • Dallas, TX • Houston, TX •
Jersey City, NJ • Los Angeles, CA •
Miami, FL • New York, NY • Philadelphia,
PA • Princeton, NJ • Salt Lake City, UT •
San Francisco, CA • Seattle, WA •
Tampa, FL • Washington, DC

International: Auckland • Bangalore •
Bangkok • Beijing • Buenos Aires •
Calgary • Dubai • Dublin • Frankfurt •
Geneva • Hong Kong • Johannesburg •
London • Madrid • Melbourne • Mexico
City • Milan • Moscow • Mumbai • Paris
• São Paulo • Seoul • Shanghai •
Singapore • Stockholm • Sydney • Taipei
• Tokyo • Toronto • Zurich

Diversity Leadership

Lance LaVergne
Vice President, Global Head of Diversity
Recruiting

Employment Contact

Martin Rodriguez
Vice President

Gina Moore
Associate
www.gs.com/careers

Recruiting

Please list the schools/types of schools at which you recruit.

- *Ivy League schools:* Harvard University, Princeton University, University of Pennsylvania, Columbia University, Brown University, Dartmouth College, Yale University, Cornell University

- *Other private schools:* Stanford University, New York University, University of Chicago, Northwestern University, Duke University, Georgetown University, Massachusetts Institute of Technology, Boston College, Villanova University, St. John's University, University of Southern California, University of Notre Dame, Emory University, Vanderbilt University

- *Public state schools:* University of Illinois, University of California – Los Angeles, University of California – Berkeley, University of Michigan, University of Virginia, University of Texas, Rutgers University, City University of New York – Baruch College, University of North Carolina – Chapel Hill, University of Indiana

- *Historically black colleges and universities (HBCUs):* Howard University, Morehouse College, Spelman College, Hampton University

- *Hispanic serving institutions (HSIs):* University of Puerto Rico

- *Other predominantly minority and/or women's colleges:* Barnard College, Wellesley College, Smith College, Mt. Holyoke College, Bryn Mawr College

Do you have any special outreach efforts directed to encourage minority students and graduates to consider your firm?

- Hold a reception for minority students

- *Conferences:* National Association of Black Accountants, National Society of Black Engineers, Society of Women Engineers, Society of Hispanic Professional Engineers, National Black MBA Association, National Society of Hispanic MBAs, National Association of Women MBAs, Association of Latino Professionals in Finance and Accounting, Hispanic Alliance for Career Enhancement

- Advertise in minority student association publication(s) or other minority-focused publications

- Participate in/host minority student job fair(s) or other minority-focused job events

- Sponsor minority student association events
- Firm's employees participate on career panels at school
- Outreach to leadership of minority student organizations
- Scholarships or intern/fellowships for minority students
- *Other:* Host workshops for graduate and undergraduate students through programs such as undergraduate and MBA Camps

What activities does the firm undertake to attract minority and women employees?

- Partner programs with women and minority associations
- *Conferences:* National Black MBA Association, National Society of Hispanic MBAs, National Society of Black Engineers, Society of Hispanic Professional Engineers, National Association of Black Accountants, Association of Latino Professionals in Finance and Accounting, Hispanic Alliance for Career Enhancements, Consortium for Graduate Studies in Management, Society of Women Engineers
- Participate at minority job fairs
- Seek referrals from other employees

Internships and Co-ops

Summer Analyst Program

Deadline for application: Winter 2007 (varies by school)

Length of the program: 10 weeks

Web site for internship/co-op information: www.gs.com/careers

Summer analysts join a 10-week comprehensive program, where they are given the opportunity to learn critical business skills while gaining fundamental experience in their respective divisions. Goldman Sachs seeks highly motivated candidates who have demonstrated outstanding achievements in academic and extracurricular activities. We are looking for self-motivated team players who have excellent organizational and communication skills. While a background in finance or accounting is not required, candidates should have an interest in business and financial markets.

The following divisions hire summer analysts:

- Equities
- Fixed income, currency and commodities
- Finance (includes controllers, credit and corporate treasury, and firmwide risk)
- Global investment research
- Human capital management
- Investment banking/corporate finance
- Investment management—asset management and private wealth management
- Global compliance
- Legal and management controls
- Merchant banking/private equity
- Operations (includes global operations)
- Services
- Technology

Scholarships

Scholarship for Excellence

Deadline for application for the scholarship program: December

Scholarship award amount: $5,000 for sophomores; $7,500 for juniors

Web site or other contact information for scholarship:

www.gs.com/careers/about_goldman_sachs/diversity/internships_s cholarships/index.html

The Goldman Sachs Scholarship for Excellence Program was established in 1994 as a way to attract undergraduate students of black, Hispanic and Native American heritage to careers at Goldman Sachs. Students of all majors and disciplines are encouraged to apply.

Recipients of the scholarship will receive:

- A cash award to cover tuition and fees: sophomores—$5,000; juniors—$7,500
- An internship as a summer analyst in which the scholarship recipient will gain insight into the financial services industry, the firm and our unique culture
- A coach/mentor that will help ensure a successful summer experience
- Exposure to senior level managers and participation in firmwide networking opportunities

Sophomores who successfully complete their summer internship have an opportunity to receive an additional award and an offer to return for a second summer internship.

The following are criteria we will consider when selecting our scholarship recipients:

- Black, Hispanic or Native American heritage
- Minimum cumulative grade point average of 3.4 or above on a 4.0 scale
- Interest in the financial services industry
- Community involvement—service to campus and community
- Demonstrated leadership and teamwork capabilities

Affinity Groups

At Goldman Sachs, we recognize that our ability to maintain and strengthen our position as a market leader requires a diverse workforce

that can offer the widest possible range of perspectives. Through our diversity efforts, we work to provide a supportive and inclusive environment where all individuals, regardless of age, gender, race, religion, national origin, sexual orientation, gender identity, disability or other classification or characteristic can maximize their full potential.

Our affinity networks are an important part of the firm's diversity strategy because they serve as a forum to share ideas, concerns and successes, and provide opportunities for professional development. The primary focus of the networks is to:

- Promote the firm's business principles
- Foster leadership development and offer guidance on career management
- Increase the engagement and retention of historically underrepresented groups and women
- Facilitate relationship-building between network members
- Create business development opportunities
- Enhance recruitment efforts for historically underrepresented groups and women
- Raise awareness, share ideas and create a sense of collaboration and community among everyone at Goldman Sachs
- Raise the visibility of our leadership and diversity commitment to external communities

The firm currently sponsors the following Networks in the Americas:

- Asian Professionals Network
- Firmwide Black Network
- Firmwide Hispanic/Latin Network
- Gay and Lesbian Network
- Goldman Sachs Women's Network

Each network operates on a firmwide level and has chapters in divisions where greater interest and participation exists. Members of the firm's Management Committee and Partnership Committee sponsor each firmwide network. Network members meet on an ongoing basis and participate in network events throughout the year. Each network also organizes and participates in history and heritage months throughout the year. Every network has an internal web site which serves as a source of information for all Goldman Sachs employees on the network's mission, leaders, key initiatives and events.

Entry-Level Programs, Full-Time Opportunities and Training Programs

Full-time Analyst Program
Geographic location(s) of program: Opportunities are available in the majority of our global offices

The main purpose of the analyst program is to provide analysts with critical business skills while gaining fundamental skills in their respective divisions. Goldman Sachs seeks highly motivated candidates who have demonstrated outstanding achievements in academic and extracurricular activities.

We are looking for self-motivated team players who have excellent organizational and communication skills. While a background in finance or accounting is not required, candidates should have an interest in business and financial markets.

Goldman Sachs hires full-time analysts for the following divisions:
- Equities
- Fixed income, currency and commodities
- Financing group
- Finance (includes controllers, credit and corporate treasury, and firmwide risk)
- Global investment research
- Human Capital Management
- Investment banking/corporate finance
- Investment management—asset management
- Investment management—private wealth management
- Global compliance
- Legal and management controls
- Merchant banking/private equity
- Operations (includes global operations)
- Services
- Technology

Please visit our web site for specific divisional overviews at: www.gs.com.

Strategic Plan and Diversity Leadership

How does the firm's leadership communicate the importance of diversity to everyone at the firm?
The Internal Communications Group focuses on reinforcing the culture of Goldman Sachs, keeping our people informed about news of the firm, our viewpoints on the global markets, our diverse businesses and management announcements. We use a variety of channels to communicate information throughout the firm—including GS Web (the firm's official Intranet site), "To All" memorandums, firmwide voicemails, global town halls and briefing toolkits.

The office of global leadership and diversity partners with the Internal Communications Group to ensure that diversity messages are communicated effectively firmwide. As such, critical diversity messages are woven into senior leadership's announcements as well as in town halls. Key communications vehicles managed by GLD include:

Global leadership and diversity web site: Goldman Sachs' global leadership and diversity internal web site provides a visible, informative and globally inclusive forum to share diversity-focused messages. The site, global in scope, is comprised of a homepage that highlights articles from each region as well as separate sections dedicated to the Americas, Europe and Asia. The web site also houses all affinity network homepages globally.

GLD newsletters: Goldman Sachs distributes formal global leadership and diversity newsletters to employees across the globe. These newsletters inform people about current initiatives and events such as history and heritage months, encourage them to become involved in affinity networks and highlight best practices and accomplishments across the firm.

In addition to the GLD web site, we also highlight diversity-related initiatives and events on GS Web, the firm's global internal website.

Who has primary responsibility for leading diversity initiatives at your firm?

Edith Hunt, managing director

Does your firm currently have a diversity committee?

Yes

If yes, please describe how the committee is structured, how often it meets, etc.

In 1990, Goldman Sachs formed the Firmwide Diversity Committee (FDC) to support and promote an inclusive work environment that recruits, retains, develops and rewards the best and brightest individuals and successfully supports a diverse workforce. Today, the FDC is led by our Chairman and CEO Lloyd Blankfein, and consists of members of the firm's Management Committee and other senior leaders. The FDC meets on a quarterly basis.

If yes, does the committee's representation include one or more members of the firm's management/executive committee (or the equivalent)?

Yes

If yes, how many executives are on the committee?

Total Executives on Committee: 21

Does the committee and/or diversity leader establish and set goals or objectives consistent with management's priorities?

Yes. One of the Firmwide Diversity Committee's (FDC) goals is to continue to promote an environment of mutual respect, cooperation and professionalism, and foster the teamwork essential to the firm's commitment to excellence. One of our most successful tools in driving our diversity initiatives throughout the firm has been the commitment and involvement of senior management.

The FDC works closely with the firm's diversity professionals and networks to develop and approve strategies that guide the firm, divisions and regions in achieving our diversity goals. The committee's key priorities include:

• Holding managers accountable for attracting, retaining and promoting talented men and women from the widest possible range of backgrounds, cultures and experiences

• Ensuring that people are appropriately rewarded and compensated for their performance in this area, as well as other aspects of citizenship

• Expanding the vision and execution of our leadership and diversity efforts

The FDC is not only accountable for diversity activities throughout the firm, but it is also a body that encourages serious debate and discussion on important diversity-related issues. To date, the FDC has endorsed numerous programs that enable employees to manage personal commitments, enhance career development and heighten sensitivity to diversity issues in the workplace. These programs range in scope from training and professional development programs to generous family leave policies.

Has the firm undertaken a formal or informal diversity program or set of initiatives aimed at increasing the diversity of the firm?

Yes, formal. Goldman Sachs' office of global leadership and diversity directs the firm's diversity strategy and translates the firm's diversity commitments into specific actions. Aligned with both the executive office and human capital management, the office of global leadership and diversity is led by Edith Hunt, a managing director, and is driven by a central team that works collaboratively with divisional and regional leadership and diversity managers who ensure our diversity efforts are supported, coordinated and effective across the globe.

The office of global leadership and diversity seeks to drive leadership, commitment and accountability from top to bottom. In order to fulfill this commitment, a structured set of annual priorities are set, and division and region heads are held responsible for achieving them as well as communicating them in key forums. Ultimately, the Firmwide Diversity Committee is responsible for the state of diversity at Goldman Sachs and answers to our board of directors.

The office of global leadership and diversity employs a focused strategy that seeks to create real change and traction by (1) affecting cultural transformation, (2) advancing leadership and management skills across the firm, and (3) integrating diversity considerations into our key business and people processes such as: recruiting, training, career development, compensation, promotions, succession planning and other key retention strategies as a means to achieve our objectives. To accomplish this, we leverage four key catalysts: (i) leadership commitment; (ii) education and training; (iii) communication and involvement; and (iv) accountability.

To drive our diversity efforts deeper into our organization, Goldman Sachs has developed and implemented various formal systems which focus on short-and long-term priorities as well as measuring progress. These leading initiatives have played a significant role in advancing our diversity efforts.

How often does the firm's management review the firm's diversity progress/results?

Quarterly

How is the firm's diversity committee and/or firm management held accountable for achieving results?

Senior management reports to the board of directors annually on the state of the firm's diversity initiatives.

The Stats

	NUMBER OF EMPLOYEES		REVENUE	
	2006	2005	2006	2005
Total in the U.S.	15,477	14,466	$20,361 million	$14,639 million
Total outside the U.S.	10,990	9,157	$17,304 million	$10,599 million
Total worldwide	26,467	23,623	$37,665 million	$25,238 million

Diversity Mission Statement

Goldman Sachs aims to be the employer, advisor and investment of choice by attracting and retaining the best and most diverse talent. Through our leadership and diversity efforts, including the affinity network program, we work to provide a supportive and inclusive environment where all individuals, regardless of gender, race, ethnicity, national origin, sexual orientation, gender identity, disability or other classification can maximize their full potential, which in turn leads to strengthening the firm's position as a leader in the industry.

The firm's commitment to diversity is evident at the most senior levels and is driven down through the firm by way of our seventh business principle:

"We offer our people the opportunity to move ahead more rapidly than is possible at most other places. Advancement depends on merit and we have yet to find the limits to the responsibility our best people are able to assume. For us to be successful, our men and women must reflect the diversity of the communities and cultures in which we operate. That means we must attract, retain and motivate people from many backgrounds and perspectives. Being diverse is not optional; it is what we must be."

We know that to manage diversity well, we have to manage people well. We realize that successful formal processes have a particularly positive influence on women, historically underrepresented groups and non-U.S. nationals. The office of global leadership and diversity reinforces our culture of meritocracy by advancing leadership and management skills, and integrating diversity considerations into our key business and people processes, such as recruiting, training, career development and other retention strategies.

Additional Information

At Goldman Sachs, we recognize that having a diverse workforce encourages increased creativity and innovation. This is crucial to improved performance and continued business success. To that end, we are committed to creating an environment that values diversity and promotes inclusion. Goldman Sachs recruits individuals from diverse cultures and backgrounds. The result is a wealth of talent and creativity where exceptional individuals work together to provide a world-class service to a broad spectrum of corporate, government, institutional and private clients.

In our search for outstanding individuals, we partner with organizations promoting diversity. Through our work with INROADS, Sponsors for Educational Opportunity, the Jackie Robinson Foundation, the Forte Foundation, the Employers Forum on Disability and others, we increase our commitment to recruiting women, students from ethnic minorities and those with disabilities.

Further, we have initiated and manage a number of programs designed to increase awareness of the firm and our industry. These programs allow us to offer academic scholarships, educational opportunities, summer internships and full-time positions to many outstanding students. Not all of these students have a finance or business background; we actively seek candidates from a broad array of academic disciplines and concentrations such as liberal arts, applied math, sciences and engineering in order to reach a wide spectrum of strong candidates.

We invite to take a closer look at our firm and learn more about the different programs and opportunities available to you: www.gs.com/careers.

Hallmark

Relationships are woven like fine fabric,

in colors of beauty and patterns of truth,

strengthened by *many distinct threads*.

AT HALLMARK, OUR COMMUNITY IS A WORK OF ART.

Visit www.hallmark.com for information on Hallmark career opportunities.

Hallmark Cards, Inc.

2501 McGee Street
Kansas City, MO 64108
Phone: (816) 274-5111
Fax: (816) 274-5061

Diversity Leadership
Vickie Harris
Corporate Diversity Director

Employment Contact
Dawn Harp
Corporate Staffing Manager
www.hallmark.com/careers

Recruiting

Please list the schools/types of schools at which you recruit.

• *Public state schools:* Central Missouri State Univ., Iowa State Univ., Kansas State Univ., Univ. of Kansas, Univ. of Missouri—Columbia, Univ. of Oklahoma

Do you have any special outreach efforts directed to encourage minority students to consider your firm?

• Participate in/host minority student job fair(s)
• Sponsor minority student association events
• Firm's employees participate on career panels at school
• Outreach to leadership of minority student organizations
• Scholarships or intern/fellowships for minority students

What activities does the firm undertake to attract minority and women employees?

• Partner programs with women and minority associations
• *Conferences:* NSBE, SWE, NABA
• Participate at local and regional minority job fairs
• Seek referrals from other employees
• Utilize online job services

Do you use executive recruiting/search firms to seek to identify new diversity hires?

Occasionally

Internships and Co-ops

Summer Internship

Deadline for application: October for all but creative, which does not have a deadline

Number of interns in the program in summer 2007 (internship) or 2007 (co-op): 40

Pay: $13.50 to $18.50 per hour

Length of the program: 12 weeks

Percentage of interns/co-ops in the program who receive offers of full-time employment: Approximately 80 percent

Web site for internship/co-op information:
www.hallmark.com/careers

Our program includes rich assignments, many networking opportunities and social events for the interns. We search for interns for our marketing, finance, operations, retail, IT and creative divisions. The qualifications are that the student be obtaining a degree within the area of discipline appropriate to the division, strong .GPA, leadership and strong communication skills. Typically we look for students entering their senior year.

Affinity Groups

Hallmark African-American Leadership (HAAL)

Mission is to ensure there is value for cultural differences and that those differences add value to the company by identifying solutions concerning education and awareness; recruitment, development and retention of African-Americans, product development and retail for African-Americans and maintaining community alliances with organizations who have similar business interests to Hallmark.

Hispanic Education Awareness Resource Team (HEART)

Mission is to enable our company to reach Hispanic consumers and to educate employees on Hispanic culture. Additionally, HEART focuses on the retention, recruitment and development of Hispanic employees, and leveraging the Hispanic culture, traditions and opportunities through local community involvement.

Hallmark Employees Reaching Equality (HERE)

Mission is to provides Hallmark's gay, lesbian, bisexual and transgender (GLBT) employees with a support network, as well as a forum to work with management and peers on education and awareness of issues that affect them.

Asian American Resource Community at Hallmark (AARCH)

Mission is to serve as a resource for Hallmark on Asian-American issues to ensure there is value placed on cultural differences and that those differences add value to the company by identifying solutions concerning education and awareness, recruitment, development and retention, product development and stronger retail presence, and building community alliances with organizations that have similar business interests as Hallmark.

All affinity groups are open to all employees of Hallmark Cards, Inc. and meet monthly and host additional activities outside of monthly meetings.

Strategic Plan and Diversity Leadership

How does the firm's leadership communicate the importance of diversity to everyone at the firm?

By hosting events at Hallmark (e.g. CEO Walking the Talk Diversity Awards and Supplier Diversity Awards) and through articles in the daily company newsletter.

Who has primary responsibility for leading diversity initiatives at your firm?

Vickie Harris, corporate diversity director

Does your firm currently have a diversity committee?

Yes

The Corporate Diversity Council (CDC) is made up of senior leaders from across Hallmark. They have bimonthly meetings to set the diversity strategy for the company and ensure that this strategy is executed both at corporate and division levels.

If yes, does the committee's representation include one or more members of the firm's management/executive committee (or the equivalent)?

Yes

Does the committee and/or diversity leader establish and set goals or objectives consistent with management's priorities?

Yes, the strategy uses marketplace, workplace and workforce as the framework for setting goals and objectives which naturally fit with the priorities of the business and with HR. Also, since the CDC is

comprised of business leaders, they are instrumental in ensuring that the objectives are aligned with the business goals.

Has the firm undertaken a formal or informal diversity program or set of initiatives aimed at increasing the diversity of the firm?

Yes, formal

We: a) attend at least four diversity recruiting conferences every year, b) have division diversity councils who often make increasing the diversity of their division a key goal, c) do targeted development, such as using Inroads interns, and d) have awareness raising programs for all employees.

How often does the firm's management review the firm's diversity progress/results?

Quarterly

How are the firm's diversity committee and/or firm management held accountable for achieving results?

They are held accountable via their annual performance reviews.

Retention and Professional Development

Please identify the specific steps you are taking to reduce the attrition rate of minority and women employees.

- Develop and/or support internal employee affinity groups (e.g., minority or women networks within the firm)
- Increase/improve current work/life programs
- Adopt dispute resolution process
- Succession plan includes emphasis on diversity

Diversity Mission Statement

The corporate diversity department exists to support Hallmark's goal of creating an environment that fully taps the potential of all individuals in pursuit of corporate objectives. We strive to accomplish this by:

Developing a critical mass of change agents throughout the company who value diversity and will assist in driving a change process.

Offering programs that build awareness regarding diversity and the business success that results from effectively managing diversity.

Developing and supporting systems, processes and programs that serve to eliminate artificial barriers, which prevent individuals from achieving full potential.

Sustaining a positive image as a company that values diversity.

Additional Information

Hallmark's Diversity Vision

Our corporate diversity vision is centered on providing shareholder value through:

• Our people create an environment that taps the full potential of every employee. We attract, develop and retain the best and brightest of a diverse talent pool.

• Our consumers, present and future, look to Hallmark to provide superior products and services that help them express their thoughts, feelings, and emotions.

• Our products and services help all people express their heritage and enrich their own lives and the lives of others.

Hallmark's Business Case for Diversity

Hallmark Cards, Inc. recognizes diversity as central to its success in the marketplace and as a key component of creating a competent workforce and an inclusive workplace.

Marketplace

Business success in the 21st century means responding to increasingly diverse consumer markets, which demand that companies understand them and be willing and able to address their specific needs through their products and services. As the industry leader in the personal expressions business, Hallmark has a distinct relationship with its consumers, who trust Hallmark to enrich their lives and enhance their relationships. Hallmark's brand and core competencies uniquely position it to meet the needs of all of its consumers in ways that are meaningful and memorable. Similarly, success as a retailer depends on Hallmark's ability to meet the needs of diverse consumers and to provide products and services that link positive emotion to the retail experience for them.

Workplace

An environment in which diversity is embraced and diverse traits leveraged as strengths is one where every employee can perform to his or her potential and in which his or her contributions are respected and appreciated. Hallmark leaders demonstrating inclusiveness in all they do and challenging others to do the same will help employees contribute to a positive workplace for everyone.

Workforce

More than affirmative action, Hallmark focuses on attracting, developing, and retaining a competent and diverse work force to improve productivity and ensure innovative problem solving and the development of relevant product solutions, all of which are good for business and help Hallmark meet consumer needs. This strength is drawn from differences in ethnic origin, religion, gender, age, sexual orientation, ability, lifestyle, economic background, regional geography, employment status, thinking style and more.

Additionally, Hallmark has an award-winning work/life balance program that includes the following:

• Adjusted workday/workweek

• Backup child care

• Compressed work week

• Dependent care discounts and referral services

• Educational programs

• Elder care consultation and referral

• Flex-time

• Job sharing

• Leaves of absence

• Part-time schedules

• Telecommuting

• Voluntary time off

HCA, Hospital Corporation of America

One Park Plaza
Nashville, TN 37203
Phone: (615) 344-9551
Fax: (615) 344-2830
www.hcahealthcare.com

Diversity Leadership
Kim Sharp
VP, Diversity

Employment Contact
Danielle Craig
Corporate and Campus Recruiter
E-mail: Danielle.craig@hcahealthcare.com

Recruiting

Please list the schools/types of schools at which you recruit.

• Private schools
• Public state schools
• Historically black colleges and universities (HBCUs)
• Other predominantly minority and/or women's colleges

Do you have any special outreach efforts directed to encourage minority students and graduates to consider your firm?

• Hold a reception for minority students
• Advertise in minority student association publication(s) or other minority-focused publications
• Participate in/host minority student job fair(s) or other minority-focused job events
• Sponsor minority student association events
• Firm's employees participate on career panels at schools
• Outreach to leadership of minority student organizations
• Scholarships or intern/fellowships for minority students

What activities does the firm undertake to attract minority and women employees?

• Partner programs with women and minority associations
• *Conferences:* National Black MBA Association Conference, National Society of Hispanic MBA Conference, National Association of Health Services Executives, National Association of Black Accountants
• Participate at minority job fairs
• Seek referrals from other employees

Do you use executive recruiting/search firms to seek to identify new diversity hires?

No

Internships and Co-ops

Minority Internship Program

Deadline for application: April 14, 2006/April 13, 2007

Number of interns in the program in summer 2006 (internship) or 2006 (co-op): Summer 2006 interns—10

Pay: Varies based on students classifications/paid biweekly

Length of the program: 12 weeks

Percentage of interns/co-ops in the program who receive offers of full-time employment: 10 percent

Web site for internship/co-op information: www.hcahealthcare.com

Mission

To provide talented minority students with an enriching internship experience that will help prepare them for a professional career and expose them to health care as a career option.

Program Objectives

• To provide exposure to the business world and health care as a profession
• To provide a quality experience that will enhance and allow students to prosper in their future professional careers
• To show that we impact patient care even outside the hospital
• To allow students to gain greater insight into the health industry
• To create and deliver a meaningful internship experience that is as close to reality as possible

Intern Qualifications

• College student (freshman, sophomore, junior, senior)
• Ethnic minority
• Minimum of 3.0 GPA
• Open to all majors, but general interest in healthcare management preferred
• Recommendation letter from school advisor/professor

- Excellent communication skills
- Strong interpersonal skills
- Must have the ability to work with all levels of management
- Working knowledge of Microsoft Office
- Must be available to work during the summer months (June to August)
- Will complete an online application which will include responding to essay questions and submitting a cover letter along with resume

Target Departments

- Design and construction
- Diversity—human resources
- Internal audit
- IT & S
- Patient account services
- Quality
- Supply chain
- TriStar Marketing

Intern responsibilities vary based on the assigned department. In 2006, interns worked on marketing and public relations projects, research and field study observations with our quality department and creating and facilitating training programs to HCA employees. These projects were in addition to daily administrative tasks, data entry, interdepartmental rotations and presentation development.

Scholarships

The minority scholarship program is in its first year of planning and implementation.

Entry-Level Programs, Full-Time Opportunities and Training Programs

Executive Development Program (COO, CNO, Controller/CFO Development Programs)

Length of program: COODP—three to five years, CNODP—12 to 18 months, CDP—12 to 18 months

Geographic location(s) of program: Candidates must be geographically flexible and willing to be placed at any one of HCA's hospitals throughout their development during the program and once they are promoted to executive level positions

An associate's development in the program is based on the 80-10-10 model. Eighty percent of an associate's development is based on targeted work assignments at the facility. Ten percent of an associate's development is based on the mentoring experience with the CEO, CFO or CNO. The final 10 percent is based on participation in formal learning seminars. The associates will assume line management roles with hands-on application to include operations, quality, staffing, budgeting, capital management, and developing leadership and management skills.

Strategic Plan and Diversity Leadership

How does the firm's leadership communicate the importance of diversity to everyone at the firm?

Weekly newsletters highlighting diversity tools, web sites and resources. Internal diversity web site. The diversity team also has monthly presentations educating the corporate campus on various cultures and cultural competence (i.e., Black History presentation, Women's History Program, language appreciate series, etc.).

Who has primary responsibility for leading diversity initiatives at your firm?

Each department is responsible for developing diversity initiatives for their respective areas. These initiatives are assisted by the corporate office of diversity and inclusion. Kim Sharp is VP, diversity.

Does your firm currently have a diversity committee?

Yes

If yes, does the committee's representation include one or more members of the firm's management/executive committee (or the equivalent)?

Yes

Does the committee and/or diversity leader establish and set goals or objectives consistent with management's priorities?

Yes

Has the firm undertaken a formal or informal diversity program or set of initiatives aimed at increasing the diversity of the firm?

Yes, formal

How often does the firm's management review the firm's diversity progress/results?

Quarterly

How is the firm's diversity committee and/or firm management held accountable for achieving results?

The success of HCA's diversity and inclusion initiatives is part of executive's performance evaluations.

The Stats

	NUMBER OF EMPLOYEES	
	2006	**2005**
Total worldwide	185,240	187,750

2006 DEMOGRAPHIC PROFILE	
Female	76 percent
Minority	35 percent

HCA is the nation's leading provider of healthcare services, composed of locally managed facilities that include 173 hospitals and 108 outpatient centers in 20 states and Europe. At its founding in 1968, Nashville-based HCA was one of the nation's first hospital companies.

Retention and Professional Development

Please identify the specific steps you are taking to reduce the attrition rate of minority and women employees.

• Increase/improve current work/life programs

• Succession plan includes emphasis on diversity

• Work with minority and women employees to develop career advancement plans

• Strengthen mentoring program for all employees, including minorities and women

• Professional skills development program, including minority and women employees

Diversity Mission Statement

At HCA, we provide cross-cultural competent care to all patients we serve. We will foster a culture of inclusion across all areas of our company that embraces and enriches our workforce, physicians, patients, partners and communities.

Additional Information

HCA Mission and Values Statement

Above all else, we are committed to the care and improvement of human life. In recognition of this commitment, we strive to deliver high quality, cost-effective health care in the communities we serve.

In pursuit of our mission, we believe the following value statements are essential and timeless:

• We recognize and affirm the unique and intrinsic worth of each individual

• We treat all those we serve with compassion and kindness

• We act with absolute honesty, integrity and fairness in the way we conduct our business and the way we live our lives

• We trust our colleagues as valuable members of our healthcare team and pledge to treat one another with loyalty, respect and dignity

HCA Diversity and Inclusion Vision

At HCA, we will provide culturally competent care to every patient we serve.

We will foster a culture of diversity and inclusion across all areas of our company that embraces and enriches our workforce, physicians, patients, partners and communities.

HCA's diversity and inclusion vision provides a view for creating a diverse and inclusive organization where:

• Culturally competent care is the standard

• Performance excellence is expected, developed and reinforced

• Employees, patients/families and physicians are respected and valued for their contribution to business successes

HDR, Inc.

8404 Indian Hills Drive
Omaha, NE 68114
Phone: (402) 399-4872
Fax: (402) 548-5002
www.hdrinc.com/careers

Locations

More than 5,200 employee-owners in
over 130 locations worldwide in 36
states including Ontario, Canada, and the
United Kingdom.
HDR has worked in all 50 states and
more than 60 countries.

Diversity Leadership

Judy Webster
Vice President, Employee Relations Director
Phone: (402) 399-4993
Fax: (402) 548-5002
E-mail: judy.webster@hdrinc.com

Employment Contact

Geralyn Bryant
Human Resources Representative
Phone: (402) 926-7052
Fax: (402) 548-5015
E-mail: geralyn.bryant@hdrinc.com

Recruiting

Please list the schools/types of schools at which you recruit?

• Ivy League schools

• Other private schools

• Public state schools

• Historically black colleges and universities (HBCUs)

• *Other predominantly minority and/or women's colleges:*
Hampton University, Howard University, Morgan State University,
Southern University, Grambling State University, Tennessee State
University, Tuskegee University

Do you have any special outreach efforts directed to encourage minority students to consider your firm?

• *Conferences:* NSBE (National Society of Black Engineers)

• Advertise in minority student association publication(s)

• Participate in/host minority student job fair(s)

• Firm's employees participate on career panels at school

• Outreach to leadership of minority student organizations

• Scholarships or intern/fellowships for minority students

HDR, Inc. has partnered with INROADS for seven years, sponsoring one to three interns annually. The company made a decision to expand its corporate diversity initiative and in 2006 placed 24 INROADS interns in 13 locations. HDR received the Corporate Plus Award at the Ninth Annual Awards Banquet held in Omaha in July 2005.

The first HDR/AMIE (Advancing Minorities' Interest in Engineering) scholarships were awarded to students at Morgan State University in Baltimore, Md., and Hampton University in Hampton, Va. The scholarships are a direct benefit of HDR's platinum membership in AMIE, which is a coalition of industry, government agencies and the ABET certified historically black colleges and universities (HBCUs) schools of engineering that seek to forge corporate/academic partnerships that serve to promote and support quality engineering programs.

HDR Howard University Fellowship Program: This program was created to support graduate students through their two-year education in the Howard Department of Civil Engineering and to give them opportunities for real-world experience in the field of water and wastewater treatment engineering. The $20,000 fellowship is awarded to a graduate student with exceptional technical talent in the field of water and wastewater. As part of the fellowship program, the recipient serves as a research assistant on HDR projects involving such innovations as membrane technology, and may intern at an HDR office over the summer.

HDR, Engineering, Inc. Diversity Scholarship Fund for students attending the Peter Kiewit School of Engineering or the University of Nebraska.

What activities does the firm undertake to attract minority and women employees?

• Partner programs with women and minority associations

• Conferences

• Participate at minority job fairs.

• *Seek referrals from other employees:* HDR has an employee referral program for employees to submit candidates for open positions and receive a referral bonus

• *Utilize online job services:* Utilize BlackCollegian.com and NSBE (National Society of Black Engineers) to list job postings

Do you use executive recruiting/search firms to seek to identify new diversity hires?

No

Internships and Co-ops

HDR Internship and Cooperative Education Programs

Deadline for application: Recruiting for internships and co-ops runs year round. Typically recruiting begins in the fall and most students are hired and start their internship in May. HDR posts current open internship opportunities year round on its web site.

Pay: Salary ranges vary by location from $11 to $16 per hour, based on academic placement, experience and discipline

Length of the program: Summer internships typically run a 12-week period

Percentage of interns/co-ops in the program who receive offers of full-time employment: Offers are made to qualified students at a rate of 85 percent or more

Web site for internship/co-op information: www.hdrinc.com/careers

At HDR, we offer professional opportunities in many career fields. Engineering, architecture, planning, design, environmental or consulting jobs make up the majority of our available positions, but we are also looking for talented individuals with accounting, human resources, legal, marketing, information technology and safety backgrounds. Through the internship program, HDR will typically employ students for two consecutive summers as interns.

Interns will be selected from a variety of schools and programs throughout the country. HDR accepts interns who apply on their own for an internship. Other interns are referred to HDR from programs with universities and other organizations such as INROADS and MESA.

Internships

• Open to currently enrolled full-time students
• Students work full-time during the summer or part-time during the semester
• Students are provided with career-related experience
• Students are compensated for work

Co-ops

• Open to currently enrolled full-time students
• Students alternate university enrollment with terms of full-time employment
• Students are provided with career-related experience
• Students are compensated for work
• Students receive college credit

Strategic Plan and Diversity Leadership

How does the firm's leadership communicate the importance of diversity to everyone at the firm?

Through the companies' 2008 business plan and business meetings.

Does your firm currently have a diversity committee?

No

Does the committee and/or diversity leader establish and set goals or objectives consistent with management's priorities?

Yes

Has the firm undertaken a formal or informal diversity program or set of initiatives aimed at increasing the diversity of the firm?

Yes, informal

How often does the firm's management review the firm's diversity progress/results?

Monthly, through the management dashboard.

Annually, through performance reviews.

How is the firm's diversity committee and/or firm management held accountable for achieving results?

Through goals and objectives and management dashboard.

Retention and Professional Development

Please identify the specific steps you are taking to reduce the attrition rate of minority and women employees.

• Work with minority and women employees to develop career advancement plans
• Strengthen mentoring program for all employees, including minorities and women
• Professional skills development program, including minority and women employees

Additional Information

HDR (hdrinc.com) is an architectural, engineering and consulting firm that excels at managing complex projects and solving challenges for clients. More than 4,500 employee-owners, including architects, engineers, consultants, scientists, planners and construction managers, in 130 locations worldwide, pool their strengths to provide solutions beyond the scope of traditional A/E/C firms. Headquartered in Omaha, Nebraska, HDR serves the communities throughout all of it's locations through volunteer service, outreach, education and leadership.

A few of these include:

• In one city, busloads of HDR employees travel to locations throughout the community to prepare meals for the homeless, renovate homes for the poor, rebuild community parks and escort underprivileged children to a science center.

• In another, a team of employees crosses the border into an impoverished area of Mexico, where they build a day care center for children who are often victimized by crime.

• And in still another, employees spend their free time cleaning up a community park.

• *Support for the following programs:* MESA—Math, Engineering & Science Achievement; and INROADS, an international career development organization. HDR is a longtime supporter of grade school and high school MESA programs, even bringing it to the college level in one city, and is a founder of INROADS in Omaha, Nebraska.

• Also participates in local Habitat for Humanity and Paint-a-thon efforts.

• HDR locally supported Creighton University's 2006 All-Nations Pow Wow.

Below are a few of the diversity efforts that HDR has been recognized for:

• Ranked Fourth in Top Supporters of Black Engineering Schools (April 5, 2006)

• HDR's Chicago Office Receives Employer Of The Year Honors From Women's Transportation Group (January 18, 2006)

• First HDR/AMIE Scholarships Awarded To Students At Morgan State, Hampton Universities (October 26, 2005)

• HDR Ranks Among Top Corporate Supporters of Black Engineering Schools (March 11, 2005)

• HDR Employees to Participate in Brush Up Nebraska (July 26, 2005)

• HDR Donates Aluminum Cans to Habitat for Humanity (July 18, 2005)

• *The Black Collegian* Top 100 Employers for the Class of 2006; No. 39—Top Employer (2006)

• *US Black Engineer & Information Technology* Among top 51 corporate supporters of black engineering schools *(*2005 and 2006)

• *Howard University Dean Attends Alexandria Office Event:* Dr. James H. Johnson Jr., dean of Howard University's College of Engineering, Architecture and Computer Sciences, and HDR Architecture President Merle Bachman joined the Alexandria office staff on Wednesday, November 9, 2005 for a surprise reception to celebrate Kathryn Prigmore's National Women of Color Lifetime Achievement Award. The award was presented during the 10th Annual National Women of Color in Technology Awards Conference, sponsored by the career communications group, held October 20 to 22, 2005 in Atlanta, Georgia. The conference supports and recognizes minority women in technology careers and connects them with mentors and employers to help launch or re-energize their careers.

• *Abad-Fitts Honored as Technology All Star:* San Antonio assistant department manager Carmen Abad-Fitts received a national Women of Color Technology Award for her accomplishments in advancing technology and science. (October 28 to 30, 2004)

Hershey Company, The

100 Crystal A Drive
Hershey, PA 17033
www.hersheys.com

Diversity Leadership
Andre Goodlett
Senior Director of Diversity & Inclusion

Employment Contact
Tonia Anderson
Director of Talent Acquisition, Integration &
 Retention
100 Crystal A Drive
Harrisburg, PA 17110
Phone: (717) 508-3886
Fax: (717) 534-8053
E-mail: tanderson@hersheys.com

Recruiting

Please list the schools/types of schools at which you recruit.

- Ivy League schools
- Public state schools
- Historically black colleges and universities (HBCUs)
- Hispanic Serving Institutions (HSIs)

Do you have any special outreach efforts directed to encourage minority students to consider your firm?

- Firm's employees participate on career panels at schools
- Scholarships or intern/fellowships for minority students

What activities does the firm undertake to attract minority and women employees?

- Partner programs with women and minority associations
- Participate at minority job fairs
- Seek referrals from other employees
- Utilize online job services

Do you use executive recruiting/search firms to seek to identify new diversity hires?

Yes

Internships and Co-ops

Hershey's Intern Professional Program (HIPP)

Deadline for application: Ongoing all year

Number of interns in the program in summer 2006 (internship) or 2006 (co-op): 157 interns

Pay: Ranges from $11.75 to $21.60 per hour, depending on major and year in school

Length of the program: Typically interns 12 weeks, co-ops 12 months, though possibly longer, depending on a student's availability and department needs.

Percentage of interns/co-ops in the program who receive offers of full-time employment: Company-wide the figure is less than 10 percent. In the sales department it's 20 percent or more.

Web site for internship/co-op information: www.hersheys.com

Typically engineering, sales, human resources and finance have the majority of undergrad interns/co-ops.

Hershey's Inter Professional Programs (HIPP) formally began in 1978. Over the years, HIPP has grown to become a critical element in Hershey's strategic recruiting and hiring plans. The program provides students with opportunities to develop and apply their skills in a challenging, exciting and industry–leading corporate environment. Many interns have moved right into great jobs with Hershey's upon graduation. Future job offers have also been extended to some interns before returning to school to finish their senior year!

Scholarships

Hershey Scholar Program

Deadline for application for the scholarship program: February 15th

Scholarship award amount: $500 to $3,000—Paid in two equal installments on August 15th and December 30th.

Scholarships are available only for children of employees.

UNCF/Hershey Scholar Program

Deadline for application for the scholarship program: April 30th

Scholarship award amount: $5,000

Scholarships are only available to minority Pennsylvania residents attending one of UNCF's 38 member colleges, or one of 14 institutions under the Pennsylvania state system of higher education.

Affinity Groups

All affinity groups within The Hershey Company are established with chairs and committees and have held several events in 2006. The Women's Council won a 2006 Hershey Company Executive Award of Excellence for Organizational Excellence.

- African-American Affinity Group
- Asian Affinity Group
- Hispanic Affinity Group
- Minorities in Sales
- Network of Young Professionals
- Prism—GLBT Affinity Group
- Sales Diversity Council
- Women's Council
- Women in Sales

Entry-Level Programs, Full-Time Opportunities and Training Programs

New Employee On-Boarding

Length of program: Two days

Geographic location(s) of program: Hershey, Penn.

The program gives an overview of company heritage, organizational departments/functions, diversity, human relations, as well as a performance overview.

The role of the Hershey Leader

Length of program: Two days

Geographic location(s) of program: Hershey, Penn.

Leadership training, diversity overview, HR overview.

Strategic Plan and Diversity Leadership

How does the firm's leadership communicate the importance of diversity to everyone at the firm?

The Hershey Company has a dedicated diversity web site with a cultural calendar to help educate and share diversity-related information. In addition, the public relations department sends out monthly e-mails to employees highlighting diversity events and activities that are both internal and external.

Who has primary responsibility for leading diversity initiatives at your firm?

Senior Director of Diversity and Inclusion, Andre Goodlett

Does your firm currently have a diversity committee?

Yes. The committee consists of several small councils, e.g., manufacturing plants, field sales diversity councils in addition to multiple affinity groups. The leads of each group meet to form the corporate council.

If yes, does the committee's representation include one or more members of the firm's management/executive committee (or the equivalent)?

Yes

If yes, how many executives are on the committee, and in 2006, what was the total number of hours collectively spent by the committee in furtherance of the firm's diversity initiatives?

Total Executives on Committee: Six

There are approximately 80 hours devoted to diversity initiatives. The full council consists of 21 members and they convene as a full council four times a year.

Does the committee and/or diversity leader establish and set goals or objectives consistent with management's priorities?

Yes

Has the firm undertaken a formal or informal diversity program or set of initiatives aimed at increasing the diversity of the firm?

Yes, formal

How often does the firm's management review the firm's diversity progress/results?

Quarterly

The Stats

	NUMBER OF EMPLOYEES		REVENUE	
	2006	2005	2006	2005
Total worldwide	Over 13,000	N/A	$4.944 billion	$4.429 billion

Retention and Professional Development

How do 2006 minority and female attrition rates generally compare to those experienced in the prior year period?

Lower than in prior years

Please identify the specific steps you are taking to reduce the attrition rate of minority and women employees.

- Develop and/or support internal employee affinity groups (e.g., minority or women networks within the firm)
- Increase/review compensation relative to competition
- Increase/improve current work/life programs
- Succession plan includes emphasis on diversity
- Work with minority and women employees to develop career advancement plans

Diversity Mission Statement

At The Hershey Company, diversity is a key ingredient in making us one of the finest companies in the world. We value the differences that make each individual, supplier, community, customer and consumer unique. Our success is a product of our ability to recognize, understand and incorporate those differences into everything we do. Hershey's strength and future success lie in its diversity—the diversity of thought, management styles, experience and abilities that only can come from bringing together people with different backgrounds and different ways of seeing the world. Hershey's approach to diversity emphasizes four areas: customer and consumer align-

ment, employee involvement and support, supplier diversity and community involvement.

Additional Information

Hershey's Initiatives:

Customer and Consumer Alignment: Hershey has significant opportunity in a diverse U.S. marketplace with an estimated ethnic buying power of $1 trillion. Hershey's multifaceted partnership with Latina superstar Thalía and acquisition of Mexican candy company Grupo Lorena and its top brand, Pelon Pelo Rico, are significant steps in reaching these consumers. Hershey has introduced a new line of co-branded, Latin-inspired candies to build an awareness of a preference for its brands with this fast growing, dynamic population.

Employee Involvement and Support: Reaching out to employees through various diversity councils, affinity groups, continuous diversity education and internal cultural awareness campaigns are all vehicles through which The Hershey Company demonstrates its commitment to diversity.

Supplier Diversity: One of the most important aspects of our business is our interaction with our suppliers. Like our employees, our suppliers make our success possible. Maintaining a diverse network of suppliers makes us a more efficient company while contributing to the economic development of the communities in which we live and work. Our approach is to partner nationally and locally with organizations to identify diverse suppliers. We also aim to open up opportunities at all levels and in all categories of spending to certified diversity suppliers and, in areas where the diversity supplier is limited, to mentor promising minority and women businesses.

Community Involvement: The Hershey Company has a long history of community leadership. Central to who we are as a company is our belief in making a difference in the lives of youth. We demonstrate our commitment through our participation with The Milton Hershey School, UNCF scholarships and the Hershey Youth Track and Field program. We also believe in the value of maintaining strong relationships with diversity focused organizations nationally and locally. We partner nationally with organizations like NAACP, La Raza and the United Way and in the Hershey, Penn. area with organizations like the Urban League, Y Black Achievers and Junior Achievement.

Houlihan Lokey

1930 Century Park West
Los Angeles, CA 90067
Phone: (310) 553-8871
Fax: (310) 553-2173
www.hlhz.com

Recruiting

Please list the schools/types of schools at which you recruit.

- *Ivy League schools:* A variety including the University of Pennsylvania, Cornell, Columbia Business School, Columbia University, Princeton and Stanford
- *Public state schools:* A variety including University of Virginia, University of Southern California, University of Wisconsin-Madison, and the University of Texas
- *Private schools:* A variety including Notre Dame, Georgetown, Emory and NYU
- *Historically black colleges and universities (HBCUs):* Morehouse, Spelman and Howard

Do you have any special outreach efforts directed to encourage minority students to consider your firm?

- Conferences
- Participate in/host minority student job fair(s)
- Sponsor minority student association events
- Firm's professionals participate on career panels at school
- Outreach to leadership of minority student organizations

What activities does the firm undertake to attract women and minorities?

- Partner programs with women and minority banking associations
- Seek referrals from other professionals
- Utilize online job services
- *Other:* Conduct workshops

Internships

Summer Analyst and Associate Program

Deadline for application for the internship: Depends on school but typically January and February

Number of interns in the program in summer 2006: 50

Pay: Prorated full-time base salary

Length of the program (in weeks): 10

Percentage of interns in the program who receive offers of full-time employment: Ideally all

Web site for internship information: careers.hlhz.com

The internship program is structured to give each student an opportunity to explore the areas that interest him or her the most, whether that be in a general sense (corporate finance, financial restructuring, financial advisory) or a more product-group-oriented one (health care, aerospace, finance). The interns are considered to be part of the deal teams and accordingly accompany the teams to meetings both in and out of the office. They are mentored and guided throughout the summer to give them the best possible summer internship experience.

Entry-Level Programs, Full-Time Opportunities and Training Programs

Orientation and Technical Training

Length of program: Currently just over two weeks

Geographic location(s) of program: New York

All analysts and associates begin their careers with an Orientation and Training program. Orientation consists of two days of senior management presentations allowing new employees to understand the firm strategically. Orientation also represents an opportunity to meet financial staff at all levels.

Technical training is two weeks and includes accounting, modeling, financial valuation techniques, research skills, credit, capital markets, M&A and distressed situations/restructuring, as well as specific group training and internal work processes.

Following the classroom training, analysts return to their respective offices and group and are quickly exposed to live deals to gain relevant training and experience. In addition, the firm provides ongoing educational opportunities in the form of a Speaker Series.

Strategic Plan and Diversity Leadership

Who has primary responsibility for leading overall diversity initiatives at your firm?

The Operating Committee

Who has primary responsibility for diversity recruiting initiatives at your firm?

Director of Recruiting Cynthia Bush

Does the committee(s) and/or diversity leader establish and set goals or objectives consistent with management's priorities?

Yes

Has the firm undertaken a formal or informal diversity program or set of initiatives aimed at increasing the diversity of the firm?

Yes. While the program is informal, we do actively recruit at several diversity schools.

The Stats

Employees

2006: 800

Humana Health Plans

500 West Main Street
Louisville, KY 40202
Phone: (502) 580-1000
www.humana.com

Diversity Mission Statement

At Humana, we aspire to create a diverse and inclusive workforce that connects us with the consumer, drives innovation and engagement in the workplace, supports a multicultural community and promotes opportunity for our enterprise in the marketplace.

Our goal is for Humana to become the employer, health solution and community partner of choice.

Building talent at Humana is essential to achieving this goal. Therefore, we are using INROADS and other internship/professional development programs to infuse diverse talent into our workforce. Our hope is that many of these interns will go on to be full-time associates. We believe that having the right talent in place at all levels of our organization will drive Humana's business success.

Integrys Group (Wisconsin Public Service Corporation)

700 N Adams St.
P.O. Box 19002
Green Bay, WI 54307-9002
Phone: (920) 433-1673
Fax: (920) 430-6366
www.integrysgroup.com

Diversity Leadership
Ka Youa Kong
Corporate Recruiter

Employment Contact
Bobbie Vlies
Corporate Recruiter
E-mail: bjvlies@integrysgroup.com

Recruiting

Do you have any special outreach efforts directed to encourage minority students and graduates to consider your firm?

• Advertise in minority student association publication(s) or other minority-focused publications

• Participate in/host minority student job fair(s) or other minority-focused job events

• Outreach to leadership of minority student organizations

• Scholarships or intern/fellowships for minority students

• *Other:*

– Relationships with multicultural centers

– Strong partnership with our surrounding colleges to get minority and female students to enroll in programs that we are hiring from

– Work with middle and high school students (targeting schools that are more diverse) to prepare them for our careers (hosting on-site tours and classroom presentations)

What activities does the firm undertake to attract minority and women employees?

• Participate at minority job fairs

Do you use executive recruiting/search firms to seek to identify new diversity hires?

No

Internships and Co-ops

Deadline for application: March 1st

Number of interns in the program in summer 2006 (internship) or 2006 (co-op): 54 interns and co-ops

Pay: $10.19 to $17.67 per hour

Length of the program: 10 to 14 weeks

Percentage of interns/co-ops in the program who receive offers of full-time employment: 25 percent

Web site for internship/co-op information: www.integrysgroup.com

We have an internship program which includes education and social events throughout the summer. We believe our program does a wonderful introduction to the utility industry and allows you to network within and outside of your department. We hire in the following areas for interns and co-ops: engineering, accounting and finance, IT (computer science and MIS), business management and public affairs.

Scholarships

Business and Technology Scholarships
Deadline for application for the scholarship program: February 1st
Scholarship award amount: $1,500 renewable per year
Web site or other contact information for scholarship: www.wisconsinpublicservice.com

Open to current sophomore and junior college students, and minority or female students.

Entry-Level Programs, Full-Time Opportunities and Training Programs

Emerging Leaders Program
Length of program: At employees' pace

The Emerging Leaders Program uses a blended learning approach with a combination of classroom workshops and eLearning courses.

Upon completing all six courses, which can be done in any order, individuals will receive a certificate of completion for the program.

Strategic Plan and Diversity Leadership

How does the firm's leadership communicate the importance of diversity to everyone at the firm?

Various communications through our Diversity Council and task force.

Who has primary responsibility for leading diversity initiatives at your firm?

Ka Youa Kong, corporate recruiter

Does your firm currently have a diversity committee?

Yes

If yes, please describe how the committee is structured, how often it meets, etc.

The committee meets on a monthly basis and discusses and develops ideas to bring in diverse talent and to recognize existing diverse employees.

If yes, does the committee's representation include one or more members of the firm's management/executive committee (or the equivalent)?

Yes

If yes, how many executives are on the committee?

Total Executives on Committee: Four

Does the committee and/or diversity leader establish and set goals or objectives consistent with management's priorities?

Yes

Has the firm undertaken a formal or informal diversity program or set of initiatives aimed at increasing the diversity of the firm?

Yes, formal—hiring a recruiter to spend 50 percent of her time building these efforts.

How often does the firm's management review the firm's diversity progress/results?

Quarterly

Retention and Professional Development

How do 2006 minority and female attrition rates generally compare to those experienced in the prior year period?

About the same as in prior years.

Please identify the specific steps you are taking to reduce the attrition rate of minority and women employees.

• Develop and/or support internal employee affinity groups (e.g., minority or women networks within the firm)

• Increase/review compensation relative to competition

• Work with minority and women employees to develop career advancement plans

• Strengthen mentoring program for all employees, including minorities and women

Diversity Mission Statement

At Integrys Energy Group and our companies, we respect and value diversity. Integrys defines diversity as all the dimensions that make one person different from another. It includes differences in our ethnic heritage, race, gender, language, age and beliefs. It also includes family, financial and educational background as well as life experience, personality type and diversity of thought.

Additional Information

We celebrate diversity at Integrys Energy Group and our companies by:

• Offering diversity learning for all leaders and employees. In addition, a diversity component is woven into all workshops. Diversity lunch sessions scheduled quarterly, with topics ranging from veterans benefits to intercultural communication to Native American organic foods

• Making community involvement a priority for ourselves in all of the communities we serve. Events include the Hispanic Fair, Hmong New Year Celebration and more

• Focusing on supplier diversity

• Expanding our talent pool through ongoing recruiting of qualified, diverse individuals for all companies and business units

• Partnering with local and national diversity organizations

• Using fair and consistent processes and practices

International Business Machines Corporation (IBM)

New Orchard Rd.
Armonk, NY 10504
Phone: (914) 499-1900
Toll Free: (800) 426-4968
Fax: (914) 765-7382
www.ibm.com/careers

Locations

170 locations in North America, South America, Asia Pacific, Europe, Middle East and Africa.

Diversity Leadership

Bill Lawrence
Senior Diversity Program Manager

Employment Contact

Vera Chota
Manager, University Programs

Recruiting

Please list the schools/types of schools at which you recruit.

• Ivy League schools

• Other private schools

• Public state schools

• Historically black colleges and universities (HBCUs)

• Hispanic serving institutions (HSIs)

• Native American tribal universities

Do you have any special outreach efforts directed to encourage minority students to consider your firm?

• Hold a reception for minority students

• *Conferences:* American Indian Science and Engineering Society (AISES), Grace Hopper Conference for Women in Computing. HENAAC, National Association of Asian American Professionals (NAAAP), National Association of Women MBAs (NAWMBA), National Black MBA Association (NBMBAA), National Society of Black Engineers (NSBE), National Society of Hispanic MBAs (NSHMBA), Reaching Out, Society of Hispanic Professional Engineers (SHPE), Society of Mexican American Engineers and Scientists (MAES), Society of Women Engineers (SWE), Women In Technology International (WITI)

• Advertise in minority student association publication(s)

• Participate in/host minority student job fair(s)

• Sponsor minority student association events

• Firm's employees participate on career panels at school

• Outreach to leadership of minority student organizations

• *Scholarships or intern/fellowships for minority students:* INROADS, National GEM Consortium, National Action Council for Minorities in Engineering (NACME), Sponsors for Educational Opportunity (SEO), Project View, Project Able and Entry Point (focused on People with Disabilities)

Web site: www.ibm.com/employment/us, click on "University", then "Diversity Recruitment Programs"

What activities does the firm undertake to attract minority and women employees?

• Partner programs with women and minority associations

• *Conferences:* American Indian Science and Engineering Society (AISES), Grace Hopper Conference for Women in Computing. HENAAC, National Association of Asian American Professionals (NAAAP), National Association of Women MBA (NAWMBA), National Black MBA Association (NBMBAA), National Society of Black Engineers (NSBE), National Society of Hispanic MBAs (NSHMBA), Reaching Out, Society of Hispanic Professional Engineers (SHPE), Society of Mexican American Engineers and Scientists (MAES), Society of Women Engineers (SWE), Women In Technology International (WITI)

• Participate at minority job fairs

• Seek referrals from other employees

• Utilize online job services

Do you use executive recruiting/search firms to seek to identify new diversity hires?

Yes

Internships and Co-ops

Employment Pathways for Interns and Co-ops (EPIC)

Deadline for application: Applications accepted year round

Pay: Competitive with industry (pay varies by hire type e.g. undergrad, grad student)

Length of the program: Internships are typically 10 to 14 weeks; co-ops are typically six or seven months

Web site for internship/co-op information: www.ibm.com/careers

A student employment assignment at IBM gives you real-world experience that offers you a competitive edge when you enter the workforce. Student employment assignments provide you the opportunity to become familiar with IBM's organization, work style and corporate culture. Co-op and internship programs are an important recruiting channel for IBM because they help management identify high-potential prospective employees. Participating students are often considered for a long-term commitment of regular employment. Our philosophy is recruit once, hire twice. As an IBM intern or co-op, you will be assigned to a paid technical or nontechnical position related to your major or career goals.

Extreme Blue

Deadline for application: Applications accepted year round

Pay: Competitive with industry

Length of the program: Typically 10 to 14 weeks

Web site for internship/co-op information: www.ibm.com/extremeblue

The Extreme Blue™ internship program—IBM's incubator for talent, technology and business innovation—challenges project teams of technical and MBA interns (along with their technical and business mentors) to start something big by developing new high-growth businesses.

Scholarships

IBM-INROADS Scholarship

Scholarship award amount: $1,500 tuition scholarship (one-time scholarship)—several scholarships awarded

Web site or other contact information for scholarship: Available to INROADS interns at IBM only

The IBM-INROADS Scholarship provides $1,500 tuition scholarships to IBM INROADS interns who have demonstrated both academic and professional excellence.

Affinity Groups

Over 172 affinity networking groups globally.

Global Affinity Groups at IBM:

• Asian

• Black

• Gay, Lesbian, Bisexual, Transgender (GLBT)

• Hispanic/Latino

• Men

• Native American

• People with disabilities

• Women

Diversity Network Groups consist of employees who voluntarily come together with the ultimate goal of enhancing the success of IBM's business objectives by helping their members become more effective in the workplace through:

• Community outreach

• Developing professional skills

• Enhancing recruitment and welcoming

• Meeting and teaming

• Mentoring and coaching

• Networking

• Social, cultural and educational events

Entry-Level Programs, Full-Time Opportunities and Training Programs

International Business Machines Corporation, headquartered in Armonk, N.Y., is the world's largest information technology (IT) company. While we are the IT leader, the solutions and services we deliver to our clients span all major industries, including financial services, health care, government, automotive, telecommunications and education, among others. It is the breadth of our portfolio—across hardware, software, services, consulting, research, financing and technology—that uniquely separates IBM from other companies. We have a rich history of driving innovations that help our clients transform themselves into on-demand businesses through our professional solutions, services and consulting businesses. IBM has a diverse and talented workforce that conducts business in 170 countries. For more information about IBM career opportunities, including our business areas and geographic locations, please visit www.ibm.com/careers.

Strategic Plan and Diversity Leadership

How does the firm's leadership communicate the importance of diversity to everyone at the firm?

The importance of diversity is communicated at all levels in IBM via electronic communication.

Who has primary responsibility for leading diversity initiatives at your firm?

Ron Glover, vice president, global workforce diversity

Does your firm currently have a diversity committee?

Yes, a global diversity council governs over 70 local diversity councils around the world. Additionally, there are executive task forces for eight constituencies: Asian, black, gay, lesbian, bisexual, transgender, Hispanic/Latino, men, women, Native American and people with disabilities.

If yes, please describe how the committee is structured, how often it meets, etc.

Diversity councils are located at multiple IBM-based locations worldwide.

If yes, does the committee's representation include one or more members of the firm's management/executive committee (or the equivalent)?

Yes

Does the committee and/or diversity leader establish and set goals or objectives consistent with management's priorities?

Yes

Has the firm undertaken a formal or informal diversity program or set of initiatives aimed at increasing the diversity of the firm?

Yes, formal

How often does the firm's management review the firm's diversity progress/results?

Annually

How is the firm's diversity committee and/or firm management held accountable for achieving results?

Through the annual chairman's review, senior-level executives report on year-to-year progress.

Retention and Professional Development

Please identify the specific steps you are taking to reduce the attrition rate of minority and women employees.

- Develop and/or support internal employee affinity groups (e.g., minority or women networks within the firm)
- Increase/review compensation relative to competition
- Increase/improve current work/life programs
- Adopt dispute resolution process
- Succession plan includes emphasis on diversity
- Work with minority and women employees to develop career advancement plans

- Review work assignments and hours billed to key client matters to make sure minority and women employees are not being excluded
- Strengthen mentoring program for all employees, including minorities and women
- Professional skills development program, including minority and women employees

Diversity Mission Statement

IBM leaders, in every generation, have believed that an inclusive workplace is right for the company, no matter what the prevailing views of the day represented. That kind of leadership didn't just happen—it is a natural companion to our shared beliefs and values. Diversity and the concept of workforce inclusion are key factors in helping define how we do business. "Diversity policies lie as close to IBM's core as they have throughout our heritage," says Sam Palmisano, IBM chairman and CEO. "Today we're building a workforce in keeping with the global, diverse marketplace to better serve our customers and capture a greater share of the on-demand opportunity."

Additional Information

Project View is IBM's award-winning diversity recruitment program that offers black, Hispanic/Latino, Native American, Asian, women and people with disabilities the chance to be considered for IBM career opportunities nationally. Travel, meals and lodging are included in this unique one-and-a half-day visit. Only IBM makes a job search this much fun! Selection is based on work experience, skills and overall academic achievement. This program is open to students receiving a BA, BS, MS or PhD. Project View is open to U.S. citizens or nationals; permanent residents, refugees, asylum seekers, or those authorized to work under the amnesty provisions of the U.S. immigration law.

Multicultural People in Technology (MPIT) is a multicultural IBM employee initiative that focuses on:

- Supporting the growth, development, advancement and recognition of IBM's current multicultural technical talent

- Attracting and recruiting technical multicultural talent to IBM

- Encouraging more multicultural youths (K-12) to pursue education and careers in science and technology

Currently, MPIT manages internal and external programs that address these needs in six multicultural constituencies: Asian, black, gay/lesbian/bisexual/transgender, Hispanic/Latino, Native American and people with disabilities.

EXploring Interests in Technology and Engineering (EXCITE) Camps are an extension of IBM's commitment to reach groups that are underrepresented in the technical workforce and to train and recruit individuals from those constituencies for technical careers. Through its EXITE Camps, IBM identifies 12- and 13-year-old girls with an interest or proficiency in math and science and prepares them to fill the technical pipeline by introducing them to the potential of technology, as well as the fun and exciting things they can do with it right now, and exposing them to women who have successful technology careers. Nearly 2,000 IBM volunteers, female and male, will participate in the EXITE Camps, developing, coordinating and overseeing such activities as web page design, computer chip design, laser optics, animation, robotics, and working with computer hardware and software. The volunteers will also introduce the girls to a variety of IBM technologies, including TryScience.org, an award-winning web site designed to make learning science more fun for kids. In addition, they will serve as e-mentors, corresponding with participants during the school year via e-mail, providing tutoring and encouraging the students to further pursue their interests in math, science and technology.

MentorNet is a not-for-profit educational organization focused on furthering women's progress in engineering and science fields through the use of an e-mentoring network. MentorNet matches protégés from various colleges and universities with mentors from industry and academia. IBM is a strategic partner of MentorNet, and IBMers comprise the program's largest source of professional mentors.

International Paper Company

6400 Poplar Avenue
Memphis, TN 38197
www.internationalpaper.com

Locations

United States
China • Belarus • Belgium • Brazil •
Canada • Chile • Columbia • Czech
Republic • Dominican Republic • El
Salvador • Finland • France • Germany •
Guadeloupe • Hong Kong • Hungry •
Israel • Italy • Japan • Latvia • Mexico •
Netherlands • Norway • Poland • Russia •
Saudi Arabia • South Korea • Spain •
Sweden • Switzerland • Taiwan •
Thailand • Turkey • Ukraine • United
Kingdom • Venezuela

Diversity Leadership

Cheryl Kern
Director of Diversity & Inclusion

Employment Contact

Gabrielle Frase
Talent Manager, Global Talent Acquisition
6400 Poplar Avenue
Memphis, TN 38197
Phone: (901) 419-7783
Fax: (901) 419-7329
E-mail: gabrielle.frase@ipaper.com

Recruiting

Please list the schools/types of schools at which you recruit.

• *Public state schools:* University of Alabama, University of Arkansas, Auburn University, Florida A&M University, Georgia Institute of Technology, Louisiana State University, Mississippi State University, North Carolina State University, Ohio State University, Penn State University, Purdue University, University of Tennessee, University of Texas – Austin

Do you have any special outreach efforts directed to encourage minority students and graduates to consider your firm?

• *Conferences:* SWE, NSBE, NBMBAA, NSHMBA, SHPE, NAWMBA

What activities does the firm undertake to attract minority and women employees?

• Partner programs with women and minority associations
• *Conferences:* SWE, NSBE, NBMBAA, NSHMBA, SHPE, NAWMBA
• Utilize online job services/job boards

Do you use executive recruiting/search firms to seek to identify new diversity hires?

Yes

Internships and Co-ops

Finance, Manufacturing, Global Sourcing, IT, and Sales & Marketing

Deadline for application: Spring (March)

Number of interns in the program in summer 2006 (internship) or 2006 (co-op): 25 internships, 25 co-ops

Pay: Paid every two weeks, but varies by function/position

Length of the program: 10 to 12 weeks for interns, 25 weeks for co-ops

Percentage of interns/co-ops in the program who receive offers of full-time employment: 75 percent

Web site for internship/co-op information: www.careers-ipaper.com

Strategic Plan and Diversity Leadership

Who has primary responsibility for leading diversity initiatives at your firm?

Cheryl Kern, director of diversity and inclusion

Does your firm currently have a diversity committee?

Yes

If yes, please describe how the committee is structured, how often it meets, etc.

Committee is comprised of the company's senior executives and meets six times a year (every other month).

If yes, does the committee's representation include one or more members of the firm's management/executive committee (or the equivalent)?

Yes

If yes, how many executives are on the committee, and in 2006, what was the total number of hours collectively spent by the committee in furtherance of the firm's diversity initiatives? How many employees are on the committee?

Total Executives on Committee: 12 executives and three employees

Total number of hours collectively worked by committee: 600 hours of executives' time and 750 hours of employees' time.

Does the committee and/or diversity leader establish and set goals or objectives consistent with management's priorities?

Yes

Has the firm undertaken a formal or informal diversity program or set of initiatives aimed at increasing the diversity of the firm?

Yes, formal

How often does the firm's management review the firm's diversity progress/results?

Quarterly

How is the firm's diversity committee and/or firm management held accountable for achieving results?

Balance scorecard objectives tied to annual reward/compensation.

The Stats

	NUMBER OF EMPLOYEES		REVENUE	
	2006	2005	2006	2005
Total in the U.S.	42,057	47,237	N/A	N/A
Total outside the U.S.	19,900	21,257	N/A	N/A
Total worldwide	61,957	68,494	$22 billion	$21.7 billion

Diversity Mission Statement

To accelerate efforts towards building and maintaining a more diverse community of highly engaged employees. This will be accomplished through:

• Employee engagement, inclusion and development

• Diversity education and training

• Recruiting and representation

Additional Information

The Value of Many Voices

International Paper's diversity initiative, Many Voices, One Vision—"A Blue Print for Success," targets the workforce and workplace with strategies to create an awareness of the importance of diversity in every aspect of the business and encourages the culture to create an environment of trust and openness where every person can realize their full potential. Our intention is to accelerate efforts toward building and maintaining a more diverse community of highly engaged employees. This will be accomplished through:

• Employee engagement

• Diversity education and training

• Recruiting and representation—the cornerstones of our diversity blueprint

We define diversity as the hiring, developing, retaining and promoting of talented individuals from many races and cultures. It includes race, gender, age, religion, marital status, disability, sexual orientation, national origin and veteran status, but goes beyond that by focusing on creating an environment that leverages the talents and diverse thinking of all employees which will improve IP's competitive position.

Today's global business environment is complex and ever-changing. Companies wanting to maintain their competitive advantage must be aware of changing demographics and strive to maximize the contributions of every employee. At International Paper, we recognize that a competitive advantage will be impossible if we do not value and encourage diversity of thought, experience, backgrounds and talents in our employees. We recognize that a diverse, engaged workforce is able to deliver successful business results that are critical to our company's success.

Through the power of people, we will succeed with customers and deliver operational excellence to achieve our goal of making International Paper one of the best companies worldwide. Change within International Paper has already begun. Look for your opportunity to participate!

J.C. Penney Company, Inc.

6501 Legacy Drive
Plano, TX 75024
Phone: (972) 431-1000
Fax: (972) 431-2320
www.jcpenneycareers.com

Locations

Plano, TX (HQ)
Store locations nationwide

Diversity Leadership

Fernando Serpa
VP of Diversity

Employment Contact

Juna Jones-Moore
College Relations
6501 Legacy Drive
Plano, TX 75024
Phone: (972) 431-1000
Fax: (972) 431-2320
E-mail: jjone31@jcpenney.com

Recruiting

Please list the schools/types of schools at which you recruit.

• Ivy League schools
• Public state schools
• Historically black colleges and universities (HBCUs)
• Hispanic serving institutions (HSIs)
• Native American tribal universities

Do you have any special outreach efforts directed to encourage minority students to consider your firm?

• *Conferences:* BEEP—Black Executive Exchange Program through National Urban League
• Advertise in minority student association publication(s)
• Participate in/host minority student job fair(s)
• Sponsor minority student association events
• Firm's employees participate on career panels at school

What activities does the firm undertake to attract minority and women employees?

• Partner programs with women and minority associations
• *Conferences:* NUL, NAACP, LULAC, plus others
• Participate at minority job fairs
• Seek referrals from other employees

Do you use executive recruiting/search firms to seek to identify new diversity hires?

Yes

Internships and Co-ops

Various ranging from sales manager interns, marketing interns, logistics interns, IT interns

Deadline for application: May 1st
Length of the program: Summer program—10 weeks; co-op—six months
Percentage of interns/co-ops in the program who receive offers of full-time employment: 75 percent
Web site for internship/co-op information:
www.jcpenneycareers.com

Description

The 10-week summer intern program provides a realistic overview of the activities related to the specific departments: IT, marketing, sales, logistics, HR, procurement, legal. The main emphasis of this program is spent in the home office gaining a basic understanding of the process and a working knowledge of the departments that support the process.

Structure

The J.C. Penney Internship Program will provide a training schedule consisting of activities, training and projects designed to improve your knowledge of the specific department. A final written report or oral presentation will be made to marketing senior management.

Qualifications

Students between junior and senior years with a 3.0 minimum GPA are preferred. Most interns are marketing, HR, CIS, finance, supply change, management and business majors, but any student with a sincere interest in pursuing a career with J.C. Penney who has strong leadership and analytical skills can be successful.

Entry-Level Programs, Full-Time Opportunities and Training Programs

- Merchandising Training Program
- Direct Merchandising Training Program
- Assistant Designer Training Program
- Logistic Training Program
- Sales Manager Training Program

Length of program: Six months

Geographic location(s) of program: Varies; regional stores—all 50 states and corporate office in Plano, Texas

Employee benefits and employee discounts are also provided.

Description

The six month training program provides a realistic overview of the J.C. Penney process and operations. The main portion of the program is spent in the home office gaining a basic understanding of the process and a working knowledge of the departments that support the process. Upon successful completion of the training program and promotion into a full-time position, the annual salary will be increased.

Structure

The program will provide a training schedule, manual and web-based materials to facilitate the program. The schedule consists of activities, training and projects designed to improve your knowledge of J.C. Penney specific operations. Assignments, written reports and oral presentations will be made to senior executives.

Qualifications

College graduates with a 3.0 minimum GPA are preferred. Most graduates are business, finance, HR, management, marketing and/or fashion merchandising majors, but any student with a sincere interest in pursuing a career in retail who has strong leadership and analytical skills and a flair for retail concepts can be successful. Retail experience is strongly preferred, plus a willingness to relocate.

Strategic Plan and Diversity Leadership

How does the firm's leadership communicate the importance of diversity to everyone at the firm?

The firm communicates diversity initiatives through mailings, the company web site, newsletters, meetings and pep rallies.

Who has primary responsibility for leading diversity initiatives at your firm?

Fernando Serpa, VP of diversity

Does your firm currently have a diversity committee?

Yes

If yes, does the committee's representation include one or more members of the firm's management/executive committee (or the equivalent)?

Yes

How many employees are on the committee, and how often does the committee convene in furtherance of the firm's diversity initiatives?

Total Executives on Committee: Four

The committee meets quarterly.

Does the committee and/or diversity leader establish and set goals or objectives consistent with management's priorities?

Yes

Has the firm undertaken a formal or informal diversity program or set of initiatives aimed at increasing the diversity of the firm?

Yes, formal

How often does the firm's management review the firm's diversity progress/results?

Twice a year

The Stats

	NUMBER OF EMPLOYEES	REVENUE
	2006	2006
Total in the U.S.	149,245	$18,781,000

Diversity Mission Statement

Our Commitment

JCPenney is committed to valuing the diversity of our associates and the customers we serve. The goal of this positioning statement is to reinforce our commitment to valuing diversity and incorporating it into the Penney culture and the way we do business.

Additional Information

What is diversity?

Diversity refers to the uniqueness of each human being. Each person is an original, a one-of-a-kind combination of characteristics—physical, personality, gender, ethnicity, race, religion, skills, cultural background and sexual orientation—that makes each person special and different.

Valuing diversity means appreciating the many advantages of diversity and behaving in a way that reflects respect for individual differences, while treating each person based on his or her own merit. For the company, valuing diversity means the inclusion of all our associates' and customers' differences as part of our overall business strategy.

Valuing diversity is in keeping with the Penney idea and philosophy

The Golden Rule was the company's original name and the principle by which James Cash Penney intended the business to be guided. The Penney Idea, adopted in 1913, set as its fifth principle, "To improve constantly the human factor in our business." We continue to broaden this vision by building more cultural diversity into our population. Our goal is to ensure that no gaps exist between our principles and our achievements.

Diversity is part of our business strategy

As our company has grown and prospered, it has become a citizen of the communities in which it operates worldwide. This has made it even more important for us to value and appreciate our diversity—because the successful retailer of the future will recognize diversity as a competitive strategy.

Valuing diversity is part of our strategic business plan and an important part of strengthening our competitive position. As we plan and run our business with customer diversity in mind, we will enhance our ability to gain and keep market share and increase sales and profits. Being customer driven requires that we have a mix of merchandise and workforce that are responsive to the customers we serve.

Our associate base represents a tremendous resource that we must continue to tap. We are committed to supporting diversity in our workforce through all of our personnel actions.

We believe a diverse workforce will enhance the quality of the decision-making process. This is, in fact, the essence of our team process.

Our vision

We see a J.C. Penney that is:

- Known by our associates as the place to work because we have an environment that makes it possible for all associates to contribute, be productive, receive recognition, grow and succeed

- Known by our customers as the place to shop, since we can meet their needs through our stores, catalog and other businesses

- Known by our suppliers as a company that provides and demands fair and equitable practices in all our business dealings

- Known by our shareholders as a company that maximizes its diverse resources to provide a fair return

Diversity is a shared responsibility

All associates share responsibility for respecting and utilizing the strengths of diversity in their actions with customers, suppliers and other associates.

Management must create an environment that encourages diverse viewpoints. This is accomplished through positive action, such as attracting, hiring, training, developing, promoting and retaining a diverse workforce. Every level of management is accountable and responsible for accomplishing this.

JEA

21 W. Church Street
Jacksonville, FL 32202
Phone: (904) 665-6000
Fax: (904) 665-7245

Location

Jacksonville, FL

Diversity Leadership

Walette Stanford
Labor Relations Coordinator
E-mail: stanwm@jea.com

Employment Contact

Maria Salgueiro
Manager—Talent Acquisition and Retention
E-mail: salgme@jea.com
www.JEA.com/careers

Co-op Program

Carol Higley
Manager—Corporate Workforce Planning
E-mail: higlca@jea.com

Recruiting

Please list the schools/types of schools at which you recruit.

• *Private schools:* Jacksonville University

• *Public state schools:* Clemson University, Florida State University, Georgia Institute of Technology, Penn State University, Purdue University, Rutgers University, Rensselaer Polytechnic Institute, University of Central Florida, University of Florida, University of North Florida

• *Historically black colleges and universities (HBCUs):* Bethune Cookman University, Edward Waters College, Florida A&M University

Do you have any special outreach efforts directed to encourage minority students and graduates to consider your firm?

• Advertise in minority student association publication(s) or other minority-focused publications

• Participate in/host minority student job fair(s) or other minority-focused job events

• Firm's employees participate on career panels at schools

• Outreach to leadership of minority student organizations

What activities does the firm undertake to attract minority and women employees?

• *Conferences:* AABE

• Participate in minority job fairs

• Utilize online job services

Do you use executive recruiting/search firms to identify new diversity hires?

Yes

Internships and Co-ops

JEA Co-op

Deadline for application: May 1, 2008

Pay: $10.50 to $15 per hour

Length of the program: Summer, 12 to 15 weeks or part time, year round, and semester on/off also available

Percentage of interns/co-ops in the program who receive offers of full-time employment: New formalized program for 2007 (TBD)

Web site for internship/co-op information: www.jea.com/careers/recruitment

JEA is interested in college students who make a long-term commitment to integrate classroom studies with learning through productive work experience in a field related to their academic/career goals.

The desired skill sets generally include:

• *Engineering:* Chemical, civil, electrical, environmental, industrial and mechanical

• *Chemistry/natural science:* Environmental support, environmental/fuels analysis, process chemistry, sampling, technical support, permitting and compliance.

- *Finance:* Accounting, audit, budget, planning, risk management and treasury services

- *Information technology:* Business intelligence, development, enterprise architecture, information security, infrastructure and project management

- *General business:* Communications, human resources, marketing and public affairs

Qualifications

- Must be currently enrolled in an accredited institution
- Undergraduate student in related field of study
- Graduate student in related field of study
- Successful completion of standard JEA recruitment processes

Schedule

We offer co-op/internship opportunities year-round with flexible start and end dates, semester on/off, as well as full-time summer or part time.

Environment

The co-ops participate as a group in an employee orientation, networking/feedback sessions, including JEA subject matter expert speakers and facility tours throughout their duration of employment, and community outreach.

Participation in individually challenging projects, while training on the job, will improve the co-ops' technical skills, in addition to strengthening their behavioral competencies.

Strategic Plan and Diversity Leadership

What trends in your industry affect your corporate diversity goals, strategies and/or internal or external alliances?

Building company bench strength to prepare for the pending aging workforce retirements.

How does the firm's leadership communicate the importance of diversity to everyone at the firm?

Web site, corporate meetings and senior leadership meetings

Who has primary responsibility for leading diversity initiatives at your firm?

Bill Hegeman, director, employee services

Does your firm currently have a diversity committee?

No

Does the committee and/or diversity leader establish and set goals or objectives consistent with management's priorities?

Yes

Has the firm undertaken a formal or informal diversity program or set of initiatives aimed at increasing the diversity of the firm?

Yes, informal

How often does the firm's management review the firm's diversity progress/results?

Quarterly

How is the firm's diversity committee and/or firm management held accountable for achieving results?

JEA is committed to the success of the Equal Opportunity/Equal Access Program. The program applies without regard to race, creed, color, religion, political affiliation, sex, national origin, disability, age, veteran status, marital status or related personal characteristics. It pertains to every level of city government and all city implemented and/or sponsored programs and service related to employment. This includes, but is not limited to: recruitment, hiring, compensation, training, placement, promotion, discipline, demotion, layoff, recall, termination, working conditions and related terms and conditions of employment.

The Equal Opportunity/Equal Access Program is designed to challenge all city employees to achieve equality, accessibility and equal opportunity throughout all levels of city government. Consistent with this commitment, every manager, appointed staff member and employee is encouraged to join together in an effort to achieve the full realization of a better, more open and equitable society. A variety of approaches, programs and tools will be used by JEA to promote and utilize diversity.

The Stats

	NUMBER OF EMPLOYEES		REVENUE	
	2006	2005	2006	2005
Total worldwide	1,903	1,858	$1.427 billion	$1.199 billion

Retention and Professional Development

How do 2006 minority and female attrition rates generally compare to those experienced in the prior year period?

Approximately the same as in prior years

Please identify the specific steps you are taking to reduce the attrition rate of minority and women employees.

• Increase/review compensation relative to competition

• Increase/improve current work/life programs

• Adopt/dispute resolution process

• Succession plan includes emphasis on diversity

• Work with minority and women employees to develop career advancement plans

• Strengthen mentoring program for all employees, including minorities and women

• Professional skills development program, including minorities and women.

John Deere

One John Deere Place
Moline, IL 61265
www.JohnDeereCareers.com

Diversity Leadership
Deb Taylor
Director Global Diversity & Inclusion

Employment Contact
Erin Kennedy
Staffing Project Administrator
Phone: (309) 765-0421
Fax: (309) 749-2665
E-mail: KennedyErinE@JohnDeere.com

Heidi Ciha
Manager Recruiting & Staffing

Recruiting

Please list the schools/types of schools at which you recruit.

Augustana College • Bowling Green State University • Colorado State University • Drake University • Ferris State University • Florida A & M University • Georgia Institute of Technology • Illinois State University • Indiana University • Iowa State University • Kansas State University • Luther College • Michigan State University • Michigan Tech University • Milwaukee School of Engineering • North Carolina A&T • North Carolina State University • North Dakota State University • Northern Illinois University • Ohio State University • Pittsburg State University (Kansas) • Purdue University • South Dakota School of Mines • Southern Illinois University • St. Ambrose University • Texas A&M University • Tuskegee University • University of Illinois • University of Iowa • University of Michigan • University of Missouri-Rolla • University of Northern Iowa • University of Wisconsin-Madison • University of Wisconsin-Platteville • Washington State University • Western Illinois University • Western Michigan University • Bradley University • Central Missouri State University • Georgia State University • Murray State University • Ohio University • Oklahoma State University • Saint Mary's College • Tennessee Tech • University of Arizona • University of Tennessee • University of Tulsa • Virginia Tech

Do you have any special outreach efforts directed to encourage minority students to consider your firm?

• *Conferences:* Currently participate in SWE, NSBE, SHPE, NABA & MANRRS at the national and regional conferences

• Advertise in minority student association publication(s) or other minority-focused publications

• Participate in/host minority student job fair(s) or other minority-focused job events

• Sponsor minority student association events

• Firm's employees participate on career panels at school

• Scholarships or intern/fellowships for minority students

What activities does the firm undertake to attract minority and women employees?

• Partner programs with women and minority associations

• *Conferences:* See list above

• Participate at minority job fairs

• Seek referrals from other employees

• Utilize online job services

Do you use executive recruiting/search firms to seek to identify new diversity hires?

Yes

Internships and Co-ops

John Deere Student Program

Deadline for application: Accept applications year round

Number of interns in the program in summer 2006 (internship) or 2006 (co-op): 285 students

Pay: Pay varies by year in school and major course of study

Length of the program: 13 weeks. We ask our students to work 500 hours during their session to receive one-year service credit with John Deere.

Percentage of interns/co-ops in the program who receive offers of full-time employment: From the 2006 student program, 95 percent of the students received either a full-time offer or an offer for a returning internship.

Web site for internship/co-op information:
www.deere.com/en_US/careers/collegejobs/student_programs.html

The following are the majors John Deere recruits: accounting/finance (minimum GPA 3.25), engineering, information technology, marketing/ag business, supply management (minimum GPA 3.0).

The John Deere Student Program refers to the collective group of students hired in the Internship Program (interns) and the Cooperative Education Program (co-ops). The recruiting department provides staffing process support to the business units and coordinates the internship and co-op programs.

The Student Program is utilized as a recruiting tool, marketing the John Deere brand on campuses to attract future employees, and as a feeder to full-time employment needs. The Student Program also assists the company's goals in developing interns and co-ops and assessing their potential for full-time employment, and in building an effective, diverse and inclusive workforce. Managers of interns and co-ops are responsible for providing assignments that are project-oriented and developmental so the experience is valuable for both the student and the company.

Scholarships

Scholarship opportunities exist at various universities. Scholarship criteria, award amounts and application deadlines vary by univer-sity.

Affinity Groups

John Deere recognizes that one of the drivers for a diversity strategy is to align high-performance teamwork. There is a need to tap the creative, cultural and communicative skills of all employees and to use those skills to improve the company policies, products and customer experiences.

Employee networks are company supported, employee-driven, resource groups that are all inclusive and are implemented around a common interest, identity, gender or ethnicity. They are utilized to connect employees to each other, the community and to engage them in the business. Each network group holds monthly meetings and plans numerous events to encourage career development, networking, and community service. As of spring 2007, John Deere has 16 network groups located through out North America, and three internationally.

African-American

An inclusive group dedicated to developing the skill sets of its members to lead, assist and excel professionally and to help improve recruitment and retention through personal relationships. This network accomplishes its objectives through the creation of a collaborative environment. In 2006, this network group was responsible for securing $1.6 million in new sales through relationships developed with the National Conference of Black Mayors.

Asian/Pacific Islander or LOTUS (Lead, Organize, Teach Unite and Support)

This groups aims to promote an inclusive, collaborative environment for all employees within John Deere in order to help them accomplish outstanding business results. This group leads, assists and supports the company's efforts to employ, develop and retain Asian/Pacific Islanders.

New Employees or NEON (New Employee Organizational Network)

This network welcomes new employees or those who are early in their careers, with the aim of helping them acclimate to the company, build networks and socialize.

Women REACH (Relating, Enriching, Achieving, Challenging and Helping)

This network has regular meetings, forums, and educational events and conferences to help women share, grow and build professional relationships. The aim of this group is to help female employees reach their full potential.

Entry-Level Programs, Full-Time Opportunities and Training Programs

Development programs have been established within functional areas of the business that have ongoing hiring needs. These programs provide new or recent college graduates with exposure to the company via rotational, entry-level work assignments. Many graduating interns and co-ops begin their full-time career by entering a development program that aligns with their educational discipline. New and recent college graduates are also hired to fill permanent entry-level positions within John Deere business units.

Engineering Development Program

Length of program: One year

Geographic location(s) of program: Midwest

The Engineering Development Program is a one-to-two year rotational program. The program was designed to give new engineers exposure to different aspects of the business. The program consists of three rotations in different areas of engineering (customer related, manufacturing, and product development/design).

Finance Development Program

Length of program: Three to four years

Geographic location(s) of program: All John Deere locations through out the United States

The Finance Development Program is a three to four year rotational program consisting of two or three, 12 to 18 month work assignments. Rotations will be structured to provide opportunities for early career employees to develop an understanding of John Deere's products and services, establish a network of people to support personal and professional growth, and to gain experience in one or more of the following focus areas: cost management, financial analysis, functional assignments, and strategic planning. The work assignments are generally available in cost accounting, financial planning and reporting, funding and other treasury operations, general accounting, internal audit, SAP information system implementation, supply management, and tax.

IT Development Program

Length of program: Three years

Geographic location(s) of program: All John Deere locations throughout the United States.

The IT Development Program is designed to develop John Deere's talent pool in the early career period with business and technical skills that will enhance IT's competitive advantage. The IT EDP is a three-to-four-year rotational program consisting of approximately two, 12-month work assignments with the third and final assignment lasting from 12 to 18 months. Rotations will be structured to provide opportunities for early career employees to develop an understanding of John Deere's products and services, establish a network of people to support personal and professional growth, and to gain experience in one or more of the following focus areas: architecture, infrastructure, application development, data and security.

Supply Management Development Program

Length of program: Three years

Geographic location(s) of program: All John Deere locations through out the United States.

The Supply Management Development Program (SMDP) is designed to develop a supply management talent pool, in the early career time period, building on business and technical skills to enhance the supply management function's competitive advantage. The SMDP is a three-year rotational program consisting of two 18-month work assignments. Rotations are structured to provide opportunities for early career employees to develop an understanding of John Deere's products and services, establish a network of people to support personal and professional growth, and to gain experience in one or more of these areas: OFP, logistics, cost management, service parts and indirect materials and services.

All employees can participate in John Deere's tuition reimbursement program to further their education.

Strategic Plan and Diversity Leadership

What trends in your industry affect your corporate diversity goals, strategies and/or internal or external alliances?

Our corporate diversity goals are part of our ongoing business strategy. We feel it is not an industry trend, but a global demographic issue of workforce shortage. In the future, seven out of 10 workers entering the workforce will be people of color and women.

How does the firm's leadership communicate the importance of diversity to everyone at the firm?

We have a newly introduced strategy called Team Enrichment, which is a strategy improvement that we are taking globally.

Who has primary responsibility for leading diversity initiatives at your firm?

Laurie Simpson, director team enrichment

Deb Taylor, director, global diversity and inclusion

Does your firm currently have a diversity committee?

Yes

If yes, please describe how the committee is structured, how often it meets, etc.

Team Enrichment Councils meets frequently, since it's a new initiative.

If yes, does the committee's representation include one or more members of the firm's management/executive committee (or the equivalent)?

Yes

Executives on the Team Enrichment Councils (TEC): One per TEC

Employees on the TEC: Seven to 10

Frequency of meetings: Too new into initiative to answer

Since we are dealing with global team members, meetings are virtual.

Does the committee and/or diversity leader establish and set goals or objectives consistent with management's priorities?

Yes

Objectives consistent with John Deere's High Performing Teamwork strategy.

Has the firm undertaken a formal or informal diversity program or set of initiatives aimed at increasing the diversity of the firm?

Yes, formal

Team Enrichment strategy

How often does the firm's management review the firm's diversity progress/results?

Quarterly

How is the firm's diversity committee and/or firm management held accountable for achieving results?

Will be part of John Deere's global performance management (appraisal) process.

Johnson & Johnson

501 George Street
New Brunswick, NJ 08901
Phone: (732) 524-1958
Fax: (732) 524-2587
www.jnj.com/careers

Locations

Worldwide

Employment Contact

Caridad Arroyo
Manager, Diversity Outreach
E-mail: carroy1@corus.jnj.com

Recruiting

Does your firm annually recruit at any of the following types of institutions?

• Ivy League schools

• Other private schools

• Public state schools

• Historically black colleges and universities (HBCUs)

• Hispanic serving institutions (HSIs)

Do you have any special outreach efforts directed to encourage minority students to consider your firm?

• Hold a reception for minority students

• *Conferences:* National Society of Black Engineers, Society of Hispanic Professional Engineers, CGSM, GEM, National Society of Hispanic MBA, NBMBAA, Reaching Out, Disco, MBA Diversity Forum

• Advertise in minority student association publication(s)

• Participate in/host minority student job fair(s)

• Sponsor minority student association events

• Firm's employees participate on career panels at schools

• Outreach to leadership of minority student organizations

• Scholarships or intern/fellowships for minority students

What activities does the firm undertake to attract minority and women employees?

• Partner programs with women and minority associations

• *Conferences:* SWE chapter level, see list above

• Participate at minority job fairs

• Seek referrals from other employees

• Utilize online job services

• *Other:* Advertising

Do you use executive recruiting/search firms to seek to identify new diversity hires?

No

Internships and Co-ops

Over 1,000 interns yearly and 90 + INROADS participants

Length of the program: Varies based on the student schedule, program

Percentage of interns/co-ops in the program who receive offers of full-time employment: 60 percent INROADS; the other programs are run by the operating companies—decentralized recruitment

Johnson & Johnson offers numerous internships. Please contact us for more information.

Scholarships

• Consortium for Graduate Studies in Management

• GEM

• Historically black colleges and universities

• Hispanic serving institutions

• National Society of Black Engineers

• Penn State

• Society of Hispanic Professional Engineers

Scholarship award amount: Varies

Affinity Groups

• African-American Leadership Council (AALC)

• Association of Middle Eastern & North African

Heritage (AMENAH)

- Community of Asian Associates at Johnson & Johnson (CAAJJ)
- Gay & Lesbian Organization for Business and Leadership (GLOBAL)
- Help our Neighbors with our Resources (HONOR)
- Hispanic Organization for Leadership and Achievement (HOLA)
- South Asian Professional Network & Association (SAPNA)
- Women's Leadership Initiative (WLI)

Entry-Level Programs, Full-time Opportunities and Training Programs

- Finance Leadership Development Program
- IM Leadership Development Program
- Engineering/Operations Leadership Development HRLDP
- HR Leadership Development Program

Length of program: Two years

Geographic location(s) of program: Across the U.S. and Puerto Rico

Strategic Plan and Diversity Leadership

How does the firm's leadership communicate the importance of diversity to everyone at the firm?

Office of diversity, diversity minute "webinar," in-house conferences, e-mails, newsletters, web sites, meetings.

Who has primary responsibility for leading diversity initiatives at your firm?

Joann Heisen, vice president, office of diversity

Does your firm currently have a diversity committee?

Yes

If yes, does the committee's representation include one or more members of the firm's management/executive committee (or the equivalent)?

Yes

Does the committee and/or diversity leader establish and set goals or objectives consistent with management's priorities?

Yes

Has the firm undertaken a formal or informal diversity program or set of initiatives aimed at increasing the diversity of the firm?

Yes, formal

The Stats

	NUMBER OF EMPLOYEES	REVENUE
	2005	2005
Total worldwide	115,600	$50.5 billion

Retention and Professional Development

Please identify the specific steps you are taking to reduce the attrition rate of minority and women employees.

- Develop and/or support internal employee affinity groups (e.g., minority or women networks within the firm)
- Increase/review compensation relative to competition
- Increase/improve current work/life programs
- Adopt dispute resolution process
- Work with minority and women employees to develop career advancement plans: Done for all employees
- Strengthen mentoring program for all employees, including minorities and women
- Professional skills development program, including minority and women employees

Diversity Mission Statement

Johnson & Johnson's credo sets forth our responsibilities to our employees. It recognizes their dignity and merit, their individuality and the requirement for equal opportunity in employment, development and advancement for those qualified. From these principles, modified over the years, Johnson & Johnson has fostered and encouraged the development of a diverse workforce—a workforce for the future. While we can point with pride to a commitment to diversity deeply rooted in our value system, we recognize that our employees, customers and communities were far different from those of today. However, our commitment to these core stakeholders, as they have evolved and as Johnson & Johnson has evolved, is as strong as ever. Today's customers and employees come from all over the world and represent different ages, cultures, genders, races and physical capabilities. Through their life experiences, they provide a diversity of thought and perspective that must be reflected in our corporate culture.

To achieve this vision, we must build a workforce that is increasingly skilled, diverse, motivated and committed to dynamic leadership. This workforce should reflect our diverse customer base and be knowledgeable of the markets we serve. Being the employer of choice in a dynamic global environment means embracing the differences and similarities of all our employees and prospective employees. It also means the execution of innovative diversity and marketing initiatives to ensue our ability to recruit, develop, retain and promote exceptional talent from an array of backgrounds and geographies, while continuing our pursuit of excellence. Our goal is to ensure our ability to meet the demands of a changing world with a vision worthy of our values and our commitment to be the leader in health care across the globe. When we achieve our vision, diversity becomes one of our most important competitive advantages.

Additional Information

Because of J&J's decentralized structure, there are many other diversity initiatives that take place at the respective operating company levels.

JPMorgan Chase

1 Chase Manhattan Plaza
Floor 18
New York, NY 10005
www.jpmorganchase.com

Locations

4,492

Employment Contacts

Sandra C. Dorsey
Vice President
Internship Program Manager
Phone: (212) 552-5986
Fax: (212) 552-6128
E-mail: sandra.dorsey@chase.com

Cecilia Nelson
Vice President
Diversity Relationship Manager
Phone: (212) 552-6012
Fax: (212) 552-6128
E-mail: cecilia.nelson@jpmorgan.com

Recruiting

Please list the schools/types of schools at which you recruit.

We recruit across a range of programs and campuses. Please check jpmorganchase.com/careers for events at your campus this fall and throughout the year.

Do you have any special outreach efforts to encourage minority students to consider your firm?

• *Conferences:* We participate in various industry-wide organizations and conferences. These include: Out for Undergraduates (BA), INROADS (BA), the United Negro College Fund (BA), Disability Mentoring Day (BA), JPMorgan Chase Smart Start Program (BA), the Consortium for Graduate Study in Management (MBA), the Forte Foundation (MBA), National Black MBA Association Conference, National Society of Hispanic MBAs Conference, National Association of Black Accountants (NABA) Convention and Reaching Out MBA Conference, which attracts gay, lesbian, bisexual and transgender (GLBT) students

• *Other:* We visit a range of college campuses, including historically black colleges and universities, and conduct various outreach efforts to ensure that we meet and engage a diverse student population

What activities does the firm undertake to attract minority and women employees?

In addition to the BA and MBA recruiting activities we described in the previous questions, the firm is committed to placing diverse, experienced professionals in open positions. We strive to place candidates internally and also work closely with our partner search firms to identify external candidates.

Internships and Co-ops

JPMorgan Chase has over 15 different summer internship programs, all of which hire a significant number of diverse candidates. Those divisions hiring interns include everything from technology and credit card services to investment banking and human resources. Summer interns are given a large amount of responsibility and are expected to become integral members of their teams over the 10-week summer program.

In order to supplement our on-campus recruiting efforts, we work closely with INROADS, HACE, HBCUs and SEO to source diverse talent for our many summer programs. Deadlines vary for the internships, but most are in January and February, with interviews taking place in February and March. The pay also varies across the different lines of business within the bank and is competitive with the salaries paid by other financial service firms. The percentage of interns receiving offers of full-time employment varies from year to year, but is generally a very high percentage.

Scholarships

The JPMorgan Chase UNCF Scholars Program

As a firmwide program dedicated to finding undergraduate students who have a commitment to diversity, the program is open to all students who can demonstrate this commitment, have high academic achievement and strong leadership qualities. Each year, we select up to 20 students to join the program. Each receives up to $10,000 in scholarship money as well as a guaranteed summer internship. You can apply through the UNCF web site: www.uncf.org/internships.

Affinity Groups

JPMorgan Chase Employee Networks

The firm has more than 70 employee networks, initiated by and for employees, in locations across the globe. There are also several employee networks within the investment bank. These are groups of employees of a common cultural heritage, gender, age or interest. They are valued organizations within the firm and are actively supported by management. Employee networks provide their members with a forum to communicate and exchange ideas, build a network of relationships across the firm, get access to volunteer opportunities in the community and support for career development and mentoring. More than 20,000 of the company's worldwide employees participate in one or more employee network. Employee networks strengthen our culture by:

• Supporting employees
• Promoting professional development
• Offering mentoring opportunities
• Helping employees understand the firm's culture
• Reinforcing JPMorgan Chase's commitment to inclusiveness and diversity
• Functioning as a resource to the Corporate Diversity Council
• Acting as a forum to accelerate the pace of change and cultivate an inclusive atmosphere

Recently, employee networks have hosted notable speakers and events. For example, AsPIRE, the employee network for Asian/Pacific Islanders, hosted Indra Nooyi, president and CFO of PepsiCo, Inc. Additionally, PRIDE, the employee network for lesbian, gay, bisexual and transgender employees, hosted an appearance by acclaimed playwright Tony Kushner.

JPMorgan Chase Employee Networks (partial list)

Access Ability: A resource on disability issues and a voice for employees with disabilities.

Adelante: Promoting the development of Latino/Hispanic employees at JPMorgan Chase.

AsPIRE (Asians and Pacific Islanders Reaching for Excellence): To enhance professional development and leadership opportunities for those of Asian/Pacific Island heritage.

Investment Bank Finance and Business Management Women's Network: Formed to meet the needs of women at all levels in the investment bank finance and business management function globally, including networking, mobility, professional development and social responsibility.

Investment Bank Junior Women in Banking: Formed to promote the retention and advancement of analyst and associate women in the investment bank area. To strengthen the pipeline of female employees, Junior Women in Banking focuses on leveraging senior leader engagement, networking, career development and mentoring.

Investment Bank Women's Committee: A grassroots organization formed to address the needs and issues of women in the front office areas of the investment bank in North America. The committee's goal is to work together, and with management, to help attract, retain, develop and promote women across the businesses.

Investment Bank Women Who Trade: Formed to foster communication among female traders in the investment bank and support recruiting efforts, this group is comprised completely of female traders across all of the investment bank's businesses and product groups.

Native American Tribes Instilling Opportunities and Network Support: Native American employees and others supporting a diverse and inclusive workplace at JPMorgan Chase.

Parents Networking Group: A network to help working parents in Europe, the Middle East and Africa successfully balance family and career.

PRIDE: Supporting workplace fairness for lesbian, gay, bisexual and transgender employees.

Professional Networking Association: Enthusiastic, outgoing young and young-minded professionals who want to grow personally and professionally.

South Asian Society: A London-based network to maximize the impact of South Asians in making JPMorgan Chase successful.

ujima: A forum for JPMorgan Chase employees of African descent, ujima is Swahili for "collective work and responsibility."

Women of Color Connections: Designed to promote awareness of the unique challenges experienced by women of color.

Women's Network: A forum for women at JPMorgan Chase to collaborate and grow as professionals.

Working Families Network: A network to help JPMorgan Chase employees succeed in balancing family and career needs.

Women in Risk Exchange: Formed to help retain talented women at all levels and give women at all stages of their careers concrete opportunities, both to develop professionally and to lead.

Entry-Level Programs, Full-Time Opportunities and Training Programs

We have 11 entry-level, full-time programs for undergrads:

• Asset management
• Audit

- Card services
- Commercial banking
- Corporate finance
- Finance
- Instore sales management
- Operations, management services and technology
- Research
- Sales and trading
- Treasury and securities services

For detailed, up-to-date information, please visit us at jpmorgan-chase.com/careers.

Two aspects of our entry-level programs, in particular, differentiate JPMorgan Chase from other potential employers.

First, we take a holistic approach to managing our new BA (analyst) and MBA (associate) hires. The first few years are crucial in defining and establishing a strong career platform and mark the beginning of a road defined by targeted skills training and support. During that time, we want to ensure that training and development experiences are carefully structured so that our analysts and associates can build a strong foundation with the firm. We make significant investments in training and development, and our programs are considered to be among the best in the industry.

Second, we are serious about giving and getting clear direction and honest performance feedback. One resource available is our rites of passage roadmap, which illustrates how to get ahead, the skills that are needed for each role and function, and the training programs that are available to close any gaps. Evaluation committees review performance and promotions across peer groups.

Strategic Plan and Diversity Leadership

How does the firm's leadership communicate the importance of diversity to everyone at the firm?

At JPMorgan Chase, we have been helping our clients do business for more than 200 years. To describe our firm and our people, there is no better phrase than that of one of our founders: "To at all times conduct first-class business in a first-class way." For us, this philosophy has everything to do with our people. Along with our reputation, our people are our most valuable asset. In an industry as dynamic, innovative and complex as financial services, we need to find and retain the very best employees.

To conduct first-class business in a first-class way, we understand the importance of fostering an environment of respect and inclusiveness. Our business principles serve as a roadmap for how and

why we make decisions. As Chairman and CEO Jamie Dimon said in his 2006 annual shareholder letter, "Ultimately, we will succeed or fail based upon the talent, dedication and diligence of our management team and the people who work with them."

At JPMorgan Chase, we constantly remind ourselves that the most important thing we can do for employees is to build a healthy, vibrant company that treats people with respect and create an environment where everyone has the opportunity to succeed. Performance is recognized and rewarded based on merit.

Managers are also encouraged to participate in a range of diversity activities, including:

- Mentoring
- Leadership and/or sponsorship roles in employee networks
- Participate in college recruiting
- Sponsorship of "fireside chats" with key employee groups

Who has primary responsibility for leading diversity initiatives at your firm?

Responsibility for creating a diverse and inclusive organization begins at the top. Our Chairman and CEO, Jamie Dimon, leads the Corporate Diversity Council—a group of senior leaders from across the company, including the investment bank, who set the vision and strategy for diversity at the firm. Progress on diversity objectives is reviewed monthly by the executive management of the firm and regularly with the board of directors. In addition, managers understand that they are accountable for making measurable, sustainable progress in this regard.

The Stats

Revenue

2006: $64.5 billion

Diversity Mission Statement

At JPMorgan Chase, we constantly remind ourselves that the most important thing we can do for employees is to build a healthy, vibrant company that treats people with respect and creates opportunity. Everyone counts, and we have to remember that we all support one another. We strive to create a more inclusive work environment that draws on and develops the best talent. We want individuals of any race, nationality, gender, sexual orientation or physical ability to have the opportunity to excel based on their performance and contribution to the firm. Building a diverse and inclusive work environment requires effort and perseverance, which is why we make inclusiveness and diversity an integral part of how we manage the company.

Additional Information

What makes JPMorgan Chase a "best practice" firm?

We asked a range of JPMorgan Chase employees why they joined and why they stay. From analysts to senior managers, there was a clear consensus on the six major attractions:

• The scale, scope and prestige of the bank

• Our reputation as a business innovator

• The chance to make a personal impact

• High-quality training and development

• Exceptional quality of work and deal flow

• A spirit of cooperation and teamwork

We understand that the best and brightest come from many backgrounds, cultures and outlooks. What the best and brightest share is a will and desire to achieve. By seeking out these candidates, honoring and celebrating their diversity, and nurturing their strengths, we will stand apart from our competitors and be recognized by our clients as the best in the business.

Awards and Honors

We feel good about our efforts with regard to diversity and inclusiveness and are especially gratified when external partners recognize them through awards and honors. For example:

• Top 50 Companies for Latinas by *LATINA Style* magazine, 2006 and previous five years running

• Henry Viscardi, Jr. Legacy Award by Abilities!—an organization dedicated to empowering people with disabilities to be self-sufficient, 2006

• Top 50 Companies for Minorities by *Fortune* magazine, 2006 and previous seven years

• Leading Edge Company for GLBT Employees by Stonewall, an GLBT advocacy organization in the U.K., 2007

• Top Six Companies for African-American Women by *Essence* magazine, 2004

• Top 50 Companies for Diversity by *DiversityInc* magazine, 2006 and previous five years running

• Top MBA Employers for Women by *Fortune* magazine, 2006

• Top 10 Diversity Employers by *The Black Collegian*, 2005

• Top 50 Employer for Women in U.K. by *The Times* newspaper, 2006

• Top 10 Company for Working Parents by *Working Mother* magazine for 2006. Achieved "Top 100" list for previous 10 years.

• Workplace Excellence Award by Out & Equal for our forward-looking approach to workplace equality, safety, policies, benefits parity and community support, 2006

• Top Companies for Women of Color by *Working Mother* magazine, 2006 and previous two years running

• 100 percent rating on the Corporate Equality Index, an evaluation conducted by the Human Rights Campaign to measure how well major corporations treat their GLBT employees and customers. Perfect score for five years running, since inception of this recognition

• Top 10 Companies for Executive Women by *DiversityInc* magazine, 2006

• Top 10 Adoption-Friendly Workplaces by the Dave Thomas Foundation for Adoption, 2007

• Top 10 Companies for People with Disabilities by *DiversityInc* magazine, 2005

• Top 10 Companies for Latinos by *DiversityInc* magazine, 2005

• Corporate Responsibility Award for outstanding leadership in corporate diversity efforts in the workplace from SAGE (Services and Advocacy for Gay, Lesbian, Bisexual & Transgender Elders), 2005

• Closing the Gap Award by New Detroit, a Michigan-based civic and community group, for outstanding efforts by JPMorgan Chase to improve economic and social equity between races, 2005

• The Ron Brown Award for Corporate Leadership—a Presidential Award recognizing JPMorgan Chase for outstanding achievement in employee and community relations, 2004

• Corporate Leadership for Children award from Child Care Inc. for our "extraordinary commitment to quality child care for children", 2003

• Top company for women by the New York City Mayor's Office/Women's Commission, 2003

• Top 50 best places to work by *Savoy* magazine, 2003

• Top 10 Companies for Recruitment and Retention by *DiversityInc* magazine, 2003

• Opportunity Now Award (U.K.) for programs benefiting the careers of women, 2002

• Diversity Award for Excellence (U.K.), 2002

• CEO Diversity Leadership Award from Diversity Best Practices, 2002

• Top 50 Companies by *CAREERS & the disABLED Magazine,* 2000

• Psychologically Healthy Workplace Award from the American Psychological Association, 2003

- Top Companies for People with Disabilities by *Enable* magazine, 2002

- Corporate 100 by *Hispanic* magazine, 2003

- Work-Life Innovators Award by The Conference Board, 2002

- Catalyst Award for innovative programs that advance the careers of women, 2001

As proud as we are of our achievements and recognitions, we know that there is always more that can be done. We'll encourage you to share your interests in ways that help raise standards on all sides, giving you the challenges, experiences, development and support you need to fulfill your potential, because that's how we will achieve ours.

Kellogg Company

One Kellogg Square
Battle Creek, MI 49016-3599
Phone: (269) 961-2000
www.kellogg.com/careers

Locations
Asia Pacific • Europe • Latin America •
North America

Diversity Leadership
Velois Bowers
VP Diversity & Inclusion

Employment Contact
Byron R. Foster

Recruiting

Please list the schools/types of schools at which you recruit.

- *Public state schools:* Western Michigan University, DePaul University, Michigan State University, UTEP, UCLA, Indiana University
- *Historically black colleges and universities (HBCUs):* Lincoln University (MO), Central State University, Clark Atlanta University, Howard University, Morgan State University, Chicago State University, Alabama A&M, University of Arkansas-Pine Bluff, Hampton University, Wilberforce University
- *Hispanic serving institutions (HSIs):* Texas A&M

Do you have any special outreach efforts directed to encourage minority students to consider your firm?

- Host a reception for minority students
- Conferences
- Participate in/host minority student job fair(s)
- Sponsor minority student association events
- Outreach to leadership of minority student organizations
- Scholarships or intern/fellowships for minority students

What activities does the firm undertake to attract minority and women employees?

- Partner programs with women and minority associations
- *Conferences:* NSBE, Consortium, NBMBAA, NABA, NSHM-BA, ALPHA, SHPE, SWE, NSN, NAWMBA
- Participate at minority job fairs
- Seek referrals from other employees
- Utilize online job services
- Network with diversity organizations

Do you use executive recruiting/search firms to seek to identify new diversity hires?

Yes

Internships and Co-ops

The internship programs are in several Kellogg business groups and are typically recruit during the academic year. Most of the internships are during the summer following the close of the academic year. The internships consist of undergraduate and graduate students

Length of the program: 12 weeks

Percentage of interns/co-ops in the program who receive offers of full-time employment: 75 percent

Web site for internship/co-op information: www.kellogg.com/careers

The internships are designed as developmental tools which are meaningful projects providing a bridge to full-time positions following graduation. The quality of work and successful project completion are among the key factors to determine if an intern will receive an offer of employment.

Scholarships

Kellogg's Corporate Citizen Fund (KCCF)

KCCF has provided funding for scholarship programs that are weighted to selection of diverse students, including the following:

- *Carson's Scholars Fund:* $25,000 to support the Carson's Scholars Fund offered to Battle Creek Public Schools students
- *Consortium for Graduate Study in Management:* $15,000 to support Millenium Campaign for Educational Excellence
- *Hispanic College Fund:* $10,000
- *Hispanic Scholarship Fund:* $6,000
- *MESAB:* $10,000 scholarship support for Medical Education for South African blacks
- *National Association for Black Accountants (NABA):* $6,000
- *Women's Grocer Association:* $1,000

Affinity Groups

Kellogg employee resource groups offer opportunities for employees who are connected by some common dimension of diversity to come together to build relationships; identify and generate potential solutions to real or perceived barriers that interfere their ability to realize their full potential; and to create opportunities to aid Kellogg Company in driving positive business results. Each group meets monthly and more information about each one can be found at www.kellogs.com.

Women of Kellogg (WOK)

This community is dedicated to the personal and professional growth and development of the women within Kellogg Company. They join together to project a common voice for the shared experiences, perceptions and needs of women in the Kellogg workplace and to help members reach their full potential.

Kellogg African American Resource Group (KAARG)

This group contributes to company objectives by ensuring the professional development of its members and serving as a resource to positively influence the Kellogg environment. They provide career development strategies and activities, advise company leadership as appropriate and actively drive retention.

Kellogg Young Professionals

This group provides professional and social networking opportunities for young employees (30 years and under) to assist in their acclimation and development within the company. Professional development opportunities are focused on enhancing the understanding of Kellogg operations while providing both macro- and micro-level learning.

Other employee resource groups currently in development:

• Hispanic Employee Resource Group

• Multicultural Employee Resource Group (KMERG)

Entry-Level Programs, Full-Time Opportunities and Training Programs

Global learning and development opportunities (25 workshops offered in 2005).

Strategic Plan and Diversity Leadership

Who has primary responsibility for leading diversity initiatives at your firm?

VeLois Bowers, vice president diversity and inclusion

Does your firm currently have a diversity committee?

No

Does the committee and/or diversity leader establish and set goals or objectives consistent with management's priorities?

Yes

Has the firm undertaken a formal or informal diversity program or set of initiatives aimed at increasing the diversity of the firm?

Yes, formal

How often does the firm's management review the firm's diversity progress/results?

Quarterly

How is the firm's diversity committee and/or firm management held accountable for achieving results?

At the core of Kellogg's diversity and inclusion initiative is accountability. That is the essence and strongest component of the initiative. Performance measures were added to the evaluations of all people managers around the initiative. The success of the initiative became one of several factors that played a part in performance evaluations, promotions and bonuses.

Human resources and people managers knew that the Executive Management Council (EMC) was reviewing the overall diversity and inclusion plan quarterly. A standing agenda item for the EMC was the number of women and minorities who are being prepared for positions of increasing responsibility in the company.

A diversity scorecard was designed to allow the company to see its progress on the initiative. It had measurable objectives for hiring, retention and promotion of women and minorities. The scorecard kept track of company sponsored training of women and minorities, demographics, Affirmative Action deficiencies, and women and minority underutilization. On a quarterly basis, managers were given their scorecard to determine their progress.

Retention and Professional Development

Please identify the specific steps you are taking to reduce the attrition rate of minority and women employees.

• Develop and/or support internal employee affinity groups (e.g., minority or women networks within the firm)

• Increase/review compensation relative to competition

• Increase/improve current work/life programs

• Succession plan includes emphasis on diversity

• Work with minority and women employees to develop career advancement plans

• Strengthen mentoring program for all employees, including minorities and women

• Professional skills development program, including minority and women employees

Diversity Mission Statement

Valuing Diversity

At Kellogg Company, we're dedicated to the things that set us apart and make us better. With different backgrounds, cultures and experiences, everyone brings something valuable to our team. We thrive on the diverse talents of our employees, and we expect all of our team members to show dignity and respect to those talents. There's always a better idea just around the corner and, with support, creative thoughts become brilliant working solutions. At Kellogg Company, it's all about being yourself, being accepted and being successful.

Additional Information

People are our most important asset.

Kellogg diversity and inclusion strategy focuses on four key strategic areas:

• Build accountability for diversity and inclusion throughout the organization

• Recruit, retain and develop talented people

• Drive understanding, education and awareness

• Create the environment

Companies are constantly in flux as to who is responsible for making sure that the people of the organization are developed, trained and motivated to give their best for the success of the company. The question is continually being asked as to who is accountable for providing skill-building experiences so that employees are always learning and continually creating innovative products. At Kellogg, the world's leading producer of cereal and a leading producer of convenience foods, the answer is its strategy.

Accountability: everyone, every level.

Every management level and every people manager within the organization must have measurable accountabilities, which help to ensure that Kellogg attracts, retains and promotes people from the broad range of backgrounds that comprise the diverse global marketplace it serves.

Such accountability is broad in its scope. But the creation of the K Values made it reasonable to believe that the company could embrace and support such an initiative. The K Values, six guiding Kellogg values, encompass the way the company runs its business and builds relationships with its employees.

The K Values are:

• We act with integrity and show respect

• We are all accountable

• We are passionate about our business, our brands and our food

• We have the humility and hunger to learn

• We strive for simplicity

• We love success

The key value underpinning the diversity and inclusion initiative is "We act with integrity and show respect." K Values call for everyone in the company to show respect and value all individuals for their diverse backgrounds, experiences, styles, approaches and ideas. And, it requires every member of the organization to listen to others.

Everyone who manages people at Kellogg has measurable performance requirements around the initiative. However, three groups in particular are accountable for ensuring the integration of the initiative within the company. They are:

• The Executive Management Committee (EMC)

• Human resource professionals

• The company's people managers

The specific tasks and deliverables for each group differ, but each has accountabilities in the four key strategic focuses of the diversity and inclusion strategy:

• Build accountability for diversity and inclusion throughout the organization

• Recruit, retain and develop talented people

• Drive understanding, education and awareness

• Create the environment

Three programs help to ensure that the key accountabilities are driven throughout the organization:

• Kellogg's performance management review

• The diversity and inclusion scorecard

• Managing inclusion training

Kelly Services

999 West Big Beaver Road
Troy, MI 48084
E-mail: talentmanagement@kellyser-
vices.com
www.kellyservices.com (choose United
States to go to our US homepage)

Recruiting

Please list the schools/types of schools at which you recruit.

• Private schools

• Public state schools

• Historically black colleges and universities (HBCUs)

• Hispanic serving institutions (HSIs)

*Kelly accepts resumes from various, private, public, HBCUs and HSIs.

Do you have any special outreach efforts directed to encourage minority students to consider your firm?

Kelly Services is affiliated with the following organizations:

• American Association of Retired Persons (AARP)

• Black Data Processing Association (BDPA)

• National Association of Black Accountants (NABA)

• National Association of Colleges and Employers (NACE)

• Navy League

• National Urban League

• Operation Able

Internships and Co-ops

Kelly is dedicated to supporting INROADS, Inc. Working in one of our many Kelly offices as a member of the INROADS internship program is an exciting and rewarding opportunity for any student. In fact, it's the perfect opportunity to prepare for our College Graduate-in-Training Program. Our internships are an educational strategy designed to help students merge their career goals and classroom studies with real-world experience. This is accomplished though mentorships, professional support, guidance, training and development.

The partnership between Kelly and INROADS began in 1994 and is a cornerstone of Kelly's diversity initiative. Since starting the relationship, we have hired students to work in field and corporate capacities.

Entry-Level Programs, Full-Time Opportunities and Training Programs

Our 18-month College Graduate Manager-in-Training (CGIT) program is designed to provide career opportunities to talented individuals with the desire to grow with Kelly. Our program will train you in all aspects of our branch office operations and sales process, ultimately promoting you into a management and leadership role for your own market.

What does a Kelly manager do?

As the manager of your own branch operation, you will have complete responsibility for the business development of your market as well as the development and coaching of the inside service team. You'll consult with our clients to develop human resource business solutions, while managing a multi-million dollar portfolio of business. Our managers:

• Manage branch operations to meet and exceed financial targets

• Select, train and develop staff

• Identify potential new clients through outside business development activities

• Lead team efforts in service delivery, customer and employee retention, recruiting and expense management (e.g., workers' compensation, unemployment compensation, general operating expenses)

• Build and maintain relationships with key customers and business leaders in the community, as well as local, regional and corporate Kelly management

• Design and conduct presentations and proposals to potential customers

We'd like to meet you if you have:

• A bachelor's degree in marketing, management, liberal arts or other business majors

• GPA 3.0+

• Ability to relocate

• The ability to build relationships and communicate effectively

- The ability to collaborate effectively with others to ensure both Kelly's and the customers' business goals are met and/or exceeded
- The ability and desire to lead and contribute to the personal and professional development of others
- Knowledge of financial concepts and a keen level of awareness on current labor, business and community issues

The Stats

	NUMBER OF EMPLOYEES		REVENUE
	2006	2005	2006
Total in the U.S.	4,600	4,600	N/A
Total outside the U.S.	4,000	4,000	N/A
Total worldwide	8,600*	8,600	$5.6 billion

* Kelly corporate and field employees (globally).

Diversity Mission Statement

Kelly Services is committed to and has a long history of supporting a diverse workplace. With a workforce of more than 750,000 employees globally, we place a premium on creating a culture of inclusion in order to attract, retain and develop a diverse talent pool. At Kelly Services, an inclusive culture encompasses diversity acceptance and respect for each of our employees and their contributions. We strive to maintain a diverse workforce that reflects the population of each community in which we do business.

Kelly Services has a long history of supporting a diverse workplace and maintaining a commitment to an inclusive environment. Our shared values of diversity, individual dignity and mutual respect reflect our clear commitment to diversity throughout our organization. To strengthen our commitment, diversity is one of our core strategies in the corporate business plan, which is used as a guide for all of our employees. We are also in the process of implementing a five-part diversity strategic plan that includes the following components: recruitment, talent management, outreach, education and communication.

Our main goal is to create an environment of inclusion where diverse ideas and perspectives flourish to create the best business solutions for our customers. Our success is directly tied to the success of our employees.

Additional Information

Kelly Services, Inc. is a Fortune 500 company headquartered in Troy, Mich., that provides staffing services to customers in various industries worldwide. Kelly offers staffing solutions that include temporary staffing services, staff leasing, outsourcing, vendor on-site and full-time placement. Kelly owns and operates nearly 2,600 offices in 33 countries and territories. Kelly provides employment to more than 750,000 employees annually, with skills including office services, accounting, engineering, information technology, law, science, marketing, light industrial, education, health care and home care.

Key Bank

127 Public Square
Cleveland, OH 44114
Phone: (216) 689-6300
Fax: (216) 689-7009
www.keybank.com/html/A-3.html

Locations
950 Branches located in 23 geographic districts across 13 states

Internships and Co-ops

Key internship programs offer college students an opportunity to experience working at Key on a short-term basis. Internships prepare students for full-time opportunities in the undergraduate programs and other opportunities upon graduation. Key recruits for its internship program at college campuses across the country and targets undergraduate students who major in finance, business, accounting and information technology.

Internships also help to build a foundation of diversity at Key, as Key partners with organizations such as INROADS and the United Negro College Fund (UNCF).

Web site address for employment: www.key.com/jobs

Entry-Level Programs, Full-Time Opportunities and Training Programs

Undergraduate Programs
Key undergraduate programs help connect recent college graduates with exciting opportunities at Key. By combining on-the-job training, hands-on experience and department rotations, Key analyst program graduates are well prepared for a career with the firm.

We presently offer three rotational programs in:

• Key technology services
• Key corporate and investment banking
• Finance

Strategic Plan and Diversity Leadership

At Key, we are developing a workforce and a way of doing business that reflects the diversity of our customers and communities. Economic inclusion is part of Key's diversity strategy in order to deliver exceptional products and services to our clients. In collabo-

ration with Key Corp leaders, corporate diversity will enhance the client experience and shareholder value by fostering an inclusive work environment that reflects Key's diverse markets and serves their needs.

Corporate Diversity's Mission is to be recognized by our employees, customers, stakeholders, and peer companies as the most admired financial services organization in the practice of diversity management and inclusion. Corporate Diversity at Key develops employee program opportunities, creates and leverages new and existing brand opportunities, and enhances diversity learning opportunities. Key is honored to be named a 2007 Top 50 Company for Diversity by *DiversityInc* and a 100 Best Corporate Citizen 2007 by *Corporate Responsibility Officers Magazine.*

The Stats

	NUMBER OF EMPLOYEES		REVENUE		ASSETS	
	2006	2005	2006	2005	2006	2005
Total	19,801	19,694	$4.9 billion	$4.7 billion	$93 billion	$92 billion

Retention and Professional Development

Diversity Awareness
Key offers training, mentoring programs and partnerships to our employees and to our communities.

Training
Diversity Training: Valuing differences reinforces basic diversity concepts and provides skill-building exercises; training focuses on understanding oneself and others, cultural conflicts, resolving diversity conflicts, workplace behavior, managing diverse relationships and dealing with inappropriate humor in the workplace.

Weatherhead Executive Experience (1Key Diversity Leadership Challenge): Provides diversity training for senior-level executives as part of the Weatherhead Executive Experience.

Mentoring

Mentoring helps employees confront barriers, provides exposure to critical decision-making and helps build relationships in informal and formal organizational networks. Through mentoring, minority and female employees receive professional development coaching from executives.

Partnerships

Key partnerships include:

- *National Black MBA Association:* The National Black MBA Association, Inc. (NBMBAA) is a nonprofit organization of minority MBAs, business professionals, entrepreneurs and MBA students.

- *National Society for Hispanic MBAs:* National Society of Hispanic MBAs (NSHMBA) is a nonprofit organization whose mission is fostering Hispanic leadership through graduate management, education and professional development to improve society.

- *INROADS Program:* An international, world-class nonprofit organization that helps to recruit, source and develop talented young people of color.

- *Esperanza:* Serves the educational needs of Cleveland's Hispanic community since 1983 and offers programs for elementary, middle school and high school students.

- *United Negro College Fund (UNCF):* Oldest and most distinguished higher education assistance organization in the United States.

- *Historically Black Colleges and Universities (HBCU):* We have partnerships with the following nationally ranked HBCU colleges and universities: Hampton University, Morehouse College and Spelman College.

- *Diversity Hiring Coalition:* Active member of the Diversity Hiring Coalition in Maine where resources are shared to help Maine employers to increase, support and retain racial and ethnic diversity in the workplace.

Web site for diversity: www.key.com/html/A-3.6.1.html

KPMG LLP

345 Park Avenue
New York, NY 10154-0102
Phone: (212) 758-9700
Fax: (212) 758-9819
www.kpmgcareers.com

Locations
93 US offices

Diversity Leadership
Nereida (Neddy) Perez
Chief Diversity Officer—National Director
Diversity
Three Chestnut Ridge Road
Montvale, NJ 07645

Employment Contact
Jennifer Neal
Campus Recruiting Manager
1660 International Drive
Tysons Corner
McLean, VA 22102
Phone: (703) 286-8218

Recruiting

Please list the schools/types of schools at which you recruit.

KPMG maintains recruiting relationships with well over 100 colleges and universities across the United States at both private and public institutions.

Do you have any special outreach efforts that are directed to encourage minority students to consider your firm?

• *Conferences:* National Association of Black Accountants (NABA), Association of Latino Professionals in Finance and Accounting (ALPFA), Hispanic Student Business Association (HSBA), Ascend (National Asian Accounting Association)
• Advertise in minority student association publication(s)
• Sponsor minority student association events
• Firm's employees participate on career panels at schools
• Outreach to leadership of minority student organizations
• Scholarships or intern/fellowships for minority students
• *Other:* Host Case Study Competitions for NABA and ALPFA

Do you use executive recruiting/search firms to seek to identify new diversity hires?

Yes. KPMG does use executive search firms that focus on minority and women professionals.

KPMG's Recruiting Strategy

Recruiting is another important way the firm demonstrates that diversity is profoundly important to its success. KPMG's campus recruiting team is actively involved in recruiting at historically black colleges and universities (HBCUs) and participates at the NABA and ALPFA student chapter level on a regional basis. Campus and experienced hire recruiting participate in numerous career fairs held by diverse organizations. Recruiting literature includes messaging on the firm's commitment to being a great place to work and inclusive environment.

Our interest in increasing our presence on HBCU campuses is exemplified by our participation in the Howard 21st Century Advantage Program for the past three years. Through the program, we've worked closely with groups of 20 students each year and have provided mentoring on a one-to-one basis by minority employees from KPMG.

Internships and Co-ops

INROADS

Deadline for application: May

Number of interns in the program in summer 2006 (internship) or 2006 (co-op): 100

Pay: Varies

Length of the program: Eight weeks

Percentage of interns/co-ops in the program who receive offers of full-time employment: 100 percent of those eligible to receive offers of full-time employment did receive a full-time offer.

Web site for internship/co-op information: www.inroads.org

KPMG is a member of INROADS, a program that places minority students in intern positions in our offices throughout the country.

Through this program, we are able to offer internships at an early stage,(i.e., prior to entering college) and for as many as four years, compared to our traditional one-year internship beginning the summer before graduation.

Scholarships

KPMG Foundation/Frank Ross Professorship

Deadline for application for the scholarship program: April

Scholarship award amount: $2,500

Web site or other contact information for scholarships: Awarded through NABA

Frank Ross, a retired partner with KPMG, continues his active commitment to diversity education and recruitment in the accounting field beyond his retirement from the firm. Mr. Ross, a founder of NABA, has created, in collaboration with the foundation and the firm's Washington, D.C. office, a $650,000 endowment fund. KPMG's partners and employees can contribute to this endowment fund, and KPMG's foundation will match their contribution.

We provide four $2,500 scholarships during the national NABA convention. The students are chosen by NABA based on the criteria and weightings below:

• *GPA:* 40 percent
• *Financial need:* 20 percent
• *Essay:* 15 percent
• *Leadership:* 15 percent
• *Working for education funds:* 10 percent

Minority Doctoral Scholarship Program

The KPMG Foundation invested seven million dollars to establish a Minority Doctoral Scholarship Program, open to African-American, Hispanic-American and Native American accounting doctoral students (scholarships were also awarded to information systems doctoral students from 1997-2002). This program annually awards nearly $600,000 in scholarships. This is in addition to the teaching and research assistantship and waiver of tuition and fees normally provided by doctoral-granting institutions. To date, 50 percent of the minority doctoral scholarships have been awarded to women.

Howard University Student Business Executive Leadership Honors Program

KPMG is a part of the Howard University Student Business Executive Leadership Honors Program. In this venture, KPMG works with a team of students and provides mentoring in addition to career advice and professional development opportunities for future accounting, finance and computer professionals.

Affinity Groups

Over the past several years, KPMG has developed a number of internal networks to engage our diverse groups in career development. These networks help increase visibility of diverse people among the general workforce and enhance a feeling of inclusiveness between leadership and employees.

KPMG's diversity networks include:

• APIN (Asian Pacific Islander Network)
• African-American Network
• AALA (African-American Latino Americans)
• KNOW (KPMG's Network of Women)
• Hispanic-Latino Network
• International Circle (for those engaged on an international assignment or considering one)
• Pride@KPMG (gay, lesbian, bisexual and transgender professionals)

Women's Initiatives

Constituting nearly half of all new hires, women represent an enormous part of KPMG's talent pool. To help women realize their full potential, KPMG formed a women's advisory board in 2003, charged with developing programs and initiatives designed to help support, advance and reward women.

One such program, KPMG's network of women (KNOW), has been helping to foster women's networking, mentoring and leadership opportunities in nearly half of KPMG's U.S. offices. Further expansion is planned in the years ahead. So far, KNOW has positively affected more than 8,500 women.

In addition, the Women's Advisory Board and KNOW leaders have collaborated to develop external events that bring together senior-level executive women and showcase the firm's commitment to women.

Entry-Level Programs, Full-Time Opportunities and Training Programs

Diversity Training

KPMG has always believed strongly in setting and maintaining high standards of integrity. To promote integrity and inclusiveness, KPMG requires all employees and partners to undergo "respect and dignity and diversity in the workplace" training.

Professional Training and Development

Training is available to entry-level employees and availability continues throughout each individual's career through learning opportunities to audit, tax and advisory professionals to keep each individual technically current in their accounting discipline and fully prepared to apply their auditing and accounting knowledge to the particular industry context relevant to the clients they serve.

Complementary learning opportunities are available to increase skill in client relationship management, collaboration, leadership and other personal effectiveness skills. All told, partner and employee training averages 72 hours per person annually, which significantly exceeds the National State Boards of Accountancy (NASBA) annual and triennial requirements.

KPMG has also enhanced the curriculum available to our client service support (CSS) staff to better enable their individual skills development and career success within KPMG and beyond. Areas of training include business writing and making effective presentations, building effective relationships with colleagues and clients, problem solving and decision making, leading and mobilizing teams, performance management, project management and self-management of one's career. The overall management of learning and development is carried out by the firm's center for learning and development (CLD). The CLD is staffed with a team of experienced, dedicated professionals who are the backbone of KPMG's education and training environment. Their efforts are complemented by the contributions of hundreds of audit, tax and advisory professionals who are drawn in to develop and deliver the comprehensive curriculum that is available to employees of the firm.

KLEARN LIVE! is key to the firm's blended learning approach. It's Central software-based virtual classroom delivers training in an efficient, non-intrusive way. Individuals simply log in for the training they need. Instructors and subject matter experts lead training sessions from anywhere, using slides, multimedia, whiteboards, questions, chats and other training tools.

Strategic Plan and Diversity Leadership

What trends in your industry affect your corporate diversity goals, strategies and/or internal or external alliances?

International growth is becoming very important. Many of our clients are global in nature, so we have started to offer global assignments to interns, as well new hires, as a way to develop them for the future.

Competition for talent is a challenge, so we have launched a new career management program called the Employee Career Architecture that gives employees and interns an opportunity to project and develop a career plan online. We are looking to offer access to the program to prospective recruits online by end of 2007.

How does the firm's leadership communicate the importance of diversity to everyone at the firm?

KPMG uses a variety of communication methods to help foster a supportive and inclusive work environment such as KPMG Today, the firm's Outlook-delivered daily update on news and events both

internal and external to the firm, and *KPMGLife* magazine, which profiles our people and their accomplishments.

There are messages sent out by the employee network groups as well as messages sent on behalf of the Diversity Advisory Board, which is headed up by the chief operating officer of the organization.

Who has primary responsibility for leading diversity initiatives at your firm?

Nereida (Neddy) Perez, national director of diversity and AA/EEO serves as the firm's head of diversity for the U.S.

Does your firm currently have a diversity committee?

Yes we have a national committee/advisory board, and we have several local diversity councils, as well as employee networks in place.

If yes, please describe how the committee is structured, how often it meets, etc.

KPMG's national diversity team, led by Nereida (Neddy) Perez, drives and supports the firm's national and grassroots efforts in support of KPMG's commitment to being an all-inclusive workplace. Such programs and initiatives include events, such as national diversity celebrations in local offices, KPMG diversity networks and external minority professional organization sponsorships.

Has the firm undertaken a formal or informal diversity program or set of initiatives aimed at increasing the diversity of the firm?

KPMG's Commitment to Diversity

KPMG embraces diversity and encourages our employees to share their views and lifestyles, thereby broadening everyone's awareness of differences. We believe in fostering an environment of inclusion that encourages partners and employees to be successful. By valuing our differences, we build upon our individual, team and firm strengths. It's an approach that we believe benefits our people and our clients.

Our Team

Joseph Maiorano, Executive Director, Workplace Solutions
Phone: (201) 307-7269
E-mail: jmaiorano@kpmg.com

Nereida (Neddy) Perez, National Director of Diversity and AA/EEO
Phone: (201) 307-8368
E-mail: clydejones@kpmg.com

Kathy Rohan, Manager of Diversity & AA/EEO
Phone: (201) 307-7780
E-mail: krohan@kpmg.com

Mentoring

KPMG prides itself on its mentoring culture, with thousands of partners and employees benefiting from the mentoring experience every day. The firm has several resources to help individuals establish and maintain a mentoring relationship, and leverage it for personal growth, career development and potential advancement. People can also visit the KPMG mentoring web site, and the firm helps partners and employees initiate and develop a mentoring relationship as a mentor or mentee.

Equal Employment Opportunity

KPMG LLP reaffirms its longstanding policy of providing equal opportunity for all applicants and employees regardless of their race, color, creed, religion, age, gender, national origin, citizenship status, marital status, sexual orientation, gender identity, disability, veteran status or other legally protected status.

This policy applies to recruiting, recruitment advertising and/or other communications media, hiring, rates of pay and other compensation, benefits, overtime, promotions, transfers, demotions, terminations, reductions in force, discipline and all other terms, conditions, or privileges of employment.

How often does the firm's management review the firm's diversity progress/results?

Quarterly

The Stats

	NUMBER OF EMPLOYEES		REVENUE
	2006	2005	2005*
Total worldwide	21,128	19,600	$4.7 billion

*fiscal year ending Sept. 30, 2005

Retention and Professional Development

How do 2006 minority and female attrition rates generally compare to those experienced in the prior year period?

Attrition as a whole went down slightly in 2006.

Please identify the specific steps you are taking to reduce the attrition rate of minority and women employees.

• Develop and/or support diversity networks

• Increase/review compensation relative to marketplace

• Increase/improve current work/life programs

• Professional skills development programs

Diversity Mission Statement

Our Mission

Foster a work environment that is inclusive and embraces diversity of our people, their ideas and lifestyles, professional insights and personal perspectives. This is vital for KPMG to stand apart from other audit, tax and advisory services firms and as an employer of choice.

Our Vision

Our aim is to make enhancements to the firm's work environment by valuing our differences and including them in what we do. Our values support it, our clients value it and our success depends on it.

Our Strategy

Leveraging, valuing and encouraging diversity of thought, perspective and approach to create an open and inclusive work environment where both business and personal objectives and growth can be met through:

• Awareness: Promote KPMG's strategy and commitment to diversity and inclusion internally and externally

• Recruitment: Recruit, retain and promote the best and the brightest

• Education: Provide orientation into KPMG through consistent and ongoing messaging around our culture of values, our competencies and our diversity strategy

• Career development: Provide information regarding career planning internally, including networking and mentoring and external exposure through workshops, seminars and community involvement.

Additional Information

KPMG is committed to diversity. We embrace diversity and encourage our partners and employees to share their views and lifestyles, thereby broadening everyone's awareness of differences and creating an inclusive environment free of discrimination. The varied backgrounds and experiences of our professionals are crucial to understanding and meeting our clients' needs in an increasingly diverse marketplace. Diversity is a critical component to being an employer of choice, and one of KPMG's genuine strengths. People are KPMG's most important asset and the driving force behind its success. The firm is committed to being an inclusive work environment that is built on the firm's standards and values. These help create the trust, support and openness necessary for successful people and, in turn, a successful firm.

KPMG's Values

KPMG's values define our culture and our commitment to the highest principles of personal and professional conduct. They represent how we relate to each other, what we expect from our clients, and what our clients and the marketplace should expect from us. As such, they will continue to be at the heart of how we operate as a firm.

The following is a list of KPMG's seven values:

• *We lead by example*: We, as firms and individuals, act in a manner that exemplifies what we expect of each other and our clients, and what our clients should expect of us.

• *We work together*: Forging relationships across diverse teams, cultures, functions and practices to enhance team and business results.

• *We respect the individual*: We respect all individuals for their diversity, who they are and what they bring as individuals and as team members for the benefit of our clients and the firm.

• *We seek the facts and provide insight*: We listen to and proactively challenge different points of view in order to arrive at the right judgments.

• *We are open and honest in our communication*: We encourage timely, clear and constructive two-way communication.

• *We are committed to our communities*: We, as individuals and teams, use our time and resources to support our local communities.

• *Above all, we act with integrity*: We are professional first and foremost, take pride in being part of KPMG and are committed to objectivity, quality and service of the highest standards.

External Diversity Outreach

NABA and ALPFA

KPMG is a corporate sponsor of the National Association of Black Accountants (NABA) and the Association of Latino Professionals in Finance and Accounting (ALPFA) annual conventions. We provide financial support for and sponsor KPMG professionals to attend these conventions. Many KPMG partners and employees currently hold national and local leadership positions in these organizations.

KPMG sponsors NABA and ALPFA student case study competitions that provide finance and accounting students with the opportunity to showcase their business, accounting, research and presentation skills.

KPMG maintains memberships—and plays a leading role—in various organizations focused on promoting diversity in accounting, including:

• ALPFA/National Society of Hispanic MBAs
• American Indian Business Leaders
• Diversity Career Group
• Executive Diversity
• Hispanic Association for Career Enhancement
• National Association for Asian American Professionals
• National Council of Philippine American & Canadian Accountants
• National Urban League
• Out and Equal
• Professional Strategies LLC
• Urban Financial Services Coalition
• Women for Hire
• WorkplaceDiversity.com

Memberships

KPMG is a member of the American Institute of Certified Public Accountants (AICPA), where Clyde Jones, national director, diversity and EEO/AAP, sits on the Minorities Initiative Committee, a group that is focused on increasing the number of minority CPAs in the accounting profession. This is an appointed position and Mr. Jones is in the second year of a three-year term. The committee meets quarterly and subgroups operate throughout the year. Mr. Jones chairs the academic support taskforce, which seeks to increase the minority CPA population through innovative academic scholarship programs. Mr. Jones is also a member of the Association of Latino Professionals Business Advisory Council (ALPFA). ALPFA is the premier Latino organization dedicated to enhancing opportunities for its members in the accounting, finance and related professions.

Diversity Begins on Day One

Communicating KPMG's culture starts early and goes beyond the first day of hire. Each new employee attends a new hire orientation session, which includes information about the firm's values, culture and structure. During this orientation, new hires hear from leadership about why KPMG is a great place to work and what it takes to be successful. The orientation provides all the necessary information to help ensure the new hire has a solid understanding of KPMG's strategy, policies, benefits and programs.

Supplier Diversity Program

The firm actively seeks to promote participation of minority-owned, women-owned, Veteran-owned and special disabled veteran-owned businesses in our purchasing supplier process. Equal opportunity is given to minority-owned, women-owned, Veteran-owned and special disabled veteran-owned businesses to join our supplier base by competing and participating in the purchasing process, subject to established purchasing policies and procedures.

In this regard, KPMG is the only big four firm that supports Women Business Enterprise National Council (WBENC), a national organization dedicated to the advancement of women-owned businesses (WBEs). KPMG contributes an annual contribution of nearly $40,000 to support the group's mission through sponsorships and events. Additionally, KPMG has participated in several networking events with WBEs, where our purchasing team members network with WBEs as potential vendors. KPMG is also a member of the National Minority Supplier Development Council, Inc.

KPMG Foundation

KPMG Foundation is the creator, cofounder and administrator of The PhD Project, one of the most far-reaching and ambitious diversity programs ever conceived, to address the underrepresentation of minority Americans in business, higher education and the corporate workforce. A landmark effort, The PhD Project aims to put more minorities on business school faculties, with the goal of attracting more minority students and creating greater diversity among future business students.

In December 1994, The PhD Project, with additional funding from academia and leading corporations, held a conference to bring together 266 potential minority doctoral candidates with current doctoral students, business school faculty, deans and heads of doctoral programs for a two-day conference. Less than one year after the first PhD Project conference, the nation's business schools reported a 42 percent one-year increase in the number of African-Americans, Hispanic-Americans and Native Americans entering doctoral programs in business. Half of those newly created PhD students were individuals who had been reached by The PhD Project.

The PhD Project Statistics

Forty-five of the 266 individuals who attended The PhD Project conference in 1994 began a doctoral program the following year; 62 percent of them were women. Of the 45, 19 have finished the doctoral program and are currently teaching at a university; 13 are women.

Since 1994, 10,027 individuals have submitted an application for the annual November conference, of which 4,584 were selected and 4,233 have attended.

Of the 4,233 past conference attendees, 374 started a business doctoral program, of which 109 have finished the doctoral program and currently teaching at a university; 58 of those new faculty are women.

PhD Project Doctoral Students Associations

In August 1994, KPMG Foundation formed the first African-American Accounting Doctoral Students Association (AADSA), now known as The PhD Project Accounting Doctoral Students Association. Since 1994, the foundation has expanded the associations to include finance, information systems, management and marketing students, and membership has been extended to Hispanic-Americans and Native Americans. The PhD Project Doctoral Students Associations (DSAs) help sustain a high level of commitment and sense of connection among minority students in business through networking, joint research opportunities, peer support and mentoring. As a result, 92 percent of DSA members have completed or are continuing in their doctoral programs, compared with 70

percent among doctoral candidates generally. AACSB International reports that 60.5 percent of those who earn business doctorates have teaching positions. For The PhD Project, that number is an astounding 99 percent.

KPMG's Recognitions for Diversity

KPMG's local offices have won numerous awards for their efforts in diversity and community service, including:

- *The Black Collegian* magazine's Top 100 Employers

- American Cancer Society's National Team Program Recognition award

- Award for Excellence in Workplace Volunteer programs/Points of Light

- Human Rights Campaign Foundation's Corporate Equality Index

- *Working Mother* magazine's 100 Best Companies

- *Hispanic* magazine's corporate 100 Best Places for Latinos to Work and Top 50 Recruitment Companies

- *Asian Enterprise* magazine's 10 Best Companies for Asian Americans

- American Society of Women Accountants' Balance Award: Celebrating the Dimensions of Success

- *DiversityInc's* Top 10 Companies for Executive Women, Top 10 Companies for Asian Americans, 20 Noteworthy Companies

- Center for Companies that Care, 2005 Honor Roll Volunteerism award

- National Fatherhood Initiative (NFI) Fatherhood award

- Abilities, Inc./NBDC at the National Center for Disability Services, Making a Difference award on celebrating diversity year round

- YAI/NIPD (National Institute of People with Disabilities)— Corporation of the Year

- The Human Rights Campaign (HRC) Best Places to Work

The materials contained within this document provide a general overview of some of KPMG's programs, practices and policies.

It is important to remember that individual situations will vary. Further, the programs, policies and practices described generally herein do change from time to time, and we reserve the right to make such changes and/or discontinue any of them at any time and for any reason, subject to applicable federal, state and/or local laws.

Kroger Co., The

1014 Vine Street
Cincinnati, OH 45202
Phone: (513) 762-4000
Fax: (513) 698-1850

Locations

The company operates 2,473 supermarkets and multi-department stores in 31 states under two dozen local banners including Kroger and Kroger Marketplace, Ralphs, Fred Meyer, Food 4 Less, King Soopers, Smith's and Smith's Marketplace, Fry's and Fry's Marketplace, Dillons, QFC and City Market) and 774 convenience stores, 418 fine jewelry stores, 619 supermarket fuel centers and 42 food processing plants.

Diversity Leadership

Carver Johnson
Chief Diversity Officer

Employment Contact

Joan Harris-Graves
Corporate Manager of Recruiting & Selection
Phone: (513) 762-4063
E-mail: krogerresumes@kroger.com

Recruiting

Please list the schools/types of schools at which you recruit.

- Ivy League schools
- Other private schools
- Public state schools
- Historically black colleges and universities (HBCUs)
- Hispanic serving institutions (HSIs)
- Native American tribal universities

Our enterprise recruits at over 180 colleges and universities annually for the Store Management Training Program, Manufacturing Career Training Program, Information Systems & Services, and for engineering, auditing, human resources, accounting and pharmacy.

Do you have any special outreach efforts directed to encourage minority students and graduates to consider your firm?

- Advertise in minority student association publication(s) or other minority-focused publications
- Participate in/host minority student job fair(s) or other minority-focused job events
- Sponsor minority student association events
- Firm's employees participate on career panels at school
- Outreach to leadership of minority student organizations
- Scholarships or intern/fellowships for minority students

What activities does the firm undertake to attract minority and women employees?

- *Partner programs with women and minority associations:* Urban League, Urban League YouthWorks Program, Minority Chambers of Commerce Nationwide, UNCF, National Pharmaceutical Association
- *Conferences:* National Society of Hispanic MBA Conference, American Pharmacist Association Conference, American Society of Health System Pharmacists Mid-Year Meeting, NAACP Conferences, Rainbow/PUSH Coalition Conferences
- Participate at minority job fairs
- Seek referrals from other employees
- Utilize online job services

Internships and Co-ops

INROADS

Deadline for application: INROADS deadline

Pay: Varies depending on the position and the division

Length of the program: 10 weeks

Percentage of interns/co-ops in the program who receive offers of full-time employment: 80 percent

Web site for internship/co-op information: www.inroads.org

Kroger partners with INROADS in several of our divisions across the company.

Facility Engineering Co-Op or Intern

Deadline for application: February

Number of interns in the program in summer 2006 (internship) or 2006 (co-op): 15

Pay: Varies depending on experience

Length of the program: Summer (three months) or co-op during the school year

Web site for internship/co-op information: E-mail krogerresumes@kroger.com

Students must be working toward a four-year degree in mechanical/electrical/civil engineering or building construction, be able to travel, have basic computer skills, be able to use Microsoft Word and Excel, and have excellent communication and interpersonal skills. These positions are all over the country.

Atlanta, GA Mayor's Next Step 2007 Summer Internship Program

Deadline for application: December 2006 (Processed by the mayor's office)

Number of interns in the program in summer 2006 (internship) or 2006 (co-op): Two

Pay: $10 per hour, 30-35 hours per week

Length of the program: Eight weeks

Percentage of interns/co-ops in the program who receive offers of full-time employment: The program is for graduating high school seniors going to college

Web site for internship/co-op information: Atlanta city government web site. The mayor's office screens the students and assigns them to the employers based on student interest.

Cincinnati/Dayton Division Garnes Ward Internship Program

Deadline for application: April 1st

Number of interns in the program in summer 2006 (internship) or 2006 (co-op): Eight. Students must be going into their junior or senior year of college.

Pay: $7,000 for the entire program. Upon completion of the internship program, $3,500 is donated to the college or university.

Length of the program: 10 weeks

Web site for internship/co-op information: E-mail krogerresumes@kroger.com

Fred Meyer Internship Program (Oregon)

Deadline for application: February

Number of interns in the program in summer 2006 (internship) or 2006 (co-op): 25

Pay: $12 per hour

Length of the program: 11 weeks

Percentage of interns/co-ops in the program who receive offers of full-time employment: 63 percent

Web site for internship/co-op information: www.fredmeyer.com

Students intern in the corporate office in Portland and the stores learning purchasing, merchandising, human resources and store management. Eligible students must be juniors in college with a 3.0 GPA.

Fry's Internship Program (Arizona)

Number of interns in the program in summer 2006 (internship) or 2006 (co-op): Two

Pay: Varies based on experience

Length of the program: Summer

Web site for internship/co-op information: E-mail krogerresumes@kroger.com

The program is targeted toward students with an interest in human resources and training and development.

Great Lakes Division Internship Program

Deadline for application: March 1st

Number of interns in the program in summer 2006 (internship) or 2006 (co-op): Six

Pay: $10.50 per hour; varies based on experience

Length of the program: 12 weeks

Percentage of interns/co-ops in the program who receive offers of full-time employment: 50 percent

Web site for internship/co-op information: E-mail krogerresumes@kroger.com

The program is targeted toward students at Ohio State University and Western Michigan University.

Multicultural Business Scholars at University of Kansas

Number of interns in the program in summer 2006 (internship) or 2006 (co-op): One at Dillon Food Stores

Pay: $9 per hour, adjusting with experience

Length of the program: 13 weeks

Interns work approximately 15-20 hours per week and receive the abbreviated version of our management development training program.

Corporate Audit Internship Program (Cincinnati, Ohio)

Deadline for application: February

Number of interns in the program in summer 2006 (internship) or 2006 (co-op): 10

Pay: Varies depending on experience

Length of the program: Summer

Web site for internship/co-op information: www.krogerresumes@kroger.com

To be eligible, students must be accounting majors and have a goal of sitting for the CPA.

Information Systems & Services Internship Program

Deadline for application: Program is year around, but with a heavy emphasis on summer internships

Number of interns in the program in summer 2006 (internship) or 2006 (co-op): 25

Pay: $12 per hour and up

Length of the program: Varies

Web site for internship/co-op information: E-mail itresumes@kroger.com

To be eligible, students must be majoring in the information systems and solutions field. The internships will involve you in meaningful projects that expand your technical and business skills. Some of the areas that may have internship positions include:

• Programming

• Networking

• Data administration

• Desktop engineering

• Web development

• Information security

• E-mail engineering

• E-Commerce

• Supply chain systems

• Merchandising systems

• Scholarships

Kroger Delta Division INROADS Scholarship

Deadline for application for the scholarship program: January 15th (fall); June 1st (spring)

Scholarship award amount: $250 to $1,000

The student must be an INROADS intern that has worked for Kroger Delta division at least one summer.

Georgia Food Industry Association

Scholarship award amount: $2,500

Houston Grocery Manufacturers and Dallas Food Sales Association Scholarships

Scholarship award amount: Up to $3,000

University of Kansas Multicultural Scholars

Scholarship award amount: Sponsorship of 10 scholars

Web site or other contact information for scholarship: Please contact University of Kansas

Entry-Level Programs, Full-Time Opportunities and Training Programs

Management Development Program

Length of program: 12 to 18 weeks

Geographic location(s) of program: Nationwide

This program prepares candidates to become co-managers and ultimately store managers in our stores. This program is extremely robust and is the best way to learn the business and be promoted within the organization. As part of the training program, candidates learn the following: inventory control, merchandising and sales, conflict mediation, labor management and prioritization, accounting, problem solving, change management, performance management, customer service, and continuous self-growth and education.

Upon completion of the program, tuition reimbursement for further education is available in most divisions.

Kroger Manufacturing Career Training Program

Length of program: 12 to 18 months

Geographic location(s) of program: Nationwide

Kroger Manufacturing is the largest private-label manufacturer of grocery products in the United States. We currently operate 41 manufacturing plants across the U.S. Our mission is to become an employer of choice by valuing people and professionally managing our business. We want to further enhance the quality of our employees' careers by providing challenging, purposeful and rewarding development.

The Career Training Program is designed to give recent graduates the opportunity to gain a broad perspective of the core business functions that are critical to the manufacture of Kroger private-label brands.

Trainees will be hired into the company at a first-level management position and will complete a training program over a 12- to 18-month period.

The program provides trainees with:

• Real, challenging and meaningful assignments within a plant environment

• Structured written training program, both general and career-specific*

• Quality progress reviews

• Training in technical and managerial skills

• Coaching and career counseling with assignment managers and mentors

• A strong sense of partnership and teamwork

*Career-specific areas include:

• Human resources
• Production
• Engineering
• Sales
• Quality assurance
• Information systems
• Packaging and procurement
• Accounting

Qualifications

• Bachelor's degree in a field of discipline
• Relocation is required at the completion of the program

E-mail your resume with your present salary and future salary expectations, geographic relocation preferences, dislikes or limitations to mfggreatpeople.corp@kroger.com. For more information, visit www.kroger.com.

Western Association of Food Chains Certificate Program

Geographic location(s) of program: California, Nevada, Arizona, New Mexico, Washington and Utah

Candidates attend community college to learn in a program specifically targeted toward food retail. They focus on the following areas: supervision, business writing, business math, oral communication, introduction to management, human relations, human resource management, retailing, accounting/bookkeeping and introduction to marketing. This program prepares hourly associates in retail for management positions within the company.

Urban League YouthWorks

Length of program: Summer program for students 15 to 17 years old

Geographic location(s) of program: Kroger divisions across the country partner with the Urban League to offer young adults in the community an opportunity to work for a Kroger store.

The students train on Saturdays and learn how to interview, dress, handle financial responsibility, etc.

Kroger associates volunteer to assist with the classes.

Strategic Plan and Diversity Leadership

How does the firm's leadership communicate the importance of diversity to everyone at the firm?

Quarterly and annual communications to associates at all levels within the organization, internal inclusion web site, availability of inclusion training for associates, cultural council champions and leaders throughout the organization.

Who has primary responsibility for leading diversity initiatives at your firm?

Carver Johnson, chief diversity officer

Does your firm currently have a diversity committee?

Yes

If yes, please describe how the committee is structured, how often it meets, etc.

Every division has an inclusion council composed of associates from various levels. These councils work on many projects that reflect our core values of honesty, integrity, respect, diversity, inclusion and safety.

If yes, does the committee's representation include one or more members of the firm's management/executive committee (or the equivalent)?

Yes

If yes, how many executives are on the committee?

An executive from each division is involved with the council.

Does the committee and/or diversity leader establish and set goals or objectives consistent with management's priorities?

Yes

Has the firm undertaken a formal or informal diversity program or set of initiatives aimed at increasing the diversity of the firm?

Yes, formal. The councils have created a roadmap and have the role of ensuring the roadmap is implemented throughout the company. They also identify and remove barriers that get in the way of building a more diverse and inclusive business environment.

How often does the firm's management review the firm's diversity progress/results?

Quarterly, annually

The Stats

	NUMBER OF EMPLOYEES		REVENUE
	2006	2005	2006
Total worldwide	290,000	290,000	$66 billion

Women and people of color are slightly more than half of the managers and 60 percent of the professionals in our company. We are committed to continuous improvement in the representation of women and people of color in our management ranks, including the highest levels of the company and our board of directors. Our successor planning process requires managers and department heads to provide annual updates on progress made in the placement and promotion of women and people of color.

Key job categories with the percentage of female and minority associates as of late 2005 are:

	FEMALE	MINORITY
Officials and managers	41 percent	18 percent
Professionals	54 percent	18 percent
Sales workers	53 percent	29 percent
All associates	51 percent	28 percent

Retention and Professional Development

How do 2006 minority and female attrition rates generally compare to those experienced in the prior year period?

About the same as in prior years.

Please identify the specific steps you are taking to reduce the attrition rate of minority and women employees.

• Develop and/or support internal employee affinity groups (e.g., minority or women networks within the firm)

• Increase/review compensation relative to competition

• Increase/improve current work/life programs

• Succession plan includes emphasis on diversity

• Work with minority and women employees to develop career advancement plans

• Strengthen mentoring program for all employees, including minorities and women

• Professional skills development program, including minority and women employees

Additional Information

Supplier diversity is an important part of Kroger's business strategy as evidenced by Kroger's 2007 Induction into the Billion Dollar Roundtable. The Billion Dollar Roundtable is the premier forum for corporations that have achieved $1 billion or more in spending with minority and women-owned businesses. Our goal is always the same, to be sure that our suppliers reflect the broad diversity of the customers and marketplaces we serve. Kroger's supplier diversity program is more than 25 years old. The goal of the program is to foster the use, growth and development of qualified minority and women-owned suppliers. We work with hundreds of M/WBEs and purchase millions of dollars of services and retail goods from them. These firms, which range in size from large corporations to small entrepreneurs, play a critical role in helping Kroger understand and meet the diverse needs of our customers everyday. We also encourage our major suppliers to increase their supplier diversity efforts as well.

Lehman Brothers

745 Seventh Avenue
New York, NY 10019
Phone: (212) 526-7000
www.lehman.com/careers

Contact Person

Anne Erni
Managing Director, Chief Diversity Officer

Diversity Campus Recruiting Team Leader

Deirdre O'Donnell
Senior Vice President, Global Head of
Diversity Recruiting

Experienced Hire Contact

Erica Irish Brown
Senior Vice President, Head of Diversity
Lateral Recruiting

Recruiting

Does your firm annually recruit at any of the following types of institutions?

- *Ivy League schools:* Brown University, Columbia University, Cornell University, Dartmouth College, Harvard University, University of Pennsylvania, Princeton University and Yale University
- *Other private schools:* Amherst College, Carnegie Mellon University, Duke University, Franklin & Marshall College, Georgetown University, George Washington University, Johns Hopkins University, Massachusetts Institute of Technology, Middlebury College, New York University, Northeastern University, Northwestern University, Rider University, Rochester Polytechnic Institute, Rochester Institute of Technology, St. John's University, Stanford University, University of Maryland, University of Miami, University of Notre Dame, Villanova University, Washington University in St. Louis and Williams College
- *Public state schools:* Baruch College, North Carolina A&T State University, Rutgers University, Stony Brook University, University of California Berkeley, University of California Los Angeles, University of Florida, University of Michigan, University of Texas at Austin and University of Virginia
- *Historically Black Colleges and Universities (HBCUs):* Morehouse College and Spelman College
- *Other predominantly minority and/or women's colleges:* Barnard College and Wellesley College

Do you have any special outreach efforts directed to encourage minority students to consider your firm?

- Hold a reception for minority students

- *Conferences:* National Black MBA NBMBAA, National Society of Hispanic MBAs NSHMBA, Out for Undergraduate Business Conference, Reaching Out Conference, MBA Jumpstart, Society of Hispanic Engineers SHPE, National Society of Black Engineers NSBE, Society of Women Engineers SWE, Hispanic Alliance for Career Enhancement HACE and Management Leadership for Tomorrow ML4T
- Advertise in minority student association publication(s)
- Participate in/host minority student job fair(s)
- Sponsor minority student association events
- Scholarships or intern/fellowships for minority students
- *Other:* Resume and interview skills workshops
- Participate in diversity career panels at schools
- Maintain and execute aggressive outreach to leadership of minority student organizations

What activities does the firm undertake to attract minority and women employees?

All of the firm's diversity initiatives are aimed at attracting, hiring and retaining qualified diverse candidates and employees. In 2005, the firm hired a full-time diversity lateral recruiting team who concentrates solely on identifying top female and minority candidates for new job openings at Lehman Brothers. The group focuses on hiring qualified individuals into front, middle and back office positions at the analyst level and above.

All internal recruiters assist hiring managers in sourcing diverse candidates through various professional and charitable organizations, organization and job posting web sites, conferences and other contacts. These resources include the Financial Women's Association, 85 Broads, Toigo Foundation, LatPro.com, America's Job Bank, Hot Jobs and alumni networks, such as Columbia Business School's African American Alumni

Association. Hiring managers are encouraged to post all new openings internally and externally for all employees and others to have the opportunity to apply and to ensure that there is a diverse slate of qualified candidates for open positions before extending the offer. In addition, the firm offers a training program entitled "Interviewing Through a Diversity Lens" which helps hiring managers identify candidate strengths beyond their first impression and enables the managers to be more objective during the recruiting and interview process.

In addition to campus recruiting, the lateral recruiting team attends annual conferences for the National Black MBA Association (NBMBAA), the National Society of Hispanic MBAs (NSHMBA), the National Association of Black Accountants (NABA) and the Association of Latino Professionals in Finance and Accounting (ALPFA) as well as the National Association of Securities Professionals (NASP). Lehman participates in various professional career fairs including the Annual Diversity Career Expo sponsored by the National Association of African Americans in Human Resources (NAAAHR) and WorkplaceDiversity.com, the Hispanic Alliance for Career Enhancement (HACE), Women for Hire, the Wall Street Business and Disability Council and the TOIGO Foundation Annual Career Fair for Fellows and Alumni.

In addition to the external sources of candidates mentioned above, employee referrals for lateral professional hires are actively solicited from the firm's employee networks: Women's Initiatives Leading Lehman, Lehman Employees of African Decent, The Latin American Council, Lehman Brothers Asian Network, Lehman Brothers Disability Working Forum and Lehman Brothers Gay and Lesbian Network.

In 2005, Lehman Brothers launched Encore^{SM} , an innovative program aimed at strengthening the firm's recruiting efforts. Encore^{SM} was the firm's corporate response to the Harvard Business Review research study, "Off-Ramps and On-Ramps," published in 2005. This study, which Lehman Brothers sponsored, focused on the difficulties women face in re-entering the workforce after taking time off to have children, to care for elderly parents or to address other life responsibilities. Gathering for a unique half-day experience, 71 female participants visited Lehman Brothers looking for "on ramps" in their professional careers. The attendee list included employees who had previously worked at Lehman Brothers and former employees of other financial entities. The Encore^{SM} event included networking, self-reflection and informational sessions. Introductory screening and counseling sessions were conducted with the majority of women who submitted their resumes, and opportunities for subsequent follow-up interviews with the businesses were extended when appropriate. Encore^{SM} has since expanded globally and was launched in Europe in early 2006. The second annual Lehman Brothers Encore^{SM} event was held in November 2006 in New York and since then, the program has expanded to Hong Kong and Tokyo and a second program in Europe will be held later this year.

In addition to the firm's internal diversity initiatives, Lehman Brothers requires that search firms provide hiring managers with diverse slates for each and every job opening on which they are retained. This policy is reinforced by the firm's annual "search firm breakfast," where senior management reiterates the firm's commitment to diversity and the need for search firms who wish to do business with Lehman Brothers to be equally committed.

Do you use executive recruiting/search firms to seek to identify new diversity hires?
Yes

Internships and Co-ops

Lehman Brothers' summer analyst programs provide motivated college juniors with an internship position in one of six programs: investment banking, capital markets, investment management, finance, operations or information technology. These summer analyst programs offer an exciting opportunity for talented individuals interested in exposure to the financial services industry.

In all programs, weekly workshops and seminars are provided to expose analysts to all areas of the firm. Summer analysts are assigned junior and senior mentors to provide guidance throughout the summer. They will also benefit from contact with employees at all levels of the firm through group events and informal functions. Summer analysts are provided with detailed feedback twice during the summer—first, midway through the program and then at the end. The divisions look upon the summer analyst programs as a primary source for hiring full-time analysts.

What we look for in a summer analyst:

- Students currently pursuing an undergraduate degree in their penultimate year of graduation
- Record of distinctive academic performance
- Distinctive problem-solving skills
- Strong professional presence to include self-confidence and maturity
- Marked leadership potential
- Strong initiative—the ability to make things happen
- Ability to contribute in team-based environment

Investment Banking Summer Analyst Program

Pay: Competitive

Length of the program: Varies

Web site for internship information: www.lehman.com/careers

The Investment Banking Division (IBD) summer analyst program is managed as two separate sequential summer programs (term one and term two). Each program is eight weeks, with the exact term coinciding with the summer vacation schedules of our participating schools. As a summer analyst, you are provided with a hands-on opportunity to work as a full member of a client team on a variety of projects and transactions.

As a summer analyst, you will go through an initial one-week training program that is designed to introduce you to the firm's unique culture, and reinforce the skills necessary for a successful career in banking. You will also have the opportunity to attend presentations and networking events throughout the summer that will enable you to learn more about the different groups and meet colleagues across different areas of the firm.

The division views the summer analyst program as a primary source for hiring full-time analysts. Accordingly, if you are interested in the full-time analyst program, you are strongly encouraged to apply to the summer analyst program.

Group Placement Process

Summer analysts are assigned to a single industry, product or geography group for the summer. Group assignments are based on a matching process between your preferences, balanced against the needs of the groups.

Equities, Fixed-Income and Prime Services Summer Analyst Program

Pay: Competitive

Length of the program: Eight weeks

Web site for internship information: www.lehman.com/careers

The Capital Markets Division summer analyst program is managed as two separate sequential summer programs (term one and term two). Each program runs for eight weeks, and the exact term maps to the summer vacation schedules of our participating schools. As a summer analyst, you are provided with training and then placed in an equities, fixed income or capital markets prime services business. You are also assigned a recruiter who is responsible for tracking your performance while you are in the program.

Apart from receiving initial training, you will also have the opportunity to attend presentations and networking events throughout the summer which will enable you to learn more about the different groups and meet colleagues across different areas of the firm.

The division views the summer analyst program as a primary source for hiring full-time analysts. Accordingly, if you are interested in the full-time analyst program, you are strongly encouraged to apply to the summer analyst program.

Group Placement Process

Before beginning the summer program, you are asked to complete a placement questionnaire and rank, in order of preference, the areas in equities, fixed income and capital markets prime services in which you are interested in working in during the summer. Placement decisions are made by the capital markets program management and recruiting teams and are based on business demands and your preferences

Investment Management Summer Analyst Program

Pay: Competitive

Length of the program: 10 weeks investment management

Web site for internship information: www.lehman.com/careers

The Investment Management Division (IMD) summer analyst program is an eight-week program which begins in late May with a three-day training program. This is a direct placement program designed to give you experience in one or two of the four areas in the division:

• Investments and Research
• Client Advisory and Solutions
• Strategy and Business Management
• Private Investment Management

At the end of the summer, individual business groups extend direct offers for the full-time program to exceptional performers.

Group Placement Process

As a summer analyst, you will spend your entire summer in one or two business groups in the division. Placements are based on your preferences and balanced against the overall business needs of the groups.

Finance Summer Analyst Program

Pay: Competitive

Length of the program: 10 weeks

Web site for internship information: www.lehman.com/careers

The finance division summer analyst program is a 10-week program that provides you with the opportunity to work with experienced professionals, obtain insight into the work and culture of the firm as a whole, and build marketable skills. Summer analysts will also have the opportunity to contribute as valued members of the group to which they are assigned.

To ensure that summer analysts receive the best possible development experience, we supplement on-the-job experience with a comprehensive training curriculum. The curriculum spans professional skills and industry knowledge that will enable you to achieve success within the finance division. The modules include:

• Presentations on communicating and operating effectively within the finance industry
• Management-led overviews
• Presentations by internal and external experts on relevant financial products and market topics
• New York Stock Exchange tour

Group Placement Process

Placement decisions are made based on business needs and skill sets demonstrated during the interview process. Placements are made into the following groups:

- Accounting and external reporting
- Equity product control
- Fixed income product control
- Global interest control
- Investment management finance
- Tax compliance
- Treasury management

Operations Summer Analyst Program

Pay: Competitive

Length of the program: 10 weeks

Web site for internship information: www.lehman.com\careers

The operations division summer analyst program is a 10-week program in which you are trained, placed in a business and encouraged to develop your skills on an ongoing basis. As a summer analyst, you have the opportunity to contribute as a full and valued member of the team to which you are assigned, and assume responsibilities similar to those of a first-year analyst.

To ensure that you receive the best possible exposure to the division during the summer program, we supplement on-the-job experience with a comprehensive curriculum designed to provide you with professional skills, industry knowledge and development opportunities. This training includes attending management-led overviews and presentations by internal and external experts on relevant financial products and market topics, and a tour of the New York Stock Exchange.

The division views the summer analyst program as the primary source for hiring full-time analysts. Accordingly, if you are interested in the full-time analyst program, you are strongly encouraged to apply to the summer analyst program.

Group Placement Process

As a summer analyst, you are placed into one area for the entire 10-week program. Similar to the full-time operations analyst program, placement decisions are made based on business needs and your preferences; skill sets that you demonstrated during the interview process are also taken into account. Placement decisions are made based on business needs in the following groups:

- Equity operations
- Fixed-income operations
- Investment management division operations
- Information and exposure management
- Clearance and custody services
- Operations control
- Business analysis group

Information Technology Summer Analyst Program

Pay: Competitive

Length of the program: 10 weeks

Web site for internship information: www.lehman.com/careers

The Information Technology (IT) Division summer analyst program is a 10-week work experience offered to students in their junior year who are majoring in computer science, electrical engineering or management information systems. You will join either an application development or infrastructure technology team and take an active role in developing the technology that drives our businesses. Weekly meetings, social events and seminars provide you with exposure to senior management of the division and the businesses of Wall Street. As a summer analyst, you will gain valuable experience while meeting new people and learning new skills.

IT summer analysts attend a weekly breakfast speaker series where senior managers address varying subjects on technology on Wall Street. Additionally, you will have an opportunity to network with their managers and colleagues throughout the summer and to hear about different areas in technology.

The division views the summer analyst program as a primary source for hiring full-time analysts. Accordingly, if you are interested in the full-time analyst program, you are strongly encouraged to apply to the summer analyst program.

Group Placement Process

All summer analysts are placed directory in a specific group and begin working in their group on the first day of the program. Placements include:

- Equities technology
- Fixed-income technology
- Investment management technology
- Operations technology
- Enterprise information services (EIS)
- Enterprise architecture services (EAS)
- Infrastructure engineering and support (IES)
- Finance technology
- Risk technology
- Corporate advisory technology
- Investment banking technology
- Human resources technology
- Capital Markets Prime Services technology

Affinity Groups

Lehman Brothers' diversity initiatives is aimed at attracting the best people and providing a culture and work environment that helps maximize that having a diverse workforce encourages increased creativity and innovation, which are crucial drivers for continued business success. To help achieve our diversity goals, the firm endorses

employee networks. Networks are encouraged to meet as often as necessary; the frequency is determined by the networks. Meetings take the form of steering committee meetings, subcommittee meetings, town halls, general events and monthly network leader meetings with the global diversity and inclusion office. In 2005, network leaders were invited to present to the firm's CEO on issues relevant to their constituencies and the firm. In the U.S., Europe and Asia there is active participation in one or more of the following networks:

Lehman Brothers Asian Network (LBAN)

LBAN enhances professional development opportunities, increases awareness of various Asian cultures and fosters collaboration among our colleagues globally.

Lehman Brothers Disability Working Forum (LBDWF)

LBDWF works both to develop a strategy to educate and raise awareness about disabilities, and to develop relationships with external disability-related organizations.

Lehman Brothers Employee & Family Network (LEAF)

LEAF aims to provide education and support for employees who are caregivers of all ages and family situations.

Lehman Brothers Gay & Lesbian Network (LBGLN)

LBGLN is committed to enhancing the firm's profile in all places where we conduct business and ensuring that the firm is the employer of choice for gay, lesbian, bisexual and transgender (GLBT) people. To achieve this mission, LBGLN will work to maintain a positive and inclusive environment at the firm, sustain an atmosphere where GLBT employees are respected and valued and provide a community and career development network to GLBT employees. LBGLN will also build greater awareness beyond our network on issues important to the GLBT community.

Lehman Brothers Multicultural Network (LBMCN)

LBMCN works to embrace and enrich the cultural fabric of the firm by providing a supportive environment for the firm's black and ethnic minority employees to enhance career development and retention.

Lehman Employees of African Descent (LEAD)

LEAD is dedicated to promoting diversity and inclusion at the firm through recruiting, mentoring, philanthropy, cultural initiatives and educational programs. LEAD is committed to helping every employee have an impact, engage their passion and achieve their greatest career potential.

The Latin American Council (TLAC)

TLAC works to create career, educational and social opportunities for Latin American/Hispanic professionals within Lehman Brothers. TLAC seeks to help Lehman Brothers identify, retain and develop the firm's Latin American/Hispanic talent by fostering an environ-

ment for professional and personal advancement that contributes to the firm's growth and continued success.

Women's Initiatives Leading Lehman (WILL)

WILL works to encourage, inspire and support women in their career development at Lehman Brothers, with the goal of attracting and retaining women who can contribute to the firm's long term success.

For more information, visit our diversity networks web site at: http://www.lehman.com/who/diversity/networks.htm

Entry-Level Programs, Full-Time Opportunities and Training Programs

Investment Banking Analyst Program

Length of program: Two to three years

Geographic location(s) of program: New York, Los Angeles, Menlo Park, Chicago, Houston

The Investment Banking Division (IBD) analyst program is a two-year program (with a third-year option) in which you are trained, placed in a group and developed professionally on an ongoing basis. Analyst program managers guide you through the group placement process and monitor your career development by facilitating the feedback and review process, as well as the advancement process.

As an analyst, you will perform a wide variety of roles. Most assignments involve some form of financial analysis, including those necessary for debt and equity financings, mergers and acquisitions, divestitures and strategic financial advisory. You will have the opportunity to work with colleagues at different levels and from different areas within the firm, as well as to attend client meetings with senior bankers. As your experience grows, so will your level of responsibility.

The IBD analyst program targets candidates with a high level of academic and leadership achievement, who are able to withstand the rigors of a rapidly changing and demanding, but ultimately rewarding environment. In return, we strive to provide you with exceptional professional exposure and the opportunity to work with some of the most talented bankers in our industry.

Group Placement Process

New York analysts are hired into the generalist pool and then participate in the group placement process. As a new analyst, you will attend a series of group presentations and networking events during the initial training program. These events give you the opportunity to learn about each group and meet bankers from a variety of business areas. Program managers will then place you in a group by

matching your preferences and skill set with the specific business needs of the groups.

Analysts in other regional offices in the U.S., who are directly placed into specific groups, do not participate in the group placement process. Pre-placed regional analysts begin working in their groups directly after completion of the initial training program.

Following the group placement and the completion of the initial training program, analysts attend group-specific training, which corresponds to the industry/product group in which they will work.

Training

The initial training program for the U.S. IBD analysts is a four- to five-week program held in New York.

The primary objectives of the training programs are to:

• Provide an overview of Lehman Brothers' products and businesses

• Develop an understanding of the role of the analyst and the nature of investment banking work

• Enhance finance/technical skills essential to investment banking

• Introduce Lehman Brothers' specific technologies and internal processes

• Promote social interaction and networking among offices and regions

Some of the topics that will be covered include:

• Accounting

• Corporate finance/valuation

• Financial modeling

• Capital markets

• Computer training

• Regulatory training

• Overview of the investment banking groups

Equities, Fixed Income and Prime Services Analyst Program

Length of program: Two to three years

Geographic location(s) of program: New York

The Capital Markets Analyst Program is a two- to three-year program in which you are trained, placed in a business within capital markets (unless directly placed) and developed professionally on an ongoing basis.

You are assigned a program manager who is responsible for your career development while you are in the program. The program manager guides you through the rotation and group placement process, and monitors your career development by facilitating the feedback, review and advancement process.

Rotation and Group Placement Process

Prior to participating in the initial training program, analysts and senior analysts hired as generalists will rotate through businesses in the equities, fixed income and capital markets prime services divisions to find a permanent position within the firm. Analysts who are directly hired into specific positions (typically in real estate, structured finance, public finance and analytics) do not participate in the rotation process.

The generalist rotation process begins with career fairs, where generalists will learn about the various equities, fixed income and capital markets prime services businesses seeking to hire analysts. Following the career fairs, generalists will follow rotation schedules, consisting of several four-hour interactive rotations through various desks, enabling them to explore different roles and functions within all three divisions.

Upon completing these intensive and interactive rotations, placement decisions are made by the regional heads of the equities, fixed income and capital markets prime services divisions, based on overall business needs, appropriate fit and your preferences.

Once placement decisions are made, you will participate in an eight-week training program, after which you will begin working on your assigned desk. From this point forward, your progress is carefully managed by your program manager.

Training

Capital markets analysts are offered a seven- to eight-week sales, trading and research initial training program, held in New York. Instructors include both Lehman Brothers speakers and third-party consultants. The general curriculum includes the following modules:

• Capital markets fundamentals—accounting and bond math

• Divisional product training in equities, fixed income and capital markets prime services

• Regulatory certification training for the NASD Series 7 and Series 63 licensing exams

Investment Management Analyst Program

Length of program: Two to three years

Geographic location(s) of program: New York, with some positions available in Chicago and other branch offices

The Investment Management Division (IMD) analyst program is a two- to three-year program in which analysts are placed in diverse jobs across three groups in the division: investments and research, client advisory and solutions, and strategy and business management.

Rotation and Group Placement Process

Our program is primarily a direct hire program. Throughout the interview process we determine the best fit for you within our division and we extend you an offer for a specific group placement.

This allows you to prepare for your position as necessary during your final year of school. In some cases we may hire a few generalist analysts. For generalists, group placements will be determined upon your arrival at the firm, and after a period of rotations through various investment management businesses.

Training

The Investment Management analyst initial training program is an eight-week program held in New York. Beginning with the "One Firm" training, IMD analysts join their associate colleagues for a week and one-half of division-specific training, designed to provide you with a thorough understanding of the division and how its diverse business units work together.

In addition, IMD analysts receive intensive investment analysis initial training. Topics include:

- Financial statement analysis
- Building integrated financial statement forecasts
- Power Excel® a modeling
- Valuation and portfolio performance analytics
- U.S. IMD analysts receive training for the Series 7 and Series 66 securities licensing exams. This training takes place over the course of two weeks and finishes with the analysts sitting for both exams.

Finance Analyst Program

Length of program: Two years

Geographic location(s) of program: New York and New Jersey

The finance division analyst program is a two-year program consisting of three eight-month rotations through the finance division. The program begins with an orientation to Lehman Brothers, followed by a three-week comprehensive training curriculum. The curriculum is designed to provide you with the professional skills, industry knowledge and development opportunities that will enable you to achieve success within the finance division.

Group Placement Process

At the end of training, you will be assigned to the first of your three rotations. Placement decisions are made based on business needs and the skill sets you demonstrated from your time as a summer analyst or during the interview process. Placements are made into the following groups:

Accounting and external reporting

- Equity product control
- Fixed-income product control
- Global interest control
- Investment management finance
- Tax compliance
- Treasury management
- Training

The U.S. finance analysts are required to complete an online training course before the program begins. Upon joining, the program offers three weeks of initial training for the analysts. The general curriculum for the first two weeks includes the following modules:

- Bond math
- Accounting
- Fixed-income and equity markets overview
- Derivatives and structured products

Instructors include both Lehman Brother speakers and third party consultants, who cover topics such as communication skills, Microsoft Excel and Access training. The program also includes team-building events, diversity events and employee roundtables. The third week is held in conjunction with capital markets training. Additional training courses are held periodically throughout the two-year program.

Operations Analyst Program

Length of program: Two years

Geographic location(s) of program: New York, New Jersey

The operations analyst program is a two-year program in which you are trained, placed in a business and developed professionally on an ongoing basis. The program begins with an orientation to Lehman Brothers, followed by a comprehensive overview of our capital markets business and professional development training curriculum. The program is designed to provide you with the professional skills, industry knowledge and development opportunities that will enable you to achieve success within the operations division.

Group Placement Process

During orientation, you will learn about the various placements that are available within the operations division. Placement decisions are made based on business needs and your preferences. After one year of successful performance in your initial placement, you are eligible to explore other opportunities within the operations division to include, but not be limited to:

- Equity operations
- Fixed-income operations
- Investment management division operations
- Information and exposure management
- Clearance and custody services
- Operations control
- Business analysis group
- Training

Following an initial orientation to the firm, operations training includes a comprehensive overview of our capital markets business and professional development training curriculum.

Training courses are held periodically throughout the two-year program. They cover topics including:

- In-depth overviews of all operations departments
- Brokerage operations processing I and II
- Debt Securities I and II
- Introduction to equities, introduction to forwards and futures, introduction to options, introduction to swaps
- Compliance 101
- Managing operational risk
- Effective teamwork

In addition to these classes, we encourage you to take courses offered to the entire capital markets division. These courses are added periodically to the general training curriculum for operations employees.

Information Technology Development Program

Length of program: Three months

Geographic location(s) of program: New York, London, Tokyo and India

The Information Technology (IT) analyst program is an excellent platform to begin your career at Lehman Brothers. The Technology Development Program (TDP) consists of an initial training program in which all new IT analysts participate. It is designed to help you develop as a highly skilled IT professional who will partner with our businesses to help drive the productivity of the firm and to enable the businesses to meet their strategic objectives.

Group Placement Process

As an IT analyst, you can expect to work in one of the following roles:

- Infrastructure support and engineering

- Systems development and support

- You will be directly placed into a specific group and begin working in your group immediately after completion of the IT analyst training program.

Training

Initial training typically begins in July of each year, and the curriculum includes the following modules:

- Introduction to working at Lehman Brothers
- Capital markets and corporate finance seminars
- Technical skills training
- Divisional technology presentations
- Professional development classes
- Team-building and networking activities
- Final project and presentation

Instructors include both Lehman Brothers speakers and third-party consultants. You will spend the last five weeks of training on a final

project sponsored by a Lehman technology group. The project is designed to integrate all aspects of your training and help ease the transition into your future technology group.

The training culminates with a formal presentation for the CIO and other IT senior managers discussing the architecture, business requirements, and development challenges of the project. Additional training that the division makes available to you includes: technical, project management and business analysis skills classes, and a wide array of capital markets training.

Strategic Plan and Diversity Leadership

The firm's leadership communicates the importance of diversity utilizing all avenues available, including divisional town hall meetings, general e-mails to all employees from senior leaders, awards and recognition e-mails, postings to the firm's Intranet (known as LehmanLive) and Global Home Page, the *Lehman Brothers Quarterly Newsletter,* invitations to diversity events, periodic diversity fact sheets, recruiting updates, diversity-related poster series displayed in office elevators and floor lobbies, and various brochures—including the Global Diversity & Inclusion brochure.

Who has primary responsibility for leading diversity initiatives at your firm?

Anne Erni, managing director, chief diversity officer

Does your firm currently have a diversity committee?

Yes

If yes, please describe how the committee is structured, how often it meets, etc.

Yes, the firm has regional and divisional councils chaired by their representative business leaders.

If yes, does the committee's representation include one or more members of the firm's management/executive committee (or the equivalent)?

Yes

If yes, how many executives are on the committee, and in 2006, what was the total number of hours collectively spent by the committee in furtherance of the firm's diversity initiatives? How many employees are on the committee, and how often does the committee convene in furtherance of the firm's diversity initiatives?

There are approximately 15 to 18 members of each of the regional and divisional diversity councils, all of whom are vice presidents, senior vice presidents or managing directors.

The councils meet on average eight to 10 times during the year.

Does the committee and/or diversity leader establish and set goals or objectives consistent with management's priorities?

Yes

Has the firm undertaken a formal or informal diversity program or set of initiatives aimed at increasing the diversity of the firm?

Yes, formal

How often does the firm's management review the firm's diversity progress/results?

Twice a year

How is the firm's diversity committee and/or firm management held accountable for achieving results?

Lehman Brothers holds all managers, including those at the top of the organization accountable for diversity. Each business division is responsible for developing an annual diversity plan which addresses their particular opportunities and defines measurable action steps for achieving results. Regional CEO's and the firm's president review the diversity plans. Our performance management system incorporates criteria on diversity practices for all employees.

Diversity Mission Statement

Chairman and Chief Executive Officer, Richard S. Fuld, Jr.'s statement on diversity and inclusion:

"At Lehman Brothers, we have achieved momentum across our businesses and regions because we have built a culture where our people come together as a team to deliver all of the firm's resources to our clients. Our firm has come a long way by many measures. One of the greatest changes is in the wide variety of perspectives and backgrounds of our people today. We have made substantial progress in recruiting and developing the very best people, creating a diverse and inclusive culture and establishing ourselves as leaders in the community.

"To reach our next level of success, we must continue to foster a culture that is full of opportunity, where exceptional people want to build their careers. Our commitment to being a world class organization goes hand in hand with our commitment to building a truly diverse and inclusive culture and to ensuring that all employees are valued for their unique abilities and contributions and their diversity of thought and perspective.

"Our diversity efforts are integral to strengthening our 'One Firm' culture and to delivering on the firm's client-focused strategy. A truly diverse and inclusive culture enables us to deliver the best service and products and to generate the most innovative ideas for our clients. There are remarkable opportunities for us to take this firm to its next level of success. I am confident that the people here at

this firm and those who will join us in the time ahead will help us build on that success."

Additional Information

At Lehman Brothers we are committed to attracting, retaining and developing the best people from the broadest backgrounds, and to nurturing our inclusive culture that fosters employee development and contributes to our commercial success.

Each of our employees comes from a unique background and each brings a diverse perspective to the firm based on his or her variety of life experiences. This variety of thought and perspective is of intrinsic value to us in our talent evaluation process.

To assist in the retention and development of our people, we emphasize tools such as networking opportunities, mentoring programs, employee and management education and training, and corporate citizenship.

Following are a sample of our employee programs:

• Employee networks in all geographic regions open to all employees

• Over 500 employees act as mentors in one of over 20 mentoring programs

• Over 15,000 employees have taken part in our Awareness Training program, in the U.S., Europe and in Asia since 2004, with another 2,000 more slated for this year

• The firm and its networks partner with over 70 diversity related community organizations each year, either through financial or volunteer sponsorship. These include:

Community organizations: Robin Hood, Harlem's Children Zone, Girl Scouts

Professional organizations: New York Women's Foundation, National Association of Asian Professionals, The Hispanic Federation, The Twenty First Century Foundation

In summary, why are diversity and inclusion such imperatives at Lehman Brothers? In very simple terms, it's because they are commercial imperatives for our business. We are part of a very competitive industry, where firms succeed or fail based solely on the quality of the ideas and solutions that their employees bring to their clients. To succeed, Lehman Brothers has to attract the very best people from 100 percent of the available talent pool. We need to make sure that each and every one of our employees feels welcomed and valued in an environment where they can reach their potential and do their best work. Anything less and we aren't giving our clients our very best.

At Lehman Brothers, diversity is an integral part of our vision, and we pride ourselves on bringing together diverse groups of people who work to produce extraordinary outcomes for our clients, shareholders and our firm. We integrate diversity into every aspect of our business—from dealing with our clients to managing our workforce.

We're focused on making a great firm even better. At Lehman Brothers, you will find what you want, a place where individual approach and perspective are celebrated, the need to find life balance is valued and creative solutions are the norm.

Liberty Mutual Insurance Company

175 Berkeley Street
Boston, MA 02129
Phone: (617) 357-9500

Locations

Boston, MA (HQ)
900 locations worldwide

Employment Contact

Shawn Tubman
Director, University Relations
175 Berkeley St.
Boston, MA 02129
Phone: (617) 357-9500
Fax: (617) 574-5616
E-mail: campus.recruiting@libertymutual.com
Career web site:
www.libertymutual.com/getstarted

Recruiting

Please list the schools/types of schools at which you recruit.

Liberty Mutual visits campuses throughout the U.S., including HBCUs and HSIs, as well as private and public institutions of higher education. If we are not on a particular campus, we welcome resumes through our web site.

Do you have any special outreach efforts that are directed to encourage minority students to consider your firm?

• Conferences
• Advertise in minority student association publication(s)
• Sponsor minority student association events
• Firm's employees participate on career panels at schools
• Outreach to leadership of minority student organizations
• Scholarships or intern/fellowships for minority students

Liberty Mutual is eager to meet minority students on the campuses we visit and will participate in activities, association meetings and job fairs. Scholarship opportunities are also available through the Hispanic Scholarship Fund and the United Negro College Fund, as well as to students at Morehouse College.

What activities does the firm undertake to attract minority and women employees?

• Partner programs with women and minority associations
• Participate at minority job fairs
• Utilize online job services

Internships and Co-ops

Liberty Mutual Internship Program

Deadline for application: Early spring semester

Number of interns in the program in summer 2007 (internship) or 2007 (co-op): 400

Pay: Competitive

Length of the program: 10 to 12 weeks

Percentage of interns/co-ops in the program who receive offers of full-time employment: 85 percent

Web site for internship/co-op information:
www.libertymutual.com/getstarted

Liberty Mutual will hire approximately 400 undergraduate interns each summer and approximately 25 MBA-level interns. Approximately one third of these undergraduate interns will come from the INROADS program. Pay is competitive and positions are throughout the U.S. Internships are based on business needs, so interns work in a variety of functional areas throughout the organization, including traditional business jobs, accounting, finance, IT and HR. Positions also exist in the functional areas specific to the insurance industry, including claims, underwriting, sales, loss prevention and actuarial. During the summer, interns participate in training programs to learn about the business of insurance as well as the organization. Undergraduate rising seniors have the opportunity to visit the Boston headquarters and meet with senior executives and interview for positions. Development plans are developed for each student so that returning interns see a progression through a job family. MBA interns will meet with senior executives to gain a perspective on strategic initiatives.

Scholarships

Target School Scholarship Program

Liberty Mutual has a scholarship program at a number of our targeted undergraduate campuses.

Deadline for application for the scholarship program: Spring of sophomore year

Scholarship award amount: Varies by school

Web site or other contact information for scholarship: www.libertymutual.com/getstarted

UNCF

Deadline for application for the scholarship program: See web site for details

Web site or other contact information for scholarship: www.uncf.org

HSF

Deadline for application for the scholarship program: See web site for details

Web site or other contact information for scholarship: www.hsf.net

Entry-Level Programs, Full-Time Opportunities and Training Programs

Liberty Mutual anticipates hiring 800+ college grads during the upcoming academic year. Opportunities exist in accounting, finance, IT, sales, claims, underwriting and HR. Some of the development programs include:

Fellowship in Finance and Accounting (FIFA)

Length of program: Two years (three eight-month assignments within the corporate finance, accounting and strategic business units)

Geographic location(s) of program: Boston

Training opportunities include a two-week employee orientation, professional development, on-the-job training and technical training programs.

Foundations for Sales Success

Length of program: Four to 12 months

Geographic location(s) of program: Field-based

Includes technical classroom training and field experience.

Technical Development Program (TDP)

Length of program: Three to five years

Geographic location(s) of program: Portsmouth, Wausau (some opportunity for rotations in Indianapolis)

Three phases of your development include a classroom orientation, a business assignment, technical immersion and up to four information systems rotations.

Corporate Real Estate Rotational Program

Length of program: 18 to 24 months

Geographic location(s) of program: Boston

Within rotations, on-the-job training will develop participants' skills. Rotations include: strategic planning, budget preparation and monitoring of office relocation projects within corporate real estate, tenant services and procurement.

HRDP—Human Resource Development Program

Length of program: 18 to 24 months

Geographic location(s) of program: Boston

Individual rotations include all areas of HR, benefits, HR systems and compensation within the corporate and business groups—strategic plan and diversity leadership.

Strategic Plan and Diversity Leadership

Has the firm undertaken a formal or informal diversity program or set of initiatives aimed at increasing the diversity of the firm?

Liberty Mutual has a strategy in place to attract and retain minority representation and to build a more inclusive work environment as part of each individual business unit workforce plan. The strategy is multi-pronged and includes implementation of a mentoring program across business units, training for all new managers on inclusion, increased financial support to professional minority organizations, enhanced college relations and recruitment programs, and improved communications to external candidates and our internal employee population to better articulate our employment value propositions. Visit our web site at www.libertymutual.com/aboutus for more information.

How often does the firm's management review the firm's diversity progress/results?

Quarterly

How is the firm's diversity committee and/or firm management held accountable for achieving results?

Business unit heads are held responsible for effective implementation of their inclusive workforce plans to meet the respective business needs.

The Stats

As of December 31, 2006, Liberty Mutual Group had $85.5 billion in consolidated assets and $23.2 billion in annual consolidated revenue. The company ranks 95th on the Fortune 500 list of largest corporations in the United States based on 2006 revenue.

LMG offers a wide range of insurance products and services, including personal automobile, homeowners, workers compensation, commercial multiple peril, commercial automobile, general liability, global specialty, group disability, assumed reinsurance, fire and surety.

LMG (www.libertymutual.com) employs over 39,000 people in more than 900 offices throughout the world.

Additional Information

Liberty Mutual has a strong promote-from-within philosophy; therefore, it is critical that we bring strong talent into the organization from college campuses. This initiative includes working with diversity associations on campus, INROADS and professional associations including NBMBAA, NSHMBA, ALPFA, NABA, the Consortium, NAACP and Urban League, among others. Our recruiting on campus includes visits to HBCUs.

Inclusion is critical to our success. By tapping all available pools of talent, we will better serve the needs of our customers in the communities we serve and want to serve. An inclusive company also treats people with dignity and respect and provides the opportunity to grow and succeed based on ability, performance and aspirations.

Liz Claiborne Inc.

1441 Broadway, 20th Floor
New York, NY 10018
Phone: (212) 354-4900

Locations

US: Arleta, CA • Atlanta, GA • Commerce, CA • Dallas, TX • Los Angeles, CA • New York, NY • North Bergen, NJ • Vernon, CA • Wakefield, MA

International: Amsterdam, The Netherlands • Hong Kong, China • Huxquilucan, Mexico • Jakarta, Indonesia • Madrid, Spain • Manila, Philippines • Montreal, Quebec, Canada • Ontario, Canada • Shanghai, China • Sri Lanka • Taiwan • Voorschoten, The Netherlands

Distribution Center Locations: Breinigsville, PA • Dayton, NJ • Lincoln, RI • North Bergen, NJ • Ontario, Canada • Montreal, Canada • Mt. Pocono, PA • Santa Fe Springs, CA • West Chester, OH • Vernon, CA

Employment Contact

Marla Schwartz
College Relations
1441 Broadway, 20th Floor
New York, NY 10018
Phone: (212) 626-5447
Fax: (212) 626-5527
E-mail: marla_schwartz@liz.com
www.lizclaiborneinc.com

Recruiting

Please list the schools/types of schools at which you recruit.
• Ivy League schools
• Other private schools
• Public state schools
• Historically black colleges and universities (HBCUs)
• Other predominantly minority and/or women's colleges

Do you have any special outreach efforts directed to encourage minority students to consider your firm?
• Advertise in minority student association publication(s)
• Participate in/host minority student job fair(s)
• Firm's employees participate on career panels at schools
• Scholarships or intern/fellowships for minority students

What activities does the firm undertake to attract minority and women employees?
• Partner programs with women and minority associations
• Participate at minority job fairs
• Seek referrals from other employees
• Utilize online job services
• *Other:* Black Retail Association Group (BRAG) and INROADS

Do you use executive recruiting/search firms to seek to identify new diversity hires?
No

Internships and Co-ops

Liz Claiborne Inc. Summer Internship Program
Pay: Undergraduate—$10 per hour; IT/IS undergraduate—$12 per hour; MBA—$1,500 for 10 weeks
Percentage of interns/co-ops in the program who receive offers of full-time employment: Of the ones we identify as stand-outs, we hire at least 50 percent depending on business needs (head count)
Web site for internship/co-op information:
www.lizclaiborneinc.com

The Summer Internship Program starts in mid-June and runs through mid-August for 10 weeks. We offer internships in the following areas:

design, merchandising/planning, production/manufacturing, sales, finance, information systems, human resources and legal.

Each intern is also given a summer project that will take six to eight weeks to complete. The summer project will create a hands-on experience for each intern to gain better exposure to the area in which they have been placed.

The Summer Internship Program also provides exposure to different areas of the company as the interns complete their assignments. There are weekly activities that include brown bag lunches, field trips and other activities for the interns to interact with each other as well as gain more exposure to other areas of the organization.

Affinity Groups

We do not currently have any affinity groups, although every intern is paired with a mentor/buddy to help them with the transition into Liz Claiborne Inc. and our corporate environment.

Entry-Level Programs, Full-Time Opportunities and Training Programs

Our two programs, the Finance Management Training Program and the Accounting Management Program, are both four-month rotations through our finance and accounting divisions. Once the rotation is completed, a full-time opportunity is identified.

Through our organizational development department, an extensive list of training programs and classes for Liz Claiborne associates are offered.

Classes included are: Civil Treatment® for Employees, Civil Treatment® for Managers, ValuEthics™, Basic Retail Math, Presentation Skills for Designers, Presentation Skills for Sales Associates, Business Simulation, Business Writing 1, Business Writing 2, Coaching & Counseling for the Experienced Manager, Dale Carnegie, Executive Presentation Skills, Focus - Time Management, Frontline Leadership, Management Effectiveness, Positive Power & Influence Skills, The Accounting Game and The Finance Game. Also, see below for Attraction, Retention, Professional and Leadership. Development.

Strategic Plan and Diversity Leadership

How does the firm's leadership communicate the importance of diversity to everyone at the firm?

Our diversity and inclusion efforts are our CEO's number one non-financial initiative. There is constant discussion and reminders of the importance of expanding our diversity and inclusion efforts at all lev-

els. Our CEO's diversity and inclusion statement is featured on our Intranet.

Who has primary responsibility for leading diversity initiatives at your firm?

Dennis Butler, vice president of associate relations. Diversity is a company-wide effort and initiative, so every manager, executive, etc. is committed to its growth.

Does your firm currently have a diversity committee?

Yes. Currently, the diversity committee includes an executive VP, a group president, the senior VP of HR, the VP of associate relations and a director of HR. We are currently in the process of identifying 10 to 15 additional members at the VP level or higher from a cross section of our organization.

If yes, does the committee's representation include one or more members of the firm's management/executive committee (or the equivalent)?

Yes

How often does the committee convene in furtherance of the firm's diversity initiatives?

Currently, the committee is meeting monthly.

Does the committee and/or diversity leader establish and set goals or objectives consistent with management's priorities?

The most senior members of the committee (EVP, GP and SVP) have non-financial objectives relative to increasing and valuing the diversity of our workforce.

Has the firm undertaken a formal or informal diversity program or set of initiatives aimed at increasing the diversity of the firm?

Yes, informal. As a federal contractor, we are an affirmative action employer with written AAPs that are reviewed and updated annually. Where underutilization exists, specific formal goals are set.

Additionally, we recognize that having a diverse workforce that reflects the diversity of our marketplace makes good business sense. Accordingly, we are actively working to increase awareness and the valuing of diversity.

How often does the firm's management review the firm's diversity progress/results?

Quarterly.

How is the firm's diversity committee and/or firm management held accountable for achieving results?

Key executive non-financial objectives reflect inclusion goals.

The Stats

	NUMBER OF EMPLOYEES	REVENUE
	2006	2006
Total in the U.S.	25,400	$4.85 billion

DEMOGRAPHICS	
Female	76 percent
Minority	36 percent
Female leadership council	60 percent
Leadership council	9 percent
Female executive council	40 percent

Retention and Professional Development

Please identify the specific steps you are taking to reduce the attrition rate of minority and women employees.

- Increase/review compensation relative to competition
- Increase/improve current work/life programs
- Succession plan includes emphasis on diversity
- Work with minority and women employees to develop career advancement plans
- Strengthen mentoring program for all employees, including minorities and women
- Professional skills development program, including minority and women employees
- Attraction, Retention, Professional and Leadership Development:

The survival of any organization depends on the attraction, retention and development of quality associates. The stewardship review and talent management process provide the opportunity to review the performance of key executives and other high-potential associates. HR generalists and executives meet on a regular basis (formally and informally) to discuss cross-functional, promotional and other developmental opportunities for high-potential employees. During this process, we make a conscious effort to identify minorities as candidates for these opportunities. By recognizing these outstanding performers, we are able to strategically develop and create a diverse pipeline for the future leadership of Liz Claiborne.

In addition to many internal and external training/leadership development courses offered, following are programs we have established to enhance the developmental opportunities, retention and promotability of all associates. In implementing these programs, specific attention is given to assuring that the current and future leadership of our organization appropriately reflects the diversity of the labor pool and marketplace.

Last year, we introduced the "Leader Studio." This three-phase program includes an experiential learning opportunity and on-the-job practice using concepts of adult learning styles and generational influences which can be effectively applied to managing a diverse workforce. As part of the learning, participants visit the Civil Rights Museum in Memphis, Tenn. This event enhances their appreciation of peoples' differences by encouraging them to better understand the experiences of those who were involved in the Civil Rights Movement.

We have increased funding and support for associates' participation in networking conferences specific to women of color. Last year, the Working Mother Women of Color Conference (New York, NY), the Hispanic Women's Conference (Phoenix, AZ) and the NAFE Conference (New York, NY) were attended by female associates of various ethnic backgrounds and at all levels.

Additionally, we have implemented the following:

Senior Executive Stewardship Reviews: Annually, the chairman/CEO and human resources meet with each of the division presidents and corporate department senior vice presidents to discuss their direct reports and any high-potential associates that should be considered part of our strategic succession planning process. Developmental needs and opportunities are discussed as part of this process. The process also helps uncover and address skill gaps and to surface any other real or perceived barriers that may be blocking the advancement or development of associates. As part of this process, the chairman specifically charges his executive team with assessing their recruiting, retention and development strategies to be sure they adequately address the needs of our diverse workforce and marketplace.

Organizational Reviews: Annually, each division and corporate department, in partnership with human resources, reviews their organization to identify high potentials/promotables, performers/technical experts and any non-performers. Managers discuss their subordinates with their supervisors to ensure that appropriate development plans exist and are being executed. This process follows the setting of individual performance and development plans by associates and their managers.

Talent Management: As an expansion and enhancement of the existing organizational review process, the talent management process was developed. All human resources generalists, recruiters and organizational development leadership meet formally several times throughout the year to review the internal talent pool in great detail. The group discusses career paths, strengths, development needs and explores any existing and future, new and/or cross-functional opportunities for each high potential/potential employees (approximately 500 of whom are women). The opportunity to share information regarding top and emerging talent—our future leaders—results in more efficient and timely promotion of internal movement and development. As part of this process, we annually conduct all-day talent management summits.

Diversity Mission Statement

From our CEO:

February 7, 2005

To: All Liz Claiborne Associates

Subject: Diversity & Inclusion

The creation of a diverse portfolio has been a cornerstone of our strategy. Multiple brands that are sold in multiple channels and geographies and that touch multiple consumer demographics have generated an enviable record of consistent performance and growth. In order to be successful in this environment, we must be innovative, responsive, dynamic and adaptable to the demands of a global marketplace. While it is our consistency of execution that creates our competitive advantage, it is our ability to understand and translate the distinct differences of our consumers, brands and channels of distribution that distinguishes us.

We are a global corporation and take pride in a culture of achievement and excellence. Among our standards of excellence is the consistent goal to create a workplace in which our behaviors, practices and policies promote respect, opportunity and advancement for all our associates. A key to these standards in our culture is inclusion.

Inclusion reflects the diversity of backgrounds, experiences and outlooks our associates bring to the workplace. More importantly, inclusion focuses on behaviors and actions that reflect our value for diversity in our workplaces, communities and markets.

In our workplace, inclusion must be embodied in everything we do and be a vital part of our cultural fabric from ideas, concepts and processes to training, development, mentoring and our day-to-day relationships. Inclusion will allow us to attract and retain the best talent.

In our communities and the workforce from which we draw our associates, inclusion must be evident in our recruiting outreach and community involvement.

In our marketplace, inclusion is visible in our suppliers and in our sales and marketing initiatives.

Most of all, inclusion is a shared responsibility. My senior executives and I have a responsibility as leaders of our company to demonstrate a visible commitment to fostering an environment of inclusion. As associates of this company, we all have a responsibility to model behaviors that honor and celebrate the unique contributions and perspectives our associates bring to this work we share.

Great companies accelerate the pace of change and push beyond the status quo to uncover new ideas, concepts and opportunities. Great companies fuel that acceleration by increasing inclusion initiatives and renewing the values and beliefs that guide their actions.

We are a great company that I believe can be greater. Embracing differences, leading change through innovation, committing to common goals, valuing integrity in everything we do and engaging the minds and energies of each and every associate—these will enable us to realize that greatness.

—Paul R. Charron

Additional Information

We are a visionary and progressive company that actively supports the advancement of qualified minorities and women. We have a workforce that mirrors the diversity of our marketplace. Women and minorities are well-represented throughout all levels of the company.

CEO commitment to inclusion has resulted in the establishment of a Diversity Steering Committee and the communication of the CEO's inclusion statement to all associates. We have increased representation of Latinas across the company. Additionally, key executive non-financial objectives reflect inclusion goals, our intern program has successfully targeted and recruited more minorities, and we have expanded funding to support associate attendance at conferences for Latinas and other women of color.

Our programs give associates the opportunity to focus on professional development while balancing their work and family needs. We offer a very generous paid time-off program, alternative work arrangements, summer hours, steep clothing discounts and more. Additionally, our "traditional" benefits are very competitive, including healthcare, employee assistance programs, 401(k) matching, tuition reimbursement and gym membership discounts (including an onsite facility).

The focus of the Liz Claiborne's Foundation is women's issues, and we have implemented corporate initiatives relative to domestic violence and helping women, including minorities, achieve their life goals for safety, professional achievement and family.

We continue to develop strategic approaches for creating a more inclusive culture in which behaviors, values and practices promote respect, representation, career development and success across all forms of diversity. Our culture, which empowers associates to achieve their full potential, attracts and retains loyal, dedicated, promotable associates, including women and minorities.

Lockheed Martin Corporation

6801 Rockledge Drive
Bethesda, MD 20817
www.lockheedmartin.com/careers

Locations

Major sites in:
Dallas/Fort Worth, TX area • Denver, CO
area • Orlando, FL area • Palmdale, CA •
Philadelphia, PA area • San Jose/Bay, CA
area • Washington, DC area • Marietta, GA
As well as many other national and international sites.

Diversity Leadership

Sonya Stewart
Vice President for Diversity and Equal
Opportunity Programs

Employment Contact

Leslie L. Chappell
Director, University Relations

Recruiting

Please list the schools/types of schools at which you recruit.

• Ivy League schools

• Other private schools

• Public state schools

• Historically black colleges and universities (HBCUs)

• Hispanic serving institutions (HSIs)

• Other predominantly minority and/or women's colleges

Do you have any special outreach efforts directed to encourage minority students to consider your firm?

• Hold a reception for minority students

• *Conferences:* HACU, HENAAC, NSBE, SWE, SHPE, AISES, MAES, NAMEPA, BEY

• *Advertise in minority student association publication(s): Minority Engineer, Women Engineer*

• Participate in/host minority student job fair(s)

• Sponsor minority student association events

• Firm's employees participate on career panels at schools

• Outreach to leadership of minority student organizations

• Scholarships or intern/fellowships for minority students

• Internship/co-op opportunities, workshops, special speakers, mentors

What activities does the firm undertake to attract minority and women employees?

• Partner programs with women and minority associations

• *Conferences:* HACU, HENAAC, NSBE, SWE, SHPE, AISES, MAES, NAMEPA, AMIE

• Participate at minority job fairs

• Seek referrals from other employees

• Utilize online job services

Do you use executive recruiting/search firms to seek to identify new diversity hires?

Yes

Internships and Co-ops

Deadline for application: Ongoing

Pay: Varies by academic level, major and geographic location

Length of the program: Typically, nine to 11 weeks

Percentage of interns/co-ops in the program who receive offers of full-time employment: 52 percent

Web site for internship/co-op information: www.lockheed-martin.com/careers

Lockheed Martin seeks students at all academic levels in the following majors:

• Aeronautical engineering

• Computer engineering

• Computer science

• Electrical engineering

• Mechanical engineering and systems engineering

We also have limited opportunities in:

• Finance

• Human resources

• Accounting and business

Scholarships

Lockheed Martin participates in the following scholarship programs aimed at women and minority students, please see their web sites for details on deadlines, amounts and eligibility requirements:

• *American Indian College Fund -Tribunal Scholarships:* http://www.collegefund.org/

• *American Indian Science and Engineering Society:* http://aises.org/highered/scholarships/

• *Hispanic Association of Colleges & Universities (HACU) Scholarships:* https://scholarships.hacu.net/applications/applicants/

• *Hispanic Scholarship Fund:* http://www.hsf.net/scholarships.php

• *League of Latin American Citizens Scholars (LULAC):* http://www.chci.org/chciyouth/scholarship/listofscholarships.htm

• *Mexican-American Engineering Society (MAES) Scholarship:* http://www.maes-natl.org/index.php?module=ContentExpress&func=display&ceid=237&meid=241

• *National Society of Black Engineers Corporate Scholarships:* http://www.nsbe.org/programs/nsbescholarships.php

• *Society of Women Engineers Scholarship:* http://www.swe.org/stellent/idcplg?IdcService=SS_GET_PAGE&nodeId=9&ssSourceNodeId=5

• *Society of Hispanic Professional Engineers Foundation (Scholarships):* www.shpe.org/index.php/docs/239

Lockheed Martin also offers many scholarships for diversity students that are administered directly by the schools with whom we partner, most are in engineering. These scholarships have a wide range of eligibility requirements, deadlines and award amounts.

Entry-Level Programs, Full-Time Opportunities and Training Programs

Leadership Development Program (LDP) (various specialties)

Length of program: Two to three years of rotational assignments

Geographic location(s) of program: Nationwide

Employees receive weeklong training each summer and periodic communications throughout the year. Most large worksites have dedicated LDP managers who help guide the employees.

Tuition reimbursement is provided so that employees in this program can pursue a master's degree. In some cases, paid time off is provided in order to attend classes or to study for examinations. In some cases, flexible work schedules can be arranged so that the employee can attend day classes if necessary.

Strategic Plan and Diversity Leadership

Who has primary responsibility for leading diversity initiatives at your firm?

Sonya Stewart, vice president for diversity and equal opportunity programs

Does your firm currently have a diversity committee?

Yes. Our Executive Diversity Council (EDC) is chaired by our chairman, president and CEO, Robert J Stevens and vice-chaired by our CFO, Chris Kubasik. The members consist of 26 of the top leaders of the corporation, including executive vice presidents, operating business unit presidents, the chief information officer (CIO) and senior vice president of human resources. The EDC serves as an advisory function to our executive management council. It is their vision and strategy that is driven down through out the corporate via the diversity councils at our business units.

If yes, does the committee's representation include one or more members of the firm's management/executive committee (or the equivalent)?

Yes

Does the committee and/or diversity leader establish and set goals or objectives consistent with management's priorities?

Yes. We have aligned our business processes with our people management process to ensure our goals and objectives are consistent with management's priorities.

Has the firm undertaken a formal or informal diversity program or set of initiatives aimed at increasing the diversity of the firm?

Yes, formal. Lockheed Martin views diversity in a broad sense of the term that goes beyond race and gender. While those are two aspects of our view on how we define diversity, we look at things like educational background, geographic location, personal style, etc. Our efforts at creating a more inclusive environment focuses on all aspects of diversity. When we talk about increasing the number of women and minorities, we use the term increasing representation. Our approach to increasing representation is maintaining a positive compliance posture, as defined by the affirmative action regulations to address underutilization.

How often does the firm's management review the firm's diversity progress/results?

Quarterly

How is the firm's diversity committee and/or firm management held accountable for achieving results?

We have put an assessment process in place to measure the performance of a business unit in the area of diversity inclusion. The assessment process takes employee opinion, as well as the kinds of processes and practices in place to foster inclusion. The business unit receives a numeric score associated with the assessment and BU leaders are held accountable for results through their incentive compensation plan.

The Stats

	NUMBER OF EMPLOYEES		REVENUE	
	2006	2005	2006	2005
Total worldwide	140,000	135,000	$39.6 billion	$37.2 billion

Of our total workforce, 24 percent is female and 20 percent is minority.

Retention and Professional Development

Please identify the specific steps you are taking to reduce the attrition rate of minority and women employees.

• Develop and/or support internal employee affinity groups at some locations and with our company executive leadership
• Increase/review compensation relative to competition for all employees
• Increase/improve current work/life programs, alternative work schedule, telecommuting, flexible work schedules, etc.
• Adopt dispute resolution process and a corporate policy statement to address dispute resolution
• Succession plan includes emphasis on diversity
• Work with minority and women employees to develop career advancement plans and review work assignments and hours billed to key client matters to make sure minority and women employees are not being excluded

Diversity Mission Statement

Lockheed Martin is committed to creating one all-inclusive company and team where diversity contributes to mission success. Diversity at Lockheed Martin is an inclusive team that values and leverages each person's individuality.

Additional Information

At Lockheed Martin, we recognize that diversity is not just a short-term trend—it is a business imperative. Our long-term success depends on a commitment to diversity. We have to leverage the individuality of each employee as a competitive advantage by eliminating barriers to inclusiveness. Diversity is about creating an environment that welcomes, respects and develops our individual differences as a competitive strength. It begins with our core values of Ethics, Excellence, "Can-Do" Attitude, Integrity, People and Teamwork. It extends to every activity involved in attracting and retaining a talented workforce that reflects the diversity of our customers, suppliers and our world.

There's a difference between stating our commitment to diversity and living it. We are dedicated to a process that listens to the voices of our employees and partners to help shape our course. It is through this process that we set goals and develop a strategy that will hold us accountable for making Lockheed Martin a place of "institutionalized inclusion."

Our approach to diversity is analogous to our work as system integrators. Each element and each subsystem must do its job, but function as part of a larger, integrated whole, will achieve astounding results. The whole is definitely stronger than its individual parts. In similar fashion, Lockheed Martin is made stronger by the combined efforts of each employee and each operating business unit working as one team.

The Lockheed Martin team is naturally diverse, encompassing 130,000 people with a wide variety of skills, backgrounds, perspectives and lifestyles. We draw from this tremendous source of talent to forge a great company and one team that is committed to the success of our customers on projects of profound significance to our world. As a world-class advanced technology leader, we must continually reach out to new and different points of view to succeed in the global marketplace. This means we must have an environment that attracts the best people with the biggest dreams and the highest standards, and give them the support and encouragement they need to reach their full potential. It also keeps us focused on assuring the widest possible circle of suppliers with whom we do business.

Diversity must be more than words. Having an inclusive environment really demands an engagement process that starts at the top—in the office—and extends throughout the corporation to each and every employee and stakeholder in this enterprise. We share in this commitment as a team because it is right for people and right for business.

That's what diversity is all about for Lockheed Martin and the people and institutions we serve. Diversity is a journey, and we are on this journey together.

L'Oréal USA

575 Fifth Avenue
New York, NY 10017
Phone: (212) 984-4000
www.lorealusa.com

Diversity Leadership
Ed Bullock
Chief Diversity Officer

Employment Contact
Ann McAtee
Director Corporate Strategic Recruitment

Malvina Complainville
Director Corporate Strategic Recruitment

Recruiting

Please list the schools/types of schools at which you recruit.

• Ivy League schools
• Other private schools
• Public state schools
• Historically black colleges and universities (HBCUs)
• Hispanic serving institutions (HSIs)
• Native American tribal universities
• Other predominantly minority and/or women's colleges

Do you have any special outreach efforts directed to encourage minority students and graduates to consider your firm?

• Hold a reception for minority students
• *Conferences:* NBMBAA, NSHMBA, Reaching out
• Advertise in minority student association publication(s) or other minority-focused publications
• Participate in/host minority student job fair(s) or other minority-focused job events
• Sponsor minority student association events
• Firm's employees participate on career panels at schools
• Outreach to leadership of minority student organizations
• Scholarships or intern/fellowships for minority students

What activities does the firm undertake to attract minority and women employees?

• Partner programs with women and minority associations
• Conferences
• Participate at minority job fairs
• Seek referrals from other employees
• Utilize online job services

Do you use executive recruiting/search firms to seek to identify new diversity hires?
Yes

Internships and Co-ops

L'Oréal Summer Internship Program

Deadline for application: Early October deadline to apply to the L'Oréal Brandstorm NYC Weekend recruitment event held in November; most offers are finalized by end of November

Number of interns in the program in summer 2006 (internship) or 2006 (co-op): 110 undergraduate interns

Pay: Competitive

Length of the program: 10 to 12 weeks

Web site for internship/co-op information: www.lorealusa.com

The L'Oréal Summer Internship Program consists of three main elements:

• Day to day functional job assignments as part of an existing team
• A business-related individual strategic project to be presented to management
• Educational and professional development sessions

Interns may be placed in the following areas: marketing, sales, finance, accounting, information systems, logistics, manufacturing, research and development.

Scholarships

L'Oréal SoftSheen-Carson Scholarship program

In keeping with the group's commitment as a champion of education and diversity, the L'Oréal SoftSheen-Carson Scholarship Fund was established in 2002. Its purpose is to assist young African-Americans, who attend selected HBCUs, achieve their dream of a higher education.

The program will recognize African-American students who have demonstrated significant academic achievements during their years in high school. These students must also have shown outstanding leadership qualities as indicated by their participation in school and community activities.

The L'Oréal SoftSheen-Carson Scholarships, in the amount of up to $10,500, will be awarded each year to qualifying freshmen-year students entering a designated HBCU in the fall. Each scholarship is renewable for three years or completion of their bachelors' degree, whichever comes first. Qualifying students are selected by the schools to apply for the scholarship funds.

Entry-Level Programs, Full-Time Opportunities and Training Programs

Management Development Program for Marketing, Sales, Finance, Information Systems, Manufacturing, or Research & Development

Length: 18 months to two years

Location: New York or New Jersey

The Management Development Program is designed for students graduating with a bachelor's degree who want to pursue a career in marketing, sales, finance, information systems, manufacturing or research and development. L'Oréal USA's Management Development Program has been designed to develop our future leaders.

As part of the L'Oréal USA Management Development Program, students are placed into one of the channels of trade at L'Oreal USA—consumer products, luxury products, professional products, active cosmetics or one of our corporate functions, i.e. finance, accounting, manufacturing or research and development. The program is designed to give you the opportunity to gain exposure and hone your skills through hands-on assignments and puts a strong emphasis on professional development through formal training held at our management development center and individual check points with members of the HR community. L'Oréal USA takes a three-pronged approach to the program whereby successful candidates will experience a period of integration, participate in training rotations and ultimately be placed in an entry-level management position.

Strategic Plan and Diversity Leadership

What trends in your industry affect your corporate diversity goals, strategies and/or internal or external alliances?

L'Oréal is dedicated to serving all expressions of beauty and well-being, which it seeks to make accessible to women and men all over the world.

How does the firm's leadership communicate the importance of diversity to everyone at the firm?

A diversity video featuring Lindsay Owen-Jones, chairman of L'Oréal, has been created to convey the L'Oréal diversity philosophy. This video is featured at all orientations and leadership programs.

Who has primary responsibility for leading diversity initiatives at your firm?

CEO Laurent Attal supported by the office of diversity

Does your firm currently have a diversity committee?

Yes

If yes, does the committee's representation include one or more members of the firm's management/executive committee (or the equivalent)?

Yes

Does the committee and/or diversity leader establish and set goals or objectives consistent with management's priorities?

Yes

Has the firm undertaken a formal or informal diversity program or set of initiatives aimed at increasing the diversity of the firm?

Yes, formal—two programs that are delivered at employee orientation and global executive leadership forums, as well as mandatory diversity for all employees.

How is the firm's diversity committee and/or firm management held accountable for achieving results?

Management is held accountable through the employee performance assessment process.

The Stats

	NUMBER OF EMPLOYEES	REVENUE
	2006	2006
Total in the U.S.	7,533	3.954 billion Euros
Total outside the U.S.	60,851	€15.8 billion consolidated sales
Total worldwide	52,403*	14.53 billion Euros*

* 2005 employee and revenue totals

Retention and Professional Development

Please identify the specific steps you are taking to reduce the attrition rate of minority and women employees.

- Increase/review compensation relative to competition
- Increase/improve current work/life programs
- Succession plan includes emphasis on diversity
- Strengthen mentoring program for all employees, including minorities and women
- Professional skills development program, including minority and women employees

Diversity Mission Statement

Our business is a celebration of diversity. Diversity, in all its forms, is a business imperative for L'Oréal. Our ability to embrace diversity will shape, define and add clarity to our shared vision for success in the 21st century.

Additional Information

L'Oréal is dedicated to serving all expressions of beauty and well-being, which it seeks to make accessible to women and men all over the world. We believe our approach to diversity and inclusion must stand on a firm foundation of respect for the individual as stated in our L'Oréal code of business ethics. We embrace the philosophy of first being diverse from within, and in order to become more diverse, we have established the office of diversity reporting to the president of L'Oréal USA and supporting global initiatives. This position will ensure our steady progress toward a more inclusive and innovative organization.

Our Definition of Diversity

Diversity is the mosaic of people who bring a variety of backgrounds, styles, perspectives, values, beliefs and differences as assets to the groups and organizations with which they interact.

Our Thoughts on Diversity

"At L'Oréal, success starts with people. Our people are our most precious asset. Respect for people, their ideas and differences is the only path to our sustainable long-term growth."

Laurent Attal, president and CEO, L'Oréal USA

"At L'Oréal, we manage diversity by giving value and respect to our employees, our consumers and our business partners as core ingredients in the formula for our success. We respect the talents, creativity and diversity they bring to our entire brand portfolio.

"We are committed to the recruitment, retention and development of a diverse workforce without regard to gender, ethnicity, religion, disabilities or sexual orientation."

– Edward W.Bullock, VP diversity and inclusion, L'Oréal USA

Marriott International, Inc.

Marriott Drive
Washington, DC 20058
Phone: (301) 380-3000

Diversity Leadership
Maruiel Perkins Chavis
Vice President, Workforce Effectiveness &
 Diversity
Phone: (301) 380-8391
Fax: (301) 380-4202
marriott.com/careers/default.mi

Employment Contact
Stacey Veden
Director, Recruiting Operations
Phone: (301) 380-5475
Fax: (301) 380-4202

Recruiting

What activities does the firm undertake to attract minority and women employees?

Marriott maintains a strong commitment to national recruitment advertising, with placements in such publications as *Black Collegian, Black Enterprise, Black MBA, CAREERS* and the *disABLED, DiversityInc, Hispanic Business* and *Working Mother.* Our strategic relationships with dozens of affinity organizations and media outlets help us get the word out that minorities and women have a great future at Marriott as associates, vendors, franchisees and guests. Examples include: the National Association of Black Accountants, the National Black MBA Association, the National Society of Minority Hoteliers, the Organization of Chinese-Americans, National Council of La Raza, the Women Business Enterprise Council, National Hispanic Corporate Council, the U.S. Hispanic Chamber of Commerce, the NAACP and the National Urban League.

Internships and Co-ops

Marriott International Internship Program
Deadline for application: No deadline
Number of interns in the program in summer 2006 (internship) or 2006 (co-op): Over 370
Pay: Varies by location and discipline
Length of the program: Typically between eight and 12 weeks; six-month and 12-month internships are also available.

Percentage of interns/co-ops in the program who receive offers of full-time employment: Over 30 percent
Web site for internship/co-op information: careers.marriott.com

Marriott offers internships that provide true hands-on work experience to prepare students for leadership in the professional world.

Students will focus on one professional area, with possibilities to explore other business operations. Internships are offered in the following areas:

• Accounting and finance
• Banquets/event services
• Culinary
• Front office
• Housekeeping
• Human resources
• Recreation
• Restaurants
• Sales

The majority of these positions will be at one of our lodging properties in North America, though some opportunities do exist at our corporate office.

Scholarships

Marriott is actively involved in the Emerging Markets Program of the International Franchise Association. The company contributes monetary, in-kind and management executive talent resources to IFA and has partnered with the association to launch a Minority Entrepreneurs Scholarship program.

Contact information for scholars:

Mr. John Reynolds, president

IFA Educational Foundation

1350 New York Ave. NW

Suite 900

Washington, DC NW 20005

Phone: (202) 662-0764

E-mail: johnr@franchise.org

The J. Willard and Alice S. Marriott Foundation announced in February 2007 the launch of the Marriott Scholars Program at both the Hispanic College Fund (HCF) and the United Negro College Fund (UNCF). The Marriott Foundation will award grants of up to $500,000 annually to HCF and UNCF in support of scholarships for students pursuing degrees within the hospitality management, hotel management, culinary, and food and beverage fields. Eligible Hispanic and African-American students can apply for renewable scholarships of up to $9,000 annually in tuition support for up to four years.

As a part of the program, Marriott International managers and executives from the hotels and corporate offices, including Chairman and CEO J.W. "Bill" Marriott Jr., will provide career guidance, mentoring, development and internship opportunities to scholarship recipients. Applicants interested in applying for the Marriott Scholars Program must meet the following eligibility requirements. Candidates must be:

- Enrolled full-time in an accredited four-year college or university with a hospitality management program as an incoming college freshman, first-year freshman or community college transfer

- Pursuing or planning to pursue a degree within the hospitality management, hotel management, culinary or food and beverage field

- Possess a cumulative grade point average of 3.0 or better on a 4.0 scale.

Those interested can apply online at www.uncf.org/scholarships or www.hispanicfund.org.

Strategic Plan and Diversity Leadership

Does your firm currently have a diversity committee?

The Marriott board of directors has established a subcommittee on diversity, which meets regularly to set significant goals and monitor progress at every level of the corporation.

Has the firm undertaken a formal or informal diversity program or set of initiatives aimed at increasing the diversity of the firm?

Three regional diversity councils drive our corporate diversity message home in the field with implementation of diversity-related initiatives to include strategic partnerships, targeted recruitment campaigns, leadership development programs, internships, conferences and other outreach to women and minorities.

The Stats

Our commitment to diversity begins at home. Marriott's 151,000 associates hail from dozens of nations, speak more than 50 languages and work under the Marriott banner in 66 countries and territories around the world. Sixty percent of our associates are minorities and 54 percent are women, many of whom take advantage of the company's professional development programs to move up and map out long-term careers with the company.

Nearly 3,000 of Marriott's current managers began their careers with Marriott in hourly positions. Currently, 55.7 percent of the company's supervisors—the first step toward achieving a management post—are minorities.

Of the new managers hired during 2006, 27 percent were minorities and 46 percent were women.

Diversity Mission Statement

At Marriott International, diversity is more than a goal ... it's our business. From our global workforce and vendors to our franchisees, our customers and communities, we thrive on the differences that give our company its strength and competitive edge.

In the process, we've set the standard for the entire hospitality industry. And it shows:

- *DiversityInc* ranked Marriott among the Top 50 Companies for Diversity. Marriott was the highest-ranking lodging company on the list and placed number four in the Top 10 companies for People with Disabilities category. (March 2007)

- The National Association of Female Executives has named Marriott one of the Top 10 companies for Executive Women. (March 2007)

- *Hispanic Trends* magazine has recognized Marriott as one of the Top 50 Corporations for Supplier Diversity. (Feb. 2007)

- The National Society of Minorities in Hospitality presented Marriott International with its first ever Lifetime Commitment Award as a result of our work and support of the association.

Retention and Professional Development

Based on monthly retention reports, minority and female attrition rates between the present time and the same period last year have not changed. Marsh has continued to retain female and diverse candidates, losing very few employees within the two groups.

Please identify the specific steps you are taking to reduce the attrition rate of minority and women employees.

• Develop and/or support internal employee affinity groups
• Increase/improve current work/life programs
• Succession plan includes emphasis on diversity
• Work with minority and women employees to develop career advancement plans
• Review work assignments and hours billed to key client matters to make sure minority and women employees are not being excluded

• Strengthen mentoring program for all employees, including minorities and women
• Professional skills development program, including minority and women employees

Diversity Mission Statement

Marsh will foster an environment in which each colleague values what every other colleague has to offer. We expect all of our people to view differences—whether they are race, ethnicity, gender, age, sexual orientation, function, geography or other facets of experience—as a powerful source of organizational strength. We will creatively leverage these different experiences and perspectives into a rich collection of skills and knowledge to provide innovative approaches to our business and unparalleled service to our clients. We will continue to ensure that all Marsh colleagues are valued and respected so that they are able to apply their unique capabilities in the pursuit of personal and organizational effectiveness.

• *Essence* magazine named Marriott as one of the publication's Top 25 Places to Work for African-American Women.

• *The Black Collegian,* a career and self development magazine targeted to African-American students named Marriott to its list of Top 100 Diversity Employers 2006. One of only three hospitality companies, Marriott ranked highest on the list.

• *Hispanic Business* magazine ranked Marriott No. 11 on the list of the Top 50 Companies for Hispanics. (Sept. 2006)

• *Black Enterprise* magazine named Marriott International one of the 40 Best Companies for Diversity. Marriott was recognized in two important categories: 10 Best in Workforce Diversity and 10 Best in Board Diversity.

• The NAACP has ranked Marriott the highest of any global lodging company for the seventh time in its lodging industry report card.

• *LATINA Style* magazine has named Marriott to its list of The 50 Best Companies for Latinas to Work for in the U.S. the eighth year in a row.

• *Working Mother* magazine has listed Marriott among its 100 Best Companies for Working Mothers for 14 years.

• *Fortune* magazine recognized Marriott as one of the 100 Best Companies to Work For for the last 10 consecutive years.

Additional Information

Our stakeholders know we're serious about diversity.

Marriott International's stakeholders know that our commitment to diversity can be summed up in one word: absolute.

Marriott Chairman and CEO J.W. Marriott Jr., sits on the board of trustees of the National Urban League.

In February 2003, J.W. Marriott Jr. was awarded the Lifetime Achievement Award by the Hospitality Industry Diversity Institute for his commitment to recognizing and including women, minorities and people with disabilities in the hospitality industry.

Suppliers and vendors: A world of opportunity at Marriott

Every big company begins as a small business. Marriott did ... back in 1927. We've never forgotten the opportunities that others gave us to succeed. Today, we proudly continue the tradition by reaching out to a whole new generation of entrepreneurs.

Marriott is on track to exceed the minority ownership and supplier diversity goals it set itself in 2005. The 2010 goal to have 500

minority- and women-owned Marriott hotels is well on its way to being met with over 400 minority- and women-owned hotels in the Marriott system.

In 2006, through our companywide supplier diversity program, Marriott purchased and facilitated spending of more than $400 million in goods and services, or 12.9 percent, with minority- and women-owned suppliers.

In 2006, NABHOOD (National Association of Black Hotel Owners, Operators and Developers) presented Marriott with the organization's first annual Champion Award for diversity leadership, as well as the Supplier Diversity Award for efforts to expand business opportunities to minority suppliers.

Minority franchisees and owners grow with us.

As Marriott pursues its growth plan and continues to expand, we want diverse partners and stakeholders to grow and prosper alongside us.

Our minority ownership initiative helps us attract and develop relationships with quality-minded minority and female owners and franchisees, and support them through every step of the development process. Today, 15 percent of franchise units are owned by minorities. As of July 2006, more than 400 Marriott hotels are owned, operated or under development by women or ethnic minorities.

Marriott International, Inc., received the 2006 Ronald E. Harrison Award by the International Franchise Association (IFA) for its significant contributions to minorities in franchising.

In 2006, Marriott announced that RLJ Development, owned by Black Entertainment Television (BET) founder Robert L. Johnson, became one of its largest hotel owners with the acquisition of 90 hotels.

Mirroring our stakeholders and our communities

We won't be satisfied until every aspect of our business reflects the rich diversity of the people and communities that touch Marriott's world.

For more information:

External diversity initiatives: Priscilla Hollman at (301) 380-1223

Supplier diversity: Michael Tobolski at (301) 380-7699

Owner/Franchisee Diversity: Norm Jenkins at (301) 380-2102

University relations and recruiting: Stacey Veden at (301) 380-5475

Media inquiries: Corporate communications at (301) 380-7770

Marsh Inc.

1166 Avenue of the Americas
New York, NY 10036
Phone: (212) 345-6000

Locations

Worldwide

Employment Contact

College Recruiting
1166 Avenue of the Americas
New York, NY 10036
Phone: (212) 345-6000
Fax: (212) 345-2088
www.marsh.com

Recruiting

Please list the schools/types of schools at which you recruit.

• Ivy League schools
• Other private schools
• Public state schools
• Historically black colleges and universities (HBCUs)

Do you have any special outreach efforts directed to encourage minority students to consider your firm?

• Hold a reception for minority students
• Conferences
• Advertise in minority student association publication(s)
• Participate in/host minority student job fair(s)
• Sponsor minority student association events
• Firm's employees participate on career panels at school
• Outreach to leadership of minority student organizations
• Scholarships or intern/fellowships for minority students

What activities does the firm undertake to attract minority and women employees?

• Partner programs with women and minority associations
• Conferences
• Participate at minority job fairs
• Seek referrals from other employees
• Utilize online job services

Do you use executive recruiting/search firms to seek to identify new diversity hires?

No

Internships and Co-ops

Summer Risk Analyst Program

Deadline for application: February 1, 2008

Number of interns in the program in summer 2006 (internship) or 2006 (co-op): 2006: 62 interns, 2007: 86 interns

Length of the program: 10 weeks

Percentage of interns/co-ops in the program who receive offers of full-time employment: 85 percent

Web site for internship/co-op information: www.marsh.com (careers/college recruiting)

All majors are considered.

Scholarships

Marsh Diversity Scholarship Program (Tuskegee University)

Deadline for application for the scholarship program: February 28, 2008

Scholarship award amount: $2,000 for the entire scholarship

Web site or other contact information for scholarship: Available in the career office.

All majors are considered.

Marsh Diversity Scholarship Program (Howard University)

Deadline for application for the scholarship program: February 28, 2008

Scholarship award amount: $8,000 for the entire scholarship

Web site or other contact information for scholarship: Available in the career office.

All majors are considered.

Marsh Diversity Scholarship Program (Temple University)

Deadline for application for the scholarship program: February 28, 2008

Scholarship award amount: $3,000 for the entire scholarship

Web site or other contact information for scholarship: Available in the career office.

All majors are considered.

Qualification:

• Must be a U.S. citizen or have unrestricted authorization to work for an employer in the U.S.
• Progress toward a BA/BS degree with a 3.0 GPA
• Proficient in Microsoft Office
• Ability to work in a fast-paced team environment with rapidly changing priorities and demands
• Candidates must be prepared to discuss work location preferences during the on-campus/first interview.
• Qualified candidates must be highly motivated and demonstrate a strong interest in business.
• Candidates must possess superior detail orientation and excellent communication and interpersonal skills. Candidates should also be service-oriented individuals with strong analytical, research and problem-solving skills.
• Some previous business experience is preferred.

Entry-level Programs, Full-time Opportunities and Training Programs

Risk Analyst Program

Length of program: Two years

Geographic location(s) of program: Atlanta, Boston, Chicago, Detroit, Houston, Los Angeles, New York and San Francisco

The Risk Analyst Orientation Curriculum is a development program that integrates formal learning, on-the-job experiences, networking, recommended books and performance support. The orientation program takes place during the first year of the risk analyst's employment with Marsh. After two years in a role, colleagues will be eligible for a future development program based on a nomination process.

Strategic Plan and Diversity Leadership

How does the firm's leadership communicate importance of diversity to everyone at the firm

Yes, through broadcast e-mail communications and Intranet web site.

Who has primary responsibility for leading div tiatives at your firm?

Susan Reid, managing director

Does your firm currently have a diversity con

Yes

If yes, does the committee's representation i one or more members of the firm's managen utive committee (or the equivalent)?

Yes

Does the committee and/or diversity leader e and set goals or objectives consistent with r ment's priorities?

Yes

Has the firm undertaken a formal or informa program or set of initiatives aimed at increas diversity of the firm?

Yes, formal

How often does the firm's management rev firm's diversity progress/results?

Quarterly

The Stats

	NUMBER OF EMPLOYEES		RE
	2006	2005	2006
Total worldwide	26,000	30,000	$5 billion

Marshall and Ilsley Corporation

770 N. Water Street
Milwaukee, WI 53202
Phone: (414) 765-7700
www.micorp.com

Diversity Leadership

Walt A. Buckhanan
Vice President, Corporate Diversity/Inclusion
Manager
770 N Water Street
Milwaukee, WI 53202
Phone: (414) 765-7771
Fax: (414) 765-7514
E-mail: Walt.Buckhanan@micorp

Recruiting

Please list the schools/types of schools at which you recruit.

• Private schools
• Public state schools

Do you have any special outreach efforts directed to encourage minority students to consider your firm?

• *Conferences:* Black MBA and NEON
• Participate in/host minority student job fair(s)
• Sponsor minority student association events
• Firm's employees participate on career panels at school

What activities does the firm undertake to attract minority and women employees?

• Partner programs with women and minority associations
• *Conferences:* Black MBA, NEON, M&I Milwaukee and You
• Participate at minority job fairs
• Seek referrals from other employees
• Utilize online job services

Do you use executive recruiting/search firms to seek to identify new diversity hires?

Yes

Internships and Co-ops

INROADS

Deadline for application: February 28th
Pay: TBD (Based on experience and grade level.)

Length of the program: 12 weeks
Web site for internship/co-op information: www.micorp.com

Jr. Associate Program

Deadline for application: February 28th
Pay: TBD (Based on experience and grade level.)
Length of the program: 12 weeks
Web site for internship/co-op information: www.micorp.com

Each manager develops a job description on an annual basis.

Affinity Groups

We are in the process of developing criteria for employee resource groups.

Entry-Level Programs, Full-Time Opportunities and Training Programs

Financial Sales Program

Length of program: Seven to 12 months
Geographic location(s) of program: Arizona, Minnesota, Missouri and Wisconsin

Treasury Management Sales Program

Length of program: Seven to 12 months

Geographic location(s) of program: Arizona, Minnesota, Missouri and Wisconsin

Retention and Professional Development

Based on monthly retention reports, minority and female attrition rates between the present time and the same period last year have not changed. Marsh has continued to retain female and diverse candidates, losing very few employees within the two groups.

Please identify the specific steps you are taking to reduce the attrition rate of minority and women employees.

- Develop and/or support internal employee affinity groups
- Increase/improve current work/life programs
- Succession plan includes emphasis on diversity
- Work with minority and women employees to develop career advancement plans
- Review work assignments and hours billed to key client matters to make sure minority and women employees are not being excluded
- Strengthen mentoring program for all employees, including minorities and women
- Professional skills development program, including minority and women employees

Diversity Mission Statement

Marsh will foster an environment in which each colleague values what every other colleague has to offer. We expect all of our people to view differences—whether they are race, ethnicity, gender, age, sexual orientation, function, geography or other facets of experience—as a powerful source of organizational strength. We will creatively leverage these different experiences and perspectives into a rich collection of skills and knowledge to provide innovative approaches to our business and unparalleled service to our clients. We will continue to ensure that all Marsh colleagues are valued and respected so that they are able to apply their unique capabilities in the pursuit of personal and organizational effectiveness.

Corporate Banking Program

Length of program: Seven to 12 months

Geographic location(s) of program: Arizona, Minnesota, Missouri and Wisconsin

Trust Operations Program

Length of program: Seven to 12 months

Geographic location(s) of program: Arizona, Minnesota, Missouri and Wisconsin

Audit analysis Program

Length of program: Seven to 12 months

Geographic location(s) of program: Arizona, Minnesota, Missouri and Wisconsin

Strategic Plan and Diversity Leadership

How does the firm's leadership communicate the importance of diversity to everyone at the firm?

Corporate newsletter, e-mails, meetings and training

Who has primary responsibility for leading diversity initiatives at your firm?

Walt A. Buckhanan, VP corporate diversity/inclusion manager

Does your firm currently have a diversity committee?

Yes

If yes, please describe how the committee is structured, how often it meets, etc.

It is made up of business line managers representing key areas of responsibilities.

If yes, does the committee's representation include one or more members of the firm's management/executive committee?

Yes

If yes, how many executives are on the committee? How many employees are on the committee, and how often does the committee convene in furtherance of the firm's diversity initiatives?

Our diversity council make up is apprised of: one executive sponsor, the CEO and nine business line managers. The council meets quarterly

Does the committee and/or diversity leader establish and set goals or objectives consistent with management's priorities?

Yes

Has the firm undertaken a formal or informal diversity program or set of initiatives aimed at increasing the diversity of the firm?

Yes, formal

How often does the firm's management review the firm's diversity progress/results?

Quarterly

Retention and Professional Development

Please identify the specific steps you are taking to reduce the attrition rate of minority and women employees.

• Increase/review compensation relative to competition

• Succession plan includes emphasis on diversity

• Work with minority and women employees to develop career advancement plans

• Strengthen mentoring program for all employees, including minorities and women

Diversity Mission Statement

Marshall & Ilsley Corporation is committed to a diverse workforce that reflects the communities we serve. We value our employees' talents and support a work environment that is inclusive and respectful.

Mattel, Inc.

333 Continental Boulevard
El Segundo, CA 90245
Phone: (310) 252-2000

Locations

With worldwide headquarters in El Segundo, CA, Mattel employs more than 25,000 people in 42 countries and sells products in more than 150 nations throughout the world.

Diversity Leadership

Graciela Meibar
VP Global Diversity

Employment Contact

Teresa Newcomb
Corporate Staffing
333 Continental Boulevard
El Segundo, CA 90245
Phone: (310) 252-2000
E-mail: teresa.newcomb@mattel.com
www.mattel.com

Recruiting

Please list the schools/types of schools at which you recruit.

• Ivy League schools

• Other private schools

• Public State schools

• Historically black colleges and universities (HBCUs)

• Hispanic serving institutions (HSIs)

• Other predominantly minority and/or women's colleges

Do you have any special outreach efforts that are directed to encourage minority students to consider your firm?

• *Conferences:* NSHMBA and NBMBAA

• Firm's employees participate on career panels at school

What activities does the firm undertake to attract minority and women employees?

• Partner programs with women and minority associations

• *Conferences:* NSHMBA and NBMBAA

• Seek referrals from other employees

Do you use executive recruiting/search firms to seek to identify new diversity hires?

No

Scholarships

Mattel offers scholarships to the children of employees.

Affinity Groups

None at this time, although the company is starting a women's network.

Strategic Plan and Diversity Leadership

How does the firm's leadership communicate the importance of diversity to everyone at the firm?

The firm communicates diversity information via e-mails and newsletters.

Who has primary responsibility for leading diversity initiatives at your firm?

Graciela Meibar, VP global diversity

Does your firm currently have a diversity committee?

No

Does the committee and/or diversity leader establish and set goals or objectives consistent with management's priorities?

Yes

Has the firm undertaken a formal or informal diversity program or set of initiatives aimed at increasing the diversity of the firm?

Yes, informal

How often does the firm's management review the firm's diversity progress/results?

Quarterly

The Stats

	NUMBER OF EMPLOYEES
	2005
Total in the U.S.	5,000
Total outside the U.S.	20,000
Total worldwide	25,000

Retention and Professional Development

Please identify the specific steps you are taking to reduce the attrition rate of minority and women employees.

• Develop and/or support internal employee affinity groups

• Strengthen mentoring program for all employees, including minorities and women

• Professional skills development program, including minority and women employees

Diversity Mission Statement

Diversity is a strategic business plan imperative to Mattel, Inc. As we get closer to our consumers, we will become more successful. The best way to do so is by having a workforce that reflects our worldwide consumers.

McDonald's Corporation

2111 McDonald's Drive, Dept. 147
Oak Brook, IL 60523
Phone: (630) 623-4833
Fax: (630) 623-7232
www.mcdonalds.com

Locations

Oak Brook, IL (HQ)

Diversity Leadership
Pat Harris
Chief Diversity Officer

Employment Contact
Lynda DuBovi
Admin., Diversity & Inclusion

Recruiting

What activities does the firm undertake to attract minority and women employees?

• Partner programs with women and minority associations

• *Conferences:* NAACP, NUL, NCLR, NAAAP, WFF, HACU, LULAC, JASC, NBMBA, ALPFA, Bennet College for Women

• Seek referrals from other employees

Do you use executive recruiting/search firms to seek to identify new diversity hires?

No.

Scholarships

RMHC/African American Future Achievers Scholarship Program

Commitment to Education

The RMHC/African-American Future Achievers Scholarship Program is a program of Ronald McDonald House Charities global office and its U.S. chapters. It is one of several RMHC scholarships designed to assist specific students who face a widening education gap. The goal of this RMHC program is to provide scholarships to graduating high school seniors who may need an extra hand getting in and staying in college. Studies show that the more difficult it is for a student to get into college, the less likely they are to graduate. Funding from RMHC can sometimes make the difference between attending and not attending the college of someone's choice. During the 2003-2004 RMHC/African-American Future Achievers program, over $1.3 million was awarded in scholarships.

The RMHC/Future Achievers Scholarship Program provides financial support to students who are committed to pursuing postsecondary education in their chosen field at an accredited institution. The RMHC/Future Achievers Program recognizes young peoples'

education accomplishments, their potential and their commitment to serve the community. Local chapters of RMHC operate the program in their respective geographic areas with support from the global office of RMHC, local McDonald's restaurants and other businesses and organizations in the community.

To apply for a RMHC/Future Achievers scholarship, students must:

• Have at least one parent of African-American origin

• Be eligible to enroll in and attend a two-year or four-year accredited college with a full course of study

• Attend college in the U.S.

• Reside in a participating local chapter's geographic area

• Scholarships are generally a minimum of $1,000 and are designated for graduating high school seniors, although some local programs may award different scholarship amounts.

Scholarship recipients are selected based on:

• Academic achievement

• Financial need

• Community involvement

• Personal qualities and strengths as portrayed in a required essay

Recipients must enroll in and attend an accredited institution in the academic year after their selection and provide verification of enrollment. Scholarship funds are paid directly to the schools and no funds will be dispersed to students directly.

Additional eligibility information and instructions are provided on the scholarship application.

RMHC/ASIA (Asian Students Increasing Achievement) Scholarship Program

Commitment to Education

The RMHC/ASIA Scholarship Program is a program of Ronald McDonald House Charities global office and its U.S. chapters. It is one of several RMHC scholarships designed to assist specific students who face a widening education gap. The goal of this RMHC

program is to provide scholarships to graduating high school seniors who may need an extra hand getting in and staying in college. Studies show that the more difficult it is for a student to get into college, the less likely they are to graduate. Funding from RMHC can sometimes make the difference between attending and not attending the college of someone's choice. During the 2003-2004 RMHC/ASIA program, over $600,000 was awarded in scholarships.

The RMHC/ASIA Scholarship Program provides financial support to students who are committed to pursuing postsecondary education in their chosen field at an accredited institution. The RMHC/ASIA program recognizes young peoples' education accomplishments, their potential and their commitment to serve the community. Local chapters of RMHC operate the program in their respective geographic areas with support from the global office of RMHC, local McDonald's restaurants and other businesses and organizations in the community.

To apply for a RMHC/ASIA scholarship, students must:

• Have at least one parent of Asian-Pacific origin (any major Asian-American, Southeast Asian, South Asian or Pacific-Islander group)
• Be eligible to enroll in and attend a two-year or four-year accredited college with a full course of study
• Attend college in the U.S.
• Reside in a participating local chapter's geographic area

Scholarships are generally a minimum of $1,000 and are designated for graduating high school seniors, although some local programs may award different scholarship amounts.

Scholarship recipients are selected based on:

• Academic achievement
• Financial need
• Community involvement
• Personal qualities and strengths as portrayed in a required essay

Recipients must enroll in and attend an accredited institution in the academic year after their selection and provide verification of enrollment. Scholarship funds are paid directly to the schools and no funds will be dispersed to students directly.

Additional eligibility information and instructions are provided on the scholarship application.

RMHC/HACER (Hispanic American Commitment to Educational Resources) Scholarship Program
Commitment to Education

The RMHC/HACER Scholarship Program is a program of Ronald McDonald House Charities global office and its U.S. chapters. It is one of several RMHC scholarships designed to assist specific students who face a widening education gap. The goal of this RMHC program is to provide scholarships to graduating high school seniors who may need an extra hand getting in and staying in college.

Studies show that the more difficult it is for a student to get into college, the less likely they are to graduate. Funding from RMHC can sometimes make the difference between attending and not attending the college of someone's choice. During the 2003-2004 RMHC/HACER program, more than $2 million was awarded in scholarships.

The RMHC/HACER Scholarship Program provides financial support to students who are committed to pursuing postsecondary education in their chosen field at an accredited institution. The RMHC/HACER program recognizes young peoples' education accomplishments, their potential and their commitment to serve the community. Local chapters of RMHC operate the program in their respective geographic areas with support from the global office of RMHC, local McDonald's restaurants and other businesses and organizations in the community.

History of the Program

As a former educator, McDonald's franchisee Richard Castro from El Paso, Texas, was keenly aware of the alarming number of Hispanic students who dropped out of high school in his hometown and across the country. Driven by his commitment to give back, Castro acted to change the situation by leading the effort to create a scholarship program that would serve as encouragement for young Hispanics to complete high school and continue their education.

Castro rallied his fellow McDonald's franchisees and McDonald's Corporation and secured the support of Ronald McDonald House Charities to establish the RMHC/HACER program in 1985. An initial fund of $97,000 served to launch the program, providing $1,000 awards to high school seniors in various communities. Today, the RMHC/HACER Scholarship Program has become the largest high school-to-college scholarship program for Hispanic students and a nationally-recognized program.

To apply for a RMHC/HACER scholarship, students must:

• Have at least one parent of Hispanic origin
• Be eligible to enroll in and attend a two-year or four-year accredited college with a full course of study
• Attend college in the U.S.
• Reside in a participating local chapter's geographic area

Scholarships are generally a minimum of $1,000 and are designated for graduating high school seniors, although some local programs may award different scholarship amounts.

Scholarship recipients are selected based on:

• Academic achievement
• Financial need
• Community involvement
• Personal qualities and strengths as portrayed in a required essay

Recipients must enroll in and attend an accredited institution in the academic year after their selection and provide verification of enrollment. Scholarship funds are paid directly to the schools and no funds will be dispersed to students directly.

Additional eligibility information and instructions are provided on the scholarship application.

www.rmhc.org/mission/scholarships/index.html

Affinity Groups

• Asian Employee Network

• Hispanic Employee Network

• Hispanic Leadership Council

• McDonald's African-American Employee Network

• Women's Leadership Network

Entry-Level Programs, Full-Time Opportunities and Training Programs

LAMP

Length of program: 12 months

Geographic location(s) of program: U.S.

The purpose of the Leadership at McDonald's Program (LAMP) is to accelerate the development of high-potential leaders in a way that drives results, shapes organizational culture and builds leadership depth.

Development focuses on leveraging on-the-job experiences, while providing appropriate skills that can be applied and practiced in each participant's day-to-day job. It will also focus on developing the leadership abilities of each participant. The framework that will be used to guide leadership development is based upon three leadership challenges: leading oneself, leading high performance teams and leading the organization.

Strategic Plan and Diversity Leadership

Who has primary responsibility for leading diversity initiatives at your firm?

Pat Harris, chief diversity officer

Does your firm currently have a diversity committee?

Yes, we have a diversity council

If yes, please describe how the committee is structured, how often it meets, etc.

The council was started in 2004 under the direction of the CEO of McDonald's USA. With a focus on diversity and inclusion, the council participants represent diversity thought leaders throughout our corporation.

If yes, does the committee's representation include one or more members of the firm's management/executive committee (or the equivalent)?

Yes

If yes, how many executives are on the committee? How many employees are on the committee, and how often does the committee convene in furtherance of the firm's diversity initiatives?

There are five executives on the council. There are an additional 28 employees on the council and they meet on a quarterly basis.

Does the committee and/or diversity leader establish and set goals or objectives consistent with management's priorities?

Yes

Has the firm undertaken a formal or informal diversity program or set of initiatives aimed at increasing the diversity of the firm?

Yes, formal

How often does the firm's management review the firm's diversity progress/results?

Twice a year

Retention and Professional Development

Please identify the specific steps you are taking to reduce the attrition rate of minority and women employees.

• Develop and/or support internal employee affinity groups (e.g., minority or women networks within the firm)

• Succession plan includes emphasis on diversity

• Strengthen mentoring program for all employees, including minorities and women

Diversity Mission Statement

Ensure our employees, owner/operators and suppliers reflect and represent the diverse population McDonald's serves around the world. Harness the multi-faced qualities of our diversity—individual and group differences among our people—as a combined complimentary force to run great restaurants.

Additional Information

Diversity—it's everybody's business

It is our belief that diversity is a shared accountability across the U.S. business.

The diversity initiatives department provides the strategic direction for diversity. This department is charged with developing the internal framework to integrate diversity into business strategies. This framework is delivered through consulting with the divisions and home office departments to ensure the alignment of diversity initiatives with the "plan to win" key business strategies. The diversity initiatives department serve as a brand ambassador with external organizations to strengthen and optimize McDonald's national partnerships with diverse community, political and educational organizations.

In the spirit of "Diversity—It's Everybody's Business" partnerships across the U.S field and the U.S. corporate departments, diversity has become a part of the fabric of the organization. These partnerships have positioned core diversity strategies to leverage our current strengths and to develop actionable initiatives for areas of diversity development.

Medco Health Solutions, Inc.

100 Parsons Pond Drive
Franklin Lakes, NJ 07417
Phone: (201)269-3400

Locations

Franklin Lakes, NJ (HQ)
Cincinnati, OH • Columbus, OH •
Dallas/Fort Worth, TX • Memphis, TN •
Nashville, TN • Las Vegas, NV •
Pittsburgh, PA • Spokane, WA • Tampa,
FL • Willingboro, NJ

Diversity Leadership

Karin Princivalle
SVP, Human Resources
www.medco.com/careers ("Our commitment
to diversity")

Employment Contact

Laurie Lawsky
Director, Staffing
www.medco.com/careers

Recruiting

Please list the schools/types of schools at which you recruit.

• Ivy League schools

• Other private schools

• Public state schools

• Historically black colleges and universities (HBCUs)

Medco visits campuses throughout the U.S., including Harvard University, University of Pennsylvania, New York University, University of Rochester, Bucknell University, Villanova University and Rutgers University. We also recruit at many HBCUs, including Florida A&M and Xavier University. If we are not on a particular campus, we welcome resumes through our web site where we post all opportunities.

Do you have any special outreach efforts directed to encourage minority students and graduates to consider your firm?

• Conferences

• Advertise in minority student association publication(s) or other minority-focused publications

• Participate in/host minority student job fair(s) or other minority-focused job events

• Firm's employees participate on career panels at school

Medco participates in many conferences and job fairs, such as NABA and NAACP. In addition, we are closely associated with Operation Link Up, a nonprofit organization that provides support, direction and financial assistance to high school students in low-income neighborhoods. We provide material support to many schools of pharmacy, including several at historically black colleges and universities, and we provide career counseling at Florida A&M and Xavier's School of Pharmacy. Our vice president of operations chairs the Deans Advisory Council for the Xavier University College of Pharmacy.

What activities does the firm undertake to attract minority and women employees?

• Partner programs with women and minority associations

• Conferences

• Participate at minority job fairs

• Seek referrals from other employees

• Utilize online job services

Medco partners with a variety of organization and conferences to attract minority and woman employees. We support Operation Link Up, INROADS, NAACP career fairs and NABA, and we are members of the Diversity Best Practices and Workforce Diversity Networks. Every one of our open positions, including our internships, is posted to over 95 diversity job sites. Medco encourages its employees to refer minority candidates through its Diversity Network Employee Referral Program. When a member of our diversity network refers a candidate who is then hired, Medco rewards the referring employee with its standard referral bonus and also makes a matching contribution to the diversity network in their honor.

Do you use executive recruiting/search firms to seek to identify new diversity hires?

Yes

Internships and Co-ops

MBA Management Leadership Development Program (MLDP)

The MLDP program is a highly selective management rotation opportunity that provides participants with a range of business and leadership experiences that accelerate the leadership path of high-potential employees. Graduates who are selected to enter this program typically rotate through two highly visible business units over a two-year period and receive executive-level mentoring. This program prepares participants for key management roles across the entity.

First-year MBA students will spend the summer with us and work alongside experienced, knowledgeable managers, manage assigned deliverables, participate and present in departmental meetings and complete a critical, long-term project. Offers to summer associates to enter our MLDP program after finishing their second year will be extended at the conclusion of the summer.

Application deadline is early March through campus career services.

Technology Operations and Architecture Co-op

The technology co-op plays an important role on the team that develops Medco's system applications, and provides hands-on experience in the development and implementation of mainframe and client/middleware based applications. Successful candidates will be sponsored throughout their college career, in accordance with guidelines set by their institution. College credits and pay will also be set according to individual campus guidelines. Students in the metropolitan New York and New Jersey areas are encouraged to contact their career services office for more information

Account Management/Installation Management AC/IC Internship

Medco's Account Management/Installation Management (AC/IC) program's objective is to accelerate the learning, growth and performance of potential leaders through high-impact assignments, targeted learning activities and cross-business opportunities.

The AC/IC Program is a two- to three-year rotational program that includes two 12- to 18-month assignments, the first of which is in account management and the second in installation services. Each assignment offers opportunities for career growth and culminates in a management-level position at program's end.

Undergraduate summer interns spend eight weeks working directly with an account team at Medco's corporate headquarters. The program enables them to make an immediate contribution and provides them with practical professional skills and business acumen. Offers to enter our AC/IC Program upon graduation will be extended and the conclusion of the summer.

Application deadline is early March through campus career services or via www.medco.com/careers.

Summer Internship—Accounting

Medco's summer internship in accounting trains college juniors to work independently, prioritize projects and set goals while preparing them for an entry-level role within a fully functional accounting department. Interns spend eight weeks at Medco's corporate headquarters, during which time their work contributes to all departmental goals and objectives. The successful candidate must exhibit problem solving and analytical capabilities, effective communication skills and have a passionate desire to contribute to a large, dynamic and fast-growing organization.

Application deadline is early March through campus career services or via www.medco.com/careers.

Scholarships

The University Level Support Program (ULS)

The mission of Medco's ULS Program is to advance pharmacy training and research in cooperation with selected colleges and universities. The target schools' philosophies are consistent with Medco's overall recruitment strategy—to attract minority and women, and to support academic excellence and leadership in our industry. In 2006, Medco selected the following colleges of pharmacy to participate: Washington State University, University of Montana, University of Arizona, University of Cincinnati, University of Kentucky, Ohio State University, University of Toledo, SWOSU, St. John's University, Philadelphia College of Pharmacy, Rutgers State University, University of Texas at Austin, Texas Tech University, University of Florida and Florida A&M University.

We also support Xavier University in New Orleans through the Centers for Health Disparities an initiative of the XU College of Pharmacy and to Katrina Hurricane Damage Relief designated for XU related renovations.

Affinity Groups

Medco's diversity network is a key element of the company's efforts to promote a diverse work environment. Its goals include helping develop a strong and diverse organizational culture, conducting effective community outreach and providing positive role models for Medco employees of all backgrounds. Just as important, the network provides a forum for social interaction and an environment where work-related issues and concerns can be safely raised and addressed. Glenn Taylor, Medco's group president of key accounts, is the organization's executive sponsor.

The diversity network conducts regular quarterly meetings, at which it invites high-profile members from various minority communities to speak about their career experiences. Community outreach, though, is among the most important of the network's activities, and it either sponsors or takes part in a wide variety of events throughout the year.

Strategic Plan and Diversity Leadership

What trends in your industry affect your corporate diversity goals, strategies and/or internal or external alliances?

Medco recognizes that diversity initiatives improve the quality of the workforce, increase employee satisfaction and loyalty, lower turnover and improve business performance. We believe that our workforce should mirror the increasingly diverse demographics of the country, our clients and our members. Most importantly, we believe that diversity of thinking encourages creativity.

Our goal is to be recognized by our employees and the external community as a company that values diverse talents, skills and perspectives. Further, we seek to become known as an organization that provides an inclusive culture that integrates, recognizes and rewards diverse, individual approaches.

How does the firm's leadership communicate the importance of diversity to everyone at the firm?

Broadly communicating our diversity mission to all Medco's employees is a top-level priority. Our leadership communicates through the company's robust training curriculum, Intranet site, weekly newsletter and state-of-the-art digital television studio.

Who has primary responsibility for leading diversity initiatives at your firm?

Karin Princivalle, SVP human resources, has primary responsibility for leading Medco's diversity initiatives and reports on their progress directly to the company's executive board. Medco believes that the person responsible for diversity leadership should personify the benefits of such diversity in his or her career, and Karin was recently honored by Operation Link Up for her personal contribution to their organization.

Retention and Professional Development

Please identify the specific steps you are taking to reduce the attrition rate of minority and women employees.

Medco offers a number of additional programs that help promote its commitment to a diverse workforce.

The company's Diversity Mentoring Program focuses on developing the leadership abilities and business knowledge of women and diverse males. Participants gain considerable exposure to senior leaders in the business while they further develop their leadership skills through a structured mentoring experience and development opportunities over a nine-month period.

Medco is an active sponsor of Women Unlimited, and Medco's high-potential women have participated in this external program for more than 10 years. Approximately 12 to 16 female employees participate every year, meeting monthly for structured learning sessions throughout the United States. In addition, each woman has two external business mentors (both male and female). Many Medco leaders continue to develop their skills by also participating as a mentor for other women in this program

The Women Unlimited Alumnae Network is a Medco-based organization focused on "giving back" to the organization. The network organizes companywide learning events that focus on building leadership skills and broadening employees' exposure to other business issues.

Diversity Mission Statement

Our Commitment to Diversity

At Medco, we are committed to a diverse work environment. Our goal is to hire the best people, foster a work environment that allows them to achieve their full potential, support them through training and job flexibility, and treat everyone with dignity and respect. Together, we are building an environment that expands our thinking, challenges for all to reach new levels and values our ideas, creativity and individuality.

The Stats

	NUMBER OF EMPLOYEES	
	2006	2005
Total worldwide	13,112	13,095

Monsanto Company

800 No. Lindbergh Boulevard
St. Louis, MO 63167
www.monsanto.com

Employment Contact

Jack Nesbitt
University Relations Lead
Employment Marketing Lead
800 No. Lindbergh Boulevard
St. Louis, MO 63167

Recruiting

Please list the schools/types of schools at which you recruit.

- Private schools
- Public state schools
- Historically black colleges and universities (HBCUs)
- Hispanic serving institutions (HSIs)
- *Other:* Several Big 10 schools

Do you have any special outreach efforts directed to encourage minority students to consider your firm?

- *Conferences:* FFA, AFA, HACE, MANRRS
- Advertise in minority student association publication(s)
- Firm's employees participate on career panels at school

What activities does the firm undertake to attract minority and women employees?

- Partner programs with women and minority associations
- *Conferences:* HACE, MANRRS
- Participate at minority job fairs

Internships and Co-ops

IT Coop Program & Internships

Deadline for application: April

Pay: Based on completed year in school—pay is every two weeks

Length of the program: IT co-op—six months; interns—10 to 12 weeks

Percentage of interns/co-ops in the program who receive offers of full-time employment: Varies

Web site for internship/co-op information: www.monsanto.com

The Monsanto Intern Program (in St. Louis or other U.S. locations)

This program offers college students on-the-job experience through paid temporary, full-time positions. Participants gain valuable professional experience and develop an insider's understanding of how Monsanto operates. Students typically participate in the intern program during their summer semester break. Interns generally work 40 hours per week and assignments may vary in length from 10 to 12 weeks during the summer. Internships are for students who wish to explore a career at Monsanto. If you are interested, we encourage you to respond online.

Children of employees can be considered for internships, but must go through the same selection process as all other candidates. If selected, children may not work in any direct or indirect reporting relationship to their parent.

Program requirements

You must be currently enrolled as a full-time student in a bachelor's, master's or PhD degree program at an accredited university. In most cases, you must have completed at least the freshman year.

Preferred candidates should have:

- Demonstrated leadership, communication and business acumen

- *One of the following majors:* Accounting, finance, human resources, law, information systems, agronomy, animal science, agricultural business, plant breeding, plant physiology, genetic engineering, chemical engineering, biological sciences, botany, chemistry or other agricultural-oriented majors

- *Interns could be assigned to work in one of the following functional areas:* Engineering, operations, research and development, finance/accounting, sales, animal agriculture, manufacturing/seed operations or technology

Selection

Selection is based on student credentials, behavioral-based interview results and the matching of student's skills to available openings.

Program details

Dates: The intern program typically begins in May and continues through August. We usually fill positions by mid-February.

Locations: We have opportunities located throughout North America. Our headquarters are located in St. Louis, Mo.

Logistics

Transportation: Students are primarily responsible for securing their own transportation to and from the work site on a daily basis. Monsanto is able to provide information to students regarding carpools, rental cars and public transportation.

Travel Lump Sum: The Travel Lump Sum provision of the program provides a relocating student with a predetermined dollar amount based upon the mileage traveled round trip between the city in which the school is located and the city in which the work site is located.

Why you should consider a Monsanto internship for the summer?

Networking: You'll interact with senior executives at a variety of meetings and receptions, and interact with each other at First Day Welcome, volunteer activities and social events.

Professional development: Your work will be measurable and realistic and allow you to stretch your ability. To give you practice interacting with managers and demonstrating your business acumen, you may be chosen to present a summary of your project work to managers and peers at the end of your internship.

Guidance: At the start of the summer, we'll help you develop a career development plan, and you'll receive a midpoint and end-of-summer performance evaluation. We'll also pair you with a mentor on an individual basis.

Compensation: Internship compensation is very competitive.

Lunch and learn: Senior executive presentations.

Affinity Groups

- African-Americans in Monsanto
- Hispanic Network
- Asian Network

The Stats

	NUMBER OF EMPLOYEES	REVENUE
	2006	2006
Total worldwide	17,833	$7.3 billion

Retention and Professional Development

Please identify the specific steps you are taking to reduce the attrition rate of minority and women employees.

- Develop and/or support internal employee affinity groups
- Increase/review compensation relative to competition
- Increase/improve current work/life programs
- Adopt dispute resolution process
- Succession plan includes emphasis on diversity
- Work with minority and women employees to develop career advancement plans
- Review work assignments and hours billed to key client matters to make sure minority and women employees are not being excluded
- Strengthen mentoring program for all employees, including minorities and women
- Professional skills development program, including minority and women employees

Diversity Mission Statement

Monsanto's goal is to build an inclusive and diverse organization, which values and engages all of our people's talents and perspectives. We also strive to leverage our diversity to achieve outstanding business success overall, and to ensure the growth and acceptance of biotechnology. This commitment has launched a number of actions. In addition, the importance of diversity is also reflected in our external pledge under the heading of respect.

Specifically, we will respect the religious, cultural and ethical concerns of people throughout the world. We will act with integrity, courage, respect, candor, honesty, humility and consistency. We will place our highest priority on the safety of our employees, the communities where we operate, our customers, consumers and the environment.

Additional Information

At Monsanto, we believe diversity is a business imperative. We have created a culture that reinforces diversity. As part of Monsanto's ongoing "Create a Winning Environment" initiative, all employees are encouraged to recognize, appreciate and leverage diversity. People managers and employees alike are trained to look for and appreciate the unique value that each individual brings to work and strive to create a more inclusive environment where everyone can contribute what they can to the collective goals of the organization.

To foster a highly inclusive environment for all, the company offers several different training experiences that range from basic diversity awareness to advanced relationship skills for people managers. In addition, each employee is expected to set at least one DPR goal related to how they will create a more inclusive work environment. Our innovative staffing process seeks to provide a slate of diverse candidates for available positions.

We fundamentally believe that diversity leads to outstanding business success. Our commitment is driven by an urgency to create a Monsanto that better reflects the skills and perspectives required for continued global success.

Some creative examples of our diversity efforts are listed below:

- The global diversity web site
- Quarterly featured employee called "Who Am I"
- Town halls
- Demonstration by African dancers to increase cultural awareness
- Visibility for network leads to update organization on activities
- Viewing of CBTs created by employees on local diversity issues
- Pledge report
- Examples of fostering participation and collaboration
- Diversity fairs
- Networking and sharing
- Poster sessions on what's happening around the world
- Speaker series
- Leadership skills for Asian Pacific professionals
- Dale Carnegie training
- Language lessons
- French and Spanish classes offered by employees

Nationwide

One Nationwide Plaza 1-01-20
Columbus, OH 43215
Toll Free: (800) 882-2822

Locations
All 50 US states, District of Columbia,
Virgin Islands, Asia, Europe & Latin
America

Diversity Leadership
Candice Barnhardt
VP Organizational Effectiveness Practice

Employment Contact
One Nationwide Plaza 1-01-20
Columbus, OH 43215
Toll Free: (800) 882-2822
www.nationwide.com/nw/careers/university-relations.index.htm

Recruiting

Please list the schools/types of schools at which you recruit.
- Ivy League schools
- Other private schools
- Public state schools
- Historically black colleges and universities (HBCUs)

Do you have any special outreach efforts that are directed to encourage minority students to consider your firm?
- Hold a reception for minority students
- Advertise in minority student association publication(s)
- Participate in/host minority student job fair(s)
- Sponsor minority student association events
- Firm's employees participate on career panels at school
- Outreach to leadership of minority student organizations
- Scholarships or intern/fellowships for minority students

What activities does the firm undertake to attract minority and women employees?
- *Conferences:* National Urban League Conference (NUL)
- Participate at minority job fairs
- Utilize online job services
- *Other:* The firm participates in the following organizations: National Association for the Advancement of Colored People (NAACP), National Black MBA Association (NBMBAA), National Society of Hispanic MBAs (NSHMBA), National Association of Asian American Professionals (NAAAP)

Do you use executive recruiting/search firms to seek to identify new diversity hires?
Yes

Internships and Co-ops

Tom Joyner/Nationwide, "On Your Side" internship program
Deadline for application: March 31st
Number of interns in the program in summer 2006 (internship) or 2006 (co-op): 10 undergraduate and graduate interns
Pay: Range $13 to $27 per hour
Length of the program: 10 weeks
Web site for internship/co-op information: www.nationwide.com/nw/careers/university-relations/index.htm

INROADS
Number of interns in the program in summer 2006 (internship) or 2006 (co-op): Five interns
Pay: $13 to $16 per hour
Length of the program: 12 weeks
Web site for internship/co-op information: www.nationwide.com/nw/careers/university-relations/index.htm

Leader Development Institute (LDI) graduate-level internship program
Deadline for application: Driven by manager's request (no later than March 31st). Students can post their resume for internship opportunities year round.
Number of interns in the program in summer 2006 (internship) or 2006 (co-op): 20 interns
Pay: $22 to $27 per hour

Length of the program: 12 weeks

Web site for internship/co-op information:
www.nationwide.com/nw/careers/university-relations/index.htm

Qualifications for our graduate-level internship program

LDI consist of: completion of first year at an accredited MBA program, minimum 3.2 GPA, at least three years work experience, competitive academic performance, coursework concentration in finance, marketing, actuarial science, risk management business or information technology. Features of the LDI program include a variety of activities to enhance learning.

Interns Today ... Leaders Tomorrow (Corporate Internship Program)

Deadline for application: Driven by manager's request (no later than March 31st). Students can post their resume for internship opportunities year round.

Number of interns in the program in summer 2006 (internship) or 2006 (co-op): 100 (includes Tom Joyner, INROADS and LDI programs)

Pay: $13 to $16 per hour

Length of the program: 10 to 12 weeks

Percentage of interns/co-ops in the program who receive offers of full-time employment: 40 percent

Web site for internship/co-op information:
www.nationwide.com/nw/careers/university-relations/index.htm

Interns are placed in various business units across Nationwide. Placement stems from our managers' request. Once they've identified a hiring strategy, university relations works to identify and recruit the best and brightest for that area. Qualified candidates should have at least a 3.0 GPA, status as rising junior or senior, solid academic achievement, strong oral and written communication skills, involvement in various student organizations and prior internship experience (preferred but not required). Each business unit identifies projects and assignments for their intern.

Our Tom Joyner program requires same qualifications, with one addition: the student must be enrolled at a historically black college or university.

Scholarships

Tom Joyner/Nationwide, "On Your Side" Scholarship

Deadline for application for the scholarship program: March 31st

Scholarship award amount: Entire scholarship up to $2,500, based on unmet financial need

Web site or other contact information for scholarship: Only interns selected to participate in the Tom Joyner/Nationwide, "On Your Side" internship program are eligible. The scholarship amount is up to $2,500 and is based on the student's unmet financial need.

Affinity Groups

Asian Awareness Network

This group works to network and create awareness and understanding of the Asian cultures within Nationwide through business, social and multicultural activities.

Pride Gay & Lesbian Club

This club meets to network on social, service and cultural activities. In addition, the group provides support and other resources for members who seek to improve their relationship with friends or family members who are gay or lesbian.

Raising Interest in Spanish Awareness (RISA)

This group is for those interested in building a more inclusive environment through education, social and business networking. The members participate in a variety of activities including: mentoring Hispanic students, child car seat inspections, job fairs, Latino Festival, and educational and cultural events.

Umoja Network

The mission of the Umoja Network is to recognize, celebrate, educate and raise awareness of the African-American contribution. The group promotes a message of inclusion and shares knowledge about topics that are important to success in the workplace and as members of the larger community.

Entry-Level Programs, Full-Time Opportunities and Training Programs

Financial Leadership Rotation Program (FLRP)

Length of program: Two years

Geographic location(s) of program: Columbus, Ohio

This program includes a two-week tailored orientation, mentoring partnerships, project assignments, coaching and feedback, professional networking and recognition through placement.

Nationwide Financial Leader Development Program (NFLDP)

Length of program: 12 months

Geographic location(s) of program: Columbus, Ohio

Components include but are not limited to:

• Coaching sessions
• Team building
• Presentation skills
• Surveys/assessments

- 360 feedback
- Mentoring

Strategic Plan and Diversity Leadership

Who has primary responsibility for leading diversity initiatives at your firm?

Candice Barnhardt, vice president, organizational effectiveness practice

Does your firm currently have a diversity committee?

Yes

Nokia

North American Headquarters:
6000 Connection Drive
Irving, TX 75039
Phone: (972) 894-5186
Fax: (972) 894-5814

Locations

Argentina • Austria • Brazil • Canada •
Chile • Columbia • Czech Republic •
Denmark • Ecuador • Egypt • Ethiopia
Finland • France • Germany • Greece •
Hungary • India • Indonesia • Iran • Japan
• Kazakhstan • Kenya • Kuwait • Lebanon
• Mexico • Morocco • Netherlands • Nigeria
• Pakistan • Philippines • Poland • Portugal
• Russia • Saudi Arabia • Singapore •
South • Africa • Spain • Switzerland •
Taiwan • Thailand • Tunisia • Turkey •
Ukraine • UK • US • Venezuela

Diversity Leadership

Catherine Simin Rousteau
HR Manager/University Relations
6000 Connection Drive
Irving, TX 75039
Phone: (972) 894-5186
Fax: (972) 894-5814
E-mail: simin.rousteau@nokia.com
www.nokia.com/careers

Recruiting

Please list the schools/types of schools at which you recruit.

• *Ivy League schools:* Columbia, Cornell, Harvard, University of Pennsylvania/Wharton, Yale

• *Other private schools:* MIT SMU, TCU, USC, Carnegie Mellon University, Duke, University of Chicago, Stanford

• *Public state schools:* UT, UTD, UTA, UCLA, University of California Berkeley, University of San Diego, University of Maryland

Do you have any special outreach efforts directed to encourage minority students to consider your firm?

• *Conferences:* National Society of Black Engineers, Society of Hispanic Professional Engineers

• Advertise in minority student association publication(s)

• *Participate in/host minority student job fair(s):* National Society of Black Engineers, Society of Hispanic Professional Engineers, National Society of Black MBAs, Society of Women Engineers, National Society of Hispanic MBAs

• Sponsor minority student association events

• Firm's employees participate on career panels at schools

• Outreach to leadership of minority student organizations

• *Other:* We advertise in the minority issue of NACE's campus publication. We also advertise extensively in several minority publications, in addition to posting our open jobs on DiversityInc, LatPro and other diversity job boards.

What activities does the firm undertake to attract minority and women employees?

• Partner programs with women and minority associations

• *Conferences:* Society of Women Engineers, National Society of Black Engineers, Society of Hispanic Professional Engineers

• Participate at minority job fairs: Society of Women Engineers, National Society of Black Engineers, Society of Hispanic Professional Engineers

• Seek referrals from other employees

• Utilize online job services: LatPro, SWE, NSBE online

Do you use executive recruiting/search firms to seek to identify new diversity hires?

Yes

Internships and Co-ops

Nokia hires interns to fill specific positions, based on need. Most interns are hired at the beginning of the fall, spring and summer semester, corresponding with most university calendars. Assignments/projects generally last three months or 1,000 hours.

Qualifications to be an intern:

• Currently be enrolled in a degree program (bachelor's, master's, PhD) at an accredited university
• Preferably at least junior level
• Preferably at least a 3.0 GPA

Intern benefits:

• Competitive hourly wages
• Holiday pay
• Additional perk benefits, based on position
• If an intern is hired as a regular employee, he/she will be given credit for time as an intern
• Access to other Nokia perks

Entry-Level Programs, Full-Time Opportunities and Training Programs

As with the intern positions, specific entry-level positions are based on business group need. Our networks group does have a rotational program for entry-level technical service managers.

Strategic Plan and Diversity Leadership

Who has primary responsibility for leading diversity initiatives at your firm?
Catherine Simin Rousteau, manager, diversity, North America

Does your firm currently have a diversity committee?
Yes

If yes, does the committee's representation include one or more members of the firm's management/executive committee (or the equivalent)?
Yes

Total Executives on Committee: Five

Does the committee and/or diversity leader establish and set goals or objectives consistent with management's priorities?
Yes

Has the firm undertaken a formal or informal diversity program or set of initiatives aimed at increasing the diversity of the firm?
Yes, formal

How often does the firm's management review the firm's diversity progress/results?
Annually

How is the firm's diversity committee and/or firm management held accountable for achieving results?
Diversity results and next-year plans have to be presented to Nokia's CEO on an annual basis by the head of each Nokia business group.

The Stats

	NUMBER OF EMPLOYEES	REVENUE
	2005	2006
Total in the U.S.	5,863	N/A
Total outside the U.S.	51,033	$34.2 billion
Total worldwide	56,896	$29.3 billion

Retention and Professional Development

Please identify the specific steps you are taking to reduce the attrition rate of minority and women employees.

• Succession plan includes emphasis on diversity
• Work with minority and women employees to develop career advancement plans
• Strengthen mentoring program for all employees, including minorities and women
• Professional skills development program, including minority and women employees

Diversity Mission Statement

Our main goal is to evolve the company culture toward a more inclusive work environment. This means, among other things, that we're committed to seeking, respecting and harnessing the broad range of diversity at Nokia, including gender, race, age, cultural background, physical ability, religion, sexual orientation and/or any other attribute that shapes an individual's perspective.

Norfolk Southern Corp.

Locations
22 states

Diversity Leadership
Kisah Hutchings

Employment Contact
Kisah Hutchings
Employment Specialist—Co-op/Intern Recruiting
www.nscorp.com/careers

Recruiting

Please list the schools/types of schools at which you recruit.

- Ivy League schools
- Other private schools
- Public state schools
- Historically black colleges and universities (HBCUs)
- Other predominantly minority and/or women's colleges

Do you have any special outreach efforts directed to encourage minority students and graduates to consider your firm?

- Advertise in minority student association publication(s) or other minority-focused publications
- Participate in/host minority student job fair(s) or other minority-focused job events
- Sponsor minority student association events

What activities does the firm undertake to attract minority and women employees?

- Partner programs with women and minority associations
- Participate at minority job fairs
- Seek referrals from other employees
- Utilize online job services

Do you use executive recruiting/search firms to seek to identify new diversity hires?

No

Internships and Co-ops

We have 50 different co-op/intern positions.

Deadline for application: *Summer:* April 1, 2007; *fall:* August 1, 2007; *spring:* November 1, 2007

Number of interns in the program in summer 2006 (internship) or 2006 (co-op): 71

Pay: $1,920 to $2,835 per month

Length of the program: 12

Percentage of interns/co-ops in the program who receive offers of full-time employment: 10 percent

Web site for internship/co-op information:
www.nscorp.com/careers

Norfolk Southern: Co-op and Internship Program

Our co-op and internship programs are designed to allow students to gain work experience during their college academic career. Our co-op program requires an individual to be a full-time college student, have a formal arrangement with their academic institution and be able to alternate full-time work and school semesters for two terms. Our internship program typically requires an individual to work one summer semester, but we do have opportunities available during fall and spring semesters as well. For additional information and specific job descriptions, please visit our careers web site at www.nscorp.com/careers.

Monthly salary is as follows:

Freshman: $1,920
Sophomore: $2,125
Junior: $2,335
Senior: $2,545
Graduate: $2,835

Entry-Level Programs/Full-Time Opportunities/Training Programs

Management Trainee Program
Length of program: 15 months

Geographic location(s) of program: Varies

The Management Training Program trains recent college graduate effective leadership abilities. Tuition reimbursement is available.

The Stats

Employees

2006: 30,000

North Carolina Office of State Personnel

1331 Mail Service Center Diversity Leadership
Raleigh, NC 27699-1331

Diversity Leadership

Nellie Riley
Human Resources Managing Partner
Phone: (919) 807-4800
Fax: (919) 733-065

Employment Contact

Charlene Shabazz
HR Partner
116 West Jones Street
Raleigh, NC 27603
E-mail: Charlene.shabazz@ncmail.net
Phone: (919) 807-4800

Recruiting

Please list the schools/types of schools at which you recruit.

• Public state schools

• Historically black colleges and universities (HBCUs)

• Other predominantly minority and/or women's colleges

Do you have any special outreach efforts directed to encourage minority students to consider your firm?

• Participate in/host minority student job fair(s)

• Firm's employees participate on career panels at schools

• Outreach to leadership of minority student organizations

• Scholarships or intern/fellowships for minority students

What activities does the firm undertake to attract minority and women employees?

• Partner programs with women and minority associations

• Participate at minority job fairs

• Seek referrals from other employees

Do you use executive recruiting/search firms to seek to identify new diversity hires?

No

Internships and Co-ops

INROADS

Deadline for application: December

Number of interns in the program in summer 2007internship: 13

Budget for the entire program: $89,975

Length of the program: 12 weeks

Percentage of interns/co-ops in the program who receive offers of full-time employment: 2 percent

Web site for internship/co-op information: www.inroads.org

Qualifications for the INROADS program is at least a 2.5 grade point average and selection is competitive based on interviews by INROADS staff. Participants must major in courses specified by the position description. Supervisors in departments and agencies select students.

NC state government participating departments include:

• Commerce

• Insurance

• Juvenile Justice and Delinquency Prevention

• Revenue

• Administration

• State Treasurer and the Office of State Personnel

• State Controller

• Environment and Natural Resources

• Model Cooperative Education

Deadline for applications: Varies by semester

Number of interns in the program in summer 2006 (internship) or 2006 (co-op): 11 interns

Budget for the entire program: $21,000

Length of the program: 12 weeks

Percentage of interns/co-ops in the program who receive offers of full-time employment: 3 percent

Qualifications:

• At least a 2.0 grade point average

• Majoring in the area specified on the position announcement

• Resident of North Carolina

Students are referred from college placement offices/co-op coordinators. Supervisors in departments and agencies select co-op students.

Summer Assistance Department of Transportation

Deadline for application: April 1st each year

Number of interns in the program in summer 2006 (internship) or 2006(co-op): 90 interns

Budget for the entire program: $75,000

Length of the program: 12 weeks

Percentage of interns/co-ops in the program who receive offers of full-time employment: 60 percent

Web site for internship/co-op information: www.NCDOT.org

Qualifications:

This program is for students majoring in civil engineering. Must have at least a 2.5 grade point average and 21 semester hours and be a legal resident of North Carolina.

Summer Internships: NC Youth Advocacy and Involvement Office—Department of Administration.

Deadline for application: January each year

Number of interns in the program in summer 2007 (internship) or 2007 (co-op): 100

Budget for the entire program: $82,500

Length of the program: 10 weeks

Web site for internship/co-op information: www.ncyaio.com

Summer internships are offered in virtually all areas of state government.

Qualifications:

• Students must have completed their first year of college

• Be enrolled in a community college, law or graduate school in or out of state for the semester following the internship

• Be a legal resident of North Carolina and have at least an overall 2.5 GPA on a 4.0 scale

Department of the Controller—Beacon Project College Internship Program

Deadline for application: Accept applications throughout the year

Number of interns in the program in summer 2006 (internship) or 2006 (co-op): Six students; salaries are $12.89 per hour

Budget for the entire program: $110,592. This amount will expire July 2007. Anticipate a new budget after that date

Length of the program: 12 weeks in summer and during the spring and fall semesters; length varies

Web site for internship/co-op information: www.beacon.nc.gov

Qualifications:

Applicants should be juniors, seniors or graduate students majoring in business management, public administration or management information systems.

Affinity Groups

No specific names, but affinity groups/networks have been established for females and African-American males. Opportunities to network and career development are the reasons the groups have been established. The groups meet at least every other month.

Entry-Level Programs, Full-Time Opportunities and Training Programs

DOT Transportation Engineering Associate Program

Deadline for application: November 30th and March 30th each year

Number of associates slots: 100 slots continuously. Hire at least 20 December grads and 20 May grads.

Length of the program: 18 months

Geographic location of program: Statewide

Web site for internship/co-op information: www.NCDOT.org (employment opportunities—recruitment programs)

This program is for new engineers. These engineers rotate assignments throughout the department during the 18-month training cycle.

This program provides tuition reimbursement and career development assistance with the professional engineering license.

Strategic Plan and Diversity Leadership

How does the firm's leadership communicate the importance of diversity to everyone at the firm?

E-mails, web site, newsletters and meetings are used to promote and communicate the importance of diversity. Diversity is part of the mission statement for the Office of State Personnel—the headquarters for the state personnel system that has approximately 88,000 employees subject to the State Personnel Act.

Who has primary responsibility for leading diversity initiatives at your firm?

Nellie Riley, HR managing partner—EEO and diversity expert for the state.

Does your firm currently have a diversity committee?

Yes. The council includes representatives from most demographic groups (women, veterans, American Indians, Hispanics/Latinos, African-Americans, the disabled and older workers), the director of civil rights, department of transportation and the director of the human relations commission and the state's historically underutilized business director.

If yes, does the committee's representation include one or more members of the firm's management/executive committee (or the equivalent)?

Total Executives on Committee: Three

In 2006, the executives spent 24 hours in furtherance of the state's diversity initiatives. The council meets at least quarterly for at least two hours. There are 14 committee members. Collectively, the committee spent 104 hours in 2006 on the furtherance of the state's diversity issues.

Does the committee and/or diversity leader establish and set goals or objectives consistent with management's priorities?

Yes, the council established a purpose and mission statement and objectives. Its mission is to develop and support diversity initiatives to ensure that North Carolina state government delivers effective services to citizens by recognizing, optimizing and championing a diverse work force. Further, the mission statement of the Office of State Personnel includes attracting and retaining a diverse work force.

Has the firm undertaken a formal or informal diversity program or set of initiatives aimed at increasing the diversity of the firm?

Yes, formal. The Special Emphasis Project for African-American males, females, older workers, the disabled and people of color includes initiatives to increase the representation, career development and retention of different demographic groups.

How often does the firm's management review the firm's diversity progress/results?

Annually

How is the firm's diversity committee and/or firm management held accountable for achieving results?

Through work plans

The Stats

Employees

2006: 88,000

Retention and Professional Development

How do 2006 minority and female attrition rates generally compare to those experienced in the prior year period?

About the same as in prior years.

Please identify the specific steps you are taking to reduce the attrition rate of minority and women employees.

• Develop and/or support internal employee affinity groups (e.g., minority or women networks within the firm)

• Increase/review compensation relative to competition

• Increase/improve current work/life programs

• Adopt dispute resolution process

• Work with minority and women employees to develop career advancement plans

• Strengthen mentoring program for all employees, including minorities and women

• Professional skills development program, including minority and women employees

Note: All of these initiatives are being undertaken in the Special Emphasis Project.

Additional Information

The state of North Carolina is committed to diversity through several means which include:

• A requirement that all new managers and supervisors attend the Equal Employment Opportunity Institute within the first year of appointment

• Executive Order Number Five, that requires that all occupational categories reflect diversity of the state's working population

• Statewide Diversity Council (Diversity Advocacy Partnership) that was organized by the Office of State Personnel

• A specific project entitled Special Emphasis, which focuses on the needs of all demographic groups (women, African-American males, older workers, the disabled, people of color and white male inclusion)

ACHIEVEMENT STARTS WHEN
YOU HARNESS THE POWER
OF MANY PERSPECTIVES.

WE KNOW GREATNESS IS OFTEN THE PRODUCT OF PEOPLE BRINGING FRESH PERSPECTIVES TO THE TABLE

Achievement can take you places. Northrop Grumman professionals work on the cutting edge of global defense and technology, and at every level we've made strong commitments to workforce diversity — because we know that diversity fuels innovation, and innovation fuels achievement. Our commitment is visible — Northrop Grumman was recently selected #7 in Woman Engineer magazine's Top 50 Companies Hiring Women Engineers, and 15th in NSBE's Top 50 Preferred Employers. At Northrop Grumman, we foster a breadth of perspectives to power our world-class projects. Perspectives like yours.

Achievement never ends.

www.careers.northropgrumman.com

NORTHROP GRUMMAN

DEFINING THE FUTURE™

Northrop Grumman Corporation

1840 Century Park East
Los Angeles, CA 90067-2199
Phone: (310) 553-6262
Fax: (310) 553-2076
www.careers.northropgrumman.com

Recruiting

Please list the schools/types of schools at which you recruit.

• Ivy League schools

• Other private schools

• Public state schools

• Historically black colleges and universities (HBCUs)

• Hispanic serving institutions (HSIs)

• Native American tribal universities

• Other predominantly minority and/or women's colleges

Do you have any special outreach efforts that are directed to encourage minority students to consider your firm?

• Hold a reception for minority students

• *Conferences:* SHPE, NSBE, HENAAC, SWE

• Advertise in minority student association publication(s)

• Participate in/host minority student job fair(s)

• Sponsor minority student association events

• Firm's employees participate on career panels at school

• Outreach to leadership of minority student organizations

• Scholarships or intern/fellowships for minority students

• *Other:* UNCF, INROADS, United Negro College Fund; provide speakers for minority targeted luncheons and banquets, workshops

What activities does the firm undertake to attract minority and women employees?

• Partner programs with women and minority associations

• *Conferences:* SHPE, AISE, NSBE HENAAC, SWE

• Participate at minority job fairs

• Seek referrals from other employees

• Utilize online job services

• *Other:* Host/sponsor regional diversity organization monthly meetings

Do you use executive recruiting/search firms to seek to identify new diversity hires?

Yes

Internships and Co-ops

NASA-Sharp & Cams CA. Academy Math & Science, Monster Diversity Leadership Program

Deadline for application: Varies

Pay: Varies by location

Length of the program: Flexible to meet student's needs

Percentage of interns/co-ops in the program who receive offers of full-time employment: Varies by business area

Web site for internship/co-op information: www.definingthefuture.com

Typically a 3.0 GPA and sophomore status from an accredited college or university is required. Requirements may vary by business unit.

Scholarships

• UNCF/NG Diversity Scholarship

• HIP Scholarship

• Diversity ENS Scholarship Program

Affinity Groups

• Community Practice

• WINGS

• Women's Networking Group

Entry-Level Programs, Full-Time Opportunities and Training Programs

Engineering & Business Prof. Dev. Programs (ES); Leadership Training Program

Length of program: 15 months

Geographic location(s) of program: Baltimore, Md.

Please describe the training/training component of this program: Rotational assignments supported by internal and external course-work

Please describe any other educational components of this program: Tuition reimbursement; mentoring programs

Strategic Plan and Diversity Leadership

Does your firm currently have a diversity committee?

Yes

Does the committee and/or diversity leader establish and set goals or objectives consistent with management's priorities?

Yes

Has the firm undertaken a formal or informal diversity program or set of initiatives aimed at increasing the diversity of the firm?

Yes, formal

The Stats

	NUMBER OF EMPLOYEES	REVENUE
	2005	2005
Total in the U.S.	125,000	$30.721 billion

Retention and Professional Development

Please identify the specific steps you are taking to reduce the attrition rate of minority and women employees.

Support to local chapters of minority organizations such as SHPE, WSBE, etc.

ODDS ARE, YOU'RE NOT GOING TO HAVE A TOP TEN SONG.

BUT YOU CAN HAVE A TOP TEN INTERNSHIP.

Northwestern Mutual Financial Network

720 East Wisconsin Avenue
Milwaukee, WI 53202
Phone: (414) 271-1444
www.careers.nmfn.com

Locations
350 locations nationwide

Employment Contact
www.internship.nmfn.com

Recruiting

Please list the schools/types of schools at which you recruit.

- Public state schools
- Historically black colleges and universities (HBCUs)
- Hispanic serving institutions (HSIs)
- Other predominantly minority and/or women's colleges

Do you have any special outreach efforts directed to encourage minority students to consider your firm?

- Conferences
- Advertise in minority student association publication(s)
- Participate in/host minority student job fair(s)
- Sponsor minority student association events
- Firm's employees participate on career panels at schools
- Scholarships or intern/fellowships for minority students

What activities does the firm undertake to attract minority and women employees?

- *Advertise on diverse Internet sites:* Yahoo, Careerbuilder, Monster.com
- *Conferences:* Host the national Graduate Career Enrichment Conference in 22 markets
- Local office scholarships
- *Other:* Sponsorships: Women in Insurance and Financial Services, NAACP, U.S. Hispanic Chamber of Commerce, Black and Hispanic MBA associations
- Partner programs with women and minority associations
- Participate at minority job fairs
- Seek referrals from other employees
- Utilize online job services

Do you use executive recruiting/search firms to seek to identify new diversity hires?

No

Internships and Co-ops

Financial Representative Internship Program*

Deadline for application: Ongoing

Pay: Performance-based plus training stipends

Length of the program: Both summer and yearlong can lead to full-time opportunity

Percentage of interns/co-ops in the program who receive offers of full-time employment: 35 percent

Web site for internship/co-op information:
www.internship.nmfn.com, www.nminternships.com

Financial representative interns with the Northwestern Mutual Financial Network have the opportunity to experience the career by addressing the needs of individuals and businesses in the areas of retirement, insurance and investment services, estate analysis, education funding and employee benefits. Interns can develop their own practice, but they are not alone. They are supported by our network of specialists, a variety of training programs and mentors.

*Financial representatives and financial representative interns are independent contractors, and not employees of Northwestern Mutual.

Strategic Plan and Diversity Leadership

Has the firm undertaken a formal or informal diversity program or set of initiatives aimed at increasing the diversity of the firm?

Yes, formal

Northwestern Mutual strives to build a field force that represents the diversity within the communities where we do business. Company-driven initiatives focus on increasing diversity of the Northwestern Mutual Financial Network. Our field recruiting area seeks to recruit and retain more women and minorities as financial representative interns, full-time financial representatives and in-field leadership roles. Programs include national sponsorships and a variety of campus recruiting programs designed to reach women and minority candidates.

How often does the firm's management review the firm's diversity progress/results?

Quarterly

How is the firm's diversity committee and/or firm management held accountable for achieving results?

Results are tracked as part of our recruitment and marketing balance scorecard. This includes the number of diverse employees that are financial representatives, interns and in-field leadership roles.

Additional Information

Northwestern Mutual is the market share leader in individual life insurance in the U.S. and has more than and $1 trillion of individual life insurance in force. Although the company has offered insurance since 1857, today, through its subsidiaries, it also provides financial guidance, estate planning, trust services and a variety of investment products. With $145 billion in assets the company was ranked 112 by revenue in the 2007 Fortune 500. In March 2007, *Fortune* named Northwestern Mutual the "most admired life insurance company" for the 24th straight year.

The Northwestern Mutual Financial Network is the marketing name for the sales and distribution arm of Northwestern Mutual.

The company, its subsidiaries and affiliates provide life insurance, annuities, mutual funds, long-term care insurance and disability income insurance. Among its affiliated companies are those that comprise the Russell Investment Group, which provide investment management and advisory services; Northwestern Mutual Investment Services, LLC (NMIS), a wholly-owned company of Northwestern Mutual, broker-dealer and member NASD and SIPC; and Northwestern Mutual Wealth Management Company, a wholly-owned company of Northwestern Mutual, limited purpose federal savings bank and a registered investment adviser which provides financial planning, investment management and trust services. A subsidiary, Northwestern Long-Term Care Insurance Company, offers long-term care insurance.

Office Depot, Inc.

2200 Old Germantown Road
Delray Beach, FL 33445
Phone: (561) 438-4800
Fax: (561) 438-8246
www.officedepot.com/links/jobs

Locations

Delray Beach, FL (HQ)
Worldwide locations

Diversity Leadership

Daniela Saladrigas
Recruiter

Jewell Crute
College Recruiter
E-mail: collegerelations@officedepot.com

Employment Contact

Daniela Saladrigas
Recruiter

Recruiting

Does your firm annually recruit at any of the following types of institutions?

• Ivy League schools

• Other private schools

• Public state schools

• Historically black colleges and universities (HBCUs)

Do you have any special outreach efforts directed to encourage minority students to consider your firm?

• Sponsor minority student association events

• Firm's employees participate on career panels at school

• Outreach to leadership of minority student organizations

• *Other:* Work with INROADS

What activities does the firm undertake to attract minority and women employees?

• Partner programs with women and minority associations

• *Conferences:* Office Depot Success Strategies for Business Women Conference

• Participate at minority job fairs

• Seek referrals from other employees

• Utilize online job services

Do you use executive recruiting/search firms to seek to identify new diversity hires?

No

Internships and Co-ops

Retail Management Internship Program

Deadline for application: March 15th

Pay: $10 to 12 per hour

Length of the program: 10 weeks

Web site for internship/co-op information:
www.officedepot.com/links/jobs

Corporate Internship Program

(Openings vary from year to year and often exist in IT, marketing/merchandising, HR, finance/accounting/tax and others)

Deadline for application: March 15th

Pay: $11 to $18 per hour

Length of the program: 12 weeks

Web site for internship/co-op information:
www.officedepot.com/links/jobs

Office Depot offers several types of paid undergrad internship programs. The programs are highly structured and individualized. Our interns work on meaningful projects, contribute to business units and achieve amazing results. All interns own a project which they ultimately present to senior management. We strive to place successful interns as full-time Office Depot employees after graduation.

Our Retail Management Internship Program is offered at store locations throughout the country. It is designed to expose the intern to the day-to-day life of retail management. The program offers hands-on experience in a fun, fast-paced environment and helps build skills in management, customer service, time management, problem-solving and relationship-building that the intern can utilize in all future endeavors.

The Corporate Internship Program is based at our corporate headquarters in Delray Beach, Fla. Each intern is assigned to a specific division within the company and follows a curriculum created by the specific intern's manager. Opportunities vary from year to year and often exist in the following areas: information technology, e-commerce, merchandising/replenishment, marketing, finance/accounting/tax, internal audit, customer relations and human resources.

Entry-Level Programs, Full-Time Opportunities and Training Programs

Onboarding Program

Length of program: One week

Geographic location(s) of program: Delray Beach, FL

The one-week program to orient and acclimate new college hires into Office Depot consists of:

- Buddy programs
- Exposure to executives
- Company history, values and culture
- Benefits
- Diversity and ethics workshops
- Systems training
- Team building activities
- Transition to work discussion
- Store and warehouse visits
- Touch-base meetings/feedback surveys quarterly for up to 12 months after date of hire

Strategic Plan and Diversity Leadership

How does the firm's leadership communicate the importance of diversity to everyone at the firm?

Web sites, monthly calendars, corporate cultural celebrations, newsletters and e-mails

Who has primary responsibility for leading diversity initiatives at your firm?

Virginia Rebata, vice president of organizational development and diversity for Office Depot.

Does your firm currently have a diversity committee?

Yes. The EVPs, VPs and directors meet quarterly.

If yes, does the committee's representation include one or more members of the firm's management/executive committee?

Yes

If yes, how many executives are on the committee?

Total Executives on Committee: Seven

Does the committee and/or diversity leader establish and set goals or objectives consistent with management's priorities?

Yes

Has the firm undertaken a formal or informal diversity program or set of initiatives aimed at increasing the diversity of the firm?

Yes, formal

How often does the firm's management review the firm's diversity progress/results?

Quarterly

How is the firm's diversity committee and/or firm management held accountable for achieving results?

We utilize a balance score card to measure all of our executives. The Diversity Committee is an integral part of that score card.

The Stats

	NUMBER OF EMPLOYEES	REVENUE
	2005	2005
Total in the U.S.	47,000	$141 billion

Diversity Mission Statement

At Office Depot, we are committed to creating an inclusive environment where all people are valued and respected. Diversity is an important dimension of respect for the individual—one of our core values—and a key to our success in a global marketplace.

Olin Corporation, Brass & Winchester Divisions

Corporate Headquarters
190 Carondelet Plaza
Suite 1530
Clayton, MO 63105-3443

Brass & Winchester Divisions
427 N. Shamrock
East Alton, IL 62024

Locations

Brass Division:
East Alton, IL (HQ)
Bryan, OH • Cuba, MO • Waterbury, CT
Multiple production and distribution sites
throughout the US, Puerto Rico, Mexico
and China. Sales offices throughout the
US and internationally in Singapore,
Japan, China and Europe.

Winchester Division:
East Alton, IL (HQ)
Oxford, MS • Geelong, Australia

Diversity Leadership

Valerie Peters
Director, Human Resources

Angie Standefer
Manager, Employment & Records

Employment Contact

Angie Standefer
Manager, Employment & Records
427 N. Shamrock
East Alton, IL 62024
Phone: (618) 258-2976
E-mail: akstandefer@olin.com
www.olin.com

Additional Information

Olin Corporation's Brass & Winchester Divisions are leaders in their respective industries. Brass products include copper and copper alloy sheet, strip, foil, rod, welded tube, fabricated parts, and stainless steel and aluminum strip. Winchester products include sporting ammunition, canister powder, reloading components, small caliber military ammunition and components, and industrial cartridges.

We are an equal opportunity employer and proud of our diverse workforce. Since our birth in 1892, Olin has demonstrated a commitment to excellence. Our values are simple, but powerful: integrity, innovation, continuous improvement, our employees, our customers and our shareholders. Diversity of ideas and diversity within our workforce helps us achieve excellence.

Our efforts to encourage minority students to consider Olin as an employer include advertising in minority student association publications; participating in minority student job fairs; participating in career panels at colleges, universities and high schools; and sponsoring scholarships and internships for minority students. For more information, go to our web site at www.olin.com.

OSRAM SYLVANIA

100 Endicott Street
Danvers, MA 01923
Phone: (978) 777-1900
Fax: (978) 750-2152
www.sylvania.com

Locations

Asia • Canada • Europe • Mexico • US

Diversity Leadership

Leah Weinberg
Manager of Diversity Inclusion & the
Associate Development Program
E-mail: leah.weinberg@sylvania.com

Employment Contact

Maureen Crawford Hentz
Talent Acquisition Manager
100 Endicott Street
Danvers, MA 01923
Phone: (800) SYLVANIA
E-mail: maureen.crawford@sylvania.com or
diversity.recruiter@sylvania.com

Recruiting

Does your firm annually recruit at any of the following types of institutions?

• Ivy League schools

• Other private schools

• Public state schools

• Historically black colleges and universities (HBCUs)

• Hispanic serving institutions (HSIs)

• Native American tribal universities

* Specific schools listed for recruiting on www.sylvania.com

Do you have any special outreach efforts directed to encourage minority students to consider your firm?

• Hold a reception for minority students

• *Conferences:* NSBE, SHPE, SWE, WITI, Careers and the disABLED and Jobapalooza

• Participate in/host minority student job fair(s)

• Sponsor minority student association events

• Firm's employees participate on career panels at school

• Outreach to leadership of minority student organizations

• *Other:* Advertise in the minority college edition of *Diversity/Careers in Engineering and Information Technology*

What activities does the firm undertake to attract minority and women employees?

• Partner programs with women and minority associations

• *Conferences:* NSBE, SHPE, SWE

• Participate at minority job fairs

• Seek referrals from other employees

• Utilize online job services

Internships and Co-ops

OSRAM SYLVANIA Intern and Co-op Program

Deadline for application: Our program is year-round. We have intern and co-op positions available throughout the year; resumes are accepted on a continuous basis.

Pay: Pay schedule is according to function and year in school.

Length of the program: 12 to 52 weeks; this depends upon the intern or co-op's availability and the needs of the hiring manager.

Web site for internship/co-op information:
www.sylvania.com/aboutus/careers/jobs

Anyone interested in an intern or co-op position can apply at www.sylvania.com/aboutus/careers/jobs.

Opportunities within our intern and co-op program are available in, but are not limited to, the following areas:

• Business

• Engineering

• Finance and accounting

• Human resources

• Information technology

• Logistics and supply chain

• Marketing communications

Availability is based upon the company's needs at any given time.

Affinity Groups

We have eight active affinity groups at OSRAM SYLVANIA:

• Advocates for People with Disabilities (APWD)

• African-American Network (AAN)

• Latin Alliance for Motivation & Production (LAMP)

• Osram Sylvania Asian Network (OSAN)

• Sylvania's GLBT network (SPECTRUM)

• Women's Affinity Network

The women's network currently has two subgroups—the Sales & Marketing Women's Network and the Women In Science and Engineering (WISE) Network. The purpose of each of these groups is to embrace the unique characteristics of, empower and support the employees who compose our increasingly diverse workforce.

Examples of affinity group mission statements:

African-American Network (AAN)

The African-American Network is committed to promoting the value and benefits of diversity within OSRAM SYLVANIA, while encouraging people of African descent to achieve their full potential, professionally and personally, as they pursue careers and leadership positions within the company.

Advocates for People with Disabilities (APWD)

Advocates for People with Disabilities will create an inclusive work environment and through support, advocacy and assistance, strive to level differences toward the goal of promoting individual growth and adding value to OSRAM SYLVANIA.

Sales & Marketing Women's Network

The Sales & Marketing Women's Network will provide support and assistance to women who sell OSRAM SYLVANIA products and have either direct or indirect contact with our customers. This network will address the unique challenges that women face in the business world and give us a forum for ideas and learning. In addition, this network will provide opportunities for women across all sales channels to form alliances from the field to headquarters to make us all more effective and increase sales of OSRAM SYLVANIA products.

Women in Science & Engineering (WISE)

The Women in Science and Engineering Network encourages women to achieve their full potential in careers as scientists, engineers, technologists and leaders within OSRAM SYLVANIA.

Entry-level Programs, Full-Time Opportunities and Training Programs

Associate Development Program

Length of program: 24 months

Geographic location(s) of program: United States, Mexico, Canada and Germany

During the course of the program, associates are given three different assignments throughout the company. This rotational component of the program provides training in and exposure to various areas of our business.

The mission of the Associate Development Program is to develop both the leadership skills and professional work ethics of the highest quality college graduates, while also providing access to positions of increasing responsibility within OSRAM SYLVANIA. All of this, in turn, works with the companywide goal of leading OSRAM SYLVANIA to become the number one global lighting manufacturer in the world. The program consists of three eight-month assignments rotated over a two-year period to encourage exploration and advance leadership, problem solving, decision-making and other skills. The program is comprised of six disciplines:

1) Engineering

Engineering at OSRAM SYLVANIA is directly responsible for technological breakthroughs that have revolutionized the world of lighting and precision materials. The scope and diversity of engineering at OSRAM SYLVANIA are as far-reaching as our achievements. As an engineering associate, you will be given assignments in the areas of research and development, product development, process engineering, equipment development, materials development, or testing and analysis.

Assignments may include opportunities to:

• Assist in the transfer of technology from pilot stage to full-scale production

• Design and develop innovative processes that result in increased efficiency, quality and cost reduction

• Develop high-speed automated assembly equipment

• Introduce new materials for use in lighting and other products

Academic Requirements:

• BS or MS in material science engineering, electrical engineering, mechanical engineering, chemical engineering or ceramic engineering

2) Finance

OSRAM SYLVANIA's position of leadership in the lighting industry and its vision for the future requires the financial organization to play a key role through continuous improvement in measurement,

analysis and resource allocation. Total quality and internal and external customer satisfaction are constant goals. As a finance associate, you will be given assignments with immediate exposure to our business.

Assignments are at the corporate, division and plant level and will include diverse responsibilities in financial analysis, accounting and internal auditing such as:

- Coordinating and consolidating the development of an annual budget and analyzing results and variances

- Working closely with factory personnel to develop standards, identify cost reduction opportunities and prepare capital expenditure requests

- Developing an integrated reporting system which measures the profitability and key indicators of product lines within a division

- Analyzing historical and forecasted market price trends and recommending short- and long-term actions to enhance product profitability

Academic Requirements:

- BS in accounting, business, finance or economics

- Minimum of 12 credit hours of accounting

3) Human Resources

With a workforce of approximately 10,590 employees, OSRAM SYLVANIA believes its greatest strength is its employees. As a human resources associate, you will apply your skills and academic training toward maximizing employee commitment, satisfaction and productivity—stated goals of the OSRAM SYLVANIA's human resources charter. Your responsibilities will include:

- Recruiting and selecting new employees whose education, skills and work philosophies match the organization's needs

- Implementing performance management programs that effectively motivate and provide rewards for results

- Developing labor strategies and participating in the resolution of labor negotiations, grievances and arbitration

- Managing programs that facilitate employee involvement and team problem-solving processes

Academic Requirements:

- BS, MS or MBA in human resources management or industrial relations

4) Information Technology

Information technology that provides accurate and timely data for all levels of a corporation is essential to compete in today's business environment. OSRAM SYLVANIA's Corporate Information Technology Group is considered "leading edge" in its use of client

server technology to ensure that marketing, sales, manufacturing and financial personnel always have the right information at the right time. The Associate Development Program in Information Technology offers an unequaled opportunity to gain professional competency through real-world business exposure. As an information technology associate, you will be given assignments that focus on different facets of the information technology function such as:

- Being part of the group which is the single point of contact for all OSRAM SYLVANIA's business users for the resolution of information technology problems

- Participating as a member of a key information technology project or process team and having the opportunity to do programming, systems design, testing and implementation.

- Implementing new technologies associated with network, server or desktop design and analysis, including working with computer platforms, operating systems and various network technologies

Academic Requirements:

BS in computer information systems or related field

5) Manufacturing

The production of quality products using state-of-the art equipment in an efficient, cost-effective way is the cornerstone of success for a world-class manufacturing organization. The OSRAM SYLVANIA Associate Development Program in manufacturing offers an unequaled opportunity to experience this highly technical field, as well as to give you professional competency through real-world business exposure. As a manufacturing associate, you will be given challenging opportunities to participate in, or lead, continuous improvement programs such as:

- Analyzing manufacturing processes, recommending and implementing changes to improve material and/or labor efficiencies

- Applying new systems and measurements such as Total Cycle TimeSM, First Pass Yield and ISO 9000 to existing processes to create a streamlined, consistent means of operating departments and business

- Participating in team activities to promote involvement, share ideas and gain the commitment of employees at all levels of the organization

- Supervising a department or work area with responsibility for meeting safety, quality, production and cost targets

Academic Requirements:

- BS or MS in mechanical engineering, industrial engineering, electrical engineering, material science, ceramic engineering or chemical engineering

6) Marketing and Sales

At OSRAM SYLVANIA, we value innovation not only in product development but also in how we approach the various markets that we serve. From large city skyscrapers to the living room, from rock concerts to the operating table, lighting is an essential part of daily life. As a marketing/sales associate, you will be exposed to the realities of a competitive and rewarding marketplace. Assignments may include the following responsibilities:

• Market planning and research

• Product management

• Sales

• Advertising and promotion

• Training and education

• Competitive analysis

• Logistics and customer service

Academic Requirements:

• BS in business or marketing or BA in liberal arts

While in the program, associates receive the same benefits as all other OSRAM SYLVANIA employees. We offer multiple medical and dental plans, along with a competitive, noncontributory pension program. Here are some highlights:

• Indemnity, medical plans, dental plans and vision plan

• A company match to individual 401(k) investments

• Generous company-paid life insurance benefits with options to buy additional life insurance for oneself, a spouse and dependents at group rates

• Convenience, care and income protection benefits including:

• Discounted auto and homeowner's insurance

• Short-term and long-term disability

• Optional long-term care insurance for themselves or a family member

• Physical fitness programs—onsite or through a reimbursement program

Many OSRAM SYLVANIA employees use our educational assistance/tuition reimbursement plan for themselves and our scholarship program for their children. We match employee gifts to schools at all grade levels, and distribute cash grants to organizations with whom our employees volunteer. Relocation assistance is also available for associates who move more than 50 miles while in the program.

Strategic Plan and Diversity Leadership

How does the firm's leadership communicate the importance of diversity to everyone at the firm?

Communications include letters from executives, e-mails, internal and external diversity web sites and diversity topics being addressed at quarterly meetings held by executives. An executive advocate champions each affinity group, providing support, barrier removal and a direct conduit to the executive committee of OSRAM SYLVANIA.

Who has primary responsibility for leading diversity initiatives at your firm?

Leah Weinberg, manager of diversity inclusion and the Associate Development Program, in cooperation with the Diversity Council.

Does your firm currently have a diversity committee?

Yes. Geoff Hunt, senior vice president of human resources and communication, champions the Diversity Council. The Diversity Council was established by our company president in 2001 "to analyze the diversity situation at OSRAM SYLVANIA and to keep (management) attuned to changes that need to be made if the diversity initiative is to be successful, especially over the long term."

How many employees are on the committee, and how often does the committee convene in furtherance of the firm's diversity initiatives?

The council is comprised of 28 employees from various business units, one advisor and one champion. The council meets four times per year. The council has a chairperson, facilitator and an administrator elected by the council at large on an annual basis. It is organized into five action committees focusing on communications, recruitment and retention, and other areas identified as in need of progress.

The goals established by the council are:

• To develop measurements of success for diversity at OSRAM SYLVANIA and monitor progress

• Provide management with suggestions for improving diversity at OSRAM SYLVANIA

• Communicate the benefits of diversity within the company and provide employees with an avenue to voice their concerns or issues regarding diversity in our facilities without fear of repercussion

Has the firm undertaken a formal or informal diversity program or set of initiatives aimed at increasing the diversity of the firm?

Yes, formal. The council has been tasked with identifying systems required to support diversity, identifying enablers and barriers to success, and making recommendations to management on direction

and more specifically on programs and policies. The council has successfully recommended and implemented a mentoring program, a communications plan, an affinity group initiative and others. These programs are designed to support diversity in both employee representation and customer support.

How is the firm's diversity committee and/or firm management held accountable for achieving results?

The Diversity Council is required to present progress to the Executive Committee each quarter. This includes a review of progress on programs and initiatives as well as making recommendations for future activities. The manager of diversity inclusion is responsible for achieving the desired results.

The Stats

	NUMBER OF EMPLOYEES		REVENUE	
	2006	2005	2006	2005
Total in the U.S.	11,000	11,000	€2 billion	€1.5 billion
Total worldwide	40,000	38,000	€4.6 billion	€4.3 billion

2006 DEMOGRAPHIC PROFILE		
	EMPLOYEES	INTERNS
Male	70.37 percent	65.7 percent
Female	29.63 percent	34.3 percent
Non-caucasian	11.16 percent	37.1 percent
Caucasian	88.84 percent	62.9 percent

Retention and Professional Development

Please identify the specific steps you are taking to reduce the attrition rate of minority and women employees.

• Develop and/or support internal employee affinity groups

• Increase/review compensation relative to competition

• Increase/improve current work/life programs

• Adopt dispute resolution process

• Succession plan includes emphasis on diversity

• Work with minority and women employees to develop career advancement plans

• Review work assignments and hours billed to key client matters to make sure minority and women employees are not being excluded

• Strengthen mentoring program for all employees, including minorities and women

• Professional skills development program, including minority and women employees

Diversity Mission Statement

OSRAM SYLVANIA is committed to developing an increasingly diverse workforce with fair and open access to career opportunities. We cultivate an inclusive, supportive climate, thereby enabling us to better meet the needs of our employees and customers. We believe that variety of opinion, approach, perspective and talent are the cornerstones of a strong, flexible and competitive company.

We have established a corporate commitment to recruiting, retaining and developing the talents of employees regardless of race, national origin, gender, age, sexual orientation or any other dimension of diversity. We cultivate strategic partnerships with colleges, universities and professional organizations that have significant female and minority populations. The offering of domestic partner benefits, which will go into effect January 1, 2008, acknowledges the diversity in our workforce and the company's desire to accommodate family needs. Community partnerships are established that reflect the values of our workforce and opportunities are explored to enhance supplier diversity.

Diversity strategies include affinity groups, mentoring, as well as an intensified focus on employee development. With the powerful commitment of our senior management team, OSRAM SYLVANIA is expanding its reputation as the type of environment where every talented individual will be proud to work.

Owens & Minor

9120 Lockwood Boulevard
Mechanicsville, VA 23116-2029
Phone: (804) 723-7000

Additional Information

At Owens & Minor, our vision is to be a world-class organization that builds strength through the successful integration of the diverse cultures, backgrounds and experience of our teammates and business partners. Our inclusive environment enhances our efforts as we work to find solutions for our customers and supply-chain partners. Each of our teammates, customers, suppliers, as well as the communities we serve, has differing views. They trust that we take these views into account as we operate our business. In order for us to be the best we can be, we must clearly understand these diverse needs and perspectives. Strategically, this can be best accomplished by capitalizing on the value of a diverse workforce and supplier base.

We believe that the diversity of our teammates will help our company "deliver" the difference in this increasingly diverse market. At Owens & Minor we look toward our leadership team to:

• Establish diversity as a key component of how we conduct business

• Encourage all teammates to support Owens & Minor's diversity plan and diversity efforts

• Measure the success of the team at achieving specific goals for hiring, developing, promoting and retaining teammates in underrepresented or underutilized job groups and businesses

It is our belief that diversity and business success go hand in hand.

Owens Corning

Owens Corning Parkway
Toledo, OH 43659
www.owenscorning.com

Locations
326 offices and manufacturing locations
worldwide.

Diversity Leadership
Beth Ault
University & Diversity Recruiting Specialist
Phone: (419) 248-8090
Fax: (419) 325-4090
E-mail: beth.ault@owenscorning.com

Employment Contact
Tracy Beller
Global Talent Management Leader

Recruiting

Please list the schools/types of schools at which you recruit.

- Private schools
- Public state schools

Do you have any special outreach efforts directed to encourage minority students to consider your firm?

- *Conferences:* NBMBAA, NSHMBA, SWE, SHPE, NSBE
- Advertise in minority student association publication(s) or other minority-focused publications.
- Participate in/host minority student job fair(s) or other minority-focused job events.
- Firm's employees participate on career panels at school.
- Outreach to leadership of minority student organizations.
- *Other:* We host an annual Diversity Leadership Conference targeting diverse sophomores and juniors. This is a three-day event held at our WHQ. Students are selected via an application process. Average applicant number is 25. Students are introduced to Owens Corning businesses and senior executives and participate in various learning activities around personal and professional growth.

What activities does the firm undertake to attract minority and women employees?

- *Conferences:* NBMBAA, NSHMBA, SWE, SHPE, NSBE
- Seek referrals from other employees
- Utilize online job services

Do you use executive recruiting/search firms to seek to identify new diversity hires?

Yes (senior executive level only)

Internships and Co-ops

All of our interns work on business critical projects relating to their specific function.

We do not offer any co-ops.

Finance Intern

Deadline for application: Filled during fall recruiting. Spring if needed.

Number of interns in the program in summer 2006: 16

Pay: Competitive hourly rate based on class status (junior, senior, etc.)

Length of the program: 12 weeks

Percentage of interns/co-ops in the program who receive offers of full-time employment: 75 percent for 2006 finance interns. This number varies based on intern performance.

Web site for internship/co-op information: www.owenscorning.com/careers

Qualifications for the program: 3.5 and above GPA, rising seniors only, BSBA or BS finance or accounting

IS Intern

Deadline for application: Filled during fall recruiting. Spring if needed.

Number of interns in the program in summer 2006: Three

Pay: Competitive hourly rate based on class status (junior, senior, etc.)

Length of the program: 12 weeks

Percentage of interns/co-ops in the program who receive offers of full-time employment: 33 percent for 2006 IS interns. Varies by intern performance.

Web site for internship/co-op information: www.owenscorning.com/careers

Qualifications for the program: 2.8 and above GPA, bachelor's in IS or computer science engineering.

Supply Chain

Deadline for application: Filled during fall recruiting. Spring if needed.

Number of interns in the program in summer 2006: 10

Pay: Competitive hourly rate based on class status (junior, senior, etc.)

Length of the program: 12 weeks

Percentage of interns/co-ops in the program who receive offers of full-time employment: 50 percent for 2006 supply chain interns. Varies by intern performance.

Web site for internship/co-op information: www.owenscorning.com/careers

Qualifications for the program: 3.0 and above GPA, bachelor's in supply management or related field.

HR Intern

Deadline for application: Filled during fall recruiting. Spring if needed.

Number of interns in the program in summer 2006: One

Pay: Competitive hourly rate based on class status (junior, senior, etc.)

Length of the program: 12 weeks

Percentage of interns/co-ops in the program who receive offers of full-time employment: 0 percent for 2006 HR intern. Varies by intern performance.

Web site for internship/co-op information: www.owenscorning.com/careers

Qualifications for the program: 3.0 and above GPA, bachelor's in HR, organizational leadership or related field.

Engineering Intern

Deadline for application: Filled during Fall and Spring recruiting.

Number of interns in the program in summer 2006: One

Pay: Competitive hourly rate based on class status (junior, senior, etc.)

Length of the program: 12 weeks

Percentage of interns/co-ops in the program who receive offers of full-time employment: 100 percent for 2006 intern. Varies by intern performance.

Web site for internship/co-op information: www.owenscorning.com/careers

Qualifications for the program: 2.7 and above GPA, bachelor's in mechanical, chemical, material science, industrial engineering.

Operations Intern

Deadline for application: Filled during fall and spring recruiting.

Number of interns in the program in summer 2006: One

Pay: Competitive hourly rate based on class status (junior, senior, etc.)

Length of the program: 12 weeks

Percentage of interns/co-ops in the program who receive offers of full-time employment: 0 percent for 2006 interns. Varies based on intern performance.

Website for internship information: www.owenscorning.com/careers

Qualifications for the program: 2.7 and above GPA, bachelor's in mechanical, chemical, material science, industrial engineering or operations management.

Science & Technology Intern

Deadline for application: Filled during Fall and Spring recruiting.

Number of interns in the program in summer 2006: Six

Pay: Competitive hourly rate based on class status of degree earned (first year master's or PhD, etc.)

Length of the program: 12 weeks

Website for internship/co-op information www.owenscorning.com/careers

Qualifications for the program: 3.0 and above GPA, master's or PhD only, engineering, scientists and chemists.

Affinity Groups

• African-American Resource Group
• Hispanic Diversity Council
• Women's Information Network
• Owens Corning Multicultural Network
• Gay Lesbian Bisexual Transgender and Allies

All of our affinity groups have a senior executive sponsor and meet monthly. Their web sites are for internal use only. Their purpose is for inclusion, career development, networking, etc., for affinity group members.

Entry-Level Programs, Full-Time Opportunities and Training Programs

Finance Leadership Program

Length of program: Three years

Geographic location(s) of program: Multiple locations across U.S.

Technical and professional training is included in program plan.

Information Systems Development Program

Length of program: One year

Geographic location(s) of program: Toledo Ohio

Core technical training is included in program plan.

Supply Chain Development Program

Length of program: Three years

Geographic location(s) of program: Multiple locations across U.S.

Technical and professional training is included in program plan.

Engineering Development Program

Length of program: One year

Geographic location(s) of program: Various U.S. locations.

Technical and professional training is included in program plan.

Operations Development Program

Length of program: Two years

Geographic location(s) of program: Various U.S. locations.

Technical and professional training is included in program plan.

Science & Technology Development Program

Length of program: Three years

Geographic location(s) of program: Granville, Ohio

Technical and professional training is included in program plan.

HR Leadership Program

Length of program: Three years

Geographic location(s) of program: Multiple U.S. locations.

Technical and professional training is included in program plan.

Strategic Plan and Diversity Leadership

What trends in your industry affect your corporate diversity goals, strategies and/or internal or external alliances?

Limited diverse talent at the majority of the core schools we recruit at. Increasing number of international students who need sponsorship and increase in limited number of HB1 visas being issued. Increased number of students who want to stay close to home.

How does the firm's leadership communicate the importance of diversity to everyone at the firm?

Support of diversity initiatives, communication, executive support of affinity groups, global meetings, global newsletters, etc.

Who has primary responsibility for leading diversity initiatives at your firm? Name of person and his/her title:

Simone Hayes, director of community relations

Joseph High, senior VP human resources

Tracy Beller, global talent management leader

Beth Ault, university and diversity recruiting specialist

Does your firm currently have a diversity committee?

No

Has the firm undertaken a formal or informal diversity program or set of initiatives aimed at increasing the diversity of the firm?

Yes, informal

Support attendance and recruiting at national diversity conferences.

How often does the firm's management review the firm's diversity progress/results?

Annually

The Stats

	NUMBER OF EMPLOYEES		REVENUE	
	2006	2005	2006	2005
Total in the U.S.	13,908	14,693	$5.2 billion	$5.3 billion
Total outside the U.S.	5,641	5,193	$1.3 billion	$1 billion
Total worldwide	19,549	19,886	$6.5 billion	$6.3 billion

Retention and Professional Development

How do 2006 minority and female attrition rates generally compare to those experienced in the prior year period?

About the same as in prior years.

Please identify the specific steps you are taking to reduce the attrition rate of minority and women employees.

- Develop and/or support internal employee affinity groups (e.g., minority or women networks within the firm)
- Increase/improve current work/life programs
- Succession plan includes emphasis on diversity
- Work with minority and women employees to develop career advancement plans
- Strengthen mentoring program for all employees, including minorities and women
- Professional skills development program, including minority and women employees

Diversity Mission Statement

Diversity is inherent to our quest for becoming the preferred place of employment and attracting and retaining the very best people, is the inclusion of employees—regardless of gender, race, creed, religion, national origin, etc.

Diversity Goals

• To achieve an inclusive work place

• To achieve a representative work force

• To give OC a sustainable competitive advantage through people

Additional Information

When people think of Owens Corning, they often picture the Pink Panther™, who appears predominantly in its advertising campaigns. Best known for its PINK FIBERGLAS® home insulation and other products that conserve energy, which helps protect the environment, Owens Corning is a world leader in building materials systems and composite solutions. Owens Corning's people redefine what's possible each day to deliver high-quality products and services ranging from insulation, roofing, siding and manufactured stone to glass composite materials used in high-performance applications.

Owens Corning achieved sales of $6.5 billion in 2006 and employs more than 20,000 employees in 26 countries. The company continues to grow rapidly, with sales increasing each year since 2001.

A Fortune 500 company for more than 50 years, Owens Corning has cultivated a culture that emphasizes safety, performance and accountability, openness and stewardship. Newly hired employees report that a key reason they were attracted to the company is that the people working for Owens Corning are confident in their abilities, yet open and approachable.

Owens Corning's emphasis on its people and its commitment to its corporate values: integrity, respect, accountability, fun, sharing, candor and innovation result in a unique employment experience.

Additional information is available at www.owenscorning.com/career.

Pearson Education

One Lake Street
Upper Saddle River, NJ 07458
Phone: (201) 236-3419
Fax: (201) 236-3381

Locations

US:
Bloomington, MN • Boston, MA •
Champaign, IL • Columbus, OH •
Glenview, IL • Eagan, MN • Indianapolis,
IN • Iowa City, IA • Lawrence, KS •
Mesa, AZ • New York, NY • Old Tappan,
NJ • Parsippany, NJ • San Francisco, CA
• Upper Saddle River, NJ • White Plains,
NY

International:
Africa • Asia • Australia • Canada •
Europe • India • Middle East • New
Zealand • South America

Diversity Leadership

Francine Rosado-Cruz
Diversity Manager, Pearson

Ryan Darlington
College Recruiting

Employment Contact

Anne Adamo
Manager, Employee Relations
E-mail: anne.adamo@pearsoned.com
www.pearsoned.com/careers

Recruiting

Please list the schools/types of schools at which you recruit.

• *Ivy League schools:* Harvard

• *Other private schools:* Marist, William Patterson, Syracuse, Seton Hall, Muhlengerg, Mt. St. Mary, Quinnipiac

• *Public state schools:* Rutgers

Do you have any special outreach efforts directed to encourage minority students to consider your firm?

• *Conferences:* Monster Diversity Leadership Program, Black Wharton Undergraduate Association, Southern Christian Leadership Conference

• Participate in/host minority student job fair(s)

• Sponsor minority student association events

• Firm's employees participate on career panels at schools

What activities does the firm undertake to attract minority and women employees?

• Participate at minority job fairs

• Seek referrals from other employees

• *Utilize online job services:* Monster.com, DiversityHire.com, AmericasJobBank.com

• *Other:* Advertise in minority publications such as *Hispanic Network Magazine, Professional Women's Magazine,* Southern Christian Leadership Conference, *Black Enterprise* magazine, *Black EOE Journal*

Do you use executive recruiting/search firms to seek to identify new diversity hires?

No

Internships and Co-ops

Pearson Intern Program

Deadline for application: April 15th

Number of interns in the program in summer 2006 (internship) or 2006 (co-op): 20

Pay: Varies

Length of the program: Minimum eight weeks during June/July/August

Percentage of interns/co-ops in the program who receive offers of full-time employment: Varies by position/location

Web site for internship/co-op information:
www.pearsoned.com/careers

Pearson maintains a Summer College Intern Program that enables the company to recruit and train a diverse group of people for careers in publishing by providing students an opportunity to expand their theoretical knowledge, clarify their career goals and enhance opportunities for full-time employment. Students will be placed in departments that suit their interests as well as their major course of study. The departmental structure includes corporate functions, editorial, marketing, sales, production, design and human resources.

Entry-Level Programs, Full-time Opportunities and Training Programs

General Accounting Program

Length of program: Two years

Geographic location(s) of program: Upper Saddle River facility

Hands-on experience in four major accounting areas.

Tuition reimbursement is offered, but as company policy, not just for this program.

Strategic Plan and Diversity Leadership

Who has primary responsibility for leading diversity initiatives at your firm?

Christine Trum, senior vice president, human resources.

Does your firm currently have a diversity committee?

Yes

If yes, please describe how the committee is structured, how often it meets, etc.

The diversity council meets quarterly and includes executive management.

If yes, does the committee's representation include one or more members of the firm's management/executive committee (or the equivalent)?

Yes

Total Executives on Committee: Nine

Does the committee and/or diversity leader establish and set goals or objectives consistent with management's priorities?

Yes.

Has the firm undertaken a formal or informal diversity program or set of initiatives aimed at increasing the diversity of the firm?

Yes, formal, including:

• HR diversity team
• Internship program
• Metrics
• Training initiatives

How often does the firm's management review the firm's diversity progress/results?

Quarterly

How is the firm's diversity committee and/or firm management held accountable for achieving results?

Diversity metrics and practices are reviewed by the Pearson plc board each year. Goals are set and scrutinized annually.

The Stats

	NUMBER OF EMPLOYEES		REVENUE	
	2006	**2005**	**2006**	**2005**
Total in the U.S.	16,800	16,500*		$600 million

Total employees (7,489 Pearson Education)

Retention and Professional Development

Please identify the specific steps you are taking to reduce the attrition rate of minority and women employees.

• Develop and/or support internal employee affinity groups (e.g., minority or women networks within the firm)
• Increase/improve current work/life programs
• Succession plan includes emphasis on diversity
• Strengthen mentoring program for all employees, including minorities and women
• Professional skills development program, including minority and women employees

Diversity Mission Statement

We want to be: (1) A diverse company—to attract the very best candidates, at all levels, regardless of race, gender, age, physical ability, religion or sexual orientation. We always try to hire the best person for the job, and to ensure that our candidate pool is diverse and our hiring is nondiscriminatory. (2) A fair company—to ensure that pay, retention, promotions and terminations are determined without regard to race, gender, age, physical ability, religion or sexual orientation. (3) A company which uses diversity to help achieve its commercial goals and targets new opportunities in growing markets.

Additional Information

Pearson was awarded both a Bronze Corporate Spirit Award for leadership in fully making the INROADS mission a part of our daily work and a Growth Award for significantly increasing the number of INROADS internships. Additionally, Pearson's corporate INROADS liaison was named business advisor of the year.

Pepco Holdings, Inc.

701 Ninth Street, NW
Washington, DC 20068
Phone: (202) 872-2489
Fax: (202) 872-2897
www.pepcoholdings.com

Diversity Leadership

Joy Dorsey
Director, Diversity & HR Strategic Planning

Employment Contact

Carolyn Lomax
Diversity Specialist
E-mail: cmlomax@pepco.com

Recruiting

Please list the schools/types of schools at which you recruit.

• *Private schools:* American University, Anne Arundel Community College, Capitol College, Catholic University, Drexel University, George Mason University, George Washington University, Loyola College in Maryland, Montgomery College, PennState—Erie: The Behrend College, Prince George's Community College, Rowan University, Suitland High School, TESST College, Thomas Nelson Community College, University of Delaware, University of Maryland—College Park, University of Maryland—Baltimore County, Villanova University, Virginia Tech, Widener University

• *Historically black colleges and universities (HBCUs):* Alabama A & M University, Clark Atlanta University, Delaware State University, Florida A&M University, Hampton University, Howard University, Morgan State University, North Carolina A& T, Prairie View A&M University, Southern University, Tennessee State University, Tuskegee University, University of the District of Columbia, University of Maryland Eastern Shore

Do you have any special outreach efforts directed to encourage minority students and graduates to consider your firm?

• *Advertise in minority student association publication(s) or other minority-focused publications:* Clark Atlanta University Yearbook, Howard University Hilltop, Howard University, Bison

• *Participate in/host minority student job fair(s) or other minority-focused job events:* First Annual Hispanic Workforce Conference & Job Fair, 2006 NAACP Diversity Job Fair, Howard University Fall 2006 Career Fair, Greater Washington Urban League Career Fair, 21st Annual SHE-SWE-WCS-MEET Engineering & Computer Science Career Fair (Society of Hispanic Engineers, the Society of Women Engineers, Women in Computer Science, the Minority Engineering Education Task)

• *Other:* Firm's employees participate on career panels at various schools

What activities does the firm undertake to attract minority and women employees?

• *Conferences:* First Annual Hispanic Workforce Conference & Career Fair

• Participate at minority job fairs

• Seek referrals from other employees

• *Utilize online job services:* MiGente.com, BlackPlanet, AsianAvenue, Latpro.com, American Women's Association, National Society of Black Engineers, Hispanic National Bar Association, Ihispano.com, *San Juan Star, Society of Women Engineers Magazine*

Do you use executive recruiting/search firms to seek to identify new diversity hires?

No

Internships and Co-ops

Engineering Internship Program

Deadline for application: March 31, 2006

Number of interns in the program in summer 2006 (internship) or 2006 (co-op): 22

Pay: From $13.53 to $17.66 per hour, depending on level education completed

Length of the program: Summer program—June 1, 2006 to August 30, 2006

Percentage of interns/co-ops in the program who receive offers of full-time employment: 90 percent

Web site for internship/co-op information: Position posted on the following web sites in 2006: University of Delaware, Rowan University, Widener University, Villanova University, University of Maryland, Howard University, Virginia Tech, George Washington University, Penn State, Alabama A&M University, Florida A&M University, Hampton University, Morgan State University, North Carolina A& T University, Prairie View A&M University, Southern University, Tennessee State University, Tuskegee University, George Mason, Capitol College

Our paid internship program provides individuals with hands-on business experience and provides PHI with the opportunity to develop individuals who have the ability to remain with the company upon their graduation. The program runs from June 1st through the end of August. Housing is not provided.

Job Responsibilities:

- Provide engineering and technical consultation services in the solution of engineering problems requiring originality, initiative and independent judgment.

- Perform work of average complexity that conforms to all project/task requirements, including defined scope, schedule and budget, and that requires an independent understanding and application of engineering theories, standards, concepts, and techniques.

- Work closely with other groups within and outside the company to quickly resolve issues.

- Work under general supervision, taking ownership of project/task completion to meet scheduled due dates, identifying emerging issues and contributing solutions for problems.

Job Requirements:

- Must be a sophomore, junior or senior in an accredited four-year program.
- Electrical or civil engineering major
- Must possess a basic understanding and knowledge of the application of engineering principles, theories, standards, concepts and techniques.
- Experience using analytical, spreadsheet and word processing software packages
- Effective written and oral communication skills
- Ability and willingness to travel to various PHI locations
- Valid driver's license
- Cumulative GPA of 2.5 or above on a 4.0 scale
- Must maintain a 2.5 or higher GPA and satisfactory work performance while participating in the program.

Strategic Plan and Diversity Leadership

What trends in your industry affect your corporate diversity goals, strategies and/or internal or external alliances?

PHI realizes that in today's increasingly diverse marketplace, our long-term success depends on our commitment to providing an attractive corporate environment for recruiting and retaining the most talented, qualified, educated and motivated employees. The trends that affect PHI's corporate diversity goals are driven by such factors as the looming talent shortage, demographic shifts and enhancing career development of historically underrepresented groups.

How does the firm's leadership communicate the importance of diversity to everyone at the firm?

Corporate newsletter, biannual EEO/affirmative action meetings, management affirmative action attainment goal reports, Diversity as Haiku (diverse stories from PHI employees published monthly on Intranet and company newsletter), Diversity University (diversity dialogue sessions/workshops held companywide), Diversity Celebration Week (diverse activities/events held annually during second week in October), new employee orientation, *Managing Diversity* newsletter, diversity discussion starter modules (interactive diversity discussion sessions using customized modules), All Hand/Group meetings, diversity training videos followed by facilitated discussions, detailed reports to managers on performance in spending with diverse suppliers and executive diversity accountability scorecard based on achievement of AA goals.

Who has primary responsibility for leading diversity initiatives at your firm?

Joy J. Dorsey, director—diversity and HR strategic planning

Does your firm currently have a diversity committee?

Yes

If yes, please describe how the committee is structured, how often it meets, etc.

The PHI Diversity Council, which meets on a monthly basis, is comprised of 11 members. The council, chaired by PHI's director of diversity and HR strategic planning, includes members who represent PHI's lines of business (LOB). LOB representatives serve terms of one to three years. Oversight of PHI's diversity strategies is provided by the Diversity Steering Committee which is chaired by PHI's chairman of the board, president and CEO, chief operating officer, chief finance officer, two chief operating officers of PHI's subsidiary companies and VP human resources which comprises the executive leadership team, with the addition of PHI's director of diversity and HR strategic planning. The council serves as an advisory committee to the company on diversity and inclusion issues including developing, monitoring and implementing diversity initiatives that support PHI's organizational goals.

If yes, does the committee's representation include one or more members of the firm's management/executive committee (or the equivalent)?

Yes

Does the committee and/or diversity leader establish and set goals or objectives consistent with management's priorities?

Yes

Has the firm undertaken a formal or informal diversity program or set of initiatives aimed at increasing the diversity of the firm?

Yes, formal

How often does the firm's management review the firm's diversity progress/results?

Quarterly

How is the firm's diversity committee and/or firm management held accountable for achieving results?

The executive accountability scorecard, under the direction of PHI's CEO, the VP human resources and the director of diversity was developed in 2004 to tie a percentage of each PHI executive's incentive payout to the achievement of the company's affirmative action goals and good faith efforts. Implementation of the program effectively addresses the company's commitment to advancing and enhancing affirmative action goals and improving diverse representation of the workforce in the areas of recruitment, retention, promotions, transfers and developmental opportunities. This program adheres to ongoing quarterly reporting to the executive for affirmative action achievement. In 2005, the executive accountability scorecard was enhanced to address specific areas of good faith effort opportunities and overachievement of placement goals.

The Stats

	NUMBER OF EMPLOYEES	REVENUE
	2006	2006
Total in the U.S.	5,121	$8.4 billion

2006 DEMOGRAPHIC PROFILE	
White (non-Hispanic)	67.47 percent
Black	26.95 percent
Asian	2.79 percent
Native American/American Indian	35 percent
Latino	2.44 percent
Male	71.66 percent
Female	28.34 percent
Percentage of women in category of CEO and direct reports	22 percent
Percentage of minorities in category of CEO and direct reports	20 percent
Percentage of women in management who received promotions	40 percent

Retention and Professional Development

How do 2006 minority and female attrition rates generally compare to those experienced in the prior year period?

Lower than in prior years.

Please identify the specific steps you are taking to reduce the attrition rate of minority and women employees.

Strengthen mentoring program for all employees, including minorities and women.

Diversity Mission Statement

PHI defines diversity as the broad range of similarities and differences including, but not limited to, race, gender, age, religion, ethnicity, sexual orientation, disabilities, abilities and points of view that exist within our workforce, community, customers and suppliers.

Vision

By leveraging diversity, PHI creates a competitive advantage in our business and adds value for our suppliers and our employees. By embracing the principles of diversity, i.e., valuing and respecting the visible and invisible differences that represent the strengths and unique skills of each and every individual at PHI, we will enable PHI to achieve its vision to become the premier energy delivery and services company in the Mid-Atlantic region.

Mission

PHI will achieve its diversity vision by:

• Valuing and promoting the diversity of our workforce, customers, suppliers and the community by capitalizing on the diversity of our employees and by promoting personal, professional and regional economic development.

• Keeping up with changing demographics and best practices by attracting, developing, retaining and advancing the very best talent available.

• Designing and implementing measurable initiatives that maximize PHI's ability to promote an inclusive work environment where everyone and every group fits, feels accepted, has value and contributes to our success.

Additional Information

It is the policy of Pepco Holdings, Inc. (PHI) to incorporate business policies that reflect the company's commitment to high standards of ethical behavior and sound business principles. These corporate business policies apply to PHI's directors, employees and others working at PHI or its subsidiaries. PHI's core values center around safety, accountability, integrity, diversity and excellence. PHI's continued commitment to advancing the company's diversity efforts is supported by an executive and senior leadership adopted policy of linking employee bonus payouts and the achievement of quarterly diversity goals and good faith efforts.

PHI's diversity initiatives are solidly anchored and integrated in corporate practices and allow us to value and promote the diversity of our workforce, suppliers and the community by capitalizing on the diversity of our employees. The convergence of PHI's diversity, supplier diversity, and strategic staffing and workforce planning departments add value by providing an attractive corporate environment for recruiting and retaining the very best talented, qualified, educated and motivated employees to a corporate culture rich with diversity. Through PHI's supplier diversity initiative, the company is uniquely positioned to attract qualified, reliable and competitive diverse regional and national suppliers to provide customer service, reliability, lower costs and improve operational efficiencies.

PHI has received national recognition related to both internal/external diversity initiatives. These recognitions reinforce our commitment to foster and maintain diversity at work, in our business transactions with suppliers and the communities in which we serve. The recognitions include:

- *Black Enterprise* magazine: PHI named one of the 40 Best Companies for Diversity for the third straight year

- *Black Enterprise* magazine: PHI named one of the 15 Best in Senior Management Diversity

- *DiversityInc* magazine: PHI named as one of the 25 Noteworthy Companies for diversity

- *Veterans Business Journal:* PHI named as one of the Top 10 Companies for Veteran Businesses for its supplier diversity efforts for the second straight year

- *Women's Enterprise USA* magazine: Manager, PHI supplier diversity, recognized as one of the 100 Women Impacting Supplier Diversity

- *Fortune* magazine: PHI recognized as one of the Leading Companies for a Diverse Workforce in 2006

- *Fortune* magazine: PHI ranked as one of the Top 50 Employers for Minorities in 2004 and 2005

- AARP: PHI named as a Best Employer for Workers Age 50 and Over

- PHI named as the 2005 Corporate Small Business Advocate: PHI was awarded the 2005 Corporate Small Business Advocate award by the Asian American Business Roundtable (AABR).

Pfizer Inc.

235 E. 42nd Street
New York, NY 10017

Locations

Pfizer recruits for positions across the nation and across the globe. Our major domestic locations are:
New London, CT • St. Louis, MO • New York, NY • Peapack, NJ

Diversity Leadership

Leslie Mays
VP of Diversity & Inclusion

Employment Contact

Linda Breed
Sr. Manager, Employment Programs
E-mail: linda.breed@pfizer.com
www.pfizer.com/careers

Recruiting

Please list the schools/types of schools at which you recruit.

• Ivy League schools

• Other private schools

• Public schools

• *Historically black colleges and universities (HBCUs):* Florida A&M, University of Alabama, Howard University, Tuskeegee, Xavier University

• *Hispanic serving institutions (HSIs):* University of Puerto Rico, University of New Mexico

Do you have any special outreach efforts directed to encourage minority students and graduates to consider your firm?

• *Hold a reception for minority students:* Pfizer holds a number of activities on campus targeting diverse student populations. We involve members of our networking groups and interact with students from various demographic backgrounds.

• *Conferences:* National Black MBA Association, National Society of Hispanic MBAs, Consortium for the Graduate Study of Management and Management Leadership for Tomorrow. We also partner with the leadership of these organizations on events outside of the annual conferences. We partner with the student chapters and national organizations of the following associations: National Association for the advancement of Black Chemists and Chemical Engineers (NOBCChE), Association of Women in Science (AWIS) and National Society of Black Engineers (NSBE)

• *Advertise in minority student association publication(s) or other minority-focused publications:* Pfizer advertises in *Job Choices: Diversity* issue as well as a number of other journals focused on diversity recruitment. We also advertise on HBCUConnect.com.

• At the campuses where we recruit, we sponsor minority and women's student association events through fiscal and personnel support.

• *Scholarships or intern/fellowships for minority students:* Through Hispanic Scholarship Fund and various undergraduate fellowship programs, such as the Pfizer/UPR Fellowships and the Pfizer/XULA Fellowships.

Do you use executive recruiting/search firms to seek to identify new diversity hires?

Yes

Internships and Co-ops

INROADS Field Force Internships (Pharmaceutical Sales)

Deadline for application: Varies by school

Number of interns in the program in summer 2006: 120 to 140

Length of the program: 12 weeks

Rising juniors and seniors only. Must successfully complete two internships in order to be considered for full-time offer. Must be geographically flexible within district. All interns receive company cars, expense accounts, three to four weeks of training and four performance evaluations.

Florida A&M University Field Force Internships (Pharmaceutical Sales)

Deadline for application: Please consult FAMU career office

Number of interns in the program in summer 2006: Eight to 10

Length of the program: 24 to 36 weeks

Graduate internships in Finance, Internal Audit, Marketing, Market Analytics, Business Development, Human Resources, Product Development, Global Procurement

Deadline for application: No later than January 15th; varies by school

Number of interns in the program in summer 2006: 40

Length of the program: 12 weeks

Percentage of interns/co-ops in the program who receive offers of full-time employment: Average 50 percent

Web site for internship/co-op information: www.pfizer.com/pfizer/are/careers/mn_campus.jsp

All candidates must be first-year students at an accredited MBA program, are required to have three years of full-time work experience prior to enrolling in business school and must have permanent work authorization for the United States. They are also required to concentrate in an area of study relevant to the internship to which they apply.

Tuskeegee University Field Force Internships (Animal Health Sales)

Deadline for application: Please consult Tuskeegee career office

Number of interns in the program in summer 2006: Two

Length of the program: 26 to 36 weeks

Pfizer Global Research & Development Summer Internship Program

Deadline for application: Rolling

Number of interns in the program in summer 2006: 280

Length of the program: 12 weeks minimum

Web site for internship/co-op information: www.pfizerrdgrad.com

Pfizer global research and development's (PGRD) internship program offers a wide range of challenging projects involving issues that are critical to our research and development organization. As an intern, you will gain hands-on scientific research, business or technical experience, participating in structured projects under the guidance of a Pfizer mentor.

The goal of this program is for students to experience working in a pharmaceutical company setting, to understand the vital role of research in the drug development process and perhaps become interested in a career as a researcher.

Our summer internships typically offer full-time (40 hours per week) experiential training opportunities for a period of 12 weeks.

Program Requirements

- Be enrolled as a full-time undergraduate or graduate student in a degree program related to our primary research efforts (science, business, computer science, etc.)
- Maintain solid academic standing (3.0 GPA or above)
- Be authorized to be lawfully employed in the U.S.

If you are offered a position and you accept that position, the offer is contingent upon the satisfactory completion of a drug test, completion of a background investigation and demonstrated evidence that you are eligible to work for any employer in the United States.

Typical Opportunities

Our summer internship programs are designed to help students develop and apply their skills and knowledge to prepare for a successful career in the sciences. Pfizer recruiters periodically conduct interviews and post full-time employment and internship opportunities at numerous campuses throughout the U.S.

Summer internship opportunities are typically available in:

- Cambridge, Mass.
- Groton or New London, Conn.
- La Jolla, Calif.
- New York, N.Y.
- St. Louis, Mo.

A background in any number of disciplines prepares you for a career at Pfizer.

Scientific fields:

- Analytical chemistry
- Biochemistry
- Biology
- Biomedical engineering
- Chemical engineering
- Comparative medicine
- Drug metabolism
- Laboratory animal medicines
- Molecular biology
- Organic chemistry
- Pathology
- Pharmaceutical sciences
- Pharmacokinetics
- Pharmacy
- Physical chemistry
- Toxicology
- Vaccine discovery and development
- Veterinary medicine

Nonscience fields:

- Facilities
- Finance and procurement
- Human resources
- Information technology
- Market assessment
- Legal
- Worldwide regulatory affairs

Scholarships

Hispanic Scholarship Fund

Deadline for application for the scholarship program: Please consult www.hsf.org

Scholarship award amount: Varies

Web site or other contact information for scholarship:
www.hsf.org

Please consult www.hsf.org for specific information.

Pfizer/University of Puerto Rico Scholars Program

Deadline for application for the scholarship program: December 5th

Scholarship award amount: Varies

Please consult University of Puerto Rico LSAMP program for details.

Affinity Groups

Groups by Affiliation

Asian Networks
• Groton Asian Pacific American Group—PGRD
• Ann Arbor Pfizer Asian Network—PGRD
• Kalamazoo Asian Network Group
• La Jolla Asian Network—PGRD
• St. Louis Asian Network Group

African-American Networks
• ADVANCE Groton/New London—PGRD
• ADVANCE Ann Arbor—PGRD
• ADVANCE St. Louis—PGRD
• ADVANCE Kalamazoo
• ADVANCE Morris Plains

Gay & Lesbian Networks
• Rainbow Alliance Ann Arbor—PGRD
• Rainbow Alliance, La Jolla—PGRD
• Rainbow Alliance, Groton/New London—PGRD
• Rainbow Alliance, Sandwich—PGRD
• OPEN—Out Pfizer Employee Network
• Pfizer Rainbow Alliance Kalamazoo
• St. Louis Pfizer Rainbow

Hispanic Networks
• Groton Hispanic Network—PGRD
• VALOR—PGRD
• VALOR—St. Louis Hispanic Network Group

Women Networks
• Women's Network in Ann Arbor—PGRD
• La Jolla Women's Network—PGRD
• Women Leader's Network Groton/New London—PGRD
• Women's Network Sandwich—PGRD
• Kalamazoo Women's Network

• Japan Clinical Development (J-Clin) Mother's Network
• Working Mother Network, Nagoya, Japan PGRD
• SWNG—St. Louis Women's Networking Group—PGRD
• Disability Networks
• AVID: Focus on Abilities—PGRD

Entry-Level Programs, Full-Time Opportunities and Training Programs

Finance Rotational Program

Length of program: Two years

Geographic location(s) of program: New York, Connecticut, global

This program is open only to candidates who joined the Finance Summer Associate Program and subsequently completed their MBA.

HR Management Associate Program

Length of program: Two years

Geographic location(s) of program: New York, Connecticut, Missouri

This program is open only to candidates who joined the HR Summer Associate Program and subsequently completed their MA/MBA.

Pfizer Global Research & Development—Full-Time (Entry-Level) Hiring

Length of program: N/A—full-time

Geographic location(s) of program: New York, Connecticut, Missouri

Our new college hires typically go right to work in one of these areas:

• Pharmaceutical sciences
• Formulations
• Analytical research and development
• Organic/medicinal chemistry
• Pharmacology
• Information technology
• Drug metabolism

Strategic Plan and Diversity Leadership

What trends in your industry affect your corporate diversity goals, strategies and/or internal or external alliances?

Underrepresentation of minorities and women in science and business, government regulations and public opinions of the pharmaceutical industry.

How does the firm's leadership communicate the importance of diversity to everyone at the firm?

Diversity communication strategy through weekly employee newsletter, celebration of heritage months, diversity training for managers, sponsorship of special events, etc.

Who has primary responsibility for leading diversity initiatives at your firm?

Leslie Mays, vice president of diversity

Does your firm currently have a diversity committee?

Yes

If yes, please describe how the committee is structured, how often it meets, etc.

The committee is comprised of senior leaders (VPs and above) from each business unit. They meet quarterly.

If yes, does the committee's representation include one or more members of the firm's management/executive committee (or the equivalent)?

Yes

How many executives are on the committee?

The Worldwide Diversity and Inclusion Council sets the company-wide diversity objectives.

Total Executives on Committee: There are 19 vice presidents on the Worldwide Diversity and Inclusion Council, including three members from the executive leadership team, which is the highest governing body of the company.

Does the committee and/or diversity leader establish and set goals or objectives consistent with management's priorities?

Yes

Has the firm undertaken a formal or informal diversity program or set of initiatives aimed at increasing the diversity of the firm?

Yes, formal

How often does the firm's management review the firm's diversity progress/results?

Quarterly

How is the firm's diversity committee and/or firm management held accountable for achieving results?

The board of directors monitors progress against objectives.

The Stats

	NUMBER OF EMPLOYEES		REVENUE	
	2006	2005	2006	2005
Total in the U.S.	N/A	N/A	$25.822 million	$24.745 million
Total outside the U.S.	N/A	N/A	$22.548 million	$22.660 million
Total worldwide	Approx 105,000	Approx 120,000	$48.371 million	$47.405 million

Retention and Professional Development

How do 2006 minority and female attrition rates generally compare to those experienced in the prior year period?

About the same as in prior years.

Please identify the specific steps you are taking to reduce the attrition rate of minority and women employees.

- Develop and/or support internal employee affinity groups (e.g., minority or women networks within the firm)
- Increase/review compensation relative to competition
- Increase/improve current work/life programs
- Succession plan includes emphasis on diversity
- Work with minority and women employees to develop career advancement plans
- Strengthen mentoring program for all employees, including minorities and women
- Professional skills development program, including minority and women employees

Diversity Mission Statement

At Pfizer, we believe that a strong commitment to diversity and inclusion is key to achieving our corporate mission—becoming the world's most valued company.

Having a diverse workforce allows us to benefit from the different backgrounds and perspectives of our colleagues, and fosters more creative and innovative thinking throughout the organization. Creating a culture of inclusion where everyone is respected and valued enables us to leverage our diversity as a business driver and strengthens our global leadership position.

Pitney Bowes

1 Elmcroft Road
Stamford, CT 06854
Phone: (203) 356-5000
www.pitneybowes.com

Locations
Locations in 130 countries

Diversity Leadership
Denise Rawles-Smith
Manager, Diversity External Relationships
1 Elmcroft Road
Stamford, CT 06854
Phone: (203) 351-7910
Fax: (203) 348-1289
E-mail: denise.rawles@pb.com

Employment Contact
Michael T. Holmes
Director, Strategic Talent Management Global

Recruiting

Please list the schools/types of schools at which you recruit.

• *Ivy League schools:* Cornell, Columbia
• *Other private schools:* Rensselaer Polytechnic Institute (RPI), Rochester Institute Technology (RIT) and Fairfield University
• *Public state schools:* University of Connecticut and the University of Waterloo
• Historically black colleges and universities (HBCUs)
• Hispanic serving institutions (HSIs)
• Native American tribal universities

Do you have any special outreach efforts directed to encourage minority students to consider your firm?

• Hold a reception for minority students
• Advertise in minority student association publication(s)
• Sponsor minority student association events
• Firm's employees participate on career panels at school
• Outreach to leadership of minority student organizations
• Scholarships or intern/fellowships for minority students
• *Other:* We participate in college and university job fairs

What activities does the firm undertake to attract minority and women employees?

• Partner programs with women and minority associations
• *Conferences:* INROADS, National Society of Black Engineers, National Urban League, Association of Latino Professionals, National Society of Hispanic MBA, National Black MBA, National Sales Network and the Society of Women Engineers
• *Participate at minority job fairs:* See conference list

• Seek referrals from other employees
• Utilize online job services
• *Other:* We advertise our career opportunities in diverse publications such as *Hispanic Business, Black MBA, Asian Enterprise, Black Enterprise, Diversity/Careers, DiversityInc, Fortune, Hispanic Professional, National Society of Black Engineers, New York Times Magazine, CAREERS & THE disABLED, Society of Women Engineers, Diversity & The Bar*

Do you use executive recruiting/search firms to seek to identify new diversity hires?
Yes

Internships and Co-ops

INROADS

Deadline for application: January—candidates are interviewed in March; offers made in April
Pay: $12.50 to $16 per hour
Percentage of interns/co-ops in the program who receive offers of full-time employment: 66 percent
Web site for internship/co-op information: www.pb.com/careers

Between August and September we inform INROADS of our intern commitments for the upcoming year (that number includes students eligible to return for another internship and new students). Between October and December, we maintain communication with students we are expecting to return. We discuss their academic performance, career interests and opportunities for their next internship. Several students intern over the mid-semester break with their previous managers or potential new mangers for their next internship.

Between January and February, Pitney Bowes employees participate in INROADS Talent Pool training sessions, helping conduct mock interviews and facilitate workshops. Between March and April, Pitney Bowes' HR team interviews candidates at the annual INROADS Corporate Interview Day (CID).

After the CID, Pitney Bowes determines which candidates best fit the internship opportunities and fast-paced work environment of Pitney Bowes. Within three business days following CID, we communicate to INROADS a list of candidates to whom we will extend verbal offers.

Once our offers are accepted, we review in greater detail and agree upon starting and ending dates. Interns are matched with Pitney Bowes managers who demonstrate a strong track record of performance in coaching and employee development. As required by INROADS, all interns receive mid- and end-of-internship performance evaluations, as well as appropriate supervision and timely feedback.

All internships are designed to challenge our interns with work that allows them to make immediate contributions and demonstrate their potential for full-time professional-level employment.

Engineering Co-op/Interns

Deadline for application: Varies throughout the year

Pay: $17 to $26 per hour

Length of the program: Three to six months

Percentage of interns/co-ops in the program who receive offers of full-time employment: 5 percent

Web site for internship/co-op information: www.pb.com/careers

Most Pitney Bowes co-ops work in our technology center in Shelton, Connecticut. Our technology center project leaders hire co-ops to be on engineering teams drawing from four functional groups:

• Mechanical/electrical/systems
• Software
• Product usability and design
• Technical support/operations

Co-ops find support for their career development on the functional side while working toward specific deadlines and output goals on their various product assignments.

Pitney Bowes' Advanced Concepts in Technology, a unit dedicated to capturing the advantages of technologies likely to emerge in the next 10 years, also employs engineers on its research and development projects.

Our co-op positions are designed to challenge the students with work that allows them to make immediate contributions and demonstrate their potential for full-time professional level employment.

Scholarships

Pitney Bowes INROADS/FWC Hispanic Scholarship

Scholarship award amount: Award depends on the year the participant is in school and his or her GPA. The scholarship ranges from $500 to $2,000. Award is announced at the Annual Awards reception.

Affinity Groups

DMT Women's Forum

This forum is composed of women helping women succeed and grow. The objective is to engage women in document messaging technologies in leveraging each other to develop each woman's career by exposing them to internal and external leaders, ideas and best practices. They also learn to share best practices around managing work and personal lives. The DMT Women's Forum creates a renewed sense of employee engagement and exposure for members of the steering committee to interface with key business leaders as they organize events. This can help further the company's long-term strategic objectives and immediate business goals. They meet monthly and hold two to three evening events a year.

Entry-Level Programs, Full-Time Opportunities and Training Programs

Pitney Bowes TechCentral Professional Development Program (PDP)

Length of program: Three-year rotational program for students who just completed a bachelor's or master's degree

Geographic location(s) of program: Connecticut

The Pitney Bowes TechCentral Professional Development Program (PDP) is a rotational program to develop technical and managerial leaders within our IT organization. The program offers challenging "real job" assignments based on an individual's specific education, experience, development needs and interests. It consists of two or three assignments over a three-year period, followed by a final placement. Throughout the three years, participants can expect to be provided with:

• Exposure to business leaders across Pitney Bowes
• Work assignments with challenge and learning opportunities
• Personal development coaching and feedback
• Opportunities to network with peers

The program approach is to hire extremely talented people, nurture their growth and give them opportunities to make an impact. We are

working to identify great technical talent and to assist them in acquiring the unique skills and experiences they need to excel in their careers.

Strategic Plan and Diversity Leadership

How does the firm's leadership communicate the importance of diversity to everyone at the firm?

Our most senior level leaders (CEO, COO, CFO, chief HR officer, general counsel and business unit presidents) regularly communicate the business value of diversity via weekly voice mail power talks, town hall meetings, Intranet announcements, internal publications, diversity forums and quarterly operational reviews. These leaders also agree on collaborations with our customers and suppliers on mutually beneficial diversity initiatives.

Who has primary responsibility for leading diversity initiatives at your firm?

Susan Johnson, vice president, strategic talent management; Michael T. Holmes, director, strategic talent management and global diversity leadership.

Does your firm currently have a diversity committee?

No

Does the committee and/or diversity leader establish and set goals or objectives consistent with management's priorities?

Yes. Diversity governance is an enterprise-wide initiative, which includes accountability to the CEO and board level. The CEO receives detailed reports regarding diversity, succession planning, as well as performance assessments. In addition, business unit presidents and their direct reports, including senior corporate staff, are held accountable for the success of diversity initiatives within their individual business units. The number of employees and hours spent on these initiatives vary from business unit to business unit. Diversity is an objective of senior management and the board of directors and is enforced by tying compensation to successful completion of the diversity objective. The diversity strategic planning process outlines goals for the company and places responsibility for meeting those goals in the hands of employees organized into what is known as our Diversity Leadership Councils. Through these councils, we have diversity champions throughout all of Pitney Bowes who are actively engaged to help foster employee involvement.

Has the firm undertaken a formal or informal diversity program or set of initiatives aimed at increasing the diversity of the firm?

Yes, formal. Pitney Bowes has established a strategic architecture to define enterprise goals and objectives within the organization. Each business unit and staff function defines their goals in alignment with the company's, including:

- Strategic architecture
- Engaged workforce
- Leadership talent
- Diversity
- Business unit strategic planning process
- Staffing and recruitment
- Leadership development

How often does the firm's management review the firm's diversity progress/results?

Twice a year

How is the firm's diversity committee and/or firm management held accountable for achieving results?

We have built diversity metrics into our corporation's objectives through specific metrics. The CEO, SVP of HR and executive director of global diversity leadership have accountability to the Corporate Responsibility Committee (a subset of the board of directors). Each business leader is held accountable for furthering our diversity efforts. We have a leadership model that describes and holds leaders accountable for their behaviors (explicit and implicit). Managers are accountable for the development of their people and diversity is an objective of senior management and the board of directors and is enforced by tying compensation to successful completion of the diversity objective.

Retention and Professional Development

Please identify the specific steps you are taking to reduce the attrition rate of minority and women employees.

- Develop and/or support internal employee affinity groups (e.g., minority or women networks within the firm)
- Increase/review compensation relative to competition
- Increase/improve current work/life programs
- Adopt dispute resolution process
- Succession plan includes emphasis on diversity
- Work with all employees including minority and women employees to develop career advancement plans
- Strengthen mentoring program for all employees, including minorities and women
- Professional skills development program, including minority and women employees

To help advance women and minorities, Pitney Bowes has an initiative to augment its leadership and professional development pro-

grams into upper management. LEAD! is Pitney Bowes' multi-faceted, comprehensive initiative that provides managers with the training, tools and processes to enhance their leadership skills and help them become successful.

Pitney Bowes also believes in providing its employees opportunities to advance in the company with the flexibility to manage their time between their careers and life commitments. We offer programs such as flexible work arrangements, transportation programs, employee resources fair, on-site amenities that include fitness centers and medical clinics, an employee assistance program (EAP) and on-site financial education programs.

Diversity Mission Statement

Pitney Bowes does business in workplaces characterized by significant diversity. We value, actively pursue and leverage diversity in our employees, and through our relationships with customers, business partners and communities, because it is essential to innovation and growth. Pitney Bowes' commitment to diversity is also consistent with and further supports the company's values and practices.

Additional Information

Pitney Bowes has a long and admirable history of corporate-wide commitment to diversity dating back to the 1960s. Diversity is the foundation of our company's success. The company is consistently recognized for its ongoing commitment to building a truly diverse organization (see awards list below). The continued focus on transformation and on talent and leadership lays the foundation for future growth.

Pitney Bowes has a diverse network of strategic partnerships and alliances with over 40 key organizations. Our partners include: the National Urban League, Women's Business Enterprise National Council, National Society of Hispanic MBAs, National Black MBA Association, The Connecticut Asian Pacific American Bar Association, Society of Women Engineers, National Society of Black Engineers, Congressional Hispanic Caucus Institute, Congressional Black Caucus and National Minority Supplier Development Council.

We also have insightful strategic relationships with our internal partners and provide programs for our employees and stakeholders. Examples of some of the internal diversity related programs are:

MBA Leadership Summit

We host the MBA Leadership Summit at our world headquarters facility, in partnership with our local chapters of the National Society of Hispanic MBAs (NSHMBA) and the National Black MBA Association (NBMBAA).

Speed Networking

Speed Networking is a process Pitney Bowes uses to facilitate networking and learning. Started in 2004, Speed Networking was piloted as an initiative to help with the retention and engagement of women at middle and senior levels, and to promote the professional advancement of women in our workplace.

Prism Award

The Prism Award was created to recognize Pitney Bowes teams for strategies and initiatives that were implemented at the business or corporate level to sustain our commitment to diversity and inclusion.

Diversity Festival

The Diversity Festival is a celebration of diversity in race, religion, customs, cultures, origins and beliefs. We celebrate Pitney Bowes' employees, customers, communities and business partners worldwide, and foster greater understanding of all that we have in common.

Recognition and Awards

Pitney Bowes has earned many awards during its long history of investing in the community and partnering with nonprofits nationally and internationally. Here are some of the awards we have won that highlight our commitment to diversity:

• Awarded the Corporate Award by the Executive Leadership Council, 2005

• Ranked among the 50 Top Employers for Minorities by *Fortune* magazine, 2005

• Awarded the Brillante Award in the Corporate Award Category by the National Society of Hispanic MBAs, 2005

• Ranked among Best Employers for Workers 50 and Over by AARP, 2005, 2004

• Ranked one of the 30 Best Companies for Diversity by *Black Enterprise* magazine

• Recognized on Latin Business' 2005 Corporate Diversity Honor Roll, 2005

• Ranked among DiversityInc.com's Top 50 Companies for Diversity, 2005, 2004, 2003, 2002, 2001; ranked the No. 1 Company for Diversity in 2004

• Rated in the 100 Best Corporate Citizens by *Business Ethics* magazine, 2005, 2004, 2003, 2002, 2001, 2000

• Awarded Corporate Partner of the Year by the Connecticut Chapter of the National Society of Hispanic MBAs, 2005, 2001

• Ranked among DiversityBusiness.com's (formerly known as Div2000.com) America's Top Organizations for Multicultural Business—Opportunities, 2005, 2004, 2003, 2002, 2001

- Ranked among Top 100 Companies for Hispanics by *Hispanic Magazine,* 2005, 2004, 2003, 2002, 2001, 2000, 1999

- Ranked among *Hispanic Magazine's* Top 50 Recruitment Programs, 2005, 2004, 2003, 2002, 2001, 2000, 1999, 1998

- Awarded the Outstanding Corporate Supplier Diversity Award by the National Minority Business Council, 2005

- Named to *Asian Enterprise* Magazine's 10 Best Companies for Asian Pacific Americans, 2005, 2004, 2003, 2001, 2000

PNC Financial Services Group, Inc.

249 Fifth Avenue
Pittsburgh, PA 15222
Phone: (412) 762-2000

Locations

Pittsburgh (HQ)
Cincinnati • Delaware • New Jersey •
Maryland • Northern Virginia •
Philadelphia, PA • Washington, DC

Diversity Leadership

Davie S. Huddleston, VP, Manager, Strategic
 Talent Acquisition
249 Fifth Avenue
Pittsburgh, PA 15222
E-mail: davie.huddleston@pnc.com
www.pnc.com/careers

Employment Contact

Brian A. Rider, PHR
AVP, Manager, University Relations
249 Fifth Avenue
Pittsburgh, PA 15222
E-mail: brian.rider@pnc.com
www.pnc.com/careers

Recruiting

Please list the schools/types of schools at which you recruit.

• Ivy League schools

• Public state schools

• Historically black colleges and universities (HBCUs)

Do you have any special outreach efforts directed to encourage minority students to consider your firm?

• *Conferences:* Lead sponsor of the Minorities in Pittsburgh conference

• *Advertise in minority publications:* *Black Collegian* magazine

• Participate in/host minority student job fair(s)

• Sponsor minority student association events

• Firm's employees participate on career panels at school

• Outreach to leadership of minority student organizations

• Scholarships or intern/fellowships for minority students

What activities does the firm undertake to attract minority and women employees?

• Partner programs with women and minority associations

• Conferences

• Participate at minority job fairs

• Seek referrals from other employees

• Utilize online job services

Do you use executive recruiting/search firms to seek to identify new diversity hires?

Yes. PNC uses a broad range of executive recruiting/search firms to identify talent in the marketplace. We generally request diverse slates of candidates from both majority- and minority/women-owned firms, and have worked specifically with diversity practice groups at some of the larger firms over time.

Internships and Co-ops

PNC Internship Program

Deadline for application: No formal deadline, although the majority of our recruiting is conducted in the fall semester.

Number of interns in the program in summer 2006 (internship) or 2006 (co-op): 63 interns

Pay: 2006 ranges from $13 to $18.50 per hour

Length of the program: 10 to 12 weeks

Percentage of interns/co-ops in the program who receive offers of full-time employment: Percent is based on those eligible for hire

Web site for internship/co-op information: www.pnc.com/careers

The PNC Internship Program is a 10- to 12-week internship experience that provides meaningful work assignments and professional development exposure to senior- and executive-level management and exposure to the host city. Candidates should have a finance and/or accounting background, 3.2 GPA minimum, relevant work and/or past internship experience—preferably in a banking or financial services environment—and are involved on their campus in student-focused organizations/activities, preferably in a leadership role.

Scholarships

PNC Fellows

Deadline for application for the scholarship program: Typically mid-summer (late July)

Scholarship award amount: Ranges from $1,000 to $5,000 for undergraduates

The PNC Fellowship was initiated to help diversify our workforce by identifying and recruiting top students of color. Eligible students must maintain a high academic standing, be involved within their community and campus environment and be in good standing with INROADS (if the candidate is an INROADS intern).

Affinity Groups

PNC currently has four Employee Resource Groups (ERGs) aimed at giving a voice to specific segments of our employee population. Initial target audiences were managerial and professional-level African-Americans and senior-level women in the Philadelphia and Pittsburgh markets. These groups were charged with recommending specific business objectives, including identifying ways to increase employee and community engagement and business development in their target demographic group.

PNC's Employee Resource Groups are, by design, not traditional networks or affinity groups. Typically, networks or affinity groups are broad cross-sections of particular demographic groups that convene primarily to address employee satisfaction issues. Many diversity efforts have seen these groups devolve into social clubs that sponsor member-focused social events and relevant cultural days. They often do not reach their full potential to be catalysts for change within an organization due to a lack of strategic focus.

The ERGs at PNC, however, are positioned as strategic bodies with clear business objectives. They meet on company time to discuss the issues, often engaging in very candid dialogue. Members are provided with access to a broad range of information to help them formulate their recommendations.

The employee resource groups are small, each consisting of about 15 high-performing employees, and are sponsored by members of the executive team. Jim Rohr, PNC's chairman and CEO, and his executive team are committed to championing their recommendations. Five senior-level employees serve as sponsors for the four ERGs (one of the four groups is co-sponsored). Their active involvement with the groups not only demonstrates support, but also ensures that the ERG maintains a strategic focus.

Vision statements for the groups follow:

African-American Employee Resource Group

The African-American ERG is a catalyst that causes PNC to become an inclusive organization known for its diverse workforce and as a preferred place to work and bank for the African-American community.

Senior-Level Women Employee Resource Group

The Senior Women ERG impacts PNC's culture in a way that results in a significant number of diverse senior women holding and being actively considered for line and staff executive roles.

Strategic Plan and Diversity Leadership

Diversity is one of PNC's corporate values, and thus is an integral part of communications within the organization. Specific messages about diversity and its importance in the organization are communicated via "push" e-mail messages to the employee base (i.e., Black History Month kick-off message), via our Intranet and Internet sites, in corporate publications (including electronic and print) and as a part of other verbal communications.

Who has primary responsibility for leading diversity initiatives at your firm?

Kathleen C. D'Appolonia, senior vice president, manager, corporate recruitment and employee inclusion

Kenneth E. Spruill Jr., vice president, manager, diversity strategies

Does your firm currently have a diversity committee?

Yes. During 2006, PNC initiated a Corporate Diversity Council, made up of 19 senior- and executive-level leaders throughout the corporation and chaired by Chairman and CEO Jim Rohr. The formation of this council was based on a recommendation from PNC's Employee Resource Groups, and is charged with enhancing the visibility of and accountability for diversity results at PNC. Some of PNC's business units also have established diversity councils, which operate at the business level in conjunction with the work of corporate-level bodies like the Corporate Diversity Council.

Additionally, PNC's ERGs (mentioned above) provide a great deal of insight into diversity-related matters for the organization.

Does the committee and/or diversity leader establish and set goals or objectives consistent with management's priorities?

Yes

Has the firm undertaken a formal or informal diversity program or set of initiatives aimed at increasing the diversity of the firm?

Yes, formal

How often does the firm's management review the firm's diversity progress/results?

Quarterly

How is the firm's diversity committee and/or firm management held accountable for achieving results?

Diversity results are built into PNC's performance management process, and are a component of all employees' performance. The Corporate Diversity Council now provides an additional forum for senior- and executive-level leaders to discuss progress and further advance diversity throughout the organization.

The Stats

	NUMBER OF EMPLOYEES		REVENUE	
	2006	2005	2006	2005
Total in the U.S.	23,800	21,437	$2.6 billion	$1.3 billion

Retention and Professional Development

How do 2006 minority and female attrition rates generally compare to those experienced in the prior year period?

About the same as in prior years.

Please identify the specific steps you are taking to reduce the attrition rate of minority and women employees.

- Develop and/or support internal employee affinity groups (e.g., minority or women networks within the firm)

- Increase/review compensation relative to competition
- Increase/improve current work/life programs
- Succession plan includes emphasis on diversity
- Work with minority and women employees to develop career advancement plans
- Strengthen mentoring program for all employees, including minorities and women
- Professional skills development program, including minority and women employees

Diversity Mission Statement

PNC's corporate value of diversity is defined as follows:

We recognize the critical value of our differences and of our individual and collective strengths and skills.

Additional Information

PNC has been a proud supporter of INROADS and the local INROADS/North Central region. Through corporate representation in the INROADS Leadership Development Institute (LDI) regional conferences as well as significant financial support of LDI regional conferences held in Pittsburgh in 2001, 2004, 2005 and 2006, PNC has been recognized by INROADS as a Corporate Plus recipient in 2005 and 2006 for "true commitment to the INROADS mission." By supporting the social and developmental events during LDI, the 2005 and 2006 LDI were among the highest rated LDI experiences in the country. Each year, PNC has been recognized by INROADS nationally for its support both financially and in people-hours for planning, organizing and facilitating throughout the year. In addition, in 2007, PNC was recognized by *DiversityInc* magazine as a Top 10 Company for African-Americans and one of the 25 Noteworthy Companies to watch for its diversity efforts.

PPG Industries

One PPG Place
Pittsburgh, PA 15272
Phone: (412) 434-3131
www.ppg.com

Locations
Pittsburgh, PA (HQ)

Diversity Leadership
Managed by the Senior Diversity Leadership Council

Employment Contact
John Coyne
Director, Corporate Staffing
One PPG Place
Pittsburgh, PA 15272
Phone: (412) 434-2015
Fax: (412) 434-2011
E-mail: jpcoyne@ppg.com

Recruiting

Please list the schools/types of schools at which you recruit.

• Private schools

• Public state schools

• *Historically black colleges and universities (HBCUs):* Hampton, NC A&T, Florida A&M

• *Hispanic serving institutions (HSIs):* University of Houston, Texas A&M

Do you have any special outreach efforts directed to encourage minority students to consider your firm?

• Hold a reception for minority students

• Conferences

• Advertise in minority student association publication(s)

• Participate in/host minority student job fair(s)

• Sponsor minority student association events

• Firm's employees participate on career panels at school

• Outreach to leadership of minority student organizations

• Scholarships or intern/fellowships for minority students

What activities does the firm undertake to attract minority and women employees?

• Partner programs with women and minority associations

• Conferences

• Participate at minority job fairs

• Seek referrals from other employees

• Utilize online job services

Do you use executive recruiting/search firms to seek to identify new diversity hires?

Yes

Internships and Co-ops

We have internship programs in the engineering, chemistry, finance, IT and marketing departments each summer. Pay varies by position and we attempt to offer full-time employment if there is a fit and we have jobs.

Scholarships

We have a scholarship program available for each school at which we recruit.

Entry-Level Programs, Full-Time Opportunities and Training Programs

We hire full-time graduates in various disciplines, technical and business. They are placed across the U.S. and have a variety of training programs.

Strategic Plan and Diversity Leadership

Who has primary responsibility for leading diversity initiatives at your firm?

Tom Siegele

Does your firm currently have a diversity committee?

Yes

If yes, please describe how the committee is structured, how often it meets, etc.

The committee meets four times a year and it has all levels of employees on the committee.

If yes, does the committee's representation include one or more members of the firm's management/executive committee (or the equivalent)?

Yes

Total Executives on Committee: Eight

Does the committee and/or diversity leader establish and set goals or objectives consistent with management's priorities?

Yes

Has the firm undertaken a formal or informal diversity program or set of initiatives aimed at increasing the diversity of the firm?

Yes, formal

How often does the firm's management review the firm's diversity progress/results?

Quarterly

How is the firm's diversity committee and/or firm management held accountable for achieving results?

Reports to CEO and board of directors.

Retention and Professional Development

Please identify the specific steps you are taking to reduce the attrition rate of minority and women employees.

• Develop and/or support internal employee affinity groups (e.g., minority or women networks within the firm)

• Increase/improve current work/life programs

• Adopt dispute resolution process

• Succession plan includes emphasis on diversity

• Work with minority and women employees to develop career advancement plans

• Strengthen mentoring program for all employees, including minorities and women

• Professional skills development program, including minority and women employees

The Stats

	NUMBER OF EMPLOYEES		REVENUE	
	2006	2005	2006	2005
Total in the U.S.	31,000	30,800	$11.0 billion	$10.2 billion

Like you, we have some distinctive characteristics of our own.*

For the sixth year in a row, PricewaterhouseCoopers was voted the #1 ideal employer in our profession in the Universum Undergraduate Survey of business students.

Visit pwc.tv

*connectedthinking

 PRICEWATERHOUSE COOPERS

PricewaterhouseCoopers LLP

300 Madison Avenue
New York, NY 10017
Phone: (646) 471-4000
Fax: (646) 471-3188

Locations

PricewaterhouseCoopers LLP is a network
of professional service firms located in
148 countries.

Diversity Leadership

Roy Weathers
Chief Diversity Officer

Amy Van Kirk
Director of Diversity Sourcing
www.pwc.com/lookhere

Recruiting

Please list the schools/types of schools at which you recruit.

• *Private and public schools:* PwC actively recruits at over 200 private and public colleges and universities

• *Historically black colleges and universities (HBCUs):* Howard University, Florida A&M University, Hampton University, North Carolina A&T University, Atlanta University Center

• *Hispanic serving institutions (HSIs):* Florida International University

Do you have any special outreach efforts directed to encourage minority students to consider your firm?

• We host high school students and guidance counselors at our annual MLK Day events. This year, it included approximately 700 youths in 24 cities across the country.

• Advertise in minority student association publication(s)

• Participate in/host minority student job fair(s) and conferences

• Sponsor minority student association events

• Firm's employees participate on career panels at schools

• We offer scholarships or intern/fellowships for minority students

• Partner with universities to offer high school programs to promote accounting awareness

• Our eXceed program, which is aimed at increasing our pipeline of high-achieving minority students who are interested in pursuing a career in a professional services firm

• The PwC Challenge—a new $4 million investment over three years to fund a program targeted at 500 to 1,000 minority high school juniors in three cities, who would be invited to participate in seminars and career development training.

What activities does the firm undertake to attract minority and women employees?

• Partner programs with women and minority associations

• *Conferences:* Association of Latino Professionals in Finance and Accounting Annual Conference, National Association of Black Accountants Annual Convention, National Black MBA Association Annual Convention, National Society of Hispanic MBAs Annual Conference, *Working Mother* magazine, WorkLife Congress, National Association of Black Accountants Regional Student Conferences, National Hispanic Business Association, National Asian American Society of Accountants

• *Offer minority scholarship/leadership/internship program:* eXceed

• Platinum sponsor of the Monster Diversity Leadership Program

• Seek referrals from other employees

• Utilize online job services

• Advertise in national publications (*DiversityInc, Black Collegian,* etc.)

Internships and Co-ops

INROADS

Deadline for application: Need to apply during fall semester or early spring semester (winter quarter)

Number of interns in the program in summer 2006 (internship): 208

Pay: Varies

Length of the program: Eight to 10 weeks

Percentage of interns in the program who receive offers of full-time employment: 85 percent

Web site for internship/co-op information: www.pwc.com/lookhere

In our eight- to 10-week (may extend longer) summer program, PricewaterhouseCoopers LLP interns get a taste of what it's like to work here full time. It is an internship involving multidimensional, integrated learning coupled with a practical paid work experience. Interns attend orientation, offsite training and receive a laptop computer for the duration of their internship. All internships include social events and community service activities.

Rising freshmen, sophomores and juniors are assigned to work in an internal firm services (IFS) group—human resources/recruiting, marketing, learning and education (may require travel), finance, diversity and work/life, meeting and event services, information technology and/or sales and business development. They will receive exposure to client service through shadow days, mentor assignments, training and workshops.

Rising seniors will function in a client services role in assurance, tax or advisory. They will have responsibilities similar to a first-year associate on client engagement. They will be a part of a team of business advisors, serving diverse clients and developing optimal strategies for those clients. Interns will help advise our clients on solutions to the issues facing them, and as a member of a client service team, they'll help offer clients a thorough understanding of current and emerging issues and the underlying business concerns. Interns will be challenged to think, stimulated to grow and encouraged to contribute. If successful, interns will receive a full-time offer.

Leadership Programs

Deadline for application: Need to apply during fall semester or early spring semester (winter quarter)

Pay: None

Length of the program: Three to five days

Web site for internship/co-op information: www.pwc.com/lookhere

These are multi-event innovative programs inspiring teamwork and leadership development, geared to bridge the gap between academic education and initial intern assignments

Events may include:

• Client shadowing
• Etiquette dinners
• Social activities

Scholarships

eXceed

Deadline for application for the scholarship program: Application process runs from September through December

Scholarship award amount: $3,000

Web site or other contact information for scholarship: www.pwc.com/exceed

For PwC, diversity is a business imperative that will help it sustain its position as the U.S. professional services firm. Since 1990, PwC has awarded scholarships to some of the best and brightest African-American, Hispanic/Latino and Native American students in the U.S. Our scholarship program includes:

• A $3,000 scholarship
• An invitation to our annual Diversity in Business Leadership Conference
• A winter or summer internship with PricewaterhouseCoopers

Qualifications:

• Freshman or sophomore
• Overall GPA of 3.2 or higher
• An academic and career interest in accounting, management information systems and/or computer science

Affinity Groups

Networking Circles

At PricewaterhouseCoopers LLP, we are committed to creating an inclusive culture where everyone can succeed in achieving their professional and personal goals. We recognize that networks are critical to career success. Networks provide access to information and new business leads, as well as support and guidance in achieving career goals. Research shows that exclusion from informal networks and limited access to mentors can be barriers to advancement. A key goal of our affinity group circles is to provide that connection.

Circle members receive valuable career advice, expand skills, increase their knowledge of the firm's businesses and share best practices—all within a community of talented women and our diverse staff. Circle members meet regularly to exchange ideas, analyze developmental issues and receive feedback and guidance as a group. They also advise and mentor each other as relationships develop.

Circle goals:

• To ignite and empower women and our diverse staff to achieve their personal and professional ambitions
• To provide a sense of community and connectivity
• To create opportunities for networking and visibility
• To present opportunities for professional and personal development
• To provide role models and a mentoring environment

The following Circles in PwC offices around the country:

- Women's networking circles
- Parenting circles
- Diversity/minority circles
- GLBT circles

Entry-Level Programs, Full-Time Opportunities and Training Programs

At PricewaterhouseCoopers LLP, you'll learn on the job with your clients and in formal training programs. No matter where you are in your career, you will find the accelerated learning and coaching experiences you need to be successful. PwC invests over $235 million in training, offers over 3,500 courses for ongoing learning and provides over two million hours in training per year. We offer distinctive training programs, as well as a number of self-study programs, to further develop your skills and expand your knowledge base through a wide range of programs and resources that can be tailored to your needs.

Signature Training Programs for Assurance, Advisory, and Tax

Signature programs are comprehensive, engaging, residential programs that are offered during advancement milestones or at annual or biannual industry or line of service conferences. These programs are opportunities for you to learn valuable skills, network with colleagues and interact with leadership directly. Below are some examples of signature programs.

Go Audit: A program for first-year associates in PwC's assurance line of service around a group learning experience, Go Audit is a dynamic, two-week introduction to the way we work on audit engagements at PwC. Your team will face a variety of tasks that challenge you to demonstrate an understanding of audit and business processes, incorporating technology and critical thinking skills as a team. The program is delivered nationally at central training locations, allowing you to begin to build the professional peer network that will serve you well throughout your career.

Advisory University: This annual premier learning event for the advisory line of service brings together all advisory client service professionals across the country and several international attendees, from members of the global leadership and senior U.S. partners to associates and analysts. In addition to a full curriculum that includes both technical and professional development courses instructed by internal and external experts, this weeklong event provides everyone, from entry-level staff through partner, the opportunity to listen to leadership and obtain an understanding of the firm's strategy and goals, to acquire new relevant skills and knowledge, and to build and develop relationships across the practice.

Tax Associate Series and Tax Select: Instructor-led courses, ranging from three to ten days in length, form the cornerstone of development for tax associates in a wide variety of tax technical, professional and business skills areas. Tax associates receive in-depth technical training from both internal and external experts in the taxation of corporations, pass-through entities, individuals, international transactions and multistate transactions, supplemented with project management and relationship management skills training designed to accelerate their development into world-class business and tax advisors. Senior associates attend the annual tax select program, featuring the latest strategies, available products and services and technical developments in taxation, along with a wide array of professional skills development opportunities. Over 100 courses are offered, empowering them to take control of their professional development with a plan tailored specifically to their individual needs and interests.

Educational Support Plan

The PwC Educational Support Plan provides staff with educational support of up to $5,250 per calendar year. The program is designed to provide staff the opportunity to further their education through pursuit of a degree and/or to improve their skills by pursuing educational courses that are directly related to their current position.

Strategic Plan and Diversity Leadership

How does the firm's leadership communicate the importance of diversity to everyone at the firm?

The U.S. firm's senior partner communicates the importance of diversity in his "Weekly Wrap" e-mail communication to our partners and his bimonthly "Staff Update" e-mail to all employees. In addition, our chief diversity officer hosts web casts, goes office to office for town hall meetings and communicates through e-mails. Also, the firm's top 100 leaders underwent a two-day diversity/inclusion training session in June 2007 and diversity is a major topic at the annual partner meetings.

Who has primary responsibility for leading diversity initiatives at your firm?

Roy Weathers, chief diversity officer and member of the U.S. leadership team

Does your firm currently have a diversity committee?

Yes

If yes, please describe how the committee is structured, how often it meets, etc.

Our office of diversity is comprised of the following:

- Chief diversity officer
- Director of minority retention and advancement

- Director of women's retention and advancement
- Director of gender initiatives and dependent care
- Director of diversity for firmwide people initiatives
- Director of diversity sourcing
- Director of diversity metrics/EEO/AA
- Diversity communications leader
- Gender initiatives/dependent care manager
- Four partner diversity champions in each of the firm's major business lines
- 12 local diversity leaders in our larger markets

The national team of the office of diversity has weekly calls, and the entire team has biweekly calls to share updates, best practices and discuss strategic issues.

Has the firm undertaken a formal or informal diversity program or set of initiatives aimed at increasing the diversity of the firm?

Yes, formal. PricewaterhouseCoopers LLP is committed to creating an inclusive workplace where everyone can succeed in achieving his or her professional and personal goals. An inclusive workplace enables us to embrace the diversity and richness of backgrounds and perspectives of our people and to leverage their diverse talents to arrive at winning business solutions.

At PricewaterhouseCoopers, we believe the term "diversity" incorporates all the characteristics that make us both alike and unique: our backgrounds, cultures, nationalities, lifestyles, identities, points of view, approaches to solving problems, ways of working, and views of personal and career success. Our commitment to creating an inclusive work environment that leverages this diversity is a business imperative tied directly to our bottom line and the sustainability of our organization's success. We view inclusion as encompassing work/life flexibility and diversity. An inclusive workplace is fundamental to our business—it enhances overall business performance through global market understanding, attracting and retaining the best talent and serving clients through the most effective solutions.

PricewaterhouseCoopers continues to demonstrate its commitment to making its workplace inclusive through:

- Its chief diversity officer reporting directly to the chairman of the firm and being part of the firm's core executive leadership team
- Its office of diversity under the leadership of the chief diversity officer includes local diversity managers in 14 of the firm's major markets
- Diversity partner champions appointed in each of the firm's four lines of businesses
- National and local initiatives to recruit, retain and advance our best diverse talent
- A flexible work environment to respond in the most agile way to the demands of a client services business, while providing our partners and staff with the control and influence over their own quality of life
- Incorporating inclusion, diversity and work/life values and practices as priorities in our people strategy

- Mentoring and networking initiatives to increase leadership opportunities for women and minorities
- Learning and education opportunities for leaders, managers and staff to better manage diversity and inclusion

PricewaterhouseCoopers' diversity programs are an integral component of its strategy to identify and remove barriers to our people achieving high performance. It enhances fairness and equal employment opportunity for minorities, women, individuals with disabilities and covered veterans by ensuring that these groups have equal access to PricewaterhouseCoopers' employment opportunities.

We also believe that our people are more productive at work when they have the flexibility to successfully manage their lives outside of work. Flexibility is an individual's ability, over time, to meet the demands of his or her role and accomplish the things he or she identifies as priorities outside the office. Our senior leadership's goal is to create a flexible work environment where we can respond in the most agile way to the demands of a client service business while providing our partners and staff with control over their own quality of life.

We have created or expanded many of our work/life programs and initiatives to specifically address work/life flexibility for our people. Examples of these efforts include:

Generous vacation and time-off benefits

- Extended, paid holiday time off, when business needs allow. In 2006, this included five-and-a-half days off over the July 4th holiday and 10 consecutive days off between December 24th and January 2nd.
- A wide range of flexible work arrangements
- An employee assistance program
- Child care and elder care resource and referral services
- National child care center discounts
- Backup child care centers in many of our major markets
- Generous emergency dependent care reimbursement program
- Adoption leave and generous adoption financial assistance
- Three weeks of paternity leave for men; six to eight weeks of maternity leave (in addition to short-term disability) for women
- A dependent care expense account
- Mom's lactation program (also for partners/wives of PwC partners and staff)

The Stats

	NUMBER OF EMPLOYEES	REVENUE
	2006	2006
Total in the U.S.	More than 140,000*	$21.9 billion

*partners and staff

Retention and Professional Development

Please identify the specific steps you are taking to reduce the attrition rate of minority and women employees.

- Develop and/or support internal employee affinity groups (e.g., minority or women networks within the firm)
- Increase/improve current work/life programs
- Succession plan includes emphasis on diversity
- Work with minority and women employees to develop career advancement plans
- Review work assignments and hours billed to key client matters to ensure proportional representation on top client engagements
- Strengthen mentoring program for all employees, including minorities and women
- Professional skills development program for all employees, including minority and women employees

Additional Information

We believe an inclusive workplace enables us to take advantage of the talent of our diverse workforce to improve the quality of our services and grow our business.

—Dennis Nally, U.S. chairman

In a period of time when many organizations may have reduced their budgets, our leadership has made significant investments in our diversity effort by providing diversity leadership in each of our lines of service and supporting our diversity strategy locally with diversity leaders in 14 of our major markets. Our diversity leaders serve as change agents on the ground that collaborate with office managing partners and HR leaders to develop locally customized strategies to promote inclusion and dedicate all of their time and attention to developing diverse leaders, improving minority retention and increasing work/life quality for all our staff.

Our story is one of commitment—from the chairman's office that sets national policy to the local offices where our client teams are on the ground working with our diversity leaders. We are committed to building a culture of equity and fairness, of integrity and excellence in everything we do. We demand the best of our people and they, in turn, demand the best from us. They demand that we demonstrate a visible commitment to diversity—not just policy statements and

programs, but tangibly though the actions of their leadership and peers, and visibly by the results.

We are very proud of our diverse workforce, our leadership position in the profession and the quality service we deliver to clients. Half of our new hires each year are women, and women currently represent some 41 percent of our client service manager group, 31 percent of our client service senior manager/director group and 17 percent of the firm's senior leadership team.

People of color represent one quarter of our new hires and our client service staff. We have been recognized externally for our commitment and actions, including:

- Named one of *Fortune* magazine's 100 Best Companies to Work For three consecutive years in 2005, 2006 and 2007.
- Named one of the Top 10 Companies for Working Mothers by *Working Mother* magazine in 2006, the 11th consecutive year we were on the Top 100 list and the fourth time we've been recognized as a Top 10 company.
- Ranked No. 12 in *DiversityInc's* list of Top 50 Best Companies for Diversity in 2007, and named to three of the Top 10 Specialty Lists, including Top 10 Companies for Asian Americans, Top 10 Companies for People with Disabilities and Top 10 Companies for GLBT Employees.
- Named one of the Best Companies for Women of Color by *Working Mother* magazine in 2005 and 2006.
- Ranked No. 1 in our profession in the 2002, 2003, 2004, 2005, 2006, and 2007 Universum Business Student Survey.
- Ranked No. 1 Most Ideal Employer Overall by business students in the 2007 Universum Survey.
- Ranked No. 2 in *Training* magazine's list of Top 125 Companies
- The No. 1 employer of INROADS interns in 2006.
- Ranked No. 1 in our profession as the Most Ideal Diversity Employer in the 2006 Universum Undergraduate Survey.
- Named one of the Top Companies for Diversity by *Hispanic Business* magazine.
- Recipient of the Out & Equal Corporate Equality Award in 2006.
- Named one of the Top Companies for GLBT Employees by the Human Rights Campaign (HRC) in 2006.

We acknowledge that it is a journey, yet we are strengthened knowing that diversity is now embedded in everything we do as a firm—from recruiting to coaching and developing, from succession planning to winning clients. We know that the success of our firm depends entirely upon our people—and we can't afford not to invest in each and every one.

Procter & Gamble Company, The

One Procter & Gamble Plaza
Cincinnati, OH 45201
www.pg.com/careers

Locations

Cincinnati, OH (HQ)

US: 30 manufacturing facilities in 21 states
International: Products sold in 180 countries; operations in 80 countries

Main offices (international):
Brussels, Belgium • Caracas, Venezuela/Santiago, Chile • Frankfurt/Schwalbach, Germany • Geneva, Switzerland • Guangzhou, China • Kobe, Japan • Mexico City, Mexico • Singapore • Toronto, Canada

Contact Person

Katie Skeeters
Diversity Recruiting Specialist
One Procter & Gamble Plaza
Cincinnati, OH 45201
Phone: (513) 983-1100
Fax: 513-983-4967
E-mail: skeeters.k@pg.com

Diversity Team Leader/Diversity Campus Recruiting Team Leader

Jorge Rivera
Senior Manager, Diversity Recruiting

Experienced Hire Contact

Nicole Salisbury
Senior Recruiting Specialist

Recruiting

Please list the schools/types of schools at which you recruit.

• *Private/Public:* Procter & Gamble actively recruits at over 50 private (including Ivy colleges) and public colleges and universities throughout the U.S. However, a significant number of our entry-level new hires also come from other schools and sources (e.g., conferences, employee referrals). If you happen to attend a school where P&G doesn't have a campus presence, we encourage you to visit our career web site and, if interested in a specific opportunity, apply directly online.

• *Historically black colleges and universities (HBCUs):* Florida A&M, North Carolina A&T, Tennessee State, Tuskegee

• *Hispanic serving institutions (HSIs):* Florida International University, University of Texas – El Paso, University of Texas – Austin

Do you have any special outreach efforts directed to encourage minority students to consider your firm?

• Hold a reception for minority students
• Conferences
• *Advertise in minority student association publication(s) or other minority-focused publications:* Vault guides, *Latina, Black Collegian, Hispanic Professional*

• Participate in/host minority student job fair(s) or other minority-focused job events
• Sponsor minority student association events
• Firm's employees participate on career panels at schools
• Outreach to leadership of minority student organizations
• Scholarships or intern/fellowships for minority students

What activities does the firm undertake to attract minority and women employees?

• Partner programs with women and minority associations
• *Conferences:* National Society of Hispanic MBA's, Society of Hispanic Professional Engineers, National Society of Black Engineers, Asian Diversity Incorporated, Consortium for Graduate Studies in Management, Career Opportunities for Students with Disabilities, National Association of Asian American Professionals, National Black MBA Association, Society of Women Engineers, National Hispanic Business Association, American Indian Society of Engineers & Scientists.
• Participate at minority job fairs
• Seek referrals from other employees
• Utilize online job services
• *Other:* Hispanic Alliance for Career Enhancement (HACE)

Do you use executive recruiting/search firms to seek to identify new diversity hires?

No

Internships and Co-ops

Corporate Internship Program/Includes INROADS

Deadline for application: Applications accepted all year; most Summer Internships are staffed by March prior to the Summer.

Number of interns in the program in summer 2006 (internship) or 2006 (co-op): 450

Pay: We offer very competitive salaries based on industry benchmarks

Length of the program (in weeks): 10 to 12 weeks

Percentage of interns/co-ops in the program who receive offers of full-time employment: About 80 percent of those qualified for full-time

Web site for internship/co-op information: www.pg.com/careers

Qualifications for this program differ by function and department. We offer internship/co-op opportunities in all of our technical disciplines including customer service/logistics, engineering, information technology, manufacturing, and research and development. The intern/co-op is assigned key projects to support our brands. The intern/co-op has the opportunity to work on teams and make a contribution to the business while gaining experience that will be helpful for full-time employment. The internships and co-op assignments are designed for individuals who have completed their sophomore and junior years. We offer a one-week technical summer camp for individuals who have completed their freshman year. At the end of the camp, students have the opportunity to interview for an internship the following summer.

We offer internship/co-op opportunities in all of our commercial business disciplines including design, external relations, finance and accounting, market research, marketing and sales. The intern/co-op is assigned key projects to support our brands. The intern/co-op has the opportunity to work on cross-functional teams and make contributions to the business while gaining experience that will prove helpful for full-time employment. The internships and co-ops are designed for individuals that have just completed their junior year of college or have completed their first year of MBA school. For marketing, a one week marketing MBA summer camp is offered for students just entering MBA school. At the end of the camp, the students have the opportunity to interview for an internship the following summer. Market research offers a consumer strategy workshop that is for students just completing their sophomore year of college, with the same opportunity to interview for an internship the following summer on the last day of the camp.

Affinity Groups

Each of these teams provides its members the opportunity to network and represent themselves across the company's business units:

- Hispanic Leadership Team
- African-American Leadership Team
- Asian Pacific American Leadership Team
- Native American Leadership Team
- Hispanic Steering Team

People with Disabilities Team

Provides the opportunity to enable hiring, onboarding, retention and recognition to the contributions of people with disabilities.

Other Affinity Groups within P&G

- American Indian Science & Engineering Society (AISES)
- Asians in Marketing and CMK (AMC)
- Black Advertising Leadership Team (BALT)
- Black Women Managers within the Product Supply Organization
- Corporate Women Leadership Team
- Gay Bisexual Lesbian Employees (GABLE)
- Mentoring Program
- Multi-Cultural Multi National Team (MCMN)
- National Black MBA Association (NBMBAA)
- National Hispanic Business Association (NHBA)
- National Society of Black Engineers (NSBE)
- National Society of Hispanic MBA's (NSHMBA)
- R&D APA Team and Community
- Society of Hispanic Professional Engineers (SHPE)

Entry-Level Programs, Full-Time Opportunities and Training Programs

For the following section, please repeat this template as necessary if you have more than one full-time, entry-level program, training program or management/leadership program at your organization.

P&G's promote-from-within philosophy, places considerable emphasis on employee training, growth and development. This is critical since the people we hire at entry-level will become the future leaders of our company. In addition to on the job training, P&G utilizes a system called Rapid Learn to train and develop employees. Employees access the ongoing curriculum by using the company Intranet or attending formal training classes. The classes focus on general management subjects (i.e., time management) and functional specific subjects (i.e., negotiating for purchases).

RapidLearn

Length of program: Ongoing throughout your career at Procter & Gamble

Geographic location(s) of program: Worldwide; some classes are web-based

Please describe the training/training component of this program: Company Intranet and formal training classes.

On-Boarding

Formal on-boarding training is provided on day one, and at the six-to 12-month, and 15-to 18-month intervals after starting full-time employment.

Length of program: From start date until about 18 months with the company.

Geographic location(s) of program: Worldwide

Please describe the training/training component of this program: New hires learn about P&G, history, plans and benefits, company purpose values and principles, and an overview of the business unit they will join.

Strategic Plan and Diversity Leadership

What trends in your industry affect your corporate diversity goals, strategies and/or internal or external alliances?

Our intent is to have an organization that mirrors the composition of the consumers that we serve. Accordingly we are in touch with the shift in demographics in the U.S.A. and establish our diversity goals and strategies accordingly.

How does the firm's leadership communicate the importance of diversity to everyone at the firm?

In P&G, diversity is a business strategy. Accordingly, it is part of the company master plan and is included in the business units and functional plans. Our business and functional leaders discuss diversity results in their business reviews with their organizations. Furthermore, diversity information is available to all the employees on the P&G web site.

Who has primary responsibility for leading diversity initiatives at your firm?

Maxine Brown-Davis, vice president of diversity

Does your firm currently have a diversity committee?

Yes, the Diversity Council

If yes, please describe how the committee is structured, how often it meets, etc.

CEO and top executives. They meet quarterly and review progress versus plans, as well as high potential candidates for executive assignments.

If yes, does the committee's representation include one or more members of the firm's management/executive committee (or the equivalent)?

Yes

If yes, how many executives are on the committee? How many employees are on the committee, and how often does the committee convene in furtherance of the firm's diversity initiatives?

From 15 to 20 executives (including our CEO) are on the council. Although we don't track the hours, the quarterly reviews typically last about half a day, and there is significant time spent against agreed action plans.

Total Executives on Committee: 15 to 20

Does the committee and/or diversity leader establish and set goals or objectives consistent with management's priorities?

Yes, diversity is a shared responsibility of all our executives.

Has the firm undertaken a formal or informal diversity program or set of initiatives aimed at increasing the diversity of the firm?

Yes, formal

We have had a formal program in place for a number of years that combines comprehensive recruiting efforts with initiatives focused on continually improving retention. There are functional networks, summer camps (marketing, market research, finance and accounting, information technology, research and development researcher, and engineer). Once you attend a summer camp, you have the opportunity to interview for a summer internship.

How often does the firm's management review the firm's diversity progress/results?

We review action plan progress monthly and overall direction and future plans twice a year.

How is the firm's diversity committee and/or firm management held accountable for achieving results?

Through reviews with our senior management and use of our formal rewards system.

The Stats

	NUMBER OF EMPLOYEES		REVENUE	
	2006	2005	05/06*	04/05*
Total in the U.S.	43,500	36,500	N/A	N/A
Total outside the U.S.	95,000	73,500	N/A	N/A
Total worldwide	138,500	110,000	$68.2 billion	$56.7 billion

	2006 (FISCAL YEAR)	2005 (FISCAL YEAR)
Asian Pacific American	7 percent	6 percent
African American	8 percent	8 percent
Hispanic American	6 percent	5 percent
Native American Indian	0.2 percent	0.1 percent
Caucasian	79 percent	79 percent
Other/Unidentified	0 percent	2 percent
Female	37.5 percent	36.6 percent

Retention and Professional Development

How do 2006 minority and female attrition rates generally compare to those experienced in the prior year period?

Lower than in prior years

Please identify the specific steps you are taking to reduce the attrition rate of minority and women employees.

• Develop and/or support internal employee affinity groups (e.g., minority or women networks within the firm)

• Increase/improve current work/life programs
• Succession plan includes emphasis on diversity
• Work with minority and women employees to develop career advancement plans
• Strengthen mentoring program for all employees, including minorities and women
• Professional skills development program, including minority and women employees

Diversity Mission Statement

Our corporate diversity intent is to have a workforce that reflects the consumers and communities that we serve. We believe that this is the best way to be in touch with the world's consumers so that we can achieve our company purpose of improving their lives. We set our long term goals for workforce composition with this in mind. We hold our leaders accountable for their results on attracting, retaining and developing the diverse talent needed to achieve our diversity goals. More broadly, all employees are held accountable to the standards of appropriate behavior in the workplace as detailed in the *Worldwide Business Conduct Manual*.

Additional Information

We have initiatives tailored to attract, retain, and develop diversity talent in P&G. In attracting talent, we actively participate in campus recruiting through school teams where members of our P&G organization (including affinity group members) go to a selected group of schools and recruit top diverse talent.

We also support and participate in diversity conferences and career fairs organized by diversity associations. Examples of these are: National Society of Black Engineers (NSBE), Society of Women Engineers (SWE), Society of Hispanic Professional Engineers (SHPE), Society of Mexican American Engineers and Scientists (MAES), Asian Diversity Incorporated (ADI), and American Indian Science & Engineering Society (AISES).

In retaining talent, we have mentoring programs tailored to maintain a culture of inclusion and support. In developing talent, we offer training and growth opportunities in multiple areas in the company both in North America and in the other regions.

Progress Energy

410 S. Wilmington Street
Raleigh, NC 27601-1748
www.progress-energy.com

Locations
Florida • North Carolina • South Carolina

Employment Contact
LaTonya King
Phone: (919) 546-7622

Recruiting

Please list the schools/types of schools at which you recruit.
- Public state schools
- Historically black colleges and universities (HBCUs)
- Native American tribal universities
- Other predominantly minority and/or women's colleges

Do you have any special outreach efforts directed to encourage minority students to consider your firm?
- *Conferences:* NSBE, SWE, SHPE
- Advertise in minority student association publication(s)
- Participate in/host minority student job fair(s)
- Sponsor minority student association events
- Firm's employees participate on career panels at school
- Outreach to leadership of minority student organizations
- *Scholarships or intern/fellowships for minority students:* INROADS

What activities does the firm undertake to attract minority and women employees?
- Partner programs with women and minority associations
- Participate at minority job fairs
- Seek referrals from other employees
- Utilize online job services
- *Other:* Advertise in minority publications

Affinity Groups

- African-Americans in Progress
- Women's Insight Network (WIN)
- Latin-American Employee Alliance for Diversity (LEAD)

Strategic Plan and Diversity Leadership

How does the firm's leadership communicate the importance of diversity to everyone at the firm?
Via diversity councils, the diversity web site and internal communications.

Who has primary responsibility for leading diversity initiatives at your firm?
We have a centralized corporate diversity and inclusion office. Other key organizations include a supplier diversity organization, a recruiting organization that is responsible for diversity recruiting and corporate communications.

Does your firm currently have a diversity committee?
Yes—both corporate and business unit level committees

If yes, does the committee's representation include one or more members of the firm's management/executive committee (or the equivalent)?
Yes, the CEO leads the Corporate Diversity Council, and the business unit executives lead their respective business unit diversity councils.

Does the committee and/or diversity leader establish and set goals or objectives consistent with management's priorities?
Yes, diversity initiatives are aligned with corporate diversity and inclusion strategies and initiatives, and they are also customized for specific business needs.

How often does the firm's management review the firm's diversity progress/results?
Monthly and quarterly

How is the firm's diversity committee and/or firm management held accountable for achieving results?

Monthly discussions at our senior leaders meeting and a quarterly diversity scorecard.

Retention and Professional Development

Please identify the specific steps you are taking to reduce the attrition rate of minority and women employees.

• Develop and/or support internal employee affinity groups

• Increase/review compensation relative to competition

• Increase/improve current work/life programs

• Adopt a dispute resolution process

• Succession plan includes emphasis on diversity

• Work with minority and women employees to develop career advancement plans

• Professional skills development program, including minority and women employees

Diversity Mission Statement

Diversity at Progress Energy is more than a way to profitability. It's a way of life. Beyond simply hiring the best people into the right jobs—regardless of race, sex or creed—we have taken the goals of diversity many steps farther. In fact, few companies can match our ability to blend unique knowledge, individual interpretations, singular experiences and personal points of view across a broad workforce. Our diversity energizes our thinking, making us more flexible. It is the fuel that sparks true innovation and opens the door to new ideas. We believe in developing in our people the power to embrace and ultimately leverage their differences to attain heights impossible to reach individually.

Protective Life Corporation

2801 Highway 280 South
Birmingham, AL 35223
Phone: (205) 268-1000
Toll Free: (800) 866-3555

Locations

Alabama • California • Georgia • Illinois •
Kansas • Louisiana • Michigan •
Minnesota • Missouri •North Carolina •
Nebraska • Ohio • Tennessee •
Texas • Virginia

Employment Contact

Robert Beeman
Personnel Relations and HR Compliance
Officer
2801 Hwy 280 South
Birmingham, AL 35223
Phone: (205) 268-6034
Fax: (205) 268-7202
E-mail: Robert.beeman@protective.com
www.protective.com

Recruiting

Please list the schools/types of schools at which you recruit.

• Private schools

• Public state schools

• Historically black colleges and universities (HBCUs)

Do you have any special outreach efforts directed to encourage minority students to consider your firm?

• Participate in minority student job fair(s)

• Scholarships and internships for minority students

Internships and Co-ops

Bridges Internship Program

Length of summer program: 10 to 12 weeks

The Bridges Internship Program is designed to:

• Develop a reservoir of high potential talent for the future.

• Provide opportunities for students to accomplish tasks and projects for the business by providing challenging and meaningful work in their field of study.

• Position Protective to become the employer of choice for those interns demonstrating high potential.

We want to create and maintain an environment that is consistent with the company's mission and values and the five cardinal principles — one which will allow them to do their best work in learning about Protective.

A central component of the program is the interns producing quality work, whereby the company experiences an immediate return on its investment. Upon completion of their summer work, interns should have begun to take ownership and pride in their experience in embracing the three preeminent values:

• Quality

• Growth

• Serving people

Interns should gain a sincere appreciation for the tag line:

DOING THE RIGHT THING IS SMART BUSINESS!

Elements of Program

• Insurance business (general overview)

• How insurance companies make money (pre-work)

• Company overview/culture:

  Business seminars

  Mission and values

  Protective leadership model

  Code of business conduct

• Book review

• Self-awareness:

  Myers-Briggs Personality Type Indicator (Step I)

  Mentors

• Networking/social events

• Manager, intern, program coordinator responsibilities

• Program evaluations

Expectations

Manager responsibilities:

• Coach and provide feedback to intern

• Be an ambassador for Protective

- Develop learning agreement with intern
- Designate a mentor for the intern
- Evaluate internship performance (mid term and end)
- Provide feedback on the Bridges program
- Approve time for intern
- Set up desk, e-mail and other office necessities for intern
- Remain connected to high potentials after summer experience

Intern Responsibilities:
- Complete tasks/projects as assigned
- Participate in all developmental activities
- Participate in networking activities
- Complete all development assignments
- Evaluate/give feedback on the Bridges program
- Commit to learning about the business of Protective

Internship Coordinator(s) Responsibilities:
- Continuously look for ways to improve and market the Bridges program
- Recruit for internship positions
- Serve as primary point of contact for interns and managers
- Schedule and coordinate intern events
- Assist in all developmental activities, to the degree practicable
- Evaluate feedback from interns and managers
- Conduct exit interviews

Scholarships

Protective Life Foundation Scholarship and Academic Award Program

Purpose

The purpose of the Protective Life Foundation Scholarship and Academic Award Program is to award students who have excelled academically and/or civically and to provide financial assistance to those in need who wish to pursue a college education.

Eligibility

In order to be eligible to apply, the following criteria must be met:

The applicant must be a high school senior or one who is completing the final year of active military service.

The applicant must be a single son or daughter (adopted, natural, step or a legal ward) of a Protective Life Corporation employee. The parent must be a full-time employee of the company at the time of the student's application and when the award(s) and/or scholarship is initially awarded.

The parent must have worked on a full-time basis for at least two years by the January 1st of the year of the application.

The student must be living with the Protective parent or must be a dependent as defined by IRS guidelines and receiving his/her primary support from the Protective parent.

The applicant must be under age 22 (or 26 if applicant has been in active military service). If a scholarship is awarded, age is no longer a consideration for each renewal year's criteria.

A high school diploma or GED is required.

The applicant must be planning to attend on a full-time basis (a minimum of 12 semester hours per semester) and meet the minimum standards for admission to a public or private, accredited junior college, college or university in the United States and must be pursuing an associate or bachelor's (undergraduate) degree.

Concerning only the Protective Life Foundation Scholarship Award, applicants whose total family income is greater than $125,000 are not eligible.

Concerning only the Protective Life Foundation Scholarship Award, in order for the scholarship to be "renewed" from one year to the next (maximum of up to four years), the student must meet the scholarship renewal guidelines, plus he/she must be enrolled as a full-time student during consecutive years. Once awarded, if a student fails to apply for the scholarship during subsequent years, if continued eligibility is met, the scholarship will be considered null and void. There can be no lapses in attendance as a full-time student.

Applicants with less than a mid to high B average (or the equivalent) are normally not selected.

Awards

Doing the Right Thing Award: Open to all eligible children of ANY full-time Protective employee. Two recipients, a boy and a girl, will be named on an annual basis for outstanding service to their school, place of worship and/or community. The applicant must also maintain a good academic record. This one-time award of $1,000 will be paid directly to the student's college or university.

If eligible, an applicant may apply for the Doing the Right Thing Award, the Academic Excellence Award and/or the PLF Scholarship Award. However, he/she cannot receive both the Doing the Right Thing Award and the Academic Excellence Award.

Academic Excellence Award: Open to all eligible children of ANY full-time Protective employee. The award is determined solely on the student's ACT and/or SAT scores and overall academic record, regardless of financial need. This one-time award of $1,000 will be paid directly to the student's college or university. (Recommended minimum requirements: 25 ACT or 1100 SAT; 3.4 GPA)

If eligible, an applicant may apply for the Academic Excellence Award, the Doing the Right Thing Award and/or the PLF Scholarship Award. However, he/she cannot receive both the Doing the Right Thing Award and the Academic Excellence Award.

Protective Life Foundation Scholarship Award: Open to all eligible children of full-time Protective employees (up to and including 2nd vice presidents) whose total family income does not exceed $125,000. An applicant may receive both the scholarship award AND one of the other awards.

Up to a maximum of $2,500 will be awarded on an annual basis, depending on the student's incurred expenses related to being a full-time student at the eligible institution. The scholarship will be paid directly to the college or university towards the student's cost for tuition, student fees, room and board, books and/or school-related supplies.

The course of study is the choice of the student. If necessary, recipients may transfer from one college to another or change courses of study (while still maintaining a full-time status) without affecting the status of the scholarship.

Children of vice presidents (or an equivalent position) or above and children of Protective Life Corporation's board of directors are not eligible for the scholarship award. However, if a scholarship is initially awarded to a student whose parent is later promoted to a full vice president and/or whose total family income increases beyond $125,000, the scholarship would remain in affect, pending the student's fulfillment of the scholarship renewal guidelines and the review of the family's financial "need" status. If the Scholarship Selection Committee determines that a financial need no longer exists, the student's eligibility will not have been met and the scholarship will cease.

Scholarship Award's Responsibilities and Renewal Guidelines

The scholarship recipient must enroll for the first summer or fall term following the notification that the scholarship has been granted, and he/she must remain enrolled for the entire academic year without interruption, barring an emergency or major illness. An enrollment certificate or equivalent proof of enrollment, as supplied by the registrar's office (not downloaded from the student's college website), will be required at the beginning of each term before payment is made to the qualifying institution.

Current recipients seeking renewal scholarships must submit an official transcript of the academic year just completed AND a current invoice for the upcoming semester to the Protective Life Foundation, P.O. Box 2606, Birmingham, AL 35202 prior to the start date of the anticipated renewal period.

In order for a scholarship to be renewed, the student must maintain a good academic standing by maintaining an overall B average, as defined by an overall grade point average of at least 1.75 on a 3.0 scale, or a 2.75 on a 4.0 scale.

In order for a scholarship to be renewed, the student must demonstrate continued financial need, as to be determined through an analysis of the family's financial circumstances by the Award/Scholarship Selection Committee. Consideration will be given to all financial support that can be reasonably expected from income, assets and other resources available to the parent(s) and student.

In order for a scholarship to be renewed, the recipient must have maintained a full-time status (at least 12 semester hours per semester) and must be enrolled as a full-time student for the upcoming academic year. The submitted transcript must reflect the student's full-time status.

In order for the scholarship to be renewed, the student must meet all of the definitions described hereinbefore, plus he/she must be enrolled as a full-time student during consecutive years. Once awarded, if a student fails to apply for the scholarship renewal during subsequent years, if continued eligibility is met, the scholarship will be considered null and void. There can be no lapses in attendance as a full-time student.

Selection Process for All Awards

The Protective Life Foundation has a Selection Committee comprised of individuals who are not affiliated with the foundation or the corporation in any manner, both past and present, who are considered to be totally independent from either entity and who possess knowledge in education. The committee members will review the applications and select the recipients.

All applicants will be considered without regard to sex, race, religion or national origin. The ultimate selection will emphasize community/faith/school service, academic performance, test scores, character, leadership skills and financial need (as applicable to the Protective Life Foundation Scholarship) as demonstrated through the submitted application, references and extracurricular activities. The selection of grant recipients shall be made solely upon the substantial standards set forth herein and otherwise unrelated to the employment level of the recipient's parent(s) or to the business of Protective.

How to Apply

The application for the Protective Life Scholarship Program is available on PRISM or you may contact the Protective Life Foundation at (205) 268-4434.

Entry-Level Programs, Full-Time Opportunities and Training Programs

Managing Inclusion (managers), Exploring Inclusion (individual contributors/non-managers), online learning and knowledge builders

Length of programs: Four hours, three hours, two hours, and one and a half hours

Geographic location(s) of program: All offices

This program will provide managers and others with the right tools to acquire skills and knowledge necessary to become valuable to the company and to position others to contribute meaningfully, and thus become valuable, to the company.

Strategic Plan and Diversity Leadership

How does the firm's leadership communicate the importance of diversity to everyone at the firm?

The firm communicates diversity initiatives via training, employee communication, e-mails and leadership model.

Who has primary responsibility for leading diversity initiatives at your firm?

Opportunity Council

Does your firm currently have a diversity committee?

Yes (Opportunity Council)

If yes, please describe how the committee is structured, how often it meets, etc.

The Opportunity Council is a diverse group of current or projected company leaders. Virtually all business units are represented on the council. The purpose of the council is to facilitate and complement Protective Life's commitment to inclusion and opportunity and provide recommendations for achieving wholesale inclusion at Protective Life.

If yes, does the committee's representation include one or more members of the firm's management/executive committee (or the equivalent)?

Yes

Does the committee and/or diversity leader establish and set goals or objectives consistent with management's priorities?

Yes

Has the firm undertaken a formal or informal diversity program or set of initiatives aimed at increasing the diversity of the firm?

Yes, formal

How often does the firm's management review the firm's diversity progress/results?

Monthly

How is the firm's diversity committee and/or firm management held accountable for achieving results?

Program evaluations and feedback on exit interviews.

The Stats

Employees

2006: 2,743

Diversity Mission Statement

To encourage and facilitate opportunity for all employees by promoting a barrier-free, merit-based culture and the development of capable leaders.

Additional Information

Guidance on Opportunity at Protective

At Protective, we are firmly committed to providing equal opportunity to all individuals, regardless of a person's gender, race, age, national origin, religion, sexual orientation or other matters not relevant to job performance or career advancement. We want our company to be a meritocracy, a place where talent, hard work, good results and commitment to our values are appreciated and rewarded. This commitment to a merit-based workplace is consistent with our values and critically important to our future success.

If our company is to be a place where all employees have an equal opportunity to reach their potential as employees and human beings, Protective people must believe that they have an equal opportunity to advance. If they do not, a barrier to this goal will exist, even if equal opportunity does in fact exist. We want to make sure that no such barrier, real or perceived, exists at Protective.

One of our company's core values is growth. By growth, we mean not only growth of our company, but also the personal growth and development of Protective people within the company. As our company grows, we must also make sure that we give all Protective people the opportunity for career and personal growth.

Another of our values is serving people. To fulfill this value, we must recognize that people see the world in many different ways and that our success as a company depends upon our ability to respond to the needs of the many different types of people we serve as customers. Thus, the fact that we have a varied and diverse employee group supports our commitment to serving people and can be a competitive advantage to the extent we derive from our people the capacity to better understand the diverse needs and points of view of our customers.

This is not to say that we favor advancing a less qualified individual over a more qualified individual. Rather, it is to say that we must create an environment in which all employees will be appreciated for their unique talents and contributions, encouraged to perform at

their full potential and rewarded for doing the best job possible of satisfying the needs of the diverse customer base that we serve.

To reach our full potential as a company, we must have a highly motivated, loyal and talented workforce. We simply cannot afford to lose any talented employee because of any factor not related to job performance. We want to be the employer of choice for the best and the brightest of the people available for employment wherever we do business.

For these reasons, we encourage and embrace variety and diversity in the workplace at all levels of this company. Adherence to these principles is the right thing to do, and it is clearly smart business.

PSEG

80 Park Plaza, T21
Newark, NJ 07102
Phone: (973) 430-5257
www.pseg.com

Locations

New Jersey (HQ)

Employment Contact

Chandra Ledford
Enterprise Outreach Specialist
E-mail: Chandra.Ledford@pseg.com

Recruiting

Please list the schools/types of schools at which you recruit.

• Ivy League schools

• Other private schools

• Public state schools

• Historically black colleges and universities (HBCUs)

Do you have any special outreach efforts directed to encourage minority students and graduates to consider your firm?

• *Conferences:* Society of Hispanic Professional Engineers Region IV Conference(s), Thurgood Marshall Scholarship Fund Leadership Conference

• Advertise in minority student association publication(s) or other minority-focused publications.

• *Other:* Utility Technology Degree Program—Public Service Enterprise Group (PSEG) has teamed up with Mercer County Community College (MCCC), Essex County College (ECC), Middlesex County College (MCC) and Passaic County Community College (PCCC), to offer an exciting workforce development program to recruit new talent into technical trade positions. PSEG's associate degree in energy utility technology has generated renewed interest in trade careers within PSE&G and PSEG Power. Through a unique blend of general coursework, specialized in-class training and hands-on work experience, the degree program can also help you get started on a career in one of New Jersey's most stable and essential industries, with one of the state's oldest and most well-respected partners. The program curriculum combines regular classroom training with technical apprentice-level training at PSEG's Edison Training and Developmental Center. In addition to the general coursework, students are required to take five utility courses and complete two paid internships at PSEG field locations. Students can earn from $15 to $19 per hour in an internship. Student progress is monitored during their internships.

What activities does the firm undertake to attract minority and women employees?

• *Conferences:* See above

• Participate at minority job fairs

• Utilize online job services

Internships and Co-ops

Generation Engineer Program (three-year program)

Deadline for application: Summer/fall of each year

This program is for college graduates, not students, but the company interviews students during their senior year of school.

The successful candidate will be hired into an entry-level engineering position as a generation engineer. The new generation engineer will be involved in a three-year training and development program within the PSEG Fossil, LLC organization. During this period, the generation engineer will be assigned to various power plant locations, with subsequent other rotational assignments, along with a variety of leadership development sessions and technical training. This broad experience will aid in developing the generation engineer's skills and knowledge of PSEG Fossil, LLC and PSEG Power, LLC.

The station assignments will allow the generation engineer to understand the operation and maintenance activities associated with a power-generating station through participation in selected operating and maintenance type activities. During this period, shift-work is required and overtime compensation is offered. Other assignments will enable the engineer to understand the various roles and responsibilities of the support organizations and the services they provide to the generating stations. Throughout the three-year development period, there will be opportunities to participate in specific leadership development programs, as well as other special training.

We are looking for college graduates with:

BS degrees primarily in: electrical engineering (EE), mechanical engineering (ME), civil engineering (CE) and chemical/environmental engineering, with a GPA of 3.0 or higher. We are looking for individuals who are interested in a career at a major energy company in power generation, which includes engineering, operations and maintenance applications. A valid driver's license is also required.

PSEG Management Associate Program (MAP)

This is a three-year Rotational Development Program.

As part of the Management Associate Program (MAP), successful candidates will participated in a three-year management development program, designed to prepare recent college graduates for future decision-making roles within the enterprise. MAP associates rotate typically every nine to 12 months through various organizations to gain high-level exposure in strategic financial and operational areas of the company.

Rotational assignments have included the following areas:

- Corporate finance
- Financial risk management
- Energy trading
- Mergers and acquisitions
- Internal audit
- Accounting
- Human resources
- Marketing
- Customer services (supervisory role)
- Treasury services

New areas for rotational assignments are continuously being explored.

Program participants must be pursuing a bachelor's degree with a business major or have relevant intern/work experience. A minimum GPA of 3.25 is required. A GPA of 3.5 or higher is desired. Candidates must be authorized to work in the United States for the full length of the three-year program.

Successful applicants must be knowledgeable in core business disciplines such as accounting, economics, finance, marketing and management.

Candidates must have proven leadership potential, strong interpersonal skills and balanced quantitative and qualitative skills.

Affinity Groups

Adelante

Vision

To cultivate an environment where Hispanics/Latinos are recognized and represented at all levels throughout PSEG.

Mission

- To be a resource for PSEG employees at all levels who want to gain a greater understanding of, or contribute to, the Hispanic/Latino experience and perspective

- To communicate the collective needs of PSEG Hispanic/Latino employees and the Hispanic/Latino community

- To help PSEG leadership increase its awareness of the intellectual and technological capital provided by Hispanics/Latinos that support the successful performance and achievement of Adelante and PSEG goals

Black Data Processing Associates

The New Jersey chapter of Black Data Processing Associates (NJ BDPA) was originally established in 1981 and was known as Northern New Jersey, one of the premier chapters of the National BDPA. Chapter membership rose to over 125 members and eventually experienced a decline that resulted in the chapter becoming inactive in 1998.

NJ BDPA proudly stands with over 40 active chapters of the National BDPA, which was founded in 1975 in Philadelphia, and is currently headquartered in Washington, D.C. In the tradition of the national organization, NJ BDPA is a nonprofit, member-focused organization that exists to provide professional development programs and services to position its members at the forefront of the information technology industry.

NJ BDPA offers monthly program meetings, featuring special guest speakers who share their knowledge and professional experiences.

American Association of Blacks in Energy (AABE)

Established over 20 years ago, AABE is a nonprofit national organization comprised of energy professionals dedicated to ensuring the input of minorities in the discussion and development of energy policies, regulations, R&D technologies, entrepreneurship opportunities and environmental issues in the United States. Today, there are 32 chapters in six geographic regions in the United States.

For more information on AABE, visit the AABE web site.

Minority Interchange (MI)

Minority Interchange (MI) is a not-for-profit corporation that provides a forum for the development and nurturing of leadership ability and the promotion of career-enhancing skills and techniques. This goal is accomplished through education, employment and networking opportunities. MI is run entirely by volunteers and membership is open to everyone. MI's tone is upbeat, motivational and inspirational. To learn more about the Minority Interchange, please visit their national web site: www.mi-hq.org.

Women's Network

The PSEG Women's Network is an informal group that meets at lunchtime about eight times a year, with speakers from inside and outside of the company. Their mission is to be a forum to provide professional women at PSEG with career development insight and skills to aid in their success in both job satisfaction and advancement, as well as providing an environment that will foster collaborative mentoring and support

GaLA—Gay & Lesbian Alliances at PSEG

GaLA's vision is to assist PSEG with the creation of a safe and inclusive work environment, where GLBT (gay, lesbian, bisexual and transgender) employees and their allies are recognized and valued as part of the diverse cultural mix within all levels of the organization. Our mission is to provide opportunities for employee networking and mentoring, to raise diversity awareness, to share our collective knowledge and experiences in a learning and productive way, to expand recruitment avenues, to promote personal and professional growth, and to retain our employees—our human capital investment.

We strive to serve as a forum for education, communication and professional development that enables PSEG's GLBT associates and their allies to contribute and be recognized for their full potential. We will work separately and together with PSEG's other affinity groups to identify new recruiting and marketing opportunities and to advance corporate citizenship. GaLA will seek to build and strengthen business ties with customers, suppliers and investors within New Jersey and our operating areas.

North American Young Generation in Nuclear

The North American Young Generation in Nuclear unites young professionals who believe in nuclear science and technology and are working together throughout North America to share their passion for a field that is alive and kicking!

Our mission is to attract, retain and promote the next generation of nuclear employees. Members should have less than 10 years of service or be younger than 35 years old.

Strategic Plan and Diversity Leadership

Does your firm currently have a diversity committee?

Yes

If yes, please describe how the committee is structured, how often it meets, etc.

Structured as follows: EOG diversity steering committee; PSEG enterprise diversity council; business area councils

If yes, does the committee's representation include one or more members of the firm's management/executive committee (or the equivalent)?

Yes

Retention and Professional Development

Please identify the specific steps you are taking to reduce the attrition rate of minority and women employees.

- Develop and/or support internal employee affinity groups (e.g., minority or women networks within the firm)
- Increase/improve current work/life programs
- Strengthen mentoring program for all employees, including minorities and women
- Professional skills development program, including minority and women employees

Diversity Mission Statement

PSEG Diversity Vision

PSEG strives to be a company that truly values diversity and where all associates support each other, customers and vendors in ways that allow their unique characteristics to become enablers of, rather than barriers to, corporate success and shareholder value.

Diversity is a value that is demonstrated through mutual respect and appreciation of the similarities and differences (such as age, culture, education, ethnicity, experience, gender, race, religion, sexual orientation, etc.) that make people unique. An environment where diversity is respected is one where—as individuals and united as members of teams—we can effectively apply all of our talents, skills and experiences in pursuit of achieving business objectives.

PSEG Diversity Commitment

- Foster strong leadership, dedication and support
- Attract and recruit from a diverse pool of candidates; focus on identifying and leveraging the most effective sources for qualified talent
- Create and sustain a respectful and inclusive environment and culture to support retention of a diverse workforce
- Align diversity with human resources practices, including leadership development and training; integrate with business planning and operations
- Assure representation of the diversity of the company in internal and external communications

Pulte Homes Inc.

100 Bloomfield Hills Parkway Suite 300 Bloomfield Hills, MI 48304 **Locations** Nationwide	**Diversity Leadership** Kari Lawry National Director of Diversity & College Recruiting **Employment Contact** Kelly McGill Olin Diversity & College Recruiting Specialist E-mail: Kelly.Olin@pulte.com http://careers.pulte.com

Recruiting

What activities does the firm undertake to attract minority and women employees?

• *Conferences:* National Association of Black Accountants, National Association of Hispanic MBAs, National Association of Black MBAs

• Advertise in minority student association publication(s)

• Participate in/host minority student job fair(s)

• Sponsor minority student association events

• Firm's employees participate on career panels at school

• Scholarships or intern/fellowships for minority students

• Seek referrals from other employees

• *Other:* Outreach to middle and high schools to promote awareness of opportunities in residential construction management; partnerships with minority-focused organizations such as the Hispanic Heritage Foundation

Do you use executive recruiting/search firms to seek to identify new diversity hires?

Yes

Internships and Co-ops

Web site for internship/co-op information: http://careers.pulte.com

Our long-term investment in education and internships makes a difference—it is good for the individual student, the school, the community and the social and economic well-being of our country. It helps us to build strong relationships with tomorrow's leadership—and hopefully future Pulte homeowners—today. We are taking a direct approach to promote awareness of and interest in careers in the residential homebuilding industry, and Pulte Homes, specifical-

ly through challenging and rewarding internships. It is our way of giving back, with a keen eye toward the future!

Pulte Homes, recognized as the nation's most progressive and visionary homebuilder, is a great place to start and build your career. Our internships give students immediate exposure to what it is truly like to work for our company. Internships are offered in several areas such as:

• Sales and marketing

• Strategic marketing

• Management of construction

• Land development

• Customer relations

• Human resources

• Finance

• Technology

• And many more

In 2006, Pulte formed a strategic partnership with the Hispanic Heritage Foundation in support of their LOFT (Latinos on the Fast Track) and Team Builders Program. Beginning in summer 2007, Pulte will be hosting several Team Builders interns across the country in a variety of functions such as customer relations, land, finance, operations and construction management. Additionally, Pulte Homes actively supports the 2007 Hispanic Heritage Awards and works with INROADS for internship placement nationally.

Additionally, Pulte is a national sponsor of LEAD (Leadership Education and Development), a nonprofit organization dedicated to educating and training high-potential minority high school students and encouraging them to pursue education and careers in business. Each summer, LEAD hosts 12-month-long Summer Business Programs at top business schools throughout country. In 2007, Pulte will participate in the LEAD Summer Business Programs at the University of Michigan and Duke. Pulte will host the LEAD students on site visits and send senior executives to speak to the students on topics such as real estate and finance.

Scholarships

Pulte has established the Pulte Homes Scholarship to increase awareness among underrepresented groups about education and careers in construction management. Pulte also provides professional year-round mentoring and internship opportunities for students who are awarded the Pulte Homes Scholarship. Pulte proudly awards thousands of dollars in scholarships annually.

Affinity Groups

Local support networks are beginning to pop up in markets nationally. These networks are voluntary, employee-driven groups that are organized around inclusion and diversity initiatives, goals and programs. These employee groups have been initiated by employees and fully supported by Pulte Homes leadership at all levels. Each support network's main intent is to create an open forum for idea exchange and to strengthen the linkage to and within diverse communities.

Entry-Level Programs, Full-Time Opportunities and Training Programs

Top Gun Program

Geographic location(s) of program: Nationwide

Training is critical for your success; that's why we place so much emphasis on it. Our world-class, entry-level training program prepares you for the decisions you will eventually be making on behalf of Pulte Homes.

Our career path development cultivates your talents and prepares our new hires for promotions when opportunities arise. Our culture revolves around strong teamwork. When you join Pulte Homes, a Top Gun-trained mentor will guide you through a series of on-the-job and classroom trainings with the goal of enhancing your technical skills and building your confidence.

As your career progresses at Pulte Homes, we have a distinctive leadership training program called Top Gun that allows employees the opportunity for professional growth—trying out new responsibilities—in a risk-free environment. Becoming a Top Gun at Pulte is considered one of the highest possible honors for a front-line employee. Pulte's Top Gun Program is unique and widely acclaimed throughout the homebuilding industry. This program was

created in 1995 to provide training to high potential front-line employees on how to become successful mentors for our new employees. The goal was to provide a method to mentor new hires, both experienced and inexperienced, and provide them with a "safety net" as they learn the Pulte culture and the proven skills of their discipline. We believed that this would be an effective way to combat high turnover and loss of high potential people who often failed and left the organization because they had little support.

Not only has Top Gun achieved our goal of mentoring new hires so that they can be more successful; it also provides our high potential Top Guns substantial personal growth opportunities. After a highly charged weeklong training program, they go back to their divisions and start mentoring new hires, leading training sessions and becoming more involved in decision making as members of Top Gun councils. These councils are tasked with solving problems in divisions or tackling special initiatives, such as increasing long-term customer satisfaction or developing new procedures for opening multiple communities. The range of topics addressed by Top Gun councils vary from division to division, but the positive experience of contributing to key initiatives is consistent.

Strategic Plan and Diversity Leadership

Who has primary responsibility for leading diversity initiatives at your firm?

National Director of Diversity and College Recruiting Kari Lawry

Does your firm currently have a diversity committee?

Yes

If yes, please describe how the committee is structured, how often it meets, etc.

Pulte Homes not only has a Diversity Council, but a Women's Leadership Council as well. Both councils' members were nominated by their division's leadership and then strategically selected by Pulte's CEO, Pulte's executive vice president of human resources, and Pulte's national director of diversity and college recruiting.

When selecting council members, it was important to have at least one representative from each area (including home office, Pulte mortgage, etc.) on each council. From there, they wanted to create the most diverse mix possible in terms of function, experience, level, background, etc. After weeklong discussions, Pulte had 14 appointments to the Diversity Council and 16 appointments to the Women's Leadership Council. These councils are supported and coached by two very senior level executives and the Home Office Diversity Team.

Councils have face-to-face meetings three times per year and have broken down into separate subgroups to tackle key initiatives.

These subgroups communicate biweekly via telephone conferences. Key focuses for the councils are:

• Increasing representation, development and retention of women and diverse employees at all levels of the organization through focused training, development, mentoring and retention plans

• Increasing our technical capabilities and business results by maximizing the full capabilities and potential of every employee of our Pulte family

• Creating a strong, innovative and inclusive environment for all employees

• Heightening and increasing employee and management awareness of inclusion and diversity

If yes, does the committee's representation include one or more members of the firm's management/executive committee (or the equivalent)?

Yes

Does the committee and/or diversity leader establish and set goals or objectives consistent with management's priorities?

Yes

Has the firm undertaken a formal or informal diversity program or set of initiatives aimed at increasing the diversity of the firm?

Yes, formal

Retention and Professional Development

Please identify the specific steps you are taking to reduce the attrition rate of minority and women employees.

• Develop and/or support internal employee affinity groups (e.g., minority or women networks within the firm)

• Increase/improve current work/life programs

• Succession plan includes emphasis on diversity

• Work with minority and women employees to develop career advancement plans

• *Other:* All-employee diversity awareness training

LifeWorks! Flexible Work Program

Pulte Homes recognizes that flexible work arrangements are a way to meet employees' need for balance and flexibility while continuing to meet the company's business goals. We established our LifeWorks! program to give managers and employees choices enabling them to personally create better work/life balance while still getting the job done. LifeWorks! consists of several flexible work programs such as flex-time, compressed work week, part time and job share. Additionally, Pulte is proud to offer all full-time employees an additional two days paid time off each year for them to pursue their charitable passions. Many employees use these days for Habitat for Humanity projects, breast cancer walks and soup kitchen or shelter volunteering.

Sed de Saber

Pulte is the first national homebuilder to partner with and pilot Sed de Saber (Thirst for Knowledge). This new self-paced, learn-at-home English as a Second Language (ESL) program (based off of Leap Frog technology) empowers workers to learn English in just four months! The Home Builders Institute (HBI) created Sed de Saber—Construction Edition to help builders address the language barrier and improve safety, quality and communication on the job site. The fully interactive, learn-at-your-own-pace format gives workers the opportunity to learn general and residential construction-specific English in about 16 weeks. By empowering our Hispanic workers to learn English, we can cultivate a higher skilled, more productive and promotable workforce. Pulte will pilot the program in two markets in 2007—Florida and Arizona.

Diversity Mission Statement

To become a stronger, more competitive company by fostering an inclusive culture that recognizes the value and competitive advantage of a diverse workforce, thus realizing our full potential—not only as a company but also as individuals.

Additional Information

In the summer of 1950, 18-year-old Bill Pulte built and sold his first home in Detroit, Michigan. It was the inception of today's Pulte Homes Inc., a Fortune 200 company and one of the largest, most diversified homebuilders in the United States, with revenue exceeding $14.3 billion in 2006 and noted as one of *Fortune's* Most Admired Companies. Today, Pulte Homes has expanded across 27 states and constructed more than 450,000 homes, with experience that ranges from luxury homes, to urban in-fill projects, to active adult communities and virtually everything in between. The Pulte Homes family of brands includes:

• *Pulte Homes:* Traditional homebuilding operations from entry-level homes to million dollar homes to urban communities

• *Del Webb:* The nation's leading brand of active adult communities

• *DiVosta Homes:* One of Florida's leading and most recognized home brands

• *Pulte Mortgage:* Pulte's mortgage lending arm, financing over 90 percent of Pulte homes sold

At Pulte, we view diversity as a business priority; it is critical to our success. Innovation is one of our core business strategies, so leveraging diversity just makes sense! We believe in the value of each other's differences and in treating one another fairly and with respect and dignity. We are working hard to ensure that our future workforce reflects the diversity of our customers, partners, trade contractors, stockholders and the communities around the nation that have embraced our beautiful homes and neighborhoods. We need the insight, creativity and perspectives that a range of diverse employees bring to the table in order to become a stronger, smarter and more innovative company.

As our workforce continues to evolve to reflect the growing diversity of our communities, our ability to understand, value and incorporate differences has become increasingly important. Diversity, like any other part of our long-term business plan, requires focus and resolve. Our commitment starts at the top and filters through every geographic area.

At Pulte, our employees may all look different, but they share one thing in common: an unbridled passion for what we do … we deliver the homes that people dream of!

If you are excited about opportunities at Pulte Homes, we want to talk to you!

Please visit us at www.pulte.com.

Qwest Communications International Inc.

1801 California Street
Denver, CO 80202
Phone: (800) 899-7780
www.qwest.com/careers

Internships and Co-ops

Qwest has partnered with the INROADS organization to provide internships for minority youth across the nation for 20 years. The locations vary each year, as do the number and type of opportunities. For more information regarding INROADS, please visit their website at www.inroads.org.

Affinity Groups

Qwest has a number of employee diversity groups. These groups are comprised of current Qwest employees with a common interest in promoting the Qwest diversity philosophy. Qwest recognizes the following self-governing groups:

• ABTP (Alliance of Black Telecommunications Professionals)
• Qwest Women
• Voice of Many Feathers (Native American)
• SOMOS (Qwest Hispanic Resource Network)
• Qwest Friends (Persons With Disabilities))
• EAGLE (Employee Association for Gays and Lesbians)
• Qwest Veterans
• PAAN (Pacific Asian American Network)

The focus of these groups is to:

• Act as a resource and/or mentor to their membership
• Provide a unique cultural perspective to Qwest on how to increase market share and improve performance
• Provide a link between Qwest and the diverse communities it serves

Qwest provides each resource group an operating budget, meeting space and an Intranet site for member communications. In addition, each resource group has an annual Qwest Foundation budget of $5,000 to be used for grants to community organizations recommended by the resource groups that meet foundation guidelines. Activities of the resource groups are open to all Qwest employees and are publicized through the company's employee communications channels.

Additional Information

Qwest Communications International Inc. (NYSE: Q) is a leading provider of voice, video and data services. The company's employees are committed to the "Spirit of Service" and providing world-class services that exceed customers' expectations for quality, value and reliability. Whether you're a single household, a small business or a global corporation, from voice to data to video, Qwest has a solution just for you.

Diversity awareness is an important part of Qwest's values and has been incorporated into each management employee's annual objectives. Our business culture promotes mutual respect, acceptance, cooperation and productivity among employees who are diverse in age, color, race, national origin, veteran status, religion, sex, sexual orientation, ethnicity, marital or family status, disability and any other legally protected category.

Our diversity philosophy extends to our customers and states, "At Qwest, we embrace diversity in all aspects of the business. We meet competitive challenges by understanding and valuing all our existing and potential customers and the dedicated employees who meet their needs each day."

At Qwest, we meet competitive challenges by understanding and valuing all our customers and the dedicated employees who meet their needs each day. What makes Qwest's approach to the advancement of diversity in the workplace unique is that it is accomplished within the context of—not at the expense of—the company's overall corporate strategy.

For more information about Qwest, please visit our web site at qwest.com. If you are interested in career opportunities available at Qwest, please visit our career web site at qwest.com/careers.

RR Donnelley

---

111 South Wacker Drive
Chicago, IL 60606-4301
Phone: (312) 326-8000

Employment Contact
Dr. Damayanti Vasudevan
Vice President, Diversity & Inclusion
E-mail: Damayanti.Vasudevan@rrd.com
www.rrdonnelley.com, or e-mail your resume
to rrdonnelley@trm.brassring.com

Recruiting

Please list the schools/types of schools at which you recruit.

• Private schools

• Public state schools

• Historically black colleges and universities (HBCUs)

• Other predominantly minority and/or women's colleges

Do you have any special outreach efforts directed to encourage minority students and graduates to consider your firm?

• Advertise in minority student association publication(s)

• Participate in/host minority student job fair(s)

• Firm's employees participate on career panels at school

• Outreach to leadership of minority student organizations

• Scholarships or intern/fellowships for minority students

• *Other:* Sponsor professional development associations that would target graduate students, e.g., Black MBA, Executive Leadership Conference

What activities does the firm undertake to attract minority and women employees?

• Partner programs with women and minority associations

• *Conferences:* INROADS, UNCF, Rainbow Push, Executive Leadership Council (midlevel managers) Symposium, Catalyst, Global Summit for Women, Empowering Women Network, Black MBA Conference

• Participate at minority job fairs

• Seek referrals from other employees

• Utilize online job services

Internships and Co-ops

INROADS and UNCF

Deadline for application: Spring

Pay: $1,800 to $2,700 per month

Length of program: Eight to 10 weeks

Diversity is a critical factor in RR Donnelley's business success. Through effective recruiting, we have the opportunity to make a significant difference and improve diversity in the organization.

These are the internship programs we partner with in our diversity recruiting efforts:

INROADS

25 East Washington Avenue, Suite 801

Chicago, IL 60602

Phone: (312) 553-5000

www.inroads.org

The mission of INROADS is to develop and place talented minority youth in business and industry and prepare them for corporate and community leadership.

The United Negro College Fund (UNCF)

8260 Willow Oaks, Corporate Drive

Fairfax, VA 22031

Phone: (703) 205-3400

www.uncf.org

The United Negro College Fund mission is to enhance the quality of education by providing financial assistance to deserving students, raising operating funds for member colleges and universities, and increasing access to technology for students and faculty at historically black colleges and universities (HBCUs). Since its inception in 1944, UNCF has grown to become the nation's oldest and most successful African-American education assistance organization.

Scholarships

RR Donnelley contributes scholarship support by sponsoring external organizations like N'DIGO Foundation, UNCF, ELC Foundation and PUSH Excel.

Affinity Groups

RR Donnelley has site and regional active Inclusion Councils throughout the U.S.

Inclusion Councils at RR Donnelley strive to be a diverse representation of the employee population. They advocate for and promote an inclusive workforce by implementing programs, activities and education resources that address workplace culture, community partnerships and marketplace relationships.

Entry-Level Programs, Full-Time Opportunities and Training Programs

Corporate Mentoring Program

Length of program: One to three years

Geographic location(s) of program: Primarily domestic United States

Protégés in the program participate in various development opportunities, including training, personal career management, goal-setting, special projects and mentor assignment.

Strategic Plan and Diversity Leadership

How does the firm's leadership communicate the importance of diversity to everyone at the firm?

RR Donnelley promotes the importance of diversity through efforts of the Inclusion Councils, external/internal web site, online resource library, e-learning courses, management and sales training, CEO and executive commitment, community relations and supplier diversity program.

Who has primary responsibility for leading diversity initiatives at your firm?

Dr. Damayanti Vasudevan, vice president, diversity and inclusion

Does your firm currently have a diversity committee?

Yes

If yes, please describe how the committee is structured, how often it meets, etc.

Conducts a quarterly review of progress and annual review of strategy and progress.

If yes, does the committee's representation include one or more members of the firm's management/executive committee (or the equivalent)?

Yes, the CEO, COO and SVP of HR

If yes, how many executives are on the committee and how many employees are on the committee, and how often does the committee convene in furtherance of the firm's diversity initiatives?

Strategy committee does not have employees. Inclusion Councils are sponsored by executives and have employee participation.

Does the committee and/or diversity leader establish and set goals or objectives consistent with management's priorities?

Yes

Has the firm undertaken a formal or informal diversity program or set of initiatives aimed at increasing the diversity of the firm?

Yes, formal

How often does the firm's management review the firm's diversity progress/results?

Quarterly

How is the firm's diversity committee and/or firm management held accountable for achieving results?

RR Donnelley leaders are held accountable through MBO goals. All employees are held accountable via performance management competency of "Promoting Inclusion."

The Stats

Employees

2005: 35,510 (U.S.)

2005: 50,000 + (worldwide)

Retention and Professional Development

Please identify the specific steps you are taking to reduce the attrition rate of minority and women employees.

• Develop and/or support internal employee affinity groups (e.g., minority or women networks within the firm)

• Increase/review compensation relative to competition

• Increase/improve current work/life programs

• Adopt dispute resolution process

• Succession plan includes emphasis on diversity

• Work with minority and women employees to develop career advancement plans

• Strengthen mentoring program for all employees, including minorities and women

• Professional skills development program, including minority and women employees

Diversity Mission Statement

RR Donnelley will build strong and lasting relationships with diverse partners in the workplace, marketplace and community. We will create a workplace in which behaviors, practices and policies promote respect, inclusion, utilization, career development and success across all forms of diversity.

Additional Information

Diversity and Inclusion at RR Donnelley

To be a successful leader in the 21st century, our business practices must align with the changes in our world. The demographics of our business and workforce partners are changing rapidly, and we must stay ahead of the changes. This means we need to be diligent in ensuring that our workforce and business practices reflect the diversity and needs of the customers we serve around the world today and in the future.

Employment

RR Donnelley is building an inclusive workforce through our employment practices, such as internal and external recruiting, hiring, employee development, evaluation, promotion and retention. This includes opportunities for training, development, recognition and advancement for all employees.

Workplace Quality

RR Donnelley is committed to providing an environment in which everyone can contribute fully, feel valued and respected, and are rewarded for their contributions to the company's goals.

RR Donnelley's policy on discrimination is simple: We do not tolerate it.

Each of us is responsible for pointing out actions that are inconsistent with our company's values. Through our open door policy, employees are encouraged to bring concerns, issues or complaints to any member of management, with the assurance that they will receive prompt, thorough attention without fear of retaliation. Our managers and supervisors are responsible for investigating complaints and taking prompt and appropriate disciplinary action if these standards are violated.

Every action we take—in everything we do every day—supports our goal of building a better workplace. Our Inclusion Councils engage employees at all levels to address diversity and inclusion issues and concerns. Our focus on shared responsibility and accountability is essential to our progress in diversity.

Through education and training on diversity and inclusion, we enable cultural change and integration of diverse talent.

Supplier Relationships

RR Donnelley is committed to building relationships with a variety of business partners.

Our supplier diversity program has been in place for more than 20 years. We seek out opportunities to conduct business with underutilized organizations, such as minority-owned and female-owned businesses.

We strive to identify and develop qualified underutilized suppliers, cultivating relationships with these businesses and monitoring our progress in these areas. In establishing these relationships, RR Donnelley contributes to the economic growth and development of diverse businesses.

Customers

In the dynamic world of business, we know our customers are changing.

Our increasingly diverse customers rely on us, on our insight and knowledge to deliver the right solutions at the right time and at the right price. Meeting these expectations is a priority for RR Donnelley.

We continually assess our strategies, capabilities, practices and policies to ensure that we can serve all of our customers.

Community Involvement

RR Donnelley strives to be the neighbor of choice. We believe in being a good corporate citizen of society and the communities in which we operate.

With programs focused on literacy, youth and families, our company has a longstanding tradition of supporting a wide range of organizations, many of which serve underrepresented and nontraditional groups.

Raymond James & Associates, Inc.

880 Carillon Parkway
St. Petersburg, FL 33716
Phone: (727) 567-1000
E-mail: employment@raymondjames.com

Locations

More than 2,200 locations in North
America, Europe, Asia and South America

Entry-Level Programs, Full-Time Opportunities and Training Programs

Raymond James partners with various organizations to help develop students and prepare them for work life. We provide development, mentoring, career shadowing, technical assistance, on-site visits, job placement, networking, coaching and guest lecturing/teaching.

Our programs help provide a smooth transition from high school and college to the corporate world by providing hands-on experience in the financial services industry.

INROADS

Raymond James is proud to partner with the INROADS Internship Program. The INROADS program at Raymond James offers the best and brightest ethnically diverse high school and undergraduate college and university students an opportunity to intern each summer throughout their college career. A career development program is designed for each intern, along with the assignment of a mentor who will offer guidance to the intern while they adjust to the corporate environment.

The Stats

	NUMBER OF EMPLOYEES	REVENUE
	2006	2006
Total in the U.S.	5,500	$2.63 billion

Realogy Corporation

1 Campus Drive
Parsippany, NJ 07054 (Parent Company)

Locations

Business Units:

Cartus
40 Apple Ridge Road
Danbury, CT 06810
www.cartus.com

NRT Incorporated
1 Campus Drive
Parsippany, NJ 07054
www.nrtinc.com

Realogy Franchise Group (RFG)
1 Campus Drive
Parsippany, NJ 07054
www.realogy.com

Title Resource Group (TRG)
3001 Leadenhall Road
Mt. Laurel, NJ 08054
www.trgc.com

Diversity Leadership

Kellie Molin Kenol
Manager Diversity & Community Relations

Employment Contact

Liz Maynor
Recruiting Manager

Recruiting

Does your firm annually recruit from any of the following types of institutions?

- *Private colleges:* Marist College, Fairfield University, Sacred Heart University, Quinnipiac University, Mount Saint Mary College, Pace University, Western Connecticut State University, UCONN, Lehman College

- *Public state schools:* Montclair State, Rutgers University, and Fairleigh Dickinson University

- *Participate in/host minority student job fair(s) or other minority-focused job event:* Realogy Franchise Group has hosted events for INROADS and the NBMBAA (National Black MBA Association)

We participate in recruitment through our local colleges. Presently we are working on formalizing and establishing a college recruiting program throughout our business units.

What activities does the firm undertake to attract minority and women employees?

In addition to attending college job fairs, our main activity for recruiting minorities and women has been through our sponsorship activities and participation in the conferences of minority real estate organizations such as NAHREP (National Association of Real Estate Professionals), NAREB (National Real Estate Brokers), NGLCC (National Gay Lesbian Chamber of Commerce) and AREAA (Asian Real Estate Association of America). At these conferences, we sponsor dinners, attend conference expos and hand out recruiting materials specifically targeted to a diverse applicant pool. Realogy is taking active steps to create a culture of inclusiveness in all of its offices in order to better attract minorities and women.

NRT Incorporated has created a *Diversity Resource Guide* in order to assist our 1,000 local sales offices in 35 major markets in creating a multicultural environment that will attract minority applicants.

Title Resource Group participates in the Drexel University program. This program is a partnership with Drexel University for TRG employees to receive a discount on undergraduate or graduate online courses.

Realogy Franchise Group and Title Resource Group currently utilize the following online services to post jobs:

• Hire Disability Solutions LLC
• Hispanic Online
• Kappa Alpha Psi Fraternity, Inc.
• MiGentle.com
• NAACP
• One Economy
• The Retired Enlisted Association
• Women's Sports Services, LLC
• Advisors
• NAHREP (National Association of Real Estate Professionals)
• Job Bank

Do you use executive recruiting/search firms to seek to identify new diversity hires?

Realogy and its companies work with search firms and establish requirements that include the presentation of a diverse applicant pool.

Internships and Co-ops

Realogy has recently created a formal internship program, which includes recruiting from INROADS. The pay is competitive and the internship will last between 12 and 16 weeks.

CARTUS has two well-established summer internship programs:

CARTUS Co-op programs for the fall and spring

Deadline for application: Summer deadline is April 28th, 2007/Fall deadline is September 15 2007 and Spring deadline is January 25, 2007

Number of interns in the program in summer 2006 (intern) or 2006 (co-op): 60 interns are hired for summer program and a minimum of five are from INROADS for each of the three sessions.

Length of the program: Summer: eight to 10 weeks; *fall:* three months; *spring:* three months

Percentage of interns/co-ops in the program who receive offers of full-time employment: Since 2003, we have hired over 23 interns full-time

Internship program with Loyola University International Studies department (Cartus' Chicago office)

Deadline for application: None

Number of interns in the program in summer 2006 (internship) or 2006 (co-op): Two

Pay: Unpaid, but amounts to six credit hours

Length of the program: 12 weeks

Percentage of interns/co-ops in the program who receive offers of full-time employment: 30 percent

This internship was established eight years ago and accepts undergraduate students majoring or minoring in international studies. It is a year-round program. The Interns usually have multicultural backgrounds and/or diverse religious backgrounds. The interns are assigned to the training and language departments of global performance solutions.

In addition to what is listed, Cartus offers a formal program for interns. The Cartus program offers training: "Resume Writing," "Leadership Skills" and "Professionalism in the Workplace." Also included are reward and recognition events and scholarships. Every intern is assigned a "mentor" and is introduced to senior leaders. The interns attend a leadership forum as well as other events with senior leaders throughout the term.

Affinity Groups

Cartus has affiliations with the Women's Leadership Network, Women's Network and Gay Straight Alliance.

Cartus' affinity groups are employee networks designed to create affinity and loyalty to the organization and to promote an environment of inclusion. They provide education, support and camaraderie to employees and the community. They are employee-led with an executive sponsor and typically meet monthly.

Entry-Level Programs, Full-Time Opportunities and Training Programs

The Realogy Franchise Group has a training program focused on working effectively across generations and working effectively across cultures. The course length is three hours. It is offered at one Campus (N.J.) and through distance learning (WebEx—nationally). Each year, managers must attend diversity training.

TRG has a diversity awareness training program, which is required for all levels of leadership.

NRT's diversity awareness program, M.E.E.T. on Common Ground, is presented at new-hire orientation to help promote a "mutual respect" working environment from day one. In addition, training is provided to real estate agents through the National Association of Realtor's program, At Home with Diversity.

Cartus provides a formal diversity awareness program which includes M.E.E.T. on Common Ground. This program is mandatory for all employees and leaders in the company.

RFG has several diversity awareness programs that focus on inclusion, mutual respect and emerging markets. The programs are offered to employees as well as brokers.

Strategic Plan and Diversity Leadership

As a large company whose primary focus is real estate services, we are affected by anything that impacts the real estate market, including changing demographics of the communities we serve. We strive to ensure that our workforce and agent base reflect the diversity in the communities we serve and we aim to meet the customer needs of emerging nontraditional markets. We are also committed to establishing an environment of inclusion in all of our offices so that diversity is appreciated.

One of the first steps taken by Realogy as a brand new company was to create the Realogy Diversity and Inclusion Council (RDIC). The RDIC provides a forum for council members to leverage and implement diversity and multicultural marketing best practices and processes throughout the organization. Specifically, the council provides ideas and recommends solutions within three pillars: workforce, community outreach and supplier diversity. The council includes Realogy's chief administrative officer, the heads of human resources for each of its business units, and senior leaders and employees from various departments across the company. In addition, Cartus and NRT have their own Diversity Councils, which focus on business unit-specific diversity initiatives. The Realogy Franchise Group and the Title Resource Group will be establishing their own councils this year.

One of the primary ways in which Realogy fosters an environment of diversity and inclusion is through its monthly recognition of different minority groups. During each of the following monthly observances, facts and information will be posted to the company's Intranet site and included in the weekly newsletter *What's New At Home*. In many of our locations throughout the country, historical and educational videos will be displayed and events are conducted to foster diversity throughout our company. We have a "monthly planning committee" made up of employee volunteers who will plan activities in recognition of those months.

The Cartus Diversity Council, which is the largest in existence, is led by its president and CEO. The council and its local subset councils support educational programs and activities to educate our workforce on the value of a diverse workforce and inclusive work environment. Each year, the council provides a gift to employees; the 2006 gift was a calendar of artwork created by employees' children representing their vision of diversity and inclusion.

Who has primary responsibility for leading diversity initiatives at your firm?

The Realogy Diversity and Inclusion Council (RDIC) members lead the diversity initiatives for Realogy. The chairperson role of the RDIC is rotated among its members on an annual basis. These RDIC members also lead the diversity initiatives at their respective business units as follows:

• *Cartus:* Amy Meichner, SVP global HR

• *NRT LLC:* Lauren De Simon Johnson, SVP HR and Kellie Molin Kenol, director, diversity and community relations

• *Title Resource Group:* Amanda Mullan, SVP HR

• *Realogy Franchise Group:* Tanya Reu, VP HR

• *Realogy Corporate:* Marie Armenio, SVP HR

Diversity Mission Statement

At Realogy, diversity is a business imperative. It is the core value that underscores our strategic foundation and promotes an inclusive culture by recognizing, appreciating and respecting differences. Championing diversity not only strengthens our commitment to providing exceptional opportunities for our workforce and customer base, but it also provides us with the creativity and innovation that gives us the competitive edge that will secure our reputation as the industry leader in the areas of brokerage, franchising, relocation and settlement services.

Additional Information

As a brand new company, this is an exciting time for us. We are in the process of developing policies, designing new programs and creating our own culture. At Realogy, diversity is a core value and an inherent part of our company's culture.

Grow with Us!

Robert Half, the leader in specialized staffing services since 1948, invites you to learn more about exciting career opportunities as a member of our internal sales management team.

We are seeking Account Executives with accounting, finance, technology, legal, marketing or administrative backgrounds to work within one of our multiple lines of business. Our people are the core of our business. If you are interested in learning more about career opportunities in the United States and Canada, please forward your resume to **hqpemployment@rhi.com**.

Robert Half International Inc.

2884 Sand Hill Road, Suite 200
Menlo Park, CA 94025
www.rhi.com

Locations
More than 350 staffing locations throughout North America, Europe and the Asia-Pacific region

Employment Contact
Ranelle Dunnam
Manager, Diversity Programs
Phone: (925) 598-8475
Fax: (925) 598-8943
E-mail: ranelle.dunnam@rhi.com

Recruiting

Please list the schools/types of schools at which you recruit.
- Private schools
- Public state schools
- Historically black colleges and universities (HBCUs)
- Hispanic serving institutions (HSIs)

Do you have any special outreach efforts directed to encourage minority students and graduates to consider your firm?
- Hold a reception for minority students
- *Conferences:* National Association of Black Accountants, National Black MBA Association, National Society of Hispanic MBAs, National Asian American Society of Accountants, National Association of Asian American Professionals, Black Data Processors Association, National Society of Black Engineers, Minority Corporate Counsel, Association of Latino Professionals in Finance and Accounting
- Advertise in minority student association publication(s) or other minority-focused publications
- Participate in/host minority student job fair(s) or other minority-focused job events
- Sponsor minority student association events
- Firm's employees participate on career panels at schools
- Outreach to leadership of minority student organizations
- Scholarships or intern/fellowships for minority students

What activities does the firm undertake to attract minority and women employees?
- Partner programs with women and minority associations

- *Conferences:* National Association of Black Accountants, National Black MBA Association, National Society of Hispanic MBAs, National Asian American Society of Accountants, National Association of Asian American Professionals, Black Data Processors Association, National Society of Black Engineers, Minority Corporate Counsel, Association of Latino Professionals in Finance and Accounting, National Sales Network, Working Mother Media (Women of Color Conference)
- Participate at minority job fairs
- Seek referrals from other employees
- Utilize online job services

Scholarships

RHI sponsors or provides support for scholarship programs with many organizations, including American Institute of Certified Public Accountants Minority Scholarship Program, National Association of Black Accountants, Association of Latino Professionals in Finance & Accounting, National Association for the Advancement of Colored People, National Hispanic University, Hispanic Scholarship Fund, International Association of Administrative Professionals, National Black MBA Association, National Hispanic Business Association and United Negro College Fund.

Entry-Level Programs, Full-Time Opportunities and Training Programs

Robert Half International Inc. makes it a priority to provide its employees with the tools, resources, training and learning opportunities to be successful. New employees participate in a structured series of training programs that combine online learning with hands-on coaching. Training is continued to a wide range of facilitated programs that foster professional growth. To accommodate schedules of employees, RHI's training resources include an extensive library of online, video and audio courses, and a comprehensive electronic university called RHI University. Educational programs are provided for employees at all stages of their careers, and the investment in training and development programs continues throughout employees' careers.

Strategic Plan and Diversity Leadership

How does the firm's leadership communicate the importance of diversity to everyone at the firm?

E-mail, meetings and training sessions

Who has primary responsibility for leading diversity initiatives at your firm?

Manager, Diversity Programs, Ranelle Dunnam

Does the committee and/or diversity leader establish and set goals or objectives consistent with management's priorities?

Yes

Has the firm undertaken a formal or informal diversity program or set of initiatives aimed at increasing the diversity of the firm?

Yes, formal

How often does the firm's management review the firm's diversity progress/results?

Quarterly

The Stats

	NUMBER OF EMPLOYEES		REVENUE	
	2006	2005	2006	2005
Total in the U.S.	13,400	11,000	$4 billion	$3.3 billion

Diversity Mission Statement

To be the premier provider of specialized staffing services in all markets we serve while adhering to the highest professional standards. This includes identifying, recruiting, retaining and promoting a diverse workforce. We value an environment that respects differences and leveraging these differences allows us to be competitive in an increasingly changing global market. We believe these differences, along with an inclusive environment, will continue to make Robert Half International Inc. an employer of choice.

Additional Information

RHI is recognized as a leader in the global business community for our commitment to the highest professional standards. As a leader, RHI's diversity strategy goes far beyond simply valuing individual differences or developing human resources policies. Our diversity strategy builds on our strong commitment to "ethics first," takes into account the globalization of the world economy and leverages dynamic changes in the demographic characteristics of the population (diversity) in our talent and business markets. We actively recognize these changes as a business and social opportunity to increase productivity and growth, and have developed a diversity strategy that will have a positive effect on our business, employees, suppliers, customers, products and services, and thereby position us to gain a competitive advantage. Our strategy incorporates the following major fundamentals for building our business, growing our talent and expanding our markets:

• Maximize our ability to identify, hire and deploy professional talent

• Support commitment to our company's guiding principles which include "ethics first"

• Contribute to our continued success as a global employer of choice

• Develop new client markets and win market share in new, emerging client communities and markets

Robert W. Baird & Co. Incorporated

777 E. Wisconsin Avenue
Milwaukee, WI 53202
Phone: (800) RW-Baird

Locations
More than 80

Employment Contact
Carla Nelson
Corporate Recruiter
www.bairdcareers.com

Recruiting

Please list the schools/types of schools at which you recruit.

- *Ivy League schools:* Top 20 Ivy League schools
- *Public state schools:* Top 20 state schools
- Private schools
- *Historically black colleges and universities (HBCUs):* Hampton College, Morehouse College, Spelman College

Do you have any special outreach efforts directed to encourage minority students and graduates to consider your firm?

- Participate in/host minority student job fair(s)
- Sponsor minority student association events
- Firm's professionals participate on career panels at school
- Outreach to leadership of minority student organizations
- Scholarships or intern/fellowships for minority students
- *Other:* Additional initiatives and programs are currently in the developmental stage

What activities does the firm undertake to attract minority and women employees?

- Partner programs with women and minority banking associations
- Participate at minority job fairs
- Seek referrals from other professionals
- Utilize online job services
- *Other:* Baird has established the Robert W. Baird & Co. Fellowship at the University of Chicago Graduate School of Business to inspire women to pursue leadership careers in the financial services industry by increasing their access to exceptional business education, highly regarded mentors and key business networks. Baird has also formed a partnership with the Women in Business student organization at the University of Wisconsin. Baird's platinum sponsorship of the organization provides funding to support scholarships, programming and guest speakers.

Do you use executive recruiting/search firms to seek to identify new diversity hires?

Yes

If yes, list all women- and/or minority-owned executive search/recruiting firms to which the firm paid a fee for placement services in the past 12 months:

Baird uses Pinstripe, Inc., a women-owned recruitment process outsourcing services provider, as well as Connection Strategies Enterprises, Inc., a minority-owned IT search firm.

Internships and Co-ops

Baird's Summer Internship Program
Deadline for application for the internship: Various
Number of interns in the program in summer 2006: 33
Pay: Varies by position
Length of the program: Varies
Web site for internship information: www.bairdcareers.com

Each year, Baird hires summer interns to work in our Milwaukee and Chicago offices in various business units. We recruit interns from local universities, diversity job fairs on college campuses and through INROADs, a nonprofit career development organization that trains and develops talented minority students for corporate and community leadership. Over the years, we have hired students from the INROADs program. Baird's Summer Internship Program received the 2006 Corporate Sponsorship of the Year award from INROADS.

Private Wealth Management Internship Program (Pilot)
Deadline for application for the internship: Various
Project number of interns in the program in summer 2007: 19
Length of the program: Varies
Web site for internship information: www.bairdcareers.com

Building on the success of Baird's Summer Internship Program, this program was created to increase the number of women and minorities in private wealth management by providing internship opportunities at branch offices throughout the firm. Through the program, students interested in the financial services industry gain real-world experience, as well as the mentoring and guidance they need to be successful.

Cristo Rey Jesuit High School Internship Program
Number of interns in the program: Eight

Length of the program: During the school year

Baird participates in the Cristo Rey Jesuit High School Internship Program, which gives students the opportunity to experience life in the business world while earning money toward tuition. Students spend one day each week and one extra day per month working for participating firms—including Baird's Chicago and Cleveland offices—where they gain experience to list on college applications and future resumes. Cristo Rey students working at Baird also learn about the financial services industry and career options in the field.

Scholarships

The Robert W. Baird & Co. Fellowship at the University of Chicago Graduate School of Business

Scholarship award amount: Full tuition

The fellowship is dedicated to inspiring women to pursue leadership careers in the financial services industry by increasing their access to exceptional business education, highly regarded mentors and key business networks. By leveraging matching funds for the graduate school of business, the fellowship includes full tuition as well as the opportunity to work with Baird mentors and a paid Baird summer internship.

Baird Scholarships Awarded through the University of Wisconsin's Women in Business Student Organization

Scholarship award amount: $1,000

The scholarships were created to inspire women to pursue leadership careers in the financial services industry. They include a one-time grant of $1,000 to be used for tuition or school-related expenses, as well as the opportunity to interact with a Baird mentor.

Robert W. Baird Honors College Scholarship Fund at the University of Wisconsin-Milwaukee

The scholarships were created to help students in the honors college—deserving women and minorities especially—realize their academic and professional goals. To qualify for the competitive program, students must complete 21 credits of specialized liberal arts-oriented honors coursework and graduate with a 3.5 or better to receive the university's high distinction.

Entry-Level Programs, Full-Time Opportunities and Training Programs

Baird University

Baird University (Baird U) is the firm's in-house resource for personal and professional development. Each year, Baird U meets with business unit leaders, conducts informal interviews and does a formal needs analysis with all associates to make sure its programs are aligned with both associate needs and the strategic businesses' needs for the firm. Although there are many training opportunities that are general in nature, even more are designed to meet the needs of specific business units. The extensive training curriculum is available through several mediums, including instructor-led classes, web-based eLearning and recorded sessions.

Baird Mentoring Program (Pilot)

As part of its commitment to being a best place to work, Baird created this program to help with associate retention, career development and succession planning. The intent is to provide high-achieving mentees with personal and professional development opportunities that will enrich their careers, while offering a broadening and fulfilling experience for mentors. The pilot program includes 25 pairs of mentors and mentees who meet approximately two to four hours per month for six months.

Strategic Plan and Diversity Leadership

What trends in your industry affect your corporate diversity goals, strategies and/or internal or external alliances?

To be successful in an increasingly competitive marketplace, Baird must continue to raise the bar for itself to maintain our standing as a world-class firm and as a best place to work. Our ability to attract, retain and develop the best talent, and our passion for achieving superior results for our clients and associates are all crucial to our success. These are among the many reasons why we are committed to the continued pursuit of a culture of diversity that focuses on our clients, our associates and the communities we serve.

How does the firm's leadership communicate the importance of diversity to everyone at the firm?

Firm leadership is active in communicating the importance of diversity to the entire firm at all levels, from events geared toward all associates to more intimate senior management and department meetings. The firm's diversity initiatives were discussed during Chairman, President and CEO Paul Purcell's keynote address at Baird's annual meeting for all associates in May 2006. It was also the topic of a 2006 quarterly Baird Business Update for associates led by Paul Purcell and Mary Ellen Stanek, managing director and chief investment officer of Baird Advisors. At that event, an in-depth discussion of Baird's diversity initiatives was followed by an open Q&A. In addition, the firm's commitment to diversity is reiterated in the 2006 annual report. Periodic e-mails and memos from Paul Purcell, articles in our online employee newsletter and postings on Baird's internal site—Baird Web—continue to keep associates informed of progress on the diversity front.

Who has primary responsibility for leading diversity initiatives at your firm?

Paul Purcell, Baird's chairman, president and CEO, is committed to supporting diversity initiatives at our firm. As part of that commitment, Baird established a Diversity Steering Committee and Business Diversity Council.

Does your firm currently have a diversity committee?

Yes

If yes, please describe how the committee is structured, how often it meets, etc.

Established in 2005, Baird's Diversity Steering Committee is a group of 10 senior leaders at the firm who have been charged with developing a firmwide diversity strategy. The committee meets quarterly and is chaired by Mary Ellen Stanek, managing director and chief investment officer of Baird advisors. The committee selected 20 thought leaders from throughout the firm to form the Business Diversity Council which provides direction and feedback on the firm's diversity efforts. The Business Diversity Council meets monthly.

If yes, does the committee's representation include one or more members of the firm's management/executive committee (or the equivalent)?

Yes

If yes, how many executives are on the committee?

All 10 members of the Diversity Steering Committee are senior management.

Does the committee and/or diversity leader establish and set goals or objectives consistent with management's priorities?

Yes

Has the firm undertaken a formal or informal diversity program or set of initiatives aimed at increasing the diversity of the firm?

Yes, formal

How often does the firm's management review the firm's diversity progress/results?

Ongoing

How is the firm's diversity committee and/or firm management held accountable for achieving results?

As part of their year-end reviews with Paul Purcell, Baird's chairman, president and CEO, managers are asked a series of questions related to the firm's diversity initiatives, including what they are doing to promote and develop a diverse population.

Retention and Professional Development

Please identify the specific steps you are taking to reduce the attrition rate of minority and women employees.

• Increase/review compensation relative to competition

• Increase/improve current work/life programs

• Adopt dispute resolution process

• Succession plan includes emphasis on diversity

• Work with minority and women employees to develop career advancement plans

• Strengthen mentoring program for all employees, including minorities and women

• Professional skills development program, including minority and women employees

Diversity Mission Statement.

Baird's Commitment to Diversity

Baird is committed to diversity for our clients, for Baird associates and for the communities in which we live and work. This commitment is in keeping with our culture of integrity, our genuine concern for clients and fellow associates and our respect for the individual.

Our commitment to diversity includes providing opportunities for every individual to advance professionally and personally regardless of gender, race, color, age, religious affiliation, nationality, sexual orientation or physical ability, which are just some of the differences that make each of us unique.

Responsibility for creating a diverse organization begins with our executive management team and continues throughout our entire organization. Baird recognizes that a diverse team allows us to better understand our clients' and associates' needs and enhances our ability to develop creative solutions for how those needs can best be met. We have created an environment where differences are understood, respected and valued and where diversity unites, rather than divides, us.

Baird has long been active in helping individuals of all backgrounds achieve their personal best. For our associates, this includes initiatives in work/life balance, leadership training, recruitment, scholarships, internships, mentoring and networking. Baird and our associates also support a wide variety of community initiatives aimed at promoting diversity. Our community involvement allows us to play an active role in shaping the communities in which we live and work today and want to serve in the future.

Baird's culture, our ability to attract, retain and develop the best talent, and our passion for achieving superior results for our clients and associates are all crucial to our success. These are among the many reasons why we are committed to the continued pursuit of a culture of diversity that focuses on our clients, our associates and the communities we serve.

Additional Information

Baird is committed to being a great place to work for all associates, regardless of gender, race, color, age, religious affiliation, nationality, sexual orientation or physical ability. These efforts have earned Baird awards and recognition from a variety of third parties. Baird has been named to *Fortune's* 100 Best Companies to Work For list for four consecutive years and has also been recognized by the following publications for having a great place to work: *Milwaukee Magazine, The Business Journal* serving Greater Milwaukee and *Corporate Report Wisconsin.*

Rockwell Automation, Inc.

1201 S. 2nd Street
Milwaukee, WI 53204
Phone: (414) 382-2000

Locations
More than 450; sales and support locations in more than 80 countries.

Diversity Leadership
Joseph Tria
Director, Talent Management

Employment Contact
Kathy Ramsey
Manager, Human Resources – University Relations
www.rockwellautomation.com/careers

Recruiting

Please list the schools/types of schools at which you recruit.

- *Private schools:* Case Western Reserve, Milwaukee School of Engineering, Marquette University
- *Public state schools:* Georgia Institute of Technology, Purdue University, University of Wisconsin – Madison, University of Wisconsin – Milwaukee, University of Michigan – Ann Arbor, California Polytechnic State University, Cleveland State, Ohio State University, Texas A&M
- *Historically black colleges and universities (HBCUs):* Florida A&M, North Carolina A&T

Do you have any special outreach efforts directed to encourage minority students and graduates to consider your firm?

- Hold a reception for minority students
- *Conferences:* Participate in our Key conferences and career fairs
- Advertise in minority student association publication(s) or other minority-focused publications
- Participate in/host minority student job fair(s) or other minority-focused job events
- Sponsor minority student association events
- Firm's employees participate on career panels at school
- Outreach to leadership of minority student organizations
- Scholarships or intern/fellowships for minority students
- *Other:* Rockwell Automation University Relations philosophy is made up of Key Schools that we have identified which we focus our recruitment and relationship building with. At each of the Key Schools, we have a campus executive (Rockwell Automation leader), campus manger (alumni of school) and campus recruiting team (assists the campus manager). One of the responsibilities of this campus team is to work with the student groups and minority groups in providing them a resource for presentations, scholarships and is the main point of contact for all of the above activities.

What activities does the firm undertake to attract minority and women employees?

- *Partner programs with women and minority associations:* We are part of the SWE Corporate Partnership Council, Scholarship Sponsorships with our Key Schools
- *Conferences:* National Society of Black Engineers, National Society of Women Engineers, National Society of Hispanic Professionals, the Region H SWE and Region 6 SHPE
- *Participate at minority job fairs:* Same as above
- Seek referrals from other employees

Do you use executive recruiting/search firms to seek to identify new diversity hires?
Yes

If yes, list all women- and/or minority-owned executive search/recruiting firms to which the firm paid a fee for placement services in the past 12 months:
Division 10

Internships and Co-ops

Student Associate Program

Deadline for application: Post positions in August and January every year

Number of interns in the program in summer 2006 (internship) or 2006 (co-op): 140 students

Percentage of interns/co-ops in the program who receive offers of full-time employment: 60 percent

The purpose of the Student Associate Program is to develop a high quality, talented pipeline of diverse candidates to fill entry-level positions by providing meaningful and challenging work assignments that encourage students to consider career opportunities with Rockwell Automation.

Co-op Associates

Co-op associates work an approved work/study schedule. This is a full-time, alternating schedule where students alternate between full-time work assignments/projects and full-time college in their academic program. Co-ops are given specific work objectives each term and are evaluated against their performance of those objectives. Associates are assigned a mentor for the duration of the co-op relationship.

Intern Associates

Intern associates work an approved 10- to 12-week work schedule during the summer. This is a full-time (40 hours per week) work assignment/project. Interns are given specific work objectives each summer related to their academic program and are evaluated against their performance of those objectives. Associates are assigned a mentor for the duration of the intern relationship. Intern associates sometimes work part time during the school year if location and schedule allows.

Student associates must be enrolled in a four-year college on a full-time basis and maintain a minimum GPA of 2.75.

Opportunities are available in a variety of disciplines: engineering, finance, marketing, IT and business.

Student Associate Program Benefits

• Competitive salary

• Holiday pay

• Housing assistance*

• Medical insurance*

Service credit as a student associate counts for vacation and pension if hired

* Eligibility required

Scholarships

Rockwell Automation provides scholarships to our Key Schools and the National Society of Women Engineers, and these schools and organizations distribute the funding based on criteria that we provide them, one being a target towards women and minorities. In fiscal year 2006, we provided over $200,000 in scholarships to women and minorities.

Affinity Groups

African-American Professional Network

The African-American Professional Network (AAPN) supports the career development and interests of African-Americans while fostering a culture of inclusion at Rockwell Automation and the surrounding community.

The AAPN exists to accelerate the development of African-American employees at Rockwell Automation.

Hispanic Resource Group

The Hispanic Resource Group (HRG) is a volunteer group of Hispanic employees dedicated to supporting and strengthening the Hispanic community within Rockwell Automation. The Hispanic Resource Group identifies and helps address Hispanic issues while promoting and achieving industry leadership for a culture of inclusion at Rockwell Automation.

Professional Women's Council

The Professional Womens' Council exists to help Rockwell Automation women network with peers and continuously refresh their professional skills to achieve their career goals.

Society of Women Engineers at Rockwell

Advance – Young Professionals

Advance – Young Professionals works with Rockwell Automation young professionals and executives to shape future leaders.

The Young Professionals Network plans events to educate employees, holds focus groups to gather feedback and conducts networking sessions to share ideas. It also helps shape Rockwell Automation as the top career choice for young professionals, helps new employees adjust to the Rockwell Automation environment, links young professionals throughout Rockwell Automation business units and locations, and supports diversity initiatives and a culture of inclusion by partnering with RA.

Entry-Level Programs, Full-Time Opportunities and Training Programs

Leadership Development Programs

Length of program: Two year rotational development program

Geographic location(s) of program: U.S. and international rotations

The Rockwell Automation Development Programs are unique two-year rotationals providing experiential learning opportunities within our company's businesses. Rockwell Automation will match your background, skills and interest to current business needs. Participants establish a strong network with Rockwell Automation professionals through work and social activities, with business leaders acting as formal mentors during the program. Relocation flexibility throughout the U.S. is an important factor in this program. After completing the program successfully, members are placed at Rockwell Automation sites throughout the U.S. The program tracks consist of: business strategy track, engineering track, operations track and supply chain track.

Sales Training Program

Length of program: Nine-month training, then placed into assignment

Geographic location(s) of program: U.S., training in Milwaukee, Wisc., and then permanent assignment anywhere in the U.S., based on business need and employee interest

The America Sales Training Program is a nine-month program using a training curriculum with specific performance metrics linked to final placement in an outside sales position. Participants become involved in sales presentations, mock sales calls, projects and testing designed to develop successful sales competencies. A mid-program field assignment gives participants the opportunity to work directly with customers while continuing in a training environment. Graduates of the Sales Training Program are placed in positions after analyzing business needs and personal preferences.

Engineer – In – Training Program: Field Service

Length of program: Six-month training, then placed into assignment

Geographic location(s) of program: U.S., training in Cleveland, Ohio, and then permanent assignment anywhere in the U.S., based on business need and employee interest

The EIT program is a comprehensive six-month developmental program. EIT program participants develop required applied engineering skills as well as technical competencies on core technologies and Rockwell Automation products. In addition, participants enhance their competencies in problem solving, teamwork, project management, communications and leadership.

Strategic Plan and Diversity Leadership

What trends in your industry affect your corporate diversity goals, strategies and/or internal or external alliances?

Globalization (decisions must be based on a wide range of contributions from people with diverse ideas, backgrounds, and perspectives), changing workforce demographics (competition for talent) and increased productivity (everyone contributes to the company while growing personally and professionally).

How does the firm's leadership communicate the importance of diversity to everyone at the firm?

In 2004, we launched our culture of inclusion internal web site to communicate our commitment to workforce diversity and inclusion to employees and provide information about supporting initiatives and tools. In 2005, we began communicating our commitment to a global culture of inclusion to external audiences via our web site. We believe the external messages will help with recruiting and enable us to collaborate with customers who also share our cultural goals.

Who has primary responsibility for leading diversity initiatives at your firm?

Joseph Tria, director talent management. We recently aligned diversity initiative into the talent management office to build a more integrated approach to developing diverse talent and a culture of inclusion.

Does your firm currently have a diversity committee?

Yes

If yes, please describe how the committee is structured, how often it meets, etc.

We have five employee networks that are an important part of our diversity strategy.

Employee network structure:

- Each employee network will have a specific name
- Each employee network will have an executive business sponsor
- Each employee network will have a mission statement or statement of purpose
- Each employee network will have goals for both the short-term (next six months) and long-term (next 18 months) outlining how they will support business strategy. These goals should be fully developed within the first 90 days of operation. The group may request assistance from the executive business sponsor or the director of talent management.
- Each employee network will have a defined leadership structure, such as president, as determined by the members of the group. Where different sites have local chapters or branches of an employee network, those chapters must adhere to, and coordinate their efforts with, the mission and purpose of the originally endorsed group.

Employee networks will remain nonpartisan and secular—their sole purpose cannot be to promote social, religious, or political positions.

If yes, does the committee's representation include one or more members of the firm's management/executive committee (or the equivalent)?

Yes. Each network has an executive business sponsor. This past year, networks spent well over 600 hours (not including community outreach volunteer time) supporting our diversity strategy. On average, networks met once per month.

If yes, how many executives are on the committee, and in 2006, what was the total number of hours collectively spent by the committee in furtherance of the firm's diversity initiatives? How many employees are on the committee, and how often does the committee convene in furtherance of the firm's diversity initiatives?

Each network has an executive business sponsor. There are over 800 employees that participate in employee networks. This past year, networks spent well over 600 hours (not including community outreach volunteer time) supporting our diversity strategy. On average, networks met once per month.

Does the committee and/or diversity leader establish and set goals or objectives consistent with management's priorities?

Yes. This past year, we listened to, developed and utilized networking groups for African-Americans, Hispanics, young professionals, professional women and women engineers:

• Roundtable discussions with executives

• Career Development Series, governor keynote

• Joint event featuring Rebecca Ryan, CEO Next Generation

• New-hire orientation and networking

• Networking and cultural events open to all employees

Has the firm undertaken a formal or informal diversity program or set of initiatives aimed at increasing the diversity of the firm?

Yes, formal. Our strategy focuses on the essential requirements for a successful, diverse workforce: (1) a strong leadership committed to diversity and held accountable for results; (2) the drive to select, develop and retain the most qualified workforce in our industry by fully tapping into all sources of talent and (3) an environment and culture where all employees can contribute to the success of the business. Each year, we identify specific opportunities in these areas. We set meaningful, proactive goals and measures for improvement and monitor how goals progress through periodic reporting. We take corrective action if we appear to be off track. However, in this environment of continuous improvement, we are always alert to ways to fine-tune our efforts.

How often does the firm's management review the firm's diversity progress/results?

Quarterly

How is the firm's diversity committee and/or firm management held accountable for achieving results?

We will use quarterly reports and semiannual reviews to keep everyone engaged in the process to achieve goals.

Retention and Professional Development

Please identify the specific steps you are taking to reduce the attrition rate of minority and women employees.

• Develop and/or support internal employee affinity groups (e.g., minority or women networks within the firm)

• Increase/review compensation relative to competition

• Increase/improve current work/life programs

• Adopt dispute resolution process

• Succession plan includes emphasis on diversity

• Work with minority and women employees to develop career advancement plans

• Strengthen mentoring program for all employees, including minorities and women

• Professional skills development program, including minority and women employees

A lot of diverse thinking goes into every one of our products.

At Rockwell Collins, we believe that one of the key benefits of a highly diverse team is better, smarter solutions. That's why we're building a global workforce of men and women with different backgrounds, viewpoints and ideas. Determined to build upon our foundation of innovation. United by our singular vision – to be the most trusted source of communication and aviation electronics solutions on the planet. To find out just how far diverse thinking can take you at Rockwell Collins, visit our website.

Rockwell Collins

www.rockwellcollins.com

Building trust every day

Rockwell Collins

400 Collins Road NE
Cedar Rapids, IA 52498
Phone: (319) 295-3287
Fax: (319) 295-9347
www.rockwellcollins.com

Locations

Rockwell Collins is a global company that operates from more than 60 locations in 27 countries.

Diversity Leadership

Karen Brown
Corporate Director, Diversity

Employment Contact

Valerie Aikens
Manager, College Relations

Andrew Day
Director, Talent Acquisition
E-mail: amday@rockwellcollins.com

Recruiting

Please list the schools/types of schools at which you recruit.

• *Private schools:* Rose Hulman Institute of Technology, LeTourneau University, Embry-Riddle Aeronautical University—Prescott/Daytona campus

• *Public state schools:* Milwaukee School of Engineering, University of Wisconsin—Madison, Iowa State University, University of Iowa, Northern Iowa University, South Dakota School of Mines and Technology, North Dakota State University, University of North Dakota, University of Michigan—Ann Arbor, Michigan Tech University, Texas A&M, University of Illinois—Urbana/Champaign, University of Texas—Austin, University of Texas—Dallas, University of Texas—El Paso, Virginia Tech University, Purdue, Florida Institute of Technology, University of Florida—Gainsville, University of California—Irvine, California Polytechnic University—Pomona, Rensselaer PolyTech, California State – Fullerton, University of Minnesota, University of WI – Madison

• *Historically black colleges and universities (HBCUs):* North Carolina Agriculture and Technology

Do you have any special outreach efforts directed to encourage minority students and graduates to consider your firm?

• Host several receptions for minority students
• Advertise in minority student association publication(s) and other minority-focused publications
• Participate in/host minority student job fair(s) and other minority-focused job events
• Sponsor minority student association events
• Firm's employees participate on career panels at school
• Outreach to leadership of minority student organizations
• Scholarships or intern/fellowships for minority students

Do you use executive recruiting/search firms to seek to identify new diversity hires?

Yes

What activities does the firm undertake to attract minority and women employees?

• Host receptions for minority/women potential employees
• Advertise in minority/women association publication(s)
• Participate in/host minority/women job fair(s)
• Sponsor minority/women association events
• Firm's employees participate on career panels at school
• Outreach to leadership of minority/women student organizations
• Scholarships or intern/fellowships for minority/women students
• Partner programs with women and minority associations
• *Conferences:* SWE, NSBE, SHPE, HENAAC, National Society of Black MBAs, NSHMBA
• Seek referrals from other employees
• Utilize online job services
• *Other:* K-12 programs

Internships and Co-ops

Rockwell Collins Internship and Co-op Program

Deadline for application: Ongoing; request that students apply online at www.rockwellcollins.com/careers

Number of interns in the program in summer 2007 (internship) or 2007 (co-op): 280

Pay: Depends on number of credit hours completed for interns and number of sessions for the co-op program

Length of the program: Intern program: 12 weeks, co-op program: three work sessions that rotate with school session and total 12 months of work experience when complete

Web site for internship/co-op information: www.rockwell-collins.com

Affinity Groups

African-American Employee Network

Mission: The mission of African-Americans of Rockwell Collins is to create an environment where African-Americans can develop a competitive advantage for Rockwell, create a workplace of inclusion that promotes innovation, strengthens employee satisfaction and fosters strategies to attract/retain African-Americans.

Friends of Asia

Mission: To foster better understanding, exchange and interdependence between the East and the West.

Latino Employee Network

Mission: The mission of the Rockwell Collins Latino Employee Network is to support Rockwell Collins in its desire to embrace diversity, raise cultural awareness and increase the recruitment and retention of Latinos by promoting an environment where Latinos can grow personally and professionally.

New Hire Employee Network

Mission: To provide a business and social forum that supports new hires as they integrate into the Rockwell Collins culture and surrounding communities.

Women's Employee Network

Mission: To create a network of female employees to support professional growth through networking events, informal mentoring and career development resources.

Strategic Plan and Diversity Leadership

How does the firm's leadership communicate the importance of diversity to everyone at the firm?

- Diversity training for all employees
- Employee Network events and activities
- Community involvement
- E-mail communication and leader/employee meetings
- Newsletters
- Videos
- Posters/signage
- Internal web site and external billboards

Who has primary responsibility for leading diversity initiatives at your firm?

Karen Brown, corporate director, diversity

Does your firm currently have a diversity committee?

Yes—Executive Diversity Council and Diversity Advisory Council.

If yes, please describe how the committee is structured, how often it meets, etc.

The Executive Diversity Council meets quarterly.

The Diversity Advisory Council meets monthly via teleconference and quarterly face to face.

If yes, does the committee's representation include one or more members of the firm's management/executive committee (or the equivalent)?

Yes

Does the committee and/or diversity leader establish and set goals or objectives consistent with management's priorities?

Yes

Has the firm undertaken a formal or informal diversity program or set of initiatives aimed at increasing the diversity of the firm?

Yes, formal

How often does the firm's management review the firm's diversity progress/results?

Monthly

The Stats

	NUMBER OF EMPLOYEES		REVENUE	
	2006	2005	2006	2005
Total in the U.S.	15,254	14,562	N/A	N/A
Total outside the U.S.	2,825	2,715	N/A	N/A
Total worldwide	18,079	17,277	$3.9 billion	$3.45 billion

Retention and Professional Development

How do 2006 minority and female attrition rates generally compare to those experienced in the prior year period?

Attrition rates have remained relatively stable, year over year.

Please identify the specific steps you are taking to reduce the attrition rate of minority and women employees.

• Support the formation and sustaining of employee network/affinity groups (e.g., minority or women networks within the firm).

• Annual compensation review and adjustment relative to competition

• Participate in development and execution of programs in the Cedar Rapids, Iowa community through Diversity Focus, a nonprofit diversity organization founded by CEO/President/Chairman/CDO of Rockwell Collins

• Succession plan includes emphasis on diversity

• Strengthen mentoring program for all employees, including minorities and women

• Professional skills development program, including minority and women employees

Diversity Mission Statement

Valuing and leveraging differences to fuel innovation and build a stronger company.

Additional Information

At Rockwell Collins, workforce diversity is essential to our growth and long-term success. By establishing a diverse, talented and motivated workforce, our company increases its ability to develop innovative solutions by embracing diversity of thought, opinions, backgrounds and styles.

Since we began our diversity journey in 2004, we have had a number of accomplishments. We formed our Diversity Advisory Council, expanded our office of diversity and created employee networks.

Rockwell Collins places an importance on engaging our leadership in our diversity journey. As a result, our leaders are responsible for participating in diversity-related activities such as board memberships, speaking engagements and sponsorships or actively supporting our employee networks each year.

Our efforts also include helping to foster inclusive environments in all of the locations where we reside. We are partnering with local groups to ensure that our communities provide a welcoming atmosphere for our employees to work and play.

As we continue to grow our company, it is critical that we focus on diversity efforts as part of our strategic business imperative.

Awards and Recognitions

• A best Aerospace and Defense company for diversity by readers of *Diversity/Careers in Engineering & Information Technology* magazine

• One of 20 Great Employers for New College Graduates by Experience Inc., and *Fortune* magazine

• No. 8 of the Top 100 Employers in Electronic Design by *Electronic Design* magazine

• No. 15 of 100 companies on *Corporate Responsibility Officer* lists

• List of Top 25 Aerospace companies by *Black EOE Journal*

Russell Corporation

3330 Cumberland Suite 800
Atlanta, GA 30339
Phone: (678) 742-8810
Fax: (256) 500-9064
employment@russellcorp.com

Locations

Asia • Australia • Canada • Continental
Europe • Honduras • Japan • Mexico •
UK • US

Employment Contact

Jackie Parker
Director, Diversity

Diversity Leadership

Nina Choudhuri
3330 Cumberland Suite 800
Atlanta, GA 30339
Phone: (678) 742-8810
Fax: (256) 500-9064
E-mail: parkerjackie@russellcorp.com

Recruiting

Please list the schools/types of schools at which you recruit.

• Ivy League schools

• Historically black colleges and universities (HBCUs)

• Hispanic serving institutions (HSIs)

Do you have any special outreach efforts directed to encourage minority students to consider your firm?

• Hold a reception for minority students

• Firm's employees participate on career panels at school

• Scholarships or intern/fellowships for minority students

What activities does the firm undertake to attract minority and women employees?

• Partner programs with women and minority associations

• Participate at minority job fairs

• Seek referrals from other employees

Do you use executive recruiting/search firms to seek to identify new diversity hires?

Yes

If yes, list all women- and/or minority-owned executive search/recruiting firms to which the firm paid a fee for placement services in the past 12 months:

• Pathfinders, Inc.

• Diversity Search Inc.

• Staff Source

• First Pro

• Ingenium Partners, Inc.

Internships and Co-ops

Although Russell Corporation does not have a formal undergraduate internship program, we have been pleased to provide internship opportunities to both minority and non-minority undergraduate students from a variety of Southeastern regional colleges and universities.

Pay: Hourly rate paid bimonthly

Length of the program: Typically 12 weeks

Percentage of interns/co-ops in the program who receive offers of full-time employment: None, as these are full-time students returning to college.

Russell has had the pleasure of hosting summer undergraduate interns in our finance, IT and marketing departments. Students are channeled into appropriate departments based on their vocational interests/majors. They work closely with managers on a day-to-day basis to gain critical hands-on experience in a fast-paced corporate environment.

Affinity Groups

• African Heritage Leadership Council (AHLC)—Atlanta

• African Heritage Leadership Council (AHLC)—Alexander City

• Russell Latin American Heritage Network (RLAHN)—Atlanta

• Russell Women's Leadership Network (RWLN)—Atlanta

• Russell Women's Leadership Network (RWLN)—Alexander City

The objective of the employee networks is to assist the company in identifying opportunities and issues that uniquely exist within these segments of the Russell employee population. They meet monthly on company time to address and manage these issues. Their main goals are focused against four pillars: workplace, workforce, community and marketplace strategies.

Strategic Plan and Diversity Leadership

How does the firm's leadership communicate the importance of diversity to everyone at the firm?

Communication is done through monthly operating meetings, newsletters, e-mails and the company web site.

Who has primary responsibility for leading diversity initiatives at your firm?

Kevin Clayton, VP of diversity, and Jackie Parker, director of diversity

Does your firm currently have a diversity committee?

Yes

If yes, please describe how the committee is structured, how often it meets, etc.

The team is comprised of Russell's most senior managers who meet on a quarterly basis. The purpose of the team is to remove barriers that may get in the way of the organization's diversity vision/goals.

If yes, does the committee's representation include one or more members of the firm's management/executive committee (or the equivalent)?

Yes

Does the committee and/or diversity leader establish and set goals or objectives consistent with management's priorities?

Yes

Has the firm undertaken a formal or informal diversity program or set of initiatives aimed at increasing the diversity of the firm?

Yes, formal

• To create awareness and confirm diversity as a business imperative

• To increase the representation of women and minorities in mid to senior-level professional and management positions

• To integrate diversity into the talent management initiative and processes

• To increase the use of women- and minority-owned enterprises as suppliers of products and services to SunTrust

• To create management accountability for diversity

How often does the firm's management review the firm's diversity progress/results?

Monthly

How is the firm's diversity committee and/or firm management held accountable for achieving results?

All bonus eligible employees' compensation is tied to a diversity scorecard.

The Stats

	NUMBER OF EMPLOYEES	REVENUE
	2006	2006
Total in the U.S.	Approximately 14,000	Approximately $1.3 billion

Retention and Professional Development

Please identify the specific steps you are taking to reduce the attrition rate of minority and women employees.

• Develop and/or support internal employee affinity groups (e.g., minority or women networks within the firm)

• Increase/review compensation relative to competition

• Succession plan includes emphasis on diversity

• Work with minority and women employees to develop career advancement plans

Diversity Vision Statement

To create a fair and equitable culture in which every member of the global Russell team reinforces our values and contributes to achieving our business goals.

Additional Information

Russell also has a strong workplace diversity initiative with a goal of creating an environment where each employee is respected and valued, a place where people can celebrate his or her similarities and his or her differences. In today's competitive global marketplace, Russell feels its greatest strength is its people and that it needs all employees willing and able to contribute to move the company forward. Our focus areas are:

Workforce: To attract and retain superior talent

Workplace: To foster an empowering culture that respects both differences and similarities

Marketplace: To leverage our diversity to capitalize on unique revenue opportunities

Communities: To support the communities where we live and operate

Ryder System, Inc.

11690 NW 105th Street
Miami, FL 33178
Phone: (305) 500-4049
Fax: (305) 500-5758
www.ryder.com

Diversity Leadership

Gerri Rocker
Group Director, Corporate Diversity & CSS
HR
E-mail: Gerri_Rocker@Ryder.com

Employment Contact

Vivian Bier
Sr. Manager, Corporate Diversity

Recruiting

Please list the schools/types of schools at which you recruit.

• Ivy League schools
• Public state schools
• Historically black colleges and universities (HBCUs)

Do you have any special outreach efforts directed to encourage minority students to consider your firm?

• *Conferences:* National Hispanic MBA, National Black MBA
• Scholarships or intern/fellowships for minority students

What activities does the firm undertake to attract minority and women employees?

• *Conferences:* National Hispanic MBA, National Black MBA
• Participate at minority job fairs
• Utilize online job services

Do you use executive recruiting/search firms to seek to identify new diversity hires?

Yes

Internships and Co-ops

INROADS

Length of the program: 11 weeks

Web site for internship/co-op information: Inroads.org

Scholarships

The INROADS internship program's mission is to develop and place talented minority youth in business and industry and prepare them for corporate and community leadership. INROADS seeks high performing African-American, Hispanic and Native American students for internship opportunities with some of the nation's largest companies. The INROADS Internship is typically a 10 to 12 week paid summer program.

Interns are expected to maintain a 3.0 GPA or higher; they actively participate at the INROADS training and development sessions, attend monthly coaching sessions and complete 40 hours of community service annually.

There are two interns actively participating in the program at Ryder. One of the interns is working in the accounts payable/receivables department processing paperwork, monitoring invoices and interpreting various reference reports. The other intern is assigned to the recruiting department, assisting with various initiatives involving retention analysis and also working with the relocation department reviewing various relocation cases for employees.

Affinity Groups

There are four company sanctioned groups: Ryder Administrative Professionals Association (APA), Ryder Black Employee Network (RBEN), Ryder Hispanic Network (RHN), and Ryder's Women Management Association (WMA).

The overall mission of the network groups is to provide professional growth for participants, provide education and awareness for employees and promote the company's mission, values and corporate goals.

Strategic Plan and Diversity Leadership

How does the firm's leadership communicate the importance of diversity to everyone at the firm?

• *Mandatory diversity education awareness training for all U.S. based employees:* "The Inclusion Journey—Delivering on the Potential of a Diverse Workforce"

• *Diversity Internet site:* Maintain information on the Ryder.com web page for diversity. The site features highlights, best practices and facts/information to enhance communication and build awareness of diversity and work/life efforts for internal and external groups

• *Cultural Recognition Events:* Host a variety of multi-cultural events, i.e., Black History Month, Women's History Month and Hispanic Heritage Month activities

• "Diversity Spotlight," a series of articles written and communicated to employees that highlight various diversity topics. Information disseminated company-wide via Lotus Notes e-mail

• *Lunch and Learn Seminars:* Develop and sponsor monthly seminars related to diversity and work/life issues, i.e., stress management, dealing with differences, consumer credit counseling, elder care, wellness, etc.

Who has primary responsibility for leading diversity initiatives at your firm?

Gerri Rocker, group director, corporate diversity and work/life planning.

Does your firm currently have a diversity committee?

No. The organization does not have a committee; however, there is a department that is staffed to provide diversity and work/life resources company-wide.

The Stats

	NUMBER OF EMPLOYEES		REVENUE	
	2006	2005	2006	2005
Total in the U.S.	23,500	22,500	$5.1 billion	$4.7 billion
Total outside the U.S.	5,100	5,300	$1.2 billion	$1.0 billion
Total worldwide	28,600	27,800	$6.3 billion	$5.7 billion

Retention and Professional Development

How do 2006 minority and female attrition rates generally compare to those experienced in the prior year period?

Lower than in prior years.

Please identify the specific steps you are taking to reduce the attrition rate of minority and women employees.

• Develop and/or support internal employee affinity groups (e.g., minority or women networks within the firm)

• Increase/improve current work/life programs

• Succession plan includes emphasis on diversity

• Strengthen mentoring program for all employees, including minorities and women

Diversity Mission Statement

Create a supportive environment which values individual differences and enables all employees to contribute their full potential in pursuit of business objectives.

The diversity and work/life department provides services company-wide and is responsible for building and sustaining an inclusive culture that recognizes, understands, values and utilizes the unique talents, contributions and perspectives of its diverse workforce to maximize employee/customer satisfaction and business profitability.

Additional Information

The diversity and work/life planning department is responsible for building and sustaining an inclusive culture that recognizes, understands, values and utilizes the unique talents, contributions and perspectives of its employees. Our diversity mission is to leverage diversity to garner shareholder value and maximize the full potential of all our employees. We believe that proper training, development and coaching are key success factors for retaining and advancing employees within the organization.

Ryder has a variety of strategies and practices implemented to attract, retain and promote a diverse employee base, including:

• Balance scorecard program that tracks company-wide diversity measures linking to the business strategy

• Diversity education and awareness training for all U.S. employees

• Electronic staffing processes for internal and external candidates capitalizing on a diverse talent pool

• Community involvement in local initiatives, awareness campaigns, cultural observances and charitable activities and events

In order for us to compete in the global marketplace, we must utilize and engage every employee and leverage and value all employees for their experiences as well as their skills. We believe the value of diversity, of an inclusive workplace instilled with integrity in every action, makes us a better place to work, increases our value in the marketplace and makes us the preferred brand of our customers.

Ryland Group Inc., The

24025 Park Sorrento, Suite 400
Calabasas, CA 91302
Phone: (818) 223-7500

Locations

Ryland has operations in the following 28 markets throughout the country:

North Region: Baltimore, MD • Delaware • Chicago, IL • Cincinnati, OH • Indianapolis, IN • Minneapolis, MN • Washington, DC

Texas Region: Austin, TX • Dallas, TX • Houston, TX • San Antonio, TX

Southeast Region: Atlanta, GA • Charleston, SC • Charlotte, NC • Myrtle Beach, SC • Greensboro, NC • Greenville, NC • Jacksonville, FL • Orlando, FL • Southwest Florida • Tampa, FL

West Region: Central Valley • Coachella Valley • Denver, CO • Inland Empire • Las Vegas, NV • Phoenix, AZ • Sacramento, CA

Employment Contact

Karen Ball
Recruiter
E-mail: campushires@ryland.com
www.ryland.com/home/career.html

Recruiting

Please list the schools/types of schools at which you recruit.

• Ivy League schools
• Other private schools
• Public state schools
• Historically black colleges and universities (HBCUs)
• Hispanic serving institutions (HSIs)
• Native American tribal universities
• Other predominantly minority and/or women's colleges

Do you have any special outreach efforts directed to encourage minority students and graduates to consider your firm?

• Participate in/host minority student job fair(s) or other minority-focused job events.
• Firm's employees participate on career panels at school
• Outreach to leadership of minority student organizations

What activities does the firm undertake to attract minority and women employees?

• Participate at minority job fairs
• Seek referrals from other employees
• Utilize online job services

Do you use executive recruiting/search firms to seek to identify new diversity hires?

No

Entry-Level Programs, Full-Time Opportunities and Training Programs

Ryland Homes Management Training Program
Length of program: Three years
Geographic location(s) of program: Nationwide opportunities

Ryland Mortgage Management Training Program

Length of program: Three years

Geographic location(s) of program: Scottsdale, Ariz., plus one rotation at a mortgage branch

Ryland's Management Training Programs are company diversity initiatives created to increase the number of women and ethnically diverse employees within our management team. By providing participants with a 360-degree view of the residential construction or mortgage industry, Ryland will create a strong pool of employees from which future leaders can emerge.

Ryland's three years of on-the-job training expose management trainees to all aspects of the residential construction or mortgage industry. Through each rotation, a mentor and performance evaluations will provide ongoing guidance and feedback to address a management trainee's needs and interests.

The Stats

	NUMBER OF EMPLOYEES		REVENUE	
	2006	2005	2006	2005
Total in the U.S.	2,810	3,200	$4.8 billion	$4.8 billion

Safeway, Inc.

5918 Stoneridge Mall Road
Pleasanton, CA 94588-3229

Diversity Leadership
Chris Nenoff
Human Resources Planning Manager,
 Diversity & Inclusion

Employment Contact
Claudia Rosa
Campus Relations, Corporate Talent
Acquisition
Phone: (925) 469-7926
Fax: (925) 467-2612
E-mail: Claudia.rosa@safeway.com
www.safeway.com/employment

Vickie Panko
Director of Talent Acquisition

Recruiting

Please list the schools/types of schools at which you recruit.

• Ivy League schools

• Other private schools

• Public state schools

• Historically black colleges and universities (HBCUs)

• Hispanic Serving Institutions (HSIs)

• Other predominantly minority and/or women's colleges

Do you have any special outreach efforts directed to encourage minority students and graduates to consider your firm?

• Hold a reception for minority students

• Advertise in minority student association publication(s) or other minority-focused publications

• Participate in/host minority student job fair(s) or other minority-focused job events

• Sponsor minority student association events

• Firm's employees participate on career panels at school

• Outreach to leadership of minority student organizations

• Scholarships or intern/fellowships for minority students

What activities does the firm undertake to attract minority and women employees?

• Partner programs with women and minority associations

• Conferences

• Participate at minority job fairs

• Seek referrals from other employees

• Utilize online job services

Do you use executive recruiting/search firms to seek to identify new diversity hires?

Yes

Internships and Co-ops

Corporate Summer Internship Program

Deadline for application: Open

Number of interns in the program in summer 2006 (internship) or 2006 (co-op): 27 undergraduate, eight MBA interns

Length of the program: 12 weeks

Web site for internship/co-op information:
www.safeway.com/employment

Internship areas: financial planning and analysis, marketing, initiatives and innovations, supply chain, corporate logistics, category management, information technology, pricing, procurement, consumer brands.

Internships in all areas within Safeway's corporate headquarters vary from year to year. Resumes in all areas are accepted, especially business, math, statistics, food science, nutrition, marketing, IT and finance.

Scholarships

Safeway offers undergraduate scholarships through DECA and graduate scholarships through NSHMBA.

Affinity Groups

The following affinity groups exist within Safeway:

• African-American Leadership Network

• Asian-American Leadership Group

• Hispanic Leadership Network

• Lesbian, Gay, Bisexual and Transgender Leadership Group

• Women's Leadership Network

Entry-Level Programs, Full-Time Opportunities and Training Programs

Finance Leadership Program—Jr. Analyst

Length of program: 12 months

Geographic location(s) of program: Pleasanton, Calif.

The Finance Leadership Program is a 12-month training and development program in which recent graduates work within a business unit to maximize the opportunity to learn and advance within the company. Junior analysts will be supported throughout the process with formal mentoring and on-the-job training to help build the financial acumen and skill set needed to be successful. This 12-month learning opportunity will allow the junior analyst to work within the financial planning and analysis organization, and to help develop strategies and analysis for expanding the business. Designed to attract top-tier undergraduate candidates, the leadership program provides rich analytical experience and career development. After successful completion of the training program, finance junior analysts will be placed as an analyst within the organization.

Marketing Trainee Program

Length of program: Six to nine months

Geographic location(s) of program: Pleasanton, Calif.

The Marketing Trainee Program is a three- to nine-month training program in which recent graduates will be introduced to marketing functions including pricing, procurement and category management. After successful completion of the trainee program, marketing trainees are placed in one of three areas of marketing.

Strategic Plan and Diversity Leadership

How does the firm's leadership communicate the importance of diversity to everyone at the firm?

Statement from CEO, training, diversity intranet site, diversity library and cultural heritage videos, and sponsored events by our affinity network groups.

Who has primary responsibility for leading diversity initiatives at your firm?

Chris Nenoff, human resources planning manager, diversity and inclusion.

Does your firm currently have a diversity committee?

Yes

If yes, please describe how the committee is structured, how often it meets, etc.

Yes, 13 diversity advisory boards with over 150 members. One senior-level board for all of Safeway, and 12 division boards. Individual advisory boards determine frequency of meetings, ranging from every month to once a quarter.

If yes, does the committee's representation include one or more members of the firm's management/executive committee (or the equivalent)?

Yes

Does the committee and/or diversity leader establish and set goals or objectives consistent with management's priorities?

Yes

Has the firm undertaken a formal or informal diversity program or set of initiatives aimed at increasing the diversity of the firm?

Yes, formal

How often does the firm's management review the firm's diversity progress/results?

Quarterly

	NUMBER OF EMPLOYEES		REVENUE	
	2006	2005	2006	2005
Total in the U.S.	201,000	172,905	$38 million	$34 million
Total outside the U.S.	N/A	32,115	N/A	$38 million
Total worldwide	N/A	205,020	N/A	$72 million

Retention and Professional Development

Please identify the specific steps you are taking to reduce the attrition rate of minority and women employees.

- Develop and/or support internal employee affinity groups (e.g., minority or women networks within the firm)
- Increase/review compensation relative to competition
- Increase/improve current work/life programs
- Succession plan includes emphasis on diversity
- Work with minority and women employees to develop career advancement plans

- Strengthen mentoring program for all employees, including minorities and women
- Professional skills development program, including minority and women employees

Diversity Mission Statement

Diversity is not simply a corporate initiative; it is a living attitude deeply embedded in the Safeway culture. At Safeway, we feel that our team should reflect the diversity of the people who shop in our stores. That is why we are pleased that *Fortune* magazine has recognized our dedication to hiring and promoting qualified people from all backgrounds. Our team brings you the quality and service that you expect from Safeway every day.

507

Diversity and Inclusion in Action

At Schering-Plough, we thrive on diversity. In fact, diversity and inclusion are key drivers of our work to create new medicines for the future.

The more than 33,500 men and women who work for Schering-Plough around the world represent a range of racial, ethnic and cultural backgrounds, ages, gender orientations and physical abilities. Our diversity and inclusion strategy recognizes the value of the various perspectives our colleagues bring. By learning from each other, we are better able to serve the doctors, patients and other customers who are counting on us.

Schering-Plough Corporation
2000 Galloping Hill Road
Kenilworth, NJ 07033-0530
www.schering-plough.com

An Equal Opportunity Employer Committed to Diversity

Schering-Plough

Schering-Plough Corporation

2000 Galloping Hill Road
Kenilworth, NJ 07033
Phone: (908) 298-4144
Fax: (908) 298-3505

Locations

We have a presence in more than 100 countries in North America, Europe, Asia, Africa, Australia and Latin America.

Diversity Leadership

Beth Timmons
Director, EEO & Workforce Diversity
1095 Morris Avenue
Union, NJ 07083
Phone: (908) 629-3238
Fax: (908) 629-3266
E-mail: Elizabeth.timmons@spcorp.com
www.schering-plough.com/careers

Recruiting

Please list the schools/types of schools at which you recruit.

• Ivy League schools

• Public state schools

• Historically black colleges and universities (HBCUs)

• Hispanic serving institutions (HSIs)

Do you have any special outreach efforts directed to encourage minority students to consider your firm?

• Hold a reception for minority students

• Advertise in minority student association publication(s)

• Participate in/host minority student job fair(s)

• Sponsor minority student association events

• Firm's employees participate on career panels at school

• Outreach to leadership of minority student organizations

• Scholarships or intern/fellowships for minority students

What activities does the firm undertake to attract minority and women employees?

• Partner programs with women and minority associations

• Participate at minority job fairs

Do you use executive recruiting/search firms to seek to identify new diversity hires?

Yes

Internships and Co-ops

INROADS, Research, Manufacturing and Finance

Deadline for application: February of each year

Pay: Depends on the education major of the intern; weekly pay

Length of the program: 11 weeks

Web site for internship/co-op information: Same as above

Strategic Plan and Diversity Leadership

How does the firm's leadership communicate the importance of diversity to everyone at the firm?

The firm communicates diversity information via the company web site, newsletter and meetings.

Who has primary responsibility for leading diversity initiatives at your firm?

Paul Graves, vice president, global staffing, diversity and public affairs.

Does your firm currently have a diversity committee?

Yes

Does the committee and/or diversity leader establish and set goals or objectives consistent with management's priorities?

Yes

Has the firm undertaken a formal or informal diversity program or set of initiatives aimed at increasing the diversity of the firm?

Yes, formal

How often does the firm's management review the firm's diversity progress/results?

Quarterly

How is the firm's diversity committee and/or firm management held accountable for achieving results?

Performance evaluations

The Stats

Employees

2007: 14,000 (U.S.); 19,500 (outside U.S.); 33,500 (worldwide)

Revenue

2006: $10.6 billion

Women represent 47 percent and minorities represent 25.6 percent of the U.S. population. There are a total of 10 board members. Women represent 20 percent and minorities represent 20 percent. The management team consists of 35 members. 14.3 percent are women and 11.4 percent are minority.

Retention and Professional Development

Please identify the specific steps you are taking to reduce the attrition rate of minority and women employees.

• Develop and/or support internal employee affinity groups (e.g., minority or women networks within the firm)

• Increase/review compensation relative to competition

• Increase/improve current work/life programs

• Succession plan includes emphasis on diversity

• Work with minority and women employees to develop career advancement plans

• Strengthen mentoring program for all employees, including minorities and women

• *Other:* Talent planning includes emphasis on diversity

ServiceMaster Company, The

860 Ridge Lake Boulevard
Memphis, TN 38120
Phone: (901) 597-1814
Fax: (901) 597-7002

Locations
Memphis, TN (HQ)
Branches nationwide

Diversity Leadership
Heath Russell
HR Compliance Programs Manager
E-mail: heath.russell@servicemaster.com

Recruiting

Please list the schools/types of schools at which you recruit.

• Private schools

• Public state schools

• Historically black colleges and universities (HBCUs)

• Hispanic serving institutions (HSIs)

• Native American tribal universities

Do you have any special outreach efforts directed to encourage minority students and graduates to consider your firm?

• Advertise in minority student association publication(s) or other minority-focused publications

• Participate in/host minority student job fair(s) or other minority-focused job events

• Outreach to leadership of minority student organizations

What activities does the firm undertake to attract minority and women employees?

• Participate at minority job fairs

• Seek referrals from other employees

• Utilize online job services

Do you use executive recruiting/search firms to seek to identify new diversity hires?

Yes

If yes, list all women- and/or minority-owned executive search/recruiting firms to which the firm paid a fee for placement services in the past 12 months:

DHR International Executive Search

Entry-Level Programs, Full-Time Opportunities and Training Programs

ACCEL

Length of program: Six months

Geographic location(s) of program: On-the-job training takes place at the branches; there are classroom sessions that take place in Memphis, Tenn.

The ServiceMaster ACCEL Leadership Program is a multi-faceted training program over a six-month period to prepare management candidates (MCs) for a leadership position in a ServiceMaster branch/service center. MCs develop skills as a leader of employees and customers in accordance with the business unit policy of providing superior service. Each MC is partnered with an assigned coach to develop an understanding of the business unit services through on-the-job training. The ACCEL Program consists of four intermittent practice-based sessions on orientation, engaging the employee, engaging the customer, and graduation with preparatory and performance assignments in the field between class meetings. All in-class training is conducted in Memphis, Tenn., and in business unit branches/service centers nationwide. Upon completion, management candidates will be assigned to a branch or service center and may be required to relocate.

Strategic Plan and Diversity Leadership

What trends in your industry affect your corporate diversity goals, strategies and/or internal or external alliances?

ServiceMaster is undertaking efforts to attract the growing Hispanic workforce through relationships with minority organizations.

Who has primary responsibility for leading diversity initiatives at your firm?

Heath Russell, HR compliance programs manager

Does your firm currently have a diversity committee?

No

The Stats

	NUMBER OF EMPLOYEES	
	2006	2005
Total in the U.S.	37,542	24,306

Demographic profile

Male: 76 percent, including management positions, laborers, operatives/service positions and sales

Female: 24 percent, including management positions, office and clerical, accounting and sales

ServiceMaster is 40 percent minority.

Retention and Professional Development

How do 2006 minority and female attrition rates generally compare to those experienced in the prior year period?

Lower than in prior years.

Please identify the specific steps you are taking to reduce the attrition rate of minority and women employees.

• Increase/review compensation relative to competition

• Increase/improve current work/life programs

• Adopt dispute resolution process

• Professional skills development program, including minority and women employees

Diversity Mission Statement

ServiceMaster recognizes that a diverse workforce enriches the company by broadening its employee base to include those with diverse skills and experiences and attracts clients by having an associate population that reflects its customer base. ServiceMaster values diversity among its associates and the positive effects of diversity on company culture and employee morale. We strive to recruit, retain and support associates from diverse backgrounds in order to create an inclusive work environment that recognizes the value of each individual.

Additional Information

With the goals of increasing diversity among our associate population, ServiceMaster is focusing its efforts on recruiting and retaining associates from diverse backgrounds. We are taking steps to attract minorities nationwide—in particular, members of the growing Hispanic population. We are presently in the process of translating our web site into Spanish, including providing information about career opportunities at ServiceMaster. We are also expanding our relationships with minority and women's outreach organizations in the communities where our branches are located.

Our leadership development program, ACCEL, trains future branch managers through a six-month program that includes classroom training, mentoring and in-field assignments. The program consists of two classroom sessions in Memphis, Tenn., lasting approximately four days each, and on-the-job training which requires the completion of online assignments. ACCEL develops a wide range of essential management skills including marketing, financial planning and budgeting, technical skills, recruiting and retention, and payroll procedures and processes.

One particular strength of our program is the mentoring component. Each management candidate is paired with an experienced coach who is a seasoned branch manager. The trainee benefits from the experience and knowledge of their coach and mentor. In fact, the program as a whole focuses on peer networking and support as the management candidates go through the program with the same group of peers and mentors, and therefore benefit from the collective experience and insight of the group at large.

Our leadership development program, our extensive minority recruitment efforts and our relationships with minority and women's organizations are just a few of the ways ServiceMaster demonstrates its commitment to diversity. We are always searching for new ways to attract and retain diverse and talented associates. As the makeup of the workforce in the U.S. grows and changes, we will, through our diversity efforts, keep pace with the changing needs of our current and future associates.

ServiceMaster is the parent company of Terminix, the TruGreen Companies, Merry Maids, American Home Shield, ServiceMaster Clean, Furniture Medic, AmeriSpec and InStar Services Group.

Shell Oil Company

910 Louisiana
Houston, TX 77002
www.shell.com

Diversity Leadership

Jeff Wallace
Diversity Outreach Administrator

Carmen Wright
Manager, Graduate Recruitment &
 University Relations

Employment Contact

Julie A. Sacco
Attraction & Branding Consultant
www.shell.com/careers

Recruiting

Please list the schools/types of schools at which you recruit.

• Private schools

• Public state schools

• Historically black colleges and universities (HBCUs)

• Hispanic serving institutions (HSIs)

Do you have any special outreach efforts directed to encourage minority students to consider your firm?

• Hold a reception for minority students

• Conferences

• Advertise in minority student association publication(s)

• Participate in/host minority student job fair(s)

• Sponsor minority student association events

• Firm's employees participate on career panels at schools

• Outreach to leadership of minority student organizations

• Scholarships or intern/fellowships for minority students

What activities does the firm undertake to attract minority and women employees?

• Partner programs with women and minority associations

• Conferences

• Participate at minority job fairs

• Seek referrals from other employees

• Utilize online job services

Do you use executive recruiting/search firms to seek to identify new diversity hires?

Yes

Internships and Co-ops

Shell Internship Program

Deadline for application: Year round, best availability October to March

Length of the program: 10 to 12 weeks

Web site for internship/co-op information: www.shell.com/careers

Come and experience working with us

What's working life like at a world-class company? Could Shell be the place to start your career? If you're a talented and promising individual, you could get a taste of working with us during the summer. A paid internship with Shell gives you real work responsibility and the chance to test your abilities on genuine business challenges.

To ensure that you get the maximum benefit from your experience with us, your internship will be tailored to your specific abilities and interests, and will be certain to provide you with an opportunity to prove yourself in a true business environment. The work experience also gives you the opportunity to find out whether you and Shell are right for each other.

A Great Opportunity

• See inside the energy industry

• Take part in real projects

• Try out business challenges

• Work with Shell employees or other students

• Get feedback from senior Shell managers

• Track the long-term results of your work

Throughout your time with us, your performance will be assessed and you will receive structured feedback in order to further develop your skills, knowledge and business acumen.

We have a number of summer internship opportunities available for both technical and commercial students. Most take place during the summer in the U.S. However, as a global organization, there will be always be a number of international opportunities for exceptional candidates.

Scholarships

Shell Oil Company Technical Scholarship

Deadline for application for the scholarship program: December 31st

Scholarship award amount: Undergraduate—$5,000 per year (four-year renewable scholarship or until bachelor's degree requirements are completed, whichever occurs first); technical—$2,500 total (payable over a two-year period)

Shell Oil Company offers scholarships to selected students pursuing two-year technical training in process technology or industrial instrumentation or a four-year college degree in engineering or geosciences at certain colleges. Scholarship recipients will be selected on a competitive basis by a selection committee and will be notified of their award in the early summer after the submission of their application.

To qualify you must:

- Be enrolled in an undergraduate program
- Be a U.S. citizen or a permanent resident of the United States
- Be enrolled full-time and a sophomore, junior or senior at certain institutions
- Have a minimum 3.2 GPA, which must be maintained throughout your participation in the program
- Major in one of the following disciplines: Geology, geophysics or physics; chemical, civil, electrical, mechanical, petroleum, geological or geophysical engineering

Technical Training Program

- Be a U.S. citizen or a permanent resident of the United States

- Be enrolled full time and have completed at least 12 semester hours at certain community college technical schools
- Have a minimum 3.0 GPA, which must be maintained throughout your participation in the program
- Major in process technology, industrial instrumentation or a related field within the oil industry

Affinity Groups

- Network Next (Generation X Network)
- Society Absent of Individual Limitations (SAIL)
- Shell Asian Pacific Employee Network Group (SAPENG)
- Shell Black Network Group (SBNG)
- Support, Equality, & Awareness at Shell (SEA Shell)
- Shell Hispanic Employee Network (SHEN)
- Support Equality Awareness
- Women Adding Value Everywhere (WAVE)
- Women's Information Network (WIN)
- Shell Progressive African-American Network (SPAAN)

Strategic Plan and Diversity Leadership

Who has primary responsibility for leading diversity initiatives at your firm?

Director of diversity

Does your firm currently have a diversity committee?

Yes

Has the firm undertaken a formal or informal diversity program or set of initiatives aimed at increasing the diversity of the firm?

Yes, formal

515

I started working at Sodexho after I graduated. I thought I was finding my first job, but what I found was a place I could create a lifelong career.

Making every day a better day

I found a career, a community and a future.

Sodexho is more than a place to work. It's where I'm building my career. I became part of North America's leading food and facilities management company – and part of a diverse, inclusive community of employees and customers that make each day something special. Sodexho means hard work and excellent customer service, no matter which direction I choose for my career.

www.sodexhoUSA.com

At Sodexho, we value workforce diversity. EOE. M/F/D/V.

Making every day a better day

Sodexho

9801 Washingtonian Boulevard
Gaithersburg, MD 20878
www.sodexhoUSA.com

Locations
Gaithersburg, MD (HQ)

Diversity Leadership
Michelle Thomas
Senior Manager Diversity Recruiting
Phone: (404) 635-0776
E-mail: michelle.thomas@sodexhosusa.com

Recruiting

Please list the schools/types of schools at which you recruit.

Sodexho recruits at more than 100 colleges and universities including: culinary colleges, culturally diverse colleges and universities, historically black colleges and universities, Hispanic serving institutes and women's colleges.

Do you have any special outreach efforts that are directed to encourage minority students to consider your firm?

• *Conferences:* National Society of Minority Hospitality, HBCU Hospitality Management Consortium, National Black MBA Association

• Advertise in minority student association publication(s)

• Participate in/host minority student job fair(s)

• Sponsor minority student association events

• Firm's employees participate on career panels at schools

• Outreach to leadership of minority student organizations

• Scholarships or intern/fellowships for minority students

What activities does the firm undertake to attract minority and women employees?

• Partner programs with women and minority associations

• Conferences

• Participate at minority job fairs

• Seek referrals from other employees

• Utilize online job services

• Minority trade journals

Do you use executive recruiting/search firms to seek to identify new diversity hires?

Yes

Internships and Co-ops

Deadline for application: January 31, 2008

Number of interns in the program in summer 2007 (internship) or 2007 (co-op): 40

Pay: $460/week

Length of the program: 10 weeks

Web site for internship/co-op information:
www.sodexhousa.com/careers.asp

Interns are assigned to operating locations throughout the country. They are assigned a mentor, participate in bi-weekly professional development webinars, complete a combination of our "Beginning Your Career" management training program, special projects and attend an intern orientation session.

Scholarships

• HACU (as part of internship program)

• HIRE Scholarship co-sponsor via NSMH

Deadline for application for the scholarship program: Varies
Scholarship award amount: Varies

Scholarship programs are through specific third party organizations.

Affinity Groups/Employee Networks

• African Leadership Forum (AALF)
• Sodexho Organization of Latinos (SOL)
• Women's Network Group (WING)
• Pan Asian Network Group (PANG)
• People Respecting Individual Diversity and Equality (PRIDE)

Information on Employee Network Groups is available through our home page at www.sodexhousa.com.

Entry-Level Programs, Full-Time Opportunities and Training Programs

Beginning your Career

Length of program: 90 days

Geographic location(s) of program: At individual location sites

Sodexho University offers an in-depth management orientation process that includes a three-day orientation event (Beginning Your Career) combined with a self-study managerial skills program (Building Your Career—The First 90 Days). During the three-day classroom experience, managers are introduced to Sodexho's culture and philosophies through eight workbooks from the "First 90 Days" kit.

Sodexho University offers many training programs (online and facilitated) as well as accredited degree programs. Through Sodexho University, you have access to diverse learning opportunities specially designed to help you give your best to our clients and customers. Experts from each business line contribute to learning tools designed for you, the Sodexho employee. Flexible options include self-study, instructor-led classes and online learning.

Strategic Plan and Diversity Leadership

How does the firm's leadership communicate the importance of diversity to everyone at the firm?

Sodexho uses a variety of vehicles to communicate our diversity strategy to everyone in the company. Throughout the year, we use our weekly electronic bulletin to communicate important information relative to our diversity efforts. We also have a page on our intranet for diversity. We use required training and live meetings to reinforce our message and annually report our progress with the *Diversity and Inclusion and Equal Employment Opportunity Annual Report.*

Who has primary responsibility for leading diversity initiatives at your firm?

Senior Vice President and Chief Diversity Officer Rohini Anand sets the direction and strategy. All managers, however, are responsible for the implementation of that strategy and are held accountable through a direct link to their incentive compensation for diversity results.

Does your firm currently have a diversity committee?

Sodexho has a diversity leadership council.

If yes, please describe how the committee is structured, how often it meets, etc.

Sodexho's Diversity Leadership Council (DLC) is headed up by the president and CEO, the chief diversity and chief human resources officers and several members of the executive team. The DLC meets monthly. Additionally, each market segment has a diversity council.

If yes, does the committee's representation include one or more members of the firm's management/executive committee (or the equivalent)?

Yes

Total executives on the committee: There are seven members of the executive team on the DLC. Executive team participation in market segment diversity councils varies across the country.

Does the committee and/or diversity leader establish and set goals or objectives consistent with management's priorities?

Yes

Has the firm undertaken a formal or informal diversity program or set of initiatives aimed at increasing the diversity of the firm?

Yes. Sodexho has an integrated diversity strategy. More information may be obtained on our web site: www.sodexhousa.com.

How often does the firm's management review the firm's diversity progress/results?

Diversity progress is reviewed quarterly alongside financial results.

How is the firm's diversity committee and/or firm management held accountable for achieving results?

There is a direct link to diversity performance in every bonus eligible manager's incentive plan. Progress is measured using an innovative scorecard that tracks both qualitative and quantitative results.

The Stats

	NUMBER OF EMPLOYEES	REVENUE
	2006	2006
Total in the U.S.	125,000	$6.3 billion

Retention and Professional Development

How do 2006 minority and female attrition rates generally compare to those experienced in the prior year period?

About the same as in prior years.

Please identify the specific steps you are taking to reduce the attrition rate of minority and women employees.

• Employee network groups

• Increase/improve current work/life programs

• Succession plan includes emphasis on diversity

• Mentoring

• Professional skills development program, including minority and women employees

• Candidate selection review panels

Diversity Mission Statement

Diversity and inclusion is an inherent part of our culture and business growth. The energy and talent at all levels of the organization is unleashed, resulting in innovative solutions that contribute to a spirit of team, service and progress. With diversity and inclusion as a competitive advantage, Sodexho is an employer of choice and the benchmark for customers, clients and communities domestically and globally.

Additional Information

Sodexho's diversity journey began several years ago with the goal of not only increasing diversity and inclusion within our organization, but also to become the benchmark by which all other organizations are measured. Sodexho has a clear diversity vision that provides the direction and ambition for our focused diversity strategy. This strategy takes into consideration our people, our customers, clients, shareholders and the communities we serve.

We know that our work is not yet done. We are, however, honored to join many prestigious organizations after receiving recognition for our unwavering efforts to provide a business environment that leverages the diversity of our workforce, and in providing opportunities for all individuals to contribute to the best of their ability.

Awards Received in 2006:

• Strategic Examples of Excellence in Diversity by MFHA

• Top 50 Companies for Corporate by *Hispanic Business Magazine*

• DiversityFIRST Award—Rohini Anand—by Texas Diversity Council

• International Innovation in Diversity Award by Profiles in *Diversity Journal*

• Top 50 Company for Diversity (#14) by *DiversityInc*

• Top 10 Companies for Executive Women by *DiversityInc*

• Top 10 Companies for Persons with Disabilities by *DiversityInc*

• Top Companies for Asian American Employees by *Asian Enterprise Magazine*

• Top100 Employers for 2006 by *The Black Collegian*

• PR News CSR Award—Outstanding Diversity Annual Report—Honorable Mention

• WFF Director's Award—Lorna Donatone—by The Women's Food Service Forum

• Top 10 Best Companies for Hispanics by *Hispanic Business Magazine*

• 2006 Career FOCUS Eagle Award—Emeka Okeani—by NELI

• Employer of the Year by WI Rehabilitation Association's Job Placement Division

• Community Service Award by Washington Metropolitan Area Corporate Counsel Association

Sprint Nextel Corporation

2001 Edmund Halley Drive
Reston, VA 20191
Phone: (703) 433-4000

Employment Contact

Tammy Edwards
Director, Inclusion and Diversity
2001 Edmund Halley Drive
Reston, VA 20191
Phone: (703) 433-4000
www.sprint.com/careers

Recruiting

Does your firm annually recruit at any of the following types of institutions?

- *Public state schools:* Iowa State University, Kansas State University, Truman State University, University of Nebraska–Lincoln, University of Kansas, University of Maryland, University of Missouri–Columbia, University of Missouri–Kansas City, University of Missouri–Rolla, University of Virginia, Central Missouri State University, Florida A&M University, Florida State University, Northwest Missouri State University, Pittsburg State University, Purdue University, Southwest Missouri State University, University of Florida, Virginia Tech, Kansas City, MO Community Colleges
- Historically black colleges and universities (HBCUs)

Do you have any special outreach efforts directed to encourage minority students to consider your firm?

- Hold a reception for minority students
- Advertise in minority student association publication(s)
- Participate in/host minority student job fair(s)
- Sponsor minority student association events
- Firm's employees participate on career panels at schools
- Outreach to leadership of minority student organizations
- Scholarships or intern/fellowships for minority students

What activities does the firm undertake to attract minority and women employees?

- Partner programs with women and minority associations
- *Conferences:* NABA, NSBE, SHPE, SWE, NSHMBA, NBM-BAA
- Participate at minority job fairs
- Seek referrals from other employees
- Utilize online job services

Do you use executive recruiting/search firms to seek to identify new diversity hires?

No

Internships and Co-ops

Deadline for application: Varies depending on campus interviews for fall and spring

Pay: $10 to $22 hourly wage, depending on school classification and prior intern experience

Length of the program: 10 to 12 weeks

Percentage of interns/co-ops in the program who receive offers of full-time employment: 60 percent

Web site for internship/co-op information:
www.sprint.com/hr/college_intern.html

The Internship Program is designed to enhance Sprint's recruitment efforts and reinforce the relationships developed through these efforts. The program objectives are to:

- Promote meaningful assignments to enhance the student's learning
- Provide intern program orientation materials to students and their supervisors
- Coordinate opportunities for interaction with Sprint managers, executives and other interns
- Enhance recruiting efforts with conversion to hire

Internships are 10-12 weeks in duration. During the internship, the intern learns about the company, the department functions and gains valuable work experience enhancing his or her educational goals. Sprint hires interns based on education and experience and business needs. They are placed in business sales, consumer sales, finance, information or permanent residents, through scholarships of up to $5,000 and paid summer internships at Sprint locations. The program accepts juniors majoring in accounting, business administration, economics, finance, engineering (computer, electrical, industrial, management), mathematics, statistics and management information systems.

Scholarships

Sprint Minority Engineering Scholarship Program

Deadline for application for the scholarship program: April 1st

Scholarship award amount: Full scholarship

Web site or other contact information for scholarship:
www.kcmetro.edu/pubs/campusScholarshipLists.pdf

The Sprint Minority Engineering Scholarship Program is co-sponsored by the Kansas City Metropolitan Community Colleges, the University of Missouri-Rolla and Sprint to attract, encourage and support promising minority students wishing to enter the field of engineering or computer science.

UNCF/Sprint Scholars Program

Deadline for application for the scholarship program: January 1st

Scholarship award amount: $5,000 annual award

Web site or other contact information for scholarship:
www.uncf.org

The UNCF/Sprint Scholars Program provides educational opportunities for African-Americans, American Indians/Alaskan natives, Asian Pacific Islander Americans and Hispanic American students who are U.S. citizens.

Affinity Groups

Diamond Network

The Diamond Network is an African-American-focused employee resource group whose mission is to aid Sprint in recruiting, retaining, developing and promoting African-American employees. The vision of the Diamond Network is to be recognized as an organization that promotes inclusion and diversity as a competitive advantage for Sprint. The goals of the Diamond Network are to:

• Represent Sprint in recruitment activities

• Foster professional development

• Provide networking opportunities

• Promote diversity and inclusion

Enlace

Vision: To be a Sprint resource for communicating, supporting and engaging the Hispanic community, employees and the Hispanic culture.

Mission: Enlace is committed to supporting the partnership with Sprint and the Hispanic community. From community involvement, Hispanic cultural enrichment to employee development and market initiatives, Enlace is dedicated to promoting diversity.

Our Commitments:

• *Community involvement:* To strengthen relationships and opportunities between Enlace and the Hispanic community

• *Cultural enrichment:* To encourage the learning of and appreciation for Hispanic heritage and culture

• *Employee development:* To encourage and promote self-development and career employment

• *Market initiative:* To support Sprint initiatives that provide a competitive advantage for Hispanic marketing initiatives

Entry-level Programs, Full-time Opportunities and Training Programs

The programs are currently being redesigned.

Strategic Plan and Diversity Leadership

How does the firm's leadership communicate the importance of diversity to everyone at the firm?

Sprint communicates it's commitment to inclusion via e-mail, newsletters, training, web casts and executive presentations.

Who has primary responsibility for leading diversity initiatives at your firm?

Tammy Edwards, director inclusion and diversity

Does your firm currently have a diversity committee?

Yes

If yes, please describe how the committee is structured, how often it meets, etc.

The Sprint Executive Inclusion Council is composed of executives from various business units. The council is chaired by Gary Forsee, CEO.

If yes, does the committee's representation include one or more members of the firm's management/executive committee (or the equivalent)?

Yes

Does the committee and/or diversity leader establish and set goals or objectives consistent with management's priorities?

Yes

Has the firm undertaken a formal or informal diversity program or set of initiatives aimed at increasing the diversity of the firm?

Yes, formal

How often does the firm's management review the firm's diversity progress/results?

Quarterly

How is the firm's diversity committee and/or firm management held accountable for achieving results?

The success of the company's inclusion initiatives is part of the executive's performance review evaluations.

Retention and Professional Development

Please identify the specific steps you are taking to reduce the attrition rate of minority and women employees.

• Develop and/or support internal employee affinity groups (e.g., minority or women networks within the firm)

• Increase/improve current work/life programs
• Succession plan includes emphasis on diversity
• Work with minority and women employees to develop career advancement plans
• Strengthen mentoring program for all employees, including minorities and women
• Professional skills development program, including minority and women employees

Additional Information

To learn more about Sprint's inclusion initiatives, please visit www.sprint.com/diversity.

Staples, Inc.

500 Staples Drive
Framingham, MA 01702
Phone: (508) 253-5000
Fax: (508) 253-4227

Employment Contact
Catharine Jennings
College Relations Specialist
E-mail: catharine.jennings@staples.com
www.staples.com/jobs

Recruiting

Please list the schools/types of schools at which you recruit.

• *Ivy League schools:* Harvard, Dartmouth, MIT

• *Other private schools:* Northeastern University, Babson, Bentley, Boston College, Boston University, Worcester Polytechnic Institute, Providence, Suffolk, Wentworth, Syracuse

• *Public state schools:* UMASS Amherst, UMASS Lowell, UMASS Dartmouth, Arizona State University, Ohio State University, Michigan State University, Pennsylvania State University, Framingham State, Bridgewater, Fitchburg, RISD, NEIA

• *Historically black colleges and universities (HBCUs):* Morehouse, Spelman, Clark Atlanta, Howard

Do you have any special outreach efforts directed to encourage minority students to consider your firm?

• Hold a reception for minority students

• *Conferences:* National Society of Hispanic MBAs (NSHMBA), National Black MBA Association (NBMBAA), Association of Latino Professionals in Finance and Accounting (ALPFA), National Association of Black Accountants (NABA), National Association of Asian American Professionals

• Participate in/host minority student job fair(s)

• Outreach to leadership of minority student organizations

• Scholarships or intern/fellowships for minority students

• *Other:* African American Student Union of HBS; member of Leadership Assessment Center Board at Clark Atlanta University

What activities does the firm undertake to attract minority and women employees?

• Partner programs with women and minority associations

• *Conferences:* National Society of Hispanic MBAs (NSHMBA), National Black MBA Association (NBMBAA), Association of Latino Professionals in Finance and Accounting (ALPFA), National Association of Black Accountants (NABA), National Association of Asian American Professionals (NAAAP)

• Participate at minority job fairs

• Seek referrals from other employees

• Utilize online job services

We also have our diversity team go on campus and speak to classes at local schools about diversity in the workplace. We take at least two INROADS interns each summer.

Do you use executive recruiting/search firms to seek to identify new diversity hires?

Yes

Internships and Co-ops

Deadline for application: April 30th for internships; March 1st or October 1st for co-ops

Number of interns in the program in summer 2006 (internship) or 2006 (co-op): 42 interns, 24 co-ops

Pay: $10 to $12 hourly for interns; $12 to $30 for grad interns; $16 to $20 for co-ops

Length of the program: We have spring, summer and fall internships, and some are full time for summer and continue part time into fall and spring. We also have six-month co-ops.

Percentage of interns/co-ops in the program who receive offers of full-time employment: 25 percent

Web site for internship/co-op information: www.staplescampuscareers.com

We have interns in our home office in many different functional groups, including merchandising, information systems, finance/accounting, marketing, strategy, public relations and media. Students must have a GPA of 3.0, and typically our opportunities are best suited for rising sophomores or above. In addition to the day-to-day responsibilities of the internship, Staples interns are given the opportunity to participate in the Lunch and Learn speaker series, which gives the intern the opportunity to hear from and learn from senior level executives in the company. Past luncheons have focused on learning about Staples site usability, Staples sports marketing and Staples brands. We take the interns on a tour of one of our stores and they get to collectively have lunch and Q&A with the

CEO. It is a great summer experience that is capped off with Intern Presentation Day—an opportunity for the interns to strut their stuff and give a presentation on what they did during their internship.

Scholarships

Staples participates with many national diversity organizations to give scholarships to minority students affiliated with those organizations. Students should contact Catharine Jennings to learn more about how to qualify.

Entry-Level Programs, Full-Time Opportunities and Training Programs

Logistics Rotational Program

Length of program: Two years

Geographic location(s) of program: Multiple U.S. locations

General Format:

Each participant will be placed in one of the following positions for the described period of time:

• Supervisor-in-training—fulfillment center (12 months)
• Supervisor-in-training—service delivery operation (six months)
• Project manager-in-training—corporate office (six months)

During each of the rotations, the associate will report to an operations manager who will be responsible for exposing the associate to all departments and functions of the location. Specified training plans for each piece of the rotation ensures both classroom and on-the-job learning. Also, each associate will be partnered with a mentor to provide guidance and direction throughout the entire two-year program.

Preferred Customer Account Manager

With just the right combination and innovation, Staples has grown into a $16.1 billion world-class powerhouse of the office supply industry. As part of our dedicated and talented sales force, you will be part of an industry leader.

This is an inside sales role.

The Account Management Preferred Customer Program focuses on retaining and developing above-average Staples business delivery customers. Monthly contacts range from sales calls focusing on differing products and categories to service escalation calls. The account manager is wholly responsible for the satisfaction, growth and development of his/her account base of approximately 650 accounts. Utilize internal resources to overcome obstacles. Discover and analyze prospects needs, determine which

features/benefits of Staples will appeal the most to the customer and present those features/benefits to the customer. Create a sense of satisfaction as related to purchasing with Staples based on offers presented. Meet or exceed productivity requirements. Collect marketing intelligence and customer data as required. Leverage marketing dollars used throughout Staples, Inc., to proactively sell Staples products. Generate sales dollars for Staples business delivery. Appropriately channel leads for Staples contract division. Solve all service escalation for every account managed, proactively contact the party responsible for solving the customer's dilemma and follow through to ensure customer satisfaction. Act as the customer's primary liaison to Staples with regard to product, pricing, billing, etc. Exceptional decision-making skills are necessary.

Qualifications

• Strong oral and written communication skills
• Proven ability to set and adjust priorities based on activity
• Works well in a fast-paced environment with little supervision
• Strong sales skills
• Strong customer service skills
• Proficient PC skills, including Microsoft Office

We need driven, smart sales executives who can THINK BIG to develop new and existing business, open new doors and establish and build accounts. You must be a self-starter with proven energy and motivation, willing to develop and close sales leads. You must be results-oriented, self-motivated and driven by both financial and career opportunities. Excellent verbal and written communication skills are essential objectives. Time management skills are a must! Industry knowledge is a plus. As a Staples associate, you can expect a competitive base salary, monthly commission plan, comprehensive health care benefits, 401(k), employee stock purchase plan, union reimbursement and ongoing training and development.

Customer Service Rotation

Length of program: Two years

Geographic location(s) of program: Kentucky; Hackensack, N.J.; Framingham, Mass.; Rochester, N.Y.

General Format:

Each participant will be placed in one of the following positions for the described period of time:

• Manager-in-training—Kentucky call center (12 months)
• Manager-in-training—Rochester or Hackensack call center (six months)
• Manager-in-training—Corporate office/service improvement office (six months)

During each of the rotations, the associate will report to a manager who will be responsible for exposing the associate to all departments and functions of the location. Specified training plans for each piece of the rotation ensures both classroom and on-the-job learning.

Also, each associate will be partnered with a mentor to provide guidance and direction throughout the entire two-year program.

Position Locations:

• Kentucky call center—Florence, Ky.

• Rochester call center—Rochester, N.Y.

• Hackensack call center—Hackensack, N.J.

• Corporate office—Framingham, Mass.

Strategic Plan and Diversity Leadership

How does the firm's leadership communicate the importance of diversity to everyone at the firm?

Diversity messages are interwoven within general corporate updates, either via satellite broadcast, *Staples News,* or internal communications.

Who has primary responsibility for leading diversity initiatives at your firm?

Doreen Nichols, VP of associate relations and global diversity

Does your firm currently have a diversity committee?

No

Has the firm undertaken a formal or informal diversity program or set of initiatives aimed at increasing the diversity of the firm?

Yes, informal

How often does the firm's management review the firm's diversity progress/results?

Annually

How is the firm's diversity committee and/or firm management held accountable for achieving results?

Goals are set for the recruiting department, and this is a component of each recruiter's performance appraisal.

The Stats

	NUMBER OF EMPLOYEES		REVENUE	
	2006	2005	2006	2005
Total in the U.S.	74,000	69,000	$18.2 billion	$16.1 billion

Retention and Professional Development

How do 2006 minority and female attrition rates generally compare to those experienced in the prior year period?

About the same as in prior years.

Please identify the specific steps you are taking to reduce the attrition rate of minority and women employees.

Succession plan includes emphasis on diversity.

Diversity Mission Statement

Reflecting the face of our customer through diversity is a commitment deeply embedded in Staples' corporate culture. We are dedicated to providing a work environment of inclusion and acceptance, and look for associates who will also embrace these values.

Additional Information

To understand why diversity is so important to us, you don't have to look farther than your nearest Staples store. Our customers— whether they're shopping in our stores, online, or through Staples contract or business delivery—are a mosaic of different cultures, ethnicities, genders and ages. So it's not surprising that we strive for a workforce and a supplier network that reflect the diverse multicultural "face" of our customers.

Staples has been quietly building a workforce of diverse and talented associates, developing a network of diverse suppliers and supporting diversity in our communities through the Staples Foundation for Learning. In recognition of our achievement in this area, *DiversityInc* magazine named Staples one of the Top 10 Companies for Recruitment and Retention of a Diverse Workforce in 2004.

We know that's much to do, but the results are starting to show. Our recent focus on diverse college recruitment initiatives and partnerships with professional organizations has been highly successful. Our supplier diversity program was the first in the industry to build a network of established regional Minority Women Business Enterprise (MWBE) partners, which allows customers to purchase directly from and be billed by diversity suppliers. In our local communities, we support diversity through the Staples Foundation for Learning, which provides job skills and educational opportunities for people of all backgrounds, with a special emphasis on disadvantaged youth.

At Staples, we are proud of our commitment to diversity and the great strides we've made toward achieving it. Our success is as multi-faceted as our associates and customers.

Starwood Hotels & Resorts Worldwide

1111 Westchester Avenue
White Plains, NY 10604
Phone: (914) 640-8487

Locations
Located in over 85 countries globally.

Employment Contact
Mary Anne McNulty
Manager, Staffing & College Relations
E-mail:
Maryanne.mcnulty@starwoodhotels.com
www.starwood.jobs

Recruiting

Please list the schools/types of schools at which you recruit.

• *Ivy League schools*

• *Other private schools:* Cornell University, Boston University, University of Delaware, University of Houston, University of Massachusetts, Purdue University, University of Nevada-Las Vegas, University of Hawaii

• *Public state schools:* Washington State University, Michigan State University, Penn State University

• *Historically black colleges and universities (HBCUs):* Bethune-Cookman College, Morgan State University

Do you have any special outreach efforts directed to encourage minority students to consider your firm?

• *Conferences:* NBMBAA, NSHMBA, NSMH

• Advertise in minority student association publication(s)

• *Participate in/host minority student job fair(s):* NSMH, Thurgood Marshall

• Sponsor minority student association events

• Outreach to leadership of minority student organizations

• *Scholarships or intern/fellowships for minority students:* Hispanic College Fund, NSMH scholarship support

What activities does the firm undertake to attract minority and women employees?

• Partner programs with women and minority associations

• Conferences: OCA, NSMH, NSHMBA, NBMBAA, NAACP

• Participate at minority job fairs

Internships and Co-ops

INROADS

Pay: Varies by geographic placement

Length of the program: 10 to 12 weeks

Web site for internship/co-op information: www.starwoodcareers.com

Entry-Level Programs, Full-Time Opportunities and Training Programs

Management Training Program

Length of program: Six months

Geographic location(s) of program: Across U.S.

Starwood's Management Training Program combines professional development, mentorships, and immersion into the service-oriented realm of hotel operations. Associates in this program will be poised for entry into management positions including rooms, food and beverage, sales, revenue management, human resources, catering/convention services, accounting and more. At the completion of a 12-week rotational program, each associate is placed in a position of responsibility at the same hotel where the training was completed.

Strategic Plan and Diversity Leadership

Who has primary responsibility for leading diversity initiatives at your firm?

Shelley Freeman, director of diversity

Does your firm currently have a diversity committee?

Yes

If yes, does the committee's representation include one or more members of the firm's management/executive committee (or the equivalent)?

Yes

Additional Information

What we Believe: Diversity and Inclusion

Culture of Inclusion

At Starwood, we recognize and appreciate the diversity of people, ideas and cultures, and believe that diverse experiences and people are required for our business to succeed. We strive to create an environment that embraces the diversity of all of our constituencies: associates, customers, guests, owners, suppliers and shareholders. We support a culture of inclusion where associates at every level, including the full range of backgrounds, cultures and orientations can reach their maximum potential.

We are passionate about attracting and retaining the best and the brightest talent, unleashing their potential and stretching them beyond their comfort zone. Through this diversity of viewpoints, we deliver unprecedented business results by satisfying all of our guests and customers with superior innovation and service.

Built on Diversity

Starwood Hotels & Resorts is a global organization that is built on diversity. With six distinct brands: Sheraton® Hotels & Resorts, Four Points® by Sheraton, St. Regis® Hotels & Resorts, The Luxury Collection®, Le Méridien®, W Hotels® and Westin® Hotels & Resorts. Operating in over 95 countries, we maintain an associate and customer base as diverse as the world's population. Each brand's distinctive appeal affords us a unique position in the global marketplace that caters to travelers of all backgrounds and from almost every culture. Therefore, creating an environment of inclusion for our associates, guests and suppliers isn't just the right thing to do, it is the very core of our business.

National Partnerships

Focusing on blending and mining the talents of our more than 145,000 associates from around the world and taking care of our guests who frequent our more than 850 Starwood properties is a commitment that begins at the top of our organization, but is the shared responsibility of each associate. By creating national partnerships with associations focused on serving the needs and concerns of many types of visible and invisible differences—race, gender and sexual orientation, to name a few—we hope to have a far reaching impact by making a difference in the markets in which we operate and the guests we serve.

Diversity Council

Our Diversity Council is made up of senior leaders at Starwood. Its role is to partner with other company leaders to drive the strategy forward with the support of a dedicated staff of change agents in our office of diversity and inclusion.

Just as we approach other vital business imperatives, our Corporate Diversity Council has developed a strategy and multiyear plan for accelerating change, particularly in the area of representation. As an organization, we are committed to setting the pace for the industry, raising the bar on how we deploy and develop associates and, in the process, understanding how diversity yields business success.

Positive Messages

It takes time. We are committed to the task. Our associates must know that embracing diversity and learning how to mine different talents and opinions in a business like ours improves our company, our product and all of us as individuals. Valuing individual differences is not new here; for years, we have offered domestic partner benefits for all of our associates without hesitation. Through inclusion training, we reinforce positive messages. By continuing to introduce metrics, like linking compensation to achieving diversity goals, and clarifying the diversity goals of each department, there is a shared understanding of how serious we are about making this an unconscious part of how we do business everyday, everywhere, for everyone.

This is the Starwood way.

State Street Corporation

2 Avenue de Lafayette
Boston, MA 02111

Locations

State Street has operations in 26 countries serving more than 100 markets.

Employment Contact

Maia Germain
VP College Relations and Diversity Staffing
State Street Corp.
2 Avenue de Lafayette
Boston, MA 02111
Phone: (617) 662-1080
E-mail: mgermain@statestreet.com
www.statestreet.com (Click on Careers, then Job Opportunities)

Recruiting

Please list the schools/types of schools at which you recruit.

- Ivy League schools
- Other private schools
- Public state schools
- Historically black colleges and universities (HBCUs)
- Hispanic serving institutions (HSIs)
- Other predominantly minority and/or women's colleges

Do you have any special outreach efforts directed to encourage minority students to consider your firm?

- Participate in/host minority student job fair(s)
- Sponsor minority student association events
- Firm's employees participate on career panels at schools
- Outreach to leadership of minority student organizations
- *Other:* INROADS, Posse Foundation, Year Up, Monster Diversity Leadership Conference

What activities does the firm undertake to attract minority and women employees?

- Partner programs with women and minority associations
- Conferences
- Participate at minority job fairs
- Seek referrals from other employees
- Utilize online job services

Do you use executive recruiting/search firms to seek to identify new diversity hires?

Yes

Internships and Co-ops

INROADS; PIC (Private Industry Council); Year Up; internal programs

Deadline for application: Open, depending on program

Number of interns in the program in summer 2006 (internship) or 2006 (co-op): 300+

Length of the program: Eight weeks or longer

Web site for internship/co-op information:
www.statestreet.com/careers

In the United States, State Street's eight employee affinity groups will play an active role in this process. These groups include an

- Asian Professionals Group
- Bible Study Group
- Black Professionals Group
- Chinese Affinity Group
- Disability Awareness Alliance
- PRIDE
- Jewish Professionals Network
- Indian Employee Network
- Irish-American Professionals Network
- Latin American Professional Network
- Muslim Employee Network
- Professional Women's Network.
- State Street Connect
- Working Parents Group
- Zhejiang Professionals Network

Group members meet throughout the year to share ideas and experiences, mentor and network, and sponsor internal programs around national and international events like Black History Month, International Women's Day, Asian and Latin American Heritage

Months and PRIDE. All of the affinity groups have the support of the corporation and are provided a discretionary budget to use in outreach, community service, membership promotion, etc. State Street affinity groups are publicized in employee communications, new employee orientation, meeting announcements and through the company's Intranet.

Entry-Level Programs, Full-Time Opportunities and Training Programs

Fund Accountant, Portfolio Accountant, Portfolio Administrator

Length of program: Two weeks (each)

Geographic location(s) of program: Boston/Quincy, Mass.

Strategic Plan and Diversity Leadership

State Street's global inclusion initiative brings together a team of employee opinion leaders from across the corporation representing myriad levels; cultural, professional and lifestyle backgrounds; geographic locations and walks of life. The goal of the initiative is to provide all employees and managers with the tools, guidance and opportunity to perform to their potential and be valued, engaged and productive.

A global inclusion steering committee, comprised of representatives from State Street's senior leadership globally, leads the effort and is responsible for setting strategy and ultimately driving change centered on the work environment, gender/ethnicity and culture issues, internal mobility, management development and turnover management.

The steering committee is supported by three global inclusion regional groups, representing North America, Europe and the Asia/Pacific area. These groups are actively working to complete recommendations on improving the quality of working life at the regional and corporate levels, currently focusing on management practices, recruitment and retention of a diverse work force and improved communication effectiveness.

The Stats

	NUMBER OF EMPLOYEES		REVENUE	
	2006	**2005**	**2006**	**2005**
Total in the U.S.	13,117	13,143	$3.62 billion	$3.39 billion
Total outside the U.S.	8,603	7,822	$2.7 billion	$2.13 billion
Total worldwide	21,270	20,965	$6.36 billion	$5.52 billion

Retention and Professional Development

Please identify the specific steps you are taking to reduce the attrition rate of minority and women employees.

• Develop and/or support internal employee affinity groups (e.g., minority or women networks within the firm)

• Increase/review compensation relative to competition

• Increase/improve current work/life programs

• Work with minority and women employees to develop career advancement plans

• Professional skills development program, including minority and women employees

Diversity Mission Statement

To be a place where all employees are engaged and valued.

Steelcase Inc.

www.Steelcase.com
www.steelcase.com/na/college_intern-
ships_ourcompany.aspx?f=19120

Locations

North America Manufacturing:
Athens, AL • Atlanta, GA • Grand Prairie,
TX • Grand Rapids, MI • High Point, NC •
New York, NY • Oakland, CA • Tampa,
FL • Tijuana, Mexico • Toronto, Canada

International Manufacturing:
China • France • Germany • Japan •
Malaysia • Morocco • Saudi Arabia •
Spain • Thailand

Sales offices: Located in 20 major metropolitan cities in the U.S. and Canada.

Diversity Leadership
Karen Holtsclaw
Global Diversity Consultant

Employment Contact
Sandy Swanson
Global Talent Consultant
Phone: (616) 475-2894

Experienced Hire Contact
Steve Wolfe
Human Resource Manager
P.O. Box 1967
Grand Rapids, MI 49501
Phone: (616) 246-9036
E-mail: swolfe@steelcase.com

Recruiting

Please list the schools/types of schools at which you recruit.

• *Private schools:* Boston College, Fordham, Calvin College, Cornerstone, Aquinas & Hope College

• *Public state schools:* Michigan State University, University of Michigan, Grand Valley State University, Central Michigan University, Western Michigan University, University of Georgia, Northeastern, Manhattan, Ohio University, Ohio State University, Illinois Institute of Technology

• *Historically black colleges and universities (HBCUs):* Morehouse College, Spelman College, Clark Atlanta

Do you have any special outreach efforts directed to encourage minority students to consider your firm?

• Participate in/host minority student job fair(s) or other minority-focused job events

• Sponsor minority student association events

• Outreach to leadership of minority student organizations

• Scholarships or intern/fellowships for minority students

What activities does the firm undertake to attract minority and women employees?

• Partner programs with women and minority associations

• Seek referrals from other employees

• Utilize online job services

Do you use executive recruiting/search firms to seek to identify new diversity hires?

Yes

Internships and Co-ops

Supply Chain Management Interns
Deadline for application: Spring
Number of interns in the program in summer 2006 (internship) or 2006 (co-op): Four
Pay: $1,200 weekly
Length of the program: 12 weeks
Percentage of interns/co-ops in the program who receive offers of full-time employment: Zero
Web site for internship/co-op information: www.steelcase.com

Materials Management Interns
Deadline for application: Spring
Number of interns in the program in summer 2006 (internship) or 2006 (co-op): 11
Pay: $600 weekly
Length of the program: 12 weeks
Percentage of interns/co-ops in the program who receive offers of full-time employment: Zero
Web site for internship/co-op information: www.steelcase.com

Finance Interns

Deadline for application: Spring

Number of interns in the program in summer 2006 (internship) or 2006 (co-op): Three

Pay: $1,200 weekly

Length of the program: 12 weeks

Percentage of interns/co-ops in the program who receive offers of full-time employment: Varies

Web site for internship/co-op information: www.steelcase.com

Design Interns

Deadline for application: Spring

Number of interns in the program in summer 2006 (internship) or 2006 (co-op): Six

Pay: $1,200 weekly

Length of the program (in weeks): 12 weeks

Percentage of interns/co-ops in the program who receive offers of full-time employment: 15 to 20 percent

Web site for internship/co-op information: www.steelcase.com

Engineering Co-op

Deadline for application: Spring

Number of interns in the program in summer 2006 (internship) or 2006 (co-op): Six

Pay: $600 weekly

Length of the program (in weeks): 12 weeks

Percentage of interns/co-ops in the program who receive offers of full-time employment: 15 to 20 percent

Web site for internship/co-op information: www.steelcase.com

Marketing Interns

Deadline for application: Spring

Number of interns in the program in summer 2006 (internship) or 2006 (co-op): Varies

Pay: $600 weekly

Length of the program: 12 weeks

Percentage of interns/co-ops in the program who receive offers of full-time employment: 14 percent

Web site for internship/co-op information: www.steelcase.com

IT Internship

Deadline for application: Spring

Number of interns in the program in summer 2006 (internship) or 2006 (co-op): Five

Pay: $600 weekly

Length of the program (in weeks): 12 weeks

Percentage of interns/co-ops in the program who receive offers of full-time employment: Varies

Web site for internship/co-op information: www.steelcase.com

Scholarships

Grand Valley State University
www.gvsu.edu

Michigan Colleges Foundation
www.michigancolleges.org

Northern Michigan University
www.nmu.edu

Deadline for application for the scholarship program and award amount varies.

Additionally, the Steelcase Foundation made donations to groups involving scholarships for multicultural students, such as: Jackie Robinson Foundation, Thurgood Marshall Scholarship Fund, Careers for Students with Disabilities, EntryPoint, HBCU Connect, NAMIC (National Association for Multi-ethnicity in Communications), National Association for Equal Opportunity in Higher Education and The PhD Project.

Affinity Groups

Steelcase offers two affinity groups:

1) W.I.S.E. (Women Impacting Steelcase Excellence)

Its purpose is to support Steelcase women in their career and personal development while enhancing our corporate culture and providing support to women in the community.

2) M.A.P. (Multicultural Association of Professionals)

Its purpose is to connect and retain professionals of color and their families; professional networking events; educational programs; and community resources.

Entry-Level Programs, Full-Time Opportunities and Training

PACE

Length of program: Four months

Geographic location(s) of program: Grand Rapids, Mich.

Please describe the training/training component of this program: Entry-level training for colleges primarily focused in sales. Training covers how to sell, product training, financials and how to price, networking, etc.

LEADER

Length of program: Spread over 12 months

Geographic location(s) of program: Grand Rapids, Mich.

Please describe the training/training component of this program.

Designed similarly to a management MBA program

Strategic Plan and Diversity Leadership

How does the firm's leadership communicate the importance of diversity to everyone at the firm?

Briefings by management, annual Diversity Forum, employee e-magazine, external/internal web sites, foundation report, bulletin boards, employee handbook, orientation, training workshops, and community events. Furthermore, the CEO demonstrates his commitment by:

- Chairs diversity council
- Appoints members of diversity council
- Meets regularly with employee resource groups
- Has personal quote about diversity on corporate web site
- Personally reviews and signs off on diversity metrics and progress
- Makes sure corporate vision statement incorporates diversity
- Personally signs off on goals and achievements for supplier diversity
- Has senior advisory position not-for-profit organizations that focuses on people of color

Who has primary responsibility for leading diversity initiatives at your firm?

Brian Cloyd, VP global corporate relations and diversity
bcloyd@steelcase.com

Does your firm currently have a diversity committee?

Yes, which formally meets twice per year with a management review of the firm's diversity progress/results and initiatives. Leaders are held accountable for achieving successful diversity initiatives through bonuses, raises, stock and options.

The Stats

	NUMBER OF EMPLOYEES		REVENUE	
	2006	2005	2006	2005
Total in the U.S.	7,983	8,035	2.3 billion	2.0 billion
Total outside the U.S.	5,000	6,500	644 million	600 million
Total worldwide	13,000	14,500	2.9 billion	2.6 billion

2006 U.S. Demographics are 30 percent female and 26 percent minority.

Retention and Professional Development

How do 2006 minority and female attrition rates generally compare to those experienced in the prior year period?

Lower than in prior years

Please identify the specific steps you are taking to reduce the attrition rate of minority and women employees.

- Develop and/or support internal employee affinity groups
- Increase/review compensation relative to competition
- Improve current work/life programs
- Adopt dispute resolution process
- Succession plan includes emphasis on diversity
- Work with minority and women employees to develop career advancement plans
- Strengthen mentoring program for all employees, including minorities and women
- Professional skills development program, including minority and women employees

Diversity Mission Statement

At Steelcase, we are committed to our workforce reflecting the composition of the communities where we live and work. Promoting environments where we break down barriers by understanding and respecting one another, we support:

- Hiring and promoting individuals with an appropriate mindset toward working with diverse people
- Through programs focused on students, investing in education initiatives to cultivate the spirit of diversity long before individuals are ready to work for Steelcase
- Supporting education and training on diversity—internally and externally
- Leadership taking a personal and active role in diversity efforts
- Insuring that compliance and regulatory processes and activities are consistently above expectations

Additional Information

Steelcase, the global leader in the office furniture industry, helps people have a better work experience by providing products, services and insights into the ways people work. Our company designs and manufactures architecture, furniture and technology products. Steelcase offers careers ranging from traditional fields such as operations, marketing, management and finance to dozens of other disciplines including sales, architecture, information technology, communications, aviation, healthcare and design ... just to name a few.

Along with our commitment to diversity and flexible work arrangements, Steelcase offers talented, enthusiastic individuals career opportunities commensurate with our position as the world's largest office furniture manufacturer. The first step in growing an inclusive culture is to recruit and develop a broad base of excellent employees. The next step is to do all we can as a company to support and care for our people throughout their career. At Steelcase, we treat employees as whole people and provide a comprehensive program to help them reach their full potential as they work to meet the company's goals.

Thanks for considering Steelcase!

Sun Microsystems, Inc.

4150 Network Circle
Santa Clara, CA 95054
Phone: (408) 404-7071

Locations

US: Austin, TX • Beaverton, OR •
Broomfield, CO • Burlington, MA • San
Francisco Bay Area, CA (San Francisco,
Menlo Park, Santa Clara) • San Diego, CA

International: Argentina • Athens •
Australia • Belgium • Brazil • Canada •
Chile • China • Colombia • Czech Republic
• Denmark • Finland • France • Germany •
Hong Kong • Hungary • India • Ireland •
Israel • Istanbul • Italy • Japan • Korea •
Luxembourg • Malaysia • Mexico • New
Zealand • Norway • Poland • Singapore •
Spain/Portugal • Taiwan • The Netherlands
• Thailand • Russia • Scotland • Slovakia •
South Africa • Sweden • Switzerland •
U.A.E • United Kingdom • Venezuela

Diversity Leadership

Shari Slate
Chief Diversity Officer

Employment Contact

Shari Slate
Chief Diversity Officer
E-mail: shari.slate@sun.com
www.sun.com/corp_emp/indexus.html

Recruiting

Please list the schools/types of schools at which you recruit.

• Private schools

• Public state schools

• Other predominantly minority and/or women's colleges

Do you have any special outreach efforts directed to encourage minority students and graduates to consider your firm?

• *Hold a reception for minority students:* SHPE (Society of Hispanic Engineers, University Colorado Boulder), students take tours of Broomfield, Co., location; Multicultural Engineering Program at Colorado Schools of Mines took tour of lab, and multicultural engineering program at Colorado State took tour of Louisville Lab

• *Conferences:* Sponsorship of SWE (Society of Women Engineers) Regional conference

• Advertise in minority student association publication(s) or other minority-focused publications

• *Participate in/host minority student job fair(s) or other minority-focused job events:* Colorado State Wide Multicultural Career Fair,

SWE (Society of Women Engineers) Evening with industry events at Mines

• *Sponsor minority student association events:* SWE (Society of Women Engineers)—multiple events at University of Colorado, Colorado State University, UT Austin, Colorado Schools of Mines, Santa Clara University and UC Berkeley; SHPE (Society of Hispanic Engineers)—sponsored events at University of Colorado, UT Austin and Colorado School of Mines; AISIES (American Indian Science and Engineering Society)—sponsored events at Colorado State University; NSBE (National Society of Black Engineers)—sponsored events at University of Texas Austin, Colorado School of Mines; MBSA (Multicultural Business Student Association)— sponsored events at University Colorado Boulder; ASA (Asian Student Association)—sponsored events at Colorado School of Mines; multicultural banquets at University of Colorado, Colorado State University and UC Berkeley Women of Vision Conference

• *Firm's employees participate on career panels at school:* Panel discussion for University of Colorado Multicultural Business Student Association; Sun employees Charlotte Tyson and Cathleen Wharton sit on University of Colorado's Women and Engineering Board; Sun sits on University of Colorado Multicultural Engineering Board.

• Outreach to leadership of minority student organizations

• *Other:* Sponsored outreach programs for University of Colorado engineering MEP program and Grace Hopper Conference

What activities does the firm undertake to attract minority and women employees?

• Partner programs with women and minority associations

• Conferences

• Participate at minority job fairs

• Seek referrals from other employees

• Utilize online job services

Sun participates in the following:

• EMEA: Aurora—Women's Network

• APAC

• National Association of Asian Professionals (NAAAP)

• Network of Indian Professionals (NETIP)

• Executive Women's Alliance (EWA)

• Executive Women's Forum (EFW)

• Out and Equal

• Top 50 Hispanics in Technology and Business

• Employment Access

• Grace Hopper Conference (Anita Borg Institute)

• Women of Color in Technology (WOC)

• National Society of Hispanic MBAs (NSHMBA)

• GLBT Professionals

• Executive Leadership Council (ELC) / Next Generation (NXTG)

• Women in Technology International (WITI)

• American Indian Society of Science and Engineering (AISES)

• National Association of Women MBA (NAWMBA)

• Society of Hispanic Professional Engineers (SHPE)

• Information Technology Sr. Managers Forum

• American Foundation for the Blind

• TWIN Awards YWCA

Strategic Partnership Program

Sun's Strategic Partnership Program strategically identifies and develops partnerships with a number of professional organizations and events. These targeted organizations provide professional development and career and networking opportunities to members of communities traditionally underrepresented in the high-tech industry. By supporting the efforts of these organizations, Sun gains opportunity to tap into a pool of diverse, high-caliber talent. These partnerships serve as a valuable resource in developing an employee population that effectively understands and responds to the variety of experiences, perspectives and cultures represented in the global marketplace.

Planning Sessions:

The purpose of the Sun Microsystems Talent Pipeline Planning Session is to ensure each employee resource group (ERG), global inclusion (GI),

global workforce planning and staffing (GWP&S) and global executive talent management (GETM) has input/alignment around the global talent pipeline integration processes and the FY strategic partnerships.

Do you use executive recruiting/search firms to seek to identify new diversity hires?

Yes

If yes, list all women- and/or minority-owned executive search/recruiting firms to which the firm paid a fee for placement services in the past 12 months:

CVP—Kerwin Associates

Scholarships

Grace Hopper

Deadline for application for the scholarship program: Varies

Scholarship award amount: $1,000

Web site or other contact information for scholarship: www.grace-hopper.com

Affinity Groups

• Asian American Diversity Network (AADN)

• Black Employee Network (BEN)

• Gays, Lesbians and Friends (GLAF)

• Global Inclusion Community

• Interns@Sun

• Legal Diversity Council

• Society of Latinos (SOL)

• SunWomen

Examples of activities include:

• Education of employees regarding various cultural and demographic perspectives

• Celebration of holidays and events recognized by cultures or communities

• Serving as a resource to the business in areas of language or cultural competence

• Sponsorship of community events which support the development of populations typically underrepresented in technology or which position Sun as the "Employer of Choice" in the community

• Serve as a link for recruiting of talent from non-traditional or underrepresented populations

Entry-Level Programs, Full-Time Opportunities and Training Programs

SEED (Sun Engineering Enrichment and Development program)

Length of program: One to two years

Geographic location(s) of program: All Sun locations

As one of Sun's largest mentorship programs, SEED (Sun Engineering Enrichment Development) pairs up promising new college recruits as well as established employees with senior staff at Sun (including distinguished engineers, VPs, fellows and directors) who have volunteered to be mentors. SEED provides these individuals with resources and support that gives them more opportunity to succeed and flourish in their careers. SEED participants have seen the benefits of the programs—in addition to regular meetings, events and activities, participants, as a group, earn promotions at four times the company average and receive double the number of highest performance ratings of Sun's overall employee base.

SEED participants may focus on technical mentoring or specific engineering skills. More often, the program gives mentees a chance to learn more about "soft skills," ranging from how to improve teamwork skills to navigating the complex maze of office politics. There is also a strong emphasis on reaching out to traditionally marginalized groups and attempting to ensure diverse participation across geographies, genders and professional areas. Sun's CTO, Dr. Greg Papadopoulos, is the SEED program's executive sponsor.

SunU (Sun University)

Length of Program: Year-round

Geographic location(s) of program: All Sun locations

Sun employees have access to classes worldwide through the company's internal education system, SunU. Employees can enroll in classes that extend their technical knowledge in their field, develop personal skills or help them better understand Sun's business.

SunU is open to all employees, offered year-round and at no cost.

Strategic Plan and Diversity Leadership

How does the firm's leadership communicate the importance of diversity to everyone at the firm?

E-mails, internal and external web sites, executive radio shows, town halls, employee bulletins, networking/mentoring groups and training.

Who has primary responsibility for leading diversity initiatives at your firm?

Shari Slate, chief diversity officer

Does your firm currently have a diversity committee?

Yes

If yes, does the committee's representation include one or more members of the firm's management/executive committee (or the equivalent)?

Yes

If yes, how many executives are on the committee, and in 2006. How many employees are on the committee?

There are more than 20 executives aligned to the global inclusion model. There are more than 2,000 employees aligned to the employee resource network.

Does the committee and/or diversity leader establish and set goals or objectives consistent with management's priorities?

Yes

Has the firm undertaken a formal or informal diversity program or set of initiatives aimed at increasing the diversity of the firm?

Yes, formal. An employee resource group is a network of Sun employees who share a common identity, characteristic or set of interests. Employee resource groups exist for the betterment of Sun, engaging themselves in initiatives and activities which contribute towards Sun's success and which ensure a work environment in which each candidate, employee and customer is treated with respect, dignity, fairness and cultural sensitivity.

The efforts of Sun's employee resource groups complement global inclusion's focus areas of attracting and retaining diverse top talent and the attraction and retention of a diverse global customer base.

Interested employees voluntarily subscribe to employee resource groups through established online aliases. These aliases, open to all interested employees, provide members with opportunities to exchange information and ideas, network with those sharing similar interests and plan sponsored activities. Examples of employee resource group activities include:

- Education of employees regarding various cultural and demographic perspectives
- Celebration of holidays and events recognized by cultures or communities
- Serving as a resource to the business in areas of language or cultural competence

- Sponsorship of community events which support the development of populations typically underrepresented in technology or which position Sun as the "Employer of Choice" in the community
- Serve as a link for recruiting of talent from nontraditional or under-represented populations

How often does the firm's management review the firm's diversity progress/results?

Annually

How is the firm's diversity committee and/or firm management held accountable for achieving results?

The management excellence survey provides employee feedback on Sun management behaviors (by function or by geography), which can be used to identify behaviors we wish to benchmark, as well as those we may need to modify.

We partner with process owners to create a work plan (which is assessed biannually) for global inclusion integration into key processes within each of the following components of the global inclusion model:

- Branding and communications
- Global talent pipeline
- Global leadership
- Employee resource network

The Stats

	NUMBER OF EMPLOYEES		REVENUE	
	2006	2005	2006	2005
Total in the U.S.	18,000	21,000	N/A	N/A
Total outside the U.S.	17,000	17,000	N/A	N/A
Total worldwide	35,000	38,000	$13.068 billion	$11.061 billion

Retention and Professional Development

Please identify the specific steps you are taking to reduce the attrition rate of minority and women employees.

All below are applicable:

- Develop and/or support internal employee affinity groups (e.g., minority or women networks within the firm)

- Increase/review compensation relative to competition
- Increase/improve current work/life programs
- Adopt dispute resolution process
- Succession plan includes emphasis on diversity
- Work with minority and women employees to develop career advancement plans
- Review work assignments and hours billed to key client matters to make sure minority and women employees are not being excluded
- Strengthen mentoring program for all employees, including minorities and women
- Professional skills development program, including minority and women employees

Sun is very committed to supporting and nourishing talent and skills in their employees, especially females. Sun's employee resource group, Sun Women (SunW), is a volunteer organization committed to promoting an awareness of women's strategical issues at Sun and fostering networking, mentoring and leadership opportunities which encourage personal, professional and organizational growth. In addition to regular meetings, events and training, SunW supports recognition for women at Sun through establishing top women awards to break down barriers.

About 25 percent of SEED (described above) participants are women and about 20 percent are employees in countries outside the U.S. (mostly in China, India and Europe). The SEED program provides these individuals with resources and support that give them more opportunity to succeed and flourish in their careers.

Diversity Mission Statement

Sun's vision of network computing requires that it build the most effective and powerful network for its global community of customers, partners and employees. This requires that we bring together people from every community around the world, which requires that Sun build on a foundation of open communities, based on inclusion.

Additional Information

Sun's greatest asset is its employees. Their innovative and enterprising spirit drives everything at Sun, including the company's success. Sun has a responsibility to provide them with a positive and inclusive work environment that supports their professional and personal development and rewards them for their contributions.

A Model for Global Inclusion

Sun operates in the global marketplace and serves a wide range of customers. Sun believes it's essential to cultivate a workplace that embraces people from diverse backgrounds, values a broad spec-

trum of perspectives and inspires employees to work together toward their goals and those of our business. The company is committed to cultivating this type of workplace as well as fostering a sense of inclusiveness that serves to attract and retain talented employees.

Using the global inclusion model, Sun has identified opportunities to strengthen Sun's systems and processes, which the company is now working toward. For instance, Sun is building multigenerational integration plans and establishing goals for each of the areas of the model. This comprehensive approach is intended to encourage partnerships across the company, resulting in collaboration and collective ownership of "Inclusion at Sun."

Employee Resource Network

To help foster a more inclusive workforce, Sun builds relationships with external organizations to promote hiring of diverse talent, and we support and manage an employee resource network (ERN).

The ERN is a community of Sun employees, including councils and employee resource groups, which support the work of global inclusion. It serves as an advocate for Sun and is the voice of the customer for company initiatives. The ERN promotes internal awareness, encompasses external relationships and helps retain employees, customers, partners, developers and suppliers.

Some of our global inclusion strategic partners for fiscal 2007 include:

- American Foundation for the Blind
- Anita Borg Institute
- Executive Diversity Council
- Executive Leadership Council/Next Generation
- Executive Women's Forum
- Information Technologist Senior Managers Forum
- National Association of Asian Professionals
- National Black MBA Association
- Network of Indian Professionals
- Out and Equal Summit
- Society of Hispanic Professional Engineers
- Women of Color in Technology

In addition to being a great place to bank.... we're also a great place to work.

Headquartered in Atlanta, Georgia, SunTrust operates an extensive distribution network primarily in Florida, Georgia, North Carolina, South Carolina, Tennessee, Maryland, Virginia and the District of Columbia - and also serves customers in selected markets nationally. Our primary businesses include deposit, credit, trust and investment services, and through various subsidiaries, we provide credit cards, mortgage banking, insurance, brokerage and capital markets services.

SunTrust is proud of the diversity initiatives we've implemented to raise the quality of our workforce and employee well-being. We have established several programs to support these initiatives including:

- *Mentoring and leadership development programs for minorities*
- *Work-life benefits*
- *An aggressive Diversity recruiting strategy - resulting in a diverse workforce*
- *An active Corporate Diversity Council*
- *Diversity training programs*

SunTrust makes a significant investment in the training and development of its employees. Our comprehensive, professional internship and full-time Training Program positions provide a solid platform on which to build your career.

SunTrust values its partnership with INROADS, and provides internship opportunities throughout our footprint for talented minority students.

Visit us online to learn more about our outstanding careers at:

suntrust.com/campus

SunTrust supports a diverse workforce and is a Drug Testing and Equal Opportunity Employer. M/F/V/D.

SunTrust Banks, Inc.

303 Peachtree Street
Atlanta, GA 30302

Locations
1,700 branches across the southeast and mid-Atlantic regions

Diversity Leadership
Carolyn Cartwright
Director of Diversity
Phone: (404) 588-7711
Fax: (404) 588-8047
www.suntrust.com/campus

Recruiting

Please list the schools/types of schools at which you recruit.

- *Private schools:* Duke, Emory, Rollins College, University of Richmond, Vanderbilt, Wake Forest and Washington & Lee
- *Public state schools:* Florida State, Georgia Tech, James Madison University, University of Central Florida, University of Florida, University of Georgia, University of Maryland, University of North Carolina–Chapel Hill, University of South Florida, University of Tennessee-Knoxville, University of Virginia, Virginia Commonwealth University and Virginia Tech
- *Historically black colleges and universities (HBCUs):* Florida A&M, Howard University, Spelman and Tennessee State
- *Hispanic serving institutions (HSIs):* Florida International University and University of Miami

Do you have any special outreach efforts directed to encourage minority students and graduates to consider your firm?

- Hold a reception for minority students
- *Conferences:* Howard Financial Services Institute and Monster Diversity Leadership Program
- Participate in/host minority student job fair(s) or other minority-focused job events
- Sponsor minority student association events
- Firm's employees participate on career panels at schools
- Outreach to leadership of minority student organizations
- *Other:* Participate in the Florida A&M Industry Cluster; participate in the SWEPT Program at Spelman; established an Executive Liaison Program, where we have assigned SunTrust executives to each of our core HBCUs and HSIs; participate in the 21st Century Advantage Program at Howard University

What activities does the firm undertake to attract minority and women employees?

- Partner programs with women and minority associations

- *Conferences:* Black Data Processing Associates, Career Opportunities for Students with Disabilities (COSD), Emerging Leaders Program, Monster Diversity Leadership Program, National Black MBA, National Society of Hispanic MBAs, Urban Financial Services Coalition, Women for Hire and Women of Color Technology Awards Conference
- Participate at minority job fairs
- Seek referrals from other employees
- Utilize online job services
- *Other:* Partnership with INROADS; send SunTrust representatives to facilitate sessions at the INROADS Leadership Development Institute events

Do you use executive recruiting/search firms to seek to identify new diversity hires?

No

Internships and Co-ops

INROADS

Number of interns in the program in summer 2006 (internship) or 2006 (co-op): 25 interns

Pay: Intern pay varies based on geographic location, department placement, and year in school.

Length of the program: 10 to 12 weeks

Percentage of interns/co-ops in the program who receive offers of full-time employment: Approximately 60 percent

Web site for internship/co-op information:
www.suntrust.com/campus

SunTrust typically places INROADS interns throughout the company's footprint, in the following lines of business: business banking, commercial banking, commercial real estate, mortgage banking, retail banking, and wealth and investment management. Interns generally spend from two to four summers with the organization, learning analytical and/or sales skills through direct, hands-on participation. The summer experience includes some combination of client exposure, job, shadowing and classroom training. In addition, all interns complete a summer project and presentation that reflect appropriate research and analysis for their particular function.

All INROADS interns are paired with a mentor and human resources local coordinator. They also participate in special programming activities throughout the summer, including a variety of professional development seminars. Rising seniors are invited to participate in SunTrust's annual INROADS Senior Summit. This two-day event, which is held at our corporate headquarters in Atlanta, gives interns the opportunity to interact with senior management, gain exposure to our business strategies and network with other interns and recent college hires.

Qualifications: Vary by line of business and functional area.

Client Management Corporate Finance Internship Program

Number of interns in the program in summer 2006 (internship) or 2006 (co-op): Eight

Pay: Intern pay varies based on geographic location, department placement and year in school.

Length of the program: 10 to 12 weeks

Web site for internship/co-op information:
www.suntrust.com/campus

The Summer Internship Program provides the possibility to gain exposure to a number of disciplines within client management corporate finance. The intern will be assigned to a specific group to work on various analyses, modeling and underwriting assignments for the bank's corporate clients. Interns will sharpen financial analysis skills, develop an understanding of corporate markets and clients, and build expertise in corporate finance and investment banking products through on-the-job training. The overall goal of the program is for the intern to develop a solid understanding of our industry, organization and strategy. Assignments will be with one of our specific industry or geographic segments. The 10 to 12-week internship program will begin in May and end in August. Most of our opportunities will be in Atlanta; however, there is a potential for positions in Nashville, Orlando or Richmond.

Qualifications:

• Accounting or finance coursework preferred

• Completed junior year of a BA/BS degree in any major

• Overall minimum GPA of 3.0 required

• High degree of academic and extracurricular achievement

• Proven ability to work well in a fast-paced team, environment

• Proven analytical ability and attention to detail

• Solid leadership and interpersonal skills

• Strong interest in finance and investment banking

• Superior written and oral communication skills

• Willingness to commit substantial time and energy to the program

Debt Capital Markets Summer Internship Program

Number of interns in the program in summer 2006 (internship) or 2006 (co-op): 15

Pay: Intern pay varies based on geographic location, department placement and year in school.

Length of the program: 10 to 12 weeks

Web site for internship/co-op information:
www.suntrust.com/campus

The Summer Internship Program provides the possibility to gain exposure to a number of disciplines within Debt Capital Markets. The intern will be assigned to a specific group to work on various analyses, modeling and underwriting assignments for the bank's corporate clients. Interns will sharpen financial analysis skills, develop an understanding of corporate markets and clients and build expertise in corporate finance and investment banking products through on-the-job training. The overall goal of the program is for the intern to develop a solid understanding of our industry, organization and strategy. Assignments will be with one of our specific product segments. The 10 to 12-week internship program will begin in May and end in August. Most of our opportunities will be in Atlanta; however, there is a potential for positions in Nashville, Orlando or Richmond.

Qualifications:

• Completed junior year of a BA/BS degree in any major

• Overall minimum GPA of 3.0 required

• Finance coursework preferred

• Proven analytical ability and attention to detail

• Strong interest in finance and investment banking

• Solid leadership and interpersonal skills

• High degree of academic and extracurricular achievement

• Ability to work well in a fast-paced, team environment

• Superior written and oral communication skills

• Willingness to commit substantial time and energy to the program

Equity Capital Markets—M & A—Summer Internship Program

Number of interns in the program in summer 2006 (internship) or 2006 (co-op): Three

Pay: Intern pay varies based on geographic location, department placement and year in school.

Length of the program: Eight weeks

Web site for internship/co-op information:
www.suntrust.com/campus

A summer intern will work as a key member of a transaction team, typically comprised of two to three professionals, assist in transactions and work with clients on a day-to-day basis. Upon successful completion of the eight-week summer program, interns will be considered for a full-time intern position in equity capital markets/M&A upon graduation. Interns will be placed at our headquarters in Atlanta. SunTrust Robinson Humphrey also has satellite investment banking offices in Nashville and Orlando.

Qualifications:

- Completed junior year of a BA/BS degree in any major
- Overall minimum GPA of 3.0 required
- Accounting or finance coursework preferred
- Proven analytical ability and attention to detail
- Strong interest in finance and investment banking
- Solid leadership and interpersonal skills
- High degree of academic and extracurricular achievement
- Proven ability to work well in a fast-paced, team environment
- Superior written and oral communication skills
- Willingness to commit substantial time and energy to the program

Affinity Groups

We do not have formal affinity groups at SunTrust. However, we do have diversity site councils located across the enterprise in 20 geographic regions. These diversity site councils have subcommittees that focus on certain dimensions of diversity (i.e., women, GLBT, African-Americans, Hispanics, Asians and people with disabilities). These subcommittees focus on some of the same issues as affinity groups. Their purpose is to represent diversity in action at the local market level. Their activities include cultural celebrations, networking, recruiting new employees, mentoring, business development and community outreach. For example, our councils across the enterprise participated in Disability Employment Awareness Month by creating subcommittees to develop programs to support Disability Mentoring Day. The site councils also established African-American subcommittees to observe Black History Month. The groups sponsored events like "Juneteenth" and internal and external events around the documentary "Summer Hill," a first-person narrative describing Jim Crow. The councils meet at least once per quarter. They have market or regional web sites where they can report their local information. Additionally, each site council has a page on the corporate web site.

We also have two informal/unofficial affinity groups in place—a group that supports GLBT issues called Diversity Works, and an African-American group called SunTrust League of Employees (SALE). Meeting frequency varies from monthly to quarterly. The groups focus on employee support, mentoring, community outreach, business development and recruiting.

Entry-Level Programs, Full-Time Opportunities and Training Programs

Business Banking Associate Program

Length of program: Approximately six months

Geographic location(s) of program: SunTrust Business Banking has offices throughout the company's footprint in Georgia, Florida, Maryland, North Carolina, South Carolina, Tennessee, Virginia and the District of Columbia.

SunTrust Business Banking focuses on providing a full range of financial products and services to small businesses throughout the southeast and mid-Atlantic regions. Business bankers are sales specialists who focus on new business development of clients and prospects with annual revenue of $1 to $5 million. Associates participate in a six-month training program that begins their progression towards a business banker position within the retail line of business. The program focuses on three key areas: sales abilities, analytical skills and product knowledge. Associates participate in classroom training in Atlanta, Ga., and complete on-the-job rotations in the bank location where they were hired. Associates support business bankers and managers by analyzing a wide variety of companies, industries and markets, performing financial statement analysis and assisting with call preparation. Associates are equipped with the tools needed to be successful contributors by participating in on-the-job rotations reinforced by classroom training. SunTrust Business Banking has offices throughout the company's footprint in Georgia, Florida, Maryland, North Carolina, South Carolina, Tennessee, Virginia and the District of Columbia.

Qualifications:

- BA/BS required
- All majors accepted; accounting, finance, or equivalent analytical coursework strongly preferred
- Overall GPA of 2.8 or above required
- Strong sales orientation
- Solid interpersonal skills and communication skills
- Motivation to succeed
- Analytical aptitude

Commercial Banking Associate Program

Length of program: Approximately 11 months

Geographic location(s) of program: SunTrust Commercial Banking has offices throughout the company's footprint in Alabama, Florida, Georgia, Maryland, North Carolina, South Carolina, Tennessee, Virginia and the District of Columbia.

The SunTrust Commercial Banking Line of Business focuses on providing comprehensive financial solutions, superior value and outstanding services to targeted companies throughout the Southeast and Mid-Atlantic regions. The majority of commercial banking clients are privately-held companies with annual revenue between $5 million to $250 million. Commercial banking associates participate in a training program that begins their progression towards a relationship manager position. The program focuses on three key areas: sales skills, analytical ability and product knowledge. Associates have the opportunity to build a professional network with their peers and commercial banking managers throughout the SunTrust system by participating in central-

ized classroom training in Atlanta, Ga. Associates also complete on-the-job training in their local banking units where they support relationship managers and portfolio specialists in financial statement analysis, industry research and client call preparation.

Qualifications:

- BA/BS required
- All majors accepted; accounting, finance, or equivalent analytical coursework strongly preferred
- Overall GPA of 2.8 or above required
- Interest in business and finance
- Strong sales orientation
- Solid interpersonal and communication skills
- Analytical aptitude

Commercial Real Estate Associate Program

Length of program: Approximately 11 months

Geographic location(s) of program: SunTrust Commercial Real Estate has offices throughout the company's footprint in Alabama, Florida, Georgia, Maryland, North Carolina, South Carolina, Tennessee, Virginia and the District of Columbia.

SunTrust Commercial Real Estate is a specialized, full-service banking group dedicated to providing financial solutions to commercial developers, real estate investors, national and local residential homebuilders, affordable housing groups and real estate investment trusts. Commercial real estate clients are a combination of privately-held and publicly-traded companies ranging in size and complexity, and a number of them have market capitalization over $1 billion. Commercial real estate associates participate in a training program that begins their progression toward a relationship manager position. The program focuses on three key areas: sales skills, analytical ability and product knowledge. Associates participate in centralized classroom training in Atlanta, Ga., and complete on-the-job assignments in the bank location where they were hired. Associates support relationship managers and portfolio specialists by analyzing companies, industries, markets and real estate projects, performing financial statement analysis and reviewing the clients' current credit relationship with SunTrust.

Qualifications:

- BA/BS required
- All majors accepted; accounting, finance, or equivalent analytical coursework strongly preferred
- Overall GPA of 2.8 or above required
- Interest in business and finance
- Strong sales orientation
- Solid interpersonal and communication skills
- Analytical aptitude

Client Management Corporate Finance Analyst Program

Length of program: Two- to three-year analyst position

Geographic location(s) of program: Program is based in Atlanta; however, potential rotation and placement opportunities exist in Atlanta, Nashville, Orlando and Richmond.

Client managers in corporate finance are organized along both industry and geographic lines. Their mission is to utilize their expertise, along with that of the various product specialists and risk managers, to deliver creative ideas and solutions to their clients. The client management corporate finance track of the Corporate and Investment Banking Analyst Training Program combines relevant classroom training in Atlanta with practical on-the-job assignments. Assignments may be in any of our specialty groups—asset-based lending, energy, healthcare, financial institutions, financial services and technology, food and beverage, media and communications—or in one of our diversified industry groups located in Atlanta, Nashville, Orlando and Richmond. Analysts will sharpen financial analysis skills, develop an understanding of corporate markets and clients and build expertise in corporate finance and investment banking products.

Qualifications:

- BA/BS required
- Any major (business major preferred)
- Overall GPA of 3.0 required
- Accounting or finance coursework preferred
- Proven analytical ability and attention to detail
- Solid leadership and interpersonal skills
- High degree of academic and extracurricular achievement
- Proven ability to work well in a fast-paced team environment
- Superior written and oral communication skills
- Willingness to commit substantial time and energy to the program

Debt Capital Markets Analyst Program

Length of program: Two- to three-year analyst position

Geographic location(s) of program: Program is based in Atlanta

The debt capital markets track of the Corporate and Investment Banking Analyst Training Program combines a brief classroom schedule on the front end, followed by group assignments with product specialists during the initial two- to three-year analyst appointment. Analysts will support both external and internal clients in various industries with an assortment of capital markets products. Analysts will sharpen their corporate finance and modeling skills, as well as develop a broad understanding of capital markets and investment banking products and learn how they are leveraged in a vast number of industries. The majority of analysts will complete their assignments in Atlanta. Other assignments may include Nashville, Orlando or Richmond.

Qualifications

- BA/BS required, any major

- Overall minimum GPA of 3.0 required
- Finance coursework preferred
- Proven analytical ability and attention to detail
- Strong interest in finance and investment banking
- Solid leadership and interpersonal skills
- High degree of academic and extracurricular achievement
- Proven ability to work well in a fast-paced, team environment
- Superior written and oral communication skills
- Willingness to commit substantial time and energy to the program

Investment Banking Analyst Program

Length of program: Two years

Geographic location(s) of program: Atlanta, GA

SunTrust Robinson Humphrey's Investment Banking Analyst Program is a two-year program designed to provide recent college graduates with an introduction to investment banking through an intensive learning experience. Analysts play integral roles on project teams by working closely with senior bankers on all aspects of investment banking transactions. After a four-week classroom training period, analysts work as generalists for the first six months, serving clients in various industries, providing merger and acquisition advisory and equity capital raising services. This generalist orientation offers analysts the opportunity to develop a broad base of skills while also gaining exposure to a wide variety of industries. After six months, analysts join industry-specific teams, providing them the opportunity to develop industry and product knowledge and make significant contributions to transaction teams. The majority of analysts will be placed at our headquarters in Atlanta. SunTrust Robinson Humphrey also has satellite investment banking offices in Nashville and Orlando.

Qualifications:

- BA/BS required, any major
- Overall minimum GPA of 3.0 required
- Accounting or finance coursework preferred
- Proven analytical ability and attention to detail
- Strong interest in finance and investment banking
- Solid leadership and interpersonal skills
- High degree of academic and extracurricular achievement
- Proven ability to work well in a fast-paced, team environment
- Superior written and oral communication skills
- Willingness to commit substantial time and energy to the program

Strategic Plan and Diversity Leadership

How does the firm's leadership communicate the importance of diversity to everyone at the firm?

- New Employee Orientation Program

- Company web site: www.suntrust.com
- Employee web site
- Employee newsletter
- Annual report on diversity
- Diversity brochures
- Diversity commitment statements in Employee Handbook
- Collateral materials for marketing, benefits and new-hire orientation
- Diversity training

Who has primary responsibility for leading diversity initiatives at your firm?

Our diversity initiatives are led by Carolyn Cartwright, senior vice president.

Does your firm currently have a diversity committee?

Yes

If yes, please describe how the committee is structured, how often it meets, etc.

We have a Corporate Diversity Council made up of 20 senior executives across the enterprise who are responsible for setting the strategic direction as thought leaders, monitoring activities and evaluating the overall effectiveness of the initiative. The chairman/CEO and the president/COO co-chair the Corporate Diversity Council. The corporate council has subcommittees that serve as the working arms for moving ideas into action. The corporate council meets at least quarterly. The 20 diversity site councils (previously described) report to the Corporate Diversity Council.

If yes, does the committee's representation include one or more members of the firm's management/executive committee (or the equivalent)?

Yes

If yes, how many executives are on the committee?

Total Executives on Committee: 20

Does the committee and/or diversity leader establish and set goals or objectives consistent with management's priorities?

Yes. Diversity is a business imperative at SunTrust. It aligns and supports SunTrust's strategic intent. Specifically:

We intend to be recognized as the leading provider of high value financial services to consumers, businesses and institutions within our designated geographies.

Our success and financial market recognition will flow from our ability to enhance the economic well-being of our customers, our shareholders, our people and our communities.

Our diversity mission and goals are tied to the mission, goals and values of the organization. The Corporate Diversity Council objectives are to:

- Confirm diversity as a business imperative in our workforce, marketplace and community
- Convey management accountability for a diversity inclusive business environment
- Maintain management accountability for increasing diversity representation
- Create and sustain diversity awareness among all employees
- Deliver diversity education and training

SunTrust recognizes that we are in the midst of a changing landscape. We identified four areas for marketplace changes that we will address in our diversity strategy. They include Hispanic, female, African-American entrepreneurs and the 50+ age group.

Has the firm undertaken a formal or informal diversity program or set of initiatives aimed at increasing the diversity of the firm?

Yes, formal. Our diversity initiatives focus on the five previously stated diversity objectives. Some of the programs related to these objectives include an emerging and ethnic markets strategy, a development program for high potential people of color (POC) that is designed to accelerate the promotion rate of POC, the maintenance of a diversity representation scorecard, education and training for managers, a web-based training program for employees and a diversity recruiting strategy.

How often does the firm's management review the firm's diversity progress/results?

Programmatic review of diversity events and strategies occurs at least quarterly, and an annual evaluation is made on progress-to-date against goals. Goals are maintained or new ones established during annual planning meetings.

How is the firm's diversity committee and/or firm management held accountable for achieving results?

Managers are held accountable for their diversity efforts and representation scorecard results. The bank's performance appraisal system has a diversity performance factor. Additionally, diversity is one of the leadership elements of the Management Incentive Program.

The Stats

	NUMBER OF EMPLOYEES		REVENUE	
	2006	2005	2006	2005
Total in the U.S.	33,599	33,406	$8.22 million	$7.8 million

There are two women and two people of color, or 17 percent, on the SunTrust board of directors. (Note: One female is also a person of color.) Our workforce is made up of 69 percent females and 34 per-

cent minorities. Women account for 62 percent of all promotions to executive, senior and middle management positions. Women make up 36 percent of senior vice presidents and 75 percent of entry-level managers. People of color account for 16 percent of middle managers and senior professionals.

Retention and Professional Development

How do 2006 minority and female attrition rates generally compare to those experienced in the prior year period?

About the same as in prior years. Our turnover for women and people of color is about the same as it is for white males.

Please identify the specific steps you are taking to reduce the attrition rate of minority and women employees.

- Increase/review compensation relative to competition
- Increase/improve current work/life programs
- Adopt dispute resolution process
- Succession plan includes emphasis on diversity
- Work with minority and women employees to develop career advancement plans
- Review work assignments and hours billed to key client matters to make sure minority and women employees are not being excluded
- Strengthen mentoring program for all employees, including minorities and women
- Professional skills development program, including minority and women employees
- *Other:* Diversity training for managers and associates, employee assistance programs, tuition reimbursement program, SunTrust University—SunTrust's training and development division

Diversity Mission Statement

Vision

To create an inclusive environment and culture at SunTrust that emphasizes respect and leverages diversity in our marketplace, workforce, workplace and communities, so that we can beat our competition in making SunTrust a superior employer and financial services provider, thus enhancing shareholder value.

Mission Statement

To be recognized as being among the best financial service providers in developing a diverse employee base that successfully meets the needs of our clients within our designated geographies.

Additional Information

SunTrust has development programs in place that focus on providing exceptional work experiences and mentoring opportunities. We have both formal and informal mentoring throughout the organization. We have also established a focused Leadership Development Program for minorities. The goal of the program is to accelerate the representation of ethnic minorities in key leadership and management positions. Fifteen participants were selected for a two-year program which includes structured development activities, a business project, mentoring, coaching, 360 degree feedback and networking opportunities. It is a high-level program to support SunTrust's talent management and diversity goals related to attracting, developing, promoting and retaining a diverse workforce.

We have targeted recruiting efforts which allow us to maintain strong relationships with minority colleges and organizations. Some of our college connections include Florida A&M, Howard, Spelman and Tennessee State University. For example, SunTrust is a participant of the 21st Century Advantage Program (CAP) at Howard University. A key element is the Corporate Team Adoption Program. SunTrust has 21 business students at Howard. Adoption means regular contact between STI executives and the 21 students. The students learn about culture, history and business dynamics through case studies and site visits at SunTrust. A SunTrust executive, who acts as a corporate liaison, has been assigned to each of our core HBCUs and HSIs. Our hope is that their relationships with key faculty and staff will allow us to identify top talent from these institutions. We have also established a national partnership with INROADS and currently have 25 interns working with us.

To attract the best and brightest employees who reflect the diversity of our communities, we have established networks with key professional organizations, to include:

- Black Data Processing Associates
- Hispanic Chamber of Commerce
- National Black MBA Association
- National Society of Hispanic MBAs
- Women for Hire
- Women of Color in Technology
- Urban Financial Services Coalition

SunTrust has achieved many successes through our Diversity Initiatives Program. Some of our accomplishments include:

- Ranked 1st place by NAACP in the Economic Reciprocity Survey
- Ranked number 28 of 50 by *DiversityInc* magazine as one of the Best Places to Work for Minorities
- Ranked 25 of the Top 50 Companies for Black MBAs to work for by *Black MBA Magazine*
- Presented the Corporate Award of the Year for support of diversity in the financial services industry
- 2004 recipient of the New Freedom Initiative Award presented by the Dept. of Labor, as an initiative of President Bush for employers with practices that address the needs of people with disabilities
- We placed in the top 100 of *Fortune* magazine's Best Places to Work for Minorities
- Awarded the best diversity web site by *DiversityInc* magazine
- Given a grade of 100 (out of 100) by the Human Rights Campaign for our programs for the GLBT community
- Ranked as one of the best places to work by *The Atlanta Tribune* and *The Atlanta Business Chronicle*

SunTrust is known as a good corporate citizen in the communities where we operate. We give time and financial support to organizations like:

- 100 Black Men
- Asian American Chamber of Commerce
- Asian American Heritage Foundation
- Career Opportunities for Students with Disabilities
- Hispanic Chamber of Commerce
- Human Rights Campaign
- Jack and Jill Organization
- Latin American Association
- M.L. King Centers
- Minority/Women Business Owners' Councils
- Rainbow PUSH Coalition
- SCLC
- Urban League
- Women in Finance
- Women's Resource Center to End Domestic Violence
- YWCA

Symbol Technologies, Inc.

One Symbol Plaza, MS A-2
Holtsville, NY 11742
Phone: (631) 738-2400

Locations
Holtsville, NY (HQ)
Locations in over 50 countries.

Employment Contact
Margaret-Ann Douglas
Manager, Human Resources
One Symbol Plaza, MS A-2
Holtsville, NY 11742
Phone: (631) 738-4086
Fax: (631) 738-4763
E-mail: Margaret-ann.douglas@symbol.com
www.symbol.com/about/careers/careers.html

Recruiting

Please list the schools/lists of schools at which you recruit.
• Ivy League schools
• Other private schools
• Public state schools
• Historically black colleges and universities (HBCUs)
• Hispanic serving institutions (HSIs)

Do you have any special outreach efforts directed to encourage minority students to consider your firm?
• Participate in/host minority student job fair(s)
• Sponsor minority student association events

What activities does the firm undertake to attract minority and women employees?
• Participate at minority job fairs
• Seek referrals from other employees
• Utilize online job services

Do you use executive recruiting/search firms to seek to identify new diversity hires?
No

Affinity Groups

Symbol Women's Action Team (SWAT)
SWAT is a channel through which women can achieve their full potential professionally and personally. By serving as a network of professionals, SWAT engenders an environment in which its members communicate successes and share solutions available to women in the workplace.

SWAT meets monthly. The group's main goals are as follows:

• Recruitment and retention of women at Symbol Technologies, Inc.
• Promote and enhance relationship-building among females in the Symbol workforce
• Provide an environment for women professionals to network and form support structures among female colleagues

Strategic Plan and Diversity Leadership

How does the firm's leadership communicate the importance of diversity to everyone at the firm?
• The Intranet—diversity web site
• Diversity training for managers
• Staff meetings
• Memos

Does your firm currently have a diversity committee?
No

Has the firm undertaken a formal or informal diversity program or set of initiatives aimed at increasing the diversity of the firm?
Yes, informal

How often does the firm's management review the firm's diversity progress/results?
Annually

The Stats

	NUMBER OF EMPLOYEES	REVENUE
	2005	2005
Total in the U.S.	2,391	$1.1 billion
Total outside the U.S.	2,842	$.6 billion
Total worldwide	5,233	$1.7 billion

The figure in the US column represents revenue for TASS (the Americas international—Mexico, Latin America and Canada).

Retention and Professional Development

Please identify the specific steps you are taking to reduce the attrition rate of minority and women employees.

- Develop and/or support internal employee affinity groups
- Increase/review compensation relative to male non-minorities
- Increase/improve current work/life programs
- Adopt dispute resolution process
- Succession plan includes emphasis on diversity and identifies diverse candidates

Diversity Mission Statement

At Symbol, we know it is our associates that make us a great company. We respect and value diversity and are committed to creating a culture of inclusion where all of our associates can thrive—a culture that unlocks our enormous reservoirs of talent, innovation and commitment and tears down barriers to collaboration.

We are actively working toward creating a workforce that mirrors and responds to the communities in which we operate and reflects the growing diversity of the marketplace—increasing our competitiveness, living our values and assuring our position as the enterprise mobility company.

Additional Information

Symbol's diversity program is currently under review. We have quite a few activities planned for this year, including the provision of five scholarships to Stony Brook University, two of which must go to women; targeted outreach to women and minority colleges and we are working closely with the Hispanic Association on Corporate Responsibility to promote Hispanics in the workforce. The following are just a couple of the activities in which we have been involved in the community:

In 2005, we provided a grant of $50,000 to the Urban League of Long Island to support the development of a computer resource room to provide educational services to youths—vocational exploration programs, college prep programs and youth development and leadership programs.

A grant of $10,000 was provided to Pronto to support Hispanics. The program includes ESL classes and job placement for youth and adults.

A grant of $15,000 was provided to the Long Island Fund for Women and Girls to support "Smart Careers for Girls," a program designed to expand the interest of girls and young women in science, technology and engineering and math careers through increasing their exposure to specific information directly from women in these fields.

Synovus Financial Corp.

1000 5th Avenue
Columbus, GA 31901
Phone: (706) 644-0679
Fax: (706) 649-5793
www.synovus.com

Locations
Worldwide

Diversity Leadership
Audrey D. Hollingsworth
Senior Vice President, Director, HR Services

Employment Contact
Jeff Hart
Manager, Employment Services

Recruiting

Please list the schools/types of schools at which you recruit.
• Public state schools
• Historically black colleges and universities (HBCUs)
• Other predominantly minority and/or women's colleges

Do you have any special outreach efforts directed to encourage minority students to consider your firm?
• Advertise in minority student association publication(s)
• Participate in/host minority student job fair(s)
• Sponsor minority student association events
• Firm's employees participate on career panels at schools

What activities does the firm undertake to attract minority and women employees?
• Participate at minority job fairs
• Seek referrals from other employees
• Utilize online job services

Do you use executive recruiting/search firms to seek to identify new diversity hires?
No

Internships and Co-ops

Synovus Inter/CO-OP PROGRAM
Deadline for application: Varies depending on the position
Pay: $8 to $12 per hour
Length of the program: 10 to 12 weeks
Percentage of interns/co-ops in the program who receive offers of full-time employment: 40 percent
Web site for internship/co-op information: www.synovus.com

The internship program encompasses several departments within our family of companies. It varies from year to year.

Scholarships

Jack Parker Scholarship Fund (internal scholarship program)
Deadline for application for the scholarship program: Applications for the scholarship will be accepted each spring, with the award winners announced in the summer. Applications are reviewed and ranked by an independent, external scholarship selection committee.

Number and size of the awards to be granted will be determined each year by the board of directors of the Jack B. Parker Foundation, Inc., based on available funds. The most outstanding applicant is chosen to be the Jack Parker Scholar.

Our company strives to assist the families of our team members through the Jack Parker Centennial Scholarship Program. The Jack Parker Scholarship Program was established in 1988, as a part of the commemoration of the 100th anniversary of Columbus Bank and Trust Company. The scholarship program is managed by the Jack B. Parker Foundation, Inc., to award college or vocational institution scholarships to the children of Synovus family team members. The scholarship program and the foundation were named in memory of Jack B. Parker, whose career with our family of companies spanned 44 years. Jack's enthusiastic attitude, keen sense of duty and good heart were evident throughout his career. He served as resident historian, confidant and trainer for countless team members. Less well known was the role Jack played as an anonymous benefactor. Children of current, retired or deceased employees are eligible to submit an application for the scholarship program.

Entry-Level Programs, Full-time Opportunities and Training Programs

Management Associate Program

Length of program: Six to nine months

Geographic location(s) program: Columbus, Ga., and several banks in the Southeastern U.S.

This program includes on-the-job training and classroom training encompassing several areas of retail and commercial banking.

Strategic Plan and Diversity Leadership

How does the firm's leadership communicate the importance of diversity to everyone at the firm?

Our diversity council and the president of our company provide planned communication throughout the year. We use a variety of communication vehicles and messages. The value of diversity to our organization is displayed on our company web site to communicate our commitment to external sources. We use a formal print piece that is available for our CEO population to use during community or business meetings involving external audiences. Through our Intranet (INSITE), we deliver bimonthly articles to team members regarding various topics of interest on the subject of diversity. We also conduct an annual leadership presentation that includes progress results, goals and new-year targets on diversity. Our council meets semi-monthly to address issues of diversity, develop programmatic initiatives and prepare for focus groups session with team members.

Who has primary responsibility for leading diversity initiatives at your firm?

Audrey D. Hollingsworth, senior vice president, director, financial services HR.

Does your firm currently have a diversity committee?

Yes, the Synovus Diversity Council is comprised of various senior/executive-level corporate leaders from throughout the enterprise. The council convenes every other month to discuss goals, progress and additional efforts that can be made to further our commitment to diversity.

If yes, does the committee's representation include one or more members of the firm's management/executive committee (or the equivalent)?

Yes

Does the committee and/or diversity leader establish and set goals or objectives consistent with management's priorities?

Yes, we continue to set three major goals that aligned with our leadership priorities: diversity training for all of our leaders, targeted development plans for minorities and females and representation progress in the leadership tier.

Has the firm undertaken a formal or informal diversity program or set of initiatives aimed at increasing the diversity of the firm?

Yes, formal. There are five areas that we use to measure and assess progress toward improving representation in our organization. Those areas are workforce, leadership, top salaried, new hires and board of directors (we are substituting board of directors for termination results). We measure our progress against our community statistics, establish targets and measure progress. This year, we will introduce a report card to assess individual company results.

How often does the firm's management review the firm's diversity progress/results?

Quarterly

How is the firm's diversity committee and/or firm management held accountable for achieving results?

There is no formal accountability that is specifically directed at the council; however, the council holds itself accountable by publishing our goals to our team members and providing the team members with updates on progress toward our diversity goals. Essentially, our total workforce holds the council accountable for delivering on the expectations that are established. It is about our credibility for doing what we say we will do.

The Stats

	NUMBER OF EMPLOYEES	REVENUE
	2006	2006
Total in the U.S.	12,351	$2.6 billion

Diversity Mission Statement

We are committed to creating an environment that appreciates individuality. And now, more than ever, we're renewing our commitment to diversity. We continue to recognize diversity as a broad collection of differences that encompasses many elements: beliefs, race, work styles, age, education, ethnic origin, gender, ideas, physical ability, perspectives and more.

We believe that a wide "band of inclusion" helps to increase team member performance, empowerment, satisfaction, productivity, equity, creativity, respect and fairness. Our focus on diversity will also position us to better promote diverse business partnerships, expand our customer base, attract and retain the top talent in the market, make the company a better place to work, better understand our diverse customers' unique needs, give customers and communities outstanding service, and deliver greater value to our stakeholders. At Synovus, valuing and leveraging our differences is an essential part of our organization's success.

Our diversity strategy includes:

• *Business partnerships:* Developing relationships with diverse business partners

• *Development:* Establishing mentoring and networking models that facilitate the continued growth and development of our team members

• *Education:* Discussing the benefits, value and management of diversity

• *Representation:* Visible diversity at all levels of the organization

• *Workplace practices:* Modifying our recruiting and hiring strategy to position us to compete for a diverse talent pool

Diversity creates an environment where team members can contribute innovative ideas, seek challenge, assume leadership and continue to focus on and exceed business, professional and personal objectives. One approach toward individual success is to give people meaningful, challenging work and mentors to help them along the way.

Target Corporation

<table>
<tr><td>

1000 Nicollet Mall, TPS-0955
Minneapolis, MN 55343

Locations

Target's headquarters is located in Minneapolis, Minnesota. Target has over 1,500 store locations in 47 states, more than 30 distribution centers and import warehouses and offices in over 40 countries throughout the world to support our global sourcing initiatives.

</td><td>

Employment Contact

Yvonne Harris
Diversity Recruitment Manager
www.target.com/careers

</td></tr>
</table>

Recruiting

Please list the schools/types of schools at which you recruit.

- Ivy League schools
- Other private schools
- Public state schools
- Historically black colleges and universities (HBCUs)
- Hispanic serving institutions (HSIs)
- Other predominantly minority and/or women's colleges

Do you have any special outreach efforts directed to encourage minority students and graduates to consider your firm?

- Hold a reception for minority students
- Conferences: National Black MBA, National Society of Hispanic MBAs, National Hispanic Business Association, Monster Diversity Leadership Program, National Association of Asian American Professionals, National INROADS Alumni Association, Consortium for Graduate Study in Management
- Advertise in minority student association publication(s) or other minority-focused publications
- Participate in/host minority student job fair(s) or other minority-focused job events
- Sponsor minority student association events
- Firm's employees participate on career panels at school
- Outreach to leadership of minority student organizations
- Scholarships or intern/fellowships for minority students

What activities does the firm undertake to attract minority and women employees?

- Partner programs with women and minority associations
- Conferences
- Participate at minority job fairs
- Seek referrals from other employees
- Utilize online job services

Internships and Co-ops

Target Headquarters, Stores or Distribution Internship

Deadline for application: On-campus interviews—fall and spring

Number of interns in the program in summer 2006 (internship) or 2006 (co-op): Over 1,000

Pay: Depends on position

Length of the program: 10 to 12 weeks

Percentage of interns/co-ops in the program who receive offers of full-time employment: 50 percent general/75 percent INROADS

Web site for internship/co-op information: www.target.com/campus

Stores Overview

10-week program with rotations in the following areas:

- Assets protection
- Guest services
- Human resources
- Logistics
- Perishables
- Pharmacy
- Sales floor
- Opportunity to complete a hands-on project within your focus area
- Executive partnership and shadow rotation
- Interact with executives and top leaders in a Fortune 100 company
- Opportunity to strengthen your leadership skills
- Learn about merchandising, guest service and inventory management to maximize sales
- Availability to attend executive level leadership training classes

Qualifications:

- *Undergrad:* Currently enrolled or accepted in a four-year degree program with strong academic performance
- Leadership and strong decision-making skills
- Ability to communicate clearly and effectively in all situations
- Team-oriented thinking
- Committed to self development and developing others
- Strong cognitive skills, including problem analysis, decision making, financial and quantitative analysis
- Desire to pursue a career in retail management

Distribution Overview

10-week program designed to provide a realistic sense of distribution operations, an executive's role and our culture

Achieved through technical and leadership training, project work, committee participation

Key training objectives:

- Gain an understanding of distribution operations and supply chain management
- Gain an understanding of Target culture
- Learn what it means to be an effective Target leader
- Gain a picture of how a world-class supply chain organization operates
- Work in a fast-paced, technologically advanced, clean, bright operation
- Become part of a leadership organization that moves boxes
- Leave an imprint on the organization

Qualifications:

- Thrives in a fast-paced, results-focused, collaborative environment
- Strong ability to develop relationships with others
- Strong communication skills
- Interested in leading others
- Approaches the opportunity with initiative
- Commitment to learning
- Ready to have fun!

Headquarters Overview

The 10-week HQ internship is designed to give hands-on real world experience in the following areas:

- Target technology services
- Property development (real estate, construction, architecture, engineering, store planning and design, building services)
- Target sourcing services
- Finance/accounting
- Merchandising/merchandising presentation
- Target.com

- Graphic design marketing
- Store support/assets protection
- Target financial services
- Housing and airfare available for out of state interns

Interns will:

- Work with a team, manager and mentor
- Play a significant role in analyzing/developing company strategies
- Responsible for completing a project and presenting results at the conclusion of the internship
- Receive developmental feedback through classroom training, on-the-job application and the formal review process
- Participate in social networking events, executive lunches, Metro Intern Exchange, volunteer opportunities and involvement with Target's Diversity Business Councils

Qualifications:

- Demonstrated leadership skills
- Excellent analytical skills
- Outstanding verbal and written communication skills
- Strong computer skills
- Superior planning and organizational skills

Target also hires interns from INROADS at the corporate, store and distribution center levels. Target is a founding member of the INROADS Retail Management Institute, aimed at attracting more students of color to retail careers. In addition, Target has the Executive-In-Training Program, where a priority is placed on sourcing and staffing positions with diversity candidates.

Scholarships

We fund undergraduate scholarships through general scholarship funds of the schools where we recruit, as well as provide graduate scholarships through our partnerships with NBMBAA, NSHMBA and CGSM. We also provide funding to the United Negro College Fund and the Hispanic Scholarship Fund.

Affinity Groups

- African-American Business Council
- Asian American Business Council
- GLBT Business Council
- Hispanic Business Council

Target's Diversity Business Councils aim to create an inclusive environment and provide a forum to exchange information, share common interests and establish mentoring relationships. Each business council is focused on helping team members grow professionally and has specific programs and objectives centered on retention and development.

Entry-Level Programs, Full-Time Opportunities and Training Programs

Target Training Programs:

• Team Leader In-Training (distribution centers, business analyst (HQ/merchandising)

• Human Resources In Training (distribution, HQ, and stores)

• Executive Team Leader-In-Training (stores)

• Target Technology Leadership Program (HQ)

Length of program: 12-week training program

Geographic location(s) of program: Nationally

Our extensive training program involves classroom and on-the-job experience and a mentor who works with the team member throughout the training.

Tuition reimbursement is available.

Strategic Plan and Diversity Leadership

How does the firm's leadership communicate the importance of diversity to everyone at the firm?

Target uses all of the corporation's communication channels to share diversity information, including e-mails, web site, newsletters, posters, brochures, etc. Furthermore, Target annually administers an internal communication campaign centered on diversity awareness.

Who has primary responsibility for leading diversity initiatives at your firm?

The director of diversity

Does your firm currently have a diversity committee?

Yes

If please describe how the committee is structured, how often it meets, etc.

Target has a cross-functional Diversity Steering Committee chaired by a member of senior management. The committee meets quarter-

ly and is comprised of leaders from throughout the corporation. The objective of the committee is to provide direction, feedback and guidance on Target's corporate diversity efforts.

If yes, does the committee's representation include one or more members of the firm's management/executive committee (or the equivalent)?

Yes

If yes, how many executives are on the committee?

Total Executives on Committee: 20 executives and employees

Does the committee and/or diversity leader establish and set goals or objectives consistent with management's priorities?

Yes

Has the firm undertaken a formal or informal diversity program or set of initiatives aimed at increasing the diversity of the firm?

Yes, formal

How often does the firm's management review the firm's diversity progress/results?

Monthly

How is the firm's diversity committee and/or firm management held accountable for achieving results?

Management is required to report annually to the Target board of directors on its progress in achieving our diversity goals and objectives.

The Stats

	NUMBER OF EMPLOYEES	
	2006	2005
Total in the U.S.	374,566	348,914
Total outside the U.S.	2,624	2,317
Total worldwide	376,883	351,5358

The Stats cont'd

2006 DEMOGRAPHIC PROFILE (EEO report for 2006)	
FEMALE TEAM MEMBERS	
Officials and managers	45 percent
Professionals	59 percent
Sales workers	63 percent
All employees	59 percent

DIVERSE TEAM MEMBERS	
Officials and managers	24 percent
Professionals	16 percent
Sales workers	45 percent
All employees	41 percent

Diversity Mission Statement

Our diversity statement

Target is a performance-based company with equal opportunities for all who perform.

Our commitment

We respect and value the individuality of all team members and guests. We know that valuing diversity makes good business sense and helps to ensure our future success.

Our definition of diversity

We define diversity as individuality. This individuality may include a wide spectrum of attributes like personal style, age, race, gender, ethnicity, sexual orientation, language, physical ability, religion, family, citizenship status, socioeconomic circumstances, education and life experiences. To us, diversity is any attribute that makes an individual unique that does not interfere with effective job performance.

Additional Information

Discrimination based upon race, color, religion, sex, age, national origin, disability, sexual orientation or other characteristics protected by law is not tolerated in our work place. In addition to prohibiting such discrimination, we attempt to create an environment that recognizes the value of diversity and enhances the opportunity for success of all team members regardless of their differences.

The following are examples of initiatives within Target that are intended to promote diversity throughout our organization:

• Minority recruitment: Employees of diverse backgrounds are sought by attending minority job fairs (National Black MBA)

• Association, National Society of Hispanic MBAs and Consortium for Graduate Study in Management), placing ads in minority media, posting jobs and looking for candidates on minority-focused web sites (such as *DiversityInc* and *HireDiversity*), posting positions at schools and other public places with high minority populations, attending national meetings of minority organizations and publishing and distributing recruitment literature emphasizing our commitment to diversity.

Target is committed to providing job opportunities for people with disabilities. Target participates in community-based training by seeking out agencies, school programs and government incentive programs in an effort to hire people with disabilities.

Diversity training: Target provides training programs to all its employees and leadership development to all supervisory level team members—and diversity training is an integral part of that development. We provide training that is intended to enhance awareness of diversity in the workplace and to build the skills necessary to promote that diversity and the benefits it offers.

Diversity team: Target has an internal diversity team that is solely dedicated to leveraging diversity throughout the organization. The team focuses on recruitment and retention, awareness and communication, and measurement and works with business partners throughout the company to provide diversity guidance and drive change.

Involvement and partnerships: Target has partnerships with many diversity-focused organizations, including:

• INROADS
• The Consortium For Graduate Study in Management (CGSM)
• Monster Diversity Leadership Program (Monster DLP)
• National Association of Asian American Professionals (NAAAP)
• The National Black MBA Association Conference (NBMBAA)
• The National Society of Hispanic MBAs (NSHMBA)
• National Hispanic Business Association (NHBA)
• The National Minority Supplier Development Council (NMSDC)
• The Women's Business Enterprise National Council (WBENC)
• The Urban League
• The United Negro College Fund (UNCF)
• The Hispanic College Fund (HCF)

Diversity has been one of the strengths of our company and will continue to be an important part of our business strategy as we expand into new and different markets. We are committed to promoting and reinforcing diversity throughout our company as we position our business for continued success in the 21st century.

Use the Internet's
MOST TARGETED
job search tools.

Vault Job Board

Target your search by industry, function, and experience level, and find the job openings that you want.

VaultMatch Resume Database

Vault takes match-making to the next level: post your resume and customize your search by industry, function, experience and more. We'll match job listings with your interests and criteria and e-mail them directly to your in-box.

VAULT
> the most trusted name in career information™

Tech Data Corporation

5301 Tech Data Drive
Clearwater, FL 33760
Phone: (727) 539-7429
Fax: (727) 539-7429

Locations

Clearwater, FL (HQ)

Diversity Leadership

Ed Krauss

Contact Person

Amy Blake
Manager, Employment
5301 Tech Data Drive
Clearwater, FL 33760
Phone: (727) 539-7429
Fax: (727) 539-7429
www.techdata.com/careers

Recruiting

Please list the schools/types of schools at which you recruit.

- *Public state schools:* University of South Florida, University of Florida, Florida State, University of Tampa, Eckerd College, University of Central Florida
- *Historically black colleges and universities (HBCUs):* Florida A&M University

Do you have any special outreach efforts directed to encourage minority students to consider your firm?

- Advertise in minority student association publication(s)
- Participate in/host minority student job fair(s)
- Scholarships or intern/fellowships for minority students
- INROADS internship program

What activities does the firm undertake to attract minority and women employees?

- Partner programs with women and minority associations
- Participate at minority job fairs
- Seek referrals from other employees
- Utilize online job services

Do you use executive recruiting/search firms to seek to identify new diversity hires?

Yes

Internships and Co-ops

INROADS

Deadline for application: Fall

Pay: $10 to $12 per hour (full-time), paid biweekly

Length of the program: 12 weeks

Percentage of interns/co-ops in the program who receive offers of full-time employment: 100 percent

Strategic Plan and Diversity Leadership

How does the firm's leadership communicate the importance of diversity to everyone at the firm?

E-mail, quarterly employee meetings, web site and town hall meetings.

Who has primary responsibility for leading diversity initiatives at your firm?

Ed Krauss, senior manager, employment operations

Does your firm currently have a diversity committee?

Yes

If yes, please describe how the committee is structured, how often it meets, etc.

14 members who meet once a month.

If yes, does the committee's representation include one or more members of the firm's management/executive committee (or the equivalent)?

Yes

Does the committee and/or diversity leader establish and set goals or objectives consistent with management's priorities?

Yes

Has the firm undertaken a formal or informal diversity program or set of initiatives aimed at increasing the diversity of the firm?

Yes, formal

How often does the firm's management review the firm's diversity progress/results?

Twice a year

Retention and Professional Development

Please identify the specific steps you are taking to reduce the attrition rate of minority and women employees.

• Increase/improve current work/life programs

• Succession plan includes emphasis on diversity

• Work with minority and women employees to develop career advancement plans

• Professional skills development program, including minority and women employees

• We also analyze exit interview data to identify opportunities for improvements and trends

Diversity Mission Statement

Tech Data's philosophy has always striven to place the greatest emphasis on the role of the individual within the company. That emphasis on the individual, at the same time, requires Tech Data to pay attention to the fact that each employee brings a wealth of different perspectives to the work environment. Tech Data and its employees need to be respectful not only of those differences, but learn how to make difference, in itself, an additional value which can be incorporated into how others are treated and customers are approached.

The concept of meaningful sameness and meaningful difference is not a new one. Meaningful sameness is needed in order for people to operate within the context of a common set of standards and values for everyday operation. Employees also need to contribute meaningfully to the company in the performance of their jobs. Concurrently, Tech Data and its employees must respect and encourage meaningful difference, with the assumption that people from different perspectives provide vitality, creativity, new ideas and growth.

Multiculturalism seeks to look at difference in the broadest parameters. Culture is often defined to include terms of race, gender and national origin, and these specific indices are, of course, vital in shaping values.

Additionally, culture also involves values derived from considerations relating to one's age, marital status, religion, sexual orientation, gender identity and/or expression and disability. All of these factors, and more, shape an individual's value system, and all of these have actual potential value to Tech Data as a company.

Tech Data provides equal opportunity for all employees and applicants for employment regardless of race, color, creed, religion, national origin, sexual orientation, age or sex. Similarly, Tech Data has stated that individuals with physical and mental limitations are evaluated on their ability to perform a specific job rather than on stereotypical assumptions about their disability, and that reasonable accommodations are made when appropriate. Tech Data continues to hold steadfast to this philosophy.

A policy limited to equal opportunity, however, is not sufficient to attract and retain members of historically underrepresented groups. While Tech Data has attracted an immensely talented workforce, the nets must be cast much more widely to attract available talent. The process Tech Data uses for that purpose is affirmative action; it is a means for Tech Data to achieve multiculturalism, i.e. the existence and valuing of difference. Tech Data's operating assumption is that talent is randomly distributed in all populations, and that Tech Data benefits by the participation of different groups in its workforce.

Affirmative action is a concept misunderstood by many. In many people's minds, it has meant lowered standards or preferential treatment. Tech Data's position is that we can behave affirmatively while retaining the highest standards, but that more energy, planning and commitment must be dedicated to the inclusion of competitive talent from all segments of the population. That effort requires dedication, personal responsibility and investment of resources. Tech Data needs to continue to find ways to encourage and support hiring managers to make the extra efforts needed to attract the best people.

Multiculturalism is crucial to Tech Data domestically within the United States and as a global corporation. Tech Data's future success in the United States depends heavily upon the ability to harness and include the vitality of the burgeoning minority populations, both as employees and customers. No one group will have majority status within 10 years, and demographic factors will have major implications for the workforce composition, as well as customers.

Globally, the world is getting smaller and Tech Data's presence internationally becomes more prominent every day. Tech Data has always sought local talent in order to compete effectively, and Tech Data needs to be open to and inclusive of ideas and values that originate outside the United States. Tech Data will continue to seek ways to incorporate different perspectives in global operations.

Managing multiculturalism is a critical part of success for any 21st century company, and it is a challenge Tech Data is ready to pursue.

Thomson Corporation, The

One Station Place, Metro Center
Stamford, CT 06902
Phone: (651) 687-7924
Fax: (651) 687-2091

Locations

US: Ann Arbor, MI • Boston, MA •
Dallas, TX • Dexter, MI • Eagan, MN •
Los Angeles, CA • San Francisco, CA •
Stamford, CT

International: Brazil • Canada • Japan •
London • New Zealand • Singapore •
Switzerland • Toronto

Diversity Leadership

David Luna
Vice President, Global Diversity

Employment Contact

Jolie Chehadeh
Campus Recruiter
E-mail: jolie.chehadeh@thomson.com

Laurie Randall, Nancy Roe, Jim MacDonald,
John Qudeen, Barry Nimmich
Directors of Recruiting for the Strategic
Business Units
www.thomsoncareers.com

Recruiting

Please list the schools/types of schools at which you recruit.
• *Ivy League schools:* UPenn Wharton, Columbia, MIT, Harvard
• *Other private schools:* NYU, Boston University, Lehigh, Lafayette, Carnegie Mellon, Duke
• *Public state schools:* University of Minnesota, University of Michigan, MSU, ISU

Do you have any special outreach efforts directed to encourage minority students and graduates to consider your firm?
• *Participate in/host minority student job fair(s) or other minority-focused job events:* Multicultural and diversity fairs

What activities does the firm undertake to attract minority and women employees?
• Participate at minority job fairs
• Seek referrals from other employees
• Utilize online job services

Do you use executive recruiting/search firms to seek to identify new diversity hires?
Yes

If yes, list all women- and/or minority-owned executive search/recruiting firms to which the firm paid a fee for placement services in the past 12 months:
Adecco

Internships and Co-ops

West Technology Internship Program

Deadline for application: Spring 2007 (April)

Number of interns in the program in summer 2006 (internship) or 2006 (co-op): 50 to 60 students

Pay: $20/hour

Length of the program: 12 weeks

Percentage of interns/co-ops in the program who receive offers of full-time employment: 50 percent

Web site for internship/co-op information: www.thomsoncareers.com

It is a formalized internship program for technology interns (software and systems engineers). Students are in their freshman, sophomore or junior year of undergraduate studies and pursuing a degree in computer science or computer engineering.

Affinity Groups

Rather than corporate-wide affinity groups, the various business locations have specific affinity groups relevant to the employee-base needs (work/life balance, photo clubs, etc.).

Entry-Level Programs, Full-Time Opportunities and Training Programs

Management Associates Program

Length of program: Two years

Geographic location(s) of program: Various U.S. and international locations (opportunity is based out of Stamford, Conn.)

Orientation into Thomson Corporate structure, networking with senior executives and quarterly training programs focusing on analytical skills, personal skills and team-building.

Tuition reimbursement is a corporate-wide component for all employees. The Management Associates Program also provides relocation assistance. Most importantly, the opportunity provides a formal mentor within the organization (senior management) and an external professional coach for professional and personal development over the two-year period.

Strategic Plan and Diversity Leadership

What trends in your industry affect your corporate diversity goals, strategies and/or internal or external alliances?

Changing lives of working professionals, changes in technology, new acquisitions in new markets and geographic locations.

How does the firm's leadership communicate the importance of diversity to everyone at the firm?

Company web site (Intranet)

Who has primary responsibility for leading diversity initiatives at your firm?

David Luna, vice president, global diversity

Does your firm currently have a diversity committee?

No

Does the committee and/or diversity leader establish and set goals or objectives consistent with management's priorities?

Partially. It is a new initiative and it is a work in progress as David Luna establishes a Thomson-wide diversity program.

Has the firm undertaken a formal or informal diversity program or set of initiatives aimed at increasing the diversity of the firm?

Yes, informal (hoping to make it more formalized in the future).

How often does the firm's management review the firm's diversity progress/results?

Annually

How is the firm's diversity committee and/or firm management held accountable for achieving results?

That is to be determined as we recognize the importance of diversity initiatives and work to build out a formalized, corporate-wide accepted program.

The Stats

	NUMBER OF EMPLOYEES		REVENUE	
	2006	2005	2006	2005
Total in the U.S.	44,000	44,000	$6.6 billion	$6.1 billion

Retention and Professional Development

How do 2006 minority and female attrition rates generally compare to those experienced in the prior year period?

About the same as in prior years.

Please identify the specific steps you are taking to reduce the attrition rate of minority and women employees.

• Develop and/or support internal employee affinity groups (e.g., minority or women networks within the firm)

• Increase/improve current work/life programs

• Work with minority and women employees to develop career advancement plans

• Professional skills development program, including minority and women employees

Toyota Motor Company

19001 S. Western Ave, A134
Torrance, CA 90501
Phone: (310) 468-2083
Fax: (310) 381-6842
www.toyota.com/talentlink

Locations

Torrance, CA

Diversity Leadership

Fabiola Gonzalez
College Recruiter

Employment Contact

Jenn Gonzalez
HR Representative
E-mail: jennifer_gonzalez@toyota.com

Recruiting

Please list the schools/types of schools at which you recruit.

• Other private schools

• Public state schools

• Historically black colleges and universities (HBCUs)

• Other predominantly minority and/or women's colleges

Do you have any special outreach efforts directed to encourage minority students to consider your firm?

• *Conferences:* Atlanta University Center (AUC) and National Hispanic

• Advertise in minority student association publication(s)

• Participate in/host minority student job fair(s)

• Sponsor minority student association events

• Outreach to leadership of minority student organizations

• Scholarships or intern/fellowships for minority students

What activities does the firm undertake to attract minority and women employees?

• Partner programs with women and minority associations

• *Conferences:* NHBA and AUC

• Participate at minority job fairs

• Seek referrals from other employees

• Utilize online job services

Internships and Co-ops

Corporate Summer Intern Program

Deadline for application: September 1st to February 28th

Pay: $14 per hour

Length of the program: 10 weeks

Percentage of interns/co-ops in the program who receive offers of full-time employment: 67 percent

Web site for internship/co-op information: www.toyota.com/talentlink

The program is designed to provide the intern with exposure to the automotive industry while working in a corporate environment. While internship assignments vary based on company business need, specific functions will revolve around project-based work aimed at supporting the work group. Examples of past internships include:

• Advertising

• Business

• Distribution operations

• Financial planning

• Interactive marketing

• Market representation

• Scion

• Supplier diversity

• Toyota certified used vehicles

• Toyota dealer consulting

• Toyota Rent-A-Car (TRAC)

• Vehicle marketing

Location: TMS national headquarters, located in Torrance, Calif.

Qualifications:

• Must have only one semester/year left of school

• Candidates should be pursuing a BA/BS in business, communications, marketing, liberal arts or other related degrees

Customer Relations Internship

Deadline for application: September 1st to March 15th

Pay: $17 per hour

Length of the program: 10 weeks full time in the summer, part-time during final school year

Percentage of interns/co-ops in the program who receive offers of full-time employment: 50 percent

Web site for internship/co-op information: www.toyota.com/talentlink

The customer relations intern program provides college students with exposure to the automotive industry while working in a corporate environment. As a customer relations intern, you will receive an initial three-and-a-half weeks of classroom training that includes comprehensive training on all Toyota vehicles, products, services and policies. Training in the areas of communication, problem solving, negotiation and customer satisfaction is also provided.

After training, your primary responsibility will be communicating with customers who contact the customer experience center's toll-free number. You will work within a team environment where you will act as a liaison between Toyota owners, prospective consumers, dealerships, Toyota region offices and Toyota headquarters. You will be required to analyze customer concerns (i.e. requests for financial assistance, dealer sales or service-related complaints, or product-related concerns) and determine the appropriate action to positively impact owner satisfaction and retention.

Customer relations is one of the key entry-level positions for Toyota and offers a tremendous opportunity to learn about Toyota products, the inner workings of the company and how to work effectively with a diverse customer base. As a CR intern, your overall mission is to document the voice of the customer and build lifetime advocates for Toyota. The skills you acquire will be invaluable for your career in business.

Location: Torrance, Calif.

Qualifications:

• You should have achieved junior status and be within two semesters or three quarters of graduation.

• You must exhibit sound customer service orientation and the ability to work within a professional corporate setting, along with the following skills: written and oral communication, time management, negotiation and problem-solving, initiative, teamwork, planning and organization.

• You should have direct experience in dealing with customers in challenging situations and the ability to make appropriate decisions when considering the interests of both the customer and Toyota.

• A desire to work in the automotive industry long-term, and previous automotive experience is a plus.

Additional Information:

• This internship is designed as a 12-month program. During the summer months, you will work full time (40 hours per week).

• During the school year, you will work part-time (approx. 15 hours per week) on a flexible schedule, but with a commitment to work a minimum of four hours every Monday.

• Upon completion of the internship, consideration for full-time Toyota openings will be available to you.

Automotive Technology Internship

Deadline for application: September 1st to February 28th

Pay: $16 per hour

Length of the program: 10 weeks

Percentage of interns in the program who receive offers of full-time employment: 70 percent

Web site for internship/co-op information: www.toyota.com/talentlink

The program is designed to provide the intern with exposure to the automotive industry while working in a corporate environment.

The intern will be assigned various duties to support the activities of the department. Focus is primarily on projects scheduled for completion over the summer. Internship assignments vary based on the business need of the company. Examples of past internships and possible projects include:

• *Lexus technical support:* Provide support to product engineers for model launch activities, including preparing support materials for region or area offices and dealership technical associates

• *North American production support:* Assist with new vehicle launch activities

• *Product quality assurance body:* Support TAS operations with call volume analysis, conduct hands-on body department problem investigations and conduct field report analysis to determine extent of problems

• *Product quality assurance chassis:* Gather and report technical information on customer concerns reported by Toyota-Lexus field offices, investigate recovered parts to determine root cause of customer complaint, update and maintain technical databases

• *Product quality assurance electrical:* Gather and report technical information on customer concerns reported by Toyota-Lexus field offices, coordinate part recovery and parts test requests assigned to the department

• *Product quality assurance powertrain:* Warranty analysis, warranty part recovery, assist in the development of powertrain TSBs, and assist with the installation and evaluation of test parts on fleet vehicles

• *Service technology:* Support of scan tool software development activities and perform tool and equipment group support activities

• *Technical training:* Assist in the development of training curriculum for dealership service technicians, which includes researching, drafting and proof-reading of technical material, photo and video shoots for new model training

• *Vehicle service center:* Greet customers and dispatch repair orders to available technicians, process Toyota and Lexus warranty claims, inventory Toyota special tools and perform parts inventory

Location: Torrance, CA

Qualifications:

- One semester/year of school left before graduation
- Major in automotive technology or related degree
- Proficiency in MS Word, Excel and PowerPoint

Summer Relocation Assistance:

For candidates more than 50 miles away, Toyota will cover the following expenses:

- Round trip airfare or driving reimbursement
- Subsidized housing
- Subsidized lease car for out of state
- Shipping of 50 lbs to and from Torrance, CA

INROADS Summer Internship

Deadline for application: INROADS deadline

Pay: $13 to $14 per hour, depending on year in school

Length of the program: 10 weeks

Percentage of interns/co-ops in the program who receive offers of full-time employment: 100 percent

Web site for internship/co-op information: www.toyota.com/talentlink

The program is designed to provide the intern with exposure to the automotive industry while working in a corporate environment. While internship assignments vary based on company business need, specific functions will revolve around project-based work aimed at supporting the work group. Examples of past internships include:

- Advertising
- Financial planning
- Toyota certified used vehicles
- Vehicle marketing
- Scion
- Market representation
- Supplier diversity
- Toyota dealer consulting
- Distribution operations
- Toyota Rent-A-Car (TRAC)
- Interactive marketing
- eBusiness

Location: TMS national headquarters, located in Torrance, Calif.

Qualifications:

- Must have only one semester/year left of school
- Candidates should be pursuing a BA/BS in business, communications, marketing, liberal arts or other related degrees

Affinity Groups

African-American Collaborative (AAC)

We, as a group of dedicated associates of Toyota North America, have elected to form an organization to support Toyota's success by encouraging, through information and education, an environment that recognizes and respects diversity in the workplace, thereby creating a positive environment for all associates.

AAC is currently active in the Greater Kentucky/Cincinnati area

Gay and Lesbian (Bisexual Transgender and Friends) Alliance at Toyota (GALA)

As a group of dedicated associates of Toyota Motor Sales, we have chosen to form an organization to support the success of TMS by developing and supporting an environment that recognizes and respects diversity in the workplace, thereby creating a positive environment for all associates.

Toyota Asian American Society in Alliance (TAASiA)

Represent the diverse Asian American cultures and heritages within Toyota and in the broader community. We will leverage the strength and growing population of Asian Americans to foster an environment and corporate culture of diversity and inclusion in order to become the most respected automotive company in the world.

Toyota Organization for the Development of Latinos (TODOS)

TODOS is dedicated to the enhancement of the personal and professional development of its members. Our goal is to provide opportunities for mentoring, networking and community involvement. Furthermore, we represent a community that values diversity and inclusion. This community will foster creativity and thoughtful risk-taking to assist Toyota in becoming the most successful and respected car company in America.

Women's Business Partnering Group (Torque)

Torque is a catalyst to advance the personal and professional development of women at Toyota, enabling our full contribution by influencing systemic change, while increasing inclusion opportunities and human capital.

Entry-Level Programs, Full-Time Opportunities and Training Programs

Sales, Marketing and Service Trainee (MT) Program

The Sales, Marketing and Service Trainee Program is designed to provide you with broad exposure to automotive wholesale and retail operations prior to becoming a field traveler in a Toyota, Scion or Lexus field office. Through this rotational training program, you will gain hands-on experience in several departments within Toyota's national headquarters. The program incorporates on-the-job training as well as classroom training in time management, computer skills and retail operations.

Field analyst: Following successful completion of training, you will interview for an open position as a field analyst and be relocated to one of the Toyota of Lexus field sales offices throughout the United States. As an analyst, your function may vary as a merchandising or customer satisfaction analyst, among others.

Field traveler: After one to two years as a field analyst, you will be assigned to a position as a field traveler. As a field traveler, you will be the primary contact for a district of eight to twelve dealerships, representing TMS to assist dealers in achieving business objectives. The field traveler position typically requires heavy travel (80 to 90 percent) during the week and possible weekend assignments.

In preparation for the field analyst and field traveler positions, you will spend six to 12 months in a rotational training program involving two to three job rotations within corporate headquarter departments, such as the Toyota or Lexus customer assistance center, warranty, marketing, advertising, product education, sales administration or service and parts operations.

Location: Training takes place at Toyota's national headquarters, located in Torrance, Calif. Upon completion of corporate rotational assignments, trainees transition to one of our nationwide field offices (Portland, San Francisco, Los Angeles, Denver, Cincinnati, Chicago, Boston, New York or Atlanta). Candidates must be willing to relocate within the U.S. Placement is determined by business need.

Qualifications:

• Candidates should possess a BA or BS in business administration, marketing, management, automotive technology or related degree. Desired skills include strong interpersonal skills; ability to think on one's feet; effective customer relationship management skills; and proficiency in Word, Excel and PowerPoint. Dealership experience and/or automotive industry internship is helpful but not required.

Technical Service Corporate Trainee

Twelve- to 24-month training program in the product technical services department, which consists of six month rotations. This allows trainees to immerse themselves in projects resulting in a stronger understanding of the technical aspects of Toyota and Lexus products, as well as current dealer vehicle repair practices.

Rotations (Possible assignments include):

• Product quality assurance (four groups include: body, chassis, electrical and powertrain)

• This department reports and tracks vehicle technical issues from the first reports of a potential concern until the issue has been researched and, if necessary, resolved with a field fix or production change.

Technical and body training

This department is responsible for the development of technical and body-training courses offered to Toyota and Lexus dealership associates.

Accessory product quality assurance

This department is responsible for all aspects of accessory quality. Accessory product quality works to establish and maintain stringent accessory quality standards for companies producing accessories for Toyota and Lexus vehicles.

Service technology

This department is responsible for developing and researching special tools which dealerships will be required to purchase.

Duties include project-oriented assignments within one of three program tracks: product quality assurance, technical training or technical operations. At the beginning of the program, you will also be matched with a mentor.

Location: Torrance, Calif.

Qualifications:

• BA or BS automotive technology, industrial management, automotive service management or related degree.

• Proficiency in MS Word, Excel and PowerPoint

Information Technology Corporate Trainee

Toyota offers a 24-month training program in the information systems division, which consists of four six-month rotation assignments. The program allows corporate trainees to immerse themselves in IT projects, resulting in a technical understanding of IT systems for Toyota, Lexus and Scion divisions.

Rotation assignments:

A variety of rotation assignments for corporate trainees are available, including technical, business and field rotations. Examples of possible rotation assignments include:

Technical rotations

Enterprise data management (EDM): EDM's long-term strategy is to create single databases that encompass a particular subject area, enabling all users of data to use data from a single source—eliminating redundancy and creating efficiency.

Automotive or Toyota customer services: These groups provide support for large-scale, multi-platform applications—defining, developing and delivering enhancements projects for the vehicles business

units. Rotations through various phases of IT system enhancements or implementations provide corporate trainees the ability to learn about the various lifecycles of a system. Project management skills are developed during this rotation.

Business rotations

IS strategy and governance: This department is responsible for the IS strategic planning and governance processes, providing strategic research, process improvements, project recommendations and executive presentations.

Field rotation for technical and business programs

Toyota technology field operations: The IT field rotation offers exposure to the sales organization from an IT perspective. Field rotations may include Georgia, Illinois, Iowa, Maryland, New Jersey or Oregon.

Location: Rotation assignments located in Torrance, Calif. and U.S. field location.

Qualifications:

• BA or BS in computer engineering or technology, information systems, business administration or related degree

• Proficiency in MS Word, Excel and PowerPoint

• Strong written and verbal communication skills

Logistics training and development program

An 18-month on-the-job training program which develops high-performing logistics professionals into leaders who model Toyota values and continually challenge existing systems to improve quality, costs and lead times within Toyota's North American parts logistics division operations.

Tracks:

Candidates hired for the program will be matched with one of the following tracks and locations:

• *Procurement and inventory control:* Headquarters located in Torrance, Calif.; North American parts center in Ontario, Calif.; North American parts center in Hebron, Ky.

• *Physical distribution management:* A parts distribution center in a metropolitan location—Los Angeles, Chicago, Boston, Cincinnati, Kansas City, New York, Portland, Baltimore or San Francisco

• *Planning and strategy:* Headquarters located in Torrance, Calif.

Duties may include on-the-job training plan to be completed at the rotational training site. This training is designed to provide the trainee with hands-on learning, leadership opportunities and business insight within one of the three tracks listed above. Included in overall training program will be a short departure from the individual's assigned track to gain insight into the other two tracks, which are also key operating areas of the division. In addition, each indi-

vidual will receive core standardized training courses, which include, but are not limited to, Toyota production system, total quality management, total parts logistics, kaizen and leadership development.

Typical Career Path:

Operations: Logistics trainee > group leader > warehouse supervisor > operations supervisor > manager

Procurement: Logistics trainee > procurement analyst > procurement administrator > manager

Locations: Toyota has warehouse operations in Chicago, Cincinnati, Baltimore, Kansas City, Boston, Portland, San Francisco, Los Angeles and New York. Procurement positions are at the Hebron, Ky., and Ontario, Calif., locations. Planning and strategy positions are located at Toyota's headquarters in Torrance, Calif.

Qualifications:

• Bachelor's degrees in supply chain management, operations management or general business degrees are preferred for all tracks. Individuals with other degrees (psychology, education, etc.) but possessing supervisory experience are considered for the physical distribution track. Operations research and purchasing or procurement-related degrees are considered for procurement track.

• Proficiency in MS Word, Excel and PowerPoint

Strategic Plan and Diversity Leadership

How does the firm's leadership communicate the importance of diversity to everyone at the firm?

• Availability of diversity and inclusion training for everyone

• Champions for diversity and inclusion effort

• E-mails

• Internal diversity web site

• Speaking engagements at business partner group meetings

Who has primary responsibility for leading diversity initiatives at your firm?

Jerome Miller, VP, diversity and inclusion

Does your firm currently have a diversity committee?

Yes. The Diversity Steering committee comprises five senior executives who meet on a periodic basis to provide oversight and guidance on diversity opportunities and initiatives.

Has the firm undertaken a formal or informal diversity program or set of initiatives aimed at increasing the diversity of the firm?

Yes, formal

• Champions for diversity and inclusion

• Partnering with officers and department heads to enhance inclusion and leverage diversity within their division/department

• Moving the organization forward to diversity and inclusion awareness through formal and informal education

• Applying diversity and inclusion subject matter expertise to business priorities, objectives and opportunities

How often does the firm's management review the firm's diversity progress/results?

Monthly

The Stats

	NUMBER OF EMPLOYEES	REVENUE
	2006	2006
Total in the U.S.	260,000	$7.4 billion

Retention and Professional Development

Please identify the specific steps you are taking to reduce the attrition rate of minority and women employees.

• Develop and/or support internal employee affinity groups

• Strengthen mentoring program for all employees, including minorities and women

Diversity Mission Statement

Mission

To guide TMS in making diversity and inclusion an integral part of every aspect of our business to support Toyota in becoming the most respected and successful car company in America.

Vision

In an inclusive environment, all associates are respectfully and fully engaged in the work and life of the organization.

At TMS, diversity is our competitive advantage; understanding, embracing and leveraging our differences enables us to achieve our business goals.

Additional Information

Company Overview

Toyota Motor Sales, U.S.A., Inc. (TMS) is a wholly-owned subsidiary of Toyota Motor Corporation, one of the largest automotive manufacturers in the world. TMS is the marketing, sales, distribution and customer service arm of Toyota, Lexus and Scion in the United States, marketing products and services through a network of 1,415 Toyota, Lexus and Scion dealers in 49 states. Established in 1957, TMS and its subsidiaries also are involved in distribution logistics, motor sports, R&D and general aviation.

Travelers Companies, Inc. The

One Tower Square
Hartford, CT 06183

Diversity Leadership

Joelle M. Hayes
Director Talent Acquisition Diversity
One Tower Square
Hartford, CT 06183
Phone: (860) 954-8422
Fax: (860) 277-1970
E-mail: jmhayes@travelers.com

Employment Contact

Jessica Leifert
College Relations Consultant
One Tower Square, 1 MN
Hartford, CT 06183
E-mail: jleifert@travelers.com
Phone: (860) 277-1480
Fax: (800) 325-4672

Recruiting

Please list the schools/list of schools at which you recruit.

• Ivy League schools

• Private Schools

• Public state schools

• Historically black colleges and universities (HBCUs)

Do you have any special outreach efforts directed to encourage minority students and graduates to consider your firm?

• *Conferences:* National and regional

• Advertise in minority student association publication(s) or other minority-focused publications

• Participate in/host minority student job fair(s) or other minority-focused job events

What activities does the firm undertake to attract minority and women employees?

• *Partner programs with women and minority associations:* On-campus organizations (Women in Information Technology, etc)

• Conferences

• Participate at minority job fairs

• Seek referrals from other employees

• *Utilize online job services:* Diversity.com

Do you use executive recruiting/search firms to seek to identify new diversity hires?

No

Internships and Co-ops

The following internship programs are available at Travelers:

• Actuarial Leadership Development Program

• Finance Management Leadership Development Program

• Fixed Income Investments

• Human Resources Leadership Development Program

• Information Technology Leadership Development Program

• INROADS

• Personal Insurance Product Management Development Program

• Underwriting Development Program/ Bond Trainee

Deadline for application: No deadline

Number of interns in the program in summer 2006 (internship) or 2006 (co-op): 127 interns

Pay: Varies by program

Length of the program: 10 to 12 weeks

Percentage of interns/co-ops in the program who receive offers of full-time employment: Varies by program

Web site for internship/co-op information:
http://www.travelers.com/careers/new_grads/interns

Our internships offer:

- Work assignments for students with career aspirations in actuarial, finance, fixed income investments, human resources, IT, personal insurance product management
- Formal mentoring program
- Business learning events with executive presenters
- Subsidized housing for qualified students
- Intern-run committees: networking, community outreach and web site
- Social opportunities to meet other interns including picnics, summer gatherings and more

Requirements:

- GPA of 3.2 or greater
- Related major to applicable internship
- Demonstrated leadership skills
- Related experience to career interest
- Involvement in extracurricular activities is preferred
- Work availability from mid-May through August (10 to 12 weeks)
- Legally eligible to work in the United States

Entry-Level Programs, Full-Time Opportunities and Training Programs

Leadership Development Programs

- Actuarial Leadership Development Program
- Finance Management Leadership Development Program
- Information Technology Leadership Development Program
- Human Resources Leadership Development Program

Travelers Leadership Development Programs (LDP) are highly selective and engaging programs. From their inception in the early 1980s, they have attracted hundreds of talented participants, many of whom now hold crucial leadership and/or technical positions throughout the company and across the United States. Travelers Leadership Development Programs are available in the following areas: actuarial, financial management, human resources and information technology.

Travelers LDP core curriculum consists of multiple enrichment opportunities including:

Rotational Assignments: Individuals take part in multiple rotations that, depending on the program, last from six to 12 months each. Rotations become increasingly complex as individuals take on greater roles within the organization. LDP rotations provide individuals with a broad base of experience and skill sets which one can continually build upon.

Networking Opportunities: Travelers LDP provides individuals with numerous networking opportunities with program alumni and senior and executive-level leaders.

Mentoring Relationships: LDP participants take advantage of the knowledge and experience of both a peer and senior management mentor. These mentors guide and assist participants with their exposure to leadership opportunities and career development.

Ongoing Training: Training is imperative for building a successful career. Travelers multi-year educational program provides LDP participants with technical training, interpersonal and management skills, project management skills, as well as other managerial and technical skills training.

We understand that you've consistently worked hard and have the right to select from many opportunities. That's why if you seek to contribute at a high level, if you understand the rewards that come from constantly challenging yourself and if you desire to impart only the customer but the entire company that surrounds you, we invite you to explore the tremendous opportunities that Travel Leadership Development Program has to offer.

Length of program: Two to five years

Geographic location of program: Hartford, Conn. and St. Paul, Minn.

Web site for more information: http://travelers.com/careers/dp

Other Development Programs:

- BOND Trainee
- Claim Trainee
- Personal Insurance Product Management Development Program
- Personal Insurance Sales Specialist
- Underwriting Development Program

Length of program: Varies by program

Geographic location(s) of program: Programs have openings across the country except for the Personal Insurance Product Management Development Program (Hartford, Conn., only)

Web site for information: http://travelers.com/careers/dp

Tuition reimbursement, Actuarial Program—bonuses for each exam passed, paid study time.

Strategic Plan and Diversity Leadership

What trends in your industry affect your corporate diversity goals, strategies and/or internal or external alliances?

Baby boomers retiring, increase with marketing towards diverse groups.

How does the firm's leadership communicate the importance of diversity to everyone at the firm?

Web site

Who has primary responsibility for leading diversity initiatives at your firm?

Joelle M. Hayes, director, talent acquisition diversity

Does your firm currently have a diversity committee?

Yes

If yes, please describe how the committee is structured, how often it meets, etc.

Senior management and working groups. Meetings are biweekly.

If yes, does the committee's representation include one or more members of the firm's management/executive committee (or the equivalent)?

Yes

Does the committee and/or diversity leader establish and set goals or objectives consistent with management's priorities?

Yes

Has the firm undertaken a formal or informal diversity program or set of initiatives aimed at increasing the diversity of the firm?

Yes, formal

The Stats

	NUMBER OF EMPLOYEES	REVENUE
	2006	2006
Total in the U.S.	32,000	$24.365 million

Diversity Mission Statement

Our Commitment

At Travelers, we believe that by recognizing differences and encouraging the active participation of all employees, agents and customers in our business processes, we make better decisions, build more positive relationships, improve our opportunities and contribute to Travelers' success.

We hire a diverse workforce to reflect the communities we serve.

Travelers values the unique abilities and talents each individual brings to the organization, and recognizes that we benefit in numerous ways from differences in culture, ethnicity, national origin, race, color, religion, gender, age, disability and sexual orientation. We also believe it's important to strengthen our skilled, diverse workforce to respond to an increasingly diverse customer base.

We foster an inclusive environment for all employees.

Travelers supports a work environment where all employees feel they can work together to achieve their full potential.

We provide learning and development opportunities to advance diverse leaders.

Travelers provides opportunities for employees to seek career planning and mentoring assistance that will help them prepare for advancement. In addition, the company offers challenging job opportunities to help employees reach their personal potential.

We explore diverse markets today to tap into tomorrow's opportunities.

The insurance business depends on good relationships. To foster these relationships, Travelers is committed to acknowledging and valuing the diversity that exists among our workforce, our business partners, our customers and our communities. Our diverse workforce also better enables us to identify and capitalize on a wide range of business opportunities in diverse markets. We are committed to diversity in everything we say and do. Stated plainly, Travelers is progressive, professional and strongly committed to a diverse workforce.

Unilever US Inc.

800 Sylvan Avenue
Englewood Cliffs, NJ 07632
Phone: (800) 272-6296
Fax: (201) 541-5230

Locations
Global

Diversity Leadership
Lois Rubin, Diversity Manager
700 Sylvan Avenue
Fax: (201) 541-5230
Englewood Cliffs, NJ 07632
www.unileverusa.com

Employment Contact
Jennifer Feuer
University Relations Manager
700 Sylvan Avenue
Englewood Cliffs, NJ 07632
Phone: (800) 786-6988
Fax: (201) 541-5230
www.unileverusa.com

Recruiting

Please list the schools/list of schools at which you recruit.

• Ivy League schools
• Other private schools
• Public state schools
• Historically black colleges and universities (HBCUs)
• Hispanic serving institutions (HSIs)

Do you have any special outreach efforts directed to encourage minority students to consider your firm?

• Hold a reception for minority students
• Advertise in minority student association publication(s)
• Sponsor minority student association events
• Firm's employees participate on career panels at schools
• Outreach to leadership of minority student organizations
• Scholarships or intern/fellowships for minority students

What activities does the firm undertake to attract minority and women employees?

• Partner programs with women and minority associations
• Conferences
• Seek referrals from other employees
• Utilize online job services
• Various minority scholarship programs

Internships and Co-ops

Summer Internship Program, Supply Chain Co-op Program

Number of interns in the program in summer 2006 (co-op): 77

Length of the program: 10 weeks

Percentage of interns/co-ops in the program who receive offers of full-time employment: 65 percent

Web site for internship/co-op information: www.unileverusa.com

We hire interns from various campuses in the following fields: marketing, finance, IT, sales, supply chain and R&D for a 10- to 12-week summer internship program. Additionally, we hire INROADS and Jackie Robinson Foundation Scholars and recruit from SIFE competitions. We also have a supply chain co-op program.

Scholarships

• Jackie Robinson Foundation Legacy Award
• National Merit Scholarship Program

Affinity Groups

• African-American Business Network
• Asian Business Council
• Gay and Lesbian Business Network
• Hispanic Business Network

• Women's Interactive Network

Entry-Level Programs, Full-Time Opportunities and Training Programs

• Customer Development
• Finance
• IT
• Marketing
• R&D
• Supply Chain Management Leadership Program

All of Unilever's programs are full-time opportunities.

Strategic Plan and Diversity Leadership

How does the firm's leadership communicate the importance of diversity to everyone at the firm?

The firm's leadership communicates diversity initiatives through e-mails, the company Intranet, newsletters and meetings, training, diversity speakers/events, posters, banners and inter-office communications.

Who has primary responsibility for leading diversity initiatives at your firm?

Lois Rubin, diversity manager

Does your firm currently have a diversity committee?

Yes

If yes, please describe how the committee is structured, how often it meets, etc.

The committee is multileveled, multiethnic and composed of both men and women. The committee meets in person three times a year, in addition to holding three conference calls per year. The committee is chaired by our president.

If yes, does the committee's representation include one or more members of the firm's management/executive committee (or the equivalent)?

Yes

Does the committee and/or diversity leader establish and set goals or objectives consistent with management's priorities?

Yes

Has the firm undertaken a formal or informal diversity program or set of initiatives aimed at increasing the diversity of the firm?

Yes, formal

How often does the firm's management review the firm's diversity progress/results?

Quarterly

Retention and Professional Development

How do 2006 minority and female attrition rates generally compare to those experienced in the prior year period?

About the same as in prior years.

Please identify the specific steps you are taking to reduce the attrition rate of minority and women employees.

• Develop and/or support internal employee affinity groups
• Increase/improve current work/life programs
• Succession plan includes emphasis on diversity
• Strengthen mentoring program for all employees, including minorities and women
• Professional skills development program, including minority and women employees
• *Other:* Organization assessments, functional diversity plans, strategy-into-action plan that includes accountability for diversity inclusion success

United Parcel Service (UPS)

<table>
<tr><td>
World headquarters
55 Glenlake Parkway, N.E.
Atlanta, GA 30328
Phone: (404) 828-6000
Fax: (404) 828-6562
www.ups.com
</td><td>

Employment Contact

For information concerning employment opportunities at UPS, please go to www.upsjobs.com. UPS is an equal opportunity employer.
</td></tr>
</table>

The Stats

	NUMBER OF EMPLOYEES		REVENUE	
	2006	**2005**	**2006**	**2005**
Total in the U.S.	360,600	348,400	N/A	N/A
Total outside the U.S.	67,100	58,800	N/A	N/A
Total worldwide	427,700	407,200	$47.5 billion	$36.6 billion

Diversity Mission Statement

Founded: August 28, 1907 in Seattle, Wash.

Chairman & CEO: Michael L. Eskew

Diversity and UPS People

UPS's workforce is multicultural, multidimensional and reflective of the broad attributes of our global communities. In fact, each year since 1999, UPS has been consecutively ranked by *Fortune* magazine as one of the 50 Best Companies for Minorities.

UPS understands that diversity encompasses more than ethnicity, gender and age. It's how employees think, the ideas they contribute and their general attitude toward work and life.

Diversity is encouraged by recognizing the value of people's different experiences, backgrounds and perspectives. Diversity is a valuable, core component of UPS because it brings a wider range of resources, skills and ideas to the business.

Long-standing company policies—such as employee ownership, equal opportunity, promotion from within and teamwork—have helped make UPS a preferred employer. Diversity impacts UPS's business from many perspectives, whether it's in meeting the needs of a diverse customer base, working with a diverse supplier network or gaining momentum from the varied contributions of our diverse workforce.

African-Americans, Hispanics, Asian-Pacific Americans and other minorities make up 35 percent of the company's 360,600 employees in the United States.

Minorities accounted for half of UPS's new employees in 2003.

Women represent 27 percent of the U.S. management team and 21 percent of the overall workforce, holding jobs from package handlers, to drivers, to senior management and to the UPS board of directors.

Among the company's 58,000 U.S. managers, minorities hold nearly 30 percent of those executive positions. Positions held include district managers, the UPS management committee and UPS board of directors.

UPS Diversity Steering Council

UPS expects diversity to be fostered and encouraged by every UPSer in their daily commitment to the company. UPS also has a Diversity Steering Council whose vision is to "ensure that workforce, customer and supplier diversity remain a visible core value that is integral to our business, our community relationships and The UPS Charter."

The UPS Diversity Steering Council is co-chaired by Chairman and CEO Mike Eskew and Senior Vice President, Human Resources Allen Hill. This cross-functional council consists of internal and external representatives.

Employer of Choice

UPS is frequently recognized for its commitment to diversity. Since 1999, UPS has been consecutively ranked by *Fortune* magazine as one of the 50 Best Companies for Minorities.

UPS was profiled as a leader in *Hispanic* magazine's 13th annual Corporate 100 list, "a list of the top U.S. companies that excel in creating business and job opportunities for Hispanic Americans, as well as donating to philanthropies that target Latino communities."

Since 2000, UPS has been consecutively named a top corporation for Women's Business Enterprises (WBEs) by the Women's Business Enterprise National Council (WBENC).

UPS was honored with the coveted NAACP (National Association for the Advancement of Colored People) Corporate Citizen of the Year Award.

UPS placed third in *DiversityInc's* Diversity Top 30 poll. The poll rates corporations on a range of criteria from employment and advancement of people of color to advertising in ethnic media.

Community

Throughout our history at UPS, we've found that we grow by not only investing in our business but also in the communities where we live and work.

UPS does extensive work and partners with various organizations to improve social conditions that exist within the communities we serve. Below is a sample of the organizations UPS and UPS people partner with:

- 100 Black Men of America (100 BMOA)
- Family and Workplace Literacy Programs
- Hispanic Chamber of Commerce (HCC)
- INROADS
- National Association for the Advancement of Colored People (NAACP)
- NASCAR
- National Urban League (NUL)
- National Council of La Raza (NCLR)
- Native American Business Alliance (NABA)
- Organization of Chinese Americans (OCA)
- The National Newspapers Publishers Association (NNPA)
- Special Olympics
- UNCF Corporate Scholars
- Women's Business Enterprise National Council (WBENC)

Customers

UPS understands that customer diversity requires understanding the differences in cultural backgrounds and the unique needs of each customer.

Every day, more than 370,000 UPSers serve nearly eight million customers in over 200 countries and territories worldwide. Because of its global impact, UPS has many unique opportunities to reach a broad range of diverse customers. UPS understands that diversity is essential as the company expands and finds ways to solve the individual needs of all customers.

Supplier Diversity

Formally launched in 1992, the UPS Supplier Diversity Program is committed to providing business opportunities to minority- and women-owned businesses.

UPS strives to have diversity among its business partners. In addition to developing strategic relationships with minority- and women-owned businesses, UPS encourages majority suppliers to support women- and minority-owned firms. We are committed to ensuring that our supplier diversity process strengthens the minority- and women-owned businesses that drive economic development in our communities. More than 25,000 businesses across America are partners in the UPS supplier network.

United States Steel Corporation

600 Grant Street
Pittsburgh, PA 15219
Phone: (412) 433-6920
Fax: (412) 433-6917

Locations

US: Chicago, IL • Detroit, MI • Fairfield, AL • Gary, IN • Granite City, IL • Lorain, OH • Michigan • Minnesota • Pittsburgh, PA

International: Kosice, Slovak Republic • Serbia

Diversity Leadership

F. David Coleman
General Manager of Corporate Diversity
www.ussteel.com

Employment Contact

Lisa Sullivan
Manager of Diversity Recruiting & Communications
E-mail: lasullivan@uss.com

Recruiting

Please list the schools/types of schools at which you recruit.

• *Private schools:* Case Western Reserve University, Gannon University, LaRoche College, Rose Hulman Institute of Technology, University of Notre Dame, Valparaiso University, Duquesne University, Dayton University, Lehigh University, St. Vincent College, Vanderbilt University, Northwestern University, Marquette University, Thiel College, Waynesburg College, Westminster College

• *Public state schools:* Auburn University, California University of Pennsylvania, Cleveland State, Colorado School of Mines, Georgia Institute of Technology, Michigan State University, Michigan Tech Houghton, Mississippi State, North Dakota State University, Oakland University (Michigan), Penn State University, Purdue University Calumet (Indiana), Robert Morris University, Southern Illinois University-Edwardsville, Southern Illinois University - Carbondale, University of Alabama Birmingham, University of Alabama-Tuscaloosa, University of Illinois- Champaign, University of Michigan-Dearborn, University of Minnesota-Twin Cities, University of Minnesota-Duluth, University of Missouri - Rolla, University of Missouri-Columbia, University of North Dakota-Grand Forks, University of Pittsburgh, University of Toledo, West Virginia University, Youngstown State University (Ohio), Wayne State University (Michigan), Bradley University, Carnegie Mellon University, Grove City College, Indiana University-Bloomington, Indiana University of Pennsylvania, Ohio State University, Ohio University, Slippery Rock University, South Dakota School of Mines, St. Louis University, Tennessee Tech University, University of Alabama- Huntsville, University of Cincinnati, University of Michigan - Ann Arbor, University of Missouri-St. Louis, University of South Alabama, University of St. Francis-Joliet, Virginia Tech, Western Michigan, Bowling Green University, Eastern Michigan, Ferris State University, Indiana State University, Iowa State, Milwaukee School of Engineering, New Mexico State, Ohio Northern University, Rensselaer Poly Institute, Tri-State University-Angola, University of Akron, Washington University-St. Louis, Georgia Institute of Technology

• *Historically black colleges and universities (HBCUs):* Alabama A&M, Howard University, Southern University, Tennessee State, Tuskegee University, Hampton University, Morgan State, University of Illinois-Chicago, North Carolina A&T

• *Hispanic serving institutions (HSIs):* University of Texas - El Paso

• *Other predominantly minority and/or women's colleges:* Carlow University

Do you have any special outreach efforts directed to encourage minority students and graduates to consider your firm?

• Advertise in minority student association publication(s) or other minority-focused publications

• Participate in/host minority student job fair(s) or other minority-focused job events

• Sponsor minority student association events

• Outreach to leadership of minority student organizations

What activities does the firm undertake to attract minority and women employees?

• Participate at minority job fairs

• *Other:* U.S. Steel offers a program for women who are or once were in the steel business called Ciloets. U.S. Steel participates in job fairs for both woman and minority employees.

• Established guidelines for Affinity/Resource Groups

Do you use executive recruiting/search firms to seek to identify new diversity hires?

Yes

Internships and Co-ops

INROADS

U.S. Steel has a well-defined co-op/internship program, and all open positions/opportunities are posted online for spring, summer and/or fall semesters.

Pay: $15.00 per hour. Interns are paid every two weeks

Length of the program: Approximately 12 weeks

U.S. Steel is proud to have been affiliated with INROADS for the past 30 years. In support of their efforts, we have hired two to five interns from INROADS to work for us each summer. Each year, interns from INROADS have proven themselves as positive assets not only for our company, but also for our community. Several interns are now successful full-time employees. In response to the positive contributions of the INROADS program, U.S. Steel hosted and participated in a mock interview day at our corporate headquarters in Pittsburgh, Pennsylvania.

Scholarships

Employee Sons & Daughters Scholarship

Deadline for application for the scholarship program: November 30th

Scholarship award amount: The amount is up to 15 individual $10,000 scholarships, payable in four annual installments of $2,500. Payments are made direct to colleges and universities by Scholarship America and designated for tuition, room and/or board. The college or university is instructed to return unused funds to the United States Steel Foundation at the end of each academic year.

The scholarship program is limited to sons and daughters of active, full-time employees of U.S. Steel. Applicants must be high school seniors who have applied for full-time admissions to an accredited, four-year college or university. Foreign colleges and universities are excluded.

Affinity Groups

U. S. Steel has finalized the guidelines for its resource groups, and there are currently five groups finalizing their mission/charter.

Entry-Level Programs, Full-Time Opportunities and Training Programs

New Managers Program

Length of program: The program is a five-day seminar to provide a broad picture of United States Steel Corporation.

Geographic location of program: Pittsburgh, Pennsylvania

Included are presentations on United States Steel Corporation history and organization, steel business simulation, communications, personnel planning as well as an orientation to what is required of managers. This workshop shows participants how a new manager's life changes, both personally and professionally, on becoming a manager. The program also includes presentations by executives and general managers who provide updated information on subjects like general business conditions, key customers, United States Steel Corporation strategies, business ethics and human resources policies.

Management Associate Program

Length of program: Up to one-year program that not only provides a broad picture of United States Steel Corporation, but focuses on specific aspects of your job assignment, related jobs and overall communications/leadership skills training.

Geographic location of program: At and/or near current work location

Strategic Plan and Diversity Leadership

How does the firm's leadership communicate the importance of diversity to everyone at the firm?

The leadership at U.S. Steel communicates diversity by making diversity a business imperative and core value. Diversity and inclusion is communicated to the organization through internal publications, and it is incorporated into our training initiatives, such as the New Managers Program. Diversity and inclusion is also a part of our *Corporate Citizenship Report* which was published and distributed to our external stakeholders for the first time this year.

Who has primary responsibility for leading diversity initiatives at your firm?

F. David Coleman, general manager of corporate diversity

Does your firm currently have a diversity committee?

Yes

If yes, please describe how the committee is structured, how often it meets, etc.

The committee meets every other month.

If yes, does the committee's representation include one or more members of the firm's management/executive committee (or the equivalent)?

Yes

If yes, how many executives are on the committee? How often does the committee convene in furtherance of the firm's diversity initiatives?

U.S. Steel's Diversity Committee consists of a diverse group of 16 high level managers from across the company. The committee convenes every other month.

Does the committee and/or diversity leader establish and set goals or objectives consistent with management's priorities?

Yes. U.S. Steel as a company has made diversity a primary focus. When it comes to making the workforce a more diverse environment, both the Diversity Committee and management see diversity as an important issue for the future of the company.

Has the firm undertaken a formal or informal diversity program or set of initiatives aimed at increasing the diversity of the firm?

Yes, formal

How often does the firm's management review the firm's diversity progress/results?

Quarterly

How is the firm's diversity committee and/or firm management held accountable for achieving results?

U.S. Steel holds itself accountable for achieving results by building diversity into the metrics of the corporation. U.S. Steel employees are trained in diversity.

Retention and Professional Development

How do 2006 minority and female attrition rates generally compare to those experienced in the prior year period?

About the same as in prior years.

Please identify the specific steps you are taking to reduce the attrition rate of minority and women employees.

• Develop and/or support internal employee affinity groups (e.g., minority or women networks within the firm)

• Increase/review compensation relative to competition

• Work with all employees, including minority and women employees, to develop career advancement plans

• Strengthen mentoring program for all employees, including minorities and women

• Professional skills development program, including minority and women employees

Diversity Mission Statement

In order to attract and retain employees with the talents and skills needed for the company to achieve its vision—*Making Steel. World Competitive. Building Value.*—U.S. Steel is committed to creating an environment that values people's differences.

The Stats

	NUMBER OF EMPLOYEES		REVENUE	
	2006	2005	2006	2005
Total in the U.S.	22,000	20,000	$11.75 billion	$10.69 billion
Total outside the U.S.	22,000	26,000	$3.96 billion	$3.34 billion
Total worldwide	44,000	46,000	$15.71 billion	$ 14.03 billion

United Technologies Corporation

One Financial Plaza, MS 504
Hartford, CT 06101
Phone: (860) 728-7000

Locations

Hartford, CT (HQ)

UTC is the parent company for the following companies:
Carrier Corporation (HQ–Farmington, CT) •
Pratt and Whitney (HQ–East Hartford, CT) •
Hamilton Sundstrand (HQ–Windsor Locks,
CT) • Otis Elevator (HQ–Farmington, CT) •
Sikorsky Aircraft (HQ–Stratford, CT) • UTC
Fire and Security (HQ–Farmington, CT) •
UTC Power (HQ–South Windsor, CT) • UTC
Research Center (R&D) (HQ–East Hartford)

All companies have multiple international
and domestic operation locations.

*Our U.S. presence beyond the Hartford,
CT, metropolitan area is in:*
Carrier: Syracuse, NY • Athens, GA •
Collierville, TN • Charlotte, NC
Hamilton Sundstrand: Rockford, IL • San
Diego, CA • Miramar, FL
Sikorsky and Pratt & Whitney: West
Palm Beach, FL
Otis: Every major city
Otis and Carrier: Many satellite sales and
distributions offices.

Diversity Leadership

Grace Figueredo
Director, Workforce Diversity
The diversity campus recruiting aspect for the
corporation falls under Joelle Hayes.

Contact Person

Joelle Hayes
Manager, Corporate Recruiting and Diversity
Partnerships
One Financial Plaza, MS 504
Hartford, CT 06101
Phone: (860) 728-6516
Fax: (860) 660-9260
E-mail: joelle.hayes@utc.com
www.utc.com/careers

Recruiting

Please list the schools/types of schools at which you recruit.

We recruit at the following schools: Cornell University, Purdue University, Rensselaer Polytechnic Institute, MIT, UCONN, GA Tech, University of Michigan, Penn State, University of Illinois-Champaign-Urbana, Howard, North Carolina A&T State, University of Puerto Rico - Mayaguez

Do you have any special outreach efforts directed to encourage minority students to consider your firm?

• Hold a reception for minority students
• *Conferences:* NSBE, SHPE, SWE, BEYA

• Advertise in minority student association publication(s)
• Participate in/host minority student job fair(s)
• Sponsor minority student association events
• Firm's employees participate on career panels at schools
• Outreach to leadership of minority student organizations
• Scholarships or intern/fellowships for minority students

What activities does the firm undertake to attract minority and women employees?

• Partner programs with women and minority associations
• *Conferences:* NSBE (national and regional), SWE, SHPE, BEYA (entry level), NSHMBA, NBMBAA, NAWMBA (MBA hires); an additional 11 focus schools for MBA hires
• Participate at minority job fairs

• Seek referrals from other employees

• Utilize online job services

• *Other:* Career services, job boards

Do you use executive recruiting/search firms to seek to identify new diversity hires?

Yes, mostly executive hires, some manager and professional-level hires.

If yes, list all women- and/or minority-owned executive search/recruiting firms to which the firm paid a fee for placement services in the past 12 months:

Granville and Webb, Millette Granville and Principal. At one particular business unit, 30 percent of all search firms retained are women- and minority-owned.

Internships and Co-ops

INROADS is UTC's only internship program outside of its internal internship programs. Hamilton Sundstrand has an extremely robust co-op/experiential education program.

INROADS

Pay: Varies by major (technical/non-technical) and classification

Length of the program: 10 to 12 weeks

Percentage of interns/co-ops in the program who receive offers of full-time employment: 75 percent

Web site for internship/co-op information: www.inroads.org

Scholarships

UTC INROADS Scholarship

Deadline for application for the scholarship program: July (varies each year)

Scholarship award amount: $20,000 total annually (award amount varies); two awards at $3,500, two at $2,500, two at $1,000, five at $500

Web site or other contact information for scholarship: Only for eligible returning INROADS interns employed by UTC

Affinity Groups

• African-American Forum

• Asian Pacific Forum

• Hispanic Leadership Forum

• New Hire Forum

• Veteran's Forum

• Women's Finance Forum

• Women's Leadership Forum

UTC has established operating guidelines for affinity groups within its business units. Most of them meet on a monthly/quarterly basis. They have executive champions, who support/sponsor their activities and related events. The groups have charters, which support the overall diversity mission/vision of UTC. Most of the groups are focused on supporting the recruitment, development, advancement and retention of UTC's minority employees. In addition, these groups mentor and participate in various community outreach activities. They have web sites that inform membership of their mission, upcoming events, resources, etc.

Entry-Level Programs, Full-Time Opportunities and Training Programs

• *UTC Financial Leadership Program:* 24 months; Connecticut

• *UTC Information Technology Leadership Program:* Three nine-month rotations (27 months); Connecticut

• *Hamilton Sundstrand HR Rotational Program:* 24 months; various locations

• *Pratt and Whitney Manufacturing Engineering Development Program:* 24 months; Connecticut

• *Carrier Technical Sales Management Trainee Program:* Various locations

• *Career Engineering Leadership Program:* Various locations

All full-time and part-time UTC employees are eligible for the Employee Scholar Program, which pays full tuition, fees and books toward degree study in any area.

Strategic Plan and Diversity Leadership

How does the firm's leadership communicate the importance of diversity to everyone at the firm?

UTC has a decentralized, cascade-down approach to diversity. At the start of the year, each respective business unit sets key objectives, and diversity is embedded into these. The senior leadership of each business unit utilizes various communication vehicles to share, monitor and report on the progression of these objectives throughout the course of the year, e.g. roadmaps, scorecards, etc. These are posted on web sites and discussed through meetings, e-mail communiqués and town hall meetings, etc., which are conducted to discuss the performance and results in these areas. The CEO reviews diversity metrics at senior level operating management meetings quarterly.

Who has primary responsibility for leading diversity initiatives at your firm?

Grace Figueredo, director, workforce diversity. In addition, each business unit has a diversity manager, who makes up the UTC Diversity Council.

Does your firm currently have a diversity committee?

No. However, some of the business units do have diversity committees that were formed at the grassroots level.

Has the firm undertaken a formal or informal diversity program or set of initiatives aimed at increasing the diversity of the firm?

Yes, formal. UTC has a decentralized, cascade-down approach to diversity. At the start of the year, each respective business unit sets goals regarding representation. In addition, we track, monitor and report on the associated activity, such as hiring, promotions and attrition. Each business unit sets a strategic approach to addressing their opportunities; HR has the responsibility of partnering with line leaders to develop action and implementation plans. Every quarter, at operating management meetings, each of the business unit presidents presents a status update to the CEO, and diversity performance/results are reported, reviewed and discussed.

How often does the firm's management review the firm's diversity progress/results?

Quarterly

How is the firm's diversity committee and/or firm management held accountable for achieving results?

As stated above, the UTC diversity progression metrics are reviewed at operating management meetings quarterly by the CEO with the divisional presidents. At the conclusion of each year, executive incentive compensation is linked to their respective performance/results in all business deliverables, with diversity being one of the elements.

The Stats

	NUMBER OF EMPLOYEES	REVENUE
	2006	2006
Total in the U.S.	72,600	$16.6 billion
Total outside the U.S.	147,000	$26.1 billion
Total worldwide	220,000	42.7 billion

2006 DEMOGRAPHIC PROFILE (U.S.)	
Executive female population	9.2 percent
Executive minority population	7.9 percent
Managerial level female population	17.1 percent
Managerial level minority population	12.8 percent
Professional female population	16.6 percent
Professional minority population	13.6 percent

Over 55 percent of our employees are outside the U.S.

Retention and Professional Development

Please identify the specific steps you are taking to reduce the attrition rate of minority and women employees.

Currently standardizing and taking a more proactive and strategic approach to retention and other related drivers that affect turnover.

Diversity Mission Statement

UTC Diversity Vision

Our diversity vision is to create an environment where people want to work and contribute their fullest potential. It defines the value that is placed on the differences in the workforce and recognizes that diversity is key in broadening our experience and technical competency base to compete effectively in the global marketplace.

UTC Diversity Mission

To create an environment where all associates are encouraged to reach their fullest potential and where everyone values, accepts and respects the differences in our workforce.

Additional Information

Since 1995, United Technologies Corporation has made significant progression in its diversity representation goals and has been recognized for numerous awards and honors regarding the area of diversity—most recently, the Brillante Award from NSHMBA (National Society of Hispanic MBAs), the Golden Torch Award for Corporate Diversity Leadership from NSBE (National Society of Black Engineers) and an Innovator Award from INROADS, to name a few.

UTC believes that innovation springs from knowledge and is committed to supporting a highly educated workforce. Currently, more than 13,000 employees participate in the UTC Employee Scholar Program, which provides pre-paid tuition and fees, time off to attend classes and study and the award of UTC common stock upon graduation. The company encourages all employees to enroll in college classes to broaden their horizons, expand their thinking and sharpen their skills. Employees are free to explore their own interests, which need not be directly related to their work. The program is open to all UTC employees and the response is enthusiastic. Since the program's inception in 1996, UTC has invested more than $450 million in the Employee Scholar Program. Approximately 16,000 employees have received their degrees through the program. Retention among employees in the Employee Scholar Program is greater than for those that are not.

In 2005, UTC granted $20,000 to fund scholarships for INROADS students to prepare them for positions of leadership in corporate America. Further, through the efforts of the UTC African-American Forum, $40,000 was provided in scholarship support to INROADS interns who were impacted by the effects of Hurricane Katrina. UTC also supports several historically black colleges and universities, such as North Carolina A&T, Howard University and Tuskegee.

In order to address employees' needs for resource and referral services, the Lifechoices program was established through the support of a consulting firm to provide employees with a variety of services, including child and elder care referral services, emergency dependent care referral services, fertility and adoption consulting services, and a homework hotline. Last year, more than 22 percent of UTC's U.S. employees used the resources of Lifechoices.

UTC employees value the corporation's role in strengthening our communities through innovative and significant monetary contributions. Each year, UTC donates more than $16 million to organizations around the world that support community programs, the arts, education and the environment. This money is supplemented by the priceless contributions of time and effort made by thousands of employee volunteers. Each year, our employees spend more than 50,000 hours volunteering their time and expertise to their communities and nonprofit organizations. Like many companies, UTC matches the donations of their employees to nonprofit organizations. The company also recognizes and encourages volunteer activities by contributing to specific organizations to which employees donate a significant amount of their personal time. UTC is a leader in its support for Special Olympics. In 2005, UTC celebrated its 28th year of partnership with Special Olympics Connecticut. As a title sponsor of the state Summer Games, UTC supports Special Olympics Connecticut with more than 2,000 volunteers and $100,000 annually.

UnitedHealthcare

9900 Bren Rd. East
Minnetonka, MN 55343
www.unitedhealthgroup.com

Locations
Minnetonka, MN (HQ)

Employment Contact
Heather Cooper
Account Executive, Recruitment Services
E-mail: heather_cooper@uhc.com

Recruiting

Please list the schools/types of schools at which you recruit.

• Ivy League schools
• Other private schools
• Public state schools
• Historically black colleges and universities (HBCUs)

Do you have any special outreach efforts directed to encourage minority students to consider your firm?

• Participate in/host minority student job fair(s)
• Sponsor minority student association events
• Firm's employees participate on career panels at schools
• Scholarships or internships/fellowships for minority students

What activities does the firm undertake to attract minority and women employees?

• Partner programs with women and minority associations
• Conferences
• Participate at minority job fairs
• Seek referrals from other employees
• Utilize online job services

Do you use executive recruiting/search firms to seek to identify new diversity hires?
No

Internships and Co-ops

INROADS Internship Program

Deadline for application: March 31st
Number of interns in the program in summer 2006 (internship) or 2006 (co-op): 24

UnitedHealthcare (formerly PacifiCare) has been a national partner of INROADS since 2004, offering internship programs throughout the nation in the primary functions of underwriting, sales and finance.

Corporate MBA Internship Programs

Our corporate MBA internship program offers general management internships nationwide.

Actuarial Summer Internship Program (ASIP)

Deadline for application: March 31st
Pay: $13 to 15 per hour
Length of the program: 10 weeks
Percentage of interns/co-ops in the program who receive offers of full-time employment: Since inception in 1999, approximately 50 percent of the interns have been offered full-time positions.
Web site for internship/co-op information: www.pacificare.com, employment, college recruitment

The Actuarial Summer Internship Program (ASIP) at PacifiCare, a UnitedHealthcare Company, is a 10-week program from June to September, with flexible start and end dates depending on each intern's summer schedule. Interns will work 40 hours per week at either the Cypress or Santa Ana office in Orange County, California. Salary is competitive and will take into account any actuarial exams passed.

Interns will work on projects ranging from product pricing, provider contract analysis, reserves calculation to financial reporting. During the process, interns will go through various training programs to learn more about the managed care industry, PacifiCare's business models, and how to use database query language and Microsoft applications to perform actuarial calculations. Interns will also be guided through the examination preparation process in a full-time work setting, and study materials will be provided for the November exam sitting.

Qualifications:

• Working toward a bachelor's or master's degree in mathematics, statistics, actuarial science or other major with relevant experience

• At least junior standing with minimum 3.2 GPA

• Strong computer, analytical and communication skills

• Completion of one actuarial exam preferred; however, candidates with high GPA and analytical skill will be considered

Scholarships

Latino Health Scholars Program

* The scholarship program outlined below is for high school seniors who are entering college.

Deadline for application for the scholarship program: May 29th annually (scholarship opportunity at least through 2006)

Scholarship award amount: 70 $2,000 total scholarships and two $25,000 total scholarships available

Web site or other contact information for scholarship: www.pacificare.com; www.pacificarelatino.com

PacifiCare, a UnitedHealthcare Company, introduced the PacifiCare Latino Health Scholars Program in 2003 to address the critical shortage of Spanish speakers in the educational pipeline for health professions. Under the program, PacifiCare offers annual scholarships of $2,000 each for bilingual, bicultural high school students interested in pursuing careers in the health care industry. In 2004, PacifiCare increased the number of scholarships available from 33 to 50, for a two-year total scholarship opportunity of $166,000. Through this program, PacifiCare hopes to reverse what is currently a widening gap between the Latino population and the number of bilingual and bicultural professionals in the health care field.

For 2005 and 2006, PacifiCare further expanded its Latino Health Scholars program to include—in addition to the 70 $2,000 scholarships the company will award this fall—two $25,000 scholarships for the most deserving bilingual and bicultural students dedicated to pursuing careers in health care. These two scholarships, entitled the PacifiCare Freedom Award, recognize outstanding individuals and organizations that have demonstrated tremendous sacrifice and commitment to make a positive difference in our communities. The award was inspired by the heroic actions of U.S. Marine Sgt. Rafael Peralta who was killed by enemy action in Iraq. Fighting alongside his fellow marines in Falluja, Peralta, wounded by gunshots, reached out for a grenade that was hurled by an insurgent and cradled it to his body to protect others from the blast. His heroism saved the lives of five of his fellow Marines.

Strategic Plan and Diversity Leadership

Does your firm currently have a diversity committee?
No

Does the committee and/or diversity leader establish and set goals or objectives consistent with management's priorities?
Yes

Has the firm undertaken a formal or informal diversity program or set of initiatives aimed at increasing the diversity of the firm?
Yes, informal

How often does the firm's management review the firm's diversity progress/results?
Monthly

The Stats

	NUMBER OF EMPLOYEES	REVENUE
	2005	2005
Total in the U.S.	18,717	$27 billion

Retention and Professional Development

Please identify the specific steps you are taking to reduce the attrition rate of minority and women employees.

• Increase/review compensation relative to competition

• Succession plan includes emphasis on diversity

• Work with minority and women employees to develop career advancement plans

• Strengthen mentoring program for all employees, including minority and women employees

Diversity Mission Statement

Diversity creates a healthier atmosphere. UnitedHealthcare is an equal opportunity employer.

Additional Information

UnitedHealth Group is a Fortune 50 company listed as one of the top two most admired health care companies in *Fortune* magazine since 1995. We have the privilege each day—directly or indirectly—to make a significant difference in someone's life.

Although our employees have diverse cultural backgrounds, beliefs and lifestyles, they have one thing in common: their ability to excel.

At United, we not only respect diversity—we believe diverse viewpoints are assets. We depend on our employees' broad range of talents, personalities and ideas to help us design services specifically tailored to meet the needs of the diverse communities we serve and generate the innovations of tomorrow.

US Airways Inc.

<table>
<tr><td>

Corporate Headquarters
4000 East Sky Harbor Boulevard
Phoenix, AZ 85034
Phone: (480) 693-0800
Fax: (480) 693-8664
www.usairways.com

</td><td>

Diversity Leadership

Linda Garza Kalaf
MA, SPHR, GPHR
111 Rio Salado Parkway
Tempe, AZ 85281
Phone: (480) 693-8631
Fax: (480) 693-8664
E-mail: linda.kalaf@usairways.com

</td></tr>
</table>

Recruiting

Please list the schools/types of schools at which you recruit.

- Ivy League schools
- Private schools
- Public state schools
- *Other:* Technical schools

Do you have any special outreach efforts that are directed to encourage minority students to consider your firm?

- *Conferences:* Hispanic Women's Conference, National Black MBA Association, National Society of Hispanic MBAs, Organization of Black Airline Pilots, Women in Aviation
- Participate in minority student job fairs
- Advertise on minority web sites: www.latinosforhire.com

What activities does the firm undertake to attract minority and women employees?

- Partner programs with women and minority associations
- Participate at minority job fairs
- Utilize online job services

Do you use executive recruiting/search firms to seek to identify new diversity hires?

No

Internships and Co-ops

INROADS: A number of interns participated in 2005 and returned in 2006, and participated in human resources, engineering and accounting.

US Airways' Summer Internship Program, "Intern With Us," commenced in 1998 and is designed to provide students with airline experience that aligns with their educational and career interests.

Deadline for application: April 14th

Pay: $10 to $12 per hour (depending on school level)

Length of the program: 10 to 12 weeks

Affinity Groups

Management Club

The US Airways Management Club is an organization that fosters cooperation, communication and understanding between all members of the corporate management team by providing opportunities for education, information and interaction in an environment which, in turn, stimulates personal and corporate growth.

Minority Professional Association

MPA was organized in 1993 to provide an opportunity for management-level African-American professionals to network and further their career development via a variety of seminars and workshops. Through the years, the scope of the organization has expanded to include all minority professionals at US Airways. The MPA has hosted several annual conferences.

Professional Women's Group

PWG was organized in 2000 as a networking organization for professional women. The PWG works to recognize, develop and promote women in the company. One of the biggest successes of the organization is the creation of the Speaker Series, which provides an opportunity for our members to hear from and interact with successful women within and outside of US Airways.

Spectrum

Spectrum is a networking organization that is open to all gay, lesbian, bisexual, transgender and straight employees. Spectrum was organized in 2003 and is committed to promoting equality and recognition of sexual identity as it relates to the workplace through awareness, education and communication. Spectrum has conducted focus group meetings and membership drives in the corporate office and Philadelphia.

Strategic Plan and Diversity Leadership

Who has primary responsibility for leading diversity initiatives at your firm?

Linda Garza Kalaf, manager, diversity programs

Does your firm currently have a diversity committee?

Yes. Since the US Airways and America West Airlines merger in 2005, US Airways has recently re-established the Diversity Council to further expand the newly merged company's commitment to diversity. The Diversity Council meets on a quarterly basis.

Does the committee's representation include one or more members of the firm's management/executive committee (or the equivalent)?

No. The Diversity Council consists of a cross-section of frontline management, frontline employees and a designee from each affinity group/employee network.

How many employees are on the committee?

The Diversity Council consists of 15 employees.

Does the committee and/or diversity leader establish and set goals or objectives consistent with management's priorities?

Yes

Has the firm undertaken a formal or informal diversity program or set of initiatives aimed at increasing the diversity of the firm?

Yes, formal

How often does the firm's management review the firm's diversity progress/results?

Monthly

How is the firm's diversity committee and/or firm management held accountable for achieving results?

• Department profile (affirmative action goals)

• Inclusion of a diverse slate of qualified candidates in selection processes

• Diversity initiatives (training and outreach) completed annually

• Completion of diversity education to leadership team and front-line employees

• Summer internship program conversation to hires

Diversity Mission Statement

Creating a culture that values diversity by maximizing and embracing the talents, skills, backgrounds, experiences and perspectives of all employees, thereby reflecting the diversity of customers served by US Airways.

Valero Energy Corporation

One Valero Way
San Antonio, TX 78249
Phone: (210) 345-2000
www.valero.com

Diversity Leadership

Kim Griffin
Employment Services Manager
One Valero Way
San Antonio, TX 78249
Phone: (210) 345-2028
Fax: (210) 345-2778

Employment Contact

Ruth Pina
Staffing & Employee Services
One Valero Way
San Antonio, TX 78249
Phone: (210) 345-2000
Fax: (210) 345-2646
Toll Free: (800) 531-7911

Recruiting

Please list the schools/types of schools at which you recruit.

• Private schools
• Public state schools
• Historically black colleges and universities (HBCUs)
• Hispanic serving institutions (HSIs)

Do you have any special outreach efforts directed to encourage minority students and graduates to consider your firm?

Advertise in minority student association publication(s) or other minority-focused publications.

What activities does the firm undertake to attract minority and women employees?

• Participate at minority job fairs
• Seek referrals from other employees
• Utilize online job services

Do you use executive recruiting/search firms to seek to identify new diversity hires?

No

Internships and Co-ops

Valero Internship Program

Deadline for application: Spring 2007

Length of the program: 10 to 12 weeks

Percentage of interns/co-ops in the program who receive offers of full-time employment: 70 percent of interns are offered full-time positions

Web site for internship/co-op information: valero.hrdpt.com/college/

The Valero College Internship Program is really on the move. If you crave an internship that is more than filing papers and making copies, you are in the right place. We are big believers in giving our interns a meaningful and memorable experience, like providing hands-on training and real-life projects that impact our business. In less than two years, the number of interns throughout the Valero organization has more than tripled, and we are committed to continued growth.

Description

Valero offers three distinct intern groups: summer interns, ongoing interns and engineering co-ops. Summer interns work for a specified period during the summer months, while ongoing interns work part-time while attending school and full-time during the summer. Engineering co-ops work on a rotating schedule that involves going to school for one semester, then working full-time the next.

Whatever path you choose, an internship with Valero is a great opportunity to gain valuable experience while pursuing your education.

Requirements

You must attend a four-year accredited university and complete your sophomore year before coming on board. Also, you must have at least a 3.0 GPA (both overall and major) in order to qualify for an internship with Valero.

Departments

Various—engineering, accounting, IT, HR

Benefits

Below are the benefits that you can expect to receive while you are an intern or co-op:

- Competitive salary and relocation assistance for qualified students
- Wellness programs that help you maintain a healthy work/life balance
- Education and training opportunities that encourage your growth and development
- A mentor who will be your guide throughout your intern experience.
- Several intern events throughout the summer, including a large intern symposium where all interns are invited to the corporate office to meet company leaders and interact with each other

Ongoing interns

In addition to the benefits offered above, ongoing interns receive:

- 20 to 30 hours per week work schedule while attending school
- Medical and dental coverage
- Life insurance coverage
- Paid company holidays
- Eligibility to contribute to a company-matched 401(k) plan
- Educational Reimbursement Program—After completing three months of service, 80 percent of your tuition, fees and books for up to six semester hours paid for by Valero.

Scholarships

Since Valero began the scholarship program in 1981, the company has recognized outstanding children of all demographics, including minority groups, in support of their efforts to obtain a college education. Valero has awarded 309 scholarships totaling more than $2.3 million dollars.

In addition, for the past three years, Valero has awarded scholarships to children of Aruban employees and members of the Aruban community. Twenty-four Aruba scholarships have been granted, totaling $240.000.

Strategic Plan and Diversity Leadership

Who has primary responsibility for leading diversity initiatives at your firm?

Collective responsibility of HR group

Does your firm currently have a diversity committee?

No

Has the firm undertaken a formal or informal diversity program or set of initiatives aimed at increasing the diversity of the firm?

Yes, informal

How often does the firm's management review the firm's diversity progress/results?

Annually

The Stats

The corporate office in San Antonio, Texas, and operational sites throughout the United States are located in geographically diverse areas that enable the company to hire personnel of all demographics, including minorities and females. As of December 2006, Valero employed a total of 17,380 individuals, which included 39 percent minorities and 37 percent females. In addition, the CEO's leadership team consists of six executives, including one female. Valero generated $82 billion in revenue in 2005 and over $90 billion in 2006.

Retention and Professional Development

Please identify the specific steps you are taking to reduce the attrition rate of minority and women employees.

- Adopt dispute resolution process
- Succession plan includes emphasis on diversity
- Strengthen mentoring program for all employees, including minorities and women
- Professional skills development program, including minority and women employees

Valero is participating in Linkage conferences, which target high-potential employees as well as women and minorities. These conferences are pre-paid by the company and are made available to female managers and above. The sessions focus on diversity, women's issues in the workplace and effective leadership strategies.

Valero has an executive development program which was implemented in August 2004. This program is comprised of a three-day live simulation and feedback experience for current and emerging senior leaders throughout the organization. Graduate school incentives are also available to all employees. Costs for graduate school are reimbursed at a rate of 80 percent, contingent upon sustaining a B average or above.

Valero strives to maximize retention of all managers within the organization, including minority and female managers. This is accomplished through one-on-one coaching, training, online educational tools, HR generalist services, employee performance reviews, 360 performance reviews and ongoing performance feedback. Valero believes that retention really begins during the selection and hiring process and puts a great deal of time and effort into maximizing the effectiveness of this process and thus minimizing efforts on the retention side. Through commitment to our affirmative action plans, minority-targeted succession planning efforts and behavior-based interviews and personality assessments, Valero's selection process very effectively supports the hiring of minority managers as well as ongoing promotion of managers from within the minority talent pools.

Diversity Mission Statement

Valero has a comprehensive competency model that specifies the competencies required for success in positions throughout the organization. The model provides valuable information to employees regarding the areas most relevant to success in their current job and for jobs that they might want to consider in the future. The model includes core competencies—such as diversity—required for all Valero employees, core supervisor competencies for all Valero supervisors, and organization and contributor-level competencies.

These competencies are incorporated into many of the Valero human resources functions, including behavioral interviewing, employee performance review, 360 assessment, training and development, career planning and the development library. Within this model, "value diversity" is defined as someone who shows and fosters respect and appreciation for each person whatever their background, race, age, gender disability, values, lifestyle, perspectives, or interests; seeks to understand the worldview of others; and sees differences in people as opportunities for learning about and approaching things differently. Valuing diversity is being receptive to a wide range of people unlike oneself, according to any number of distinctions: national origin, physical ability, age, race, color, gender, class, native language, religion, sexual orientation, veteran status, professional experience, personal preferences and work style.

These initiatives are a commitment to all employees and promote practices that demonstrate respect, trust and the value of each individual to ensure a pleasant work environment for all personnel. Valero demonstrates its fair treatment to all employees by providing everyone the opportunity to be considered for promotions through company-wide job postings. Diversity training is incorporated in "What Do Great Managers Do?," "Promises, Promises," "Sexual Harassment," retail new employee orientation, retail assistant and store manager training, and the AIM training for retail area managers. These programs are provided for the purpose of maintaining a workplace that respects and dignifies each and every employee.

Additional Information

Affirmative Action Program

Valero's affirmative action program supports the company's diversity initiatives through the consistent and accurate administration of activities throughout the company's locations. The corporate human resources department works with a human resources representative from each location during the planning and preparation of their respective affirmative action plan.

Activities include:

• Communication of goals to hiring supervisor when a job is posted.

• Dissemination of quarterly reports to human resources representatives at each location, which include a summary of personnel activities and updates on progress toward meeting their site's goals.

• Annual presentations are conducted for corporate human resources managers to the management teams at each of the 19 refinery locations, highlighting the company's yearly affirmative action activities and goals.

• Completion of internal audits of affirmative action procedures at randomly selected Valero locations.

• Past recipient of the Department of Labor's prestigious Exemplary Voluntary Efforts (EVE) Award based on Valero's successful recruitment of minority and female college interns, high retention rate post graduation in professional positions at Valero, and notable progression into supervisory roles.

Names of Minority Associations which Valero Supports:

• Avance Corpus Christi
• Avance San Antonio
• Avendia Guadalupe Association
• Corpus Christi Hispanic Chamber
• Guadalupe Cultural Arts Center
• La Prensa
• National Hispanic Institute
• San Antonio Hispanic Chamber of Commerce
• Texas Diversity Council

Awards and Recognition

- Valero ranked No. 22 overall and No. 1 on its new Best Big Companies to Work For list among large companies on *Fortune's* list of the 100 Best Companies to Work For in America in 2007.

- Ranked among *Hispanic* magazine's Corporate 100 in 2002, 2003, 2004, 2006 and 2007, for providing business and job opportunities for Hispanic Americans.

- One of just five companies honored, Valero received the U.S. Department of Labor's prestigious Exemplary Voluntary Efforts (EVE) Award for exemplary and innovative equal employment opportunity programs in 2002.

- Valero is proud to have earned a number of industry awards over the years, including spots on *Forbes'* Platinum 400 Best Big Companies list, the BusinessWeek 50 and BusinessWeek Best Performing Companies lists, and the 2006 Convenience Store Chain of the Year award by Convenience Store Decisions magazine. Valero also has ranked No. 1 among the world's refining and marketing companies for the past two years at the *Platts* Top 250 Global Energy Company awards.

Verizon Communications

1095 Avenue of the Americas
New York, NY 10036
Phone: (212) 395-2121
Fax: (212) 869-3265
Toll Free: (800) 621-9900
www22.verizon.com/about/careers

Diversity Leadership

Monice Sanders
Director, Staffing and Diversity, Telecom
1095 Avenue of the Americas
New York, NY 10036
Phone: (301) 236-1281
E-mail: monice.h.sanders@verizon.com

Diversity Contact

Dianne Campbell
Senior Staff Consultant, Workforce Diversity
Telecom Human Resources

Employment Contact

Mesha Mendenhall Mott
Manager, College Relations & Recruitment
Telecom Human Resources

Recruiting

Please list the schools/types of schools at which you recruit.

- *Ivy League schools:* Cornell
- *Private schools:* Carnegie Mellon, Devry University, Georgia Tech, ITT Technical Institute, Purdue University, Rensselaer Polytechnic Institute, Stevens Institute of Technology
- *Public state schools:* City University of New York, Rutgers University, University of Illinois–Urbana-Champaign, University of Maryland-Baltimore & College Park, University of Massachusetts-Amherst, University of North Texas, University of Oklahoma, Texas A&M-College Station, University of California -Los Angeles, University of California-Riverside, University of South Florida, University of Southern California, University of Texas-Austin, University of Texas-Arlington
- *Historically black colleges and universities (HBCUs):* Clark University, Florida A&M, Hampton University, Howard University, Morehouse, Morgan State University, Norfolk State University, North Carolina A&T, Spelman
- *Hispanic serving institutions (HSIs):* City University of New York colleges, University of Texas-San Antonio

Do you have any special outreach efforts directed to encourage minority students to consider your firm?

- Participate in/host minority student job fair(s)
- Sponsor minority student association events

- Firm's employees participate on career panels at schools
- Outreach to leadership of minority student organizations

What activities does the firm undertake to attract minority and women employees?

- Partner programs with women and minority associations
- *Conferences:* National Black MBA Association, Hispanic Business Student Association, Hispanic Engineer National Achievement Awards Conference, Society for Women Engineers, Society for Hispanic Professional Engineers, National Society of Black Engineers, American Indian Science & Engineering Society, National Society of Hispanic MBAs, Organization of Chinese Americans
- Participate at minority job fairs
- Seek referrals from other employees

Do you use executive recruiting/search firms to seek to identify new diversity hires?

No

Internships and Co-ops

Verizon Young Leaders Program

Deadline for application: Candidates are sent directly from the Hispanic Association of Colleges and Universities and the Hispanic College Fund

Pay: Varies depending on location and class level

Length of the program: 12 weeks

The Verizon Young Leaders program is a partnership with the Hispanic Association of Colleges and Universities and the Hispanic Scholarship Fund to increase the number of Hispanic summer interns at Verizon. In addition to the summer internship, each student is awarded a need-based scholarship. The departments that hire will vary each summer and the responsibilities will be based on the needs of the business.

INROADS

Deadline for application: Candidates are sent directly from INROADS

Pay: Varies depending on location and class level

Length of the program: Approximately 12 weeks; however, there may be an opportunity for internship(s) to extend throughout the year in a part-time capacity

Percentage of interns/co-ops in the program who receive offers of full-time employment: 4.5 percent

Verizon has been a major participant and supporter of the INROADS Internship Program. Recruiting interns is integral to identifying talented, diverse candidates. A key to our company's long-term success is to identify challenging and mutually beneficial internship positions within Verizon each year. We are working to enhance the INROADS relationship and the number of interns we will employ for 2006 and going forward.

Scholarships

Verizon College Scholarships

Deadline for application for the scholarship program: Varies. Scholarships are awarded during the fall. Candidates are then selected during the spring or over the summer for the following school year by the colleges.

Scholarship award amount: Scholarship amounts per school vary from $1,000 to $14,000

Web site or other contact information for scholarship: Candidates apply directly with the department for the school that was awarded the scholarship.

Scholarships are awarded to all of Verizon's targeted colleges and universities. They are awarded to students majoring in engineering (electrical, mechanical, industrial, computer), computer science, math or business. The criteria for scholarships: students must possess a minimum of a 3.0 GPA and must have a specific major. Scholarships will be awarded to students that are underrepresented in the field that Verizon is targeting.

Affinity Groups

Our Employee Resource Groups (ERGs) are Verizon-supported and employee-run and organized affinity groups that promote personal and professional growth for employees with common interests. Through networking, mentoring, special initiatives, seminars and conferences, ERGs promote personal and professional growth of employees, enhance career advancement and provide a stronger sense of community within the company and externally. More than 10,000 employees are affiliated with our ten Employee Resource Groups.

Asian/Pacific Employees for eXcellence (APEX)

APEX aims to provide personal and professional development programs for its members. In addition, APEX strives to fulfill its social responsibilities by reaching out and supporting the communities in which they serve and by increasing cultural awareness and championing the corporation's response to issues facing the Asian/Pacific Islander community.

Consortium of Information and Telecommunications Executives (CITE®)

CITE provides employee advocacy, issue awareness and professional development within Verizon. CITEÒ serves as a resource for the African-American community at large. CITEÒ makes a positive impact by hosting annual conferences, providing scholarships, implementing training and development programs and being actively involved in communities. Visit CITE's web site at www.forcite.com to learn more about their history, initiatives, state chapters and upcoming events.

Disabilities Issues Awareness Leaders' (DIAL)

DIAL's mission is to recognize the talents and develop the maximum potential of Verizon employees with disabilities. DIAL provides insight, recommendations and support to individuals with disabilities and to Verizon, in keeping with the stated corporate commitment to universal design principles, the spirit of the Americans with Disability Act (ADA) and to managing diversity.

Gay, Lesbian, Bisexual, and Transgender Employees of Verizon and Their Allies' (GLOBE)

GLOBE's purpose is to address the needs and concerns of employees of Verizon who are gay, lesbian, bisexual or transgender, or who have family, friends or colleagues who are gay, lesbian, bisexual or transgender, thereby creating a working environment in which each individual is treated with respect and dignity. For more information, visit GLOBE's web site at globe-of-verizon.org.

The Hispanic Support Organization (HSO)

HSO is the voice of the Hispanic employee who is committed to increasing opportunities for professional and personal development. HSO counsels and educates leaders to raise the awareness and increase responsiveness to issues affecting the Hispanic community within and outside Verizon Communications. To learn more about HSO, visit their website at www.hispanicsupportorganization.org.

The National Jewish Cultural Resource Group (NJCRG)

NJCRG strives to create and maintain an environment in which members are encouraged to grow, participate and contribute to the company's overall success. NJCRG provides a unique cultural perspective to Verizon on various issues, which will increase our competitive advantage with our changing customer base.

Native American People of Verizon (NAPV)

NAPV has a mission to support, educate and acknowledge, through cultural exchange, the historical and contemporary contributions of American Indians/Alaskan Natives; to enhance development, advancement and recruitment of American Indians in Verizon; and support Verizon corporate values in our diverse workplace and community.

South Asian Professionals Inspiring Cultural Enrichment (SPICE)

SPICE is committed to sharing the rich heritage of South Asian cultures, providing a forum for communication of common interests and goals, and strengthening the fabric of diversity throughout the corporation. Verizon serves a diverse customer base externally and, hence a multicultural perspective internally, can prove invaluable. SPICE seeks to provide and refine that perspective throughout Verizon with respect to the South Asian community it serves.

Veterans Advisory Board of Verizon (VABVZ)

VABVZ has a mission to provide to senior management, assistance, guidance and representation, regarding veterans issues, i.e., employment, health care, changes in health care as directed by the U.S. Veterans Administration and legislation passed by U.S. Congress.

Women's Association of Verizon Employees (WAVE)

WAVE encourages an environment for learning new skills, addressing real women-in-the-workplace issues, networking and mentoring. Reaching out to women from associates through senior-level executives in Verizon, WAVE works within the consortium of resource groups to address issues such as child care, harassment in the workplace and opportunities for advancement.

Entry-Level Programs, Full-Time Opportunities and Training Programs

The Company: Verizon is one of the world's leading providers of high-growth communications services. Verizon is a major wireline carrier, wireless service provider, directory supplier and leader in data networking. To win in the marketplace, Verizon needs top talent. We seek the best people (those with diverse experience, perspectives, knowledge and backgrounds) and continue to provide the training they need to develop new or stronger skills, advance in the company and achieve their goals while contributing to Verizon's success.

The Benefits: Verizon provides an outstanding employee benefits package, including medical and dental plans, company-match 401(k) savings plan, life insurance, short- and long-term disability coverage, pension plan, personal lines of insurance, employee assistance program, domestic partner benefits, employee resource groups, flexible spending accounts and generous educational assistance program.

Contact Information: If you are interested in the following programs and meet the designated qualifications, contact your college placement office. For more information and to submit your resume online, please visit www.verizon.com/college. Verizon is an equal opportunity employer and supports workforce diversity.

The Verizon Development Program

Length of program: This two-year rotational program consists of two hands-on staff marketing assignments, each lasting about six months, plus a one-year assignment in a supervisory or customer contact role. The initial six-month assignments may involve any aspect of business-to-business or consumer marketing, including product management, product development, product launch, market analysis, promotional campaigns, distribution and pricing.

Geographic location(s) of program: These assignments are typically based in a headquarters environment. Locations include, but are not limited to: D.C., Mass., N.Y., Pa., Md., Va., N.C., Fla., Ohio, Ind., Texas and Calif. Marketing provides a solid early career foundation to outstanding individuals who can address Verizon's marketing challenges, manage others and ultimately assume leadership roles in one of Verizon's largest business units—retail markets. The focus of this program is Verizon consumer and business customer segments. The program is designed to provide broad exposure to Verizon's consumer and business-to-business marketing initiatives, complemented by customer contact experiences and the opportunity to supervise a team—an unbeatable formula for launching a successful career.

Participants then transition from this headquarters exposure to the front line, where they may experience the dynamics of customer interaction and the challenges of supervising others. They gain both line and staff, headquarters and field perspectives, which will serve them well throughout their careers. Along the way, they are exposed to a broad array of telecommunications products and services—voice and data, network and hardware. At program completion, the career path typically leads to frontline management, with career progression to general marketing management in Verizon Retail Markets.

The program provides abundant training, with coursework in telecom technology, project management, presentation skills, leadership, supervision, customer relations, financial skills and time management. Participants also attend Verizon Development Program Orientation. Orientation includes presentations by business leaders, team-building exercises, workshops and social activities that provide opportunities to meet and network with peers.

Qualifications:

- BS in marketing
- Excellent academic preparation and achievement with a minimum of 3.0 out of 4.0 overall GPA
- Superior oral and written communications, leadership, analytical and interpersonal skills
- Evidence of mature, flexible and innovative approaches to work experiences
- Potential to assume supervisory responsibilities
- Willingness to relocate during the program experience
- Must have authorization to work permanently in the United States

Software/Systems Architect Development Program
Verizon Information Technology (VZIT)

Length of program: The program format typically entails two rotational assignments, each lasting about six to nine months.

Geographic location(s) of program: Including, but not limited to Dallas, TX; Tampa, FL; Boston, MA and the D.C. metro area

The Verizon Software/Systems Architect Development Program (SSADP) provides innovative, technically sophisticated MS and PhD graduates the opportunity to immerse themselves in the dynamic environment of Verizon Information Technology (VZ-IT). Verizon IT represents the best of both worlds for technical professionals. We are a company that successfully takes advantage of the resources and security of a big corporation while maintaining a spirited and highly educated workforce. What this program offers you is the opportunity to make an impact on the future—to work within a financially stable but technologically creative environment.

You will be part of a brave new world, as the overarching Verizon IT goal is to become a technical innovator in developing and marketing information technology and eBusiness solutions. You can be part of this growth: contribute to it, develop and learn from it, establish your place in the industry and refine your career as an IT professional.

The Software/Systems Architect Development Program is designed to perpetuate your academic success by developing well-rounded software engineers with a broad technology foundation, strong Verizon systems knowledge, and potential to ultimately assume technical leadership and/or general management roles at Verizon. These assignments provide exposure to different phases of the software development life cycle (i.e. requirements, design, development and testing), different technologies and different sides of the Verizon business. SSADP participants are also exposed to various facets of software design including, but not limited to: data (logical modeling, physical database, DBMS), applications (object modeling, systems development/integration, high-level object-oriented design) and infrastructure computing (networking platforms, operating systems and software). Technologies include Java, .Net, XML, J2EE, C# and Web Services, among others. These hands-on assignments

enable you to gain valuable experience in the design and development of large-scale systems applications with mentorship from Verizon project leads.

Qualifications:

- MS/PhD in computer science, electrical/computer engineering or related fields
- Excellent academic preparation and achievement with a minimum of 3.0 out of 4.0 overall GPA
- Software design or development experience; experience with various platforms
- Exceptional analytical, interpersonal, teamwork, leadership and communications skills
- Willingness to relocate during the program experience

Verizon Finance Professional Development

Geographic location(s) of program: N.Y./N.J.; Philadelphia; Boston; D.C.; Md.; Va.; Tampa, Fla.; and Irving, Texas

This comprehensive development program, which encompasses special orientation to Verizon and the finance function, is a personal development and training plan with a targeted competency-based curriculum. Participants have access to extensive Verizon training opportunities via Verizon's NetLearn programs and access to the Verizon educational assistance program, as well as ongoing performance feedback and coaching.

Mentoring circle participation is used to encourage creating opportunities for collaborative learning experiences, exchanging ideas as a group, analyzing developmental issues, receiving feedback and guidance, providing ongoing support and a sense of community and developing a strong peer network.

Developmental forums will include exposure to senior leadership, business issues and technology, skill assessment and creation of formal development/career plans and coming face-to-face with mentoring circles.

In addition, possible rotational assignment opportunities will help participants gain knowledge and experience of other finance disciplines, understand interrelationship and dependence between the finance organizations and develop and sharpen additional finance skills and interests. These jobs will also give them the chance to demonstrate strengths and skill sets to other managers and supervisors.

Qualifications:

- *Most roles:* BS/MBA in finance/accounting
- *Technical financial analysis roles:* BS in MIS/IT/computer engineering.
- *Verizon Capital Corp. role:* Math, operations research and engineering majors will be considered
- *For all roles:* Minimum 3.3 out of 4.0 GPA preferred

- In-depth knowledge of MS Office products (and knowledge of Hyperion for some positions)
- Superior organizational, analytical, critical thinking skills, communication and interpersonal skills
- Excellent quantitative skills for some roles
- Outstanding modeling and operations research skills
- Able to work effectively under pressure to meet critical deadlines
- Must have authorization to work permanently in the United States

Verizon Finance & Accounting Full-Time/Internship Positions

Geographic location(s) of program: N.Y./N.J., Pa., Ma., D.C., Md., Va., Texas, Fla.

Verizon financial and accounting roles provide excellent opportunities to apply your finance/accounting/technical background in a corporate finance setting.

Sample internships and full-time positions are in the areas of:

- *Consolidations:* Analyze subsidiary financial reports; prepare consolidated subsidiary financial statements

- *External reporting:* Prepare and file periodic financial reports (Forms 10Q, 10-K); track, analyze impacts of SEC, GAAP developments

- *Staff accounting:* Assist with monthly closing procedures, financial analyses, journal entries, account reconciliation; report results

- *Financial performance and assurance, specialist-business development:* Evaluate business operations, financial projections, strategies, budgets and opportunities by developing financial models and conducting market/industry research

- *Line of business expenses:* Handle expense budgeting, planning and reporting for a Verizon line of business

- *Billing and collections:* Handle billing for telecom industry customers, including adjustments, negotiations, settlements, documentation, tracking and accruals

- *Financial planning & analysis:* Develop and execute financial presentations, analysis and supporting documentation; support assigned business units

- *Financial policies:* Assist with the operational implementation of new FASB and SEC accounting standards; support assigned business units, encompassing mergers and acquisitions, financial instruments, business combinations, etc.

- *Financial reporting:* Prepare comparative financial data for quarterly earnings release; review trends, unusual items and variances to present a complete, accurate and balanced view of Verizon's financial performance to Wall Street analysts

- *Corporate consolidations:* Review business unit data submissions for data integrity, including consistency, comparability and GAAP

compliance; prepare, process inter-segment elimination activity and topside adjustments; perform inter-segment out-of-balance reviews and reconciliation; generate consolidated financial statement

- *Financial planning & analysis (Verizon Capital Corp):* Provide pricing, valuation and transaction support of existing VCC portfolio using sophisticated financial modeling and forecasting tools

- *Technical financial analysis:* Implement, maintain sophisticated support systems; conduct economic cost studies; make entry and exit decisions for product lines; perform ad hoc analyses and studies; develop models for policymakers and executives

Qualifications:

- Same as those for the Verizon Finance Professional Development Program above

Full-Time Regular Positions Only:

The professional development: Members of the Verizon finance team participate in special developmental and mentoring activities, including an orientation to Verizon and the finance function.

Contact information: If you are interested and meet specified qualifications, please submit your resume to sandra.magwood@verizon.com; please reference "FT" or "Intern" in the subject field of your e-mail. For more information, please visit www.verizon.com/college. Verizon is an equal opportunity employer and supports workforce diversity.

Strategic Plan and Diversity Leadership

How does the firm's leadership communicate the importance of diversity to everyone at the firm?

Advocacy for Verizon's diversity strategy incorporates various communications vehicles including corporate/line of business-specific Intranet web sites and diversity-specific forums/meetings. Examples include, but are not limited to:

Verizon executives feature or incorporate diversity into their speeches and presentations to an internal employee audience and external groups.

Verizon's Development and Leadership Initiative (DLI) Symposium provides the opportunity for Verizon's executives to articulate Verizon's diversity strategy and engage DLI participants in discussion.

Employee Resource Group (ERG) events and activities, i.e., seminars, conferences, cultural celebrations, mentoring, etc., provide the opportunity to communicate Verizon's diversity strategy and its commitment to having an aligned and integrated workplace where

diversity is transparent, and where Verizon is an inclusive organization that leverages the diversity of employees, customers and suppliers for increased productivity, profitability and an enhanced reputation. Each of the 10 ERGs receive assistance in promoting their events and activities through the corporate e-mail systems.

HR Weekly is an online publication available through the human resources communications web page. In addition to an ongoing calendar of events, stories highlighting the ERG program are also featured. Weekly distribution to all employees is utilized through the corporate e-mail systems.

The individual lines of business and ERGs design and deploy Intranet web sites/web pages, showcasing their support and commitment to Verizon's diversity strategy.

Who has primary responsibility for leading diversity initiatives at your firm?

Tracey Edwards, vice president, staffing and diversity, domestic telecom—human resources, has the primary responsibility for the overall design, implementation and program management of various diversity initiatives within the domestic telecom lines of business in support of Verizon's diversity strategy.

Does your firm currently have a diversity committee?

Yes

If yes, please describe how the committee is structured, how often it meets, etc.

Verizon strives for diversity at every level within the company from the top down. To make progress through diversity and to ensure that it remains an integral part of our business, each business unit across the company relies on its diversity councils to help them develop and implement customized diversity plans. Those plans are designed to meet the specific requirements of that business unit and help them execute the Verizon diversity strategy.

Each council chooses a chair. The chair can be anyone from a senior leader within a line of business, to a human resources business partner, to a member of the diversity council. Councils meet at least once a month via conference call and at least once a year in person to set goals and objectives, to strategize and to implement the various diversity initiatives.

Each council is required to create and implement a diversity plan that includes diversity goals for their specific lines of business. Verizon's diversity goals include, but are not limited to:

(1) Employee Development—Encourage employees to take advantage of the specific leadership/management training classes available, including the affinity workshops; advocate continuous learning, including enrollment in diversity training offered by Verizon through various mediums such as free online or classroom-based diversity classes; ensure all director-level and above managers mentor lower-level employees

(2) Communication—Ensure all employees have a clear understanding of Verizon's diversity strategy; encourage employees to get involved with all diversity efforts and to let them know that the senior leaders stand behind diversity; host diversity weeks, panel discussions, etc.

(3) External Outreach and Partnerships—Work within the communities Verizon serves to educate people on diversity, technology and humanitarian projects

If yes, does the committee's representation include one or more members of the firm's management/executive committee (or the equivalent)?

Yes

If yes, how many executives are on the committee? How many employees are on the committee, and how often does the committee convene in furtherance of the firm's diversity initiatives?

Executive representation and the number of employees on each committee vary by each line of business diversity council. Councils meet at least once a month via conference call and at least once a year in person to set goals and objectives, to strategize and to implement the various diversity initiatives.

Total Executives on Committee: Varies by line of business

Does the committee and/or diversity leader establish and set goals or objectives consistent with management's priorities?

Yes. Corporate diversity sets the overall Verizon diversity strategy, and workforce diversity provides the councils with the human resources focus for the year (e.g. employee development for 2006). However, each line of business council creates action plans and initiatives in support of those plans depending on the needs of their particular line of business. These plans are created with input for the line of business senior management team.

Has the firm undertaken a formal or informal diversity program or set of initiatives aimed at increasing the diversity of the firm?

Yes, formal. To ensure that diverse members of our multicultural workforce are prepared for career advancement, we have established mentoring and leadership development programs, such as the Verizon Development and Leadership Initiative (DLI). The DLI provides tools that help participants identify professional goals and network with Verizon executives, while helping Verizon identify and develop a diverse pool of high-potential candidates.

The DLI and Verizon's employee development resources have strengthened Verizon's leadership team by developing high-quality managers from diverse backgrounds who are prepared to assume new job assignments and additional responsibilities.

Verizon's mentoring initiative is critical to our strategy to win in the global marketplace and be the premier telecommunications company in the world. Mentoring helps drive this strategy because it fosters the development, growth and contributions of our most important asset—our people. Mentoring achieves this objective by leveraging informal work relationships, and enhancing the skills and capacity of our people to achieve their professional and personal objectives, while adding value to the business.

How often does the firm's management review the firm's diversity progress/results?

Quarterly

How is the firm's diversity committee and/or firm management held accountable for achieving results?

We have a commitment to diversity that stems from the top of the business. In addition to a leadership team that is becoming more and more diverse, we are also governed by a diverse board of directors representing a variety of industries and experiences.

Our management executives are held accountable for promoting diversity in their organizations, and our diversity performance incentive links our employment efforts to recruit, retain and develop a diverse population of employees to meet the needs of the diverse marketplace that we serve.

Retention and Professional Development

Please identify the specific steps you are taking to reduce the attrition rate of minority and women employees.

• Develop and/or support internal employee affinity groups (e.g., minority or women networks within the firm)

• Increase/review compensation relative to competition

• Succession plan includes emphasis on diversity

• Work with minority and women employees to develop career advancement plans

• Strengthen mentoring program for all employees, including minorities and women

• Professional skills development program, including minority and women employees

Diversity Mission Statement

Verizon is committed to maintaining an inclusive corporate culture that embraces and leverages the diversity of employees, customers and suppliers for increased productivity, profitability and an enhanced reputation. The culture of inclusion that defines our com-

pany will earn the trust of our employees and the diverse customers and communities we serve.

Additional Information

Verizon is at the forefront of the transformation of the telecommunications industry and we remain committed to creating and fostering an inclusive culture that values the diversity of our employees. Competition in our industry is pervasive, and we recognize that in order to meet the ever changing and growing demands of our customers, we must rely on the innovation and creativity that a diverse employee base provides. Verizon is proud of the broad range of products and services we offer and prouder still of our ability to foster, promote and preserve the diversity and human rights of our employees, customers and communities.

Awards and Recognition

Verizon has been recognized nationally for its commitment to diversity:

2006 Diversity Awards/Honors

• *Black MBA* magazine ranked Verizon 1st on the publication's Top 50 Companies for African-American MBAs to Work (2006).

• *Black Engineer and Information Technology (USBE&IT)* magazine selected Verizon as a Top Supporter of Historically Black Colleges (2006).

• *DiversityInc* magazine ranked Verizon No. 1 on the 2006 list of Top 50 U.S. Companies for Diversity.

• Moms in Business Network/The International Association of *Working Mothers* named Verizon National Company of the Year.

• *Training* magazine Verizon Communications and Verizon Wireless both made the publication's annual Training Top 100 list of organizations that excel at employee development.

• WBENC (Women's Business Enterprise National Council) selected Verizon to its annual listing of America's Top Corporations for Women in March 2006. The award recognizes a select group of companies for their "world-class" supplier diversity programs.

• *Working Mother* named Verizon one of 2006's Best Companies for Women of Color.

2005 Diversity Awards/Honors:

• *Black Enterprise* magazine named Verizon one of the 30 Best Companies for Diversity. The publication noted Verizon's commitment to diversity among senior management, board of directors and suppliers.

- *CAREERS & the disABLED* magazine named Verizon the Private-Sector Employer of the Year for its commitment to recruiting, hiring and advancing people with disabilities.

- Diversity Business.com honored Verizon with its America's Top Organizations for Multi-cultural Opportunities award.

- Employee Assistance Society of North America presented Verizon with its Corporate Award of Excellence for its innovative employee assistance program, VZ-LIFE. Verizon received the award for offering comprehensive work/life solutions to its diverse work force.

- EPA (Environmental Protection Agency) Verizon was named US EPA WasteWise Partner of the Year

- EPA and DOT (Department of Transportation) recognized Verizon as one of the Best Workplaces for Commuters

- Montgomery County MD recognized Verizon at its 6th annual Recycling Awards Week Ceremony for our comprehensive waste reduction and recycling program—Verizon surpassed the objective of 50 percent (exceeded to 70 percent).

- *Essence* magazine placed Verizon 2nd for African-American women on its list of 35 Great Places to Work.

- HESTEC (Hispanic Engineering Science and Technology) presented Magda Yrizarry, vice president, with the UTPA Foundation Latina Pioneer Award.

- *Hispanic* magazine named Verizon to its Corporate 100 list for providing opportunities for Hispanics, as having one of the Top 25 Diversity Recruitment Programs and as having one of the Top 25 Supplier Diversity Programs.

- Hispanic Association on Corporate Responsibility (HACR) ranked Verizon second on the HACR Corporate Index in 2005. The index grades the Fortune 100 companies on their commitment to the Hispanic community.

- *Hispanic Business* magazine named Verizon to list of 25 Best Companies to Work For. Verizon was ranked one of the magazine's top five companies for Hispanics.

- *Latin Business* magazine named Verizon to its Corporate Diversity Honor Roll. (2004, 2005)

- *Latina Style* magazine named Verizon to its special Top 13 list of the 50 Top Companies for Hispanic Women.

- Maura Breen, Keiko Harvey, Jerri DeVard, senior vice presidents; and Katherine Linder, Kathy Harless and Sheila Lau, presidents, were profiled as Women of Initiative by the *Diversity Journal.*

- *Scientific American* magazine named Verizon to its first list of the 55 top companies making a difference in the way people with disabilities live and work.

- *Training Magazine* named Verizon and Verizon Wireless to its list of the Top 100 companies that excel at human capital development.

- United States Pan Asian American Chamber of Commerce (USPAACC) named Verizon Corporation of the Year.

- Women's Venture Fund presented Magda Yrizarry, vice president, with the Highest Leaf Award. The award honors women whose business or professional action positively impacts their fields and exemplifies an understanding of the balance between outcome and responsibility in their workplace.

Wachovia Corporation

One Wachovia Center
Charlotte, NC 28288-0013
www.wachovia.com

Wachovia Securities
Riverfront Plaza
901 East Byrd Street
Richmond, VA 23219
www.wachoviasec.com

Evergreen Investments
200 Berkeley Street
Boston, MA 02116
Phone: (617) 210-3200
www.evergreeninvestments.com

Employment Contact
E-mail: jobs@wachovia.com, jobs@ever-greeninvestments.com
www.wachovia.com/careers

Recruitment

Please list the schools/types of schools at which you recruit.

- *Ivy League schools:* Harvard University, Princeton University, University of Pennsylvania
- *Other private schools:* Duke University, Wake Forest University, Vanderbilt University and others
- *Public state schools:* University of North Carolina, University of Virginia, University of Texas, University of Florida and others
- *Historically black colleges and universities (HBCUs):* Morehouse College, Spelman College, Hampton University, Howard University, Florida A&M University and others
- *Hispanic serving institutions (HSIs):* Florida International University and University of Houston

Do you have any special outreach efforts directed to encourage minority students to consider your firm?

- Hold a reception for minority students
- *Conferences:* National Society of Hispanic MBAs, National Black MBA Association, NABA, NAACP, ALPFA, Thurgood Marshall Career Fair, TOIGO
- Advertise in minority student association publication(s)
- Participate in/host minority student job fair(s)
- Sponsor minority student association events
- Firm's employees participate on career panels at schools
- Outreach to leadership of minority student organizations
- Scholarships or intern/fellowships for minority students

What activities does the firm undertake to attract minority and women employees?

- Partner programs with women and minority associations
- *Conferences:* National Association of Black Accountants, Black Data Processing Association,
- Association of Latino Professionals in Finance & Accounting, National Black MBA Association, National Society of Hispanic MBAs
- Participate at minority job fairs
- Seek referrals from other employees
- Utilize online job services

Do you use executive recruiting/search firms to seek to identify new diversity hires?

Yes

Internships and Co-ops

There are a variety of internship programs in eight different lines of business. The specific programs vary each year and are updated on our web site in December. Please see www.wachovia.com/college for details.

Deadline for application: February 1st

Pay: $12 to $18 per hour for undergraduate programs, based on class year and varies slightly by line of business

Length of the program: Eight to 10 weeks

Percentage of interns/co-ops in the program who receive offers of full-time employment: Varies by line of business

Web site for internship/co-op information:
www.wachovia.com/college

Scholarships

A variety of scholarships are available.

Scholarship award amount: $500 to $2,000

Entry-Level Programs, Full-Time Opportunities and Training Programs

There are a variety of entry-level associate and analyst programs in eight different lines of business. The specific programs vary each year and are updated on our web site in August and January. Please see www.wachovia.com/college for details.

Length of program: Three- to six-month rotations in various areas, two- to three-year placements, or permanent placement depending on the program

Geographic location(s) of program: In every location within the Wachovia footprint

Programs vary from six weeks initial training to ongoing training, depending on the program.

Strategic Plan and Diversity Leadership

How does the firm's leadership communicate the importance of diversity to everyone at the firm?

Wachovia's corporate Intranet has a section called Wachovia Diversity, accessible from the homepage, where CEO Ken Thompson talks about the importance of creating a diverse and inclusive workplace. Employees can also find Wachovia's values statement, diversity strategies for the current year and diversity resources on this site. In addition, twice a year, Ken provides an update on diversity to all employees through e-mail, Intranet and over Wachovia's internal television network.

Who has primary responsibility for leading diversity initiatives at your firm?

Rosie Saez, director of diversity integration practices

Does your firm currently have a diversity committee?

Yes

If yes, please describe how the committee is structured, how often it meets, etc.

The Corporate Diversity Council, headed by CEO Ken Thompson, meets approximately six times per year to determine and direct the strategic diversity effort for the entire Wachovia footprint. The council is made up of a diverse representation of leaders from across Wachovia. The purpose of the council is to convert the ideal of what we think our company stands for into processes and procedures that ensure that the ideal becomes real. The council determines the current state of diversity in the corporation, defines corporate objectives relative to diversity and works to continuously reinforce the practice of diversity at Wachovia.

If yes, does the committee's representation include one or more members of the firm's management/executive committee (or the equivalent)?

Yes

If yes, how many executives are on the committee?

Total Executives on Committee: Six

Does the committee and/or diversity leader establish and set goals or objectives consistent with management's priorities?

Yes

Has the firm undertaken a formal or informal diversity program or set of initiatives aimed at increasing the diversity of the firm?

Yes, formal

How often does the firm's management review the firm's diversity progress/results?

Annually

How is the firm's diversity committee and/or firm management held accountable for achieving results?

The CEO is a member of the committee. Also, the committee is advised by the director of diversity integration practices.

Diversity Mission Statement

Teamwork. Synergy. The collective ideas and insights of our employees forge our solid and unified vision for success.

At Wachovia, we treat people with respect, recognize them for their individuality and provide opportunity for advancement based on performance. Race, gender, gender identity, sexual orientation, work/life status, ethnic origin, culture, spiritual beliefs and practices, age, education level, physical ability, veteran status and other differences make us unique as individuals and enhance our company as a whole.

Our Corporate Diversity Council, led by CEO Ken Thompson, guides the Wachovia diversity commitment. The council meets regularly to:

• Define corporate diversity objectives

• Raise awareness and sensitivity to diversity within our company

• Determine the state of affairs within our company and prescribe strategies and action plans when needed

• Implement programs and policies effectively

• Update and improve diversity commitments on an as-needed basis

Our commitment to diversity is also felt outside of our company. Today, we have outreach programs in place that have a significant affect on the communities we serve. These include community development products and services, purchasing programs with minority-owned firms, women's financial advisory initiatives, and products and services for underserved diverse customer groups.

Wachovia is an active participant in the INROADS internship program. If interested, please contact your local INROADS office for more information.

Additional Information

National Diversity Recruiting Partner Alliances

• *National Association of Black Accountants:* www.nabainc.org

• *Association of Latino Professionals in Finance and Accounting:* www.alpfa.org

• *National Society of Hispanic MBA:* www.nshmba.org

• *Urban Financial Services Coalition:* www.ufsc.org

• *Black Data Processors Association:* www.bdpa.org/portal

• *Gay & Lesbian Professional Career Network (National Online Job Board & Professional Alliance):* www.GLPCareers.com

• *National Association of Asian American Professionals:* www.naaap.org

• *National Black MBA Association:* www.nbmbaa.org

Wal-Mart Stores, Inc.

508 SW 8th Street
Bentonville, AK 72716-0765
www.walmartstores.com/careers

Locations

Corporate Offices in Bentonville, AR; operations in 50 United States and 13 countries.

Contact Person

Jody Hestand
Diversity Recruiter
508 SW 8th Street
Bentonville, AK 72716-0765
Phone: (479) 204-8571
Fax: (479) 277-1013
E-mail: Jody.Hestand@wal-mart.com

Diversity Team Leader

Jody Hestand
Diversity Recruiter

Recruiting

Please list the schools/types of schools at which you recruit.

- Ivy League schools
- Other private schools
- Public state schools
- Historically black colleges and universities (HBCUs)
- Hispanic serving institutions (HSIs)
- Native American tribal universities
- Other predominantly minority and/or women's colleges

Do you have any special outreach efforts directed to encourage minority students to consider your firm?

- Advertise in minority student association publication(s) or other minority-focused publications.
- Sponsor minority student association events
- Firm's employees participate on career panels at schools
- Outreach to leadership of minority student organizations
- Scholarships or intern/fellowships for minority students
- *Other:* mentoring programs

What activities does the firm undertake to attract minority and women employees?

- Partner programs with women and minority associations
- *Conferences:* NBMBAA, NSHMBA, NABA, SWE, SHPE, HACU, BEYA
- Participate at minority job fairs
- Seek referrals from other employees
- Utilize online job services

Internships and Co-ops

Summer Corporate Internships

Deadline for application: January 31st

Number of interns in the program in summer 2006 (internship): 180

Length of the program: 10 to 12 weeks

Percentage of interns/co-ops in the program who receive offers of full-time employment: 85 percent

Web site for internship/co-op information: www.walmartstores.com/careers

As a Wal-Mart intern, you will have the opportunity to gain a realistic job preview of working in a dynamic, fast-paced, retail environment. Experiencing Wal-Mart's three basic beliefs: respect for the individual, striving for excellence and service to our customers, will set you on the path to success!

A Wal-Mart paid internship will teach and give you practical skills above and beyond your classroom experience. You will gain knowledge and experience from the most successful and largest retailer in the world. Interning for Wal-Mart will set you up for a bright and successful future and also give you the necessary experience to become competitive in future endeavors. We have opportunities available for job positions in a variety of areas, including but not limited to the following: merchandising, product development, replenishment, risk control, logistics and transportation, accounting and finance, information systems, store operations (corporate), real estate, legal, international, benefits/claims, Sam's Club (corporate) and human resources.

The minimum qualifications are as follows:

- Entering your junior or senior year of college or be enrolled in graduate school (but not graduating) as of May 31st
- 3.0 cumulative GPA preferred
- Interested in a career with a fast-pasted retailer who embraces change and creative thinking
- Enthusiastic, team-oriented and enjoy working with others
- Understand and appreciate diversity as the source of new ideas and better customer service
- Value high integrity and strong business ethics
- Demonstrate a working knowledge and practice of our company's three basic beliefs: respect for the individual, service to our customers and striving for excellence

Scholarships

Academic and Emerging Scholars Programs

Deadline for application for the scholarship program: Varies by school

Scholarship award amount: Varies by program

Affinity Groups

Asian Pacific Islander Resource Group (API)
Mission

The API will serve as a resource for Wal-Mart Stores, Inc. to enhance an understanding and appreciation for the Asian/Pacific Islander culture prepare members as visionary leaders and decision makers through development and networking opportunities and partner with Wal-Mart businesses to capitalize on the Asian/Pacific Islander market. Please direct questions to APIRG@wal-mart.com.

Hispanic Latino Associate Resource Group (HLARG)
Mission

Our mission is to support Wal-Mart Stores, Inc. through ongoing education and promotion of Hispanic/Latino culture and values for the mutual benefit of our company and the communities we serve. The Hispanic/Latino Associate Resource Group will meet on the third Wednesday of each month.

Associates With Disabilities Resource Group (LEAD)
Mission

We are a network for sharing of ideas to empower associates with disabilities through workplace inclusion, community education and implementation of best practices.

Gay, Lesbian, Bisexual and Transgender Resource Group (PRIDE)
Mission

Building upon the core beliefs of respect, service, excellence and partnership with company leaders. PRIDE promotes an inclusive, supportive environment for Wal-Mart's GLBT community. They meet once every two weeks. For more information, please refer to Pride's website at http://isd/pride or e-mail Pride@wal-mart.com.

Native American Resource Group (Tribal Voices)
Mission

Tribal Voices is a group of associates who reflect and embrace the many diverse sovereign nations of the Native American people and bridge the gap between corporate America and tribal cultures.

African American Resource Group (UNITY)
Mission

The African-American Resource Group will serve as a catalyst for growth and change by enhancing awareness and appreciation of African-American culture by introducing and supporting educational programs and projects, positioning African-Americans as thought leaders and decision makers through development and networking opportunities and serving as a resource to the company and associates by supporting business initiatives that represent the African-American culture.

Women's Resource Group (WRC)
Mission

Mission of the Women's Resource Council is to promote and provide opportunities for the professional and personal development of women across all business units and at all levels of the company, to advance issues effecting women and to expand and improve opportunities for women to achieve their maximum potential.

https://sharepoint.wal-mart.com/sites/ChangeMgmt/WRC/default.aspx

Entry-Level Programs, Full-Time Opportunities and Training Programs

Merchant Trainee Program Overview
Purpose

To create a talent pool capable of filling the need for assistant buyer positions in the merchandising division. Trainees should complete the program with a strong knowledge of all areas including store operations, systems, financials, reporting, negotiating and creative skills. They should accelerate quickly through the buying organization and have leadership potential.

Program Overview

For 2008 Wal-Mart Stores, Inc. will hire 42 new merchant trainees, increasing by seven over the previous year. This increase is due to the restructure of the apparel organization under Claire Watts and the addition of the product development, global sourcing, and planning and execution teams. Each team has entry-level positions and is in need of new talent.

We currently recruit from a wide variety of colleges and universities that have strong retail, apparel/fashion merchandising, fashion/technical design, food industry, and/or business programs. We also source candidates online, through referrals, and internally. Those who perform well in the prescreening process will be brought in for a final round of interviews, including one with a general merchandise manager and two with divisional merchandise managers. New trainees are selected and offered positions after this final round of interviews.

Merchant trainees are monitored by three different groups, the merchandising people division for people related issues, the merchant training team (under the Wal-Mart University umbrella) for all training needs, as well as the program management team (under the recruiting umbrella) who monitor the on- and off-boarding processes. Trainee wages are charged to the program management team through the duration of the program.

Program Design

Once accepted into the program the trainee will spend three months of training in a Wal-Mart Store local to the corporate offices. During the store training time they will work with the merchant training team and complete weekly training modules.

Upon completion of store training the trainees return to the home office and work with a sponsor designated by their general merchandise manager for the remaining six months. During this time the trainee will complete corporate classes as well as on the job training with their sponsor. They will receive monthly evaluations (touch bases) to ensure the appropriate training is taking place. These evaluations are monitored by the merchant training team.

Strategic Plan and Diversity Leadership

What trends in your industry affect your corporate diversity goals, strategies and/or internal or external alliances?

At Wal-Mart, diversity is a top priority for our company. It helps us provide a positive work environment for our 1.8 million worldwide associates. And it helps us serve the more than 4,000 communities that surround our stores in this country. For Wal-Mart, diversity is more than something we talk about; it's who we are.

As our workforce becomes more diverse, we have a responsibility to ensure we are providing an open and positive work environment for every Wal-Mart associate. As our customer base broadens, we need to make sure we are offering the products our customers want and need—at prices they can afford. As we grow to serve more and more communities, we must continue to be the kind of neighbor that working families of all walks of life value and trust.

How does the firm's leadership communicate the importance of diversity to everyone at the firm?

Associates are kept abreast of the importance of diversity through training, diversity initiatives, programs, web site and e-mail communication, corporate notices and leadership programming.

Who has primary responsibility for leading diversity initiatives at your firm?

Senior Vice President and Chief Diversity Officer, Charlyn Jarrells Porter

Has the firm undertaken a formal or informal diversity program or set of initiatives aimed at increasing the diversity of the firm?

Yes, formal

Our Diversity Goals Program is designed to promote the professional development and retention of all of our associates, enhance external business relationships, and encourage our associates to participate in the communities we serve.

Wal-Mart has experienced many positive results because of our Diversity Goals Program and other initiatives. The program evaluates the achievement of diversity goals while at the same time helping Wal-Mart attract, hire, and retain qualified associates. The program consists of placement goals and good faith effort goals.

Placement diversity goals are tied to placing women, African-Americans, Hispanics, Asians and Native Americans in parity with the qualified, interested, and available applicant pool for field management positions.

Good faith efforts diversity goals are tied to managers participating in approved diversity events, as well as mentoring at least three associates, including persons of diverse race, gender, or background. Our commitment to these initiatives will continue to create and strengthen an even more inclusive and supportive workplace for all associates.

How is the firm's diversity committee and/or firm management held accountable for achieving results?

Senior managers and officers are also held accountable financially. If they do not achieve their diversity goals, a portion of their incentive bonus may be reduced.

The Stats

	NUMBER OF EMPLOYEES	REVENUE
	2006	2006
Total in the U.S.	1.3million	N/A
Total outside the U.S.	.5 million	N/A
Total worldwide	1.8 million	$345 billion in sales

2006 DEMOGRAPHIC PROFILE (U.S.)	
Female	826,000
African American	237,000
Hispanics	154,000
Asian Americans	41,000
Native Americans	15,000
Seniors (55+)	256,000

As the world's largest private employer, we remain fully committed to nurturing a diverse workplace that provides our associates opportunities to grow and develop. Wal-Mart's total workforce is more than 60 percent female and almost 33 percent minority.

Retention and Professional Development

Please identify the specific steps you are taking to reduce the attrition rate of minority and women employees.

• Develop and/or support internal employee affinity groups (e.g., minority or women networks within the firm)

• Increase/review compensation relative to competition

• Increase/improve current work/life programs

• Adopt dispute resolution process

• Succession plan includes emphasis on diversity

• Work with minority and women employees to develop career advancement plans

• Review work assignments and hours billed to key client matters to make sure minority and women employees are not being excluded

• Strengthen mentoring program for all employees, including minorities and women

• Professional skills development program, including minority and women employees

Diversity Mission Statement

"The courage to lead and do what's right." –Sam Walton

Diversity is a way of life at Wal-Mart, and our commitment to diversity is not just something we talk about, it's who we are. Because we are committed to diversity, we can better serve our more than 127 million weekly customers and provide a positive work environment for our 1.3 million U.S. associates. We know that attracting diverse customers, associates and suppliers is critical to our success. Our dedication to diversity extends from our board of directors to our associates, from our suppliers to our customers and to every aspect of our business.

We have long maintained diversity initiatives including personnel practices and supplier programs to help build and retain a diverse workforce and supplier base along with varied community outreach programs.

We employ diversity initiatives, including personnel practices and supplier programs. These initiatives help us build and retain a diverse workforce and supplier base, along with various community outreach programs. Our executive team was also engaged in our diversity events. In 2006, more than 60 executives (vice president and above) served as board members for a diverse group of community organizations. Many more participated as speakers for conferences, workshops or guest panels.

In 2006, the Wal-Mart diversity relations team partnered with a diverse group of organizations to support more than 400 community programs across the country including:

• United Negro College Fund (UNCF)

• National Council of La Raza (NCLR)

• National Association of Women Business

• Owners (NAWBO)

• League of United Latin American

• Citizens (LULAC)

• Women Impacting Public Policy (WIPP)

• National Urban League (NUL)

• Hispanic Scholarship Fund

• Congressional Black Caucus Foundation

• Working Mother Media

In 2006, we received awards and recognition from the following publications and organizations:

• Top 50 Corporations for Supplier Diversity
  –Hispanic Trends magazine

- 100 Best Places to Work for Latinos
  –*Hispanic* magazine

- Top 10 Companies for African Americans
  –*DiversityInc*

- 25 Noteworthy Companies for Diversity
  –*DiversityInc*

- 2006 Corporate Diversity Honor Roll
  –*Latin Business* magazine

- Corporate Counsel Diversity Award
  –Dallas Hispanic Bar Association

- Top 30 Companies for Minorities
  –The Diversity Network & *Fortune* magazine

- Top 30 Companies for Diversity Recruiting
  –Diversity Best Practices

- Top 50 Companies for African American MBA
  –*Black MBA* magazine

- 40 Best Companies for Diversity
  –*Black Enterprise* magazine

- 2006 Corporation of the Year
  –Native American Chamber of Commerce

- Business of the Year Award
  –American Indian Chamber of Commerce

- Top Companies for Female Executives
  –National Assn. of Female Exeuctives

- Top Companies for Asian Americans
  –*Asian Enterprise* magazine

- Corporate Achievement Award
  –Organization of Chinese Americans

* Sample List

Wells Fargo & Company

420 Montgomery Street
San Francisco, CA 94104

Locations

Wells Fargo is headquartered in San Francisco and has offices in all 50 states

Diversity Leadership

Linda McConley
Diversity Manager
Phone: (612) 667-0643
Fax: (612) 667-5353
E-mail: Linda.k.mcconley@wellsfargo.com

Employment Contact

April Taylor
Recruitment Manager
Phone: (623) 876-5801
Fax: (415) 371-3933
E-mail: tayloraj@wellsfargo.com

Melissa Morey
Assistant Vice President, Corporate
Communications
www.wellsfargo.com/careers

Recruiting

Please list the schools/types of schools at which you recruit.

- *Ivy League schools:* Examples include Harvard and University of Pennsylvania

- *Other private schools:* Examples include USC, Knox College, Kenyon College, Pepperdine University, Claremont McKenna Schools, Emory University, Texas A&M

- *Public state schools:* Examples include UC Berkeley, UCLA, ASU, UTA, Iowa State, University of Minneapolis, UC Davis

- *Historically black colleges and universities (HBCUs):* Examples include Clark Atlanta Schools, Xaviers, Jackson State University

- *Hispanic serving institutions (HSIs):* Examples include St. Mary's College, Our Lady of the Lake & Texas A&M

Do you have any special outreach efforts directed to encourage minority students and graduates to consider your firm?

- *Conferences:* National Black MBA, National Hispanic MBA and other diversity career fairs

- *Advertise in minority student association publication(s) or other minority-focused publications:* For every event we attend or host on campus, we actively advertise our events to those student groups that have listed themselves on the campus sites.

- *Participate in/host minority student job fair(s) or other minority-focused job events:* We participate in the Diversity Career Fair in the spring at UC Berkeley. We also host a Reverse Career Fair for the SAGE scholars at UC Berkeley. If there are other specialized fairs offered at schools we sign up for them.

- *Sponsor minority student association events* We have held a resume workshop with SAGE Scholars, and their graduation dinner at UC Berkeley and sponsor events with the Latin Business Students Association at HAAS.

- *Firm's employees participate on career panels at schools:* Many of our team members volunteer to participate in career panels with their alma maters.

- *Outreach to leadership of minority student organizations:* For every event we attend or host on campus, we actively advertise our events to those student groups that have listed themselves on the campus sites.

- *Scholarships or intern/fellowships for minority students:* Provide $100,000 scholarships for approximately 90 students with the Hispanic Scholarship Fund, United Negro College Fund and with the Asian and Pacific Islander American Scholarship Fund.

What activities does the firm undertake to attract minority and women employees?

- *Partner programs with women and minority associations:* On campuses, we advertise job opportunities to clubs that are women-focused

- *Conferences:* American Indian Business Leaders, Graduate Women in Business, National Association of Black Accountants, National Black MBA Association, National Hispanic Business Association, National Society of Hispanic MBAs, National Association of

Women MBAs, Students in Free Enterprise and various regional and campus student organizations

- *Participate at minority job fairs:* Examples include NAACP, diversity fair at UCB, Alliance of Technology and Women and numerous other local fairs focused on women and minorities

- Seek referrals from other employees

- *Utilize online job services:* Examples include Monster's diversity inclusion, AsianAvenue.com, Black Planet.com, MiGente.com

Do you use executive recruiting/search firms to seek to identify new diversity hires?

Yes

Internships and Co-ops

Corporate/Wholesale Banking Undergraduate Summer and MBA Associates Program

Deadline for application: March 2007

Number of interns in the program in summer 2006 (internship) or 2007 (co-op): 80 undergraduates/10 MBAs

Length of the program (in weeks): 10 to 12 weeks

Percentage of interns/co-ops in the program who receive offers of full-time employment: We do not track how many people we offer centrally.

Web site for internship information:
www.wellsfargo.com/employment/undergraduates/summer

Internet Services Summer Intern Program

Deadline for application: March 2007

Number of interns in the program in summer 2006 (internship) or 2006 (co-op): Seven total undergraduates and MBAs

Length of the program (in weeks): 10 to 12 weeks

Percentage of interns/co-ops in the program who receive offers of full-time employment: We do not track how many students we offer internships to centrally.

Web site for internship information:
www.wellsfargo.com/employment/undergraduates/summer/internet

Scholarships

Hispanic Scholarship Fund (HSF)

Deadline for application for the scholarship program: April 2007

Scholarship award amount: Approximately 25 scholarships; ($2,000 per scholarship for each year up to four years)

Web site or other contact information for scholarship:
http://www.hsf.net/scholarships.php

Wells Fargo offers scholarship awards (as well as internships and future employment opportunities) to Latino students in partnership with the Hispanic Scholarship Fund (HSF).

Asian and Pacific Islander American Scholarship Fund (APIASF)

Deadline for application for the scholarship program: April 2007

Scholarship award amount: Approximately 30 scholars at $2,000 per scholar per year for incoming freshmen

Web site or other contact information for scholarship: www.api-asf.org

Wells Fargo is one of several founding sponsors of the Asian and Pacific Islander American Scholarship Fund (APIASF). The scholarship is designed for college-bound students from underrepresented Asian and Pacific Islander communities interested in pursuing careers in banking and financial services.

United Negro College Fund

Deadline for application for the scholarship program: April 2007

Scholarship award amount: Approximately 25 scholarships, $2,000 per scholarship for each year

Web site or other contact information for scholarship:
www.uncf.com

UC Berkeley SAGE Scholars Program

Deadline for application for the scholarship program: Varies annually

Scholarship award amount ($US): $3,800 administrative fee per scholar/per summer, plus compensation associated with participation in the intern programs detailed above

Web site or other contact information for scholarship: http://students.berkeley.edu/sagescholars

UC Berkeley's SAGE (Student Achievement Guided by Experience) Scholars Program is an academically rigorous program that combines workplace experience with the professional skills needed to succeed in a competitive economy. SAGE works with highly motivated UC Berkeley students from low-income and diverse backgrounds. SAGE promotes quality professional leadership and career development training through internships, mentoring and education. Wells Fargo, which is on the corporate advisory board for this organization, hired six interns in 2006 and two interns in 2007.

University of Texas, Austin Jumpstart Program

Deadline for application for the scholarship program: Varies annually

Scholarship award amount: Compensation associated with three years of pre-program employment, plus all tuition and fees associated with enrollment in the UT-Austin MBA program

A new program from the University of Texas at Austin's McCombs School of Business aims to meet that need by expanding the pool of top students who consider an MBA degree. The Jumpstart Program targets undergraduate seniors who are academically qualified for a top-ranked MBA but lack the required work experience. Companies agree to provide the experience by hiring the students for three years. The McCombs School then offers candidates deferred admission to the MBA program based on the completion of their job commitment.

INROADS

Deadline for application: Varies annually

Number of interns in the program in summer 2006 (internship) or 2007 (co-op): Two undergraduates/three MBAs

Pay: $13 to $13.50 per hour (group pays INROADS $4,000 per intern per year)

Length of the program: 10 to 12 weeks depending on school schedule

Web site for internship information: www.inroads.org

The Wells Fargo Foundation contributed a total of $5.6 million to various secondary education funds, events and scholarships.

Affinity Groups

Wells Fargo has over 100 Team Member Resource Groups (TMRGs) across the company. TMRGs are internal networks of individuals with a shared background, experience or other affinity which promote awareness of cultural groups and diversity. TMRGs are critical in attracting, developing, engaging and retaining team members at all levels across the company and they focus on career development, mentoring, networking and community outreach activities. Any Wells Fargo team member can join an existing group or propose to start a new group. The groups are as follows:

• Arab (Arab-American Connection)
• African-American (CheckPoint)
• Asian/Pacific Islander (Asian Connection)
• Team Members Dealing with Disabilities (disAbilities Awareness)
• Hispanic/Latino (Amigos)
• Native American (Native Peoples)
• Persian (Caspian Connection)
• Gay, Lesbian, Bisexual and Transgender (PRIDE)
• Indian Subcontinent (I.N.D.I.A.)

Entry-Level Programs, Full-Time Opportunities and Training Programs

Each year, Wells Fargo hires undergraduate and graduate students to participate in one of our 13 professional development training programs. Ranging from six to 24 months, these rotational programs

expose participants to a variety of projects and businesses as well as to leadership development opportunities to help prepare them for future management positions. Participants in these programs, like all Wells Fargo team members, are eligible for tuition reimbursement.

Corporate Banking: Credit Management Training Program (MBA)

Length of program: Six months

Geographic location of program: San Francisco

This program familiarizes participants with how Wells Fargo analyzes and evaluates credit situations. Associates work directly with corporate clients to build and strengthen relationships and recommend the appropriate financial products to meet their needs.

Corporate Banking: Financial Analyst Program (BA/BS)

Length of program: 18 to 24 months

Geographic location of program: Major cities in California, Texas and the Pacific Northwest; Chicago, Minneapolis, New York and other U.S. locations

Participants provide analytical and operational support to senior bankers during the deal making process, corporate meetings and presentations to senior managers. Receive formal training in accounting, corporate finance, treasury management and commercial credit.

Corporate Banking: Marketing Operations and Project Manager/Leadership Pipeline Program (BA/BS)

Length of program: 12 to 18 months

Geographic location of program: San Francisco, St. Paul

This program is designed to train qualified diverse candidates for management roles in corporate banking support services. It provides participants with comprehensive exposure to the Wells Fargo corporate/wholesale businesses in preparation for an individual contributor or management position within the business group.

Capital Management: Leadership Development Program (BA/BS)

Length of program: 12 to 18 months

Geographic location of program: Some cities are San Francisco and Walnut Creek, CA; Minneapolis, Minn.; and Menomonee Falls, Wisc.

This program is designed to train qualified diversity candidates for management roles in WellsCap—capital management support services. It provides comprehensive exposure to the Wells Fargo corporate/wholesale businesses in preparation for an individual contributor or management position within the business group.

Business Banking Services: Business Banking Associate Program (UG)

Length of program: 12 months (two six-month rotations)

Geographic location of program: San Francisco, Sacramento, Concord, Boise, Minneapolis, San Antonio

This rotational program includes operations/customer service, finance/credit analysis, systems, mergers and acquisitions, and human resources. Also includes formal training in technical, business and interpersonal skills.

Finance: Finance Associate Program (UG)

Length of program: 12 months

Geographic location of program: San Francisco

This program prepares recent graduates for a career in finance through a combination of hands-on experience, classroom and web-based training and peer interaction. The program moves trainees through project teams in various finance-related business lines, and one rotation in an unassociated Wells Fargo business group.

Internet Services: Internet Business Consultant Program (MBA)

Length of program: 12 months

Geographic location of program: San Francisco

Provides participants the opportunity to develop skill sets in the world of e-commerce and address key challenges in our business.

Internet Services: Information Technology Associate (BS/BA)

Length of program: 12 months

Geographic location of program: San Francisco

Includes three project-based rotations over 12 months. The ITA program uses a combination of classroom training, computer-based training, project team participation, peer interaction and working one-on-one with e-commerce technology professionals to prepare participants for their first assignment as an Internet services IT professional.

Audit Services Group: Auditor Rotational Training Program (BA/BS)

Length of program: 36 months

Geographic location of program: Des Moines, Minneapolis, Phoenix, San Francisco

A rotational program wherein individuals complete a formal training curriculum related to technical, business and behavioral skills while rotating among different audit groups.

Technology Information Group: Leadership Development Program (BA/BS)

Length of program: 12 months

Geographic location of program: Minneapolis, Phoenix and San Francisco

A rotational program providing exposure to a variety of functional enterprises within the Technology Group. Participants may work in a retail store, a phone bank center, and/or in entry-level operations and technology assignments. They also receive guidance from the program manager, a personal mentor and various assignment managers.

Customer Sales and Services Group: Leadership Development Program (BA/BS)

Length of program: 12 months

Geographic location of program: Minneapolis and Phoenix

A rotational program providing exposure to a variety of functional enterprises within the Operations and Sales Group. Participants may work in a retail store, a phone bank center, and/or in entry-level operations and technology assignments. They will also receive guidance from the program manager, a personal mentor and various assignment managers.

Corporate Human Resources: HR Leadership Program (MBA)

Length of program: 10 to 12 months

Geographic location of program: San Francisco

Participants work as consultants on projects in various corporate HR business lines/lines of business.

"Class of" Program

Length of program: Six months

Geographic location of program: Major cities nationwide

All trainees in the programs detailed above participate in the "Class of" Program. The goal of this program is to offer participants exposure to the larger company, senior management and each other, creating a sense of community and strong working relationships across business lines. The six-month curriculum includes a two-day executive exposure forum, networking opportunities with management and peers throughout the company, and web casts on professional development and Wells Fargo's visions and values.

Strategic Plan and Diversity Leadership

How does the firm's leadership communicate the importance of diversity to everyone at the firm?

Our senior leaders have a personal commitment to creating an inclusive culture. They communicate with team members through various forms, including meetings, speeches, e-mail, internal and external web sites, newsletters, brochures, videos, training courses, phone announcements and letters. They meet regularly with corporate human resources and the Corporate Diversity Council to discuss progress, share best practices and identify areas for improvement.

Who has primary responsibility for leading diversity initiatives at your firm?

Linda McConley, diversity manager

Does your firm currently have a diversity committee?

Yes

If yes, please describe how the committee is structured, how often it meets, etc.

Wells Fargo's Corporate Diversity Council is made up of 35 team members representing each Wells Fargo business line (one Diversity Council representative per 5,000 team members). The council, which meets formally 12 times per year, advises senor management on policy culture and best practices.

Wells Fargo's also has 79 diversity councils across the company which are made up of team members from business groups or local markets.

If yes, does the committee's representation include one or more members of the firm's management/executive committee (or the equivalent)?

Yes

If yes, how many executives are on the committee, and in 2006, what was the total number of hours collectively spent by the committee in furtherance of the firm's diversity initiatives? How many employees are on the committee?

Total Executives on Committee: One

Total hours spent collectively: Four hours weekly

Total Employees on Committee: 35

The Corporate Diversity Council formally meets 12 times per year but also communicates regularly on an informal basis (phone calls, e-mail, committee work).

Does the committee and/or diversity leader establish and set goals or objectives consistent with management's priorities?

Yes

Has the firm undertaken a formal or informal diversity program or set of initiatives aimed at increasing the diversity of the firm?

Yes, formal. Wells Fargo has a company-wide diversity platform called "Six Steps to Got Diversity" to guide and measure the company's progress towards becoming a more inclusive environment for everyone. It includes six initiatives (executive involvement and accountability, recruiting and retention, diverse segment marketing, diverse community giving, supplier diversity and communications), and every business in our company is accountable for developing and implementing an action plan.

How often does the firm's management review the firm's diversity progress/results?

Twice a year

How is the firm's diversity committee and/or firm management held accountable for achieving results?

Our Corporate Diversity Council reports directly to our Executive Management Committee twice a year. We discuss progress and action items within our Six Steps platform.

The Stats

	NUMBER OF EMPLOYEES		REVENUE	
	2006	2005	2006	2005
Total in the U.S.	166,533	156,320	$35.7 billion	$33 billion

2006 DEMOGRAPHIC PROFILE	
Male employees	38.8 percent
Female employees	61.2 percent
Minorities on executive team	8.2 percent
Women on executive team	17.2 percent

Retention and Professional Development

How do 2006 minority and female attrition rates generally compare to those experienced in the prior year period?

About the same as in prior years.

Please identify the specific steps you are taking to reduce the attrition rate of minority and women employees.

• Develop and/or support internal employee affinity groups (e.g., minority or women networks within the firm)

• Increase/review compensation relative to competition

• Increase/improve current work/life programs

• Adopt dispute resolution process

• Succession plan includes emphasis on diversity

• Work with minority and women employees to develop career advancement plans

- Review work assignments and hours billed to key client matters to make sure minority and women employees are not being excluded
- Strengthen mentoring program for all employees, including minorities and women
- Professional skills development program, including minority and women employees

Diversity Mission Statement

Wells Fargo team members should expect to work in an environment where each person feels valued for individual traits, skills and talents and has the opportunity to fulfill ambitions and contribute to the success of the company.

Additional Information

We believe the diversity of our 169,000 team members enables us to respond faster to the needs of our increasingly diverse communities. We view diversity not just as the right thing to do but a growth opportunity. It's essential for achieving our vision of satisfying all our customers' needs and helping them succeed financially.

Diversity is about inclusiveness: making sure everyone—team members, customers and business partners—feels welcome and included, valued for their individualism and is given the opportunity to succeed. We want to do more than just reflect or represent the diversity of our communities. We want to be the diversity of our communities.

That's why diversity at Wells Fargo is not a separate project or program—we recognize the importance of integrating it into everything we do. We accomplish this by engaging at all levels of the company. Our CEO and executive management team have a personal commitment to creating an inclusive culture. Team member engagement is also critical. We leverage our team member networks and Corporate Diversity Council to build community relationships and advise senior management on policy, culture and leadership best practices that foster diversity and awareness.

We're the 12th Most Admired Company in the World according to *Barron's* magazine, the 20th Best Company for Diversity according to *DiversityInc* magazine, among the 100 Best Companies for Working Mothers according to *Working Mother* magazine and among the Top 50 Companies for Latinas according to *Latina Style* magazine. Three years in a row, we've received a "perfect" on the Human Rights Campaign Corporate Equality Index.

We can't grow without you. And you. And you. And you.

Your ideas, your talent, your unique perspective. We've got a place for you at Weyerhaeuser, a forest products company with business strengths from forestry to manufacturing. We recognize that the fastest way to grow as a company is to seek out diverse, creative people and provide opportunities to lead. From engineering to sales, from I.T. to operations, you can have a voice in our growth. To learn more, visit us at www.weyerhaeuser.com/careers.

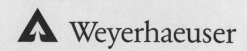

Weyerhaeuser

P.O. Box 9777
Federal Way, WA 98063-9777
Phone: (253) 924-2345
Fax: (253) 924-4151
www.weyerhaeuser.com/careers

Employment Contact
Rhonda Stickley
Director, Staffing

Diversity Leadership
Effenus Henderson
Chief Diversity Officer
Director, Recruiting

Darvi Mack
Diversity Manager

Recruiting

Please list the schools/types of schools at which you recruit.

• Ivy League schools

• Other private schools

• Public state schools

• Historically black colleges and universities (HBCUs)

• Hispanic serving institutions (HSIs)

• Native American tribal universities

• Other predominantly minority and/or women's colleges

Do you have any special outreach efforts directed to encourage minority students to consider your firm?

• Hold a reception for minority students

• *Conferences:* National Black MBA, National Society Hispanic MBA, Society Women Engineers, INROADS, CATALYST, National Association Black Accountants, National Urban League Convention, Women in Construction

• Advertise in minority student association publication(s)

• Participate in/host minority student job fair(s)

• Sponsor minority student association events

• Firm's employees participate on career panels at schools

• Outreach to leadership of minority student organizations

• Scholarships or intern/fellowships for minority students

What activities does the firm undertake to attract minority and women employees?

• Partner programs with women and minority associations

• *Conferences:* National Black MBA, National Society Hispanic MBA, INROADS, Black Data Processing Association, Association Latino Professionals & Accountants, National Association Black

Accountants, National Urban League Convention, Women in Construction, Society Women Engineers, CATALYST

• *Participate at minority job fairs all major national diversity job fairs as indicated:* National Black MBA, National Society Hispanic MBA, Black Data Processing Association, Association Latino Professionals & Accountants; National Association Black Accountants, National Urban League Convention, Women in Construction, Society Women Engineers

• Seek referrals from other employees

• Utilize online job services

Do you use executive recruiting/search firms to seek to identify new diversity hires?

No

Internships and Co-ops

Weyerhaeuser/UNCF Corporate Scholars Program

Deadline for application: End of February

Number of interns in the program in summer 2006: 25

Pay: $15.00 per hour

Percentage of interns/co-ops in the program who receive offers of full-time employment: 75 percent

Web site for internship/co-op information: www.uncf.org/internships/internshipdetail.asp?Sch_ID=16607

Weyerhaeuser/UNCF Corporate Scholars Program was established to increase student interest in Weyerhaeuser and to expand the pool of prospective diverse employees. Sophomores and juniors enrolled in the areas of engineering (chemical, mechanical, electrical, industrial, pulp & paper technology, forest), industrial manufacturing/production technology, forestry, information technology or related are eligible to apply.

Scholarships

Weyerhaeuser/UNCF Corporate Scholars Program

Deadline for application for the scholarship program: February 12th

Scholarship award amount: Up to $10,000.00 for entire scholarship

Web site or other contact information for scholarship: www.uncf.org/internships/internshipdetail.asp?Sch_ID=16607

The Weyerhaeuser/UNCF Corporate Scholars Program was established to increase student interest in Weyerhaeuser and to expand the pool of prospective diverse employees. Sophomores and juniors enrolled in participating schools in the areas of forestry, forest product sales and marketing, industrial/manufacturing/electrical engineering and operation management & supervision are eligible to apply.

Affinity Groups

- Business Support Groups
- Gay, Lesbian, Bisexual, Transgender Employees (GLBTE)
- Generation Next (Gen-Next)
- Hispanics for Outstanding Leadership and Advancement (HOLA)
- Weyerhaeuser Black Employees Alliance (WEBA)
- Women in Action (WIA)

All business support groups serve as support for its membership and are committed to assisting the company in recruiting and retention of diverse employees, group professional development and fostering a respectful inclusive workplace.

Entry-Level Programs, Full-Time Opportunities and Training Programs

Managed Entry

Length of program: Varies by program 18 months or longer

Geographic location(s) of program: National

Please describe the training/training component of this program: Accounting, engineering, sales, production, IT, HR

Please describe any other educational components of this program: All full-time employees are eligible for tuition reimbursement.

Strategic Plan and Diversity Leadership

How does the firm's leadership communicate the importance of diversity to everyone at the firm?

E-mails, company newsletters, business specific newsletters, web site, meetings, employee forums, training, brochures and via affinity groups/business networks.

Who has primary responsibility for leading diversity initiatives at your firm?

Steve R. Rogel, CEO and president, supported by Effenus Henderson, chief diversity officer

Does your firm currently have a diversity committee?

Yes

If yes, please describe how the committee is structured, how often it meets, etc.

The committee meets three times a year. Committee focuses on the firm's diversity high impact strategies areas which include leadership, governance, talent management, culture/climate and outreach.

If yes, does the committee's representation include one or more members of the firm's management/executive committee (or the equivalent)?

Yes

If yes how many executives are on the committee, and in 2006, what was the total number of hours collectively spent by the committee in furtherance of the firm's diversity initiatives?

Total Executives on Committee: Seven executives, one diversity director; meets quarterly; 25 hours

Does the committee and/or diversity leader establish and set goals or objectives consistent with management's priorities?

Yes. The executive diversity team sets the diversity goals that align with business strategy.

Has the firm undertaken a formal or informal diversity program or set of initiatives aimed at increasing the diversity of the firm?

Yes, formal. The EDT has set five high impact action areas aimed to increase diversity and retention of talent.

How often does the firm's management review the firm's diversity progress/results?

Quarterly

How is the firm's diversity committee and/or firm management held accountable for achieving results?

Accountability: 20 percent is linked to the Management Incentive Program Bonus Plan

The Stats

	NUMBER OF EMPLOYEES		REVENUE	
	2006	**2005**	**2006**	**2005**
Total in the U.S.	39,000	41,217	$21.9 billion	$22 billion

Retention and Professional Development

Please identify the specific steps you are taking to reduce the attrition rate of minority and women employees.

• Develop and/or support internal employee affinity groups (e.g., minority or women networks within the firm)

• Increase/review compensation relative to competition

• Increase/improve current work/life programs

• Adopt dispute resolution process

• Succession plan includes emphasis on diversity

• Work with minority and women employees to develop career advancement plans

• Strengthen mentoring program for all employees, including minorities and women

• Professional skills development program, including minority and women employees

• *Other:* Improve orientation and onboarding processes; work with industry attrition group to monitor attrition and turnover trends

Diversity Mission Statement

We are an employer of choice with high-performing people who are treated with respect and work together in a safe and healthy work- place where diversity, development, teamwork and open communi- cation are valued and recognized.

Additional Information

The Weyerhaeuser Way

The Weyerhaeuser Way consists of a set of statements and principles that represent our aspirations and desired culture. At the operational level, they are reflected in our Roadmap for Success. Our values statements are further amplified by Weyerhaeuser's business con- duct guidelines outlined in our code of ethics, "Our Reputation: A Shared Responsibility."

Our Vision

The best forest products company in the world and a global leader among all industries.

Our Mission

Produce superior returns for shareholders by focusing on our cus- tomers and working safely to:

• Grow and harvest trees

• Manufacture and sell forest products

• Build and sell homes

Our Values

Customers and suppliers: We listen to our customers and suppliers to improve our products and services to meet their present and future needs.

People: We are an employer of choice with high-performing people who are treated with respect and work together in a safe and healthy workplace where diversity, development, teamwork and open com- munication are valued and recognized.

Accountability: We expect superior performance and are account- able for our actions and results. Our leaders set clear goals and expectations, are supportive, and provide and seek frequent feed- back.

Citizenship: We support the communities where we do business, hold ourselves to the highest standards of ethical conduct and environmen- tal responsibility and communicate openly with Weyerhaeuser people and the public.

Financial responsibility: We are prudent and effective in the use of the resources entrusted to us to create shareholder value.

Whirlpool Corporation

2000 N. M-63
Benton Harbor, MI 49022
Phone: (269) 923-5000
Fax: (269) 923-2874
www.whirlpoolcorp.com

Locations

Corporate Headquarters: Benton Harbor, MI

European Operations Center: Comerio, Italy

Regional Headquarters: Shanghai, China & São Paulo, Brazil

Additionally, Whirlpool has 50 manufacturing and technology centers around the world.

Employment Contact

E-mail: careers@whirlpool.com
www.whirlpoolcareers.com

Recruiting

Please list the schools/types of schools at which you recruit.

• *Private schools:* University of Notre Dame

• *Public state schools:* University of Michigan, Michigan State University, Purdue University, Indiana University, Ohio State University, Western Michigan University, University of Florida, University of Miami, University of North Carolina, University of Georgia, University of Texas-Austin, Northern Illinois University, University of Arkansas, University of Arkansas-Fort Smith, Michigan Technology University, Arizona State University

Do you have any special outreach efforts directed to encourage minority students to consider your firm?

We partner with minority chapters in business and engineering at our core target programs, where we sponsor initiatives, hold learning sessions and training workshops to give minority individuals any assistance they need.

What activities does the firm undertake to attract minority and women employees?

• *Conferences:* National Society of Black Engineers, Society of Women Engineers, National Association of Black Accountants, Association of Latino Professionals in Finance & Accounting, National Hispanic Business Association, Society of Hispanic Professional Engineers

• *Other:* Referrals from campus diversity organizations and leaders, online job boards, campus job boards

Do you use executive recruiting/search firms to seek to identify new diversity hires?

No, we feel that there is no better way to reach out to new talent than to utilize existing diverse talents to target those individuals.

Internships and Co-ops

Length of the program: Nine to 12 weeks

Percentage of interns/co-ops in the program who receive offers of full-time employment: 75 percent

Web site for internship/co-op information: www.whirlpoolcareers.com/campus

Exciting internships are available in all of Whirlpool's functional departments. With an internship program of over 75 people, you create your own little beach community at one of the top 10 beaches in the nation!

Whirlpool's internship program provides real, hands-on work experience to give each intern a better understanding of the type of work they may perform as full-time employees. Whirlpool's internship program educates participants about the different areas of the company, its strategic objectives and the plans in place to achieve those objectives. We take interns to our Greenville Manufacturing site, home of the KitchenAid stand mixer, where interns tour the plant and are put on the line to test their capabilities and have a little fun!

The program also provides interns with an opportunity to experience the surrounding communities. Interns get involved in the two beach volleyball leagues, golf leagues and softball leagues to develop lasting friendships with other intern, and get to know Whirlpool employees outside of the work environment. They also enjoy the wine tours at many of the surrounding 35 wineries within a 30-minute radius.

Finally, the program evaluates each intern's work performance, as well as allows him or her to evaluate whether Whirlpool Corp. would be a good fit for his or her full-time career aspirations.

Affinity Groups

- Whirlpool African-American Network
- Whirlpool Hispanic Network
- Whirlpool Women's Network
- Whirlpool Gay, Lesbian, Bisexual and Transgender Network
- Whirlpool Asian Network
- Whirlpool Native American Network
- The Young Professional Organization

Entry-Level Programs, Full-Time Opportunities and Training Programs

Real Whirled

Length of program: Seven weeks of intensive training

Geographic location(s) of program: Training conducted in Benton Harbor, Mich. Training program graduates then relocate to various locations throughout the United States.

The Real Whirled program begins with a seven-week intensive training program, both classroom and experiential. Participants live together in a house outfitted with Whirlpool and KitchenAid appliances for the entire training program.

The purpose of the program is to provide the participants with all the necessary information and skill development required for their new positions as market brand representatives. The classroom component of the training is focused on learning about the products sold by Whirlpool Corporation throughout the United States, as well as developing leadership, communication and selling skills. The experiential component of the program is centered around activities like job shadowing, mystery shopping and using the products in the house on a daily basis. It is common for Whirlpool's senior executives to join the class discussion and to come by the Real Whirled house for dinner during the training program. Once the initial seven weeks are over, the training continues through monthly web casts, teleconferences and occasionally regionally-based face-to-face meetings.

Human Resource Leadership Development Program (HRLDP)

Length of program: Three years

Geographic location(s) of program: Primarily in Benton Harbor, Mich. Additional assignments could be in any of Whirlpool's manufacturing divisions throughout the United States or around the world.

The HRLDP is a three-year, three-rotation program that is designed to give the participants training and development through two avenues: on-the-job training and quarterly learning sessions.

First, the participants are assigned to a part of the company that has an open-staffing situation and they are given the responsibilities and objectives attached to that role. The rotational assignments are not project-based jobs. Working for and directly with a senior HR manager/director, participants take what they learned during college and transform that knowledge into practical application.

The second avenue for training is through quarterly learning sessions. Some of these sessions are focused specifically on HR topics, such as developments in the compensation system to broader business skills such as how to manage change. In addition to these learning opportunities and the feedback each HRLDP receives about their performance, HRLDPs also are assigned a senior HR leader as a mentor.

Whirlpool Technical Excellence Program (WTEP)

Length of program: Three years. Participants are assigned two six-month project assignments during their first year. The second year is based at University of Michigan completing a master's degree in engineering, and the third year is another series of two six-month assignments.

Geographic location(s) of program: The first and third year of the program can be in any of our technology and manufacturing sites in the United States (and in some cases around the world). Many of the assignments will be at our corporate headquarters in Benton Harbor, Mich. The second year of the program is spent at the University of Michigan in Ann Arbor.

Educational components: Full-time enrollment in the University of Michigan's masters of engineering program.

Global Supply Chain Leadership Development Program (GSCLDP)

Length of program: Three years

Geographic location(s) of program: Primarily in Benton Harbor, Mich., but could be at any of Whirlpool's manufacturing divisions throughout the United States.

The GSCLPD is designed to develop Whirlpool's leadership capability in the areas of logistics, procurement and operations (manufacturing). During a series of one-year rotational assignments, program participants have the opportunity to learn about the three key areas of supply-based management at Whirlpool—logistics, manu-

facturing and procurement. Besides receiving an on-the-job training program, participants also take part in learning programs designed to enhance their skills on a functional basis, as well as develop leadership skills. All program participants are assigned a mentor who is a senior leader in manufacturing, logistics or procurement.

Finance Leadership Development Program

Geographic location(s) of program: Primarily in Benton Harbor, Mich., but could be at any of Whirlpool's locations throughout the United States.

The purpose of the Finance Leadership Development Program is to develop future leaders by leveraging the finance and accounting skills learned in college and supplementing that knowledge with opportunities to develop, learn and grow as leaders. All program participants take part in functional and cross-functional training to develop required skills and enhance their current skills.

The program has two different focuses. The first is for accounting majors who will join the Whirlpool internal audit and internal controls team. The second is for finance, accounting and economics majors who will provide financial analysis skills to the company.

Strategic Plan and Diversity Leadership

How does the firm's leadership communicate the importance of diversity to everyone at the firm?

Diversity organizations are challenged by Whirlpool leaders to take responsibility for delivering business results to the Whirlpool Corporation through bottom line numbers. They believe this will help all individuals understand the value of diversity in an organization, as our customer base is diverse, and who better to reach out to them? In addition, each of these organizations is responsible for providing employee and community benefits for the diversity network being a part of this community, which has been done through community festivals, celebrity speaking engagements, high school and migrant worker mentoring, and general awareness/diversity training sessions.

Leaders have also held an innovation session surrounding breaking down barriers to success. Out of that innovation session came an action plan that has, over the course of the last year, been executed upon to ensure everyone feels included in our corporate strategy.

We also develop an annual communication plan that is part of the diversity council objectives. Primarily, we communicate through our global employee Intranet portal, on our diversity web site, through our diversity networks' newsletters, through the annual diversity and inclusion meeting for managers and employees and at our annual diversity and inclusion summit.

Whirlpool encourages diversity and inclusion throughout our global organization because diverse employees reflect our global customer base and help provide a keen understanding of our customers' needs. Simply put, diversity is about being different, while inclusion is about the respectful involvement of all people and making use of everyone's talents. We believe that differences create value. And we practice inclusion throughout our organization, not only because we believe it's the right thing to do, but also because it's a winning strategy that enables us to respond to the diverse needs of our customers.

We have a dedicated diversity web site—posted internally that is easy to find by all employees—that lists all diversity activities and events of the clubs as well as our overall strategy, accountability and network information. Some of the information included on the site is the following:

By acknowledging our diversity and practicing inclusiveness, we are able to utilize everyone's unique strengths to increase Whirlpool Corporations' productivity, profit and performance.

Our Diversity Strategy:

Build accountability:

- Align with our BFVC strategies and core competencies
- Align performance goals and behaviors
- Improve our balanced scorecard results

Connect Diversity and Inclusion to the Business:

- Build the business case around diverse consumers
- Value ideas from everywhere and everyone

Recruit and Retain Diverse People:

- Recruit and retain great diverse talent at all levels

Drive Understanding, Education and Awareness:

- Communicate the business case, opportunities learning and networking
- Provide diversity training and awareness opportunities

Create the Environment:

- Create an environment that leverages and values each person's unique strengths, allowing everyone to contribute to their fullest potential

Who has primary responsibility for leading diversity initiatives at your firm?

CEO Jeff Fettig and his Executive Committee, along with our Diversity Council—made up of our Executive Committee as well as presidents of each of the diversity networks.

Does your firm currently have a diversity committee?

Yes

If yes, please describe how the committee is structured, how often it meets, etc.

The committee is made up of the presidents of each diversity network, our three global diversity directors and nine Executive Committee members. They meet once a month to discuss the ongoing status of Whirlpool's diversity initiatives to ensure we are mimicking/advancing our consumer base and behavior.

If yes, does the committee's representation include one or more members of the firm's management/executive committee (or the equivalent)?

Yes

If yes, how many executives are on the committee?

Total Executives on Committee: Nine

Does the committee and/or diversity leader establish and set goals or objectives consistent with management's priorities?

Yes. Each year, the council reviews and measures objectives against our plan. In addition, the January meeting focuses on setting objectives aligned with our strategic business issues

Has the firm undertaken a formal or informal diversity program or set of initiatives aimed at increasing the diversity of the firm?

Yes, formal. Each region/function develops action plans and goals for increasing representation at all levels of the organization, but particularly in the feeder groups and leadership ranks. Goals are part of the overall "People Scorecard" that is directly tied to compensation of both the executives that lead the organization, as well as its employees. This ensures that everyone within the organization maintains a top-of-the-line approach to diversity.

How often does the firm's management review the firm's diversity progress/results?

Quarterly

How is the firm's diversity committee and/or firm management held accountable for achieving results?

As mentioned above with the People Scorecard, executives are rewarded for increasing diversity within the organization, and other employees have the focus as well.

Ideally, all employees will feel a personal responsibility for embracing and acting on the concepts described in this brochure. To ensure traction, the company has established clear roles and accountabilities:

Overall leadership for the effort resides in the office of the chairman.

The office of diversity is responsible for developing the strategy and related initiatives.

Our regions, business units and global functions are responsible for ensuring that our diversity strategy gets implemented.

The Diversity Council is responsible for advising leadership on matters pertaining to diversity.

Diversity networks exist for the purpose of assisting in delivering with diversity commitments.

Each employee is responsible for understanding and executing our diversity strategy.

"It is no coincidence that corporations, groups, governments and citizens all across the country are focusing on diversity initiatives and methods to make people feel more included. Whirlpool Corporation has made workforce diversity and corporate citizenship top priorities as the company has set out to bring about lasting, systemic change inside and outside of our company.

"For the past 20 years, Whirlpool has worked to make our work culture one that recognizes the benefits of a diverse employee population, as well as one that values and respects those things that make each of us unique. Our company leadership knows that diversity and inclusion are vital to our continued success and competitiveness. We hope that the strategies and high expectations we set for ourselves will truly add value to each employee's experience here."

—Corporate Director, Global Diversity

The Stats

	NUMBER OF EMPLOYEES	REVENUE
	2006	2005
Total worldwide	80,000 (30,000 salaried rolls)	$13.2 billion

U.S. EMPLOYEE DEMOGRAPHICS	
Minority	17 percent
Female	40.19 percent

Retention and Professional Development

Please identify the specific steps you are taking to reduce the attrition rate of minority and women employees.

• Develop and/or support internal employee affinity groups (e.g., minority or women networks within the firm)

• Increase/improve current work/life programs

• Strengthen mentoring program for all employees, including minorities and women

• Targeted diversity summits aimed at breaking down the barriers to inclusion and barriers to success

• Get involved with the many special events, training and activities offered to you at Whirlpool, and you'll find yourself with a new scope of knowledge, experience and networking opportunities. Events such as career workshops, leadership discussions, online learning and specialized training broaden individuals' understanding of the industry, our business and what's going on with the company right now. This page provides you with some basic tools to get involved at Whirlpool.

• Partner with established minority clubs to ensure new hires are assigned to a minority buddy from that organization to assist in on-boarding and assimilation

Diversity Mission Statement

Whirlpool Enterprise Leadership Transformation Agenda Vision

"Building a company of people passionately creating loyal customers for life."

Mission

Create and foster an environment that is inclusive and accepting, that allows and encourages diverse employees to be themselves and to participate with equality and dignity in the work environment.

Additional Information

Departments within Whirlpool:

• Communications

• Engineering

• Finance—Corporate (internal controls/audit, treasury, tax)

• Finance—North American (financial analysis in brand, channel and product delivery)

• Finance—Technology

• Human resources

• Information Systems

• Legal

• Marketing

• Operations

• Sales

• Supply chain

Williams Companies, The

One Williams Center
Tulsa, OK 74102
Phone: (918) 573-2200
Fax: (918) 573-7700
www.williams.com/careers

Locations
Tulsa, OK (HQ)
Denver, CO (Regional)
Houston, TX (Regional)
Salt Lake City, UT (Regional)
Many other field locations related to our pipeline transportation, gathering and processing, exploration & production operations

Diversity Leadership
Alison Anthony
Director, Diversity & Employee Relations

Employment Contact
Steve Beatie

Recruiting

Please list the schools/types of schools at which you recruit.
- *Private schools:* University of Tulsa
- *Public state schools:* Colorado School of Mines, University of Houston, University of Missouri-Rolla, University of Oklahoma, University of New Mexico, Oklahoma State University, Texas A&M, University of Utah
- *Historically Black Colleges and Universities (HBCUs):* Prairie View A&M

Do you have any special outreach efforts directed to encourage minority students to consider your firm?
- Sponsor minority student association events
- Outreach to leadership of minority student organizations
- Partner with minority offices and programs on campus

Affinity Groups

Presence of employee affinity groups

Do you use executive recruiting/search firms to seek to identify new diversity hires?
Rarely

Entry-Level Programs, Full-Time Opportunities and Training Programs

Rotational Program
Length of program: Two to three years
Geographic location(s) of program: Houston, Salt Lake City, Tulsa and assignments at asset bases.

These programs consist of engineering and business, and MIS OJT rotations supplemented with additional development opportunities.

Strategic Plan and Diversity Leadership

What trends in your industry affect your corporate diversity goals, strategies and/or internal or external alliances?
By the year 2010 in the oil and gas industry:

- More than 230,000 years of cumulative experience will be lost

- Almost half of the work force will be new

- Upstream companies will most likely lose more than 60 percent of all employees

- Our industry cannot afford to underutilize or overlook talent. Therefore, we have to build our capability for managing a diverse workforce just like we approach any other strategic part of the business.

How does the firm's leadership communicate the importance of diversity to everyone at the firm?

Monthly highlights of diverse populations include e-mails, presentations and a diversity Intranet site. We also have monthly Lunch and Learn education series, diversity leadership conferences, senior executive quarterly meetings and ongoing mutual respect and appropriate workplace behavior training

Who has primary responsibility for leading diversity initiatives at your firm?

Alison Anthony, director of diversity and employee relations, has functional responsibility although the primary responsibility rests with all of company leadership. Integrating diversity and inclusion into each manager's responsibility is one way we create an inclusive culture where diversity can thrive.

Does your firm currently have a diversity committee?

Yes—Enterprise Diversity Council chaired by the company's CEO.

If yes, please describe how the committee is structured, how often it meets, etc.

Meets quarterly; made of representatives across the organization, including the CEO, SVPs and VPs from each function and business unit.

If yes, does the committee's representation include one or more members of the firm's management/executive committee (or the equivalent)?

Yes

Total Executives on Committee: Nine of 20

Does the committee and/or diversity leader establish and set goals or objectives consistent with management's priorities?

Yes

Has the firm undertaken a formal or informal diversity program or set of initiatives aimed at increasing the diversity of the firm?

Yes, formal

How often does the firm's management review the firm's diversity progress/results?

Quarterly

The Stats

Williams is 15 percent minority and 27 percent female

Retention and Professional Development

How do 2006 minority and female attrition rates generally compare to those experienced in the prior year period?

Improved

Please identify the specific steps you are taking to reduce the attrition rate of minority and women employees.

• Develop and/or support internal employee affinity/business resource groups (e.g., minority or women networks within the firm)

• Increase/improve current work/life flexibility programs

• Succession plan includes emphasis on diversity

• Managerial and all-employee training focused on leading a diverse workforce and appropriate workplace behaviors

• Mentoring and career development programs

• Diversity leadership summits for women and minorities

• Participation at external development programs such as Catalyst and Executive Leadership Council

Diversity Mission Statement

At Williams, we foster an environment that attracts a high-performing, diverse workforce. All individuals are respected and valued for their contributions and have the opportunity to achieve their maximum potential.

Wyeth Pharmaceuticals

500 Arcola Road
Collegeville, PA 19426
Phone: (484) 865 - 5000
www.wyeth.com

Locations

Over 140 locations in:
Africa • Asia Pacific • Australia • Europe
• Middle East • New Zealand • North
America • South America

Recruiting

Please list the schools/types of schools at which you recruit.

- *Ivy League schools:* University of Pennsylvania the Wharton School; Johnson School at Cornell
- *Other private schools:* Vanderbilt, University of Chicago Graduate School of Business, University of Virginia Darden School of Business, Drexel University, NYU
- *Public state schools:* University of Maryland-Baltimore County, Temple University
- *Historically black colleges and universities (HBCUs):* Clark Atlanta University, Spelman College, Morehouse College, Tuskegee University, Fisk University, Cheyney, Lincoln, Howard, Hampton, Virginia State University, Virginia Polytechnic and State University, Xavier
- *Hispanic serving institutions (HSIs):* University of Miami, University of Puerto Rico

Do you have any special outreach efforts directed to encourage minority students to consider your firm?

- *Hold a reception for minority students:* National Black MBA Association Conference
- *Conferences:* SWE, NSBE, NOBCCHE, NSHMBA, NBMBAA, NMA, Urban League, SHPE, Consortium, INROADS, ISPE
- Advertise in minority student association publication
- Participate in/host minority student job fair(s)
- Sponsor minority student association events
- Firm's employees participate on career panels at schools
- Outreach to leadership of minority student organizations
- Scholarships or intern/fellowships for minority students
- *Other:* Participate in INROADS and the Leadership Development Institute, facilitate resume and interview skills workshops in the community, recruit to improve minority access to research careers

What activities does the firm undertake to attract minority and women employees?

- Partner programs with women and minority associations
- *Conferences:* SWE, NSBE, NOBCCHE, NSHMBA, NBMBAA, NMA, Urban League, SHPE, Consortium, INROADS, ISPE, BEYA, UNCF, Minorities in Research Science, HBA
- Participate at minority job fairs
- Seek referrals from other employees: Wyeth has a bonus program for internal referrals
- Utilize online job services

Do you use executive recruiting/search firms to seek to identify new diversity hires?

Yes

Internships and Co-ops

Wyeth Summer Internship Program and Co-op Program

Deadline for application: March 15th
Pay: Commensurate with year and experience
Length of the program: 12-week internships and six-month co-ops
Web site for internship/co-op information: www.wyeth.com

Wyeth's summer internship program provides valuable work experience within a pharmaceutical company to outstanding college students ranging from first year through the masters and PhD levels.

Program Objective:

The objective of the program is to provide positive work/training experience in a corporate environment, identify and track potential full-time employees and establish "ambassadors" for Wyeth on campuses. Interns receive project-focused assignments and challenging objectives consistent with their career goals. Interns are also assigned a mentor in addition to their supervisor/coach.

Interns will receive a broad orientation to Wyeth, the specific business unit and the individual work group to which they will be contributing. Developmental opportunities may include educational workshops, meetings with corporate executives, business unit information exchanges, networking events and facility tours.

Timeline:

Submit your resume before March 15th. All offers for our summer internship program will be extended by May 1st.

General qualifications:

Overall GPA of 3.0 out of 4.0 or above is required.

Full-time students will be considered from a four- or five-year accredited U.S. college or university. Interns must be enrolled to return as a full-time students following their time at Wyeth.

Wyeth MBA Summer Internship Program

Deadline for application: March 15th

Pay: Commensurate with year and experience

Length of the program (in weeks): 12 weeks

Web site for internship/co-op information: www.wyeth.com

Scholarships

Wyeth Internal Scholarship Program

Deadline for application for the scholarship program: January

Scholarship award amount: $3,000 one-time scholarship

Web site or other contact information for scholarship: Contact a local Wyeth HR representative

This scholarship program is open only to children of Wyeth employees. This program provides $3,000, one-time scholarships for up to 40 undergraduate students who are dependent children of current active full-time and part-time (who work 20 hours or more per week) employees and eligible retirees. The program is administered by National Merit Scholarship Corporation, an independent non-profit organization that selects recipients based on high school academic record, activities and contributions to school and community, test scores, the school's recommendation and a student essay.

Affinity Groups

Wyeth supports and encourages its employee networks—voluntary, employee-established groups that meet to support and facilitate professional growth and personal development of participants. Wyeth's diversity department is chartered to support all Wyeth business units in cooperation with division leaders and HR business partners in their efforts to create a more inclusive workplace environment, to attract diverse candidates for employment and to enhance managerial skills for working with an increasingly diverse and global workforce. Wyeth's employee networks help advance the professional and personal growth of all employees through networking forums, career development workshops and community service.

Wyeth Pharmaceutical's employee networks are:

- ADVANCE: African-Americans Dedicated to Adding Value-Added Networking & Corporate Excellence
- Wyeth Latin Network
- Rainbow Alliance: Supporting GLBT employees and allies
- Women's Professional Network
- Women in Leadership

To provide senior leadership and guidance to these groups, Wyeth leaders have been named executive sponsors to work closely with each group.

Xcel Energy

414 Nicollet Mall
Minneapolis, MN 55401
www.xcelenergy.com

Locations

Colorado • Michigan • Minnesota • New
Mexico • North Dakota • South Dakota •
Texas • Wisconsin

Employment Contact

Mark Sauerbrey
Recruitment Consultant
Minneapolis, MN 55401
Phone: (612) 330-5724
Fax: 612-330-7935
E-mail: mark.w.Sauerbrey@xcelenergy.com

Recruiting

Please list the schools/types of schools at which you recruit.

• Private schools

• Public state schools

• Hispanic serving institutions (HSIs)

• Other predominantly minority and/or women's colleges

Do you have any special outreach efforts directed to encourage minority students to consider your firm?

• Hold a reception for minority students

• Conferences

• Advertise in minority student association publication(s)

• Participate in/host minority student job fair(s)

• Sponsor minority student association events

• Firm's employees participate on career panels at schools

• Outreach to leadership of minority student organizations

What activities does the firm undertake to attract minority and women employees?

• Partner programs with women and minority associations

• Conferences

• Participate at minority job fairs

• Utilize online job services

Do you use executive recruiting/search firms to seek to identify new diversity hires?

Yes

List all women- and/or minority-owned executive search/recruiting firms to which the firm paid a fee for placement services in the past 12 months.

Chandler Group

Internships and Co-ops

Engineering / Business internships are posted per business unit upon approval from hiring managers. The business units run corporation wide and are open to all students per our EEO policy.

Deadline for application: Varies upon posting

Number of interns in the program in summer 2006 (internship) or 2006 (co-op): 87

Pay: $13.00 to $21.00 per hour

Percentage of interns/co-ops in the program who receive offers of full-time employment: Three to five percent are hired to full-time positions.

Web site for internship/co-op information: www.xcelenergy.com

Strategic Plan and Diversity Leadership

How does the firm's leadership communicate the importance of diversity to everyone at the firm?

The firm's leadership communicates the importance of diversity through e-mails, the company web site, newsletters and meetings.

Who has primary responsibility for leading diversity initiatives at your firm?

Paul Moore, director of diversity and staffing

Does your firm currently have a diversity committee?

Yes

Has the firm undertaken a formal or informal diversity program or set of initiatives aimed at increasing the diversity of the firm?

Yes, informal, aiming to increase the number of women and minority applicants for 2006.

How often does the firm's management review the firm's diversity progress/results?

Monthly

The Stats

	NUMBER OF EMPLOYEES		REVENUE	
	2006	2005	2006	2005
Total in the U.S.	9,700	1,000	$9 billion annually	N/A

Retention and Professional Development

How do 2006 minority and female attrition rates generally compare to those experienced in the prior year period?

No change

Please identify the specific steps you are taking to reduce the attrition rate of minority and women employees.

• Develop and/or support internal employee affinity groups (e.g., minority or women networks within the firm)

• Increase/improve current work/life programs

• Succession plan includes emphasis on diversity

• Strengthen mentoring program for all employees, including minorities and women

• Professional skills development program, including minority and women employees

Additional Information

One of Xcel Energy's core values is respecting all people. This ranks in importance with doing business in an ethical, honest manner, protecting our environment, working safely and serving our customers to the best of our ability.

When people believe that who they are and what they do is respected, morale and productivity go up. The end result is a workplace where people feel comfortable being who they are regardless of their individual differences or personal characteristics.

A number of departments and sites will also go through a training program called "M.E.E.T. on Common Ground: Speaking Up for Respect in the Workplace."

Xerox Corporation

800 Phillips Highway, Building 205-99E
Webster, NY 14580
www.xerox.com/careers

Diversity Leadership

Diversity:
Luis Martinez
Corporate HR, Diversity Programs Manager

Campus:
D. Garvin Byrd
Corporate HR, Manager of College Programs

Employment Contact

D. Garvin Byrd
Corporate HR, Manager of College Programs

Bill Graves
Corporate HR, Recruiting Manager

Dave Williams
Corporate HR, Recruiting Manager
www.xerox.com/careers

Recruiting

Please list the schools/types of schools at which you recruit.

• Ivy League schools

• Other private schools

• Public state schools

• Historically black colleges and universities (HBCUs)

• Hispanic serving institutions (HSIs)

• Native American tribal universities

• Other predominantly minority and/or women's colleges

Do you have any special outreach efforts directed to encourage minority students and graduates to consider your firm?

• Hold a reception for minority students

• Conferences

• Advertise in minority student association publication(s) or other minority-focused publications

• Participate in/host minority student job fair(s) or other minority-focused job events.

• Sponsor minority student association events

• Firm's employees participate on career panels at schools

• Outreach to leadership of minority student organizations

• Scholarships or intern/fellowships for minority students

What activities does the firm undertake to attract minority and women employees?

• Partner programs with women and minority associations

• Conferences

• Participate at minority job fairs

• Seek referrals from other employees

• Utilize online job services

Do you use executive recruiting/search firms to seek to identify new diversity hires?

No

Internships and Co-ops

Xerox College Experiential Learning Program

Deadline for application: March

Number of interns in the program in summer 2006 (internship) or 2006 (co-op): 200 interns, 20 co-ops

Pay: By week. Varies based on academic achievement

Length of the program: 10 weeks

Percentage of interns/co-ops in the program who receive offers of full-time employment: 63 percent

Web site for internship/co-op information:
www.xerox.com/careers

The internship/co-op program guidelines require the individual to be a full-time student enrolled in a college or program leading to achievement of a bachelor's or higher-level degree. Must be able to work a minimum of 10 weeks and carry a 3.0 or higher GPA.

Scholarships

Xerox Technical Minority Scholarship Program

Deadline for application for the scholarship program: September 30th each year

Scholarship award amount: $1,000-$10,000 once-per-year award

Web site or other contact information for scholarship: www.Xerox.com/employment

Requirements: Applicant must be Asian, black, Hispanic or Native American; must be enrolled in a four-year technical degree program which, when completed, will result in applicant's obtaining a bachelor's, master's or PhD degree. Applicant must have a 3.0 GPA or higher.

Affinity Groups

Asians Coming Together (ACT)

http://www.asianscomingtogether.com

Provides a voice and forum for education, professional development and interaction; to improve awareness and advocate equitable recognition and advancement opportunities for Asian employees within Xerox.

Black Women Leadership Council (BWLC)

http://www.bwlc.com

The Black Women's Leadership Council serves as a catalyst to advance professional development and address issues unique to black women in the Xerox work place. The Black Women's Leadership Council forges partnerships with senior management who facilitate the hiring, retention and development of black women and satisfy business needs.

Pride at Work (GALAXE)

http://www.galaxe.org

Galaxe Pride At Work is a formal organization for Xerox employees who are or who support gay, lesbian, bisexual or transgender (GLBT) persons. Galaxe Pride At Work's mission is to offer support and visibility within Xerox and beyond to its members and to provide an official point of contact between its membership and Xerox Corporation, as well as with other gay, lesbian, bisexual and transgender organizations external to Xerox.

The Association for Professional Advancement (HAPA)

http://www.hapa.org

The HAPA National Leadership Council is the voice to Xerox management representing Xerox Hispanics and HAPA Chapters, and it promotes Hispanic objectives that enable increased Xerox business results.

National Black Employee Association (NBEA)

http://www.nbea.net

The National Black Employees Association (NBEA) is a national caucus group of African-American Xerox employees. Ten local caucus groups covering the continental United States make up the NBEA. The NBEA is devoted to the principle that professional abilities and talents are possessed by individuals and that these traits are not the exclusive traits of any one ethnic or racial group. NBEA supports all efforts to eliminate employment and promotion practices that tend to deny this fundamental principle.

The Women's Alliance (TWA)

http://www.thewomensalliance.net

The Women's Alliance (TWA) is a catalyst to increase communications and awareness of women at Xerox, enabling women to attain their personal goals. The vision of TWA is to see that the women of Xerox are recognized and valued by the company for their significant contributions and leadership.

Entry-Level Programs, Full-Time Opportunities and Training Programs

VP Development Program

The VP Development Program provides leadership development for "ready-now" and newly appointed VPs. The content of the program is based on nine priority development objectives for VP candidates:

- Deliver more customer value
- Develop a powerful organizational vision and motivate their team to achieve it
- Explore a wide range of innovative options in the decision-making process
- Hire and retain the right people
- Make personal and organizational growth a priority
- Stay the course, walk the talk and maintain an optimistic outlook even in trying times
- Make the leap from a tactical to a strategic role
- Learn to prioritize more effectively
- Work for the benefit of the entire company

The Emerging Leader Program

This program provides leadership development opportunity for selected employees who have demonstrated the potential to move forward in the company. The program spans two years and involves four five-day face-to-face participant meetings, with independent learning opportunities between meetings.

Tuition Assistance: Another important aspect of some employees' development and work/life balance is educational pursuits. If a Xerox employee or his/her dependent is planning to attend college, Xerox offers three programs to help finance this. The tuition aid program supports an employee's professional development by reimbursing her/him for tuition and fees based upon successful completion of each course (up to $10,000 per year). The ConSern program offers employees the opportunity to apply for low-cost loans ranging from $2,000 to $20,000. The funds can be used for an accredited college or university, private secondary school or pre-approved proprietary or trade school. In addition, Xerox employees have access to an online university on our Intranet of more than 1,000 training courses, which they may pursue on their own or under the guidance of their manager at no cost.

Strategic Plan and Diversity Leadership

What trends in your industry affect your corporate diversity goals, strategies and/or internal or external alliances?

Diversity goals aren't impacted by trends. Xerox considers diversity a business imperative, therefore the goals and strategies are consistent with business objectives.

How does the firm's leadership communicate the importance of diversity to everyone at the firm?

• Town hall meetings with senior managers
• Quarterly reviews with employee caucus group leadership
• Internal and external diversity web site
• Electronic communication/announcements to all employees
• Electronic communication web board for employee stories

Who has primary responsibility for leading diversity initiatives at your firm?

Phil Harlow, chief diversity officer

Does your firm currently have a diversity committee?

Yes

If yes, please describe how the committee is structured, how often it meets, etc.

Xerox Executive Diversity Council.

Purpose: Serve as an executive leadership body and focus group for diversity and work environment initiatives and concerns. Represent the balanced needs and requirements of all employees.

Objectives: Focus efforts on the vital few; for example:
• Workforce representation
• Work environment
• Diverse customer markets
• Review, recommend and advise on Xerox diversity practices
• Support organizational efforts to address the needs of a multicultural workforce

Council composition & operation:
• Members selected by the office of corporate diversity and corporate VP of HR, and supported by the CEO
• Consists of 12 members
• Council meets two to three times per year

If yes, does the committee's representation include one or more members of the firm's management/executive committee (or the equivalent)?

Yes.

If yes, how many executives are on the committee?

Total executives on committee: Six corporate officers

Does the committee and/or diversity leader establish and set goals or objectives consistent with management's priorities?

Yes

Has the firm undertaken a formal or informal diversity program or set of initiatives aimed at increasing the diversity of the firm?

Yes, formal. In 1985, Xerox initiated its Balanced Work Force Strategy (BWF). The BWF program is intended to be a program of inclusion for all people. It is designed to achieve equitable representation with respect to race and gender at all levels, in all functions, in all disciplines and in all business divisions. All managers need to demonstrate appropriate diverse behaviors and ensure that their human resource practices are fair and equitable. This strategy has been carefully designed to improve balances in representation in the Xerox work force and to ensure a balanced work force is maintained in the event of restructuring initiatives.

Employee Caucus Groups

Primary mission:
• Employee advocacy
• Self development
• Promoters of change
• Management interface on work environment

Corporate Champions Program

- Voice at corporate level for employee concerns
- Councils and advises caucus leadership
- Serve as a communication linkage in regards to continuous improvement

Succession Planning

- Focuses on all employees
- Ensures diverse supply of talent for key management positions
- Help develops employees to meet their career objectives
- Assist in meeting the long-term business needs of the company

Minority/Female Vendor Program

Demonstrates Xerox's commitment to purchasing products and supplies and services from qualified minority-owned and women-owned businesses.

Diversity Training

Two levels:

- Awareness—introduces concepts, values and policies
- Skill building—leveraging diversity to enhance performance and productivity

Work Life Programs

- Dependent care fund
- Alternative work schedules
- Life cycle assistance (adoption assistance, mortgage assistance and partial pay replacement for FMLA leaves)
- Child care subsidy, child care resource and referral
- Employee assistance program
- Education assistance
- A matter of choice (benefits programs)
- Domestic partner benefits

How often does the firm's management review the firm's diversity progress/results?

Monthly; quarterly

How is the firm's diversity committee and/or firm management held accountable for achieving results?

Diversity is an element in each manager's performance evaluation.

The Stats

	NUMBER OF EMPLOYEES	REVENUE
	2006	2006
Total in the U.S.	28,400	N/A
Total outside the U.S.	25,300	N/A
Total worldwide	53,700	$15,701

Retention and Professional Development

How do 2006 minority and female attrition rates generally compare to those experienced in the prior year period?

About the same as in prior years

Please identify the specific steps you are taking to reduce the attrition rate of minority and women employees.

- Develop and/or support internal employee affinity groups (e.g., minority or women networks within the firm)

- Increase/review compensation relative to competition

- Adopt dispute resolution process

- Succession plan includes emphasis on diversity

- Work with minority and women employees to develop career advancement plans

- Strengthen mentoring program for all employees, including minorities and women

- Professional skills development program, including minority and women employees

Additional Information

Vision

Our vision is for everyone to treat each other with equality, dignity and respect. As individuals on a team, each member can rely on others' strengths to build on team potential and company productivity.

Goal

Our goal is to promote understanding and inclusion and to raise awareness of behaviors surrounding all types of "isms," e.g. sexism, racism.

In support of this, the company will:

- Leverage differences as a competitive advantage
- Develop leadership that values unique perspectives
- Embrace a framework around which diverse work groups can consistently perform and improve their work

YMCA of the USA

101 N. Wacker Drive
Chicago, IL 60606
www.ymca.net

Diversity Leadership
Nicole Steels
Senior Human Resources Generalist

Employment Contact
Jim Campbell
Human Resources Assistant
101 N. Wacker Drive, Suite 1400
Chicago, IL 60606
Phone: (312) 977-0031
Fax: (312) 977-3542

Recruiting

What activities does the firm undertake to attract minority and women employees?
- Seek referrals from other employees
- Utilize online job services
- *Other:* Utilize minority job boards

Do you use executive recruiting/search firms to seek to identify new diversity hires?
Yes

If yes, list all women- and/or minority-owned executive search/recruiting firms to which the firm paid a fee for placement services in the past 12 months.
We make formal written requests to each of the recruiting and search firms whose services we use to seek out diverse candidates for our open positions.

Scholarships

Scholarship Types/Categories:
- Funding limited to participation in YMCA University training
- Funding limited to undergraduate studies (bachelor's programs)
- Funding limited to postgraduate studies (master's and PhD programs)

Other YMCA-affiliated scholarships
Primary eligibility requirements for all YMCA of the USA Scholarship Funds:

Applicant's YMCA must be in compliance with Article II, Section 2 of the National Council of YMCAs Constitution (qualifications for membership), which may be viewed at www.ymcaexchange.org.

Applicant must be a full-time or part-time employee of a YMCA within the United States.

Application Process:
Apply online at www.ymcaexchange.org during open application period noted for each individual scholarship.

If further materials are required to be submitted, please forward them to the following address:

Jennifer Flannery

Scholarship Coordinator–YMCA University

YMCA of the USA

101 North Wacker Drive

Chicago, IL 60606

Toll Free: (800) 872-9622 ext. 8409

Direct Line: (312) 419-8409

E-mail: jennifer.flannery@ymca.net

Award Facts
All applying applicants will be notified by letter, directed to the applicant's name and address on their application, by June 30th of each year. Please allow 10 days for delivery.

Reimbursement Process
For scholarship monies that are awarded after completion of training or college courses, student must retain all proof of the completion of said coursework. Submission of proof must reach the YMCA of the USA by one year after awarded. Please submit paperwork to Jennifer Flannery at the above address.

YMCA STAFF SCHOLARSHIP PROGRAMS

Hispanic Staff Scholarship Program

The purpose of the YMCA Hispanic Staff Scholarship Program is to aid Hispanic staff members in obtaining additional training experiences which will impact, in a significant and positive way, their growth as YMCA professional directors and assist in their potential for upward mobility.

The minimum grant is $200 and the maximum $1,000. Applications must be completed online no later than May 31st and all applicants will be notified in writing by the Scholarship Committee no later than June 30th.

Eligibility Criteria

Any currently employed YMCA Hispanic full-time exempt staff member.

Eligible Training Events

Training events for which grants are made must be job/career-related and may be offered within or outside the YMCA University training system.

Selection Process

The YMCA University Scholarship Committee will review all applications received and will notify all applicants as to their decisions. Scholarship checks will be made payable to the recipient's local association after a verification of attendance at approved training.

YMCA Minority Staff Scholarship Program

This program is sponsored by the YMCA of the USA. The purpose is twofold: to assist minority staff members to advance in the YMCA through training experiences that help them grow as YMCA professionals and to assist them in completing their college education so they can embark on a professional YMCA career.

The scholarships operate from July 1st to June 30th. Award monies expire on July 1st the following year. Scholarships are awarded based on need and availability and are usually, but not necessarily, limited to $1,000 per person per calendar year. Scholarship awards are disbursed on a reimbursement basis only.

Eligibility Criteria

• Applicants must be active staff members of the YMCA—exempt or nonexempt, full-time or part-time.

• Applicants must be Hispanic/Latino, African-American, Asian/Pacific Islander or Native American/Alaskan Native.

• Education and training events must be career-related. They may be offered within or outside the YMCA.

• For education, scholarships are awarded only to those YMCA staff members who have taken some YMCA training towards achieving their YMCA senior director certification.

• Applicants must exhibit determination to continue work with the YMCA.

Application Deadline:

Online application must be completed online at www.ymcaexchange.org by May 31st.

William A. Hunton Fellowship Fund

The purpose of the scholarship is to help African-American staff members complete the Staff Development Program of the YMCA of the USA. The scholarship can be awarded for training toward director, professional director or senior director certification or for use toward the completion of college credit if the applicant has the director or professional director certification.

William A. Hunton became the first full-time African-American director of a YMCA in 1888 when he joined the Colored Y of Norfolk, Va., as general secretary. He later joined the national YMCA staff as head of the Colored Works Department.

The scholarship period is from July 1st to June 30th. Award monies will expire on July 1st on the following year. Scholarships are awarded based on need and availability, usually, but not necessarily, limited to $1,000 per person per calendar year. Awards are disbursed on a reimbursement basis only.

Eligibility Criteria:

• Applicants must be African-American exempt staff members currently employed at a chartered YMCA.

• Awards will be made on the basis of need, with consideration given to the applicant's tenure, position and previous staff development training.

• Applicants must exhibit determination to continue their work with the YMCA.

• For college credit, the scholarship can be awarded only to those applicants who have completed YMCA training for director certification: group work, volunteerism, and principles and practices.

UNDERGRADUATE EDUCATION SCHOLARSHIPS

Armstrong Scholarship

Earl P. Armstrong retired in June 1982 following 42 years of professional service to the YMCA. In recognition of Earl's outstanding service, a host of friends elected to pay tribute to him by establishing the Armstrong Scholarship Fund and made the initial contributions to the former South Field Office of the YMCA of the USA for that purpose.

It was his decision to use these funds for scholarship awards to deserving YMCA professionals. This was especially appropriate, as Earl was the first recipient in the YMCA of a John R. Mott Scholarship. In establishing the Earl P. Armstrong Scholarship Fund, others would benefit, as he did, in furthering their education and enhancing their contributions to the Young Men's Christian

Association. The scholarship is available for qualified YMCA directors throughout the country.

Earl continues to serve YMCAs throughout the country as a professional volunteer, especially in the field of personnel and salary administration. He is the single greatest influence in the YMCA in this field, and in 1983, served as editor of the YMCA's personnel and salary administration manual.

Gratitude is hereby expressed to those many friends whose generosity made possible the Armstrong Scholarship fund. Contributions will be gratefully accepted and will help provide more scholarships for YMCA professionals. Checks should be made to the YMCA of the USA and mailed to the YMCA University, YMCA of the USA, to the attention of Jennifer Flannery. Contributions are tax-exempt.

Eligibility Criteria for the Armstrong Scholarship:

- Must be a current, professional employee of a chartered YMCA in good standing.
- Must have at least three years of professional YMCA experience
- Must have completed all requirements for YMCA senior director status.
- Should have positive YMCA career goals, which indicate a plan for future YMCA involvement.
- Other factors that will be given consideration include personal commitment to the YMCA's basic Christian purpose, demonstrated leadership ability and scholastic aptitude.

All qualified applicants are welcome regardless of age, race or sex.

Yearly award schedule:

March 15th: Online applications available at YMCA of the USA web site, www.ymcaexchange.org

May 31st: Deadline for applications to be received (via online application process only)

June 30th: Awards announced. Notification occurs by letter, mailed directly to applicant. Please allow 10 days for delivery.

Study may begin in the summer, fall or winter semesters (must begin no later than January semester). Award must be used within 12 months of notification.

Other considerations:

- Awards will be given only for study in a recognized formal accredited academic institution.
- Grants will be made to cover tuition, fees and books, not to exceed $1,500, and will normally be paid directly to the educational institution.
- Funding will be granted for one year at a time.
- Being a recipient of any other scholarship or financial aid will not disqualify an applicant for this scholarship.

F.M.M. Richardson Fund

This scholarship was established in 1971 through a bequest by F.M.M. Richardson, general secretary from 1929 to 1939 of the YMCA in Birmingham, Ala. In accordance with his wishes, it assists Africa-American senior directors in obtaining training and education toward professional growth and greater upward mobility in the national movement. It also supports development projects at YMCAs serving black communities in the South Field YMCA and throughout the Y system.

Amount available: $600 per person per academic year

Criteria: Applicants must be African-American certified senior directors of the YMCA

Deadline: Online applications are accepted year-round

GRADUATE EDUCATION SCHOLARSHIPS

John R. Mott Scholarship

This scholarship is designed to assist YMCA senior directors in continuing their education through graduate study. It was established in honor of John R. Mott, a major YMCA leader for more than 60 years and winner of the Nobel Peace Prize in 1946. The scholarship period is from July 1st to June 30th. The award monies expire on July 1st the following year. The scholarship award is disbursed on a reimbursement basis only. A maximum of $15,000 per person per year is available.

Eligibility Criteria:

- Applicants must have YMCA senior director certification
- Applicants must exhibit determination to continue work with the YMCA
- Applicants must be enrolled in an accredited university or college
- Course of study should be in keeping with current and future YMCA duties

Application Deadline

Online application must be completed online at www.ymcaexchange.org by May 31st.

OTHER YMCA AFFILIATED SCHOLARSHIPS

Solon B. Cousins YMCA Scholarship

For Springfield College and George Williams College of Aurora University students planning a YMCA career.

Springfield College has, throughout its history, provided education and training for YMCA professionals. George Williams College of Aurora University also has a long history of educating YMCA career professionals. Today, Springfield and George Williams maintain a formal affiliation with the YMCA of the USA as the only Independent Association Colleges.

Capping a rich and varied career in the YMCA and United Way, Solon Cousins retired in 1990 after serving 10 years as national

executive director of the YMCA of the USA. The scholarship fund was created in his honor by the national board of the YMCA of the USA upon his retirement.

General information:

- Scholarships are available to Springfield College and George Williams College of Aurora University students planning a career in the YMCA.
- Applicants should have a background in YMCA or other human service endeavors.
- Applicants should exemplify the YMCA character values of care, honesty, respect and responsibility.
- Applications are accepted until May 31st online at www.ymcaexchange.org.
- Scholarship awards announced June 30th.

For more information contact:

Paul Katz
Director, YMCA Relations
Springfield College
263 Alden Street
Springfield, MA 01109
E-mail: pkatz@spfldcol.edu
Phone: (413) 748-3914

Dovetta McKee
Associate Professor & Director of YMCA Programs
Aurora University, George Williams College
347 South Gladstone Avenue
Aurora, Illinois 60506
E-mail: dmckee@aurora.edu

The Harmon O. DeGraff Memorial Scholarship

The Harmon O. DeGraff Memorial Scholarship Fund was created to assist young men with a strong human relations orientation to pursue graduate study. The selection is made by the three-person Memorial Scholarship Committee. The selection is based upon ability, motivation, objectives and human interests, similar qualifications without regard to race, creed or religion. By terms of Dr. DeGraff's will, the scholarship is restricted to males.

Details of Scholarship:

Deadline is March 31st. If scholarship monies are still available, applications may be submitted until May 1st.

Fund is restricted to those pursuing a graduate degree in sociology, social work, theology, industrial relations or any field in which human relationships can be emphasized and an integral part of the applicant's program.

Amount varies from $1,000 to $4,000 per year and is renewable for additional periods of time as required by the degree program.

Full-time course of study is expected.

For more Information, please visit www.akronymca.org/forms/general/degraffscholarship.pdf

Affinity Groups

African-American Alliance diversity group

The purpose of the group is to establish an alliance among African-American staff at YMCA of the USA.

The goal is to develop an agenda that will identify strategies and solutions to create, enhance and promote opportunities for African-American staff, both professionally and personally. The group also aims to work in establishing a more positive environment and working relationship within Y-USA.

SPEAK diversity group

Background and Justification

The YMCA of the USA SPEAK (Serving People with Equality, Acceptance and Kindness) diversity group was originally formed in 2002 to address gay, lesbian, bisexual, transgender and questioning (GLBTQ) sexuality issues of Y-USA employees and to promote a work environment where all employees—regardless of sexual orientation—are treated equally.

Mission

Our mission is to connect, serve and lead YMCAs in building a diverse culture of inclusion and respect—without discrimination, intimidation or disparate treatment—especially for GLBT individuals within Y-USA and throughout the movement.

Purpose

Our purpose is to educate national and local YMCA staff around GLBT issues, provide support, foster open discussion and create a welcoming environment for all employees.

Vision

We envision a workplace where sexual orientation plays no role in how an employee is treated and where each employee feels welcome, important and respected based on his/her own merit, efforts and actions and not on perceptions, beliefs or stereotypes.

Strategic Plan and Diversity Leadership

How does the firm's leadership communicate the importance of diversity to everyone at the firm?

Our CEO takes the time to reinforce his support of our diversity initiatives at key speaking events and in written communication to staff as part of our strategic plan. Additionally, our diversity group conducted staff focus groups and surveys specifically relating to diversity at YMCA of the USA, then released the results of the survey at a staff lunch presentation. Recently, the diversity group's strategic plan was distributed via our staff Intranet along with an invitation for staff to participate in the group. The strategic plan was also discussed at the all-staff meeting.

Who has primary responsibility for leading diversity initiatives at your firm?

Sam Evans, interim director YMCA of the USA

Does your firm currently have a diversity committee?

Yes

If yes, please describe how the committee is structured, how often it meets, etc.

The group is set to meet at least once per month, but during the development of the strategic plan, they have met approximately three to four times per month. The group is structured with a lead change agent for the group, one diversity consultant and the remaining staff members, who represent a cross-section of the organization in terms of position in the company, work location and different characteristics of diversity.

If yes, does the committee's representation include one or more members of the firm's management/executive committee (or the equivalent)?

Yes

If yes, how many executives are on the committee, and in 2006, what was the total number of hours collectively spent by the committee in furtherance of the firm's diversity initiatives? How many employees are on the committee?

The committee has three executives who are involved with the group's goals and operations. The overall committee is made up of 13 individuals, with Sam Evans serving as the primary change agent. In 2005, it is estimated that the group collectively spent approximately 150 hours to further the diversity initiative at YMCA of the USA.

Total Executives on Committee: Three

Does the committee and/or diversity leader establish and set goals or objectives consistent with management's priorities?

Yes. The diversity initiative is one of three primary initiatives for YMCA of the USA. Although the stated priority of the diversity initiative is directed toward making local YMCAs more diverse, we feel as though we need to serve as a model for local YMCA associations, and have given great attention to the issue of diversity at YMCA of the USA.

Has the firm undertaken a formal or informal diversity program or set of initiatives aimed at increasing the diversity of the firm?

Yes, formal. The YMCA of the USA is actively participating in the YMCA diversity initiative. The diversity initiative uses a six-step process for creating systemic change. Y-USA's vision for the diversity initiative is that the YMCA movement will be known for practicing inclusion by valuing the diversity of all people within its associations and the communities it serves. Through training and counsel, Y-USA helps YMCAs increase and support the cultural competence of their staff professionals, volunteers and members.

Diversity is the mosaic of people who bring a variety of backgrounds, styles, perspectives, beliefs and competencies as assets to the YMCA. By practicing inclusion, Ys not only address societal trends and remain relevant to their communities, but also remain true to the YMCA mission, goals and values.

How often does the firm's management review the firm's diversity progress/results?

Annually. There will be a diversity team progress evaluation/review component built into the completed strategic plan.

How is the firm's diversity committee and/or firm management held accountable for achieving results?

YMCA of the USA sponsors the national diversity initiative, helping local YMCAs throughout the USA and Canada to initiate their diversity initiatives. In this sense, we are held accountable by local YMCAs who expect us to lead them in diversity efforts.

Furthermore, the national executive director of YMCA of the USA has set out specific directives for his leadership team with regard to actions for their specific departments, and leadership team members are held accountable for achieving these goals as a part of the performance management process.

Additionally, YMCA of the USA has set an organizational performance goal stating that all staff must attend training in one of our three national initiatives, one of which is our diversity initiative. Thus far, over half of our staff has participated in this diversity training.

Finally, the Diversity Committee is presently finalizing the overall diversity strategic plan, and the plan will explicitly contain an accountability portion within it.

The Stats

	NUMBER OF EMPLOYEES	REVENUE
	2005	2005
Total in the U.S.	332,000	$77.15 million
Total worldwide	332,000	$77.15 million

DEMOGRAPHIC PROFILE	
Asian	4 percent
Black	17 percent
Hispanic	4 percent
White	75 percent
Female	59 percent

Retention and Professional Development

Please identify the specific steps you are taking to reduce the attrition rate of minority and women employees.

• Develop and/or support internal employee affinity groups (e.g., minority or women networks within the firm)

• Increase/improve current work/life programs

• Adopt dispute resolution process

• Professional skills development program, including minority and women employees

Diversity Mission Statement

Vision statements depict the ideal state of an organization 10 or more years in the future. Stated below is the vision for diversity and inclusion at YMCA of the USA. Imagine if we could truthfully and undeniably say this about ourselves here at Y-USA:

YMCA of the USA staff and leadership take pride in living our values of care, honesty, respect and responsibility. We live out these values by fostering a culture in which we hold each other accountable for making diversity and inclusion integral to our plans, processes, decisions and actions. Together we create a trusting, exciting atmosphere that values the diversity, contribution and talents of every individual, enabling all to reach their fullest potential.

We do this to achieve our highest level of performance, resulting in exceptional leadership and service to YMCAs and the movement.

Goals are the broad targets toward which an organization directs its efforts.

The YMCA's mission is to build spirit, mind and body for all. Therefore we will value every staff member's diverse talents and help each other develop to our fullest potential.

Because YMCA of the USA has a role in leading the movement, we will show our commitment to diversity and inclusion by moving forward with our own diversity plan and demonstrating daily policies and practices which fulfill that plan.

In keeping with YMCA traditions—fun, fellowship, community and values—we will create a vibrant and trusting environment in which all staff feel that they are respected and that they belong.

Diversity is an essential component of high-performing organizations, so we will build and maintain a diverse staff that reflects the YMCAs and communities we serve.

Strategies identify the course or path an organization will take—what it needs to do, to be or to become—in order to attain its goals.

Strategies to achieve our vision and goals include:

• Culture: Create and nurture an environment of respect, trust and inclusion.

• Access and development: Ensure equal access to opportunities and proactive development for all staff, so that we can utilize all staff to their full potential, increasing our capacity to serve YMCAs and the movement.

• Dialogue practices: Actively engage principal stakeholders in meaningful dialogue before making decisions.

• Leadership: Cultivate and reward leaders whose mindset, vision and behavior foster diversity and inclusion.

• Accountability, evaluation and celebration: Engender ownership—responsibility, accountability and pride—in Y-USA's culture of inclusion.

Additional Information

History of the National Diversity Initiative—Continuing its Priority at the YMCA

Throughout its 154-year history, the YMCA has responded to the demands and shifts of a society being transformed with ever-growing communities in its quest to build strong kids, strong families and strong communities. A new era in fulfilling that mission arose in response to changing demographics and needs in communities served by YMCAs—a comprehensive diversity initiative for the YMCA of the USA was an "idea whose time had come." At the heart of this initiative is the voice of communities across the nation that expressed the need for the YMCA to remain significant, relevant and viable servant leaders to our communities and the families in them.

In the late 1990s, the Urban Group began exploring ways that local associations could become more culturally competent and inclusive in their service areas. They formed a taskforce that assessed the cultures within YMCAs and brought back recommendations. Beginning in 1999, the taskforce convened a team of 12 people that worked with Dr. Tina Rasmussen, the Y-USA's external diversity consultant, to create a diversity plan and process that could be implemented. Their goal was to support the YMCA mission by encouraging, facilitating and supporting increased cultural competence in YMCA individuals and organizations and achieving measurable progress on locally defined diversity goals."

The Y-USA's vision for diversity is:

The YMCA will be known for practicing inclusion by valuing the diversity of all people within our associations and the communities we serve.

The taskforce transitioned to a National Diversity Steering Committee comprised of CEOs, heads of leadership development networks (formerly termed "affinity groups"), national Y support staff and the external consultant. Significant accomplishments have been made since the first YMCAs began their association-wide diversity initiatives in January 2000. Principle accomplishments are:

Championing a diversity initiative workshop, a two-and-a-half day institute was developed. This workshop guides CEOs, their association's change agents, staff and volunteers through the six-step diversity enhancement process. More than 500 individuals representing more than 100 associations (including YMCA of the USA) have graduated from this workshop with numerous Ys experiencing scorecard results as they implement the process.

Diversity module added to principles and practices training series, ImpactPlus, Teens and other national and mission strategy trainings.

The Y-USA created the diversity specialty consultant position to guide the initiative nationally and provide support to the Y-USA internal diversity team (2002).

Creation and preparation of a support network for champions through the designated diversity consultants (2003) and Diversity Initiative Advisory Team (July 2004).

Inception of an interactive, innovative diversity web site on the YMCA Exchange as of June 2004 where Ys can download tools and share program and other innovative strategies.

Received and working collaboratively with other Y-USA staff seeking corporate and foundation funding support to sponsor aspects of implementation.

Enjoyed the first issue of *Discovery Magazine* devoted specifically to the diversity initiative (June 2004).

Approximately 120 YMCAs have completed the initial workshop and are implementing the strategic model for ensuring that YMCAs serve all. Approximately 1,000 YMCA staff, executives and board members have attended the workshop.

A second level of workshop entitled "Deepening the Diversity Initiative within Your YMCA" has been designed and was launched in 2004 with tremendous results. In this two-day workshop, branch executives, other staff and volunteers become equipped to use the systemic change model in their everyday operations. To date, approximately 10 such workshops have been conducted.

In its 2005 summer issue, the Association of YMCA Professionals' publication, *Perspective,* featured the National Diversity Initiative via its challenging theme, "Is the YMCA Truly for All?"

Yum! Brands, Inc.

1441 Gardiner Lane
Louisville, KY 40213
Phone: (502) 874-8300
Fax: (502) 874-8662
www.yumcareers.com

Locations

Louisville, KY (HQ)
Dallas, TX • Irvine, CA

Diversity Leadership
Richard-Abraham Rugnao
Public Affairs, Manager, Global Diversity

Recruiting

Please list the schools/types of schools at which you recruit.

• Ivy League schools
• Other private schools
• Public state schools
• Historically black colleges and universities (HBCUs)
• Other predominantly minority and/or women's colleges

Do you have any special outreach efforts directed to encourage minority students to consider your firm?

• *Conferences:* National Society of Hispanic MBAs, National Black MBA Association, INROADS
• Participate in/host minority student job fair(s)

What activities does the firm undertake to attract minority and women employees?

• Partner programs with women and minority associations
• *Conferences:* National Urban League, NAACP, NCLR, LULAC, OCA, INROADS
• Participate at minority job fairs
• Seek referrals from other employees
• Utilize online job services

Do you use executive recruiting/search firms to seek to identify new diversity hires?

No

Scholarships

Yum! Scholarship Program

The Yum! Scholarship Program offers scholarship money to all U.S.-based restaurant and restaurant support center employees that have worked at the company for at least one year and average at least 20 hours per week. Yum awards the following: $2,500 for any field of study in a four-year or graduate program, $1,000 for any field of study at a two-year or vocational-technical school and up to 10 "bonus" awards of $1,500 for students pursuing an approved food service/hospitality degree.

In 2004, Yum! awarded more than $500,000 in scholarships for the Yum! Scholarship Program. Approximately 15 percent of the scholarships awarded went to African-American scholars.

KFC United Negro College Fund Scholars

As part of KFC's ongoing commitment to diversity and the development of its employees, KFC provides scholarships to eligible students attending UNCF schools. The KFC/UNCF scholars program is aimed towards employees who are entry-level college freshman pursuing degrees in business management, computer science or liberal arts.

Scholarships for Minorities

Yum! Brands has a number of scholarships for minorities, including the American Indian College Fund, to increase the number of American Indian graduates, and similar programs for Hispanic-, Asian- and African-Americans.

Taco Bell–Glen Bell Scholarship Program

Open to Taco Bell hourly employees, the program awards financial scholarships of up to $2,000 for accredited undergraduate, graduate and vocational-technical educations. In 2004, Taco Bell's Glen Bell awarded $100,000 in scholarships.

Language Class Reimbursement Program

Hourly or salaried employees can receive up to $500 per year for language class tuition, books and materials.

Tuition Reimbursement Program

The company will reimburse full-time, salaried employees up to a maximum of $4,000 per calendar year for graduate and undergraduate courses.

Affinity Groups

Pizza Hut has an African-American, Hispanic and women's group. Each brand is exploring the development of their respective groups.

Strategic Plan and Diversity Leadership

How does the firm's leadership communicate the importance of diversity to everyone at the firm?

Yum! takes a comprehensive approach to communicating its diversity efforts. All means of internal and external communications are utilized.

Who has primary responsibility for leading diversity initiatives at your firm?

Terrian Barnes, director, global diversity.

Does your firm currently have a diversity committee?

No

Does the committee and/or diversity leader establish and set goals or objectives consistent with management's priorities?

Yes

Has the firm undertaken a formal or informal diversity program or set of initiatives aimed at increasing the diversity of the firm?

Yes, formal

How often does the firm's management review the firm's diversity progress/results?

Quarterly

Retention and Professional Development

Please identify the specific steps you are taking to reduce the attrition rate of minority and women employees.

- Develop and/or support internal employee affinity groups (e.g., minority or women networks within the firm)
- Increase/review compensation relative to competition
- Increase/improve current work/life programs
- Adopt dispute resolution process
- Succession plan includes emphasis on diversity
- Work with minority and women employees to develop career advancement plans

- Strengthen mentoring program for all employees, including minorities and women
- Professional skills development program, including minority and women employees

Diversity Mission Statement

Diversity is not a strategy or a program at Yum! Brands. It's a shared commitment by all of us to uphold our founding truths and to live out our "How We Work Together" principles every day.

Additional Information

Yum! Brands, Inc., with more than 33,000 restaurants in over 100 countries, is the parent to A&W Restaurants, KFC, Long John Silver's, Pizza Hut and Taco Bell. As the world's largest restaurant company and the third largest employer in the world with more than 850,000 employees around the globe, our continued success in the marketplace depends on creating an environment where all people are valued, appreciated and have the opportunity to grow and learn. That is why we have built a global culture focused on respect and recognition.

Moreover, Yum! is committed to realizing the business benefits of driving diversity and inclusion by developing current and future business leaders, franchisees and suppliers that reflect the changing demographics of our customers.

Making progress in diversity is a personal priority for our Chairman and CEO David Novak and a business priority for our entire organization. David updates the system annually on the progress we are making to reflect the communities in which we operate. Everyone in the company—from our senior leadership team at the restaurant support centers to our team members in the restaurants—is accountable for fostering an inclusive, diverse workplace culture.

"Yum! Brand's commitment to diversity helps drive all aspects of our business," says David C. Novak, chairman and CEO, Yum! Brands, Inc. "It's important that our global culture is actively developing a workforce with a broad mix of backgrounds and viewpoints at all levels of management. Building on our diverse foundation at all of our brands gives us a competitive edge and helps drive 'Customer Mania.'"

For the past two years, Yum! Brands has been nationally recognized by a leading business magazine as one of the 50 Best Companies for Minorities, claiming the number-one spot for managerial diversity. The magazine ranked Yum among the top 10 companies having the highest percentage of African-American and Native American employees. In 2004, Yum! jumped 20 spots to place 15th out of 50 on the list.

In addition, Yum! also has been named the number-one company for work/life balance in Louisville, one of the Best Places to Work in Kentucky and Pizza Hut has been named the No. 1 Best Place to

Work in Dallas. We are very proud of these accomplishments because they reflect Yum's commitment to diversity and to making the company a great place to work.

Our goal is to continue to embrace and strengthen our diversity effectiveness with customers, franchise partners, suppliers and the community and to continue to build our talent pipeline with an even stronger emphasis on diversity.

Zurich North America

1400 American Lane
Schaumburg, IL 60196
Phone: (877) 847-6593
Fax: (847) 413-5206
www.zurichna.com

Locations

Complete listing on web site

Diversity Leadership

Carol Bullock
Director, Diversity

Employment Contact

Debbie Jandt
Manager, College Relations and Recruiting
1400 American Lane
Schaumburg, IL 60196
Phone: (877) 847-6593
Fax: (847) 413-5206
E-mail: debbie.jandt@zurichna.com

Recruiting

Please list the schools/types of schools at which you recruit.

• Private schools

• Public state schools

• Historically black colleges and universities (HBCUs)

Do you have any special outreach efforts directed to encourage minority students to consider your firm?

• Participate in/host minority student job fair(s)

• Outreach to leadership of minority student organizations

What activities does the firm undertake to attract minority and women employees?

• Partner programs with women and minority associations

• Participate at minority job fairs

• Seek referrals from other employees

• Utilize online job services

Do you use executive recruiting/search firms to seek to identify new diversity hires?

Yes

Internships and Co-ops

Zurich Internship Program

Deadline for application: February 15th

Number of interns in the program in summer 2006 (internship) or 2006 (co-op): 100 interns

Pay: $10 to $25 per hour

Length of the program: 10 to 12 weeks

Web site for internship/co-op information: www.zurichna.com

The objective of the internship program is to prepare individuals for careers in their field of study. In the end, participants come away with a unique and well-rounded understanding of Zurich in North America—its products, its services and its customers.

Candidates are recruited for those locations that have determined a need for interns. The program is formalized and structured; it encompasses "real work" assignments. These are formalized program assessments throughout the summer for the intern and assigned mentor. During the course of the summer program, the intern will assume the duties of the job as if it were a permanent position and work alongside the talented individuals who actually perform the roles today.

The internship program is for college sophomores and junior candidates who can demonstrate problem-solving skills in a customer-focused environment, a willingness to work hard and to learn, strong written and verbal communication skills, excellent time-management skills, flexibility, the ability to work independently, self-motivation and a minimum cumulative grade point average of 3.0. The program is from May to August, and housing in not provided.

Entry-Level Programs, Full-Time Opportunities and Training Programs

Associate Program

The Zurich Associate Program is a unique learning, mentoring and networking program that provides select individuals with an insurance education, experience in the way we do business and opportunities to build a career.

Associates participate in broad-based training sessions and work directly with experienced underwriters, risk engineers and claims professionals across the U.S. and Canada over the course of 11 months. Rigorous field preparation and comprehensive examinations are also included in the curriculum. Performance is continuously evaluated, and associates advance only when each phase is successfully completed. In addition, associates must be willing to relocate and be available to work in any one of our North American office locations.

Every new associate program class kicks off in the North American headquarters in Schaumburg, Ill., just 45 minutes northwest of Chicago. Associates first take part in a series of insurance and general business workshops. The insurance workshops focus on the core disciplines of commercial insurance: claims, risk engineering and underwriting.

To be considered for the associate program, you must be a college graduate (graduated no earlier than one year before the next class start date) and eligible to work in the U.S. for the duration and after the training program. In addition, you must have a:

• Bachelor's degree
• Minimum 3.0 cumulative GPA
• Valid driver's license and acceptable driving record documents

Strategic Plan and Diversity Leadership

What trends in your industry affect your corporate diversity goals, strategies and/or internal or external alliances?

Planning is influenced by industry competition for individuals with skills in claims, underwriting, and actuarial. Additionally, the industry has an increasing average age of professionals that could result in more retirements and loss knowledge and skill.

How does the firm's leadership communicate the importance of diversity to everyone at the firm?

Web site, presentations

Who has primary responsibility for leading diversity initiatives at your firm?

Director, Diversity, Carol Bullock

Does your firm currently have a diversity committee?

No

Has the firm undertaken a formal or informal diversity program or set of initiatives aimed at increasing the diversity of the firm?

Yes, formal

How often does the firm's management review the firm's diversity progress/results?

Annually

The Stats

	NUMBER OF EMPLOYEES	
	2006	**2005**
Total in the U.S.	11,000	8,775

Additional Information

Zurich Financial Services is an insurance-based financial services provider with a global network that focuses its activities on key markets in North America and Europe. Founded in 1872, Zurich is headquartered in Zurich, Switzerland. Through its offices in more than 50 countries, 57,000 Zurich employees serve customers in more than 120 countries. In North America, Zurich is a leading commercial property-casualty provider serving the global corporate, middle market, small business, specialties and program sectors.

Through its diversity and inclusion vision, Zurich is committed to creating a culture of inclusion consistent with Zurich Basics (values)—one that attracts top talent and that promotes the development and full contribution of all employees to achieve business goals.

We want an environment where all people are recognized, feel valued and can go as far as their talent and ambition allow. We want to create an inclusive culture that understands and values diversity in age, ethnic origin, gender, lifestyles, physical abilities, race, religious beliefs, sexual orientation, work background and other perceived differences. We encourage, recognize and reward individuals to work together toward team, company and individual goals. We believe that by leveraging diversity as a competitive advantage, we make our organization a better place to work.

About the Editors

About the Editor

Angela Entzminger is an editor at Vault. She earned her bachelor of science degree in communication studies from the University of Texas at Austin. She lives in New York City.

About Vault

Vault is the leading media company for career information. Our team of industry-focused editors takes a journalistic approach in covering news, employment trends and specific employers in their industries. We annually survey 10,000s of employees to bring readers the inside scoop on industries and specific employers.

Popular Vault titles include:

The College Buzz Book

The Law School Buzz Book

Vault Career Guide to Media & Entertainment

Vault Guide to Human Resources Careers

Vault Guide to Marketing & Brand Management

Vault Guide to Top Internships

Vault/INROADS Guide to Corporate Diversity Programs

Vault MBA Career Bible

Vault has published more than 120 titles for job seekers and professionals. To see a complete list of Vault titles, visit www.vault.com.